HTML 4.0

NO EXPERIENCE REQUIRED

AIU
BIT 2000

HTML 4.0

NO EXPERIENCE REQUIRED™

E. Stephen Mack
Janan Platt Saylor

SYBEX®

San Francisco • Paris • Düsseldorf • Soest • London

Associate Publisher: Gary Masters
Acquisitions Manager: Kristine Plachy
Acquisitions & Developmental Editor: Suzanne Rotondo
Editor: Kim Wimpsett
Technical Editor: Rima Sonia Regas
Book Designers: Patrick Dintino, Catalin Dulfu
Graphic Illustrators: Steve Brooks, Andrew Benzie
Desktop Publishers: Kris Warrenburg, Franz Baumhackl
Production Coordinator: Charles Mathews
Proofreaders: Katherine Cooley, Eryn Osterhaus, Duncan Watson
Indexer: Matthew Spence
Cover Designer: Ingalls + Associates

Screen reproductions produced with Collage Complete.

Collage Complete is a trademark of Inner Media Inc.

SYBEX is a registered trademark of SYBEX Inc.

No experience required. is a trademark of SYBEX Inc.

TRADEMARKS: SYBEX has attempted throughout this book to distinguish proprietary trademarks from descriptive terms by following the capitalization style used by the manufacturer.

Netscape Communications, the Netscape Communications logo, Netscape, and Netscape Navigator are trademarks of Netscape Communications Corporation.

The AlienFlower Poetry Workshop Home Page text and images used throughout this book are ©1995–1997 by Janan Platt Saylor and are used with the permission of Janan Platt Saylor.

Excerpts from Zeigen's Dilemma used throughout this book are ©1994–1997 by E. Stephen Mack and are used with the permission of E. Stephen Mack.

Photographs and illustrations used in this book have been downloaded from publicly accessible file archives and are used in this book for news reportage purposes only to demonstrate the variety of graphics resources available via electronic access. Text and images available over the Internet may be subject to copyright and other rights owned by third parties. Online availability of text and images does not imply that they may be reused without the permission of rights holders, although the Copyright Act does permit certain unauthorized reuse as fair use under 17 U.S.C. Section 107.

Library of Congress Card Number: 97-69202
ISBN: 0-7821-2143-8

Manufactured in the United States of America

10 9 8 7 6

Acknowledgments

We'd like to thank everyone at Sybex who made this book possible, including Acquisitions & Developmental Editors Dan Brodnitz and Suzanne Rotondo, Acquisitions Manager Kristine Plachy, Technical Editor Rima Sonia Regas, Desktop Publishers Kris Warrenburg and Franz Baumhackl, Indexer Matthew Spence, Production Coordinator Charles Mathews, and especially Editor Kim Wimpsett, whose quick work and expert skills are without peer.

Our book wouldn't exist without the World Wide Web Consortium (W3C), which maintains HTML and other Web standards, and Tim Berners-Lee, who invented the World Wide Web.

This book was greatly aided by Antiweb, a mailing list of Web experts created by Malcolm Humes in 1995. All of our friends on Antiweb helped shape this book, including Malcolm Humes, Scot Hacker, Mark Napier, Levi Asher, Phil Zampino, Kristen Ankiewicz, Phil Franks, Jody Cline, and Meg Wise-Lawrence. But most of all, we'd like to thank Christian Crumlish, who's easily the best computer book writer in the field today. Christian's generous advice and influence allowed us to write this book in the first place.

Grateful thanks to Anita M. Rowland (`http://www.halcyon.com/anitar/`) for her expert comments on Skill 14 (style sheets).

We'd also like to thank Peter Flynn, Warren Steel, Abigail, Jukka Korpela, Håkon Lie, Arnaud Le Hors, Dave Raggett, Arnoud "Galactus" Engelfriet, Liam Quinn, Brian Wilson, Benjamin Franz, Chris Lilley, Chris Wilson, Todd Fahrner, and the many other Internet experts of the `www-html@w3.org` and `www-style@w3.org` mailing lists and the `comp.infosystems.www.authoring.html` newsgroup, whose advice, Web sites, postings, and e-mail helped shape this book. (Any mistakes in this book are ours alone.)

E. Stephen Mack:

My undying appreciation goes to my co-author Janan Platt Saylor. I'd also like to thank Rich Shuey, Greg Burrell, Kyrie Robinson, John Restrick, Erin Denney, Sam Parazette, Partha S. Banerjee, and Karen Dodson for being excellent friends and for their suggestions. Rick Salsman deserves special praise for providing several Macintosh screen shots and general information on short notice. Thanks, guys!

I'm grateful for the music of Tori Amos, especially considering how many Web sites she's inspired. This book was also written to the musical accompaniment of Luscious Jackson, that dog, Pavement, Sebadoh, Blur, Radiohead, Liz Phair, Bettie Serveert, and Ajax.

My father, Ed Mack, read through the first part of the manuscript and offered his advice. Since he is a pioneer of computer networking whose designs were one of the foundations of the Internet's architecture, I owe him a double debt of gratitude.

Finally, my appreciation goes to all of my students from every class I've ever taught—for teaching me just as much as I've taught them.

Janan Platt Saylor:

It's been a delight working with my co-author Stephen. My deep appreciation goes to him because his enthusiasm was constant, he always worked so hard, and he left me with just the fun stuff to do.

And Tori, if you're reading this, Antiwebber Jody and I say, "go for it 'cause if we weren't already each married...."

My sincere thanks to all of the AlienFlower poets. Their beautiful poetry inspires my writing every day.

Contents at a Glance

Table of Contents

Introduction

The World Wide Web has become a critically important communication medium—and the language of the Web is HTML, the Hypertext Markup Language.

Our goal in this book is to teach HTML from the ground up, providing every skill necessary to create a great Web site. Making an interesting home page requires a variety of different abilities. Rather than getting caught up in the abstractions of HTML, we're going to give you all the facts, examples, and step-by-step instructions that you'll need to get the job done. Toward that goal, each chapter in this book is called a "Skill," and we've named each Skill based on the experience you'll gain.

What's in This Book?

HTML 4.0 is the newest version of HTML, which offers groundbreaking improvements in the areas of internationalization, accessibility, interactivity, and style sheets. Skill 1 will define HTML and its history in the context of the Internet and the Web, and Skill 2 will get you started if you've never used HTML before.

HTML is a language that's surprisingly simple and elegant. The Web's popularity is built on the fact that anyone can learn HTML and create attractive and compelling Web pages. There's no need to rely on a program that writes HTML for you—instead, you'll find that you get better results from knowing HTML yourself.

HTML has come a long way since its first version. HTML has been shaped by companies like Netscape and Microsoft and the opinions of Web authors and designers from all over the world. One of the strengths of this book is that we're not committed to any particular flavor of HTML—instead we'll present *all* of it, giving you the appropriate warnings when necessary and always steering you toward the best solutions. We're also up-to-date, teaching you the latest trends in HTML practices, with Skills on Cascading Style Sheets, scripting, and Dynamic HTML—the newest shakeups that are changing the way the Web looks and acts. We'll warn you about the behaviors of the two most popular browsers, Netscape's Navigator and Microsoft's Internet Explorer, as well.

In the near future, Microsoft and Netscape will both bring HTML to your desktop in important new ways. As new operating systems appear that integrate the

Internet and your desktop, HTML will become more important than ever before. You couldn't pick a better time to learn HTML or a more valuable computer language skill for your résumé.

This book is written by two authors, Janan and Stephen, and we'll both share our individual opinions and experiences and give you the benefit of a team consensus.

Each Skill ends with a section called "Are You Experienced?" that lists the topics we covered as a checklist for your newly acquired abilities.

What's on Our Web Sites?

We've also worked with Sybex to put together two Web sites for this book. At Sybex's Web site, you'll find most of the example pages and HTML code listings in this book, so you won't have to type in any code to see the examples in action.

We've also put together a separate Web site that expands on the book's examples and skills. You'll see different approaches to common problems, so you'll be able to decide which approach works best for you. We have a forum for your questions, as well as some expanded tutorials that we couldn't shoehorn into the book. We'll keep the book's Web site updated; if there are any late-breaking changes to HTML, we'll let you know.

 NOTE   To get to Sybex's Web page for this book, go to `http://www.sybex.com/`, click the Catalog graphic, and click the No Experience Required graphic. Then navigate to this book's page. To get to this book's Web site, visit `http://www.html1ner.com/` and follow the instructions there.

What You'll Need

Unlike other books where you need a specific software package from a particular software publisher to get anywhere, this book can be used with a wide range of HTML tools or even with no HTML tools at all. Skill 4 of this book will give you a lot of information about HTML tools, but it's helpful to know what you'll need up front.

To get the most out of this book, you should be able to edit files on your computer and browse the Web. (Don't worry if you don't understand any of these terms—they're explained in Skill 1.) You'll need:

- Access to some kind of computer, whether it's a PC running Windows, a Macintosh, or a UNIX workstation

- A text editor (the one that came with your computer's operating system will do fine)

- A Web browser that works with your computer, such as Netscape's Navigator, Microsoft's Internet Explorer, NCSA's Mosaic, or Lynx

- A modem and an account with an Internet service provider so that you can access the Web (or a network card with a network connection, or some other connection to the Internet)

Even if you don't have an Internet connection, you can still use this book. (We'll show you how to get an Internet account in Skill 18.) At the bare minimum, all you'll need is a text editor and a browser.

If you want to publish your pages on the Web (a process explored in Skill 18), you'll need to see if your Internet service provider gives you or your organization some Web space as part of your agreement. You might need to get:

- An account with an Internet presence provider that gives you some Web space (see Skill 19) or access to some Web space through your employer, school, or another organization

- A program that lets you send files using the File Transfer Protocol (FTP), such as Netscape Navigator, WS_FTP, CuteFTP, Fetch, Microsoft's Web Publishing Wizard, or the command-line FTP program that comes with Windows 95

To see many of the HTML 4.0 features of this book in action, it's important to be able to have access to the latest versions of Navigator (4 or newer) or IE (4 or newer). You may also want to obtain some of the HTML tools discussed in Skill 4.

Publishing Conventions

In this book, we'll follow several publishing conventions.

NOTE   Notes look like this. They present additional information and points of special concern.

TIP   This is a Tip, which provides information that will make the current task easier. We'll give you suggestions, shortcuts, and alternatives in these Tips.

WARNING   Warnings emphasize special precautions you should take or indicate some possible negative consequences to a particular approach.

Even though HTML is not a traditional programming language, it is like *code*—which means that HTML consists of a set of programming instructions that are interpreted by a browser. Sample code will look like this:

 example.html

```
<!DOCTYPE HTML PUBLIC "-//W3C//DTD HTML 4.0//EN">
<HTML LANG="EN">
  <HEAD>
    <TITLE>Welcome to HTML 4.0: No experience required!</TITLE>
  </HEAD>
  <BODY BGCOLOR="#FFFFFF">
    <H1 ALIGN="CENTER">You Made It!</H1>
    Welcome to
    <A HREF="http://www.sybex.com/">Sybex's Web Site</A> for our book.
    <IMG ALT="[Sybex Logo]" SRC="http://www.emf.net/~estephen/images/
➦smallsybexlogo.gif">
  </BODY>
</HTML>
```

 NOTE   Don't worry, we'll teach what all of this means in the book.

The code icon next to the `example.html` filename tells you that this code is available from the Sybex Web site. Also, notice in the third line from the bottom that we'll use a continuation arrow when our book's margins force us to wrap a long line of code. Any line marked with a continuation arrow should be typed at the end of the previous line. (The arrow should not be typed.)

When we refer to a piece of HTML code in the body of a paragraph, such as when we talk about the `<TITLE>` tag, it will appear in a monospaced font, like `<B>this</B>`. URLs are also presented in monospaced font; for long URLs, linebreaks will occur before a period or after a slash to avoid confusion. An item in italics marks the definition of an important concept. Also, italics show you where to substitute a value; for example, with `WIDTH="`*NUMBER*`"` you substitute a number like 50 for the word *NUMBER*. When we refer to a Web page's link text that you can click on, it will be underlined (such as <u>Sybex's Web site</u>). Any keys or text that you're supposed to type during an exercise will be in bold, such as "enter **hello.html**." Keystroke commands, like Ctrl+A, will use the plus sign to mean that you hold down the Control key while pressing the A key. And finally, any menu command is indicated like this: File ➤ Exit.

Now that our watches are in sync, it's time to learn our first skill. Skill 1 will give you thorough background information on the Internet, the Web, and HTML.

PART 1

Starting Out with HTML

Part I of this book will teach you about the basics of HTML—the skills that you'll need to know whenever you make a Web page. Skill 1 will introduce you to the Internet, the World Wide Web and its address system, and give you your first look at HTML. Skill 2 is a quick introduction to the essentials of HTML and how it works. You'll actually create a fully functional Web page using HTML and learn some of the basic HTML commands. Skill 3 teaches you about the content of an HTML document, including what characters you can use and how they can be arranged in a file. Skill 4 shows you a few examples so that you can pick the tool that's right for you.

After that, we start getting down to business. Skill 5 teaches you about the HTML elements that go in the head section of an HTML document, while Skill 6 teaches you about the ones that go in the body section. Skill 7 teaches you how to link your Web pages to other pages on the Web, and Skill 8 teaches you how to create graphics.

Learning about HTML, the Web, and the Internet

- → **Exploring the Internet and the World Wide Web**
- → **Introducing Web pages and HTML**
- → **Working with URLs**
- → **Learning the anatomy of a tag**
- → **Understanding HTML's history and philosophy**

The Internet is an international network of computers that exchange information with each other. The World Wide Web is a vast interconnected library of information, art, and commerce. Even if you've already spent some time on the Internet and the World Wide Web, it's a good idea to read through this Skill to make sure you have some basic understanding. Then we can build on this framework in the following Skills.

HTML (Hypertext Markup Language) is a computer language used to build Web pages. Before we get into HTML in detail, though, we'll make sure that you're comfortable with the Internet and the Web. We'll also introduce you to the Internet address system, which is made up of URLs (Uniform Resource Locators). Finally, before we move on to Skill 2, we'll give you a good idea of what HTML looks like to prepare you for the rest of the book.

In the Beginning: The Internet

The Internet began in the mid-1960s as a project of the United States Department of Defense's Advanced Research Project Agency. Scientists and researchers developed the Internet as a way to communicate and share information between various research institutions. To do this, they created new *protocols*, or agreements to establish how computers should talk to each other when they exchange information. The modern Internet is based on these protocols.

To understand how computers exchange information, you need to understand a key concept of the Internet: the distinction between *clients* and *servers*. A server is a computer that provides information, while a client is a tool or program on a different computer used to get information from a server. Think of calling the time service on a telephone: Your telephone is the client, and the phone company has a server that gives you the current time of day.

In fact, telephones are a good analogy for other Internet concepts. When you dial a number, the phone on the other end rings and is then answered; this is similar to the way different computers talk to each other, using the *handshaking*, or *interfacing*, that goes on with Internet protocols behind the scenes.

Internet protocols became more popular as increasing numbers of research institutions, universities, and high-tech corporations became connected. The protocols allowed Internet users to send *e-mail*, exchange files using *FTP*, and read or post news using the *NNTP*. Let's look at these key concepts one by one:

- **E-mail** Electronic messages are sent from one user to another via SMTP, the Simple Mail Transfer Protocol. (Historically, other protocols were used, but these days SMTP is the most common protocol for e-mail.) E-mail is the most popular use of the Internet. Most people use an e-mail client, such as Qualcomm's Eudora or Netscape's Messenger, to send and receive messages. Mail servers on the Internet take care of relaying e-mail.

- **FTP (File Transfer Protocol)** A way to exchange files. The way it works is fairly simple: Somewhere, someone puts a file on an FTP server; these files can be text files, programs, or images. Using your FTP client, you call up the FTP server and request that file. There are lots of different FTP client programs available. Some clients use a series of typed commands like "open" (to connect to a server) and "get" (to download a file); other FTP clients use a graphical interface where you select files that you want.

- **NNTP (Network News Transfer Protocol)** A way to distribute messages on an immense worldwide bulletin board with many different topic areas. Using a news client program, such as Forte's Agent, Netscape's Collabra, or Microsoft's Internet News, you can read and write articles in *newsgroups* such as rec.humor.funny (a joke newsgroup) or comp.infosystems.www.authoring .html (an HTML discussion newsgroup). The name for this Internet bulletin board is *Usenet*.

If you're unfamiliar with how e-mail, FTP, and Usenet are used, you may want to pick up a general-purpose Internet book, such as *The ABCs of the Internet*, also published by Sybex. Of course, there are a lot more protocols than just these three. (We'll see some others later in this Skill when we talk about URLs.) And getting connected to the Internet involves the use of protocols as well.

GETTING CONNECTED TO THE INTERNET

For your computer to be connected to the Internet, you'll need to have TCP/IP installed. *TCP/IP* is the Transfer Control Protocol/Internet Protocol that routes information from the Internet to your computer and vice versa.

Once you have TCP/IP on your computer, you'll need an Internet service provider (ISP) or online service to connect to the Internet. Most ISPs charge you around $20–30 a month and give you an e-mail account (for sending and receiving e-mail) as well as access to the Internet. Some of the best-known national ISPs are Netcom, UUNet, and Best, but there are hundreds of different ISPs.

continued ▶

If you don't have an ISP, you may be able to access the Internet through your company, school, or organization. Or you can sign up with an online service, such as America Online (AOL), Prodigy, or CompuServe. Originally, these online services were entirely separate from the Internet, but now they offer full Internet access in addition to their proprietary content and services.

If you use a modem to dial your ISP, you can have two types of accounts. The most common type of account uses PPP (Point-to-Point Protocol) or SLIP (Serial Line Interface Protocol) to connect your computer to the Internet. The other type of account is a *shell account*—using your modem and *terminal emulator* software, you connect to your ISP's computer and use the Internet from there, with typed commands. The drawback to shell accounts is that your computer isn't directly connected to the Internet, and you are limited to text with no graphics. PPP/SLIP accounts are much more popular than shell accounts. Many ISPs offer both types of accounts as a package deal.

Your modem (modulator-demodulator) receives and transmits information in the form of digital signals sent through a telephone line. TCP/IP routes the information to its destination. Along the way, your information is split into small *packets* of information that hop from one computer to another.

Modern personal-computer operating systems include TCP/IP, so if you're using a recent version of Windows, OS/2, UNIX, or the Apple Macintosh operating system (MacOS), you're all set. But if you're using an older operating system such as Windows 3.1 or System 7.0, you'll need to download or purchase a package that includes TCP/IP. Many ISPs provide this software when you sign up.

Skill 18 includes some information about choosing an ISP and getting connected to the Internet with TCP/IP.

The Internet used to be something that was largely unknown to the general public, and it was funded principally by governments and public institutions. Thanks to the rise of the World Wide Web, the Internet has evolved into what it is today—a vital medium for sharing information that is a commercial realm. The importance of the modern Internet as a communications tool cannot be over-emphasized. A few people think the current popularity of the Internet is a fad. One thing is certain: The Internet is here to stay. What remains to be seen is how it will evolve over the next few years.

Since Internet tools and protocols such as e-mail, Usenet, and FTP are so popular and effective, many companies have rushed to join. It's common to see billboards and advertisements that contain Internet addresses. Companies are now replacing or supplementing traditional means of advertising with Internet advertisements. Companies are also setting up internal sites, or *intranets,* to distribute information specifically within their organization.

 NOTE

An intranet is a corporate or organizational network that uses the same protocols used on the Internet to share files and send e-mail. The only real difference between an intranet and the Internet is that an intranet is cut off from the outside world. (Often intranets allow their users to access the Internet, but prevent outside access to internal files by hiding behind a security system called a *firewall.*)

Many people think of the rise of the Internet as the dawn of a true Information Age, or the next revolution in publishing—comparable to the invention of the printing press. Over the next several years we'll continue to see an exciting, and potentially explosive, growth period.

A Close-up Look at the World Wide Web

In the 1990s, a new Internet protocol emerged called HTTP (HyperText Transfer Protocol)—and the World Wide Web was born. The *World Wide Web* (also called "W3," "WWW," or "the Web" for short) is a vast network of HTTP servers sending files across the Internet.

 NOTE

Many people confuse the Web with the Internet itself. But the Web is just one of the many services available on the Internet. Think of it this way: The Internet is like a road that connects many different towns. You can take a bus, or you can bicycle, or you can drive. Similarly, on the Internet, you can send and receive many different types of information: e-mail, Usenet articles, chat sessions, and Web pages. Just as you wouldn't confuse your car with the highway system, don't confuse the Web with the Internet.

Introducing Web Browsers

These days, the most popular Internet tools are clients designed for accessing the Web. (You'll hear people say they're Web "browsing" or "surfing" the Web. In this book, we'll call people who look at your Web page *surfers*.) The two most popular Web clients are Netscape's Navigator and Microsoft's Internet Explorer. Web clients like these are typically referred to as *browsers*. They are popular because they are graphical and easy to use. Figure 1.1 shows Navigator 4.

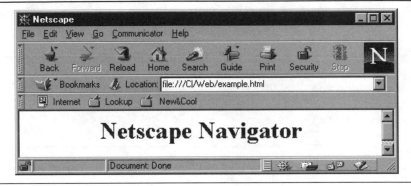

FIGURE 1.1:   Navigator 4, a Web browser from Netscape

IE is the other popular browser, shown in Figure 1.2.

FIGURE 1.2:   IE 4, a Web browser from Microsoft

The Internet was originally a text-only medium, but then along came Web browsers, which could display graphics and play sounds easily.

Both popular browsers, Navigator and IE, use a *graphical user interface* (GUI, pronounced "gooey"). With this kind of format, both browsers use mouse and menu commands, toolbar buttons, and context menus. To display a context menu, right-click if you're a Windows user; hold down the mouse if you're a Macintosh user.

An advantage of these two Web browsers (and another reason for their popularity) is that they are flexible. Netscape and IE both let you do a lot more than browse the Web. In addition to Web surfing, you can send and receive e-mail, download files from FTP servers, and read and post articles to Usenet newsgroups.

With these browsers, the Web has become a multimedia universe of interconnected documents. The Web was originally conceptualized by its inventors as "a seamless world in which *all* information, from any source, can be accessed in a consistent and simple way," and it's quickly achieving that goal.

There are many browsers aside from only Navigator and IE. Two browsers in particular that are fairly popular are Lynx (a text-only browser) and Mosaic (the first graphical browser, on which both Navigator and IE are based). Some other browsers include Amaya, UdiWWW, GNUscape, Opera, Arena, DOSLynx, Air-Mosaic, and WebTV (which runs on a television set).

Understanding Hyperlinks

The key to the Web is that files on different servers can be linked together using *hyperlinks* (also called *links*). You can also use hyperlinks to jump around to various sections within a single document. Think of hyperlinks as an interactive table of contents. Hyperlinks point you to text, graphics, audio, or other media when you simply "click" (using your mouse) on the text of the hyperlink. Images can also be hyperlinks, in which case they're usually surrounded by a blue border to show that you can click on them. Text hyperlinks are highlighted and underlined in your browser so you'll know that they're "clickable." For example, Figure 1.3 shows two text hyperlinks on a Web page.

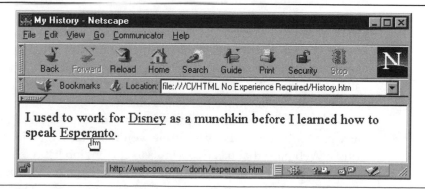

FIGURE 1.3: Notice the hyperlinks Disney and Esperanto in this sentence. Often your mouse pointer will change shape when it is over a link, as shown here.

If you click on the word <u>Disney</u>, then the hyperlink will take you somewhere else, presumably some Web site having to do with Walt Disney. Clicking on <u>Esperanto</u> would take you to a different place, perhaps a tutorial on Esperanto. Figure 1.4 shows the page you'll see after you click on <u>Esperanto</u>.

FIGURE 1.4: Clicking on <u>Esperanto</u> takes you to an Esperanto tutorial. This page uses an advanced HTML feature called *frames*, which we'll discuss in Skill 11.

Thanks to hyperlinks like the ones shown in Figure 1.3, the Web is an inconceivably vast, multidimensional set of information, already larger than all of the books in the Library of Congress. In fact, the Library of Congress itself is just one site out of the millions of individuals, institutions, organizations, governments, and businesses that have presences on the Web.

Because of hyperlinks, it's easy to find different sources of information about any particular topic. If, for example, you're looking for a job in your area, you can find a Web page that has hyperlinks to current job listings from hundreds of different employers. Or if you want to find out about a TV program you missed on PBS this week, it's easy: Just go to the PBS home page (*home page* is a synonym for

Web page, usually meaning the main page of the site). Figure 1.5 shows PBS's home page. The highlighted and underlined text are hyperlinks. For example, when you click on <u>Nova/PBS Online: Alive on Everest</u>, your browser takes you to a page of text about a Mount Everest adventure.

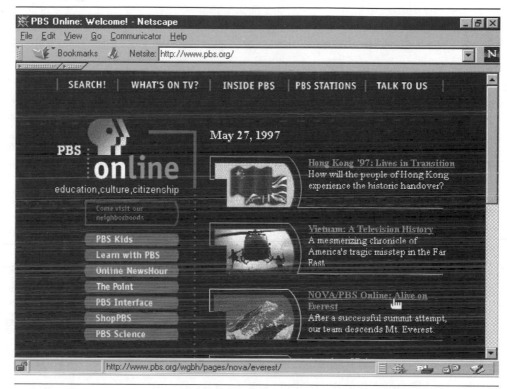

FIGURE 1.5: You can find PBS's home page at http://www.pbs.org/.

 NOTE   "Hyperlink" is a mouthful, so from now on we'll just refer to them as "links."

Discovering Web Formats

While Web servers can transfer any type of file, the Web uses the same types of files over and over again. You can usually recognize a file by its *extension*, or the code that follows the period at the end of a filename. Most extensions are three-letter codes (such as .doc for a Microsoft Word document). Web files typically fit in one of the following categories:

- Web pages are files written in HTML, as we'll see in "What Is a Web Page?" later in this Skill. HTML files have an .html or .htm extension.

- Image files are either GIF (.gif) or JPEG (.jpg) format (see Skill 8).

- Multimedia files—see Skill 9 for more information on multimedia files.

- Text files are in plain ASCII format, with an extension of .txt.

 NOTE   *ASCII* is an acronym for American Standard Code for Information Interchange. ASCII defines the 128 characters considered plain text, including lowercase and uppercase letters, numbers, and normal punctuation. ASCII doesn't allow formatting (such as bold, italic, or font size). "ASCII" and "plain text" are often used as synonyms. ASCII is only useful for English. We'll learn about character encoding for other languages in Skill 3.

The exact nature of these file formats change periodically, and new formats show up from time to time.

As you move through the rest of this book, you'll learn how to create these types of files and publish them on the Web. For now, let's continue with our discussion of the Web by defining Web pages in more detail.

What Is a Web Page?

A Web page is simply a special type of file written in HTML (don't worry, we'll be getting to HTML in just a minute).

Publishing a Web page means transferring your Web page to a place where it can be served by an HTTP server so that people all over the world will be able to read it.

 NOTE   Most Web pages are served by an HTTP server, but you can also store Web pages on a different file server (such as a gopher server, an FTP server, or a corporate network). You can keep HTML files on your personal computer's hard drive, but then no one else will be able to read them.

You can also publish Web pages on an intranet so that only people who are in your organization will be able to see your Web pages.

There's a huge variety of Web pages out there. Some types of Web pages include:

- Personal home pages describe individuals and their hobbies, interests, and projects (and posting your résumé on your personal Web page is a popular way of increasing exposure).

- Business home pages describe a business and its products or services, much like a brochure, and can also allow customers to purchase products or receive customer service.

- Directories, such as Yahoo!, WebCrawler, or Excite, list other Web pages by category.

- Search engines, such as Lycos, AltaVista, or HotBot, create huge indexes to the Web and allow you to make keyword searches for topics that interest you.

- Artistic projects, which are pages created by artists or museums, contain interesting or provocative words, images, or multimedia.

Web pages have many advantages over traditional media. They're easy to update and relatively inexpensive to maintain. Also, Web pages provide an efficient method for distributing information, files, and software. And all of this happens while you're reaching a wider, and global, audience.

In short, Web pages are many things to many people—but the one thing all Web pages have common is their underlying structure, which is written in HTML.

Earlier you read that publishing a Web page can give you global exposure. You may be wondering, "How would someone find my home page?" Well, it happens the same way they would find your house: with an address (in this case, it's called a *URL*).

Getting There: URLs

A *URL* (pronounced either as three separate letters or less frequently as "earl") is a Uniform Resource Locator. Simply speaking, it's an address for a Web page or any other file on the Internet.

Every URL on the Web is unique. Since URLs vary in format quite a bit and express a lot of different information, and since you'll need to completely understand URLs in order to link your pages to other pages on the Web, it's worth taking some time to explain them thoroughly. The best way to learn about URLs is to see them in action, so we'll look at plenty of examples in the next few sections.

Understanding Simple URLs

URLs follow a particular syntax. All URLs must be accurate; even one wrong letter or mistyped period will prevent it from working—much like using the wrong street or apartment number when you send a letter through the post office. One wrong letter in a URL, depending on where in the address it appears, could bring you to an entirely different Web page, or it could just result in an error message—just like getting a letter returned to you. There are several types of URLs, and we'll start with the simplest URLs for Web pages.

Simple Web page URLs consist of the name of the Web protocol (http), followed by a colon, followed by two forward slashes, followed by a domain name, and ending with a final slash. The *domain name* is the Internet name of the computer that is serving the information.

Let's look at a simple URL:

```
http://www.loc.gov/
```

This URL is for the Library of Congress. It specifies that this resource is served using the HTTP protocol, and that the name of the site is www.loc.gov (which refers to a machine named www in the subdomain named loc in the domain named gov). Type this URL into your Web browser and you'll see the home page for the Library of Congress.

 NOTE   Navigator and other browsers let you abbreviate URLs a little bit. For example, just typing www.loc.gov (without the http://) into Navigator's Location box would get you to the right place. However, when you create Web pages, you must always specify the full and exact URL in your links.

Domain names are not case-sensitive. HTTP://WWW.LOC.GOV/ and Http://Www.Loc.Gov/ both mean the same as http://www.loc.gov/.

This second example URL is for AltaVista, a search engine created and sponsored by the Digital Equipment Corporation:

```
http://www.altavista.digital.com/
```

Note that this domain name has four segments—when you interpret it, move from right to left: com indicates that we're looking in the commercial domain. Next, digital is the name of the company that is serving the home page we're looking for; altavista is the area or *subdomain* that has the specific information we want. Finally, www is the name of computer in the AltaVista subdomain that will actually send the information to us.

> **NOTE**
>
> There are six common generic top-level domains ("TLDs" or "gTLDs") for the United States. The .com domain is for commercial entities, .org is for organizations (including non-profit groups), .net is for network companies, .gov is for government agencies, .mil is for military divisions, and .edu is for educational institutions, including schools, colleges, and universities. New TLDs have been proposed, such as .web, .store, .firm, and .art. These new TLDs are not yet in use and may take a while to catch on when they've been approved.

Most U.S. sites use one of the TLDs, but a few geographic Web sites, like http://www.ci.berkeley.ca.us/, use the United States' country code instead of a generic top-level domain. This example has the United States' country code (us), as well as a state code (ca), a city name (berkeley), the special code for official city information (ci), and the name of a Web server (www). This URL would take you to the City of Berkeley's Civic Network (see Figure 1.6).

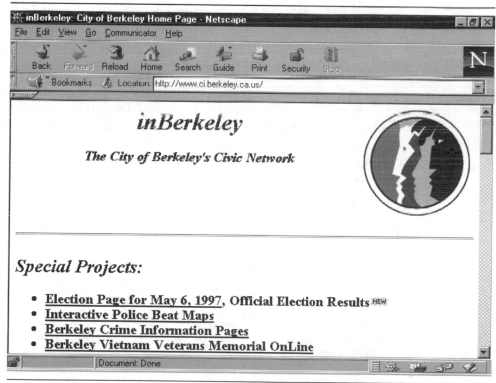

FIGURE 1.6: The City of Berkeley's Civic Network

This is a URL for Cambridge University (cam) in the United Kingdom (uk): http://www.cam.ac.uk/. The ac segment stands for "academic." As you can see, the United Kingdom subdomains are classified with different codes than United States top-level domains. There's a Cambridge College in Cambridge, Massachusetts with the URL http://www.cambridge.edu/—but don't confuse them!

 NOTE   Every country, including the United States, has a two-letter top-level domain code. You can find a list of these country codes on the Web, such as at http://www.aldea.com/bluepages/domain.html.

Not every Web server is called www, although the majority of them are. Many sites have lots of different servers, with the main or most official server being called www and the other ones with a name that reflects its function. For example, to see the official home page for Toyota, you'd visit http://www.toyota.com/. But Toyota has set up another server for the home page of their Owners Club, and that server is called owners, so the Owners Club's URL is http://owners.toyota.com/.

URLs with Account Names

The simple URLs we've seen are fine if you want to go to the main page of a domain. But often you want to go to the page created by a specific user at a particular domain. Web sites for ISPs, universities, and companies often have many different users, each with their own account. To choose a particular account, you add the *account name* to the end of the URL. Account names typically begin with a tilde (~). There's a big difference between going to http://www.pobox.com/ and http://www.pobox.com/~xian/—the first address shows you the home page for pobox itself, which lists their services and rates. The second address goes to the home page for someone whose account name is xian.

Any simple URL can have an account name added to the end. But not every Web site has different home pages for different accounts—it depends if the company lets employees create home pages, or if the domain is for an Internet service provider that lets its users create home pages. The rule of thumb is always to include the account name in the URL if you know it, but to leave it off if you want the general home page for the domain. Let's see some examples to learn how this works.

This is URL for Janan Platt's AlienFlower Poetry Workshop:

    http://www.sonic.net/~janan/

sonic is a subdomain in the net domain. Most sites that end in net are for ISPs or other network companies. If you go to `http://www.sonic.net/`, you'll get Sonic's home page, and find out that Sonic is an ISP in Sonoma County, California.

This URL is different from the ones in the previous section because it contains an account name that leads to a particular person's account area—in this case the `janan` area. This URL tells us to first look at the `net` domain in order to look up the `sonic` subdomain, and then asks for information in the `janan` account from the computer named `www` that is part of Sonic's network.

The `janan` account belongs to Janan Platt. Janan has a Web page here that is hosted by Sonic. Even though Janan's URL has Sonic's name in it, that doesn't mean that Janan works for Sonic or has any relationship with them other than as a customer of Web service.

 **WARNING**

Although domain names are not case-sensitive, many account names *are* case-sensitive. You can go to either `http://www.sonic.net/` or `HTTP://WWW.SONIC.NET/` and see the same page for Sonic. But if you try to go to `HTTP://WWW.SONIC.NET/~JANAN/` or `HTTP://WWW.SONIC.NET/~Janan/` instead of `HTTP://WWW.SONIC.NET/~janan/`, you'll get the dreaded "404 Document Not Found" error.

This URL is for something called Zeigen's Dilemma:

`http://www.emf.net/~estephen/`

which is E. Stephen Mack's home page. This URL also uses the tilde character (~). The tilde character means "home of" and the name that follows is the name of a particular account. So this URL means "go to the Internet service provider named EMF.NET and then show me the home page owned by the account named estephen."

IP Addresses in URLs

Some URLs vary from the examples we've seen up until now by including a series of numbers for the domain name. These specially formatted numbers are called *numerical IP addresses*.

Internally, each computer on the Internet is represented by a series of four numbers separated by a period; these numbers are called the *IP address*. Whenever you type in a domain name, like `ibm.com`, a search is done through a domain name server (DNS) to translate your name request into its numerical IP equivalent. (For example, the machine known as `ibm.com` has an IP address of 129.34.139.30. Whenever you refer to `ibm.com`, your DNS looks up the numerical address for `ibm.com`). Once the numerical address is looked up, your request can be sent along the Internet.

Sometimes you'll see URLs that use IP addresses instead of domain names, as in this example:

`http://205.226.156.5/`

This URL shows the numerical IP address of a machine. Using a special DNS program lookup tool, you could find out that this IP address is equivalent to the domain name of `www.accesscom.com`, so the URL `http://www.accesscom.com/` is equivalent to the numerical address.

When you use URLs, you can include either the numerical IP address or domain name (you have to have one or the other)—but domain names are much easier to remember, of course. Domain names are more reliable, since IP addresses can change from time to time. On the other hand, numerical IP addresses are a little faster since there's no lookup involved. And sometimes the domain name servers are not working, so a domain name URL wouldn't work while a numerical IP address URL would work. Overall, though, you'll find that IP addresses are not used nearly as often as domain names.

URLs with Pathnames and Filenames

URLs often refer to a specific pathname and filename. A *pathname* is a sequence of one or more directories and subdirectories, each separated by a slash. A *filename* is the name of a particular file, including its extension.

Some URLs, such as `http://www.sonic.net/web/`, include only a single pathname appended to the regular URL. This URL retrieves Janan Platt's home page. (In this case `web` happens to have been set up to be a synonym for `~janan.`) You can keep adding directory names to the path. For example, `http://www.sonic.net/web/albany/workshop/` first opens the `web` directory, then the `albany` directory, and finally a directory named `workshop`.

A large number of URLs refer to a particular file, and most of those files are HTML files:

`http://www.emf.net/~estephen/facts/lefthand.html`

This URL builds on an earlier example, by specifying that the file to be retrieved is named `lefthand.html` (case is critical here) and it resides in a directory named `facts` (again, case is vital). This URL is for "Being Left-Handed," which is part of Zeigen's Dilemma.

Even though most URLs refer to Web pages (files with an extension of `.html`), you can use URLs to point to any type of file:

`http://calbears.berkeley.edu/images/scrptgld.gif`

This example URL would display an image called `scrptgld.gif`, which is located in a directory called `images` on a server called `calbears` in the `berkeley.edu` domain.

> **NOTE**
> It's common for people to leave off the final slash in a URL like `http://www.ibm.com/` since most URLs still work without it. Technically, you need that final slash, and some URLs *don't* work properly without it. But watch out for the exception: URLs that end with the name of a specific file (such as `proteus.html`, `scrptgld.gif`, and `lefthand.html` in the previous examples) should *never* have a final slash. The rule is that any URL that *doesn't* end with a filename *should* have a slash at the end.

URLs with Port Numbers

Some URLs need to include a port number to work properly. The port number comes right after the domain name, and it's a number preceded by a colon. Most URLs don't have port numbers, which is easier to remember. But you might be saddled with a Web server that requires a port to be specified in your URL.

This URL, for Episode 7 (`e7`) of the award-winning online magazine called *Enterzone* (`ez`), shows the use of a port number after the domain name (the colon followed by 1080):

```
http://ezone.org:1080/ez/e7/
```

Port numbers are required on certain Web servers, usually when additional Web sites are being hosted on the same server. Since *Enterzone* is hosted by the American Arts and Letters Network (AALN), you can't get *Enterzone* by entering the plain URL of `http://ezone.org/` (that will get you AALN instead)—instead, you have to use the URL `http://ezone.org:1080/` to go to the right place.

Another distinctive feature of *Enterzone*'s URL is that there is no need for a machine name of www at the front of the domain name. Many URLs don't require the www machine name; some URLs work either way. But some URLs don't work if you put the www in front. The only way to know which URL is correct is to try it in Navigator or another browser.

Different Protocols in URLs

All of the URLs up until now have started with `http:` because they are Web pages and HTML documents. But URLs can point to parts of the Internet other than just the Web.

FTP is the File Transfer Protocol, used to quickly transfer files from one computer to another. Just as most Web servers are located on machines named www, most FTP servers are located on machines named `ftp` (`ftp://ftp.winsite.com/`). This URL goes to the FTP site of a Windows software archive named `winsite.com`, using the protocol named `ftp`.

This URL, `ftp://ftp.netscape.com/pub/navigator/3.01/windows/n32e301p.exe`, points to a specific filename and path from Netscape's FTP server.

At risk of getting a little too complex, you can also add user information to an FTP URL (`ftp://joe@ftp.accesscom.com/./www/`). By specifying `joe@` in front of the domain name, you are specifying that you want to log in as the user named `joe`.

The period by itself in between slashes is a special shortcut to `joe`'s normal directory. This URL (when the correct password is supplied) would display a list of the files in `joe`'s Web directory. A URL like this one can be used to publish Web pages from your computer; there's much more information about publishing in Skill 18.

This URL is for an e-mail address, to the President of the United States: `mailto:president@whitehouse.gov`. Mailto URLs are commonly used as a way of letting readers send e-mail to the creator of a Web page by simply following a mailto link to the creator's e-mail address.

 NOTE You can recognize e-mail addresses because they always have an at sign (@) that separates the name of the person from the person's domain name.

This last example URL is for a Usenet newsgroup where World Wide Web announcements are posted: `news:comp.infosystems.www.announce`.

Note that both mailto and news URLs don't include the two slashes between the protocol name and the specific part after the colon. URLs are full of strange exceptions, so it's a good idea to know the rules.

Rules for URLs

The format for a URL is:

```
protocol:address
```

Depending on the protocol you use, the address will vary. For the http protocol, URLs look like this:

```
http://sitename:port/~username/path/filename
```

The sitename is either a domain name or a numerical IP address. The port number is not required in most URLs, so you can safely skip it if you don't know it. Similarly, the username, path, and filename parts are not required for every URL. For other protocols, use a protocol keyword from Table 1.1.

TABLE 1.1: A List of Protocols Used in URLs

Protocol Keyword	Description
ftp://	File Transfer Protocol
http://	Hypertext Transfer Protocol
gopher://	Gopher protocol
mailto:	Electronic mail address (doesn't require two slashes)
news:	Usenet newsgroup (doesn't require two slashes)
telnet:	Interactive session using the Telnet protocol (doesn't require two slashes)
file://	Local filename

File protocols have a structure that depends on your computer system. We're not going to discuss them in detail in this book since your browser can supply them automatically whenever you open a local file.

URLs never have spaces in them, and if you're copying a URL from a newspaper, be careful about extraneous dashes—sometimes a newspaper will inadvertently stick in a dash because the URL is too long to fit on a single line. Also, don't confuse a period or comma that's part of a sentence as being part of a URL. In this book, we'll try to list URLs in parentheses to avoid confusion.

That was a lot of information about URLs, but working with HTML requires a thorough understanding of all of the points made here. (We'll see more about URLs, including some shortcuts for them, when we learn about how to create links in Skill 7.) Now that we've gotten URLs out of the way, we'll learn exactly what a .html extension means.

What Is HTML?

HTML stands for Hypertext Markup Language. Let's take each of those words in sequence.

Hypertext is ordinary text that has been dressed up with extra features, such as formatting, images, multimedia, and links to other documents.

Markup is the process of taking ordinary text and adding extra symbols (for example, an editor's proofreading symbols are a type of markup). Each of the symbols used for markup in HTML is a command that tells a browser how to display the text. Markup can be very simple, or it can be very complicated. Either way, the underlying text being marked up is always present and viewable.

Language is actually a key point to remember about HTML. HTML is a computer language, related to computer programming languages (like BASIC, C, and Pascal). HTML has its own syntax, slang, and rules for proper communication.

Markup languages are a special type of computer language because they are solely concerned with classifying the parts of a document according to their function—in other words, indicating which part is the title of the document, which part is a subheading, which part is the name of the author, and so on. It's not really correct to speak of "programming HTML" because HTML isn't really a programming language. Instead, HTML is a markup language that has a different goal than creating a program.

Understanding HTML's Main Goal

The main goal of HTML is to be a universal language for classifying the function of different sections of a document. In other words, HTML is used to define the different parts of your page. You indicate which part of your document is a title, which part of your document is an address, which part of your document should be emphasized, which part of your document should include an image, and so forth.

HTML is neither a page-layout language nor a printing language. The only thing HTML does is classify parts of your document so that a browser can display it correctly. This allows documents to be displayed on many different kinds of platforms.

 NOTE   Your *platform* is the combination of computer hardware and operating system that you use. You could be using a Windows platform (the combination of an IBM-compatible PC and Microsoft Windows), a Mac platform (a Macintosh computer and operating system), a UNIX platform, or something entirely different. If something is *cross-platform*, it works on more than one specific platform.

Although HTML has evolved to the point that it contains many layout and formatting commands, these functions are secondary to HTML's role in classifying the logical parts of your documents.

The important thing to remember is that HTML is designed to work on a wide variety of platforms. Not just ordinary personal-computer platforms like PCs and Macintoshes (although that's enough of a trick in and of itself), but HTML is also designed to work on a wide variety of graphical workstations, "dumb" (that is, text-only) terminals, network computers, hand-held devices, and much more.

The idea behind HTML is that if you mark up your document by indicating the parts of your document by function, then you should be able to trust that your document will be attractively and correctly displayed by any browser on any computer anywhere in the world.

This means that HTML can be used to put a document on not just computer screens, but also printers, fax machines, TV sets, game consoles, Braille devices, digital watches, and text-to-speech machines. Imagine, for example, a browser that accepts input from the touch-tone buttons on a telephone, and then reads a Web page back to you over the phone.

THE WEB DESIGNER AS AUTHOR

Since HTML lets you create documents that are viewable all over the world over a wide range of devices, you have to be flexible in your design and let go of the idea of having absolute control over a document's appearance. For an analogy, it's helpful to think of the relationship between an author and a publisher. Warren Steel, a Web author and professor at the University of Mississippi, puts this concept very eloquently in his "Hints for Web Authors" (http://www.mcsr.olemiss.edu/~mudws/webhints.html).

"A Web author is not a programmer, nor a typographer, nor a graphic designer. Since the days of Gutenberg, authors have learned to 'let go' of their cherished work ('Farewell, sweet book') when they deliver their manuscript to the publisher. The author's manuscript may include chapters, paragraphs, headings, tables, and illustrations, all clearly marked, but it is the editor who chooses the paper, page design, fonts, and other characteristics, according to a 'house style.' In the same way, a Web author prepares a document by marking up the elements, and then 'sends it to the publisher' by placing it on a Web server. The function of the editor is shared between the browser, which renders the text and graphics on the available hardware, and the human being who views the document. It is the user who configures the browser by choosing the fonts, sizes, and colors and other features of the onscreen appearance.

continued ▶

"This is the great strength of the World Wide Web. On a non-graphic browser, the user can view text descriptions in place of the invisible images. On a graphic browser, a nearsighted user can control the size of the fonts; a colorblind user can choose colors that offer enough contrast for legibility. A user on a slow line, say a dialup, can disable graphic loading, only displaying graphics individually when they contain essential information. A blind user can listen to a Web document when rendered by a speech synthesizer, or read it by means of a Braille browser. In every case, the structure of the document is the same, but the renderings are customized for the individual."

Some HTML designers neglect the logical structure of HTML and concentrate on simply making pages that look neat. However, it would be a shame if the useful information on their pages couldn't be used by a blind user with a text-to-speech Web browser. In this book, we'll teach you how to create HTML pages that are both structurally correct (and thus accessible) as well as attractive.

Why Learn HTML?

There are plenty of advantages to knowing HTML:

- **Flexibility** You can always work on your Web site even when you're away from the computer you usually work on, because no matter which computer you end up using, it will always have a text editor you can use to edit the raw HTML. You're not dependent on a particular piece of software that may not be available to you.

- **Deeper understanding** You will have a much better concept of the structure of your page and understanding of why it works the way it does, because you built the page from the ground up.

- **Troubleshooting** Since you wrote the HTML, you'll be able to troubleshoot it efficiently and have a better idea of what techniques to try if something's not working.

- **Price** Using HTML doesn't cost you a cent. There are no expensive licenses to buy and no annoying upgrades to purchase.

- **Independence** You're not stuck to any one vendor or any one program; you don't have to worry about bugs in a particular editing program or any companies going out of business and leaving you stranded.

There's no big trick to learning HTML. It's much simpler than any programming language, and several orders of magnitude simpler than human languages like French or Japanese. The reason why the Web is so popular and has such diverse content is because it was easy for so many people to learn HTML and create Web pages. You'll create your first HTML document in the very next Skill. All it takes is learning HTML's commands, which are called *tags*.

HTML's Incredible, Invisible Tags

A *tag* is a unit of markup, a set of symbols defined in HTML to have special meaning. Tags start with a less-than sign (<) followed by a keyword, and conclude with a greater-than sign (>). (These symbols are known as *angle brackets*.) For example, these are all tags:

```
<Strong>
<img>
<TITLE>
</B>
<html>
```

Every tag in HTML has a meaning, and it's usually pretty straightforward. For example, <B> is a tag that means to switch on bold, and <HR> is a tag that inserts a horizontal rule (a *rule* is just a fancy name for a decorative line).

NOTE   Tags are not case-sensitive, so <Title>, <title>, <TITLE> and <tItLE> all have the same meaning. (In this book, we'll put tags in uppercase so they stand out more clearly.)

Understanding Start Tags and End Tags

There are two types of tags: *Start tags* are used to begin an effect, and *end tags* are used to end that effect. End tags always repeat the keyword with a slash in front.

For example, text to be displayed in bold is enclosed between the <B> start tag and </B> end tag, like this:

```
I hope to <B>shout</B> at the moon all night.
```

This HTML code will be displayed with the word "shout" in bold, as in Figure 1.7.

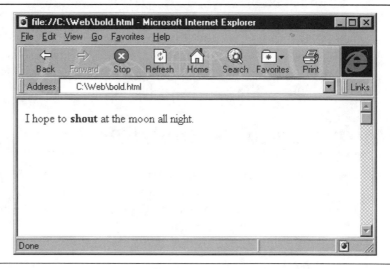

FIGURE 1.7: A line of text with the word "shout" in bold; the <B> and </B> tags themselves are invisible.

Similarly, <TITLE> indicates the beginning of a document's title, and </TITLE> indicates the end of the title, like this:

```
<TITLE>Dr. Strangelove or: How I Learned to Stop Worrying and Love the
Bomb</TITLE>
```

 WARNING   If you're a Windows user, you may be used to typing backslashes (\). Be sure to break that habit when you start using HTML. You'll never use a backslash in HTML—it's all forward slashes. Also, be careful to put the slash in *front* of the tag's name, not after it: <B/> doesn't work to end bolding, only </B> does.

Tags can be nested within each other, so if <B> is for bold and <I> is for italic, then you can combine them like this:

```
To be or not to be, <B><I>that</I></B> is the question
```

The word "that" will appear in both bold and italic. Notice that the italic start and end tags are contained completely within the bold tags.

Understanding Tag Attributes

Many start tags can take attributes that affect the tag's behavior. An *attribute* is a keyword separated by a space within the angle brackets, such as <HR NOSHADE> (which calls for an unshaded horizontal rule). Some attributes require a value, preceded by an equals sign, such as <HR WIDTH="200"> (which calls for a horizontal rule that is 200 units wide).

In a browser, the tags themselves are not displayed but their effect is. Any tags and attributes that are unknown are ignored. For example, a <HYPNOTIC> tag is not defined in HTML. The following HTML code

```
In 1993, <B><I>Wizco</I></B> first offered <HYPNOTIC>Amazing 3-D
Glasses</HYPNOTIC> to the general public.
```

would display as shown in Figure 1.8, with no special formatting for the words "Amazing 3-D Glasses."

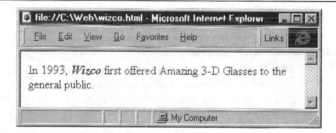

FIGURE 1.8: Gee, IE doesn't seem to make the words "Amazing 3-D Glasses" display hypnotically.

We'll teach you how to use each tag, along with any attributes for that tag, as we introduce and describe them throughout this book. In addition, the appendix contains a complete reference for every HTML tag.

You'll get a taste of how tags actually work when we create a quick example HTML document in the next Skill. But before you rush into building your first Web page, it's nice to know a little bit about HTML's history and what you can expect.

Understanding Some HTML History and Perspective

HTML is evolving quickly. It's helpful to know where it's coming from and which way it's heading. That way, if someone throws out the term "SGML" or talks about "HTML 2.0" you'll know what they're talking about. By understanding the past versions of HTML, you'll also have a better idea of why HTML behaves the way it does now, and you'll get an idea of what you can expect from future versions of HTML.

Who Invented HTML and Who Controls It?

HTML and the Web were first conceived in 1989 by a researcher named Tim Berners-Lee who worked for CERN, the European Laboratory for Particle Physics in Geneva, Switzerland. CERN researchers developed the first World Wide Web programs in 1990 and began releasing programs and specifications to Internet users in 1991. In 1992, there were only 26 Web servers; by mid-1994 there were more than 1,500. Suddenly, by the end of 1994, there were more than 10,000 Web servers. From there, the Web began to really take off: Millions of servers are operating today.

 NOTE   The Web supplanted an existing technology of linked information, called *gopher*. Gopher was a text-only global set of linked menus and files. There are still quite a few gopher servers around, but gopher is almost extinct now.

The Web pioneers, led by Berners-Lee, regrouped into the World Wide Web Consortium (W3C) in December 1994. The W3C is now responsible for the standards of HTTP, HTML, and other Web technologies.

You can find the W3C's home page at http://www.w3.org/ (see Figure 1.9).

Even though the W3C is responsible for HTML standards, they don't necessarily control HTML. Vendors such as Microsoft, Netscape, Hewlett-Packard, SGI, and Sun work with the W3C to develop HTML; and standards only work if people agree to abide by them.

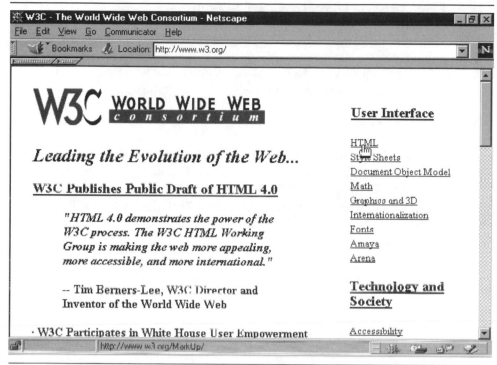

FIGURE 1.9: The people at the World Wide Web Consortium (W3C), responsible for the standards of HTML, report any new developments at their Web site.

SGML

HTML is one member (and easily the most popular member at that) of a family of markup languages called *SGML*, which stands for Standard Generalized Markup Language. SGML was developed by the International Organization for Standards in 1986 to define markup languages designed for various different purposes.

Every language in the SGML family conforms to certain requirements, the main one being that all of the symbols are strictly defined and described using a DTD, or Document Type Definition. The DTD for HTML defines what tags are available and how they can be used. The DTD answers the tricky questions about tags, such as the order in which tags can be used.

The Many Versions of HTML

HTML has evolved quite a bit since its first appearance. We'll briefly present each of the versions of HTML to give you some historical perspective. If you're anxious to build a Web page right away, you might want to head on over to Skill 2 now and come back to this section when you have the time.

HTML

The first version of HTML was not called HTML 1.0—it was just called HTML. This first version of HTML is not dissimilar to the most recent version that we cover in this book. The basic tags have not changed much, and any document written for the original version of HTML would still be usable today. (HTML has tried to stay *backward-compatible* so that new versions of HTML don't contradict old versions.)

The original HTML was never in wide use since it appeared at a time when there were only a few dozen Web servers in existence and most Web authors knew one another personally.

The first version of HTML was an excellent early attempt, and subsequent versions of HTML built on its foundation. Although HTML has always had its critics, its wild success is testament to its ability to fill a need.

HTML+

Dave Raggett worked on a successor to HTML called HTML+ in 1993. Although HTML+ was never an official specification, many of its ideas were incorporated into HTML 2.0.

HTML 2.0

A specification for HTML 2.0 was created in July 1994, and after editing by Dan Connolly, HTML 2.0 became a standard approved by the IETF (Internet Engineering Task Force) in November 1994. Consisting of most of the tags that are in use today, HTML 2.0 was more consistent and a little easier to use than HTML. HTML 2.0 was the first popular version of HTML, and the massive explosion of Web popularity took place from late 1994 to 1995 using Web pages written in HTML 2.0.

HTML 2.0 was extremely easy to learn and proved to be popular with a wide range of Web authors, who at that time were mostly students and engineers. As the Web became more popular, more professional designers took an interest, and HTML 2.0 was criticized for not containing more formatting commands.

Proprietary Extensions to HTML

Since HTML 2.0 did not contain many formatting commands (after all, formatting was not HTML's purpose), some vendors, particularly Netscape, became impatient with the pace of HTML's development. When the first version of Navigator was released in 1994, it was designed to accept certain non-standard tags (for example, tags that allowed text to blink and be centered, among other things). Newer versions of Navigator continued to add proprietary tags. When IE arrived on the scene in mid-1995, Microsoft played the same game, adding tags that were only supported by IE.

These tags, called *extensions* to HTML, were introduced despite the fact that the W3C never approved them. Many existing browsers, such as Mosaic and Lynx, did not support the tags, and a period of incompatibility dawned.

Some of the extensions to HTML 2.0 were eventually approved and incorporated into HTML 3.2. Some tags are still considered non-standard and are not as widely supported.

 NOTE   In this book, we'll let you know which tags are safe to use and which are dangerous to use because of compatibility issues.

The Orphan: HTML 3.0

Along the way to HTML 3.2, there was a slight detour: HTML 3.0, the abandoned prodigal stepdaughter. HTML 3.0, drafted in March 1995, was different from HTML 2.0. It provided many additional options over previous versions of HTML, including tables, math, and a new way of handling graphics.

Unfortunately, HTML 3.0 was too big a change for most Web authors, and it was never supported by the two most popular browsers. HTML 3.0 never became an official specification, and its new design approaches and new tags never caught on. (This book does not cover the new tags and attributes proposed by HTML 3.0 since they were never in wide use and never became an official standard.) The W3C specification for HTML 3.0 expired without ever having been approved—instead, HTML 3.2 replaced it completely.

HTML 3.2

HTML 3.2, originally codenamed "Wilbur," became finalized in January 1997. But it was popular and in use since its first release in May of 1996. (The W3C releases specifications of HTML during development; the actual standards approval process is quite drawn-out.)

HTML 3.2 was immediately popular, mostly because it supported existing practices in a logical way and was more compatible with HTML 2.0. It added support for tables and helped make many practices more consistent. IE 3 and Netscape 3 supported HTML 3.2 almost completely.

HTML 4.0

Codenamed "Cougar," HTML 4.0 is the latest version of HTML. Like HTML 3.2, HTML 4.0 incorporates common practices of Web design and formalizes some tags and HTML features (such as frames) that were previously extensions to HTML 3.2. We'll learn about frames in Skill 11.

The largest difference between HTML 4.0 and previous versions of HTML is the character set. Instead of allowing only a limited range of international characters, HTML 4.0 uses a character set called "Unicode" that allows thousands of different characters. We'll see Unicode, along with HTML's previous character set, which was called "Latin-1," in Skill 3.

Because of Unicode, HTML 4.0 takes strides in increasing the Web's usefulness for international users. HTML 4.0 also makes it easier for Web authors to create Web pages that are accessible to surfers with disabilities.

HTML 4.0's specification (which was edited by Dave Raggett, Arnaud Le Hors, and Ian Jacobs) strongly encourages the use of style sheets. A style sheet controls the appearance of a document. Since the style sheet can take of things like aligning text and formatting the appearance of fonts, HTML 4.0 discourages those HTML tags and attributes that are solely for formatting, visual appearance, and layout. We'll explain how to use style sheets in Skill 14, and throughout this book we'll indicate which HTML tags are not recommended.

HTML 4.0 also introduces the <OBJECT> tag, which is used to present multimedia (such as movies and sounds). We'll learn how to use the <OBJECT> tag in Skill 9.

Another goal of HTML 4.0 is to allow for richer, more flexible and interactive pages thanks to dynamic HTML and scripting. We'll see scripting in Skill 15 and Dynamic HTML in Skill 16. We'll learn about the future of HTML in Skill 20.

As HTML develops, better authoring tools will appear. Perhaps someday people won't need to know anything about HTML to create the most cutting-edge Web sites. For a while, though, the best HTML tool is a thorough knowledge of HTML tags and a good text editor. The next two Skills will teach you the basics of HTML. After that, we'll examine what HTML tools are available and help you decide what tools you might want to use to develop your Web pages.

Are You Experienced?

Now you can...

☑ understand the basic concepts behind the Internet and the World Wide Web

☑ recognize a Web page and Web browser

☑ use URLs and understand their formats

☑ keep in mind what HTML is and what HTML isn't

☑ tell what tags look like

☑ discuss the history of HTML knowledgeably with your friends

Starting with HTML Basics

- ➔ Creating our first HTML example
- ➔ Saving and viewing HTML pages
- ➔ Introducing HTML's basic structure
- ➔ Learning the commonly used HTML elements
- ➔ Viewing source
- ➔ Nesting elements

Skill 1 gave you a background of the Internet and the World Wide Web; it also presented HTML's philosophy and introduced HTML tags. In this Skill, we will create our first HTML document, using the traditional "Hello, World" example often used in teaching programming languages. We'll see HTML's basic structure tags (<HTML>, <HEAD>, <TITLE>, and <BODY>) in order to learn how HTML pages should be organized. Also in this Skill, we'll cover a broad range of the most commonly used HTML tags so you can "get your hands dirty."

Hello, World: Our First HTML Example

Let's hit the ground running and actually make a Web page. In teaching computer programming languages like C and Pascal, it's traditional to show how to create a "Hello, World" program—a program that simply puts the words "Hello, World" on the screen. Even though HTML isn't a programming language in the same league as C and Pascal, we'll still follow that tradition by creating a "Hello, World" HTML document.

Creating the HTML Code

To create this HTML example, just start your text editor and type in the following HTML code, which we'll refer to as `hello.html`.

 **hello.html**

```
<HTML>
<HEAD>
<TITLE>A Hello World Example in HTML</TITLE>
</HEAD>
<BODY>
Hello, World!
</BODY>
</HTML>
```

Netscape Navigator will display this code as a simple page, as shown in Figure 2.1.

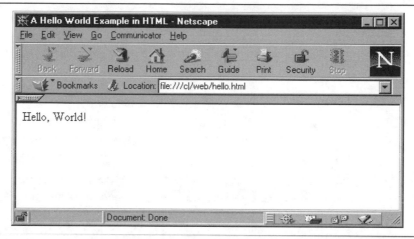

FIGURE 2.1: Navigator shows our "Hello, World" example (typed into Notepad and saved as `hello.html`). Notice how the title in the title bar corresponds to the text in between the `<TITLE>` and `</TITLE>` tags.

Microsoft Internet Explorer would show the page in exactly the same way.

WHICH TEXT EDITOR SHOULD YOU USE?

A text editor is a simple word processor: It only works with plain text—text editors don't do any character formatting. Your computer's operating system usually includes a rudimentary text editor, so the text editor you use depends on what kind of computer you're using.

You may want to use a different text editor than the one your operating system offers; we'll cover text editors in detail in Skill 4.

Here are some basic text editor instructions for some commonly used operating systems:

DOS

If you're using Microsoft DOS or another version of DOS, you'll probably have access to a text editor called Edit. (If you're using a really old version of DOS, your editor is Edlin, and you'll definitely want to get a different text editor, since Edlin is frustrating to use.)

continued ▶

To create a file named hello.htm, type **edit hello.htm** (you won't be able to call your file hello.html since DOS limits file extensions to three letters).

To get help with Edit, select Alt+H or press F1.

Windows

In any version of Windows, use the Notepad editor (which is in the Accessories group). You can get help with Notepad through the F1 command or the Help menu.

For Windows 3 users, you'll open the Accessories group and then double-click on the Notepad icon. When you save your document, you'll need to call it hello.htm instead of hello.html, since file extensions are limited to three letters in old versions of Windows.

For Windows 95 or later, click on the Start menu, choose Programs ➤ Accessories ➤ Notepad.

Macintosh

On a Mac, use SimpleText or TeachText (they're just the same, except that SimpleText is used on newer Macintosh systems). Get help by switching on Balloon Help.

UNIX

In the UNIX world, you could try the joe, pico, vi, or emacs editors (in order from simplest to most powerful). You may need to get help from the man command (for example, man vi).

Our "Hello, World" document uses eight basic structure tags: <HTML>, <HEAD>, <TITLE>, </TITLE>, </HEAD>, <BODY>, </BODY>, and </HTML>. Basic structure tags are the building blocks for everything else, so it's important you understand them. When creating an HTML document, people typically use the basic structure tags in the following order:

1. Start your document with the <HTML> tag, which declares you are writing an HTML document.

 NOTE   HTML documents contain two sections: the head section, which describes the document, and the body section, which contains the document itself. Both of these are discussed in later sections of this Skill. In addition, Skill 5 is all about the head section, and Skill 6 is all about the body section.

2. To start the head section, use the <HEAD> tag.

3. Inside the head section is the title of the document (notice how Navigator displays the document's title in the title bar at the top of the window). Start the title with the <TITLE> tag. Immediately after that (with no extra spaces), type the title you want for your document.

4. To close the title you need to use an end tag. As we described in Skill 1, end tags start with a slash. End tags are critical—if you leave off a required end tag, your document might not display at all. To end the title, use the </TITLE> tag. Again, don't put any spaces between the title itself and the end title tag.

5. To finish the head section, use another end tag, the </HEAD> tag.

6. Next, start the body section with the <BODY> tag.

7. Type the text of your document, and then close the body section with the </BODY> tag.

8. Finally, end your document with the </HTML> tag.

These tags are contained (or *nested*) within each other. The <HTML> and </HTML> tags contain the <HEAD> and </HEAD> tags, which in turn contain the <TITLE> and </TITLE> tags. Similarly, the body of your document is contained in the body section's <BODY> and </BODY> tags, which in turn are nested within the <HTML> and </HTML> tags. Figure 2.2 shows a diagram of an HTML document's basic structure and its nesting.

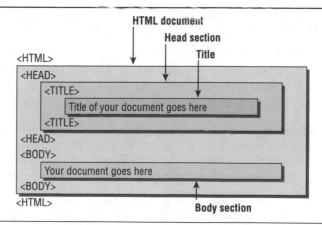

FIGURE 2.2: The basic structure of an HTML document, with elements nested inside each other in the proper order

We'll return to the topic of nesting toward the end of this Skill in "HTML's Rules of Nesting." Also, we'll be examining each of the eight basic structure tags in detail a little bit later.

When typing in the code, you don't really have to worry about the case of the HTML tags, although it's a good idea to be consistent—if you stick to a uniform case, it will make your HTML code much easier to understand. We used all caps for the tags in `hello.html` because tags stand out more clearly that way; many Web designers use all caps, but plenty use lowercase as well—it's a matter of personal preference.

Furthermore, it doesn't really matter for this example what text you put in between the <TITLE> and </TITLE> tags (you could put your name or any phrase that describes this document). You could also substitute any text you desire for "Hello, World!" For example, you could type "Welcome to Cyberdyne Systems!" and then whatever text you typed will be displayed instead of "Hello, World!"

Once you've typed in the HTML code, save the text file as `hello.html`. (If you're using an older DOS or Windows 3 system that doesn't support four-letter extensions, save it as `hello.htm` instead.)

TIP   If you're using Windows 95, make sure you're not hiding MS-DOS Extensions. Otherwise, Notepad will always save files with an extension of `.txt`—so that `hello.html` will be incorrectly saved as `hello.html.txt`. To check whether extensions are displayed, double-click on My Computer, use the View ➤ Options menu command, click on the View tab, and make sure there is *not* a check mark next to Hide MS-DOS File Extensions for File Types That Are Registered. Then choose OK.

Viewing the HTML Page in a Browser

To view the results of this HTML code in a browser, run Navigator, or whatever browser you have access to, and use the File ➤ Open Page command, or whatever seems closest. (With Navigator Gold 3, the command is File ➤ Open File in Browser; with IE, the command is simply File ➤ Open.)

TIP   For many browsers, the shortcut for the File ➤ Open command is Ctrl+O. (That's the letter "O" as in "Open," not the number 0.)

As a shortcut, try to open the folder or directory where you saved `hello.html` and then double-click on the filename. (If you're on a UNIX system, typing **lynx hello.html** instead should work.) When you double-click on an HTML file, usually your default Web browser will display the file. You should see something resembling Figure 2.1. This shortcut doesn't work on every system, so if you don't see your page, you'll have to run your browser and open files manually.

 WARNING   If you don't save an HTML file with an extension of .html or .htm (.html is preferred), then your browser won't display it correctly.

Reinforcing the Steps

To illustrate the process, here are some step-by-step instructions for creating hello.html on a Windows 95 system:

1. Click on the Start menu.

2. Select Programs ➤ Accessories ➤ Notepad.

3. Type in the HTML code. The end result should resemble Figure 2.3.

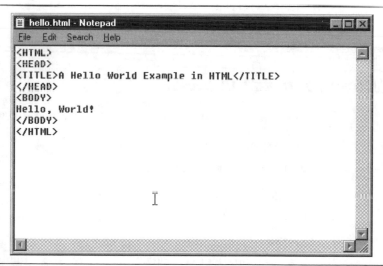

```
<HTML>
<HEAD>
<TITLE>A Hello World Example in HTML</TITLE>
</HEAD>
<BODY>
Hello, World!
</BODY>
</HTML>
```

FIGURE 2.3: Our "Hello, World" example, typed into Notepad and saved as hello.html

4. Use the File ➤ Save command. Double-click on My Computer and then the name of the hard drive where you save your files. Create a new folder (using the Create New Folder button), call it web, and then double-click on the new web folder to open it.

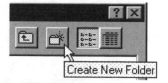

NOTE   It's a good idea to have a new folder for your Web files so you can keep all of your HTML files together. You can use an existing folder if you prefer, but creating a new folder will keep things easier to manage as you work on more HTML documents.

5. In the File Name box, replace the word "Untitled" with **hello.html**, then click on Save.

6. Click on Start ➤ Programs ➤ Windows Explorer.

7. Double-click on the web folder, where you saved hello.html.

8. Double-click on hello.html.

9. If you've installed Navigator or IE, it should display your file after a few seconds. If not, you'll need to get Navigator, IE, or another browser and install it. (You can download browsers from the Internet, get one from your Internet service provider, employer or school, or you can buy browsers from a computer store.)

DOWNLOADING A BROWSER

To download Navigator or IE, visit these respective Web sites:

http://www.netscape.com/
http://www.microsoft.com/ie/

(If you need an older version of Navigator or IE that isn't available from the official sites, you can give http://www.download.com/ a try.)

It's like the old dilemma about the chicken and the egg: The easiest way to get a Web browser is...with a Web browser. This is fine if you already have one Web browser and you're just rounding out your collection with a different one, or updating to the newest version. Most versions of Windows 95 start you off with IE (older versions of Windows 95 include IE 1, while newer versions of Windows 95 include IE 3). But if you don't have Windows 95 or later, you may not have a Web browser already—so you might have to just buy a copy of Navigator from a software store.

Mission accomplished! Sure, we're glossing over some things about `hello.html` that will be covered in more detail later, but this example gives us a good idea of the basic structure of all HTML documents. There are only eight tags in `hello.html`: `<HTML>`, `<HEAD>`, `<TITLE>`, and `<BODY>`—along with their corresponding end tags. "Learning the Basic Structure Elements of HTML" later in this Skill defines each of these tags in detail. They are the fundamental tags of HTML.

Introducing HTML Elements

In Skill 1, we talked about HTML's tags and introduced some examples of start tags, end tags, and attributes. Although many Web authors talk about tags all the time, the preferred term is *element*. An HTML element defines the structures and behaviors of the different parts of a document. We'll learn about many different elements in this Skill, such as the paragraph element (which marks a paragraph), the horizontal rule element (which creates a horizontal line), and the bold element (which makes text appear in bold). You can think of elements as the *commands* of HTML.

Most elements consist of three parts: a start tag, the content, and an end tag.

Consider, for example, the bold element we used as an example in the previous Skill: `<B>shout</B>`. Together, three things make up this bold element: The start tag, `<B>`, plus the content (in this case, the word "shout"), plus the end tag, `</B>`.

 NOTE

> If we refer to "the `<B>` tag," you know that we're talking about a start tag since there's no slash. End tags always have a slash, such as `</B>`. In this book, if we use the word "tag" by itself, it's just shorthand for "start tag."

Every HTML element has a start tag. We'll refer to elements like "the italics element" and let you know what the start tag is (for the italics element, it's `<I>`).

Some HTML elements are not required to have end tags. For example, the paragraph element uses the `<P>` start tag to mark the beginning of a paragraph. The paragraph's text is considered to be the content of the paragraph element. But you're not required to mark the end of a paragraph with a `</P>` tag (although you can if you want).

Some HTML elements have no content. For example, the horizontal rule element (which uses the `<HR>` start tag) has no content; its only role is to create a line. Elements with no content are called *empty elements*, and they never have end tags.

Some HTML elements are not required to have either start or end tags. The presence of such an element is assumed, even if its start tag and end tag don't explicitly appear in a document. We'll see some examples of these elements in the next section, when we learn about HTML's basic structure.

When we introduce an element, we'll tell you what its start tag is, whether it has an end tag, and whether it's empty. The appendix summarizes all of HTML's elements.

Remember from Skill 1 that the tags themselves are not case-sensitive. We'll show tags in uppercase in this book solely because they stand out better.

 **WARNING**

Be careful not to mix up elements and tags. To quote the HTML 4.0 specification, "Elements are not tags. Some people refer incorrectly to elements as tags (for example, "the P tag"). Remember that the element is one thing, and the tag (be it start or end tag) is another." When you talk about tags, always include the angle brackets.

Learning the Basic Structure Elements of HTML

The basic structure of an HTML document consists of the html, head, title, and body elements. In the "Hello, World" example of hello.html, we created a fully functional HTML document using this basic structure.

 NOTE

The four basic structure elements (the html element, the head element, the title element, and the body element) are always present in every HTML document. However, the actual <HTML>, </HTML>, <HEAD>, </HEAD>, <BODY>, and </BODY> tags themselves are not required. Browsers can figure out where these tags are supposed to go. Only the <TITLE> and </TITLE> tags are required to appear in your HTML document.

We'll start our discussion with the html element and work our way through the other three.

Defining HTML Documents with the Html Element

Every HTML document is simply an html element. Your document should be contained within the <HTML> and </HTML> tags. Notice how the first line of hello.html was the <HTML> tag, and the last line of hello.html closed the html element with the </HTML> tag.

The purpose of the html element is to simply declare that your document is, in fact, an HTML document.

> **NOTE**
>
> The `<!DOCTYPE>` declaration precedes the `<HTML>` tag and defines exactly what version of HTML you're using. We'll learn about the `<!DOCTYPE>` declaration in Skill 5.

When someone looks at a file, they can recognize it as an HTML document by seeing the `<HTML>` tag at the top.

Each HTML element must contain two parts: the head section, which describes the HTML document but is not displayed by the browser directly, and the body section, which contains the document itself (including the document's text and its HTML markup tags). We'll discuss the head section and the `<HEAD>` tag first, and then move onto the body section and `<BODY>` tag.

Describing Documents with the Head Element

The head element is used to mark the position of the head section. The head section contains elements that define certain information about an HTML document, such as what its title is, who the author is, and reference information about the document. To create a head element, start with a `<HEAD>` tag, then include all of the elements you want in your head section, then end the head element with a `</HEAD>` tag.

> **NOTE**
>
> See Skill 5 to learn a whole lot more about the head section's functions.

In `hello.html`, the head section contains only the title of the document. (The title of the document is contained within the `<TITLE>` and `</TITLE>` tags, as we'll see in the next section.)

Besides the title, we could have added all sorts of things to the head section, including copyright statements and author information, but it's typical for many HTML documents to contain only a title in the head section.

The head section has many important uses other than just acting as a placeholder for the title, but these other uses are more technical, like defining relationships to other documents and incorporating advanced features like style sheets and scripts, so we won't discuss these things until Skill 5. Overall, however, the most important thing to remember about the head element is that it contains the title element.

Naming Documents with the Title Element

The title element is a strict requirement of HTML. Every HTML document *must* have a title contained within a <TITLE> start tag and a </TITLE> end tag. In turn, the title *must* be contained in the head section.

For example, we put the title element in the head section of hello.html like this:

```
<HEAD>
<TITLE>A Hello World Example in HTML</TITLE>
</HEAD>
```

Titles are displayed by browsers on top of the page, usually in the title bar. Figure 2.1 showed the title bar—but it's easy to miss it since it's so small. Here is the title bar by itself (using the title of our "Hello, World" example).

Titles are important because they are used to index and refer to the document. The more descriptive a title, the more useful it will be. A generic title such as "HTML document" or "My Home Page" won't help people remember what your page is about. We'll discuss titles in more detail in Skill 5.

Wrapping Your Content with the Body Element

Following the head element is the body element. The body element contains the body section: Start with a <BODY> tag and end it with a </BODY> tag. Anything in between these two tags is the body section.

The body section is where the meat of the document is. Anything in the body section is displayed by the browser when you view the document. Notice how hello.html uses the <BODY> and </BODY> tags to contain all of the text to be displayed. In this case there's not much, only "Hello, World!" In most full-fledged HTML files, there is considerably more in the body section.

We'll learn much more about the body section in this Skill, and Skill 6 will give an organized list of all of the HTML tags that go in the body.

Now that we've seen the basic structure of HTML, it's time to see which HTML tags are most commonly used in the body of a document.

Learning the Two Categories of Body Elements

We've seen our first example and described the basic structure of HTML. Now we'll define the types and categories of tags that can be used in the body section. Our goal will be to create an example page more sophisticated than hello.html.

There are two basic categories of HTML elements used in the body section:

- Block-level elements
- Text-level elements

Block-level elements are used to define groups of text for a specific role, such as a heading, an author's address, a form, or a table. Text-level elements are for marking up bits of text, including creating links, inserting things like images or sounds, and changing the appearance of text (such as making text emphasized, small, or italic).

 NOTE The main functional difference between these two types of elements is that text-level elements don't cause line-breaks, while block-level elements do cause line-breaks.

Block-Level Elements

Block-level elements include tags that position text on the page, begin new paragraphs, set heading levels, and create lists.

Here are some commonly used block-level elements and their tags:

- Paragraph: <P> and </P>
- Heading, level one: <H1> and </H1>
- Heading, level two: <H2> and </H2>
- Horizontal rule: <HR>
- Centering: <CENTER>

 NOTE We haven't talked about headings yet. You'll see what we mean by "level one" and "level two" later in this Skill in "Understanding the Example's Headings."

We'll see each of these five block-level elements in action (see "Creating Your First Real HTML Page" below) after we discuss text-level elements.

Text-Level Elements

Text-level elements are used to mark up bits of text, including changing text appearance or creating hyperlinks. Some commonly used text-level elements are:

- Bold: `<B>` and `</B>`

- Italic: `<I>` and `</I>`

- Line-break: `<BR>`

- Link anchor: `<A HREF="`*URL*`">` and `</A>`

- Image: `<IMG SRC="`*URL*`">`

The last two elements feature attributes. (In Skill 1, we defined an *attribute* as an optional argument inside a start tag that defines the way an element works.) In these attributes, note the *URL* part. Don't actually type *URL*—instead, that's where you'd substitute an actual URL such as `http://www.yahoo.com/` or `http://www.emf.net/~estephen/images/jk.gif` and so on. (Review the "Getting There: URLS" section in Skill 1 if these two URL examples don't look comprehensible.)

It's important to keep text-level and body-level elements distinct in your mind. These two types of elements behave differently from each other; we'll see exactly how as we learn more about paragraphs later in this Skill. But for now, let's see these text-level and body-level elements at work.

Creating Your First Real HTML Page

We've now seen two types of commonly used elements. These elements might well make up about 70 percent of all the HTML tags you'll use. (However, the other elements are also important!) Using just these common tags, we can create a real HTML page. For this example, let's pretend we're creating a page for a business that sells T-shirts.

You should still have your text editor running from the "Hello, World" example at the beginning of this Skill. Switch to the text editor, create a new file (for example, using the File ➤ New command), type in the following HTML code, and save it as `rupert.html` in your web folder.

NOTE   If you don't want to type in this example, you can always browse to this book's Web page and download the HTML code. This example, `rupert.html`, is available at Sybex's Web site at `http://www.sybex.com/`. Click on the No Experience Required icon and navigate to this book's page.

rupert.html

```
<HTML>
<HEAD>
<TITLE>Rupert's Fabulous T-shirt Company</TITLE>
</HEAD>
<BODY>
<H1>Welcome to Rupert's Fabulous T-shirts!</H1>
<H2>Fabulous T-shirts Since 1752</H2>

Our company, <B>Rupert's Fabulous T-shirt Company</B>,
is your <B><I>second-best choice</I></B> for T-shirts.
(The best choice is <A HREF="http://www.inkyfingers.com/">Inky
Fingers</A>.)

Write us at:<BR>
555 Garment Way<BR>
Alameda, CA  94412

<P>
Call us at (510) 555-9912. <I><B>We're here to help!</B></I>
<IMG SRC="http://www.emf.net/~estephen/images/turtleshirt.jpg">

<HR>

<CENTER>Why not visit <A
HREF="http://www.yahoo.com/">Yahoo</A>?</CENTER>

</BODY>
</HTML>
```

Before we explain the tags that we used in `rupert.html`, let's see what this page looks like when you view it with a browser. Use your browser's Open command (from the File menu) to view the `rupert.html` file. Figure 2.4 shows the page as it is displayed by Navigator.

FIGURE 2.4: Rupert's Fabulous T-shirt Company page displayed by Navigator. (The toolbars have been switched off here to make the entire page fit on one screen.) Notice the different sizes for the two headings at the top of the page.

As you can see, this page has much more formatting than the "Hello, World" example. In the next few sections, we'll spend some time understanding the tags used in rupert.html: the headings (<H1> and </H1>, <H2> and </H2>), bold (<B> and </B>), italic (<I> and </I>), the rules of nesting, line-breaks (<BR>), horizontal rules (<HR>), images (<IMG>), paragraph breaks (<P>), centering (<CENTER>), and links (using the anchor element, <A> and </A>).

Understanding the Example's Headings

Examine the rupert.html example and pay attention to the sixth and seventh lines:

```
<H1>Welcome to Rupert's Fabulous T-shirts!</H1>
<H2>Fabulous T-shirts Since 1752</H2>
```

These lines contain heading elements. The first heading element is a level-one heading, enclosed with the <H1> and </H1> tags. The second heading element is a level-two heading, enclosed with the <H2> and </H2> tags.

There are six levels of headings. They range from level one, the most important (which uses the <H1> and </H1> tags), to level six, the least important (which uses the <H6> tag). Headings are always containers (meaning you need both a start and end tag). The more important headings are usually displayed in a larger font than less important ones.

The rupert.html example uses two headings. Notice in the Navigator display (Figure 2.4) how much difference there is in the font sizes on the first two lines.

We'll learn more about headings in Skill 6.

Nesting Bold and Italics in the Example

In the example, Navigator displays both of the headings in bold; there's nothing you can do about that—that's just how Navigator displays normal headings. But there are three other places where bold is displayed: "Rupert's Fabulous T-shirt Company," "second-best choice," and "We're here to help!" All of these three phrases appear in bold because of the presence of the bold element in the HTML code. In addition, the last two phrases also appear in italic, due to the italics element.

Interestingly, two tags are used on the same phrases: the <B> tag *and* the <I> tag both come before "second-best choice" and "We're here to help." The order in which these two text-level elements are applied doesn't matter. Consider the two different lines of HTML code that we used in the previous example, repeated here:

```
<B><I>second-best choice</I></B>
<I><B>We're here to help!</B></I>
```

In the first line, first bold is applied, then italic. In the second line, it's the reverse. The end result is the same. In both cases, one set of tags is *nested* (contained) within the other. We'll discuss nesting in more detail at the end of this Skill, in "HTML's Rules of Nesting."

Breaking Lines with <*BR*> in the Example

Notice in Figure 2.4 the line-breaks after "Write us at:" and "555 Garment Way." The line-breaks occurred in these two places because of the <BR> tag (which is short for "break").

A line-break is like a typewriter's carriage return—it just takes you back to the left margin. Line-breaks are good for ending lines after short pieces of information, such as the address in this example.

While line-breaks split text onto two different lines, they do not make that text split into two separate paragraphs. The lines of the address in this example are all part of the same paragraph that starts with "Our company." Recall our earlier definition of block-level and text-level elements: Block-level elements, by definition, separate paragraphs, but text-level elements do not. Since the line-break element is a text-level element, it doesn't cause a new paragraph—just a carriage return.

NOTE   Whether things are considered to be in the same paragraph is important, and this concept will make more sense once we are more familiar with block-level elements and how they're used. Skill 6 should help clear up any uncertainty you're having at this point.

Seeing the Example's Horizontal Rule

Near the end of the `rupert.html` file is a tag for a horizontal rule, `<HR>`. This horizontal rule is simply a line you can use to divide different sections. It is mostly for decorative purposes.

The `<HR>` tag is used by the horizontal rule element, which is a block-level element. It splits "We're here to help" and "Why not visit Yahoo?" into two separate paragraphs. Since the horizontal rule is a block-level element, you can use it to create a new paragraph automatically (splitting the text before and after the rule).

Different browsers display rules differently. For example, Navigator creates a line with a three-dimensional appearance, while IE's line is not as three-dimensional as Navigator's. Lynx, a text-only browser, displays a line with simply a row of dashes.

There are a large number of attributes that can affect how a horizontal rule is displayed; we'll spend more time on `<HR>` and its attributes in Skill 6.

Comprehending the Example's Image

Perhaps the first thing your eye catches when you view the `rupert.html` page in Navigator or IE is the image of the T-shirt. Don't worry about the image itself or how it was created; we'll talk about creating images and image formats in great detail in Skill 8. For now, let's just focus on the HTML code that causes the image to appear:

```
<IMG SRC="http://www.emf.net/~estephen/images/turtleshirt.jpg">
```

The <IMG> tag requires an attribute, SRC. This stands for the "source" of the image—that is, where the image is located. We learned in the previous Skill that whenever you need to know *where* something is located on the Web, you use a URL. The URL of the T-shirt graphic is contained in quotes and used as an attribute value.

If you were to enter the URL into your browser's location box, you'd see just the image by itself, as shown in Figure 2.5. (The image was created by Rick Salsman of Inky Fingers to incorporate a painting by musician Syd Barrett. It can be seen at http://www.emf.net/~estephen/images/turtleshirt.jpg.)

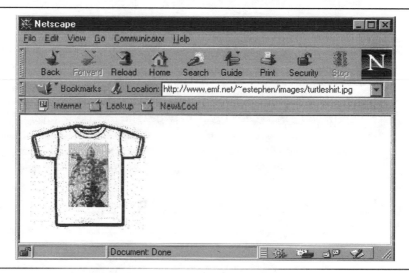

FIGURE 2.5: Navigator displaying the T-shirt image by itself

Another term for an image on a Web page is *inline image*. That's because the image is considered to be part of the line in which it appears ("in" the "line" of text). In our sample page, the paragraph that begins with "Write us at…" is pushed down because the image is taller than the line. If the image were not included (that is, if we deleted the entire <IMG> tag), then the sample page would appear as shown in Figure 2.6.

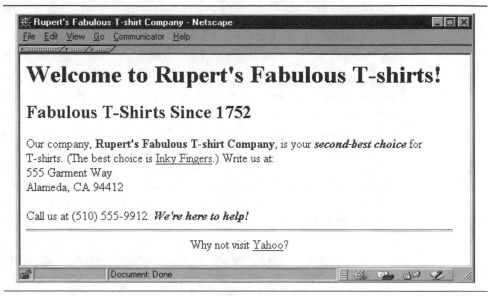

FIGURE 2.6: Navigator's display of the `rupert.html` example, without the inline image

As you can see, the break between the first paragraph and the second paragraph is much smaller than in Figure 2.4, where the image is included. Speaking of paragraphs, we've been mentioning them a bit, so now it's time for a thorough discussion. Understanding how paragraphs work is an important aspect of HTML.

Understanding Paragraph Breaks in the Example

The largest difference between the format of HTML and the format of plain text is the organization of paragraphs. In plain ASCII text, determining where paragraphs start can be a problem because of some technical details about how end-of-line characters work. (We don't really want to get mired in those ASCII technical details here, right? Thought not.) To avoid any ambiguities about paragraphs, HTML uses a specific tag to mark the beginning of every paragraph: <P>.

NOTE   Optionally, you can end a paragraph with </P>. If you want to write "strict" HTML that dots every i and crosses every t, then you should use a </P>; otherwise, you can safely omit the </P> tag.

If you don't mark the beginning of your paragraphs with the <P> tag, HTML treats everything in your document as one giant paragraph. With no paragraph breaks, documents are nearly impossible to read.

Skill 2

TIP   Newspaper articles often use a lot of paragraph breaks, since studies have shown that shorter paragraphs are much easier to read than longer ones. Consider doing the same for your Web pages, and break up long paragraphs into several shorter nuggets of wisdom.

When interpreting your HTML document's code, browsers will always ignore carriage returns. This is actually demonstrated in the rupert.html example: Notice that we put two carriage returns in between "The best choice is Inky Fingers" and "Write us at..." in the HTML code. But these two carriage returns don't have any effect on the display of this document in Navigator, or any other browser for that matter.

Browsers ignore those carriage returns and put the two phrases next to each other, in one paragraph. In fact, if we had hit Enter 100 times to create 100 carriage returns, Navigator would ignore all 100 of them. Any extra white space in your document is ignored. (We'll discuss this phenomenon in more detail in the next Skill, when we talk about the concept of white space in the "Arranging HTML on the Page" section.)

NOTE   *White space* is any character that takes up space but is itself invisible. Three characters are used to create white space: the space (created when you use the spacebar), the carriage return (created by pressing Return or Enter), and the tab (created by the Tab key).

Unlike a word processor where you simply press Enter to start a new paragraph or hit the spacebar a bunch of times to create some empty space, no amount of white space will start a new paragraph in HTML. The only way to start a new paragraph in HTML is to use an element's start tag, such as <P> or <H1>. (You can cause line-breaks with the <BR> tag, but as we said earlier, that's not the same thing as starting a new paragraph.)

The sole purpose of the <P> tag is to start a new paragraph. To see the <P> tag in action, study the rupert.html example again. Notice the <P> tag before the "Call us at" line. This tag tells the browser that a new paragraph should be started. We can see from the Navigator display that a new paragraph was in fact started at exactly the point where the <P> tag occurred.

Leaving off the <P> tag would make the document appear quite differently. Figure 2.7 shows the same document in Navigator if the <P> tag were removed.

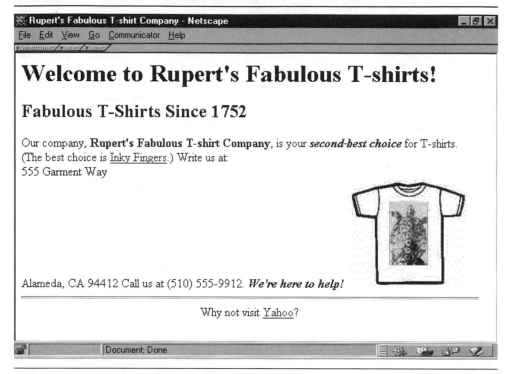

FIGURE 2.7: Navigator viewing the rupert.html example without the <P> tag. From "Our company" to "We're here to help!" is one paragraph.

All browsers, not just Navigator, would treat the text from "Our company" to "We're here to help!" as one long paragraph.

The reason for the white space in between the "555 Garment Way" line and the "Alameda, CA" line is that the image of the T-shirt is pushing down the last line. The inline image is like a giant letter that makes the entire line very tall. Imagine if the image was replaced by a giant letter T. Figure 2.8 shows what that would look like.

NOTE   We haven't taught you how to make letters bigger yet; this large capital T was created with the font element, which you'll learn about in the next Skill.

Alternately, we could take the image and the giant letter T out altogether. Figure 2.9 shows that result.

FIGURE 2.8: Navigator's display of the rupert.html example, except with the image replaced with a large capital T. Notice how the spacing for the entire line is determined by the tallest letter.

FIGURE 2.9: The rupert.html example in Navigator, with the inline image completely removed. The paragraph now has almost normal spacing.

Finally, let's take out the two line-breaks by removing the two <BR> tags. This will make the paragraph completely normal, as seen in Figure 2.10.

FIGURE 2.10: The rupert.html example in Navigator, with all paragraph marks, images, and line-breaks removed

Let's see how the HTML code for the paragraph in Figure 2.10 would look with all the changes that we've made in this section:

```
Our company, <B>Rupert's Fabulous T-shirt Company</B>,
is your <B><I>second-best choice</I></B> for T-shirts.
(The best choice is <A HREF="http://www.inkyfingers.com/">Inky
Fingers</A>.)

Write us at:
555 Garment Way
Alameda, CA 94412

Call us at (510) 555-9912. <I><B>We're here to help!</B></I>
```

The important thing to remember is that even though there are all sorts of carriage returns and white space in this HTML code, none of it counts for making a separate paragraph. Without a paragraph element's <P> tag or other block-level element, browsers will run this code together into just one paragraph. All of the tags that are present here (<B>, <I>, and <A>) are four text-level elements, which don't cause paragraph breaks.

If you look back at Figure 2.10, you'll see that Navigator is now displaying a total of four paragraphs. The two headings each count as a paragraph, and the final line, "Why not visit Yahoo?" is a separate paragraph as well. It's a separate paragraph for two reasons: First, it is separated by the <HR> tag, which is a block-level element. Second, it is contained within the <CENTER> and </CENTER> tags, and centering is also a block-level element.

Centering Text in the Example with the Center Element

The <CENTER> tag is used to begin centering, and the </CENTER> tag is used to end centering. Anything between these two tags will be centered—including images as well as text. The two tags, plus the text between them, make up the center element.

 NOTE　Technically, <CENTER> is a synonym for a block-level element called division with center alignment. The <DIV> tag for centering looks like: <DIV ALIGN="CENTER">. We'll see the <DIV> tag in more detail in Skill 6. We'll learn about other methods of centering in Skill 6.

Navigator and IE will redraw your page if the browser's window is resized, and the browser will use the new width of the page to determine where the center is, redrawing any centered paragraphs.

In the rupert.html example, only the line "Why not visit Yahoo?" is contained in the <CENTER> element so that's the only part that's centered.

If you recall our earlier discussion of nesting, you'll see that an anchor is nested inside the element along with the text "Why not visit" and the question mark. This anchor element makes the word "Yahoo" into a link. We'll discuss anchors next.

Linking to Example Web Sites with an Anchor

There are two links in the rupert.html example. The first link is to the Inky Fingers home page, and the second link is to Yahoo! (a popular Web page catalog). The relevant HTML code looks like this:

```
<A HREF="http://www.inkyfingers.com/">Inky Fingers</A>
<A HREF="http://www.yahoo.com/">Yahoo</A>
```

Both examples use the same type of tags—only the specific details differ. In both cases, the element being used is called an anchor element. "Anchor" is abbreviated to <A>.

The <A> tag requires the HREF attribute (short for "Hypertext Reference"), and HREF requires that a URL be specified after an equals sign (=). It's strongly recommended (though not a requirement) that you put the URL inside quotes. You can use double quotes or single quotes, but traditionally double quotes are used.

WARNING Make sure you don't leave off one of the quotes around the URLs in your anchors. A typo like this one will cause real problems for your page: `<A HREF ="http://www.webwitch.com/>WebWitch</A>`. The missing close quote here will cause an error that could mess up how the rest of your page is displayed. It might even make the rest of your page not be displayed at all!

Following the anchor element start tag comes some text (here, it's "Inky Fingers" and "Yahoo"). The browser will display this text as a link. (By default, link text is blue and underlined in Navigator and IE.) Your anchor text should describe what is at the other end of the link. Finally, the anchor element is closed with an end tag, </A>.

There are many more uses of anchor elements, such as for a table of contents and local files. We'll return to this topic in Skill 7 with more detail.

All told, the `rupert.html` example used 10 new types of elements, in addition to the basic structure. You now know how to use these new elements and tags, and we showed you what role they had in making the example work the way it did.

However, it's important to remember that different browsers display HTML documents in different ways. We've seen how Navigator displays `rupert.html`, and in a moment, we'll see this page in IE and in a text-only browser.

Viewing Pages in Different Browsers

It's vital to remember that different browsers will interpret your HTML code in vastly different ways. Some Web surfers may *hear* your page instead of see it, using a text-to-speech Web browser. So it's important to understand how different browsers will treat your tags.

IE and Navigator behave similarly, but not identically. Figure 2.11 shows the `rupert.html` example displayed in IE.

But not every browser is as similar to Navigator as IE. There are still a significant number of Internet users who access the Web through a command-line, nongraphical program named Lynx. Figure 2.12 shows the `rupert.html` page displayed in Lynx.

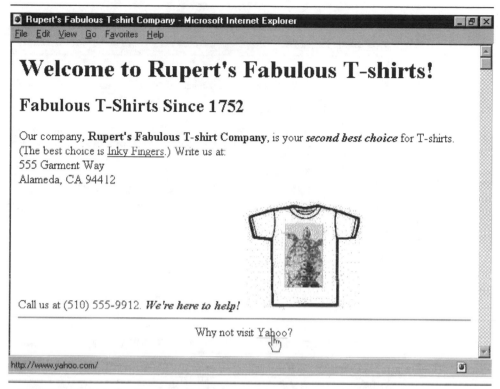

FIGURE 2.11: Rupert's Fabulous T-shirt Company page displayed by IE 4. Other than the slightly thinner horizontal rule (and the differences in the scroll bar and menu names), you'd be hard-pressed to find a difference between this version and the Navigator version we saw in Figure 2.4.

Lynx runs on many different computers, including Windows 95 and Macintosh platforms; primarily, however, Lynx is used on UNIX systems. Because Lynx is non-graphical, it displays the word "[INLINE]" (short for "inline image") where the picture of the T-shirt should be. (We'll learn a technique for alternate text in Skill 8 that's used to replace the word "INLINE" with a more helpful description of the image.)

As we mentioned in Skill 1, if you have an older type of Internet account called a *shell account*, you use a modem and a terminal emulator program to dial into the remote computer where you have your account. (Alternately, some ISPs offer both normal Internet access as well as a shell account that you can use the Telnet protocol to access.) From a shell account's command prompt, you use the Lynx browser (instead of Navigator or IE) to access the Web.

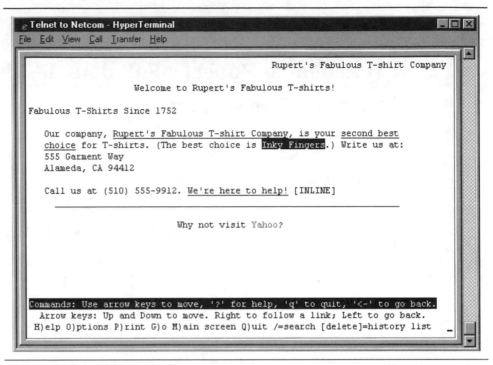

FIGURE 2.12: Rupert's Fabulous T-shirt Company page displayed by Lynx 2.7. Notice the word "[INLINE]" used as a placeholder for the T-shirt image.

NOTE   Telnet is a protocol used to log in to a remote computer. Using Telnet, you can log in to a shell account and use UNIX commands to read and send mail, work with files, and browse the Web. On Windows 95, you can use a Telnet program called simply "telnet," or you can use other Telnet clients, such as Hyper-Terminal, NCSA Telnet, and CRT. Neither Navigator nor IE have the ability to Telnet by themselves.

It's worth considering how a page looks in Lynx. Lynx is in common use in foreign countries and on older computers. Lynx is also used, along with a text-to-speech reader, to allow blind or visually impaired users to access the Web. We'll discuss design considerations for Lynx in Skill 17. It's not at all hard to make a page that looks great in Netscape, IE, *and* Lynx: Just stick to the rules of HTML as we teach them to you.

In general, our rupert.html sample page comes across just as well in Lynx as it did in Navigator. However, there are differences in how Lynx and Navigator display HTML tags. Notice the difference in the "Welcome to Rupert's Fabulous

T-Shirts!" line (Figure 2.12), which was a level-one heading: Lynx centers the heading, while Navigator just uses a larger font and bold. Many different browsers use slightly different methods for displaying headings; that's part of the power of HTML, since it allows many different types of computers and platforms to view your document. But a consequence of this flexibility of HTML is that you cannot expect to have absolute control over the appearance of your document.

Lynx, in contrast to Navigator, can't change the font size (since it can display only plain text). Instead, some versions of Lynx display the level-one heading centered and in all caps (not every version of Lynx uses all caps); Lynx shows the level-two heading as plain text, but not indented like the rest of the document.

Viewing the HTML Source

When a browser displays an HTML document, it starts by retrieving the HTML file and then it interprets the HTML tags contained in that file. As we've seen, the browser doesn't display the HTML tags—just the *results* of those tags. When you're browsing the Web, you'll often see a page that does something interesting or attractive, and you'll want to know how it was done. There's an easy way to learn how pages do what they do: Look at the HTML code. This technique is called *viewing source* (since you're seeing the "source" of the document, and because computer programming code is often called *source code*).

NOTE No one can "hide" their source and make it so that you can't see the HTML they used to create their page. Similarly, you can't hide your HTML code from anyone else. Anyone can view your source and see how your Web page was constructed.

We can view the source of our `rupert.html` example. (Even though we have access to the source on our own, through the text editor that we used to create the HTML code, it's still useful to learn the procedure of viewing source.) In Navigator 4, the command to view source is View ➤ Page Source.

NOTE For earlier versions of Navigator, the command was View ➤ Document Source instead of View ➤ Page Source. Both commands do the same thing; only the name of the command has changed.

With IE, you can use the View ➤ Source command to see the HTML tags used to display the document. IE will display the source using Notepad (or WordPad if the source is very long). In Lynx, you can view the source by pressing the backslash key (\).

If you are using IE to view a page that has *frames* (that is, a page with one or more different subdivisions), you'll have to choose the View Source command from the context menu for the frame. If you are using Navigator to view a page with frames, use the View ➤ Frame Source command. We'll learn about frames in Skill 11.

In your travels on the Web, it's a good idea to frequently view the source of pages that you find interesting and try to understand the HTML code that you see. But it's also a good idea to occasionally view your own documents' source in Navigator from time to time, since Navigator will highlight any errors it sees by making the incorrect tag blink. (We'll learn other ways to check for errors in Skill 17.)

Speaking of errors, we'll end this Skill with a discussion of one of the principal causes of HTML errors: incorrect nesting.

HTML's Rules of Nesting

Nesting is common in HTML. Consider that the entire body section of any HTML document is nested within the body element. In turn, the body element itself is nested within the html element.

Block-level elements often contain other block-level and text-level elements. For example, a paragraph block-level element might contain some bolded text (the body element text-level element):

```
<P>
Rich ate six slices of <B>Crazy Joey's Crustacean Pizza</B> and
survived! Barely!
</P>
```

There are four main rules to remember about nesting:

- Elements must be completely nested and not closed in the wrong order.

- Text-level elements may be nested within block-level elements or other text-level elements.

- Block-level elements may be nested within other block-level elements.

- Block-level elements may *not* be nested in text-level elements.

To illustrate the first rule, consider our example of bold and italic text from `rupert.html`:

```
<B><I>second-best choice</I></B>
```

```
<I><B>We're here to help!</B></I>
```

The previous two examples show: first, italic text nested within bold text; and second, bold text nested within italic text. Both of them are correct, since the inner element is entirely contained within the outer element. Be sure not to mix up the order of the end tags. Here are the two incorrect orders:

```
<B><I>second-best choice</B></I>
<I><B>We're here to help!</I></B>
```

Both lines are in error since there is no nesting. Although Navigator and IE would do their best to understand the above two incorrect lines of HTML code (and in this case, would probably succeed in doing the right thing), there's no guarantee that your document would be displayed correctly—it's possible that the bold or italic elements would not switch off correctly and spill over into the rest of your document. To prevent things like this from happening, always nest elements completely inside other elements.

Now we've learned about nesting, along with a full discussion of 10 tags in the rupert.html example. These 10 tags are the most commonly used HTML tags. A few other commonly used tags, <FONT>, <BIG>, and <SMALL>, are described in the next Skill. In addition, the next Skill will tell you more about how HTML can be arranged on the page and what special characters you can use in your HTML documents. After that, we will take a look at some attributes used in the <BODY> tag that affect the color scheme and appearance of HTML documents. By then you'll be ready to go a lot further than the "Hello, World" example you started this Skill.

Are You Experienced?

Now you can...

- ☑ **create, save, and view basic HTML pages**
- ☑ **use HTML's basic structure**
- ☑ **view source code**
- ☑ **distinguish between block-level and text-level elements**
- ☑ **master 10 of the most commonly used HTML elements (and nest them properly)**

Beautifying Your HTML Documents

- ➔ Using white space for legibility
- ➔ Adding comments
- ➔ Using special character entities
- ➔ Creating color schemes for your documents
- ➔ Using the *<FONT>* tag
- ➔ Creating and editing a more sophisticated HTML page

In Skill 2, we created our first two HTML documents, learned HTML's basic structure, and experimented with 10 of the most commonly used elements. In this Skill, we'll play with a bit of font control and a splash of color. We'll learn how to arrange and organize HTML pages, include comments in our pages, and use special characters. Finally, we'll round out our knowledge of HTML elements by creating and editing a slightly more sophisticated page.

We learned in Skill 2 during our discussion of the paragraph element that browsers ignore extra carriage returns in your HTML documents. In the next section, we'll see exactly how this works to your advantage: It helps you write HTML documents that are easy to understand.

Arranging HTML Tags

It's common to create an HTML document with all of the tags and text jumbled together in one big block. The trouble is, this may not be the best way to arrange your HTML, especially when you or another person want to go back and revise a specific section. It's simply too hard to read and understand.

A long HTML page, especially one that's complicated or includes advanced features, can benefit by a consistent structure of indentations (tabs) and carriage returns. This white space makes the code more readable. People call this practice following "code formatting conventions."

Code formatting conventions are normally a custom employed by computer programmers. But even if you're not a programmer, it doesn't hurt to adopt some of their conventions for your HTML code right from the start.

The basic idea is to keep different sections separated by carriage returns and to indent sections that are nested. To illustrate these concepts, let's use the example of rupert.html that we created in Skill 2, except with the code arranged in a structured way:

```
<HTML>
    <HEAD>
        <TITLE>Rupert's Fabulous T-shirt Company</TITLE>
    </HEAD>

    <BODY>
        <H1>Welcome to Rupert's Fabulous T-shirts!</H1>
        <H2>Fabulous T-shirts Since 1752</H2>

        Our company,
        <B>Rupert's Fabulous T-shirt Company</B>,
```

```
                    is your
                    <B>
                        <I>second-best choice</I>
                    </B>
                    for T-shirts.
                    (The best choice is
                    <A HREF="http://www.inkyfingers.com/">Inky Fingers</A>.)
                    Write us at:<BR>
                    555 Garment Way<BR>
                    Alameda, CA 94412

                    <P>
                    Call us at (510) 555-9912.
                    <I>
                        <B>We're here to help!</B>
                    </I>
                    <IMG
    SRC="http://www.emf.net/~estephen/images/turtleshirt.jpg">

                    <HR>

                    <CENTER>
                        Why not visit
                        <A HREF="http://www.yahoo.com/">Yahoo</A>?
                    </CENTER>
                </BODY>
            </HTML>
```

With the HTML code arranged this way, it's easy to see which tags are nested within other tags, and it's easy to see the breaks between the different sections.

As you surf the Internet and view the HTML source code of your favorite Web sites, you can observe how the HTML is arranged on the page and then gradually adopt the style that's best for you as you learn to work with the code.

NOTE We learned how to view source in Skill 2. If any of this seems a bit unfamiliar, go back and brush up on viewing source code—it can take a while to get all of this down.

Every HTML designer has a different idea of how HTML should be arranged; some people use tabs, while other people use three or four spaces. Most HTML authors would probably not indent as much as we've done here, but how much indenting you use is up to you.

All of these code formatting conventions depend on the rules of how HTML understands white space, which we'll now see in detail.

HTML's Rules of White Space

The general rule of white space is that multiple spaces, tabs, and carriage returns are turned into a single space. For example, consider this code:

 **space.html**

```
<TITLE>Too Much          Space</TITLE>
<BODY>
     I've got
way


too        much

<B>
                    space           </B>
     in


                        my

house.
```

Netscape Navigator and other browsers will display this in a much more compact way than you might first expect. Figure 3.1 shows what this HTML code looks like when displayed by Navigator.

FIGURE 3.1: Navigator eliminates multiple white space to display this document as condensed as possible. (All browsers would display this document with exactly the same amount of condensing.)

NOTE This code is a valid HTML document, even though it doesn't have any basic structure tags except for <TITLE>, </TITLE>, and <BODY>. If you want to duplicate this example, type the previous code in your text editor, save it as space.html, and view the file in your browser. If you'd rather not type in the code, you can get it from Sybex's Web site at http://www.sybex.com/. Just click the No experience required icon and navigate to this book's page.

There is another rule of white space for HTML that can help you when you're creating an HTML document. Consider this code:

```
<P>
Text
</P>
```

Officially, the specification for HTML defines the following piece of code as identical to the previous one:

```
<P>Text</P>
```

Furthermore, the following piece of code is considered to be identical to the previous two arrangements:

```
<P>
Text</P>
```

The next piece of code is also equivalent:

```
<P>Text
</P>
```

Finally, because of the general white space rule, the following code is also equivalent to all of the previous examples:

```
<P>

Text

</P>
```

These five examples all use the <P> tag, but the rule holds for every HTML tag. The consequence of this white space rule is that you can put carriage returns between your tags and your text, as you see fit, in order to improve the legibility of your HTML documents.

NOTE   You can use pre-formatted text elements to get around these white space rules. In Skill 6, we'll learn the pre-formatted text element, and see how you can place <PRE> and </PRE> tags around sections of text where you don't want white space to be collapsed.

However, there are two problems with the white space rules that we need to discuss: the exception to the white space rules and the indenting dilemma.

The Exception to the White Space Rules

Unfortunately, Navigator, Internet Explorer, and most other browsers don't follow the white space rule we just described. Sometimes putting a carriage return between text and an end tag results in an erroneous space sneaking into a browser's display of your document. To illustrate this problem, we'll use the <U> tag, which is used to underline text. Consider the following HTML code:

```
<TITLE>Underline Problem</TITLE>
<BODY>
Let's look at four examples of underlining:

<P>
<U>1. This text is underlined with no carriage returns.</U>
<BR>

<U>
2. This text is underlined with carriage returns before and after.
</U>
<BR>

<U>
3. This text is underlined with a carriage return before.</U>
<BR>

<U>4. This text is underlined with a carriage return after.
</U>
```

Now let's see how Navigator displays this code (see Figure 3.2).

The error is hard to spot—but it's there, and it can show up in all sorts of documents in a way that makes them subtly different from how you'd expect. The problem may well be corrected in future versions of Navigator and other browsers, but this isn't too likely since the problem has existed in every version of Navigator and IE so far. This is just one example of how the people who create browsers don't always follow HTML specifications.

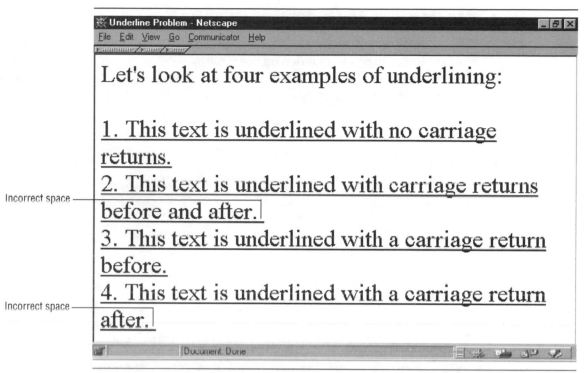

FIGURE 3.2: Navigator displays the first and third underlining samples in the same way, but a problematic and erroneous space has appeared in the second and fourth underlined phrases, after the period.

To avoid this problem, you'll want to put your end tag immediately after the text, without any extra spaces or carriage returns. For example, this code:

```
<U>King Lear</U>
```

will generate a better result than the following:

```
<U>King Lear
</U>
```

Similarly, you can avoid extraneous underlined spaces in your links if you don't put a carriage return after your anchor tag. So it's better to use:

```
<A HREF="http://www.sybex.com/">Sybex</A>
```

rather than:

```
<A HREF="http://www.sybex.com/">Sybex
</A>
```

Grappling with the Indenting Dilemma

There is an extremely unfortunate side effect of HTML's white space rules: There is no good way to create an indented paragraph.

Many documents have paragraphs with the first line indented (with a tab), like these two paragraphs from a short story called "James' Ear":

```
    James was driving through Gateshead when he began to hear a high-
pitched tone in his left ear. It started quietly but soon became
uncomfortably loud, like commercials that are much more shrill than the
TV show they sponsor.
    James turned off the radio, and stuck his pinkie in his ear. He wished
he had a Q-tip. But rubbing his ear made no difference; the noise
continued unabated.
```

To re-create these two paragraphs in HTML, you might try to type the following in an HTML document:

```
<TITLE>James' Ear</TITLE>
<BODY>
<P>  James was driving through Gateshead when he began to hear a high-
pitched tone in his left ear. It started quietly but soon
became uncomfortably loud, like commercials that are much more shrill
than the TV show they sponsor.</P>
<P>  James turned off the radio, and stuck his pinkie in his ear. He
wished he had a Q-tip. But rubbing his ear made no difference;
the noise continued unabated.</P>
```

Unfortunately, the tab (or any number of spaces) in between the <P> tag and the first word of each paragraph has no effect at all, due to the white space rules. Figure 3.3 displays the result of the previous code in Navigator.

You might imagine that there is a simple HTML tag that can be used for indenting. But actually, there isn't. You can use a number of HTML tricks to produce the desired effect of an indent—but no official HTML solution exists, and no solution exists that works for every browser. Web designers who want to use an indent are faced with the dilemma of choosing between various unsatisfactory work-arounds. We'll see the different methods of indenting that you can try in Skill 6 and discuss their merits and disadvantages. But you should simply accept that there's no easy way to indent paragraphs in HTML.

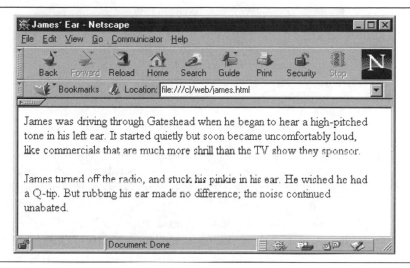

FIGURE 3.3: Navigator doesn't put any tabs or spaces at the beginning of new paragraphs. The extra spaces in our HTML source code are ignored.

 NOTE   The best way to indent paragraphs is to create a style sheet. In Skill 14 we'll learn about style sheets and briefly introduce the text-indent property.

So now we've learned about the white space rules and we know that we can use them to improve the readability of our HTML code. There's also one other technique that's used to help make HTML code understandable: comments.

Using Comments to Increase Understanding

A comment is a part of your HTML document that a browser does not display. You can think of a comment as an invisible Post-It note that is only revealed when someone looks at the HTML source code by viewing the source.

There are several reasons to include comments in your HTML code. One reason is to help remind yourself what a tag does. Secondly, comments can help other people understand your HTML document. You might also use comments as a way to put notes about your plans for a document (for example, "Update this section in June!"). Another use of comments is to temporarily remove ("comment out") a section of your document without actually having to delete the section entirely.

To create a comment, start with the <!-- characters. Then type whatever text you want to be in the comment. Then end the comment with the --> characters. (Comments are different from other HTML tags because the comment characters are really SGML, and they can be much more complicated than this. However, most browsers only understand simple comments.) Here is a sample comment tag:

```
<!-- Your comments go here -->
```

Often comments are used to give information about copyright to people in your audience who view your HTML. Remember, comments are ignored by browsers—the only way you can see a comment using Navigator or IE is to view the HTML's source.

The comment tag is often used mistakenly by HTML designers. It's easy to leave off a dash or get a character in the wrong place. The rules of comments require that you not include any greater-than signs (>) or two hyphens (--) inside your comments.

The comment doesn't have to be a single line. You could write your comment like this:

```
<!--
The Widget Family Home Page
by James P. Widget
Copyright 1998 by James P. Widget.
-->
```

They must be outside your comments

Here's a brief excerpt of commented code from the home page of the Church Divinity School of the Pacific (http://www.cdsp.edu/):

```
<BR>
<P>
<BR>
<!-- by alternating line breaks with a paragraph start, you can
     force a double-space -->
```

Here's an example of some HTML code with part of the document "commented out." Anything in between the comment start (<!--) and the comment end (-->) won't appear in the browser:

```
<B>Welcome to the Playhouse!</B>
<!-- I Call 555-1632 for updated information. /I -->
```

The advantage of commenting out code is that it's easy to delete the comment characters and restore the comment (allowing its text to be displayed by the browser again). Just delete the exclamation point and the hyphens, and make sure any tags are reconstructed. For example:

```
<B>Welcome to the Playhouse!</B>
<I>Call 555-1632 for updated information.</I>
```

One danger of using this technique is that comments aren't really hidden—anyone can view source to see them, so remember to be tasteful and don't try to hide any company secrets in a comment.

TIP   You should strongly consider using comments in your HTML documents, at the very least to indicate copyright information and when you last made changes.

So far in this section, we've learned about white space and comments. The last aspect of arranging your HTML in a file that we have to consider is what characters are illegal and how you can include special characters.

Avoiding Illegal Characters and Using Special Characters

In HTML, some characters, such as the quote ("), the ampersand (&), and the angle brackets (< and >), have special meanings other than their uses as text characters. Other characters, such as foreign letters and symbols (for example, the copyright symbol), can be included in your HTML documents if you know how. For both situations, HTML uses *entity codes*.

Keyboards don't have keys for all of the characters that you might want to use (there's no © key on your keyboard, for example), so your only option is to use an entity code.

These entity codes are taken from charts that list every legal character you can put in your HTML pages, including the foreign language characters and special symbols. You'll find copies of these charts in the appendix of this book.

In addition, with some browsers, it's not safe to use certain characters in your HTML code—these characters won't display properly unless the entity code is used in their place. If you use an "illegal" character in your HTML page, some browsers may not view your text properly or, worst of all, your page may "crash" certain browsers.

In order to create pages that are readable to the widest audience, it's a good idea to get into the habit of using entity codes for some characters in HTML character set. The *character set* is the list of all legal characters that you can use. There are two different character sets for HTML. Older versions of HTML used a character set called Latin-1, while HTML 4.0 uses a character set called either Unicode or Universal Character Set. Let's look at the Latin-1 character set first.

Introducing the Latin-1 Character Set

Every version of HTML prior to HTML 4.0 used a set of characters called the Latin-1 character set. This character set was defined by the International Organization for Standardization (ISO). Another name used to refer to the Latin-1 character set is "ISO 8859-1."

NOTE   The ISO is an international group that promotes the development of computer and trade standardization. Their home page (http://www.iso.ch/) explains that "ISO" is not an acronym, but is instead derived from a Greek word that means "equal."

Each character in the character set is called an *entity*. The numerical or code equivalent of each entity is referred to as the entity code or "escape sequence" for that entity.

The Latin-1 character set includes:

- The basic printable characters in the ASCII character set, which are numbered from 32 to 126, and include the lowercase and uppercase letters, numbers, and basic punctuation symbols that are on computer keyboards

- New characters numbered from 160 to 255, for foreign letters and special symbols

NOTE   A complete list of the entities in the Latin-1 character set is included in the appendix.

Introducing UCS and Unicode

HTML 4.0 introduces the use of Unicode as a character set for HTML. To quote from the Unicode Consortium (a non-profit group that develops Unicode, with a home page at http://www.unicode.org/), "The Unicode Worldwide Character Standard is a character coding system designed to support the interchange, processing, and display of the written texts of the diverse languages of the modern world. In addition, it supports classical and historical texts of many written languages. In its current version (2.0), the Unicode standard contains 38,885 distinct coded characters derived from 25 supported scripts. These characters cover the principal written languages of the Americas, Europe, the Middle East, Africa, India, Asia, and Pacifica."

The Universal Character Set (UCS) is the character-by-character equivalent to Unicode. UCS is defined as ISO standard 10646. Some documents about HTML refer to UCS instead of Unicode.

Understanding Character Encodings

It's one thing for us to say that HTML uses Unicode, but it's another thing for you to create documents using the full character set. For technical reasons, almost every computer system, text editor, mail program, and HTML tool uses only a subset of the entire Unicode character set. It's far more efficient for your computer to work with only that portion of Unicode that applies to your language.

When your computer system or HTML tool uses a subset of the entire character set, it's called *character encoding*. The most common character encoding is ASCII (which consist of only 128 different characters; see the appendix). Many mail programs and HTML tools only let you work with ASCII, so if you want to include other HTML characters, you'll have to use an entity (see the next section).

The second-most common character encoding is ISO-8859-1 (which is Latin-1, as we defined earlier). Other popular encodings are ISO-8859-5 (for the Cyrillic alphabet used in the Former Soviet Union), SHIFT_JIS (a Japanese encoding), and euc-jp (another Japanese encoding).

In Skill 5, we'll learn about the meta element and see how one of its uses is to specify which character encoding you're using in your HTML document.

Because HTML 4.0 is new, many browsers don't support the full Unicode character set yet. And even if you use a browser that does understand Unicode, you might not have a font on your computer that can display a particular Unicode character. (If you're using an English or American version of Windows 95, for example, most of your fonts probably can only display the shapes—or *glyphs*—for the Latin-1 characters.)

NOTE   Browsers often have a menu command to switch their display to a different character encoding. If you encounter a page with lots of accented vowels, you can try using Navigator's View ➤ Encoding command or IE's View ➤ Fonts to switch to a different character encoding.

Since you're most likely using a keyboard that only has keys for ASCII characters, you'll need to use entities to refer to Latin-1 and Unicode characters. In the next sections, we'll show you how to use entities in different ways.

Using the Basic Entities

The most commonly used entity codes are for the illegal characters that we mentioned previously. Instead of using a less-than sign (<), for example, it's imperitive to use its entity code equivalent.

There are two types of entity codes: character entity codes and numerical entity codes. The character entity code for a less-than sign is:

<

Alternately, you can use the numerical entity code for the less-than sign. If you check out the appendix, you'll find that the less-than sign is listed as character number 60. So the numerical entity code equivalent of a less-than sign is:

<

 **WARNING**   Numerical entity codes always start with an ampersand (&), followed by a number sign (#), followed by the desired number, and ending with a semicolon (;).

The other basic entities are for quote marks, greater-than signs, and less-than signs, as shown in Table 3.1.

TABLE 3.1: The Basic Entities

Character	Numerical Entity Code	Character Entity Code
"	&#34;	&quot;
<	&#60;	&lt;
>	&#62;	&gt;
&	&#38;	&amp;

NOTE

Even though " exists in HTML 4.0 and existed in earlier versions of HTML, the official specification of HTML 3.2 does not include " in its list of entities since it was removed by the W3C. But to quote from their Web site: "This disappeared in a rationalization of the entities, and with hindsight should not have been removed." Instead of using ", just use " if you're using HTML 3.2.

To summarize the basic idea: Since HTML uses ampersands and angle brackets as special symbols, it's not a good idea to use these characters as regular text in your documents. Suppose you want to type the phrase "Jules & Jim." The ampersand in that phrase could cause problems for some browsers since the ampersand is a special HTML character. Instead of typing the ampersand in that phrase, use the following code instead:

```
Jules &amp; Jim
```

Similarly, don't include the equation "X < Y" in your HTML documents. The less-than character is used for tags, and many browsers would get confused and display your page incorrectly. Instead, use the following code:

```
X &lt; Y
```

This technique is not just a nitpicky rule; it's important to use entities to prevent problems in displaying your document. It's also useful to use entity codes for including special characters in your HTML documents.

Inserting Latin-1 Entities

There are many special symbols in the Latin-1 character set that you can safely include in your HTML documents. Most of these special symbols, such as the copyright symbol and international characters, do not have a key on your keyboard. Therefore, the only way to include these characters is to use their entity code. For example, the copyright symbol is typed as either © or ©.

Other entities you may routinely use are foreign characters, such as é (the letter e with an acute accent). To include this character, use either of the following entity codes:

```
&eacute;
&#233;
```

If you want a capital E with an acute accent, É, use one of the following two entity codes:

```
&Eacute;
&#201;
```

Note that the only difference between é and É is the capital letter E. Entities are one of the few times when the case of HTML code matters. There is no such entity as &EACUTE; and most browsers would show the actual letters "&EACUTE;" in your document—so it's important to get the case of entities correct.

For other entities, check out the appendix.

There is one final special entity that we will discuss: the non-breaking space.

Using HTML 4.0's New Named Entities and Unicode Entities

In the previous section, all of the entities that we've referred to are commonly understood by the popular browsers. HTML 4.0 introduces some new named character entities for typographical symbols (such as • for a bullet and ™ for a trademark symbol), mathematical symbols (such as ∑ for a summation symbol and √ for a square root symbol), and Greek letters (such as Α for a capital Greek letter alpha and δ for a lowercase Greek delta letter).

Support for these new entities is currently a mixed bag. IE 4 can display some of these examples, but can't display others (depending on what fonts you have available) and substitutes a small hollow square. Other browsers (including Navigator 4 and earlier, along with IE 3 and earlier) simply ignore the entity and will display the entity name instead of the proper symbol. It can be disconcerting to see "Buy PowerBall™" instead of "Buy PowerBall™."

Since HTML 4.0 uses Unicode, you can also refer to Unicode characters. While Latin-1 uses only 256 different characters, Unicode has set up maps of many thousands of characters (and not all of them are yet defined).

HTML 4.0 lets you refer to entity codes for Unicode characters using either normal numbers or hexadecimal numbers (we'll learn about hexadecimal later in this Skill).

For example, suppose you want to include a Cyrillic capital I (which looks sort of like a backward N). Using a Unicode reference, you could find this character as number 1048 on the charts. (A small subset of these charts is included in the appendix of this book.) HTML 4.0 specifies that you could use either of the following numerical entities: И or И. The latter notation uses an x to indicate that the number is in hexadecimal format.

Unfortunately, no browser can display hexadecimal numeric character entities yet. And to make matters worse, neither Navigator nor IE have included full Unicode fonts.

Here's how IE would display some of the named and Unicode entities we've referred to in this section (along with a Chinese character and ASCII's greater-than sign just for comparison):

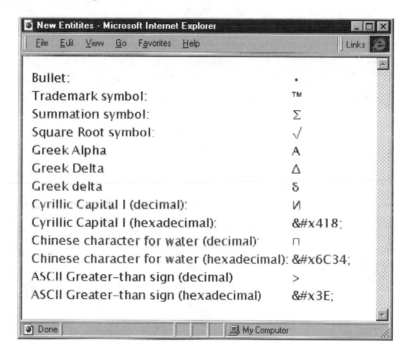

To display many of these characters, IE must be using View ➤ Fonts ➤ Universal Alphabet (instead of the default Western Alphabet). Notice how IE's default font changes when this font setting is used.

Navigator 4 also has a similar font change command, View ➤ Encoding ➤ Unicode, but Navigator 4 fares far worse in its display of these characters, as shown on the following page:

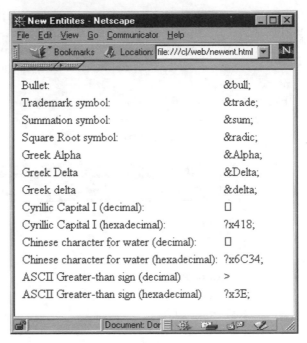

It's probably safest to avoid most of HTML 4.0's new named character entities and Unicode entities for now.

Using a Non-Breaking Space

The non-breaking space is a special space character that won't cause a line-break. Sometimes you may have information that you don't want to split between two lines. For example, suppose you have a phone number with an area code, such as (510) 555-3566, that happens to be split between two lines when it's displayed by a browser, like this:

```
We hope that you will give us a call at (510)
555-3566 soon!
```

You probably want the entire phone number to stay together as a single unit. You could add or subtract words from the line until the phone number doesn't wrap, but since every browser and every computer screen is different, you have no idea how many words to change before you've fixed the problem. You could take out the space after the area code, but that would look ugly.

There's a much better solution. Instead of using a regular space between the area code and the phone number, you can use a non-breaking space. The main difference between non-breaking spaces and normal spaces is that a browser will not wrap (or "break") a line of text at a point where there is a non-breaking space.

Here's two equivalent pieces of HTML code to create a space using the entity for a non-breaking space:

```
Hello, World!
Hello, World!
```

Both of these examples above would render a space between the word "Hello," and the word "World!" The resulting phrase "Hello, World!" would always appear together, unbroken, on a single line.

 TIP

The non-breaking space is one way around the indenting dilemma we saw earlier. So, if you want more spaces, type in a non-breaking space code for each space in your HTML text. Most browsers will not collapse multiple non-breaking spaces into a single space.

Using Soft Hyphen Entities

HTML 4.0 introduces the use of the soft hyphen entity. The soft hyphen tells a browser where a line break can occur in the middle of a word.

 NOTE

In contrast, the plain hyphen (-) is used in a variety of places, such as phone numbers, and hyphenated words like "seven-year-old." But it's not used to hyphenate normal words and cause them to break from one line to the next.

A soft hyphen is invisible unless it occurs at the end of a line.

To use a soft hyphen, use its named character entity ­ (alternately, you can use its numerical entity code, ­, or its hexadecimal Unicode entity code, ­).

 **WARNING**

Unfortunately, IE 4, Navigator 4, and earlier browsers don't yet understand the soft hyphen entity. This means that there is currently no way to reliably hyphenate a long word.

We've learned quite a bit about how HTML documents can be arranged and structured. Now we'll introduce you to a method that can change the appearance of your HTML documents: document attributes that can be included in the <BODY> tag.

Changing Your Color Scheme with Body Element Attributes

By using attributes in your document's <BODY> tag, you can define the appearance of your document. These attributes let you declare background and foreground colors for your page's text and links, as well as a background image.

The <BODY> attributes are optional. But they are worth learning because they can make your document's appearance much more attractive.

 NOTE   These <BODY> tag attributes were introduced by Netscape as an extension to HTML, and then became official in HTML 3.2. In HTML 4.0, however, the use of these attributes is *not* recommended. Instead, HTML 4.0 urges the use of style sheets. We'll learn about style sheets in Skill 14.

If you do end up changing one of the <BODY> attributes (for example, if you want to change the default text color from black to red), it's a good idea to specify *all* of the <BODY> attributes. The reason for this is that <BODY> attributes override a browser's default settings. For example, if a surfer changes their default background from gray to red, when they view your page with its red text, then they'll see only a blank page because your red text will be invisible on their red background.

There are six body attributes: BGCOLOR, BACKGROUND, TEXT, LINK, VLINK, and ALINK. However, before we learn about these attributes, it's necessary to learn how you specify colors in HTML.

Specifying Colors by Name or RGB Code

There are two ways to specify colors in HTML documents: by a color name or by a color code known as an RGB code. *RGB* stands for Red, Green, Blue.

The color names are more straightforward, so we'll show them first. There are 16 color names in HTML 4.0. These names are considered "widely understood," meaning that most browsers know how to interpret them.

The 16 colors are BLACK, SILVER, GRAY, WHITE, MAROON, RED, PURPLE, FUCHSIA, GREEN, LIME, OLIVE, YELLOW, NAVY, BLUE, TEAL, and AQUA. To see what they look like, check Sybex's Web site (http://www.sybex.com/). Click on the No Experience Required link and navigate to this book's Web page.

In addition to these 16 colors, some browsers (including Navigator) understand a much larger list of colors, with names such as "goldenrod" and "darkolivegreen" (the color names are always one word). However, since not all browsers understand these color names, it's much safer to specify colors using the RGB code.

RGB codes are always six numbers: two numbers that specify an amount of red, followed by two numbers that specify an amount of green, and ending with two numbers that specify an amount of blue. By mixing different amounts of the three primary colors red, green, and blue, it's possible to generate any color.

It would be simple if the numbers used to specify color amounts were regular numbers, but things are never that simple. Instead, RGB is measured using a *hexadecimal*, or base 16, numbering system.

In the hexadecimal system, there are 16 units, numbered from 0 to 9 followed by A to F. When you count in hexadecimal, it goes like this: 0, 1, 2, 3, 4, 5, 6, 7, 8, 9, A, B, C, D, E, F, 10, 11, 12, 13, 14, 15, 16, 17, 18, 19, 1A, 1B, 1C, 1D, 1E, 1F, 20, 21, and so on.

The number 10 in hexadecimal is equivalent to the number 16 in decimal. The number that comes after 99 in hexadecimal is not 100, but 9A. (100 comes after FF.) The number that comes after 9F is A0. FF is the highest two-digit number in hexadecimal, and it's equivalent to decimal 255.

N **NOTE**   If hexadecimal makes no sense to you, you're not alone! It's quite confusing. Instead of worrying about it, just check out the color list in the appendix.

By tradition, hexadecimal colors are preceded by a number sign (#). HTML follows this tradition, and therefore, we do too.

When you use RGB colors, you specify two-digit hex numbers for the amount of red, green, and blue. For example, to specify the color blue, you need to have blue maximized, but no red or green. In RGB, you would express that as #0000FF.

For the color lime, you need to have green maximized to #FF and red and blue minimized to #00. So the RGB equivalent of lime is #00FF00. (Most of us would call this color "green," but for historical reasons it's called "lime" instead.)

We learned in grade school that to make the color yellow, you mix red and green. That works for RGB as well; yellow is a combination of the maximum amount of red, plus the maximum amount of green, plus the minimum amount of blue: #FFFF00.

Black is represented by minimizing red, green, and blue, so black is #000000 in RGB. White is represented by maximizing red, green, and blue, so white is #FFFFFF in RGB.

Table 3.2 lists some sample colors in hexadecimal.

TABLE 3.2: A Few Sample Colors with Their RGB Value

Color	RGB Value	Color	RGB Value
white	#FFFFFF	fushia	#FF00FF
red	#FF0000	aqua	#00FFFF
green	#00FF00	navy	#000080
blue	#0000FF	gray	#808080
yellow	#FFFF00	purple	#800080

Hopefully, these RGB colors are starting to make some sense; they're commonly used on the Web. As you use RGB colors more, they'll become more familiar. It's worth understanding RGB values, since it will help you use the <BODY> tag attributes for specifying colors that we're about to see. Be sure to look at the appendix for a list of color names and RGB values.

Now that we know how to specify colors in HTML, let's see how we can change the colors of our Web pages.

Specifying the Background Color of Your Page with *BGCOLOR*

In all the examples of HTML documents that we've seen so far, the body section of the document begins with a simple <BODY> tag. But the <BODY> tag can take one of several attributes; these attributes will change the document's appearance.

For example, consider the following code:

```
<HTML>
<HEAD>
    <TITLE>Black and White Are My Favorite Colors</TITLE>
</HEAD>
<BODY BGCOLOR="BLACK" TEXT="WHITE">
<B>Hello, World!</B>
</BODY>
</HTML>
```

This code will be displayed by IE as shown in Figure 3.4.

You can use either a color name or an RGB color. The following two lines of code are equivalent to each other:

```
<BODY BGCOLOR="LIME">
<BODY BGCOLOR="#00FF00">
```

FIGURE 3.4: IE displaying a document with white text and a black background color

If you don't specify a background color in your HTML document, the browser will use the background that was specified by the user when they set up their browser. If the user has not specified a background color, then the browser will use the default color.

For older versions of Navigator and IE (3 and earlier), the default background color is silver (RGB #C0C0C0). (It looks more like gray than silver.) For newer versions of Navigator and IE (4 and later), the default background color is white instead of silver.

 **WARNING**   Don't make your background color too similar to your text color, or else your document will be hard to read. The more contrast between the foreground and the background, the better. Skill 17 discusses these design issues in more detail.

Tiling a Background Image with the *BACKGROUND* Attribute

In addition to setting a background color, you can use any image file as a background for a page. Here's an example of a background image being specified in the <BODY> tag:

```
<BODY BACKGROUND="clouds.jpg">
```

Here's how Navigator would display a document with a background image showing some clouds (see Figure 3.5).

The BACKGROUND attribute names a URL or file for an image that will be used as a background for your page. In Skill 8 we explain more about how to create these images so that the image quality and download time is optimal.

NOTE   Animated images, which we'll discuss in Skill 8, will not animate when they are used as a background image. Only the first frame of an animated image will display if it is used as a background.

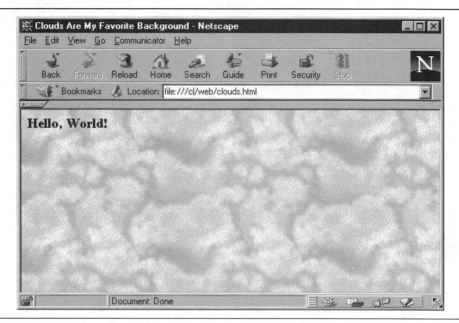

FIGURE 3.5: A cloudy background. Notice that the cloud image is tiled (repeated) to fill up the window.

The BACKGROUND attribute overrides the BGCOLOR attribute. So if you specify both a background image and a background color, the background image will appear on top of the background color. (You will see the background color briefly, however, during the time it takes for the browser to retrieve the background image.)

 **WARNING**   It's all too easy to use a background image that makes it nearly impossible to read your page. As a general rule of thumb, the more contrast that is in your background image, the harder it will be to read the text on the page.

Background images are always optional; you certainly don't have to use one if you don't want one. If you do specify a background image or background color, though, you should also specify the text color.

Setting a Color for Your Page's Text with the *TEXT* Attribute

The TEXT attribute of the <BODY> tag is used to set the *foreground,* or text color of the page. For example, use one of the following two (equivalent) HTML tags to choose a certain shade of bluish-green:

```
<BODY TEXT="TEAL">
<BODY TEXT="#008080">
```

Most browsers' default text color is black—but you can't depend on that, since many people redefine the default color to be something else.

Once you set a text color, it's a good idea to set a link color that provides a nice contrast.

TIP   If you're ever reading a page that has poor contrast between text and background, try pressing Ctrl+A. That will select all of the text in the page (for copying and pasting), and often the selection colors will be more readable.

Changing the Color for Links with the *LINK* Attribute

The LINK attribute specifies the color used for hypertext links.

Navigator and IE use a default link color of blue (#0000FF). The following <BODY> tags would both change the link color to green:

```
<BODY LINK="GREEN">
<BODY LINK="#008000">
```

However, only links that the surfer has not seen previously ("unvisited" links) will be displayed in this color; visited links are a separate attribute, described next.

WARNING   Consider carefully before changing any link colors. Many people are used to seeing links in blue, and might get confused if you change the link color to something else.

Setting a Color for Visited Links with the *VLINK* Attribute

The VLINK attribute specifies the color used for hypertext links that have been previously visited by the viewer. Either of these two <BODY> tags would specify maroon as the color to be used on a page for visited links:

```
<BODY VLINK="MAROON">
<BODY VLINK="#800000">
```

By default, Navigator and IE use a shade of purple (#800080) for visited links.

Altering the Active Link Color with the *ALINK* Attribute

The last <BODY> attribute changes the color of the *active link*—that is, the color that is briefly used for links at the moment the user clicks on the link. (This color is displayed only while the mouse is held down on the link.)

Here are two different but equivalent ways of specifying fuchsia for that fleetingly displayed link color:

```
<BODY ALINK="FUSHIA">
<BODY ALINK="#FF00FF">
```

Navigator and IE default to red (#FF0000) for the active link color.

We have now seen how to create a color scheme for an HTML document. It's easy to choose ugly colors, and the best way to arrive at a color scheme is with a lot of trial and error.

 **WARNING**   Colors vary tremendously from platform to platform, so you can never guarantee that the colors will come out the way you expect.

We'll see an example of specifying colors using the <BODY> attributes later in this Skill; first, however, we'll introduce a couple more elements to round out our knowledge of basic HTML elements. Armed with these new elements, we'll be able to finish the Skill with a more advanced sample HTML page.

Changing Fonts with the Font Element

To complete our knowledge of the most commonly used HTML tags, we'll introduce the font element (which uses the <FONT> and </FONT> tags), as well as two of the font element's cousins, the big element's <BIG> and </BIG> tags and the small element's <SMALL> and </SMALL> tags.

The font element can let you change the size, color, and typeface of text on an HTML page. The font element is probably the most controversial HTML element; HTML 4.0 discourages its use entirely (HTML 4.0 recommends that Web authors use style sheets instead). However, the font element has some practical uses. There are three ways to use the <FONT> tag, depending on the attribute that you use:

- The first attribute, COLOR, lets you specify the color of a block of text (using the color names or RGB values that we learned).

- The second attribute, SIZE, lets you specify the relative or absolute sizes of text.

- The third attribute, FACE, lets you specify a font face (such as Arial, Palatino, and so on) that you hope to use for a block of text.

Since the font element is a text-level element, it does not cause a paragraph break. It's a container element, so you'll always have to close any <FONT> start tag with a </FONT> end tag.

We'll now see some examples of each of these three uses of <FONT>.

Specifying Font Colors with the *COLOR* Attribute

You can specify a font color for a block of text by using the <FONT COLOR= "[colorname]"> or <FONT COLOR="#[RGB-value]"> tags.

For example, here's some sample HTML code with a few color changes.

splash.html

```
<HTML>
<HEAD>
    <TITLE>A Splash of my Favorite Colors</TITLE>
```

```
</HEAD>
<BODY BGCOLOR="CYAN" TEXT="#0000AA">
<H1>Enjoy The Colors</H1>
<FONT COLOR="RED">Blood</FONT> is the favorite food of vampires.
All of us enjoy a walk on the <FONT COLOR="GREEN">grass</FONT>.
The <FONT COLOR="#FFFF00">sun</FONT> beams down.
</BODY>
</HTML>
```

With practice, you'll come to recognize the RGB colors quickly. The first RGB color is used in the TEXT attribute of the <BODY> tag; it specifies that the text color should be a blue that is a little darker than normal. The second RGB color is used for the word "sun" and is directly equivalent to the color name "yellow."

The color of the document's text is used for the headings as well as the body text. The <FONT> tag is used to override the text color for specific words or phrases.

Many Web authors will embed several paragraphs within a font element, if, for example, they wanted several blue paragraphs. However, because of the container rules that say that text-level elements cannot contain block-level elements, this practice is not, strictly speaking, legal HTML. Instead, apply the font element to each paragraph separately.

It's worth considering that many Web viewers may have black and white monitors, and that many members of your audience might be color blind. While few females are colorblind, one out of 10 males has some degree of color blindness. For these two reasons, it's important to pick your font colors with good contrast.

A better way of specifying colors involves the use of style sheets (which we'll show in Skill 14). Style sheets are more graceful than the <FONT> tag because users who are viewing your page can indicate their own preferences that the style-sheet system will try to accommodate.

Sizing Text with the *SIZE* Attribute and the Big and Small Elements

Unlike word processors and desktop publishing programs, HTML does not specify the size of text using points. A word processor (as well as a newspaper editor) can specify 10-point text or 12-point text, or a headline of 60 points. In contrast, an HTML designer can only use one of seven different sizes.

We'll see the sizes in action in Skill 6; for now, suffice it to say that the smallest size is called size 1 (and it's very small indeed), and the largest size is size 7 (which is larger than even a level-one heading).

Here's a quick example of a font size command:

```
<FONT SIZE="5">Huge Blowout Sale In Progress!</FONT>
```

You can also use the font size command to change the relative size of text, that is, make text one level smaller or larger. Consider:

```
<FONT SIZE="-1">Copyright &copy; 1998 by XYZ.</FONT>
```

This markup indicates that the copyright statement should be displayed at one size smaller than the normal text size.

There are two related elements, however, that perform the same function for relative font size changes. The big element is a text-level container (using the <BIG> and </BIG> tags) that makes text one size larger. Similarly, the small element (using the <SMALL> and </SMALL> tags) makes the text that it encloses one size smaller:

```
<SMALL>Copyright &copy; 1998 by XYZ.</SMALL>
```

The <SMALL> and </SMALL> tags accomplish the exact same task as the <FONT SIZE="-1"> and </FONT SIZE="-1"> tags, but the small element is slightly easier to understand.

Changing Typefaces with the *FACE* Attribute

The final attribute for the <FONT> tag is the most controversial. Using the FACE attribute, you can try to specify a typeface to be used in displaying a block of text. An example of this is the following line of HTML code:

```
<FONT FACE="Arial">I lived in New York for several years.</FONT>
```

The main problem with this tag is that there is no guarantee that the user who is viewing your page has a font named "Arial" on their system.

We'll cover font faces, including the pitfalls and workarounds, in Skill 6.

Combining Font Attributes

You can specify more than one attribute in a single tag. For example:

```
<FONT COLOR="RED" SIZE="4" FACE="Garamond">Call me Shirley.</FONT>
```

It's possible to mix and nest different <FONT> elements to get sophisticated results, as we'll see in the next section. The next section presents an example HTML page that combines all of the techniques we've learned in this Skill.

Creating a More Advanced HTML Page

Now that we've covered all of the HTML basics, you're ready to fire up your text editor again and try out a more advanced HTML page.

Before you go any further though, you might want to review the first two Skills and practice some of the tags you've seen in this Skill to create a couple of sample documents on your own.

NOTE   At this point, it's a good idea to obtain and install the latest versions of Navigator as well as IE. In the next section, we'll practice viewing pages in both browsers. If you only have one of those browsers, it's worth getting hold of the other one, since your page's audience will be split between users of Navigator, users of IE, and users of different browsers.

For this example, let's start by typing in the four basic structure elements, and then let's add a few of the HTML basics we've talked about in this Skill:

- Colored link and text attributes in the <BODY> tag

- A copyright entity

- A <FONT> tag

- Consistent and attractive code formatting conventions

NOTE   We'll also add a link, except that this time we'll use a mailto URL instead of an http URL. (We mentioned mailto URLs in Skill 1; they allow you to send an e-mail message to the address specified in the URL.)

Type the following code into your text editor (or visit this book's Web page, find this example, and cut and paste the HTML code into your text editor instead).

invite1.html

(handwritten) ALink = Active Link
VLink = Visited link

```
<HTML>
<HEAD>
    <TITLE>The Year 2000</TITLE>
</HEAD>
<BODY BGCOLOR="YELLOW" TEXT="BLUE" LINK="MAROON" ALINK="GREEN"
VLINK="BROWN">

<!-- The body tag attributes specify the color scheme, such as the
background color of yellow. -->

<H1>The Millennium Approaches</H1>

<FONT SIZE="+5">
    <I>And You're Invited!</I>
</FONT>

<P>

<FONT COLOR="PURPLE">Please come to my
<B>Celebration of the New Millennium BBQ &amp; Poetry Reading</B> to be
held on December 31st at 7:00 p.m. Anyone reading this page is invited;
send me mail using the link below for more
details.</FONT>

<HR>
<A HREF="mailto:estephen@emf.net">Stephen Mack</A><BR>
&copy; 1999, Stephen Mack

</BODY>
</HTML>
```

Once you've gotten the code entered (and proofread it), you're ready to save it.

Saving Locally

After you've gotten this far, save your code as a text file locally on your computer in your Web directory. For example, you might call your Web directory **web** (as we did in Skill 2), and you can save this file as `invite1.html`. (Remember to use the `.html` extension, not `.txt`.)

TIP   Always use lowercase for your Web filenames. When you publish your page on the Web, it's easier for both you and your audience to remember a URL if all the characters are lowercase.

Once the file is saved, we can view it in both Navigator and IE.

Viewing the Example Page with IE

Run Internet Explorer, and use the File ➤ Open command to open your web folder, and then open the invite1.html file by double-clicking on it. IE will display the page.

TIP   You can use the Ctrl+O command as a shortcut for File ➤ Open.

IE should display a document that looks similar to Figure 3.6. Not too bad! This page is fairly complex and looks attractive. But we can improve its appearance and practice some more HTML features, so let's edit the invite1.html document.

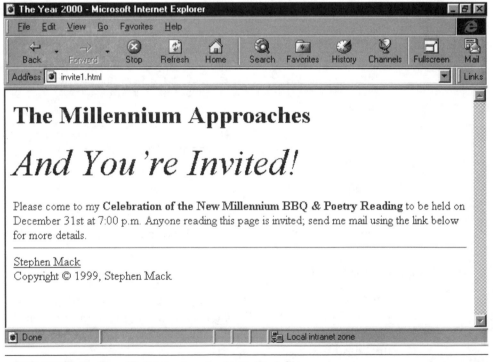

FIGURE 3.6:   IE displaying invite1.html file

Editing Our Example HTML Page

Ready to do a few edits? If you're not certain about some of the tags, don't worry, we'll go over them in more detail in Skill 6. Let's just get our hands dirty and have some fun. We'll practice:

- Centering the text

- Changing the font of a heading to "Arial"

- Adding some more text

Switch back to your text editor, and make changes to your file until it resembles the following example. Save it as invite2.html.

TIP   If you're using Windows 95, you can use the Alt+Tab command to quickly switch back to your editor. A common series of keystrokes goes like this: Alt+Tab to switch to the editor, make your changes and save them, Alt+Tab to your browser, and press Ctrl+R to redraw the page (which will show your changes).

invite2.html

```
<HTML>
<HEAD>
     <TITLE>The Year 2000</TITLE>
</HEAD>
<BODY BGCOLOR="YELLOW" TEXT="BLUE" LINK="MAROON" ALINK="GREEN"
VLINK="BROWN">

<!-- The body tag attributes specify the color scheme, such as the
background color of light yellow. -->


<CENTER>
     <H1>The Millennium Approaches</H1>

     <FONT SIZE="+5" FACE="Helvetica">
          <I>And You're Invited!</I>
     </FONT>
</CENTER>

<P>
Please come to my
<FONT COLOR="PURPLE">
```

```
        <B>Celebration of the
        New Millennium BBQ &amp; Poetry Reading</B>
</FONT>
to be held on December 31st at 7:00 p.m. Anyone
reading this page is invited; send me mail using the
link below for more details.

<P>
<CENTER>
        <FONT COLOR="BLACK" SIZE="4">
                <B>Look out!</B> Unfortunately I'll have to charge $200
                for admission.
        </FONT>
</CENTER>

<HR>
<SMALL>
        <A HREF="mailto:estephen@emf.net">Stephen Mack</A>
        <BR>
        Copyright &copy; 1999, Stephen Mack and Janan Platt
</SMALL>

</BODY>
</HTML>
```

You should be able to follow the HTML code a little more easily in the second example, since it uses more consistent indenting.

Now let's view our edits with IE and Navigator. IE renders the edited page as shown in Figure 3.7.

Navigator displays the two pages almost identically to IE. Navigator and IE will not always be this similar in displaying your HTML documents. The more complicated the document, the more differences there are likely to be. That concludes this example. In this Skill, we've spent a lot of time exploring how to arrange text on the page, using entities, and changing the color scheme. We've created a sophisticated page—however, we haven't put this page up on the Web yet. Only we can see it (for now); we'll learn how to actually publish HTML documents on the Web in Skill 18.

In the next Skill, we'll learn about HTML tools designed to make it easier to work with HTML. In the two Skills after that, we'll spend more time on first the head section, and then the body section. We'll learn all of the HTML tags in a more organized, complete, and detailed fashion. After that, we'll learn more about links (in Skill 7) and graphics (in Skill 8) to complete our knowledge of HTML basics.

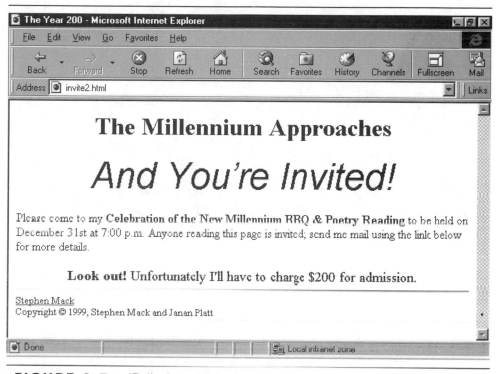

FIGURE 3.7: IE displays the invite2.html page.

Are You Experienced?

Now you can...

- ☑ arrange your HTML on the page for easier readability
- ☑ incorporate comments
- ☑ write HTML that avoids illegal characters
- ☑ change the page color scheme to add some color to your page
- ☑ use the *<FONT>*, *<BIG>*, and *<SMALL>* tags

Employing HTML Tools

- ➔ Choosing the right HTML tool for you
- ➔ Editing text (and HTML) with text editors
- ➔ Comparing HTML editors
- ➔ Evaluating the pros and cons of page- and site-creation tools
- ➔ Bringing legacy documents to the Web with conversion tools

You can use a wide range of tools to work with HTML. Some people like to use only the bare minimum: a text editor. Other people prefer a full-featured HTML editor or a program that writes the HTML for them. In this Skill, you'll see the advantages and drawbacks to the available tools so you can pick the one that works for you.

We'll discuss all of these types of tools: text editors, HTML editors, and page- and site-creation tools. Then we'll finish with a brief overview of conversion tools that will help you take existing material and put it in HTML format.

Choosing the Right HTML Tool for You

Choosing an HTML tool is a lot like choosing a method of transportation. At the high end is a Porsche or BMW, which offers a lot of speed and features but is expensive and can be a lot of trouble if you need to get repairs. At the low end is a bicycle or walking, which can take you to a lot more places and give you a better view of the scenery—but you have to do all the work.

We'll discuss the following types of HTML in this skill: text editors, word processors, page- and site-creation tools, and conversion tools.

NOTE   In addition to these tools, we'll discuss other sorts of HTML tools in later Skills. For example, all sorts of tools and programs exist for creating, editing, and enhancing images; these will be discussed in Skill 8.

Each of these tools have their uses, and you may end up using a lot of different tools. Each of the approaches is popular, and you're just as likely to find people who swear by text editors as people who recommend site-creation tools. Some projects require a hammer and others a screwdriver; similarly, you may find yourself picking FrontPage for one project and UltraEdit for another. (These two programs are described later in this Skill.)

Our own experience bears this out: For some projects, especially when a lot of simple pages are involved, we use HTML site-creation tools since they provide a lot of automation. For other projects, where the compatibility and accuracy of the HTML is more important than churning out a lot of pages quickly, we use text editors to create loving, hand-crafted HTML tags.

Ultimately, the only person who can really pick the best tool for a project is you. To help you make an informed decision, we'll look at each of the types of tools more closely and talk about some of the more popular choices in each category.

> **NOTE**   There are more than 100 different HTML editors and tools, so it's impossible for us to review all of them. You can check out Web sites that include extensive selections of HTML tools: CNET's software Web site (http://www.download.com/), Stroud's (http://www.stroud.com/), and Tucows (http://www.tucows.com/).

Using a Text Editor to Create HTML Files

A *text editor* is like a word processor, except that it only works with plain, unformatted text. Word processors are designed to help you make your document look attractive; in contrast, text editors don't care about visual presentation at all. Since every text editor saves documents in ASCII format and is designed to work with text, text editors are ideal for working with HTML.

Text editors are also inexpensive, since one is almost always provided free with your computer's operating system. DOS includes a text editor called Edit. Windows offers a text editor called Notepad. Macintosh computers have always included a text editor called either TeachText or SimpleText. UNIX and VMS systems usually are set up to offer a wide range of editors, including the joe, pico, vi, and emacs editors.

In this Skill, we'll talk about simple text editors before talking about more advanced text editors that are optimized for working with HTML. We'll now look at the two most commonly used simple text editors in more detail: Notepad (for Windows users) and SimpleText or TeachText (for Macintosh users).

Working with Windows' Notepad

If you use any version of Microsoft Windows, then you have a copy of Notepad. Notepad is a very simple text editor (see Figure 4.1). Notepad doesn't have any features specific to HTML, but nonetheless Notepad is one of the most commonly used tools to create Web pages. Since it's so simple, it's very easy to use. No matter where you go, you're likely to have access to a computer running Windows, so Notepad is almost always available.

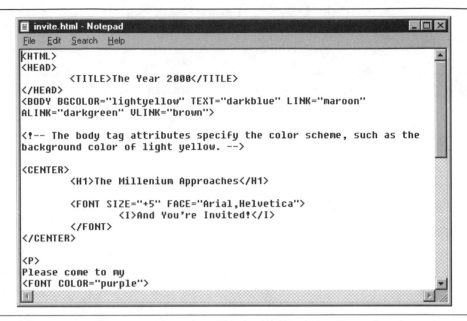

FIGURE 4.1: Notepad in action. This is the Windows 95 version, but other versions (like the Windows 3.1 version) are similar.

Notepad's strengths are in its simplicity and universality. Notepad is stable and guaranteed not to crash your system or be incompatible with other software. That's the good news.

On the other hand, Notepad has some crippling limitations: It only allows a maximum of 65,536 characters in your file, and it doesn't have many features.

 NOTE With computers, *byte* is a common unit of measurement. A byte is a single character, while 1,024 bytes is a *kilobyte*. Kilobytes are abbreviated as "k," so "64k" is the same 64 kilobytes, which works out to 65,536 characters.

If you've used a modern word processor for any length of time, you've probably come to expect such features as multiple-level undo, automatic saving, macros, and search and replace. Notepad has only a single level of undo; you have to save your files manually with the File ➤ Save command (there's not even a Ctrl+S shortcut), no macro facility, and it lets you search but not replace.

 **WARNING**   Don't confuse Notepad with WordPad. Both come free with Windows, but WordPad is a word processor, not a text editor. WordPad saves documents in Microsoft Word format by default, so if you use WordPad for HTML work, you must be careful to save your files in "Text Document" format. (WordPad comes with Windows 95; previous versions of Windows included a simple word processor called Write, which is similar to WordPad.)

Working with Macintosh's SimpleText or TeachText

Macintosh users are probably familiar with SimpleText, a rudimentary text editor included with the Macintosh operating system. (If you use an older version of the Macintosh system, you'll know SimpleText by the name "TeachText." They're virtually identical, so we'll refer to this editor as "SimpleText" for convenience.)

In many ways, SimpleText is similar to Notepad. It has most of the same abilities and some of the same limitations. Figure 4.2 shows SimpleText in action.

There's nothing really wrong with SimpleText, but on the other hand, it doesn't have much to recommend it either—other than its price and convenience.

For learning HTML, a simple text editor like SimpleText or Notepad is really the only tool you need. You can certainly create and use all of the examples of HTML in this book using just Notepad or SimpleText, but if you are designing a number of pages, you'll definitely want to investigate a more capable text editor that's aware of HTML.

Upgrading Your Text Editor to an HTML Editor

The thing to remember about the text editor that came with your operating system is "you get what you pay for." Since Notepad and SimpleText are so lacking in features, a large number of software companies and programmers offer replacements—and have been doing so long before the Web was born. Many of these replacement text editors were aimed at "power users" and computer programmers. You'll find some of these replacement text editors for sale in computer stores or on the Web. Other text editors are free (*freeware*), while many are available for you to download and try out, with the condition that you pay for the software if you end up using it (*shareware*). Most shareware and freeware programs are available from the Web.

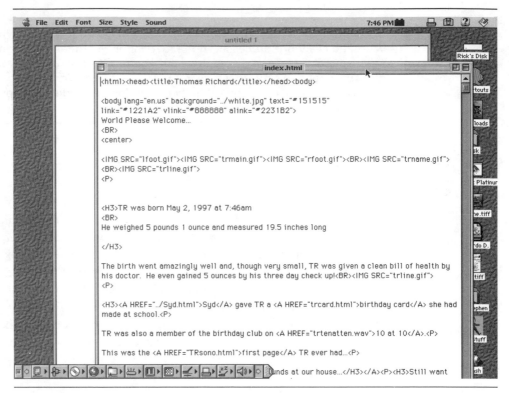

FIGURE 4.2: A Macintosh desktop with SimpleText being used to edit an HTML file

WARNING Some shareware programs only work for a limited time or only offer a subset of the features that are available if you pay for it (sometimes this type of shareware is called *crippleware*). Other shareware programs remind you constantly that you haven't paid, and keep showing dialog boxes asking for you to register the program (sometimes this type of shareware is called *nagware*). Some shareware programs are not updated reliably, or come without technical support or guarantees. On the other hand, there are a lot of great shareware programs out there. And it's not hard to beat Notepad and SimpleText.

Computer programmers and professional Web designers have high demands; they require text editors that are programmable, flexible, powerful, and feature-rich. A good text editor should be able to check your spelling, sort text, compare files, search and replace text with wildcards and across multiple files, convert text from lowercase to uppercase and vice versa, word wrap and reformat paragraphs, work with more than one file at once in different windows, and allow you to use macros.

NOTE   A *macro* is a recording of a sequence of your commands and/or keystrokes. Some text editors and word processors let you assign macros to a keystroke, to a menu command, or to a toolbar button (or some programs let you use all three methods). More advanced macros are written in a programming language so they can take different actions depending on different situations.

GETTING ADVICE ON CHOOSING AN HTML EDITOR

Web designers advocate different HTML editors with huge amounts of zeal. You'll find Web designers constantly recommending products and debating the merits of the different editors we've seen, as well as many others such as HoTMetaL PRO, WebEdit, TextPad, HTMLed, HTML Assistant, and HomeSite. It's easy to get into a discussion about the editors' relative strengths on the various Web newsgroups and mailing lists.

Some of the Usenet newsgroups where you can find discussion on HTML editors include:

comp.infosystems.www.authoring.html	alt.html
comp.infosystems.www.authoring.misc	alt.hypertext
comp.infosystems.www.advocacy	alt.html.editors.webedit
comp.infosystems.www.misc	alt.www.webmaster
alt.html.editors.enhanced-html	alt.culture

There are many different HTML mailing lists; perhaps the most well-known are the ones sponsored by the HTML Writers Guild, which are described at http://www.hwg.org/. You can find more mailing lists for Web designers (along with many other topics) by using the list of Publicly Accessible Mailing Lists (http://www.neosoft.com/internet/paml/).

When the Web came along, some of the existing programmer's text editors added special commands to aid in the creation of HTML documents. In addition, a surprisingly large number of new text editors came onto the market, intended to help you create and edit HTML files. Some text editors feature toolbar buttons or menu commands for the common HTML commands, so you can click on a

Paragraph button and the text editor simply types in the <P> tag for you. Other text editors have buttons that double-check the accuracy of your HTML code or buttons that preview your document in Netscape Navigator and Internet Explorer. You'll also see many text editors that highlight the HTML code for you.

What we're *not* talking about here are editors that create the HTML itself (that's covered in a later section, "Letting an HTML Page- or Site-Creation Tool Do the Driving"). Instead, we're talking about editors that are aware of HTML and make it easier in some way or another for you to create HTML pages or type HTML tags.

We'll look at several different text editors that are popular: BBEdit (on the Macintosh), UltraEdit (for Windows), and HotDog (available for Windows).

WHERE ON THE WEB ARE THE HTML EDITORS?

Don't be insulted if your favorite text editor isn't listed here—there are lots of them. Any text editor that offers useful features will work fine; you don't have to use one of the ones we describe. Find advanced text editors and HTML editors from any of the following URLs:

Tucows   The Ultimate Collection Of Winsock Software. Access the closest Tucows site by going to http://www.tucows.com/ and then choose your geographic location. Then pick your system (Windows 95, Windows 3.1, Macintosh, or OS/2). Your URL will vary depending on what you pick.

Stroud's Consummate List Of Winsock Apps   A Windows-only list of Internet utilities, Stroud's features fast downloads and reviews of many of its offerings. Go to http://cws.internet.com/32html.html for Windows 95 or Windows NT and http://cws.internet.com/16html .html for Windows 3.*x*.

Yahoo!   Yahoo! is not as well-suited for software listings as the dedicated software archives, but you can still find some good sites for HTML and text editors. It's easiest to go to http://www.yahoo.com/ and search for "Text Editors" and "HTML Editors" rather than trying to click your way through the different categories or typing in a very long URL.

Download.com   To check out the different editors available from CNET's download.com archive, go to http://www.download.com/ and click on the Internet category, followed by the HTML category. CNET

continued ▶

doesn't list editors separately from other HTML utilities, but you'll find a long list of HTML tools and editors in alphabetical order, including some packages not available from the other sites.

Other Relevant Web Sites   Carl Davis reviews various HTML editors and offers feature comparisons at `http://homepage.interaccess.com/` `~cdavis/edit_rev.html` (or head straight to the main list of HTML editors being reviewed by going to `http://homepage.interaccess.com/~cdavis/` `editrev/ed_list.html`).

Another set of reviews can be found at `http://cws.internet.com/` `32html-reviews.html`; both of these review sites are oriented toward Windows users.

For a more wide-ranging list of different editors, check the Tom Boutell's well-known World Wide Web FAQ's section on HTML editors (`http://` `www.boutell.com/faq/htedit.htm`).

Skill 4

Editing HTML Files with BBEdit

BBEdit is published by Bare Bones software (`http://www.barebones.com/`) and is perhaps the most widely used and well-known HTML text editor in the world. Its major limitation is that it is only available for Macintosh users.

BBEdit includes a great number of features not available with SimpleText, such as multiple-level undo, an HTML-aware spelling checker, multiple-file search and replace (with wildcards), the ability to read many different types of files, the ability to work with large files and to compare differences between files, HTML tag highlighting and error-checking, and helpful shortcuts for managing Web sites. To read more about BBEdit's features, go to `http://www.barebones.com/` `bbedit.html`.

BBEdit is commercial software (costing around $119), but a freeware version of BBEdit, called BBEdit Lite, offers a subset of BBEdit's features. You can download BBEdit Lite from `http://www.barebones.com/freeware.html`. (Macintosh users download files in either BinHex or MacBinary format. To handle either of these, you'll need to get a program such as Aladdin Systems' Stuffit Expander from `http://www.aladdinsys.com/`.)

Figure 4.3 shows BBEdit in action.

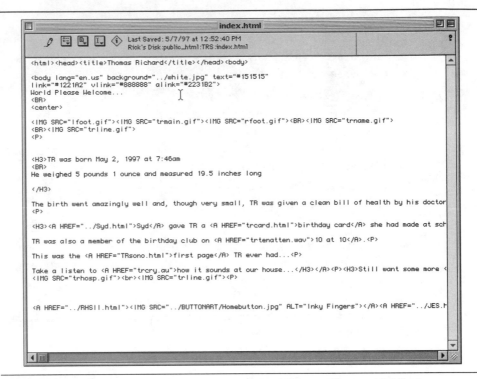

FIGURE 4:3: Bare Bones Software's BBEdit Lite editing an HTML document

If you're obtaining BBEdit Lite, you may also want to visit http://www.barebones.com/html.html to obtain a copy of the HTML Tools or HTML Extensions packages, which enhance BBEdit Lite's capabilities with toolbar buttons for HTML tags as well as other useful HTML time-savers.

Editing with UltraEdit

UltraEdit is a popular shareware text editor available for Windows. It comes in 16-bit and 32-bit versions.

NOTE   Windows 3.1 and earlier versions are "16-bit" operating systems, while Windows 95 and later versions (including Windows NT) are "32-bit" operating systems. The difference is purely technical, but you'll want to match your operating system to your software. For example, if you're using a 32-bit operating system, you'll want to download the 32-bit versions of software.

Like BBEdit, UltraEdit is a capable replacement for the default text editor. UltraEdit offers a lot more useful features than Notepad: It can edit huge files and work with columns; it includes a spell checker, highlights HTML tags, sorts text and compares files, opens and modifies multiple files at once, and lets you use macros and work with UNIX and Macintosh files.

You can read about the latest version of UltraEdit from `http://www.ultraedit.com/`, shown in Figure 4.4.

To download UltraEdit, visit `http://www.ultraedit.com/download.html` and choose the appropriate version (16- or 32-bit). These files are in zip format (an archive format that reduces file size). To unzip, you'll need to get a program such as WinZip from `http://www.winzip.com/`.

UltraEdit will work for 45 days; after that, you'll have to register it (which means that you have to pay for it—version 4.3, shown in Figure 4.4, costs $30).

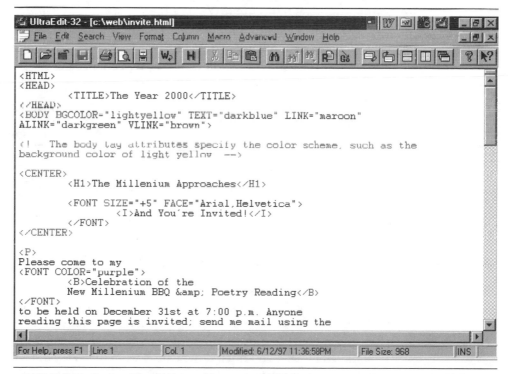

FIGURE 4.4: UltraEdit working on an HTML document we created in Skill 3. The array of menu and toolbar commands may be a little intimidating at first, but you'll quickly get used to them.

A Quick Glance at HotDog Professional

BBEdit and UltraEdit take a low-key approach, with a minimal set of toolbars and not a heavy emphasis on HTML design; they're more general-purpose text editors. Some HTML editors are exclusively designed for working with HTML. Such is the case with HotDog Professional, a well-known product that's been around for a while.

Unlike BBEdit and UltraEdit (which existed before the Web and have been expanded to include HTML capabilities), HotDog Professional, published by Sausage Software, is an HTML editor designed for Web page design from the beginning. From Sausage's Web page (`http://www.sausage.com/`) you can download HotDog Professional 3 (for Windows 95) or Hot Dog HTML Editor (for Windows 3.1).

HotDog's approach is to give you dozens of toolbars, wizards, templates, add-on programs, and buttons—to make sure there's a shortcut and tool for every possible HTML tag and action. It's certainly a valid approach, and experienced Web designers (with plenty of time to navigate their way through the learning curve of HotDog's interface) will certainly appreciate all of the bells and whistles, but for beginning authors it may be more prudent to start with a simpler text editor or HTML editor.

Figure 4.5 shows HotDog Professional in action, creating a simple Web page. The HTML tags were typed by HotDog; it can automate many simple processes and has many advanced features, but the amount of screen clutter can certainly be intimidating, as you can see.

Sausage Software includes some online tutorials to help you learn what all those buttons do. HotDog Professional can be downloaded for free; it will work for 14 days before you'll need to register it (version 3, shown here, costs $99.95).

An Even Quicker Glance at HomeSite

An HTML editor with an approach similar to HotDog is HomeSite, published by Allaire (the makers of Cold Fusion, a product that helps you connect a database to the Web). HomeSite provides toolbars and shortcuts for common and advanced HTML tasks. (A discussion of HomeSite's features is presented in the next section.) To obtain HomeSite, you must download it from the Web; the latest version is available from Allaire's site at `http://www.allaire.com/` (choose HomeSite from the Products section). Figure 4.6 shows the HomeSite editor at work; it has even more toolbars than HotDog Professional, but fortunately you can easily switch off most of them (and turn them back on only when you need them).

HomeSite is shareware; you can use it 50 times before you must register it (for $39.95).

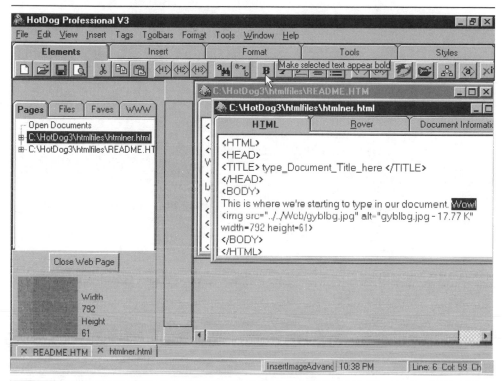

FIGURE 4.5: HotDog Professional, as it appears out of the box. Believe it or not, but you can add even more toolbars than this.

Editing HTML Files with a Word Processor

You probably already have a full-featured word processor that comes equipped with advanced features such as search and replace, macros, sorting, and so forth. Most word processors are designed for creating attractive documents (such as résumés and proposals) by formatting the text and graphics directly. But word processors are also capable of working with plain text, so there's no reason why you can't use your word processor to create HTML files. It only requires a slight change in mindset.

There are five main things to remember when creating Web pages with a word processor:

- You shouldn't use your word processor's formatting commands.

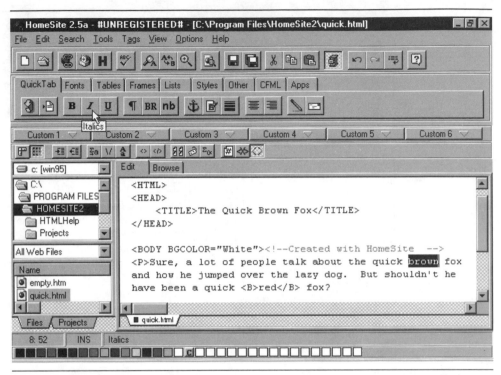

FIGURE 4.6: With Allaire's HomeSite, there are so many toolbars and doo-dads on the screen that it's hard at first to see where the HTML document is.

Your word processor has commands to make words bold, change line spacing, margins, page breaks and so forth. All of these formatting commands have no place in an HTML document. HTML documents must be in plain text (otherwise known as "ASCII text," "ASCII," or "Text Only" formats), and plain text can have no formatting at all—no bolds, no italics, no fonts, no headers, no footers, no borders, no shading, nor any other feature available from the Format menu. The font you use to type in your HTML code is irrelevant, as is the margin size and just about anything else. Just type your HTML code into the word processor without thinking about formatting at all.

- You must save your document in the correct format.

Word processors like to use their own special format. (That is, Microsoft Word saves its documents in "Microsoft Word format," WordPerfect saves in "Word-Perfect format," and so on.) This format contains all sorts of information that human beings can't understand—if you were to view the file directly by opening it in a text editor (like Notepad), it would look like gibberish. When you save your HTML documents, you must use the File ➤ Save As command (or on some word processors, the Export command or Text In/Out command). Choose "Text Only," "ASCII," "DOS Text," or whatever seems closest to that format. Text files are perfectly viewable by human beings, so you can double-check that the format is correct by trying to open the text file with your text editor.

Furthermore, you have to make sure the extension is correct. Many word processors add their own special extension (.doc for Microsoft Word, .wpd for WordPerfect, and so on). HTML files must end in .html (or .htm if your system doesn't support long extensions). When you use the Save As command, you have to remember to put in the extension. This applies even to Macintosh systems, which don't normally use extensions—you still have to type in the .html at the end of your filename.

TIP

While you're at it, remember to avoid putting spaces and special characters in your HTML filenames. Short, lowercase names are best because they're easiest to remember and type. So homepage.html, tori.html, poems.html, and index.html are good names. But HomePage.html, MyFabulousToriPage.Html, and PoEmS.HTML are bad names, because they're hard to type and remember. My Tori Page!.html is an illegal filename—because you can't have spaces or exclamation points in filenames on the Web.

Oftentimes, word processors keep trying to save your files in their special format. So if you save an HTML file in ASCII correctly and then come back and edit it later, you may still have to take precautions that your changes are not being saved in the wrong format.

- Treat HTML modes with caution.

Modern word processors (such as Word 97 as well as recent versions of WordPerfect) will let you save a document as HTML, or have special HTML authoring modes. If you use these modes, then you're using a Web page–creation tool, which we discuss later in the "Letting an HTML Page- or Site-Creation Tool Do the Driving" section.

In HTML mode, you can't enter HTML tags yourself—you have to just create your document, format it normally with the word processor's formatting commands, and then trust the word processor to do a good job of converting that formatting into HTML tags.

This would be fine if word processors did a good job of writing HTML. Unfortunately, most often they don't do a good job—in fact, they do a very poor job, and stick in all sorts of extraneous and erroneous HTML tags. You're usually much better off not using HTML mode at all and marking up the document yourself.

Skill 4

- Watch out for auto-correct and illegal characters.

Word and other word processors will often change characters and words automatically. Sometimes this is useful (for example, replacing "teh" with "the" and fixing "JAnan" with "Janan"). However, sometimes it can cause problems. For example, fancy quotes (" and " as opposed to ", and ' and ' instead of ') are not legal HTML characters and may be displayed as garbage by someone viewing your Web page.

- Treat your word processor like a text editor.

You can use macros, sorting, search and replace, spell checking, and all sorts of features that work on plain text. Just remember to treat your word processor as if it was a fancy text editor, like the ones we saw previously.

Since the world's most popular word processor is Microsoft Word, we'll take a look at how you can work with it to create HTML documents.

Using Microsoft Word as a Text Editor

No matter which version of Word you use, you can take advantage of Word's excellent spell checker; convenient keyboard shortcuts for cursor movement and cut, copy, and paste; powerful macro language; text sorting; and ability to work with multiple files and templates.

All of the precautions described previously apply to Word. If you're using Word as a text editor, be sure to switch off the AutoFormat commands for Smart Quotes (Tools ➤ Options ➤ AutoFormat, or Tools ➤ AutoFormat, depending on your version of Word).

In addition, be sure to save in "Text Only" format. Figure 4.7 shows the proper use of the File ➤ Save As command.

You can use Word's Tools ➤ Macro and Tools ➤ AutoCorrect features to help create shortcuts for HTML tags. If you're proficient with Word, you can set up toolbars with HTML shortcuts—or you can use the Web to find pre-designed Word HTML templates.

In many ways, the HTML editors that we discussed in the previous section are more powerful than Word. After all, they're already optimized for working with HTML tags—and can do tricks that Word can't handle, such as make a lot of changes to many different files at once with search and replace.

Alternately, you may decide that Word's strength is in its formatting, and use Word to create the HTML for you.

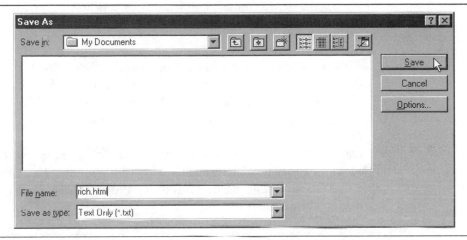

FIGURE 4.7: Use Word's File ➤ Save As command, and then select the Save as Type box to change from Microsoft Word format to Text Only format. Then type in your filename (with .html as the extension) and click on the Save button.

Using Word as a Page-Creation Tool

Word 97 added a new set of features designed to help you create and edit Web pages without knowing HTML. If you plan on using this feature of Word 97, you'll definitely want to study the Word manual or online help to get used to the Web templates and Web toolbar commands.

Word 97 can save your finished document in HTML format, and it can convert existing documents from Word format into HTML. It can also work as a rudimentary browser, opening pages on the Web and following links just like Navigator and IE do.

> **WARNING**   Depending on how Word 97 was installed, the Web Page Authoring tools may not be available. If they don't seem to be around, rerun the Setup program, choose a Custom Installation, and make sure the Web Page Authoring tools are selected.

Bear in mind that many of Word's features don't have Web equivalents, so you won't be able to use, for example, headers and footers, embossed text, columns, page numbering, revision marks, and data-entry fields.

There are two ways to create a Web page with Word:

- Open an existing document and use the File ➤ Save As command, choosing HTML Document as the Save as Type. (The finished result may differ from the existing document significantly, depending on how well Word 97 can convert its formatting.)

- Use the File ➤ New command and choose a Blank Web Page from the Web Pages section. Type your document and use the Word commands to format your document (for example, use the Style box and the commands on the Insert menu). Then use the File ➤ Save command; Word 97 will automatically save the file in HTML Document format.

When you've saved your document, be sure to open the resulting HTML file in a text editor to see what sort of HTML Word has created for you. We bet you'll be horrified. For example, Figure 4.8 shows a Word 97 HTML document being viewed in UltraEdit.

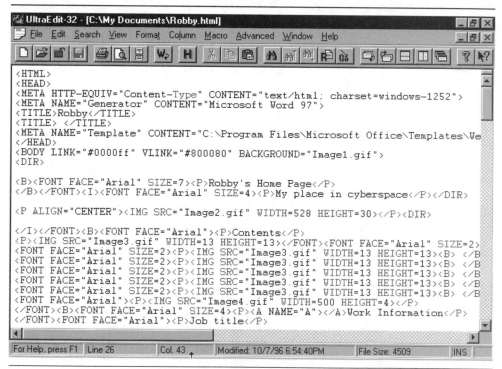

FIGURE 4.8: This HTML code was created by Word 97.

In addition to being formatted in a way that's not easy to follow, there are some strange and invalid HTML constructions, such as the extra <TITLE> tag and a bizarre fixation with the <DIR> tag (which will be discussed in Skill 6; it's supposed to be used for lists of files, not random headings).

Since Word is a Microsoft product, it tends to be biased toward another Microsoft product—IE. You may find Word using extensions to HTML that only IE understands, leaving Navigator users looking at a page very different from the one you thought you were creating. For more about extensions to HTML and the differences between IE and Navigator, see Skill 13.

On the plus side, it can be tedious to work with tables in HTML (see Skill 10), and Word 97 can do a pretty good job of converting a table you create onscreen into its HTML equivalent. In addition, Word 97 knows how to save files on the Internet directly (saving you from having to publish your files, as we'll learn how to do in Skill 19).

Although Word 97 handles the tags for you, it is possible to tinker with the tags yourself: Using the HTML Markup style, you can enter in some HTML tags. You can see the HTML tags for the entire document with the View ➤ HTML Source command. Overall, however, Word was designed to shield you from HTML tags as much as possible.

For our purposes, using Word 97 to create a page for you is not very helpful. You won't learn HTML, and you certainly won't be able to effectively take advantage of new and exciting HTML features, such as style sheets (Skill 14), scripting languages (Skill 15), and Dynamic HTML (Skill 16). Also, Word 97 can't handle any of HTML 4.0's new features.

USING INTERNET ASSISTANT

If you disagree with us and *like* the idea of creating and formatting a Word document normally and then saving it in HTML mode, you'll usually need to use Word 97. But if you have an earlier version of Word (such as Word 6 or Word 95 for Windows, or Word 6.01 for Macintosh), you can also use Microsoft's Internet Assistant.

This free add-in works much like Word 97, letting you create and save HTML pages using standard Word commands. If you are willing to trust its HTML, you can download it from http://www.microsoft.com/word/internet/ia/ and follow the instructions for installation.

If you think we sound a little leery of Word 97 and its HTML-writing capabilities, you're right. We're not nearly as strongly opposed to some of the other HTML page- and site-creation tools, such Netscape Navigator Gold and Netscape Composer. We'll see their strengths and drawbacks in the next section.

Letting an HTML Page- or Site-Creation Tool Do the Driving

Sit back, relax, and leave the HTML to the computer.

That's the general idea of page- and site-creation tools. These tools, also known as WYSIWYG (What You See Is What You Get) editors, let you type in the text of your document, format it with standard word processing commands and toolbar buttons, and then let you load in your images. As you edit, the program creates the HTML tags for you, behind the scenes.

NOTE   We're making a somewhat arbitrary distinction between page-creation tools, or tools we feel are oriented toward creating a single HTML document, and site-creation tools, or tools we feel are oriented toward creating bunches of Web pages.

The end result is that you don't have to know a thing about HTML. No tags to type, no syntax to remember. Sounds great in theory, right? In practice, it's never that easy.

Why You Should Know HTML Anyway

There are important advantages to creating the HTML yourself. You will be more aware of what HTML can and can't do, and you'll be more likely to fix problems when (not if) they occur. In addition, you'll have the added flexibility of being able to work on your Web site from any computer, not just the one where your Web-creation tool is located. (And there's no expensive software to buy and upgrade.)

It's common for these page-creation tools to advertise that they save you from "having to learn the complicated language used to create Web pages." As you've seen so far in Skills 2 and 3, HTML is not complicated at all—in fact, most of the tags are very straightforward.

In addition, there are some serious problems with the HTML code created by machine (just look at the Word 97 example in Figure 4.8). As a rule, these page- and site-creation tools don't produce very good HTML code. Not only is it bulky, inefficient, and often incorrect (not to mention difficult to follow and not aesthetically arranged), but it doesn't keep up with the newest capabilities of HTML.

Nonetheless, there are certainly times when it's easiest to use a WYSIWYG editor. But the more you know about HTML, the better you'll be able to take advantage of a page-creation tool. Whole books are written about using Composer or FrontPage, so we're not going to spend too long describing how to use them here—that would be counter-productive to our aim of teaching you HTML without crutches.

Creating Pages with Netscape Composer or Netscape Navigator Gold

Netscape Composer is part of the Netscape Communicator package (along with Navigator). It's a rudimentary editor; it doesn't have a lot of advanced features, but at the same time, it won't distract you with a lot of irrelevant toolbars. Furthermore, Composer is quite simple to use: Just start typing, and then apply styles and formatting from the Formatting toolbar, and add elements (such as images and horizontal rules) using the Composition toolbar. Figure 4.9 shows Composer in the middle of putting together a simple page.

Netscape Composer was introduced along with Netscape Navigator 4. If you use an older version of Navigator, then you can't use Composer without upgrading to the new version of Navigator as well. All is not lost however—you can use Netscape Navigator Gold, which includes a WYSIWYG page editor that's similar to Composer. About all that's different is a slight rearrangement of the toolbars, and the fact that Composer includes a spell checker and Navigator Gold doesn't.

In general, Composer and Navigator Gold turn out pretty good HTML—they don't try to get too fancy or play too many tricks with HTML. Partly this is because Netscape isn't reaching too far with these products: They don't have any method that lets you create frames, insert scripts or style sheets, or use any of the other advanced HTML features that we'll cover in later Skills.

Creating Pages with Other HTML Page-Creation Tools

A few of the other WYSIWYG page-creation tools that are out there include Atrax Web Publisher, Claris Home Page, HTML Express, Net-It Now, TrustedLink INP, and Hot Dog Express. We can't recommend any of them particularly strongly, since all of these page-creation tools have the same advantages and disadvantages found in Netscape Composer and Netscape Navigator Gold. However, each of these products have their advocates and their detractors. If you're interested, check out the comparative reviews we listed earlier, or join in on a discussion on the Web. You're free to download these tools from Tucows or Stroud's and give them a try on your own, since they're all shareware or available as demos.

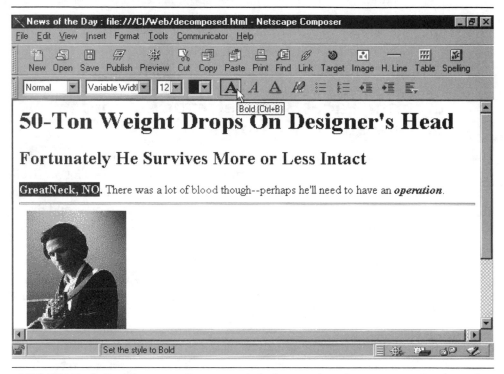

FIGURE 4.9: Netscape Composer is being used to change a couple of words into bold. Instead of typing <B> and </B>, you just click on the Bold button, similar to a word processor.

Alternately, you can give site-creation tools a try. Unlike page-creation tools, site-creation tools are designed to work on lots of different pages that are linked together to form a Web site. Suppose you have created a site for a business and need to change many different pages at once (say, for example, that you have created a new page and want to put a link to it on all of your existing pages); it would be tedious to make that change to multiple files using a simple text editor. More advanced HTML editors can do the job easily, but changing the pages with a page-creation tool would also be time-consuming since you'd need to fix them one at a time. Site-creation tools could handle the job much more efficiently.

There are three main site-creation tools in wide use: Microsoft FrontPage, Adobe PageMill (and SiteMill), and SoftQuad's HoTMetaL PRO. We'll briefly discuss PageMill and HoTMetaL PRO, and then look at FrontPage in more detail.

Managing Sites with Adobe PageMill and SiteMill

Adobe's PageMill is similar to Netscape Composer: It's a page-creation tool with toolbars for formatting. PageMill is available for both Macintosh and Windows and includes a stripped-down version of Photoshop for image editing. Unlike most WYSIWYG editors, PageMill supplies a fair degree of ability to work with the actual HTML tags, but it insists on a confusing layout for HTML tags that frustrates many Web designers.

PageMill is extremely popular, especially on the Macintosh, and has garnered excellent reviews. Its largest drawback is its price tag of $99.

For the Macintosh version, PageMill comes with SiteMill, a tool designed to help you manage sites. SiteMill offers efficient site management, allowing you to find and correct broken links, search and replace URLs across your Web site, and verify remote URLs.

To find out more about PageMill, and download a trial version, go to Adobe's site (http://www.adobe.com/), click on Products, and choose PageMill. This page includes a detailed description of PageMill as well as some sample sites created with PageMill.

Editing Pages and Managing Sites with HoTMetaL PRO

HoTMetaL PRO, published by SoftQuad (http://www.sq.com/), is something of a hybrid. It started life as an HTML editor, and grew into a WYSIWYG page creator and site manager, while still maintaining a close relationship with HTML tags. It's a flexible and powerful tool, in some ways incorporating some of the best features of HTML editors like HomeSite, as well as page-creation tools like Netscape Composer, and site managers like SiteMill or FrontPage. But it takes quite a while to learn how to use its features.

HoTMetaL PRO comes as two components: The HoTMetaL PRO Editor (which lets you create Web pages in either WYSIWYG or text modes, available for Windows, Macintosh, and UNIX), and the HoTMetaL PRO Information Manager, which lets you manage Web sites (with capabilities similar to SiteMill, but available for Windows only).

HoTMetaL PRO is a very strict editor. It tries to understand and validate every tag that you use in your HTML document so that it can display an approximation of how the browser will display the document. Figure 4.10 shows HoTMetaL PRO editing one of our examples from the previous Skill.

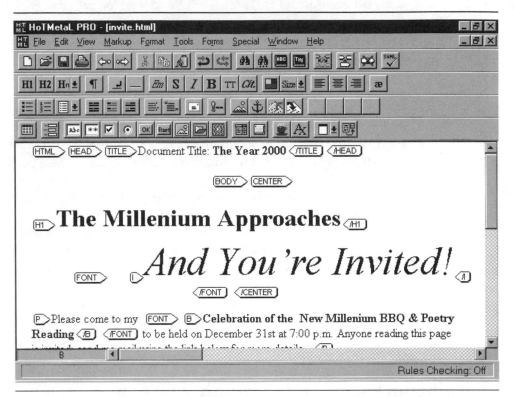

FIGURE 4.10: HoTMetaL PRO (with four rows of toolbar buttons) is displaying the `invite.html` file, and shows the fonts in an approximation of how Navigator and IE will end up displaying the file. Color information is not displayed. Notice the iconic nature of the HTML tags.

HoTMetaL PRO can be cumbersome to use, and its understanding of HTML is far from perfect (for example, it didn't understand the perfectly legal <SMALL> tag that we learned in the previous Skill).

If you do want to give HoTMetaL PRO a try, you can download a free trial version that works for 60 days from `http://www.sq.com/products/hotmetal/`; after the 60 days, you'll have to buy it for $159 if you want to keep using it.

Managing Sites with Microsoft FrontPage

Microsoft FrontPage 97 is a popular and wide-ranging site-creation tool (for Windows 95 only) that automates the process of creating and managing Web pages. You can certainly use FrontPage to create a single page, but it's more effective at managing many pages at once.

> FrontPage Express is a stripped-down version of FrontPage available as part of the complete version of IE 4.

FrontPage is part of the Office family, so it looks a little like Microsoft Word, with similar toolbars and features (such as the same spell checker). FrontPage features numerous templates and wizards that help you create your pages; and of course, it's a WYSIWYG editor that doesn't require entering HTML tags. Its editor is far more advanced than Netscape Composer, allowing you to create frames and forms, image maps, and scripts. It also includes *WebBots* designed to automate the process of creating advanced Web features, such as search engines, discussion groups, and so forth. However, these features only work on certain Web servers that are equipped with the Microsoft Server Extensions (and many Internet service providers won't install these extensions due to security considerations).

FrontPage 97 consists of several tools:

- FrontPage Explorer, which manages your Web site (allowing you to search and replace across all of your pages, check the validity of your links, and check the spelling of your entire site). The FrontPage Explorer gives you visual representation of your Web site, and lets you move and rename files similar to the Windows Explorer file tool included with Windows 95.

- FrontPage Editor, a WYSIWYG page-creation tool similar to Netscape Composer.

- To Do list, which keeps track of changes and tasks you need to complete to finish your Web site.

- Image Composer, which lets you create and edit images in many formats (behaving in some ways similar to Adobe's Photoshop, a popular—and expensive—image tool).

In addition, FrontPage 97 includes two different simple Web servers so that you can use your own computer to host your Web site (assuming it's connected to the Internet properly and you always leave it on), and a Web publishing tool so that you can transfer your Web site to the Internet easily.

Figure 4.11 shows the FrontPage Explorer managing a Web site.

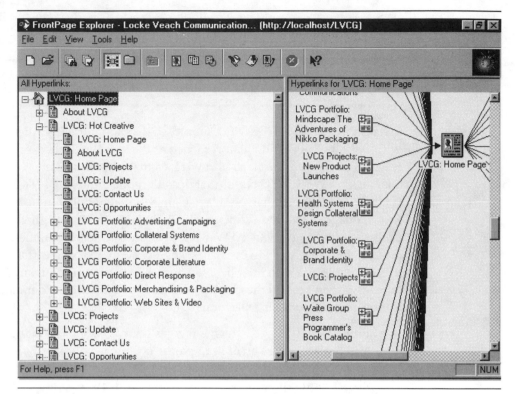

FIGURE 4.11: FrontPage Explorer displays the links between the pages that make up this site for Locke Veach Communications Group.

The largest disadvantage to FrontPage is in the FrontPage Editor, which is similar to Netscape Composer. (See Figure 4.12.)

If you edit an existing document with the FrontPage Editor, it will replace your HTML code with its own. FrontPage has some quirky ideas about how HTML code should be formatted (in one long, ugly block) and some misguided ideas about what HTML tags should be used. FrontPage code often doesn't validate as correct HTML.

Another disadvantage of FrontPage is that it is extremely biased toward IE; using FrontPage, you can insert features (such as scrolling marquees) that are exclusively IE extensions, and FrontPage will not warn you that Navigator users won't see these features. (For an overview of IE extensions, see Skill 13.)

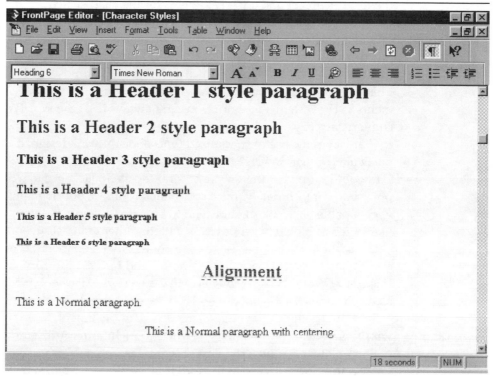

FIGURE 4.12: FrontPage Editor displays a sample document showing different headings and alignment. Notice the toolbars for formatting a Web page.

Despite these disadvantages, FrontPage is efficient at creating multiple pages, especially considering its templates and page-creation wizards.

FrontPage also excels at taking existing documents (such as Microsoft Word documents) and converting them into HTML. This is a frequent practice, and even if you don't use FrontPage, you'll want to convert documents. We'll see some methods for doing this in the next section.

Converting Existing Content to HTML with Conversion Tools

You can use several methods to convert an existing document into an HTML document. You can use the original program that created the document, and try saving it into text format (with a .html extension). Then, you must go through the text document and add HTML tags for the basic structure and the document's formatting (remembering especially to use the <P> tag before each paragraph). This is a time-consuming method.

A second approach is to copy and paste your content from the existing document into a WYSIWYG editor, such as Netscape Composer or FrontPage Editor. This technique will work, but is also time-consuming if you have many documents to convert; furthermore, you can't always trust the WYSIWYG editor to convert correctly.

That leaves the use of specialized tools and software designed to convert from a particular format into HTML.

It would be great if there were several excellent packages to which we could point you. Unfortunately, most conversion tools are poorly maintained and not very capable. In addition, they tend to be difficult to track down, so it's best to use a Web catalog that keeps track of them rather than list several here.

The best place to start a search for a good conversion tool is Yahoo! (`http://www.yahoo.com/`). Choose the Computers and Internet category, then Software ➤ Internet ➤ World Wide Web ➤ HTML Converters. After looking through the available converters listed, you can find a lot more listings by clicking on Shareware.

If you're trying to convert a Microsoft Word document, for example (and you wisely pass by the option of using Microsoft's Internet Assistant), there are several templates and converters listed.

A common approach is to use a well-understood format, such as RTF. *RTF* is the Rich Text Format designed to be a common format used by many different word processors. Many programs, including Word and WordPerfect, understand RTF and can save and read files in that format. And there are quite a few RTF-to-HTML converters listed; most likely you'll be able to select one that can meet your needs.

 NOTE   Part of the reason there are so few good conversion tools is that conversion is difficult. It's far from an exact science, and you should be prepared to edit the resulting HTML file by hand. You should also remember that the result will probably not closely resemble the original document since HTML is not a full-featured, page-description language.

In this Skill, we spent some time understanding the different available HTML tools, including text editors, HTML editors, word processors, page-creation tools, and site-creation tools. We also took a brief look at how conversion programs can be useful. It's useful to have a wide range of tools at your disposal so you can pick the appropriate tool for the job.

Now that you've chosen a tool to help you create your HTML documents (or at least decided to stick with your basic text editor for now), we'll return to our exploration of HTML tags. In the next Skill, we'll see what sorts of tags go into the head section of a document, and in Skill 6, we'll see all of the tags that are used in the body section of a document.

Are You Experienced?

Now you can...

☑ **use your text editor to edit HTML documents**

☑ **choose an HTML tool from the various options**

☑ **understand the limitations and strengths of various HTML editors and page-creation tools**

☑ **use Microsoft Word or another word processor to create HTML documents**

☑ **search for a conversion tool to translate documents**

Skill 4

Classifying Your Site with Head Section Elements

- → Using *DOCTYPE* declarations
- → Learning and using head section elements
- → Naming your pages strategically
- → Describing your page for search engines using *<META>* tags
- → Using meta refresh
- → Specifying your document's language

In Skill 2, we learned about the basic structure of HTML documents and described the difference between the head section and the body section. Now that we've seen how to arrange and beautify HTML documents (in Skill 3) and use various HTML tools (in Skill 4), it's time to examine the HTML elements in detail.

In this Skill, we'll take a close look at the head section elements, while in the next Skill we'll examine the body section elements. The head section is much more complicated than the body section, and many of its elements are for advanced features. However, since the head section comes before the body section in every HTML document, it makes sense to discuss the head section first.

In this Skill, we'll show you which head section elements are important and worth learning about, and which elements you should put off using until you have more experience with HTML. At the end of this skill, we'll talk about how you can specify language information for your HTML documents so that browsers and search engines can tell what language you've used for your document.

Before we go into the head section elements, we'll start this Skill by examining the DOCTYPE declaration, which goes before the head section and is used to define which version of HTML you're using.

Classifying Your HTML Document with *DOCTYPE*

We stated in Skill 2 that you should start your document with the <HTML> tag. Actually, there is something that should precede even the <HTML> tag: the DOCTYPE declaration.

 NOTE   The DOCTYPE declaration is not an HTML tag or HTML element; it's an SGML entity that defines what version of HTML your document uses.

There are many versions of HTML, and there will be many different future versions of HTML. (We presented an overview of the different versions of HTML at the end of Skill 1, and we take a look at future versions in Skill 20.) In addition, Netscape Navigator and Microsoft Internet Explorer understand several extensions to HTML (which are discussed in Skill 13). So with all of these different versions and dialects of HTML that exist, how can you define precisely what version of HTML you're using?

The answer is to include a DOCTYPE declaration at the very beginning of your document. You can think of the DOCTYPE declaration as a magical incantation that you should include with every document in order to specify exactly what type of HTML you're using.

Here's the DOCTYPE declaration that you should include at the top of your HTML 4.0 documents:

```
<!DOCTYPE HTML PUBLIC "-//W3C//DTD HTML 4.0//EN">
```

This declaration looks fairly complex, and it is (we'll explain it a little later). It's difficult to type in this declaration each time you're creating an HTML document from scratch and get it right, so it's probably worthwhile to create a template document that includes this DOCTYPE declaration. (We'll talk about templates in more detail in Skill 17.)

Skill 5

WHAT IF YOU DON'T INCLUDE A *DOCTYPE* DECLARATION?

As you explore the Web and view the source code of Web pages, you'll notice many HTML documents don't include a DOCTYPE declaration.

The main reason for this is that Navigator and IE don't care if the DOCTYPE declaration is there. And since these two browsers make up the majority of browsers in use, there is not a large consequence for most Web page designers if they leave out the DOCTYPE declaration.

However, some browsers (such as the HotJava browser and Softquad's Panorama Pro SGML viewer) do use the DOCTYPE declaration. Future versions of Navigator and IE might well behave differently than the current versions and may display your page based on the DOCTYPE of your document. Furthermore, the DOCTYPE declaration is required if you use any of the validation programs or sites we discuss in Skill 17.

If you want your page to be valid HTML 3.2 or 4.0, you should include the DOCTYPE. If you are using HTML 2.0, or if you don't care whether your HTML code is valid so long as it seems to work in your version of IE and Navigator, then there is no consequence to leaving off the DOCTYPE.

continued ▶

The official specification for HTML 2.0 was specific in its definition of the use of the DOCTYPE. Here's the DOCTYPE declaration for an HTML 2.0 document:

```
<!DOCTYPE HTML PUBLIC "-//IETF//DTD HTML 2.0//EN">
```

According to HTML 2.0, if you leave off the DOCTYPE, then the browser is supposed to assume that you're using HTML 2.0, as if you had entered the above DOCTYPE declaration. This statement has not been contradicted by later versions of HTML.

Since HTML 2.0 doesn't include many of the tags found in HTML 3.2 and 4.0 (including tables, fonts, and attributes in the <BODY> tag, among others), HTML 2.0 is quite limiting. It's possible that a future browser will ignore tags in your document that don't match the DOCTYPE that you've used, so if you don't use a DOCTYPE, it's possible that non-HTML 2.0 tags will be ignored or not work correctly. However, this scenario is a bit unlikely.

In practice, the only real consequence of leaving off the DOCTYPE declaration is that your pages can't be verified as valid HTML. Since validation is a worthwhile service and can point out typos in your tags or mistakes in the structure of your HTML documents, it's worth putting in the DOCTYPE declaration solely to satisfy the validation services.

By the way, the specification for HTML 2.0 is referred to as RFC 1866. This stands for "Request for Comments #1866." An official Internet specification published by the Internet Engineering Task Force—or IETF—is called a "Request for Comments" by tradition. There are many different RFCs that apply to the Web. You can see a list of RFCs (http://ds.internic.net/ds/dspg1intdoc.html), although many of them apply to other Internet functions that don't have to do with the Web. To read the official specification for HTML 2.0, go to http://www.cis.ohio-state.edu/htbin/rfc/rfc1866.html.

There are many different DOCTYPE declarations, and the one you use depends on what version of HTML that you're using. For most documents, use the HTML 4.0 DOCTYPE declaration we listed previously. If you are only using features of HTML 2.0, you may as well leave off the DOCTYPE declaration.

If you are only using features of HTML 3.2, use the following DOCTYPE declaration:

```
<!DOCTYPE HTML PUBLIC "-//W3C//DTD HTML 3.2 Final//EN">
```

(Or you can use an accepted variant such as one that leaves off the word "Final.")

If you use any of Netscape's or Microsoft's proprietary extensions to HTML (shown in Skill 13), then you need to use an appropriate DOCTYPE, such as:

```
<!DOCTYPE HTML PUBLIC "-//Netscape Comm. Corp.//DTD HTML//EN">
<!DOCTYPE HTML PUBLIC"-//Microsoft//DTD Internet Explorer 3.0 HIML//EN">
```

WHAT DO THE COMPONENTS OF *DOCTYPE* MEAN?

It's not really necessary to understand what all the elements mean, since the entire phrase of the declaration that you choose has to be included in your document without alteration. That's why it's like a magical formula—if you change even a single letter, it won't work.

You may have noticed that the DOCTYPE declaration is different from the rest of the HTML tags we've seen. That's because DOCTYPE isn't really an HTML tag—it is actually an SGML element (Standard Generalized Markup Language, a language used to define other markup languages such as HTML).

So that you're not mystified about the meaning of the DOCTYPE declaration, we'll offer this brief explanation of the components.

The first word, <!DOCTYPE, defines that this element is about to explain what *DTD*, or Document Type Definition, you are using for your HTML code. Each version of HTML has its own DTD, which defines the tags and attributes and how they can be used.

The second word, HTML, corresponds to the <HTML> tag used in your document.

continued ▶

The third word can be either PUBLIC or SYSTEM. A *public* DTD means that the next word in the DOCTYPE declaration refers to a "formal public identifier," or official label that defines the company and version of the DTD. A *system* DTD means that the next word is a URL that contains the actual DTD itself. (These DTDs are highly technical documents written in SGML that define the tags used in the markup language in a very specific way.)

The fourth word appears in quotes. If you use a URL, then this word is in a straightforward format that's already familiar to you from Skill 1; but if you use a formal public identifier, then there are a few more things to see. Each of the separate fields of an FPI are marked with two forward slashes (//). The first character after the quote can be either a plus (+) or a minus (-). A plus means the organization that wrote the DTD has registered it with ISO; a minus means the organization has not registered the DTD. As it turns out, most organizations have not registered their DTDs with ISO. The next field (after the two forward slashes) is the name of the company that created the DTD. The field after that is the official name of the DTD (including its version number), starting with the word "DTD" itself. Finally, the last field contains a two-letter identification of the language that the name of the DTD is written in (EN for "English").

Harold Driscoll (the Webmaster for the Chicago Computer Society) has an informative list of DTDs and their DOCTYPE declarations listed (`http://www.ccs.org/html/dtd/index.html`). In addition, there is usually a collection of DOCTYPE declarations available from the different HTML validation services; one such list is at the Kinder, Gentler Validator (`http://ugweb.cs.ualberta.ca/~gerald/validate/lib/catalog`). (We'll see the Kinder, Gentler Validator in action in Skill 17.)

Now that we've learned about the DOCTYPE declaration, we can proceed to a discussion of the elements that are found within the head section. We'll present them in order from most important to least important.

Understanding the Head Section Elements

The head section of your document contains information about the document. As we learned in Skill 2, the head section must include the title of the document (within <TITLE> and </TITLE> tags) and may optionally include other information, such as a description of the document, a list of keywords that help index a document, copyright information, and the name of the program used to create the HTML document.

The <HEAD> tag itself is optional. If you start your document with <TITLE> and other head section elements, and then place the body of your document next, then browsers will have no trouble understanding where the head section ends and where the body section begins.

So far in this book, all of our examples have had simple head sections, with only the title element. In this Skill, we'll create an example that has a much more complete head section. We'll spend more time on the title element, and then see the other head elements that use the following tags: <META>, <LINK>, <BASE>, <STYLE>, <SCRIPT>, and <ISINDEX>.

Using the Title Element

The title element (<TITLE> and </TITLE>) is used to contain the title of your document, as we saw in Skill 2.

 TIP   Titles should be fairly short since there's not much room on a title bar—you should keep your titles to less than 80 characters. Although there's actually no official limit to the length of your title, you'll just find that Navigator, IE, and other browsers arbitrarily cut off their display of your title after they run out of room.

Titles are always displayed as a single line. However, because of the white space rules (as defined in Skill 3), you can type your title on two lines, like this:

```
<TITLE>Sybex Books presents
HTML: No experience required.</TITLE>
```

Even though you have typed the title on two lines, it will still display as one line; the carriage return is ignored, along with any extraneous spaces. It's sometimes useful to be able to type your title on two lines if the title's first line is the same for every page on your site.

 **WARNING**   It's considered bad style to put spaces in between the title element's tags and the title itself, so don't use titles such as <TITLE> My Page </TITLE>. Instead, make sure there are no spaces in between the tags and your title, like this: <TITLE>My Page</TITLE>.

Since the title is the only general requirement of HTML, a minimum HTML document consists only of the title. (However, a minimum HTML 3.2 or 4.0 document consists of a DOCTYPE declaration and a title element.)

Our example title ("Sybex Books presents…") is just two lines of HTML. This code can be saved as an HTML document (for example, `title.html`) and displayed in a browser without problems. Figure 5.1 shows this document, which consists of only a title, in IE.

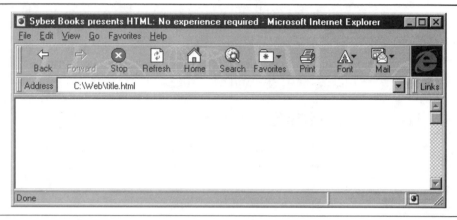

FIGURE 5.1: Just a title by itself. It's not very informative, but it's still a valid HTML document.

You are only allowed to have one title element in your document. As we've seen, most browsers display the title in the title bar at the very top of the document, where it's easy to miss; but Lynx displays the title right-aligned on the first line, and a text-to-speech browser will usually read the title of a document aloud before reading the rest of the document.

NOTE   A lot of people put the same text in their title as well as their first-level heading (<H1>, discussed in detail in the next Skill). There's nothing wrong with this, although a title should be something that's useful independent of viewing the document, whereas the first-level heading can be very particular to the document itself, perhaps even only making sense in the context of viewing the document.

Markup is not permitted in the title element, so code such as the following is invalid:

```
<TITLE>Show <B>ME</B> the Money</TITLE>
```

HTML allows you to include entities in the title element (recall our discussion of entities from Skill 3):

```
<TITLE>My R&eacute;sum&eacute; (&copy; 1997)</TITLE>
```

These entities are a little hard to read, but the above title would display quite nicely, as shown here.

WARNING Some older browsers can't display entities in the title element, so you may want to only include entities in your document's title if they're essential.

Using Advisory Titles

In HTML 4.0, almost every tag can take a TITLE attribute. For example, you could use a TITLE attribute with an anchor element (just add the TITLE attribute to the <A> tag) or to an image's <IMG> tag. These titles are called *advisory titles* and help provide additional information about individual elements of your document. We'll see some examples of advisory titles in Skill 7 and Skill 8. Don't confuse advisory TITLE attributes with the main title element of a document.

Now that we know all the rules of titles, we'll present brief tips about how you can title your documents to your advantage.

Strategically Naming Your Pages

Even though the title element is required by the HTML specification, Navigator and IE don't explode if you happen to leave it off. Instead, they simply display your document's URL in the title bar.

However, there are several excellent reasons why you want the browser to display an informative title instead of a URL (aside from the wise practice of using a title so that your document is valid HTML):

- When people are looking at a browser's list of open pages or recently visited pages, it's easier to understand a title than a URL. They can quickly choose "Philip's Photography Bookstore" page, but they might not recognize your page if it's listed as `http://www.myisp.com/~myname/photbk.html`.

- Every browser lets users create shortcuts to URLs, or *bookmarks*. (Bookmarks are saved in an easily accessible list, so people can quickly return to their favorite Web documents without having to surf or enter a URL into the browser's location bar.) When someone creates a bookmark to your Web page, it is the title of your document that is entered into their bookmark list. If your document's title is not descriptive, then someone seeing that bookmark weeks later probably won't remember what the page is about.

- Search engines (as we defined in Skill 1) help people look for pages. If you put a word in your title that's frequently searched for, then people will be more likely to see your page returned in the search list generated by AltaVista, Excite, HotBot, or other search engines.

- Directories, such as Yahoo!, often list pages in alphabetical order by title. If your page begins with "Aardvark" then it will probably be close to the top of a list. (However, don't get involved in a "I-Can-Use-More-As-Than-You-Can" race—flip to the Yellow Pages in your phone book for "Storage" and see how many companies are competing as "AAAA Storage" or "AAAAA Self-Storage.")

- Some computer alphabetization systems organize in "ASCII order"—that is, the order in which the character appears in the ASCII chart (see the appendix). ASCII puts punctuation first, and the first piece of punctuation (after the space) is the exclamation point. So if your page is called "!!! BUY NOW!!!" it has an excellent chance of being listed first (unless it's beaten out by the "!!!!!!!!!WOW!!!!!!!!!" page). However, these sorts of titles are quite obnoxious, especially when a list contains more than one page trying to be listed first in this way. (And watch out, some alphabetization systems put punctuation last.)

- Consider putting your organization or site name as the first or last part of each document's title. That way, each of your pages is "branded" as being part of your site, which helps you create a consistent identity for your pages.

- Make sure that each title for every page on your site is unique. If you give every page on your site the title "Warlock Development Corp," then people (including you!) won't be able to tell which page is which when they are listed by title. People *will* know which one is which if one page is called "Warlock Development: Company History" and the other page is called "Warlock Development: Product Catalog."

- If your document is time-specific and won't be updated in the future, you probably want to include that time information in the title (such as "Spring 1998 Course Catalog for Riverside College"). That way, people seeing your document on a list generated by a search engine will know if your document is applicable to their desired time frame.

- If your document is time-specific and is updated frequently, then you probably should *not* include the time information in the title. Titles used in Web catalogs (like Yahoo!) and people's bookmark lists are not updated easily or often. Instead, indicate in the title that the document is current: "Coolzine's Most Recent Issue" or "Current Computer Course Offerings from Diversi-Tech." (Of course, at that point you're more or less obligated to keep the page current for all eternity.)

Now that we've seen the title element in exhaustive detail, it's time to see the rest of the head section tags, starting with the meta element.

Using the Meta Element

The meta element is used to present document meta-information (that is, information about the document itself). The meta element consists of a <META> tag.

There are two ways to use the <META> tag: for named information (with the NAME attribute), and for HTTP server-equivalent commands (with the HTTP-EQUIV attribute). Both of these attributes use an accompanying CONTENT attribute.

 NOTE   Remember, an *attribute* of a tag is a keyword used within the tag to change its behavior. We defined this term in Skill 1 and used several attributes in Skill 2, such as the HREF attribute of the <A> tag: <A HREF="http://www.yahoo.com/">.

Later in this section, we'll see several uses of these two kinds of <META> tags for special purposes, including describing your site for a search engine, adding content ratings to your page, and using a special feature called *meta refresh*.

Using *<META> NAME* Tags

We'll start with some examples of <META> tags that use the NAME attribute. One common use of a named <META> tag is to indicate authorship. For example:

```
<META NAME="Author" CONTENT="William Shakespeare Jr.">
```

This tells software programs (as well as people viewing your document's source) that the document was written by William Shakespeare Jr.

There are a wide range of different values you can use in place of "Author" in the NAME attribute. For example:

```
<META NAME="Copyright" CONTENT="&copy; 1997 Philm Freax.">
```

There's no reason why you can't make up your own <META> tags that follow the same model:

```
<META NAME="LastModifiedBy" CONTENT="Mary Smith">
<META NAME="FavoriteColor" CONTENT="Red">
```

NOTE   These kinds of <META> tags aren't recognized by any general-purpose browser or software program, so you may just want to use a comment instead (as defined and illustrated in Skill 3).

HTML 4.0 recommends the use of a PROFILE attribute in the <HEAD> tag to link to a document that describes the properties of the different <META> NAME tags you use and sets their default values. For example, you could set up a group of meta elements you wish to use and link to them from each document via a <HEAD PRO-FILE="http://www.foo.com/myprofile.txt"> tag. Then, software such as an indexing program would be able to understand the custom <META> tags you use in your head section. Unfortunately, external profiles are not yet in wide use, so it's unclear if this will become an important practice. One profile that's well-defined is the Dublin Core (http://www.oclc.org:5046/research/dublin_core/).

Understanding Common *<META> NAME* Tags

Many HTML editors (of the type we saw in the previous Skill) will stick in a <META> NAME tag that indicates what program was used to create the HTML document. For example:

```
<META NAME="GENERATOR" CONTENT="Mozilla/4.01 [en] (Win95; I) [Netscape]">
```

This <META> tag indicates that the document was "generated" by the English version ("[en]") of Netscape Composer 4.01 on the Windows 95 platform. (Navigator's nickname has historically been "Mozilla," a name that refers to both the "Mosaic" browser upon which Navigator was based, and the Japanese monster "Godzilla" who habitually destroys downtown Tokyo.) Different HTML tools use their own format for their generator <META> tags.

Other common examples of <META> tags that use the NAME attribute also use an attribute new to HTML 4.0 called SCHEME. Scheme attributes define an entry in a well-known classification scheme such as the Dewey Decimal System or the ISBN numbers used for books:

```
<META NAME="DESCRIPTION" SCHEME="DDS" CONTENT="428.42 Speed reading">
<META NAME="IDENTIFIER" SCHEME="ISBN" CONTENT="0-07-882283-1">
```

These two tags place the document in either the Dewey Decimal Scheme ("DDS" in the first example) or identify the ISBN number scheme associated with the document in the second example. You could also use other schemes such as Library of Congress classification.

There are other popular <META> NAME tags used to give your page a description and keywords to control how your site is indexed; we'll see these <META> tags in the next section.

Increasing Search Hits with *DESCRIPTION* and *KEYWORDS* <*META*> Tags

Two of the most common <META> tags use the NAME="DESCRIPTION" and NAME="KEYWORDS" attributes. These two attributes can be used to help search engines list and describe your page.

Several of the most popular search engines, including Digital's AltaVista (http://www.altavista.digital.com/) and the Infoseek Corporation's InfoSeek service (http://www.infoseek.com/), will take advantage of a description <META> tag or a keywords <META> tag to help index your site.

For example, consider the following two <META> tags from The Net Net, an art and technology Web zine edited by Kristen Ankiewicz (http://www.thenetnet.com/):

```
<META NAME="DESCRIPTION" CONTENT="-=the net net=- is a weekly arts and
entertainment magazine featuring reviews, essays, art, animation, vrml,
and more.">
<META NAME="KEYWORDS" CONTENT="beer, restaurants, webgrrls,
interactivity, java, music reviews, funk, alternative books, essays,
virtual reality, animation, utilities, women on the internet,
technology revolution, new media, digital art, Negroponte, Acker,
Mekons, Haino, Boston">
```

Search engines that use these tags, such as AltaVista and InfoSeek, will display the description instead of an abstract generated from the first few words of the document. Also, a search on any of the keywords has a chance of returning The Net Net, even if that issue doesn't otherwise contain any of the words listed.

TIP   AltaVista will index the description and keywords up to a limit of 1,024 characters, so be sure to double-check that your description is short enough.

One secret of keywords is to use lots of synonyms. Another tactic is to include the names of your competitors in the keywords <META> tag.

WARNING   If you repeat keywords too much, then the search engines will penalize your attempt to manipulate them by *decreasing* the likelihood that they will display your page in a search result.

Sometimes you *don't* want to have the search engine index your page or the links leading from your page. The search engines send out "robots" that index the Web by following links. Using the robots <META> tag, you can indicate your preference to the search engine robots when they come by your page.

NOTE   The robots <META> tag is new in HTML 4.0 to allow authors to indicate to visiting robots whether a document may be indexed, or used to harvest more links. No server administrator action is required. Previous to HTML 4.0, Web site authors had to create a specially formatted text file called robots.txt. For more information about the robots.txt file, see http://info.webcrawler .com/mak/projects/robots/norobots.html. Note that the robots.txt file can only apply to an entire site, not an individual Web author's directory.

Here's an example of a robots <META> tag that tells a search engine robot that it should neither index this document nor analyze it for links:

```
<META NAME="ROBOTS" CONTENT="NOINDEX, NOFOLLOW">
```

The values allowed in the CONTENT attribute are INDEX or NOINDEX (which indicate whether the current document should be indexed) and ALL or NOFOLLOW (which indicate whether the robot should follow links in your document). The name and the content attribute values are case-insensitive, as are most attributes.

The default values for the robots <META> tag are INDEX and ALL, so if you leave off the robots <META> tag in a document, it will be indexed and all of the links on that page will be indexed as well. (Skill 18 will tell you how to command a robot to come by your site, but they do visit on their own if someone has linked to you.)

WARNING   Since the robots <META> tag is new, not all robots are programmed to obey the robots <META> tag. Also, some insidious robots are sent out to gather e-mail addresses from Web pages and add any e-mail addresses they find to commercial junk e-mail (*spam*) mailing lists. These e-mail harvesting robots just about always ignore robot <META> tags. Some people put easily decoded bogus e-mail addresses on their pages to foil these robots. (For example, you might see an address such as "estephen@NOSPAMemf.net" along with a note telling you to remove the word "NOSPAM" to get the correct e-mail address.)

Changing Server Headings with *HTTP-EQUIV* *<META>* Tags

The second type of <META> tag uses the HTTP-EQUIV attribute. These <META> tags tell the HTTP server (the computer server that transmits your Web page whenever someone requests it) to include an extra "header" of information before it sends the Web page itself. Server *headers* are normally used automatically to describe your document. For example, your HTTP server automatically sends headers that describe the date your document was last modified, among other information. HTTP headers are a complex subject, and we won't go into them in much detail in this book. Fortunately, there are not many HTTP-EQUIV <META> tags in common use. One that is used is the expiration <META> tag. By including the tag:

```
<META HTTP-EQUIV="Expires" CONTENT="Tue, 24 Dec 1997 11:38:00 GMT">
```

you are telling your HTTP server to precede your document with a header that looks like this:

```
Expires: Sun, 26 Dec 1998 11:38:00 GMT
```

HOW TO SPECIFY DATE AND TIME

You won't have to specify dates and times very often in HTML, but when you do, you have to use a very specific format. For dates and times in a head section, follow this format precisely:

```
Tue, 08 Jul 1997 09:38:23 GMT
```

The tricky part is converting your desired time into Greenwich Mean Time.

We'll see a different time format that you have to use for the <INS> and <DEL> tags, which we introduce in Skill 6.

Browsers should understand the "Expires:" header to mean that your document expires at the time specified, and that the browser should fetch a fresh copy of your document after the document has expired. Of course, this all assumes that you will know when you're going to update your document, and that you don't want people reading an old version of the document that they might have stored locally.

Another use of a meta HTTP-EQUIV tag is to provide a rating of your page's content, in order to help parents screen out material that may be harmful to children. The most common scheme for rating pages involves something called a "PICS" label, which we'll explain in the "Rating Your Pages with a PICS Label" section.

Here's a sample HTML document that combines several <META> tags together:

metaexample.html

```
<!DOCTYPE HTML PUBLIC "-//W3C//DTD HTML 3.2 Final//EN">
<HTML>
<HEAD>
    <TITLE>Vanilla Ice Appreciation Page</TITLE>
    <META NAME="Author" CONTENT="Stephen Mack and Janan Platt">
    <META HTTP-EQUIV="Expires" CONTENT="Fri, 31 Dec 1999 23:59:59 GMT">
    <META NAME="Description" CONTENT="This document describes EVERYTHING that
➥we like about the musician Vanilla Ice.">
    <META NAME="Keywords" CONTENT="Vanilla Ice, Robert Van Winkle, music,
➥rock, has-been">
    <META NAME="Copyright" CONTENT="&copy; 1997 by Winter Weather.">
    <META HTTP-EQUIV="Content-Language" CONTENT="en">
</HEAD>
<BODY>
     Yup, yup.
</BODY>
</HTML>
```

None of these <META> tags appear in the document display (only the title text and the words "Yup, Yup" appear in the browser, unless the person looking at this page decides to view its source with the View ➤ Source command). The <META> tags here don't actually affect the browser's display of this document at all; however, they do let software programs and search engines know a lot of useful information about this document, without cluttering up the way the document is displayed.

Rating Your Pages with a PICS Label

There are numerous rating services on the Internet, and parents who are concerned about their children accidentally running across inappropriate material often use software such as SurfWatch, Cyber Patrol, NetNanny, CYBERSitter, or a similar program that automatically rejects pages containing certain words or from questionable sites.

IE and Navigator support a broader approach, where you can set the browser to avoid loading pages that contain, nudity, sex, violence, or bad language. Web designers voluntarily give their sites a PICS rating, which indicates how much nudity, sex, violence, and bad language is contained in their site. When IE or Navigator are set to screen sites and come across a site with a PICS rating that meets the level that has been set as inappropriate, then the site will be rejected.

PICS is a standard established by the W3C and stands for Platform for Internet Content Selection. The PICS standard defines a complicated <META> tag format that indicates the content of a Web page. Technical information about PICS is available from the W3C (`http://www.w3.org/PICS/`).

In general, the format of the <META> tag for a PICS rating is like this:

```
<META HTTP-EQUIV="PICS-Label" CONTENT='labellist'>
```

The part that varies is represented by the word "labellist" (note that it's contained in single quotes, not double quotes; attribute values can use either single quotes or double quotes, and if the attribute value contains double quotes, you need to surround the whole value with single quotes instead of the more commonly used double quotes). You can't simply create the labellist on your own; instead, you have to visit a ratings organization and have them generate a labellist for you.

There are many different independent organizations that provide PICS-compatible ratings. Perhaps the most popular organization that provides these ratings is the RSAC, Recreational Software Advisory Council (which is well-known for its computer game rating service).

To get a rating, visit the RSAC Web site (`http://www.rsac.org/`) and go through the self-guided rating process. At the end, the RSAC will generate a <META> tag for you to copy into your HTML document.

Here's a rating that was generated for Zeigen's Dilemma:

```
<META http-equiv="PICS-Label" content='(PICS-1.1
"http://www.rsac.org/ratingsv01.html" l gen false comment
"RSACi North America Server" by "estephen@emf.net" for
"http://www.emf.net/~estephen/" on
"1997.06.05T18:51-0500" r (n 0 s 1 v 3 l 4))'>
```

The important part of this label is the list of four different ratings at the end (which are based on a scale from 0 to 4); here, it indicates that this site has no nudity, a little bit of sex, quite a bit of violence, and a lot of bad language. To actually decode the meaning of these labels, you'll need to read RSAC's ratings guidelines for yourself.

Skill 5

TIP   There's lots of useful information in the RSAC FAQ (`http://www.rsac`
`.org/faq.html`).

Creating Dynamic Documents Using Meta Refresh

A final and common use of the <META> tag is the <META> tag with a REFRESH attribute value. This allows a page to specify that the browser should retrieve a new page after a certain number of seconds. The common name for this feature is *meta refresh*.

Meta refresh was a Navigator extension to HTML that is still not fully supported by every browser, even though it is officially described in HTML 4.0's specification. Meta refresh can be used to make slide shows or guided tours.

The basic use of meta refresh is specified by HTML 4.0 with an example like this:

```
<META NAME="REFRESH" CONTENT="3,http://www.webville.com/~tori/">
```

Unfortunately, this syntax is not understood by any current browser. There's a traditional form of meta refresh (which, although it's not valid HTML syntax it actually works). For example:

```
<META HTTP-EQUIV="REFRESH"
CONTENT="10;URL=http://www.foo.com/intro.html">
```

This tag tells the browser to wait 10 seconds and then retrieve the page at the URL listed. You can use any value instead of 10 seconds; if you specify 0 seconds, then Navigator and IE will fetch the new page right away.

NOTE   Meta refresh can be used for slide shows, animation, or often-changing information, but it has some drawbacks. In particular, if you use a value of zero seconds, a surfer can no longer go back with their browser's Back button.

You can also use meta refresh to redraw the current page, but this is only useful if the page is changing often (perhaps because you have a continuously updated image or database information on the page). To use this option, you would use a tag like this:

```
<META HTTP-EQUIV="REFRESH" CONTENT="20">
```

This example refreshes the page every 20 seconds, but you can choose a different value to replace the number 20 in the example.

For an interesting example of meta refresh, read Martha Conway's story "8 Minutes" in Episode 7 of *Enterzone* (`http://ezone.org:1080/ez/e7/articles/conway/8min.html`). After going to the title page, you'll notice that after 4 seconds, the first page of the story is displayed. The rest of the story follows, taking exactly eight minutes to display in its entirety. (But watch out, the PICS rating for this story might include s3 and l4 for its frank language.)

Using the Link Element

The link element (consisting of the <LINK> tag) indicates relationships between your document and other documents or URLs. HTML 3.2 and earlier versions of HTML defined <LINK> tags but didn't actively encourage their use, and so they were not commonly used. HTML 4.0 greatly encourages <LINK> tags to help indicate how your page fits into the larger context of other pages at your site. Unfortunately, almost every browser has not yet caught up with the <LINK> tag.

You can use two possible relationships in a <LINK> tag, which are expressed as attributes: <LINK REL="*relationship-name*" HREF="*URL*"> and <LINK REV=*relationship-name*" HREF="[URL]">. The only difference between these two types is that the first one used the REL attribute, and the second one uses the REV attribute.

- The REL attribute indicates a normal relationship to the document specified in the URL.

- The REV attribute indicates a reverse relationship. In other words, the referenced document has the indicated relationship to the current document.

As an example, let's consider one type of link relationship, the "index" relationship. Suppose you are creating a page called `history.html` that describes the history of your organization. This history page is just one part of your Web site. The main page (or *index* or *home page*) of your organization is considered to be the "index." (The main page is most often named `index.html`.)

In the head section of the history page, you might include the following tag:

```
<LINK REL="INDEX" HREF="index.html">
```

This tag would let browsers and search engines know where they can find the main index for your Web site. Advanced browsers might include an Index button on a toolbar so that people viewing your organization's history Web page can click on the Index button to visit the main page for the organization itself.

To complement the <LINK> tag in the `history.html` document, you might place the following tag in the `index.html` file's head section:

```
<LINK REV="INDEX" HREF="history.html">
```

This tag would let browsers know that there is a two-way relationship between `history.html` and `index.html`—that `index.html` is the index of `history.html`, and simultaneously, `history.html` is indexed by `index.html`.

In addition to this use of the <LINK> tag, HTML 4.0 defines additional attributes, MEDIA and TYPE, to help specify the format of the resource to which you're linking.

We'll learn about the TYPE attribute in Skill 9 and the MEDIA attribute in Skill 14 (but we'll see the MEDIA attribute used in an example shortly.)

Another set of <LINK> tags can indicate the next and previous documents in a book or group of documents. For example, the 23rd document in a series might contain the following <LINK> tags:

```
<LINK REL="NEXT" HREF="doc24.html">
<LINK REL="PREVIOUS" HREF="doc22.html">
```

 NOTE   You can use PREV instead of PREVIOUS as an attribute value; they mean exactly the same thing.

Again, browsers could theoretically use these tags to put Next and Previous buttons on a toolbar that lead to the appropriate documents. A smart browser could also begin pre-loading the NEXT document to save time.

When there's a collection of separate but related HTML pages, it's helpful for search results to reference the beginning of the collection in addition to the page hit by the search. HTML 4.0 advises the use of a <LINK> tag with the REL="BEGIN" attribute, along with a TITLE, as in the following example.

```
<LINK REL="BEGIN" HREF="kibo-page1.html" TITLE="Introduction to Kibology">
```

TIP   There are a whole host of possible relationship values. HTML 4.0 specifies CONTENTS, INDEX, GLOSSARY, COPYRIGHT, NEXT, PREVIOUS (or PREV), START, HELP, BOOKMARK, STYLESHEET, and ALTERNATE. Visit http:// www.w3.org/TR/relations .html for a more complete list and definitions.

One problem with HTML is that you have little control over how the document is printed (for example, there's no way to specify where page breaks should occur). You can use a <LINK> tag to indicate the location of an alternate version of your document in a format optimized for printing (such as the Postscript format used by many different laser printers):

```
<LINK REL="ALTERNATE" MEDIA="PRINT" HREF="mydoc.ps"
TYPE="application/postscript">
```

A <LINK> tag can be used to specify a language variant of the current document. For example, if you had a French version of your document saved as mydoc-fr.html, then you could use the two-letter code for French in a <LINK> tag like this one:

```
<LINK REL="ALTERNATE" LANG="FR" HREF="mydoc-fr.html"
TITLE="My Document in French (Mon bon document)">
```

These types of links sound great in theory; however, they are completely dependent on browser and search engine support, and unfortunately, the current browsers and search engines ignore most <LINK> tags.

Fortunately, however, one browser does take advantage of a <LINK> tag. Lynx, the text-only browser in common use, will let viewers comment on a Web page (just press the letter C to send an e-mail comment to a page's author). The e-mail address for the page's author is specified with a <LINK> tag like this one:

```
<LINK REV="MADE" HREF="mailto:billg@microsoft.com">
```

Many Web validation programs recommend that you include a <LINK> tag with the REV="MADE" attribute and your e-mail address URL in the HREF attribute.

If you are creating a template file that you use a base for new Web documents, you should probably include both a DOCTYPE declaration at the top and a <LINK REV="made" HREF="mailto:you@youraddress.com"> tag in the head section.

NOTE   In addition, we'll see how you can specify a style sheet in IE using a <LINK> tag in Skill 14.

Using the Base Element

You can use the base element's <BASE> tag to indicate the full URL where a document is located. In most cases, the browser already knows exactly where the document is located; the <BASE> tag is only useful if there are problems in the links to different parts of your site, or if there are several URLs that all point to the same place and you want to indicate which one is the official URL name.

The <BASE> tag requires the use of the HREF attribute, and the full URL of the document must be specified in quotes. Here's an example of the <BASE> tag:

```
<BASE HREF="http://www.foobar.com/bookstore/">
```

 NOTE   You only need to use the <BASE> tag if your links aren't working, if search engines are using several different URLs for the same page, or if you store the same document in multiple locations.

When we learn about relative URLs in Skill 7, we'll have a better ability to understand the <BASE> tag.

(We'll also see a special use of the <BASE> tag in Skill 14, when we learn about frames.)

Using the Style Element

The style element's <STYLE> and </STYLE> tags are one of the ways you can include a style sheet in your document. Style sheets are a method of describing how your document should appear. We'll teach you how to use the <STYLE> and </STYLE> tags in Skill 14.

Using the Script Element

The script element's <SCRIPT> and </SCRIPT> tags are used to hold a script (a series of commands written in a scripting language). Scripts can perform a wide variety of different tasks, and can affect how your document is displayed. For example, you can include a script that changes the background color of a page at random intervals. The two most popular scripting languages are JavaScript (developed by Netscape) and VBScript (developed by Microsoft).

Even though we don't have enough room in this book to teach you how to program a script, we will show you how scripts work and how you can incorporate and modify existing scripts for use in your pages. We'll learn more about scripting languages and the use of the <SCRIPT> and </SCRIPT> tags in Skill 15.

Using the Isindex Element

The isindex element's <ISINDEX> tag is rarely used these days, and because of its limitations, it is no longer recommended by HTML 4.0. The presence of an <ISINDEX> tag tells a browser that the current page is a "searchable index," which means the current page is actually a script capable of performing a search or database lookup. When a browser sees the <ISINDEX> tag, the browser will display a prompt that tells the person viewing the page that they can enter in a search term.

When you create a page that uses the <ISINDEX> tag, you have to actually write a script to perform the search yourself, using a programming language such as Perl. It's not enough to simply include the <ISINDEX> tag.

 NOTE   There are newer and better ways of allowing searches than <ISINDEX>. For example, most modern sites set up a search interface using forms (see Skill 12).

The scripts that allow <ISINDEX> to search are not too complicated, as scripts go, but they are far beyond the scope of this book.

If you do have access to a search script (and your Web server is set up to allow you to put the script into place), then you can use the <ISINDEX> tag to handle the user input of the search term. The browser will usually prompt for input once it sees the <ISINDEX> tag.

Figure 5.2 shows a searchable index in action. This is the Acronym Lookup search page, run by Peter Flynn, the Webmaster of University College, Cork in Ireland (http://www.ucc.ie/cgi-bin/acronym/).

As you can see from Figure 5.2, the default prompt that Navigator displays is "This is a searchable index. Enter search keywords," but you can use an optional PROMPT attribute to change this.

 **WARNING**   Unfortunately, IE 4 no longer displays the prompt required by <ISINDEX>, making searching at sites using <ISINDEX> impossible.

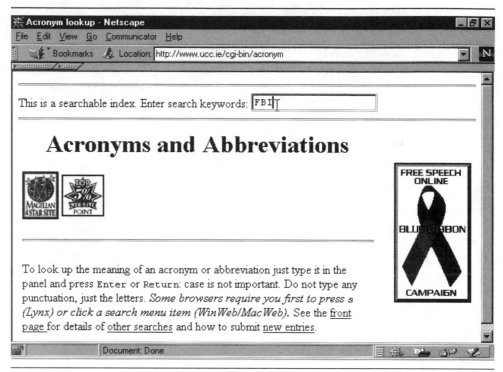

FIGURE 5.2: The Acronym Lookup page. Here we're looking up "FBI" in the searchable index prompt generated by the <ISINDEX> tag.

Specifying Language Information for Your Documents

When the Web was born, most HTML documents were written in English. As the Web became more of a worldwide phenomenon, more and more languages were used to write Web pages. Now, it's common to search for a topic such as "manifesto" and see dozens of pages returned that are written in foreign languages such as Italian or French (or even artificial languages such as Esperanto, Elfish, or Klingon).

Since different languages use different characters, and since it's important to be able to specify that you want to find pages written in English when you do a Web search, HTML 4.0 has gone to great lengths to allow for more flexibility in displaying and specifying the languages of the world.

The first major difference between HTML 4.0 and earlier versions of HTML is the use of the Unicode character set to allow many different languages' characters to be represented. Secondly, HTML 4.0 allows the use of a LANG attribute to specify the language of different parts of your document. Thirdly, HTML 4.0 introduces new attributes and elements to support right-to-left text (as used in Hebrew, for example).

You should always mark your Web documents' language so that when a search engine indexes your site, it will know what language you've used. That way, people performing searches can indicate the languages they want to read, and the search engine will be able to include or exclude the appropriate documents.

In addition, the language of a document can determine such issues as the style of quotation marks to be used and how a speech synthesizer should pronounce your document.

CHARACTER ENCODING

If you're using a foreign language with different characters than English (such as Cyrillic, Chinese, or Japanese), you may need to specify the *character encoding* (portion of the Unicode character set) that your document is written in. You can specify the character encoding with a <META> tag such <META HTTP-EQUIV="Content-Type" CONTENT="text/html; charset= euc jp">. ("EUC-JP" is a code for a type of Japanese character encoding. If you're using a language's character encoding, you'll probably already know the proper code to use here.) You may find HTML editors and page-creation tools insert a tag like <META HTTP-EQUIV="Content-Type" CONTENT="text/html; charset=iso-8859-1"> for you automatically. (Remember from Skill 3 that ISO-8859-1 refers to "Latin-1," the most popular character encoding, which is used for Western languages.) It's not necessary to specify the character encoding for normal Latin-1 documents, since most browsers will assume Latin-1 unless your document or Web server specifically says otherwise with a Content-Type header.

Specifying Languages with the *LANG* Attribute

The best way you can specify your document's language is to use HTML 4.0's new LANG attribute in the <HTML> tag that begins your document. For example:

```
<HTML LANG="EN">
```

"EN" here stands for English. If you don't specify a language for your document, then HTML 4.0 states that browsers and search engines must consider your document's language to be listed as "unknown."

There are a wide variety of language codes and subcodes. For example, you can specify LANG="IT" for Italian, LANG="EN-US" for United States English, or LANG= "EN-COCKNEY" for Cockney English.

NOTE   To learn more about the format of language codes, see RFC 1766 (ftp://ds .internic.net/rfc/rfc1766.txt) or the list of the two-character language codes (http://www.sil.org/sgml/iso639a.html).

One advantage to the LANG attribute's flexibility is that you can mark different sections of your document as being written in a different language. For example:

```
<!DOCTYPE HTML PUBLIC "-//W3C//DTD HTML 4.0//EN">
<HTML LANG="EN">
<HEAD>
<TITLE>How To Say Hello</TITLE>
</HEAD>
<BODY>
<P>I know how to say hello in three foreign languages:
French, Spanish, and Pig Latin.
<P LANG="FR">Bonjour
<P LANG="ES">Hola
<P LANG="X-PIG-LATIN">Ellohay
</BODY>
</HTML>
```

The default language for this document is English, thanks to the use of the <HTML LANG="EN> tag. Three paragraphs are marked as being in a particular language using the language code as an attribute value for the LANG attribute: French (FR), Spanish (ES), and Pig Latin (X-PIG-LATIN). Since Pig Latin isn't officially recognized as a language, it uses a special X code.

The advantage to marking the use of your languages this way is that software can automatically provide helpful translations, or allow the use of spelling checkers with an appropriate dictionary.

The LANG attribute can be used with almost any HTML tag.

SPECIFYING THE DIRECTION OF TEXT

Another language attribute that can be used with many tags is the DIR attribute, which specifies which direction a browser should use to display text. DIR="LTR" means left-to-right text (the default direction), while DIR="RTL" means right-to-left text. By using an <HTML LANG="HE" DIR="RTL"> tag at the beginning of your document, you are specifying that the document is written in Hebrew and should be displayed using right-to-left text. You could also mark a paragraph element with the same attributes to make a single paragraph display as right-to-left Hebrew text.

There's also a new HTML 4.0 bidirectional-override element (the <BDO> tag) used to override the text's direction (which is only necessary in special circumstances). Since we assume in this book that most of you are writing documents in English, we won't go into the details of bidirectional text.

Unfortunately, since language direction is such a new feature, the latest versions of popular browsers don't support right-to-left text yet.

This Skill covered three areas: the DOCTYPE declaration, the head section elements, and specifying language information. Now that we've seen how these things work, we're ready to learn about the true heart of HTML: the body section elements. Skill 6 will tell you about every body section element that you can use in your document.

Are You Experienced?

Now you can...

- ☑ use head section elements with discrimination
- ☑ add a *DOCTYPE* declaration to specify the version of HTML you're using
- ☑ give your pages appropriate titles
- ☑ use *<META>* tags to enhance your site's "findability"
- ☑ use foreign languages

Formatting the Body Section of Your Pages

- ➔ Becoming familiar with block-level elements
- ➔ Understanding text-level elements
- ➔ Playing with text-level elements
- ➔ Working with fonts and font-style elements
- ➔ Adding phrase elements to your pages

In the previous Skill, we learned about using the DOCTYPE declaration, specifying languages, and using elements in the head section of a document. In this Skill, we'll learn about the elements used in the body section. We discussed a few of the basic body section tags in Skill 2; now we'll give you the lowdown on *all* of the body section elements. We'll show you simple examples of how individual elements' tags mark up bits of text. We'll also show you examples from some of our favorite personal Web pages so you can examine other source code by "real people" and try out their HTML on your own test pages.

As we mentioned in Skill 2, there are two types of body section elements: block-level elements, used to define sections of text (such as a paragraph), and text-level elements, used to affect smaller bits of text (for example, making a word bold).

In this Skill, we'll also see that some of the text-level elements can be divided into two categories: font-style elements, which change the physical appearance of text (such a bold and italic), and phrase elements, which define certain logical roles for text (such as a citation).

 NOTE If you're just looking for a quick reference of HTML tags and their attributes, check out the appendix.

At the end of the Skill, we'll learn about two special new HTML elements that are used to mark changes to a document.

We'll start by learning about all of the different block-level elements before moving on to the text-level elements.

Using Block-Level Elements to Structure Your Documents

In Skill 2, we learned that block-level elements contain blocks of text and can organize text into paragraphs. We took a brief look at some common block-level elements: headings (<H1> and </H1>, and <H2> and </H2>), paragraphs (<P> and </P>), horizontal rules (<HR>), and centered text (<CENTER> and </CENTER>). Now we'll look at these block-level elements in more detail, as well as learn about the rest of the block-level elements.

Block-level elements, according to the W3C standard for HTML 4.0, should have a line-break or paragraph break before and after the element. (The actual method used by a browser to display the paragraph break varies from browser to browser.) When we learned about HTML's rules of nesting (at the end of Skill 2), we learned that block-level elements can be container tags for other block-level and text-level elements. We've also seen that some block-level elements are "empty," meaning that the element doesn't contain anything and the end tag is not allowed (for example, <HR> creates a horizontal rule by itself, and so the horizontal rule element can't contain text—you can't use an </HR> tag since the end tag for the horizontal rule element doesn't exist).

We'll divide the block-level elements into two categories: block-level elements used to create functional and logical divisions, and block-level elements used to create lists. We'll start with the functional and logical block-level elements.

Functional and Logical Divisions

The main purpose of HTML, as we've seen, is not so much to be a page layout and presentation language as it is to be a markup language that classifies each part of your document by its role. When you use HTML, you're indicating, for example, which part of your document is a heading and which part is a paragraph. That way, it's easy for software programs to do such tasks as create an outline of your document (by listing the headings), translate your paragraphs into foreign languages, or put paragraph breaks in between your paragraphs.

Logical HTML markup identifies the text within the start and end tags. For example, the <ADDRESS> and </ADDRESS> tags identify the words within these two tags as authorship and other contact information. The <DIV> and </DIV> tags mark up logical divisions in your text.

The basic functional units of your document are its paragraphs and headings. In this section we'll look at headings, then paragraphs, address information, forms, tables, horizontal rules, hierarchical divisions, centering, block quotations, pre-formatted text, and lists.

For each tag, we'll discuss its use and some examples. We'll also present the attributes that can be used in each element's start tag to change the element's behavior. When an element has more than one possible attribute, the attributes can appear in any order.

NOTE   You may want to review our discussion of attributes in Skill 1 and Skill 2.

Skill 6

WHEN DO YOU NEED TO PUT QUOTES IN AN ATTRIBUTE?

You may notice that in this book, we're putting quotes around attributes (for example, <FONT COLOR="RED">. On the Web, however, some authors just say <FONT COLOR=Red>.

Quotes are needed around an attribute value whenever it includes any character other than letters, digits, periods, or hyphens. This includes punctuation common to URLs (such as the colon and slash). In addition, you need quotes whenever there is any type of white space in the attribute value, such as a space.

You can use either double quotes (COLOR="RED") or single quotes (COLOR='RED'), but some browsers can get confused by single quotes.

There's no difference between saying <FONT COLOR="Red">, <FONT COLOR=RED>, and <FONT COLOR="RED"> . In this book, we'll always put the attributes in uppercase and in quotes, unless the attribute's value is case-sensitive (like a URL).

Using HTML 4.0's Generic Attributes

Before we discuss the individual elements that can be used in the body section, we'll briefly mention the generic attributes that can be used with almost every element. There are four sets of generic attributes:

- **Language attributes** At the end of the previous Skill, we learned about the LANG and DIR attributes. The LANG attribute can be used to specify what foreign language is being used within an element. The DIR attribute can specify the direction (left-to-right or right-to-left) that should be used with a language.

- **Style and identification attributes** Three attributes are used in conjunction with style sheets to specify how an element should appear. The CLASS and ID attributes mark an element as belonging to a particular class of styles or with a particular identification for an individual style. The STYLE attribute can directly apply style information. We'll learn how to use these three attributes in Skill 14.

- **Event attributes**   When we learn about scripts in Skill 15, we'll see that there is a wide class of attributes that can be used with individual elements to make documents more dynamic.

- **Advisory titles**   As we mentioned in Skill 5, many attributes can take an advisory TITLE attribute that adds more information about an element. We'll discuss this attribute in more detail in the next Skill.

In general, you can be reasonably sure that all four groups of attributes apply to all of the elements we discuss in this Skill. The best way to check to make sure that a particular attribute applies to a particular element is to check out the appendix.

With this little preamble about attributes out of the way, we can proceed to learn about the block-level elements, starting with the six different heading elements.

Adding Heading Elements

The heading elements (<H1>, <H2>, <H3>, <H4>, <H5>, and <H6>) define different levels of headings for your page, much like the headlines and subheadings in a book, newspaper article, or an essay written with an outline. There are six levels of headings, from most important to least important; for example, <H1> would be used for the largest and most important heading, and <H6> would be used for the smallest and least important heading.

Your HTML documents are certainly not required to have headings, but headings are commonly used because they help organize your document into sections.

All six headings are containers, and the end tags (</H1>, </H2>, </H3>, </H4>, </H5>, </H6>) are required. Here are the heading elements:

```
<H1>Heading Level One Text</H1>      <H4>Heading Level Four Text</H4>
<H2>Heading Level Two Text</H2>      <H5>Heading Level Five Text</H5>
<H3>Heading Level Three Text</H3>  <H6>Heading Level Six Text</H6>
```

The heading start tags can each use one of the following attributes:

```
ALIGN="LEFT"                         ALIGN="CENTER"
ALIGN="RIGHT"                        ALIGN="JUSTIFY"
```

These attributes control the horizontal alignment of the heading. For example, <H1 ALIGN="CENTER">My Heading</H1> would create a centered first-level heading with the words "My Heading."

NOTE The JUSTIFY alignment choice makes text appear with smooth margins on both the left and right side. (This is also known as "double justification," "full justification," or "justified text.") In contrast, ALIGN="LEFT" (which is the default) gives text a "ragged right" margin. The ALIGN="JUSTIFY" attribute value is a new choice in HTML 4.0, so only the very latest browsers (like Netscape Navigator 4 and Microsoft Internet Explorer 4) can display justified text.

Headings should always be used in numeric order—for example, after you've used an <H1>, the next heading tag you use should be another <H1> or an <H2>, not an <H3>. Search engines may use headings in order of importance (one is more important than two, and so on) to build an outline of your site for their search results. Heading text is rendered by Navigator and IE as bold.

Figure 6.1 shows a sample document that makes use of the six levels of heading in order to compare their sizes.

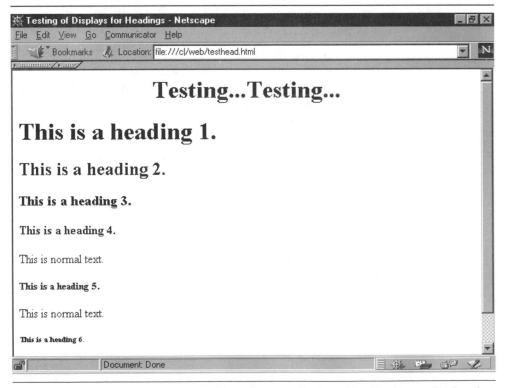

FIGURE 6.1: The six levels of headings as displayed by Navigator. Notice that the fifth and sixth-level headings are actually smaller than normal body text.

WARNING Just because Navigator and IE display headings in bold and change the font size, not every browser does so. A text-to-speech browser might represent a heading by using extra pauses or emphasis. Text-only browsers like Lynx use different levels of indentation to show headings. Other graphical browsers, like Opera and Mosaic, allow users to customize the font face, color, and size used for each heading. In short, don't use an <H1> tag just because you want some text to be large and bold—instead, use the text-level elements <B> and <BIG> for the same effect.

Here's the HTML code that produces the document displayed in Figure 6.1:

```
<!DOCTYPE HTML PUBLIC "-//W3C//DTD HTML 4.9//EN">
<HTML LANG="EN">
<HEAD>
    <TITLE>Testing of Displays for Headings</TITLE>
    <LINK REV="MADE" HREF="mailto:estephen@emf.net">
</HEAD>
<BODY>
<H1 ALIGN="CENTER">Testing...Testing...</H1>
<H1>This is a heading 1.</H1>
<H2>This is a heading 2.</H2>
<H3>This is a heading 3.</H3>
<H4>This is a heading 4.</H4>
<P>This is normal text.</P>
<H5>This is a heading 5.</H5>
<P>This is normal text.</P>
<H6>This is a heading 6.</H6>
</BODY>
</HTML>
```

NOTE Remember, headings are used to build an outline of your document. If the text isn't a heading, it doesn't belong inside a heading tag.

Headings can be modified in color or size if a <FONT> tag is nested inside the heading element. Here's another sample HTML document that makes extensive use of headings. (You can create this example and save it as headings.html, or find it on the Sybex Web site for this book.)

headings.html

```
<!DOCTYPE HTML PUBLIC "-//W3C//DTD HTML 4.0//EN">
<HTML LANG="EN">
<HEAD>
    <TITLE>Sybex presents HTML 4.0: No Experience Required</TITLE>
<LINK REV="MADE" HREF="mailto:janan@sonic.net"></HEAD>
<BODY>
<H1 ALIGN="CENTER"><FONT COLOR="RED">HTML 4.0 No Experience
Required</FONT></H1>
<H2 ALIGN="RIGHT">Skill One</H2>
<H3>The Internet</H3>
<H3>The World Wide Web</H3>
<H3>URLs</H3>
<H4>Basic URLs</H4>
<H4>Complex URLs</H4>
<H2 ALIGN="RIGHT">Skill Two</H4>
<H3>Basic Structure</H3>
<H3>Common HTML Tags</H3>
</BODY>
</HTML>
```

NOTE   Some HTML page-creation tools (like the ones we discussed in Skill 4) may get confused if you use perfectly valid tags that they don't happen to understand. For example, in headings.html, we refer to the color red by saying <FONT COLOR="RED">. Some HTML tools may only work if you use the RGB color that we saw in Skill 3 and use <FONT COLOR="#FF0000"> instead. This is a common limitation of most HTML tools: They don't know all of HTML. Browsers like Navigator and IE would display headings.html properly either way.

Navigator and IE use left alignment by default for headings, but as shown in Figure 6.2, you can change the alignment to right or center.

NOTE   You can control the appearance and alignment of headings with great precision and flexibility through the use of style sheets, which we'll learn about in Skill 14. HTML 4.0's specification does not recommend using the ALIGN attribute with a heading; it recommends that you use style sheets instead.

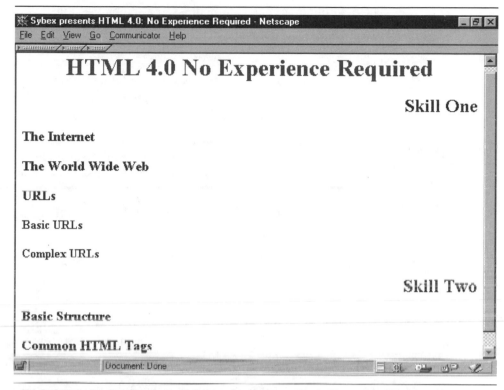

FIGURE 6.2: Navigator displays headings.html. Note the difference in font sizes for the different headings. We specified center alignment for the first-level headings; we specified right alignment for the level-two headings.

Creating Paragraphs with the Paragraph Element's <P> Tag

The paragraph element's <P> tag marks the beginning of a paragraph. The end of a paragraph can be marked with </P>. In general, the <P> tag is used to separate text into different paragraphs, such as:

```
<P>This is a paragraph.
<P>So is this.
```

(You may wish to review our extensive discussion of the <P> tag back in Skill 2.)

The paragraph element has the same alignment attributes as headings:

```
ALIGN="LEFT"
ALIGN="CENTER"
ALIGN="RIGHT"
ALIGN="JUSTIFY"
```

The default horizontal alignment is left alignment—unless your paragraph is enclosed within a <DIV> or <CENTER> element (described later) that changes the default. Browsers take care of word-wrapping your paragraphs to fit the available space.

Even though the paragraph element is a container, the end tag is not necessary. If you use any other block-level element after a <P> tag (including another <P> tag), then the </P> tag is assumed.

WARNING   Some older browsers require </P> to end the ALIGN attribute in order to make the text following the closing tag revert back to the default alignment.

Anything before the <P> start tag and after the </P> end tag is separated by two line-breaks (a paragraph break).

THE PERILS OF <P>

There are times when the presence of the <P> or </P> tags will cause a paragraph break to appear where it normally wouldn't appear, in violation of the HTML specification of how paragraphs should behave.

This is because browsers often behave a little inconsistently from the specifications of HTML. Consider this example of rules and paragraphs where <P> and </P> will create a paragraph break:

```
<HTML><HEAD><TITLE>Paragraphs andRules</TITLE></HEAD><BODY>
<HR>
<P>A wonderful paragraph describing my friends Rick and
Janet's new baby T.R.</P>
<HR>
<P>Another paragraph detailing my childhood in England,
only not closing the paragraph. (The paragraph end tag is
optional, after all.)
```

continued ▶

```
<HR>
A third and final paragraph with no p. This paragraph
mentions dinosaurs solely to make this example more popular
with children.
<HR>
</BODY></HTML>
```

When this HTML code is displayed by Navigator, IE, or older versions of Lynx, there will be a paragraph break whenever a <P> or </P> tag is used, despite the fact that <HR> is a block-level element that should cause a paragraph break in and of itself. (The same behavior occurs with other block-level elements such as <FORM> and <TABLE> substituted for <HR>.)

Figure 6.3 shows the difference in paragraph breaks depending on whether a <P> or </P> is present. As you can see from Figure 6.3, there is no paragraph break between the <HR> and the paragraph unless a <P> or </P> tag is used.

You can take advantage of this behavior by using the </P> tag only when you want a paragraph break to appear in your document.

By the way, a strict approach to HTML requires that every bit of text appears inside some kind of block-level container. The third paragraph in our previous example is only contained in the body of the document; therefore technically it is considered "Bodytext" and not a paragraph. (This distinction is important when you use a style sheet that defines how paragraphs appear. If you do use such a style sheet, only text that is nested in a paragraph element will appear in the "paragraph style.")

In practice, you might use <P> and </P> only when you want to be sure that a paragraph break will appear before and after the paragraph's text. You'll notice that some of our examples in this book have omitted the <P> tags.

Skill 6

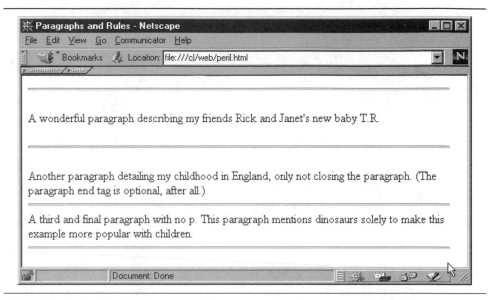

FIGURE 6.3: The <P> and </P> tags create space around the <HR> tag in this Navigator display.

As a general rule, don't use multiple paragraph tags to create vertical white space in a document because most browsers will collapse multiple paragraph breaks into a single paragraph break. For example:

```
<P>Waiting for Godot seems to take forever.
<P>
<P>
<P>
<P>In fact we're still waiting.
```

This code is treated by most browsers as if it were the following:

```
<P>Waiting for Godot seems to take forever.
<P>In fact we're still waiting.
```

In other words, the empty paragraphs are simply ignored. HTML 4.0's specification describes empty paragraphs as "bad form." You can create vertical white space by using style sheets.

You can also force an extra paragraph break by putting an invisible space in the paragraph. To use an invisible space, we'll use the non-breaking space entity that was introduced in Skill 3:

```
<P>Waiting for Godot seems to take forever.
<P> 
<P>In fact we're still waiting.
```

This code will cause an empty paragraph to appear between the first and last paragraph. However, future browsers might not allow even this construction to cause a blank paragraph and this use of a non-breaking space is a controversial area.

Another approach to causing an empty paragraph is to use a line-break tag (<BR>) after a <P> tag, as shown in this HTML code:

```
<P>Waiting for Godot seems to take forever.
<P>
<BR>
<P>
<BR>
<P>In fact we're still waiting.
```

Even this approach may not work in every browser. It's best to accept that HTML doesn't have an easy way of creating white space. The best way to create vertical white space is with style sheets (Skill 14).

Marking the Author's Address with an Address Element

The address element uses the <ADDRESS> start tag and the </ADDRESS> end tag to mark up addresses and other contact information. The text in your address element is recognized by search engines and indexers as your address information.

Navigator and IE put any text inside the address element in italics. Here's an example of an address element tag that includes a link to an e-mail address for a Web author named Malcolm Humes:

```
<ADDRESS>
<A HREF="MAILTO:mal@emf.net">Malcolm Humes: mal@emf.net</A>
</ADDRESS>
```

Here's another example of an address element showing some information that's useful to put at the end of your home page:

```
<ADDRESS>
Ankiewicz Galleries<BR>
P.O. Box 450 Kendall Square<BR>
Cambridge, MA 02142<BR>
</ADDRESS>
```

As you can see, address elements can contain a single line of text, or they can contain multiple lines (often using line-breaks created with a <BR> tag).

Getting Information with Form Elements

You can use the form element's <FORM> and </FORM> tags to mark an area where people viewing your Web page can fill in some fields and send data to you. There are all sorts of options for forms, including drop-down lists, text areas, and radio buttons (just like a dialog box). Forms are too complicated to talk about in detail in this Skill; instead, we'll give you in-depth coverage of them in Skill 12.

Presenting Data in Tables

The table element is used to create a table of data. The <TABLE> start tag and </TABLE> end tag mark the start and end of the table's position in your document. Tables have many different uses, and there are a number of special elements used to create table cells and rows. Since tables, like forms, are a little too involved to go into here, we'll come back to tables in Skill 10.

Drawing a Line with the Horizontal Rule Element

The horizontal rule element is simply the <HR> tag. Each <HR> tag in your document creates a shaded horizontal rule between text. (A *rule* is just a fancy word for a line.) This rule appears in the same color as the document background. For example, the HTML code:

```
Hello
<HR>
World!
```

would appear in IE or Navigator as shown in Figure 6.4.

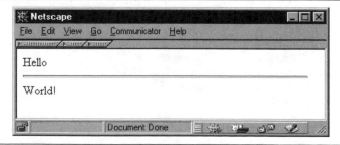

FIGURE 6.4: Navigator displays a simple horizontal rule dividing two words.

Horizontal rules have many attributes. Here's a list of the possible attributes and attribute values:

```
ALIGN="LEFT"
ALIGN="RIGHT"
ALIGN="CENTER"
NOSHADE
SIZE="NUMBER"
WIDTH="NUMBER"
WIDTH="PERCENT"
```

You can use one ALIGN attribute, a SIZE attribute, a WIDTH attribute, or a NOSHADE attribute—or a combination of these four attributes.

The ALIGN attribute positions the rule on the page either flush left, flush right, or centered. Since a rule normally fills the entire width of the screen, aligning a rule is only useful if you have changed the width of the rule with the WIDTH attribute.

The NOSHADE attribute renders the tag as an unshaded dark gray line (without the hollow and slightly three-dimensional appearance that Navigator and IE give to a rule).

The SIZE attribute is a measurement of how thick the rule is. The number must be in pixels. (*Pixels* are "picture elements," or the smallest unit of your computer screen's resolution. Each pixel is simply a dot on the screen.) If you don't specify the SIZE attribute, then Navigator and IE display the rule at size 2. Here's a fragment of HTML code that uses several sizes of horizontal rules:

```
Hello <HR> World!
<HR NOSHADE>
<HR SIZE="1">
<HR SIZE="2">
<HR SIZE="3">
<HR SIZE="4">
<HR SIZE="5">
<HR SIZE="10">
<HR NOSHADE SIZE="10">
<HR SIZE="15">
<HR SIZE="15" NOSHADE>
```

IE would display this code fragment as shown in Figure 6.5.

The WIDTH attribute can be specified with either a numeric value or a percentage value. A numeric value is measured in number of pixels, just like the SIZE attribute. Alternately, you can specify a percentage of the browser window's width, such as <HR WIDTH="50%">. Setting a percentage is a good idea in order to make your rule consistent no matter what screen resolution is being used by the surfer viewing your page.

Here's a final example of an <HR> tag that uses several different attributes:

```
<HR SIZE="4" NOSHADE WIDTH="40%" ALIGN="RIGHT">
```

 **WARNING**

The HTML 4.0 specification does not recommend using the SIZE, ALIGN, or WIDTH attributes; you should use a style sheet instead (see Skill 14).

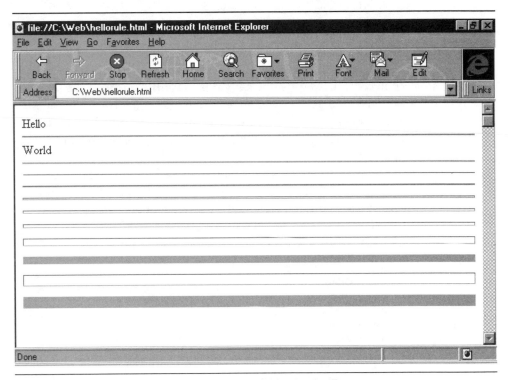

FIGURE 6.5: Various sizes of horizontal rules in IE

Dividing Sections with the Division Element

The division element divides your document into sections. The division element consists of the <DIV> and </DIV> tags, which mark the logical divisions in your text. The division element can be used to create a hierarchy of divisions within your document. In HTML 3.2, the main use of the division element was to indicate the default alignment of a section. In HTML 4.0, you can use divisions with style sheets to change the appearance of different sections of a document; we'll see how to do this in Skill 14.

The <DIV> tag's attributes are the same as those for paragraphs and headings:

```
ALIGN="LEFT"
ALIGN="RIGHT"
ALIGN="CENTER"
```

The division element can have other block-level elements, such as tables and paragraphs, nested within it. This allows you to center a big chunk of your document: You just put a <DIV ALIGN="CENTER"> tag at the beginning of the chunk and a </DIV> tag at the end. Everything wrapped within this division element will be centered.

However, just as with paragraphs and headings, HTML 4.0 does not recommend using the alignment attribute—HTML 4.0 recommends that you use style sheets instead. Unlike most block-level elements, the division element only creates a line-break instead of a paragraph break when displayed by Navigator and IE.

If you use a block-level element with another ALIGN attribute inside the division element, the innermost element's alignment will override the division element's ALIGN attribute. Here's an example called happydiv.html.

happydiv.html

```
<TITLE>HappyFunCo Divisions</TITLE>
<BODY>
HappyFunCo Presents...
<DIV ALIGN="RIGHT">
The Newly Revised
<H1>HappyFunCo Home Page</H1>
Welcome!
<P ALIGN="CENTER">We sell used junk at low prices!
</DIV>
Give us a call at 1-800-555-1223.
```

This HTML code contains six paragraphs (the title doesn't count as a paragraph, but every other line of text is separated into paragraphs by block-level elements). The <DIV ALIGN="RIGHT"> tag causes all of the following paragraphs to be right-aligned by default, until the division element is closed with the </DIV> end tag. Because the next three paragraphs ("The Newly Revised," "HappyFunCoHome Page," and "Welcome!") are within the division element, they would normally be placed aligned to the far-right side of the document. However, the "We sell used junk" line is centered, since the alignment attribute of the <P> tag here overrides the alignment attribute of the <DIV> tag.

Figure 6.6 shows Navigator's rendering of this code. The opening <DIV> tag creates a line-break between "HappyFunCo Presents" and "The Newly Revised." Similarly, there is only a line-break between "We sell used junk" and "Give us a call." However, headings and paragraphs, like most block-level elements, cause a paragraph break. You can see the distinction in Figure 6.6. Bear in mind that not every browser would show paragraph breaks in the same way.

FIGURE 6.6: Using the division element to change default alignment

Centering Items with the Center Element

The center element (<CENTER> and </CENTER>) will center large blocks of text. A line-break (and not a paragraph break) is rendered before the start tag and after the end tag. This example would center the words "Hello, World!" on a line:

```
<CENTER>Hello, World!</CENTER>
```

The <CENTER> tag is a synonym for <DIV ALIGN="CENTER">. There's absolutely no difference between them, except that <CENTER> has had a longer history (it was introduced by Netscape as extension to HTML 2.0). Since <CENTER> has been around longer, it is slightly more supported by various different browsers.

Like the division element, the center element can be used to center a whole chunk of a document, and it can be used to center tables and other block-level elements.

Quoting Sections with the Blockquote Element

The blockquote element (<BLOCKQUOTE> and </BLOCKQUOTE>) marks up quotes that take more than a few lines ("blocks of quotation"). You use this tag when you are quoting one or more paragraphs from another source. Navigator and IE indent the entire block of quoted text.

Here's some sample HTML markup for a blockquote:

```
<P>From The Bridges of New York City, Queensboro Ballads by Levi Asher
(http://www.levity.com/brooklyn/index.html):
<BLOCKQUOTE>
It isn't just that everybody hates the city; the more time I spend with
these people the more I understand that they hate everything. Or at
least they seem to, because it is the culture of Wall Street to never
show joy. Maybe some of my co-workers lead wonderful lives at home;
similarly, I bet some of the Puritans of colonial New England had great
sex behind closed doors. In public, though, we are busy, busy, busy.
</BLOCKQUOTE>
```

Figure 6.7 shows how IE renders the blockquote element.

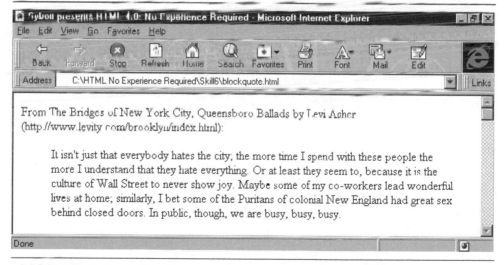

FIGURE 6.7: In this IE screen shot, you can see how Levi's blockquoted text is indented from the introductory text.

It's tempting to use the blockquote element to indent general text, but this will potentially misguide search engines and page indexers. Even though Navigator and IE indent blockquoted text, other browsers don't do this; some browsers may put quote marks around blockquoted text, or just render it in italics. (If you do want to indent text, you can use <PRE> or a style sheet setting. We'll see how to use the <PRE> tag in the next section, while style sheets are covered in Skill 14.)

NOTE   In HTML 4.0, the <BLOCKQUOTE> tag can take an optional CITE attribute to indicate where the quote came from. For example, we could have used <BLOCKQUOTE CITE="http://www.levity.com/brooklyn/index.html"> instead of <BLOCKQUOTE> in our previous example. Current browsers don't do anything with the CITE attribute, but future browsers will probably display the information in some fashion or allow you to look up the quote from the CITE attribute's URL.

We'll see another element used for quotations later in this Skill: the new HTML 4.0 quote element (which uses the <Q> and </Q> tags).

Preserving White Space with the Pre-formatted Element

The pre-formatted element (<PRE> and </PRE>) allows you to include pre-formatted text. Text contained within the pre-formatted text element defaults to a fixed pitch font (typically the Courier font). Your browser will preserve the white space (line-breaks and horizontal spacing) of your text within the <PRE> and </PRE> tags. This means that your text can continue past the screen width because your browser will not automatically wrap the text. Text is wrapped only when you include a line-break.

Most browsers will follow the HTML standard for block-level elements and create a paragraph break before the <PRE> start tag and after the </PRE> closing tag.

WARNING   It's best to use the space bar to create spaces within your text instead of the Tab key. When you or someone else goes back to edit your pages, the text editor you use may have the tab spacing set to a different value and your text may become misaligned.

As an example of pre-formatted text, we'll show a haiku by poet and teacher Tom Williams (http://www.voicenet.com/~willmar/newpage/) used with and without the <PRE> tag.

```
<P> morning wind
my hair moves
 with the clouds and trees
<PRE> morning wind
my hair moves
 with the clouds and trees</PRE>
morning wind
my          hair moves    with the        clouds
and trees
```

Figure 6.8 shows how this HTML code will be displayed by a browser.

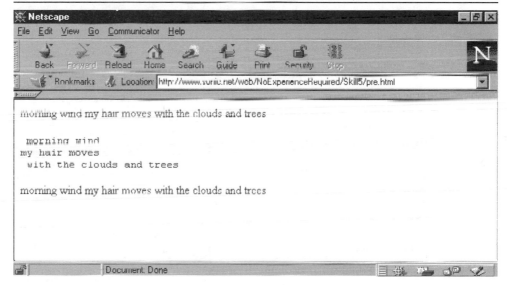

FIGURE 6.8: A haiku by Tom Williams displayed both with and without the use of a <PRE> tag

The <PRE> tag does take one attribute:

WIDTH=" *NUMBER* "

This number indicates how wide the text is (in columns). In theory, a browser would adjust the font size of the pre-formatted text to fit the <PRE> text into the entire browser window. However, this attribute isn't supported by most browsers at this time.

Stephen's ASCII art in his "Requiem for Mosaic" article in the July 1997 issue of *Enterzone* (http://ezone.org:1080/ez/e11/articles/zeigen/mosaic.html)

is a fun example of the possibilities with white space and the <PRE> tag (scroll to the bottom of the *Enterzone* Web page to view). Here is the HTML code:

<PRE WIDTH=80>

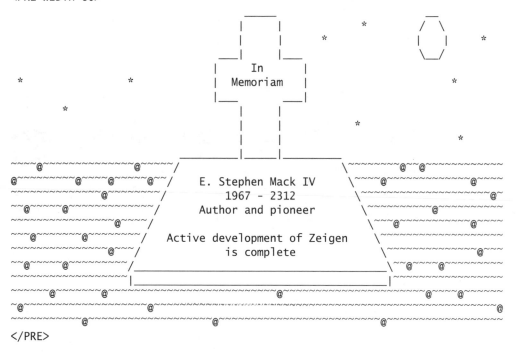

</PRE>

Using Other Block-Level Elements

HTML 4.0 introduces three new block-level elements that are used in particular types of documents:

- The noframes element (<NOFRAMES> and </NOFRAMES>) is used to indicate what should be displayed if a browser can't display frames. See Skill 11 for more information about frames and alternate content.

- The noscript element (<NOSCRIPT> and </NOSCRIPT>) allows you to specify alternate content for browsers that don't display scripts, if you're using a script (as we'll discuss in Skill 15).

- The fieldset element (<FIELDSET> and </FIELDSET>) is a special element to group different parts of a form together (covered in Skill 12).

In addition, the isindex element that we discussed in the previous Skill should normally be used in the head section of a document; in HTML 4.0, the <ISINDEX> tag can also be used as a block-level element in the body of a document.

Now that we've seen the last of the block-level elements that have to do with functional and logical divisions, it's time to see the HTML tags that can be used to create lists.

Organizing Your Text with Lists

There are three main types of lists: unordered lists, ordered lists, and definition lists. Ordered lists are numbered in some fashion, while unordered lists are bulleted. Definition lists consist of a term followed by its definition.

Both ordered and unordered lists require start and end tags as well as the use of a special element to indicate where each list item begins (the <LI> tag).

- Unordered lists can be preceded by one of several bullet styles: a closed circle, an open circle, or a square. The tags for an unordered list are <UL> and </UL>.

- Ordered lists can be preceded by Arabic numerals, uppercase or lowercase Roman numerals, or uppercase or lowercase alphanumeric characters. The tags for an ordered list are <OL> and </OL>.

- Definition lists require a start tag (<DL>) and end tag (</DL>) and two special elements: one for definition terms (the <DT> tag) and one for definitions (the <DD> tag).

In addition to these three types of lists, HTML also allows two other types of lists that are much less commonly used: directory lists (which use the <DIR> tag) and menu lists (the <MENU> tag). However, these two types of lists are not recommended.

Creating Unordered Lists and Using List Item Elements

The first of three list elements we'll see is the unordered list element, which uses the <UL> and </UL> tags.

The only element that can be contained inside the <UL> and </UL> tags is a list item, signified with the list item element. The list item element uses the <LI> tag (and optionally the </LI> tag) and contains the actual content of your lists.

Both <UL> and <LI> have the same set of attributes, which is one of the following types:

```
TYPE="CIRCLE"
TYPE="DISC"
TYPE="SQUARE"
```

The CIRCLE attribute value is used for a hollow bullet, the DISC type creates a solid bullet, and the SQUARE attribute value renders a solid block. The default appearance for a list is with a disc.

You can use an optional </LI> end tag at the end of each list item; however, the </UL> end tag is always required at the end of the unordered list.

Even though both the <UL> tag and the <LI> tag can take the TYPE attribute, it's much more common to use the attribute with the <UL> tag, so that the entire list takes on the appearance you desire. For example, here's some HTML that generates two separate lists:

```
<TITLE>Two Shopping Lists</TITLE>
<BODY>
<UL>
<LI>Eggs
<LI>Milk
<LI>Apples
<LI>Razor Blades
</UL>

<UL TYPE="SQUARE">
<LI>Hammer
<LI>Screwdriver
<LI TYPE="DISC">Screws
<LI TYPE="CIRCLE">Chainsaw
</UL>
```

Figure 6.9 shows this code in action.

FIGURE 6.9: Navigator displays two shopping lists, using the three different types of bullets.

**WARNING**   Some browsers don't recognize the TYPE attribute at all, and most browsers don't recognize that the TYPE attribute can be used with the <LI> tag. In fact, even IE 4 doesn't recognize it (although Navigator does, as we saw); IE would display the second list with all four items having square bullets.

One important aspect of lists is that you can nest one list inside another to create a sublist. The default appearance of the sublists will vary from the main list, with the first sublist using circle bullets, and the next nested list using squares. For example:

```
<UL>
<LI>Body
    <UL>
    <LI>Head
    <LI>Hand
        <UL>
        <LI>Finger
        <LI>Thumb
        </UL>
    <LI>Leg
    </UL>

<LI>Mind
    <UL>
    <LI>Brain
        <UL>
        <LI>Neuron
        </UL>
    </UL>

<LI>Spirit
    <UL>
    <LI>Soul
        <UL>
        <LI>Light body
        </UL>
    </UL>
</UL>
```

This list would be displayed with the sublists indented beneath the main list, much like we've shown in the source code for readability. There are a total of seven lists here. Each <UL> tag begins a new list. The main list (Body, Mind, and Spirit) has six sublists—two per bulleted point. Figure 6.10 shows IE's display of this code.

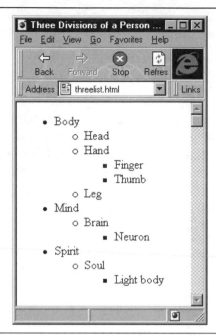

FIGURE 6.10: IE is displaying a total of seven different lists; six of the lists are sublists of the Body, Mind, and Spirit main list.

Creating Ordered Lists

The ordered list element's <OL> and </OL> tags are used to create ordered lists. Like unordered lists, ordered lists must contain list item elements (with the <LI> tag) to contain your list's text. In fact, ordered lists are identical in behavior to unordered lists except they use numbers instead of bullets, and you can use an attribute to start numbering at a number other than one.

Here are the attributes you can use with the <OL> tag:

```
TYPE="1" (Arabic numbers)
TYPE="a" (lowercase alphanumeric)
TYPE="A" (uppercase alphanumeric)
TYPE="i" (lowercase Roman numbers)
TYPE="I" (uppercase Roman numbers)
START="X"
```

The START attribute allows you establish the beginning of the list's number sequence (for example, <OL START="5"> would start your ordered list's numbering with the number five).

The TYPE attribute allows you to specify the numbering system you want to use. Arabic numbers are the default.

 NOTE Here's one of the few examples of an HTML attribute value that's case-sensitive. There's a difference between TYPE="a" and TYPE="A". The first type will count a, b, c, on up to z, and then aa, ab, ac. The second type will count A, B, C. Similarly, TYPE="i" will count i, ii, iii, iv, v; TYPE="I" will count I, II, III, IV, V.

In addition, when you are using ordered lists, the <LI> tag can use the VALUE attribute to force to make a particular list item to have a certain number.

 NOTE In theory, both <UL> and <OL> can take another attribute, COMPACT, that should tell the browser to make the list take up less space. In practice, browsers ignore the COMPACT attribute. Style sheets offer more control over list formatting, so the use of COMPACT is not recommended by the HTML 4.0 specification.

The VALUE attribute is shown here:

```
<OL>
<LI>Milk
<LI>Bread
<LI>Turkey Bacon
<LI VALUE="10">Dark Chocolate
<LT>Avocados
</OL>
```

In a browser, the order of this list would appear like so:

1. Milk
2. Bread
3. Turkey Bacon
10. Dark Chocolate
11. Avocados

Our examples of list items have just been plain text, but you can include any block-level element or text-level element as a list item, so you can make list items with multiple paragraphs, lists of links (see Skill 7), or lists of images (see Skill 8).

Defining Terms with Definition Lists

The definition list element uses the <DL> start tag and the </DL> end tag to create a definition list. This list is rendered without bullets. The <DT> tag is used for definition terms (that is, the name or title of the item you're defining). The <DD> tag is used for the definitions themselves. For example:

```
<DL>
<DT>Term A
<DD>Definition of Term A
<DT>Term B
<DD>Definition of Term B
</DL>
```

Shown here is how this code would appear in IE.

 Many Web authors have discovered that a <DD> tag when used by itself (out of the context of a definition list) is rendered by Navigator and IE as a tab. We recommend you not adopt this practice because the indenting behavior is not a part of the HTML specifications, and the indentation will not work on all browsers. For indenting text, the safest method is to use multiple non-breaking spaces ( )—although even that method is not guaranteed to work. Alternately, it's better to create indents with style sheets (Skill 14) or if you really have no alternative, you can use tables for indenting (Skill 10).

Using Directory and Menu Lists

There are two other types of lists defined in HTML: directory lists and menus. However, these two types of lists are rarely used, and Navigator and IE treat them identically to unordered lists.

The directory list element is signified by the <DIR> and </DIR> tags. This element was intended to be used for directory lists of short items (some sources recommend

20 or fewer characters so they can be listed in columns 24 characters wide). Here's a quick example of a directory list:

```
<DIR>
<LI>Item1
<LI>Item2
<LI>Item3
</DIR>
```

Similarly, the <MENU> and </MENU> tags make up the menu element, which is used for menu lists. Menus can render with different spacing results in different browsers, but Navigator and IE don't display menu lists any differently than unordered lists. Here's a quick sample menu:

```
<MENU>
<LI>Sourdough
<LI>Buttermilk
<LI>Rolls
</MENU>
```

For both directory and menu lists, the only item that should be contained is a list item element (the <LI> tag).

WARNING   Menu and directory lists have died from lack of love; the HTML 4.0 specification recommends that you avoid them entirely.

We've now finished with lists and are ready to see the different elements that HTML has for text-level markup.

Using Text-Level Elements

Text-level elements mark up bits of text, in order to change the appearance or function of that text. You use text-level elements to make words or sentences bold, for example, or turn something into a link.

NOTE   The HTML 4.0 specification uses the term inline elements to refer to text-level elements. (Older versions of HTML called these elements text-level elements as we do in this book.) To reinforce the contrast between block-level elements and text-level elements, we'll continue to use the older term.

The main contrast between text-level and block-level elements that you should remember is that text-level elements don't start new paragraphs—instead, text-level elements are usually used *within* a paragraph.

Text-level elements can only be used as containers for other text-level elements. (This structuring of tags within tags we've referred to as *nesting*.) As with any HTML element, disordered nesting, missing end tags, extra start tags, or missing portions of tag attributes (such as an ending quote or an equals sign) may cause a browser to ignore huge portions of your page.

In previous skills, we've covered some general rules. Text-level elements:

- Can define character appearance and function

- Must be nested in the proper order

- Don't generally cause paragraph breaks

- Can contain other text-level elements but not block-level elements

After examining some general purpose text-level elements (including anchors, applets, basefont, line-breaks, images, and map), we'll discuss fonts in some detail, and then see two general categories of text-level elements: font-style elements and phrase elements.

Creating Links with the Anchor Element's <A> Tag

The anchor element (<A HREF="URL"> and </A>) is used to create links. Links (otherwise known as *hyperlinks*) point to different files on the Web, and we saw the use of the anchor tag in Skill 2; we'll learn a lot more about links in the next Skill.

 **WARNING**   Anchors cannot be nested within other anchors.

The text or image enclosed within the <A> and </A> tags is a link; this link is clickable in a graphical browser. With most browsers, text within the anchor tags is displayed in a different color (the link color) and is underlined (unless the person viewing your page has customized their browser to not display links with underlines).

Here's an anchor element that leads to Mark Napier's home page:

```
<A HREF="http://www.interport.net/~napier/">Mark Napier's Home Page</A>
```

NOTE

> The NAME attribute is also used to create labels in a document, and it's possible to link to different named parts of a document (rather than always linking to the top of each document). We'll see this use in the next Skill.

To create a link, the anchor element's <A> tag requires an HREF attribute. We saw in Skill 2 how to use an HREF attribute to specify a URL. There are actually quite a few uses for anchors beyond what we've seen here. Since anchors and links are so important, we'll spend an entire Skill talking about them: Skill 7. So we'll hold off on a complete discussion of the anchor tag for now.

Inserting Java Applets with the Applet Element

The applet element is used to include Java applets in your Web pages.

 NOTE

> An *applet* is a small application that accomplishes any of a wide variety of tasks. Simple games, database references, animation, and advanced manipulation of text are all uses of applets. Java is a new and popular computer programming language created by Sun Microsystems.

Since Java is such a complicated and advanced topic, we'll put off our discussion of the <APPLET> and </APPLET> tags until Skill 15.

Specifying Default Font Information with the Basefont Element

The basefont element is simply a <BASEFONT> tag, which is placed somewhere after your document's <BODY> tag. The basefont element establishes a default font size (and optionally a default font face or font color) for your entire page. Then, within your Web page following the <BASEFONT> tag, all other text and <FONT> tags (including <BIG> and <SMALL>) are used in relation to the font size established by the <BASEFONT> tag. The <BASEFONT> tag has no effect on the size of the text in headings (such as the <H1> tag); for many browsers, it also doesn't affect text inside a table.

 NOTE

> You might want to check back to our discussion of the <FONT>, <BIG>, and <SMALL> tags back in Skill 3 at this point.

If you don't use a <BASEFONT> tag, the default font size for normal body text is 3 out of the range of possible sizes from 1 to 7; we'll see an example of the font sizes in the "Changing Font Size, Face, and Color with the Font Element" section later in this Skill. We'll also see the attributes you can use in the <BASEFONT> tag in that section.

The following bit of HTML code renders "Coffeehousebook.com" in the font size of 4:

```
<BASEFONT SIZE="2">
Welcome to
<FONT SIZE="+2">Coffeehousebook.com</FONT>
--have a cup!
```

The "Welcome to" and "--have a cup!" text would appear in font size 2, or one size smaller than normal.

The basefont element is useful because it is an empty element—that is, it doesn't have an end tag of </BASEFONT>. This makes <BASEFONT> different from <FONT>. The font element is a text-level element, and its <FONT> and </FONT> tags shouldn't be used to contain multiple paragraphs. (Remember, text-level elements can't contain block-level tags like <P>—so if you want to affect the size of several paragraphs, it's legal to use a <BASEFONT> tag in front of them, but not legal to wrap all of the paragraphs inside a <FONT> tag. Alternately, you could apply the <FONT> and </FONT> tags separately to each paragraph, but that's too much work. A single <BASEFONT> tag is simpler.)

 **NOTE**   Although you can change the default font face and font color with basefont, you must also specify the default font size, since <BASEFONT>'s SIZE attribute is a required attribute. Furthermore, both <FONT> and <BASEFONT> are not as effective as style sheets at changing the font.

Creating New Lines with the Line-Break Element

The line-break element (an empty element, consisting of the <BR> tag) forces a line-break. For example:

```
Hello<BR>
World!
```

This code would force "World!" to appear on the line after "Hello." Line-breaks are useful for addresses and other short items.

The <BR> tag was discussed in Skill 2. Since it's a very simple tag, there's not much more we can add here, except for its attributes:

```
CLEAR="LEFT"
CLEAR="RIGHT"
CLEAR="ALL"
CLEAR="NONE"
```

The CLEAR="NONE" attribute has no effect whatsoever (it's just the same as a regular <BR> tag). The other three attributes all force the line-break to be tall enough that the margin is clear on either the left side, the right side, or both sides (depending on which attribute you choose). These attributes are only meaningful when there are images (or other objects) on the page—so we'll discuss these attributes again in Skill 8, which is about images.

Using more than one <BR> tag to create vertical white space may not give the same effect in all browsers; some browsers collapse multiple <BR> tags into a single line-break. See our earlier discussion about the <P> tag for more about vertical blank space.

Adding Graphics with the Image Element

The image element is an empty element, consisting of the <IMG> tag. The image element adds images to the body of a document. These images are referred to as *inline images* because the images are often inserted within a line of text. The various attributes for the <IMG> tag tell the browser how to lay out the page so that text can flow properly around the image.

Images are a complex subject; we took a good look at the use of the <IMG> tag in Skill 2, and we'll take a much longer look in Skill 8.

Making Image Maps with the Map Element

The map element (<MAP> and </MAP>) is used for image maps. An *image map* is an image that contains *hot spots*. These hot spots can take a surfer to different URLs. So an image map is simply an image that can be used to take a surfer to different places, depending on where they click in the image. Image maps are useful, for example, with geographical maps or with an image showing the different areas of your site.

Image maps are a complex and advanced topic, and there's really no need for them any more, since you can always duplicate the effect with simpler HTML elements. We'll discuss image maps briefly in Skill 8, but for a full explanation,

Skill 5

you'll have to go to the Web site for the book. (There simply isn't room in this book for a full explanation.)

The Quote Element

A new HTML 4.0 element for citing inline quotes is the quote element. The quote element uses <Q> as a start tag and </Q> as an end tag. The quote element is very similar to the blockquote element; the main difference is that since the quote element is not block-level, it doesn't start a new paragraph. Instead, it's used within a paragraph to mark a quotation. For example:

```
<P>Churchill said, <Q>"We have chosen shame and will get war,"</Q> but
he wasn't talking about 1066.</P>
```

Since the quote element is brand new in HTML 4.0, it has not been adopted yet by the newest browsers. It's unknown whether the browsers will add quote marks automatically if they are not included within the quote element. The specification for HTML does say that style sheets should control the presence of quote marks (and that they should be appropriate for the language being used, since different languages use different quote marks than English), but there are not yet any style sheet properties that can be used for quote marks—so for now, you'll have to type them yourself.

Like the blockquote element, the quote element can take an optional CITE attribute to point to a URL from where the quote was taken.

The Subscript Element

The subscript element (_{and}) renders the enclosed text in subscript (a bit lower than regular text). This element is useful for mathematical formulas.

For example, this line of HTML code contains the chemical formula for water:

```
We all need H<SUB>2</SUB>O.
```

The Superscript Element

The superscript element (^{and}) renders the enclosed text in superscript (a bit higher than regular text). This element is also useful for mathematical formulas.

For example, here's Einstein's most famous equation:

```
E=MC<SUP>2</SUP>
```

Another good use of the <SUP> tag is for the trademark symbol:

```
Eat A Bulky Burger<SUP>TM</SUP> today!
```

WARNING Another way to get the trademark symbol is to use the ™ entity, which is one of the new "extended" entities in HTML 4.0 that we discussed in Skill 3. However, it is not yet widely supported, so the superscript method is more compatible.

We'll see an illustration of the superscript and subscript elements later in this Skill.

Using Other Text-Level Elements

In addition to the text-level elements we've seen in this section, there are a couple of other text-level elements that need to be mentioned, all of which are new to HTML 4.0:

- The object element (<OBJECT> and </OBJECT>) is used to insert images, movies, and multimedia in your document; we'll see how to use the object element in Skill 9.

- The bidirectional override element (<BDO> and </BDO>), mentioned at the end of Skill 5, controls the direction that text is displayed for foreign languages (left-to-right or right-to-left text).

- The script element (<SCRIPT> and </SCRIPT>) introduced in Skill 5 can be used as a text-level element in HTML 4.0; we'll see more about the use of the script in Skill 15.

- The span element (<SPAN> and </SPAN>) is similar to the division element in some ways (<DIV> and </DIV>); the difference is that the span element is a text-level element, and the division element is a block-level element. Both elements are commonly used with style sheets, so we'll return to the topic of the span element in Skill 14.

- There are five elements used to create buttons and other form components that are considered to be text-level elements: the input element, the select element, the textarea element, the label element, and the button element. We'll see how to use these five elements in Skill 12, which is all about forms.

- Finally, the iframe element is a text-level element used to insert another HTML document within an inline frame. We'll learn about frames and inline frames in Skill 11.

In the next section, we'll talk about the font element and how to use fonts in your documents. After that, we'll move on to the groups of elements in the font-style and phrase categories.

Changing Font Size, Face, and Color with the Font Element

The font element (<FONT> and </FONT>) is used to format the size, typeface, and color of the enclosed text. We saw the use of the <FONT> tag as well as its attributes in some detail in Skill 3.

WARNING   The font element should not be used as an alternative to the header element. If your text is actually a header, you should put it inside a header element. Indexers and search engines don't recognize <FONT> as a way to generate a hierarchical outline of your page.

Here's a haiku by Tom Williams dressed up with the use of a <FONT> tag:

```
<FONT COLOR="BLUE" SIZE="+1" FACE="VERDANA,ARIAL,HELVETICA">flock of
geese,<BR>
the same shape<BR>
as his slingshot<BR></FONT>
```

The <FONT> tag can be used with three different attributes: SIZE, FACE, and COLOR. The SIZE attribute can be specified in absolute or relative values ranging from 1 (smallest) to 7 (largest). Using a relative font size (putting a plus or a minus before the number) will change the font size relative to the BASEFONT tag or the default font size. For example: <FONT SIZE="+4"> makes the font size four steps bigger than the current size. The seven different font sizes are shown here compared to the default font size.

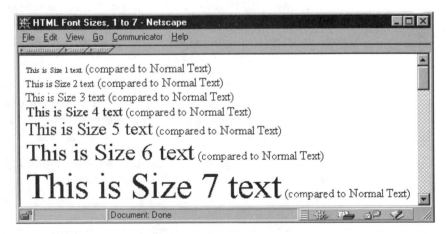

The COLOR attribute is specified with an RGB value, or you can also specify a color name. Skill 3 describes RGB color codes and names, while the appendix has a complete color reference.

The FACE attribute specifies a typeface that you'd like to use for the text enclosed by the font element; you can use a single typeface (such as ARIAL or COURIER), or you can give a list of typefaces separated by commas. We'll learn more about typefaces in the next section.

 **WARNING**

Like many of the earlier attributes and elements discussed in this Skill, the HTML 4.0 specification does not recommend the use of the font or basefont elements. Instead, the use of style sheets is recommended. HTML 4.0 uses the term *deprecated* to mean that an element or attribute has been outdated by a different method, and may become obsolete in a future version of HTML. The font and basefont elements are both deprecated.

Using Fonts Securely

Since HTML wasn't designed for page layout or word processing, there initially wasn't any way to specify a typeface for your HTML documents. After all, since HTML was a cross-platform language, there was no way to know what font faces were available—and the concept of a typeface is meaningless for a document being spoken through a text-to-speech reader. However, many Web designers pushed for a way of being able to specify the typeface in HTML. By default, most browsers used Times Roman for normal body text, and Courier for pre-formatted text. Many Web designers consider these two typefaces ugly or boring, and Navigator eventually introduced an extension to HTML in the form of the FACE attribute to the <FONT> tag. IE followed Navigator's lead.

Although HTML 3.2 did not officially recognize the use of the FACE attribute to the <FONT> tag, HTML 4.0 allows you use the FACE attribute—but at the same time, recommends that you use style sheets instead.

The current browsers don't universally agree on font properties, so the same font type might have different names on different systems, or the same font name might look different on different systems. Another deterrent to using fonts securely is that although operating systems come with default fonts, users can install additional fonts onto their computer and remove or change the default ones. You have no control over what fonts each user may have on their system. What looks beautiful on your system may look horribly ugly on someone else's system.

Arial	Comic Sans MS	Lucida Sans Unicode
Arial Black	Courier New	Times New Roman
Arial Narrow	**Impact**	Verdana

Many Windows users tend to have the same set of fonts; shown here is a list of fonts common to most Windows 95 systems.

Microsoft's Web typography site (`http://www.microsoft.com/typography/`) freely distributes several popular fonts for both Macintosh and Windows users, just in case you don't have them on your system.

One trouble with specifying font names is that similar fonts are known by different names. What is called "Helvetica" on one system may be known as "Arial" or "Univers" on a different system.

 **WARNING** Even worse, two different fonts can share the same name. And fonts can look completely different from platform to platform. Courier, for example, looks fine on Macintosh computers and UNIX workstations, but at most point sizes it is a profoundly ugly font on Windows systems.

With style sheets, font types are generic family choices. Fonts in the same general category (with similar properties) are offered as a choice so that your browser can pick the best face from its current font possibilities. Some examples of the generic font families are:

- `cursive` (Zapf-Chancery and Mistral, for example)

- `fantasy` (Western, for example)

- `monospace` (Courier, for example)

- `sans-serif` (Helvetica, for example)

- `serif` (Times New Roman, for example)

 NOTE *Serif fonts* have flags (serifs such as the main text in this book), or decorations, on the letters. *Sans serif* fonts are unadorned (without serifs as in this Note).

In Skill 14, we'll show you how to use style sheets to specify fonts in your HTML documents.

Now that we've learned about fonts, we're ready to move on to the last two categories of text-level elements: font-style elements and phrase elements.

Using Font-Style Elements

Font-style elements change the appearance of text (for example making text bold, underlined, or struck through). These font-style elements are also known as *physical* markup.

NOTE   Don't confuse "font-style elements" with the font element; they are two separate things. The font element is a text-level element that uses the <FONT> and </FONT> tags to change a font size, font face, or font color. Font-style elements are a category of elements, such as the bold and italic elements, that change the way text itself is displayed.

Among HTML purists, there is something of a stigma against font-style elements since font-style elements are device-dependent (that is, they assume that the display device is a computer screen capable of showing bold and italic and so forth). Despite this stigma, font-style elements are commonly used.

WARNING   Since you can't guarantee that your font-style elements will work on every system, make sure your document is comprehensible with even plain text. In other words, don't depend on font-style elements to convey vital information.

All font-style elements are a subcategory of text-level elements, and they all require both start and end tags. They can all be nested according to the normal rules of nesting text-level elements.

We'll look briefly at each of the seven font-style elements and the tags they use: bold (<B>), italic (<I>), underline (<U>), strikeout (<STRIKE> or <S>), big (<BIG>), small (<SMALL>), and teletype (<TT>).

The Bold Element

The bold element (<B> and </B>) causes text to appear in a bold typeface; we saw examples of the bold element in Skills 1 and 2.

The bold element does not indicate strong emphasis when read by some text-only or text-to-speech browsers. Use the strong element (a phrase element we'll see shortly) to mark important information instead.

TIP   The <B> tag is easier to type than the <STRONG> tag, so you may want to use the <B> tag when you initially create your Web pages, and then use your HTML tool's search and replace feature to change <B> tags into <STRONG> tags and </B> tags into </STRONG> tags.

The Italics Element

The italics element (<I> and </I>) marks up text in italics (text slanted diagonally upward to the right). For example: <I>Hello, World!</I>.

The italics element carries no other meaning other than that text is to be rendered in italics. It's appropriate to use the italics element to indicate text in a foreign language, for example <I>carpe diem</I>. (But using <I LANG="EL"> carpe diem</I> is even better, since this indicates that the language used is Latin, thanks to the LANG attribute we saw in Skill 5.)

There are several phrase elements that we'll see in the upcoming "Using Phrase Elements" section that are appropriately used instead of the italics element. For example, use the emphasis element (<EM> and </EM>) for emphasis or the citation element (<CITE> and </CITE>) for a citation to properly indicate why text is displayed in italics.

The Underline Element

The underline element (<U> and </U>) underlines text:

<U>Hello, World!</U>

WARNING   Readers may confuse underlined text with hyperlinked text that isn't working properly. You should avoid using the underline element.

The Strike Element

The strike element (<STRIKE> and </STRIKE> or <S> and </S>) indicates that the enclosed text should have a line drawn through the middle of the text.

<STRIKE>Yikes! I'm some helpless text and I'm struck!</STRIKE>

 **WARNING**   Not all browsers and HTML page-creation tools know how to deal with the strike element. In HTML 4.0, the use of the strike element is highly discouraged, and the new ins and del elements are recommended instead. We'll see the ins and del elements at the end of this Skill. If you do use the strike element, be aware that the <STRIKE> tag is more widely understood than the <S> tag.

Figure 6.11 shows some strikeout text in IE.

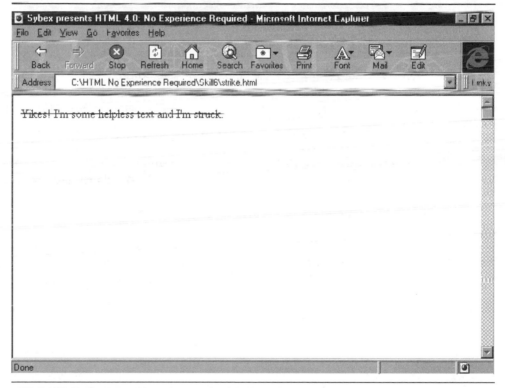

FIGURE 6.11: You can see in this IE example of struck-out text that the text, though struck, is still quite readable.

The Big Element

The big element (<BIG> and </BIG>) renders the enclosed text in a larger font (unless the document's font size is already as large as possible). The <BIG> tag has the same effect as <FONT SIZE="+1">.

```
<BIG>The Big and Tall Company</BIG>
```

More than one big element can be nested to render a larger text than with just one big element, but it might be clearer to say:

```
<FONT SIZE="+2">The Very Big and Tall Company</FONT>
```

rather than:

```
<BIG><BIG>The Very Big and Tall Company</BIG></BIG>
```

 NOTE   We saw the use of the <BIG> and <SMALL> tags in Skill 3.

The Small Element

The small element (<SMALL> and </SMALL>) renders the enclosed text in a smaller font, if possible, or ignores the tag if your text is already at size 1 (the smallest size possible). The <SMALL> tag has the same effect as <FONT SIZE="-1">.

```
<SMALL>The Small and Short Company</SMALL>
```

Like the big element, more than one small element can be nested in order to render a smaller text size than with just one small element.

The Teletype Element

The teletype element (<TT> and </TT>) renders the enclosed text in teletype font. This means that the text will be monospaced to look like a typewriter font (browsers will often use Courier font by default). For example:

```
<P>All the vowels on my typewriter are broken. I keep typing in a
standard phrase and it comes out like this: <TT>Th qck brwn fx jmps vr
th lz dg</TT>. I think I need a typewriter repairman.
```

 NOTE   Don't get confused between <TT> and <PRE>. The teletype element (<TT>) is a text-level element that doesn't affect the rules of white space, whereas the pre-formatted text element (<PRE>) is a block-level element that can be used to create indents and carriage returns, or to draw ASCII art.

Now we've seen all of the font-style elements. Before we move on to phrase elements and finish this Skill, let's see how all of these font-style elements are displayed. Figure 6.12 gives us an example of all of the font-style elements used in this section, along with the superscript and subscript elements from the previous section, as displayed by Navigator.

FIGURE 6.12: Navigator's display of all of the font-style elements and the superscript and subscript elements

Using Phrase Elements

Phrase elements are used to meaningfully mark up small sections of text. They're especially useful for readers who use a non-graphical browser, for search engines and indexers that refer to your HTML code to categorize sections of your document for their site outlines, and for other computer programs that need to interact with your Web pages to extract data for other useful purposes. For example, text rendered with the <CITE> tag may render visually the same as italicized text, but the underlying HTML code indicates the text is a citation.

Start and end tags are necessary for all phrase elements. We'll see the nine different phrase elements briefly: acronyms (<ACRONYM>), citations (<CITE>), computer code (<CODE>), definitions (<DFN>), emphasis (<EM>), suggested keyboard sequences (<KBD>), sample output (<SAMP>), strongly emphasized text (<STRONG>), and computer variables (<VAR>).

We'll see how a browser displays these elements in Figure 6.13, after we've defined all nine phrase elements.

The Acronym Element

The acronym element's <ACRONYM> and </ACRONYM> tags indicate the presence of an abbreviation (FBI, WWW, and so on). Text marked within the acronym element may not necessarily appear any differently, but spell-checkers and speech synthesizers may find it useful to know that the marked text is an acronym, and an advanced program could use the acronym element to help construct a glossary for your document.

You can use the advisory TITLE attribute to define the acronym. For example:

```
I spy for the <ACRONYM TITLE="Federal Bureau of
Investigation">FBI</ACRONYM>.
```

 **WARNING** Since the acronym element is new in HTML 4.0, it is not yet widely supported.

The Citation Element

The citation element's <CITE> and </CITE> tags are used to mark that the enclosed text is a citation (titles of excerpts, quotes, references) from another source.

 **WARNING** Don't use the <CITE> tag except to indicate the title of a cited work.

Text within <CITE> and </CITE> is usually rendered in italics (although you can't always depend that every browser will do so).

For example:

```
<P>I have read and reread <CITE>Moby Dick</CITE> but I still can't make
heads nor tails of it.</P>
```

The Code Element

The code element's <CODE> and </CODE> tags are used for examples of program code. Text nested in the code element is usually rendered in a monospaced typeface, just like text inside <TT> and </TT> tags.

 NOTE Since most of the creators of HTML are computer programmers, they're interested in having useful ways of presenting code from computer programs. Most people, who aren't computer programmers or computer trainers, will not have much use for <CODE> (or <KBD>, <SAMP>, or <VAR>).

For example:

```
<P>To use the automatic date feature in Excel, just enter
<CODE>=Date()</CODE> into a cell.</P>
```

The Definition Element

The definition element's <DFN> and </DFN> tags are intended to be used to mark the first time that you define a term. For example:

```
<P>It's not strange that <DFN>SGML</DFN> (Standard Generalized Markup
Language) is so eerily similar to HTML.</P>
```

By marking your definitions this way, special software programs can define an index or glossary for your document. Most browsers will display the definition text in italics, though not all browsers do so.

The Emphasis Element

The emphasis element is a popular way to emphasize text. Any text marked between <EM> and </EM> will be emphasized. Most browsers render the emphasized text in italics, but a text-to-speech browser knows to give spoken emphasis to text within an emphasis element.

 TIP   Many style guides recommend using the emphasis element instead of the italics element.

For example:

```
<P>I simply <EM>must</EM> get your recipe for chili, Karen Dodson!</P>
```

The Keyboard Element

The keyboard element's <KBD> and </KBD> tags indicate text that the viewer should type. Some browsers view this text as monospaced (some may also view the text as bold), though, unlike the <PRE> tag, multiple spaces within the keyboard element are collapsed.

For example:

```
<P>To start the program, hit the <KBD>S</KBD> key and press the
<KBD>Carriage      Return</KBD>, then hold onto your hat!</P>
```

The Sample Element

The sample element uses the <SAMP> and </SAMP> tags to indicate sample output text from a computer program. An example might be a directory lisitng or sample form output from a script program used to process your Web site's access log.

Like the keyboard element, the sample element's text is often rendered in a monospaced font; and multiple spaces are collapsed. The keyboard element is used for text that a user must enter, whereas the sample element is used for text that a computer generates in response to a user's action.

For example:

```
<P>Instead of giving me the expected results, the computer kept
printing <SAMP>All work and no play        makes Jack a dull boy</SAMP>
over and over again. I'm not sure what it means.</P>
```

The Strong Emphasis Element

The strong element's <STRONG> and </STRONG> tags are used to indicate strong emphasis. Text within a strong element is usually rendered as bold or given a strident pronunciation by a text-to-speech reader.

 TIP   Many style guides recommend using the strong element instead of the bold element.

For example:

```
<P>I swear, if they don't give me that raise <STRONG>tomorrow</STRONG>,
I quit.</P>
```

The Variable Element

The variable element (<VAR> and </VAR>) marks up the variables used in computer programs, or the parts of a computer command chosen by the user. The text is usually rendered as monospaced, and like the keyboard element, multiple spaces are collapsed.

For example:

```
<P>The formula for the <VAR>distance    traveled</VAR> (in miles) is
<VAR>speed</VAR> (in miles per hour) multiplied by <VAR>time</VAR> (in
hours).</P>
```

Now let's see how IE chooses to display all of the phrase elements that we've seen. Figure 6.13 shows them in action.

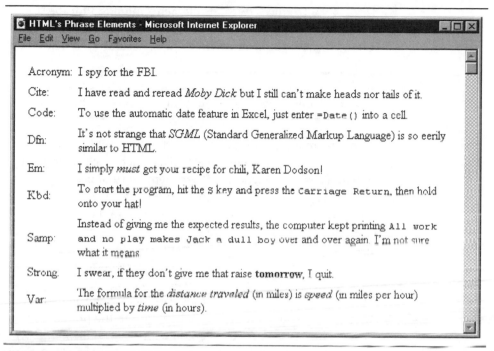

FIGURE 6.13: All the phrase elements

You can always nest multiple phrase elements. For example, you might use the following phrase elements if you were writing a Web page about the anchor element:

```
<P>When using an anchor element, make sure to use the
<CODE>HREF="<VAR>URL</VAR>"</CODE> attribute.</P>
```

Whew! That's it for phrase elements, which means we've finished the text-level elements. In the last section of this Skill, we'll introduce two new elements that are not neither text-level nor block-level elements, and are used for marking changes to a document: the ins and del elements.

Marking Changes with the Ins and Del Elements

Users of a word processor like Word or WordPerfect may be familiar with an automatic feature that compares two different document and marks the changes between them. Newly added phrases appear in a highlighted color, while deleted phrases are shown in a strikeout font.

Skill 6

HTML 4.0 introduces two new elements intended for the same purpose: The ins element (with required <INS> and </INS> tags) to mark inserted text, and the del element (with <DEL> and </DEL> tags, naturally) to mark deleted text.

 **WARNING**   Since the ins and del elements are new in HTML 4.0, they are not widely supported yet; but since they are so useful, we predict they'll catch on soon.

The actual methods used to display these elements will vary from browser to browser; but usually a section marked as deleted would either not appear at all, or appear as if it were within a strike element (that is to say, with the standard struck-out appearance—a line through the middle of the text). Newly inserted material could be highlighted with a different font color, or in italics, or with a different font face. Until new versions of browsers appear that actually make use of these elements, no one knows exactly how these elements be displayed.

The ins and del elements are neither text-level nor block-level elements. They are unique in this respect—they are the only two elements used in the body of an HTML document that aren't text-level or block-level elements.

These two elements are closest in behavior to the phrase text-level elements; however, phrase elements can't contain block-level elements, whereas the <INS> and <DEL> tags can mark the beginning of any kind of HTML body section element before they're closed with </INS> and </DEL>, for example. This makes it convenient to mark three paragraphs as being inserted.

Another difference is that while phrase elements can't take any special attributes, both the <INS> and <DEL> tags can be used with the following attributes:

```
<INS CITE="URL"> or <DEL CITE="URL">
<INS DATETIME="DATE & TIME"> or <DEL DATETIME="DATE & TIME">
```

The CITE attribute can be used to point to a URL that contains information about why a change was made.

The DATETIME attribute can be used to indicate when the change was made. However, the date and time format must be specified in a very exact way. The format is YYYY-MM-DDThh:mm:ssTZD, where:

- YYYY = four-digit year

- MM = two-digit month (01=January, and so on)

- DD = two-digit day of month (01 through 31)

- T = the letter "T"

- hh = two digits of hour (00 through 23) (A.M./P.M. *not* allowed)

- mm = two digits of minute (00 through 59)

- ss = two digits of second (00 through 59)

- TZD = time zone designator (either the letter Z to indicate UTC/GMT, or an offset such as +04:00 to indicate four hours ahead of UTC, or -02:30 to indicate two-and-a-half hours behind UTC).

Here's a quick (and quite hypothetical) example that uses the ins element to mark a new section:

```
<H2>Latest News</H2>
<INS DATETIME="1998-04-22T11:38:00-07:00"
CITE="http://www.tori.com/updatelog.html">
<P>We've just received some new information.
<P>Apparently there will be <STRONG>two shows</STRONG> on Sunday.
</INS>
<P>The show will start at 7:00 P.M.
```

This code marks the middle two paragraphs as new. They were changed on April 22, 1998 at 11:38 a.m (at 7 hours ahead of Greenwich, which is equivalent to the Pacific time zone); information about the change (perhaps who made the change or where the new information came from) can be found at the URL listed in the CITE attribute.

The ins and del elements are the last of the elements that are used in the body section. This means we're done introducing HTML tags! From here on out, the only new elements you'll see are advanced elements or extensions to HTML (such as the elements used to create tables, forms, and frames). We've now seen all of the basic elements that exist in HTML (except for a couple of obsolete tags that aren't worth worrying about).

Earlier in this Skill we looked at the anchor element briefly. In the next Skill, we'll look at anchors and links in great detail and discover some new and useful ways to link to different documents.

Are You Experienced?

Now you can...

- ☑ **create Web pages using block-level elements**
- ☑ **arrange your text to get the look you want**
- ☑ **work with fonts**
- ☑ **add phrase elements to your pages**

Stepping Out: Linking Your Way Around the Web

- Using external and internal links
- Naming and linking to sections of a document
- Using the anchor element with other HTML elements
- Maintaining and verifying links with special tools

Being able to link your Web page to other pages is the most innovative and compelling aspect of the Web, and it is certainly a huge part of the Web's success. Links are convenient—and also exciting—since they provide related information to anyone viewing your page.

In Skill 2 and Skill 6, we learned the basics of using links with an anchor element, for example `<A HREF="http://www.yahoo.com/">Visit Yahoo!</A>`.

In this Skill, we'll review link basics and then learn much more about links, including how to use advanced anchor attributes, and how to name sections of your document so you can create tables of contents with links to a particular part of your document.

We'll see the two major categories of links: *external links,* which are links to files not on your own site (created by someone else) and *internal links,* which are links to files that are part of your site (created by you). Even though you'll use the same anchor element for both types of links, it's worth looking at them separately because they involve different concepts. We'll start by looking at external links, then learn how to integrate anchors with other HTML tags, and then talk about internal links.

Finally, we'll learn how to maintain links and check automatically for faulty links.

Creating an External Link

As we saw in Skill 2, the anchor element uses the `<A>` and `</A>` tags. The anchor element is used to create both external links and internal links (both of which are otherwise known as *hyperlinks*).

NOTE   These anchor links are not to be confused with the link element (which uses the `<LINK>` tag) we discussed in Skill 5; the link element establishes different types of relationships between your document and other affiliated documents, while anchors create physical links in the body of your document.

The anchor element takes several attributes. We'll look first at the attributes `HREF`, `TITLE`, `TARGET`, and `NAME` separately, and then we'll see some other attributes, including `REL` and `REV`, and generic HTML 4.0 attributes. We'll also discuss some tips for your anchor text while we discuss the `HREF` attribute.

Since external links use the URL addressing scheme that we're already familiar with (thanks to our discussion in Skill 1), we'll talk about anchors in the context of external links first.

Unlike most HTML tags, which don't require attributes, the anchor tag requires either the HREF attribute or the NAME attribute (or both).

Using the *HREF* Attribute and Anchor Text

Most of the time, you must use the anchor element's HREF attribute to specify the Hyperlink REFerence (that is, a reference to a link's address). We've already seen a few examples of this in Skill 2. The HREF attribute must point to a URL (see Skill 1 for a discussion of URLs), and the URL should appear in quotes, like this:

```
<A HREF="http://www.construct.net/">Construct</A>
```

In this example, the HREF is pointing to a Web page at the URL http://www.construct.net/.

TIP When adding a link to your page, it's sometimes difficult to make sure that the URL is typed correctly. (One typo and it might not work at all.) You can visit the page you want to link to, copy the address from the location bar, and then paste it into your text editor in between the quotes of your HREF attribute.

You don't have to always link to Web pages—you can link to any type of file on the Web, including images, sounds, and movies. For example, here's some text that includes a link to a movie that's in Microsoft's AVI format:

```
<P>You can see a five-megabyte movie of two guys playing souped-up
<A HREF="http://www.unrealities.com/videos/roshambo.avi">Roshambo</A>.
```

(We'll learn more about images in Skill 8; we'll see more about multimedia, including movies and sounds, in Skill 9.)

TIP When linking to a format that's not usually used on the Web, it's polite to put some details about that format in your anchor text. For example, if you have a zip file containing some PowerPoint documents, your anchor might look like this:
`<A HREF="files.zip">A Zipped Archive of PowerPoint files, 104K</A>`.

You can also use links that don't use the HTTP protocol, such as the mailto link we saw in Skill 3 or links to files served by FTP (File Transfer Protocol):

```
<P>If you have trouble downloading this
<A HREF="ftp://ftp.emf.net/users/estephen/file.txt">file</A>,
then go ahead and <A HREF="mailto:estephen@emf.net">send me a message</A>.
```

Other types of URLs were presented in Skill 1, and they can all be used in anchors.

Whenever you link to a resource, the text enclosed within the anchor element is highlighted as a link, and serves as the *anchor text* that somehow introduces the resource to which you are linking. For example, in the link `<A HREF="http://www.suite101.com/">Visit Suite 101</A>`, "Visit Suite 101" is the anchor text.

 NOTE   In Skill 3, we learned how to specify the color of anchor text in your document using the three different link attributes of the `<BODY>` tag.

You might want to review Figures 1.3 and 1.7 from Skill 1 of this book to see some examples of anchor text in Microsoft Internet Explorer and Netscape Navigator. By default, anchor text is blue and underlined in Navigator and IE.

 **WARNING**   Users of browsers can set the link color to whatever color they want (even overriding the link color you've specified in your document). Browser users can also select whether they want links to be underlined. Therefore, you shouldn't include a statement like, "Click on the blue and underlined word 'Next' above to see the next page!"—the word "Next" may not be underlined or blue at all.

It's best not to use device-specific terms in your anchor text. For example, it's common to see Web authors use statements like:

```
<P>Click <A HREF="http://www.tori.com/">here</A> to read about Tori Amos!
```

However, not everyone viewing your page has a mouse, so what if they can't click anything? Also, the anchor text is just the word "here," which isn't much of a description—some browsers remember pages you visit by their anchor text. Anyone viewing a list of recently visited pages may see your document listed as just the word "here," which won't help them remember what the "here" document is about.

Instead, use the anchor element to surround the most relevant description of the resource to which you're linking:

```
<P>Read about <A HREF="http://www.tori.com/">Tori Amos</A>!
```

Now the person viewing your page can select the link (whether by mouse or another method) and also knows exactly what page they're visiting; the page's description will appear in any lists of visited documents, and this approach is more concise than the "click here" approach.

To continue our discussion of anchor text, some links use straightforward anchor text.

```
<P>Kyrie works for <A HREF="http://www.sgi.com/">SGI</A>.
```

In this case, "SGI" (Silicon Graphics, Inc.) is the name of the company, and clicking on the company name would lead to SGI's main Web site. It might be misleading for the word "SGI" to lead anywhere other than a main SGI home page.

Sometimes, Web authors create anchor text that is subtle so that people are surprised when they follow the link. For example:

```
<P>Partha told me he thought we should sue
<A HREF="http://www.ticketmaster.com/">those jerks</A>.
```

It's not clear from the context of the page who "those jerks" is meant to refer to—until you point to the words "those jerks" and see Ticketmaster's URL on the status bar. At that point, you understand the object of Partha's ire.

This "misleading" use of anchor text is all part of the fun of the Web and is quite common.

 **WARNING**

Some corporations do not take kindly to the appropriation of their logos or people "misrepresenting" their name. One Web author, John Klopp, actually received a nasty phone call from a Pacific Bell lawyer for putting a link similar to this one on his page: `<A HREF="http://www.playboy.com/">Pacific Bell</A>`. Some companies have been known to threaten to sue Web authors who use their company name in a disparaging way. Your chances of being successfully sued depend on if you are misusing a trademarked logo and whether you are running a commercial page that makes money—as well as the truth of your claims about the company.

Creating Advisory Titles for Your Links with the *TITLE* Attribute

One anchor attribute that expands on the information available about a link is the TITLE attribute. The TITLE attribute allows an "advisory title" that explains the resource in more detail. To use our previous example, you can make it clearer who Partha dislikes by using the following HTML code, which differs only by including a TITLE attribute in the anchor element:

```
<P>Partha told me he thought we should sue
<A HREF="http://www.ticketmaster.com/" TITLE="Ticketmaster">those
jerks</A>.
```

Browsers may choose different methods of showing the advisory TITLE attribute, such as displaying the title in a *tool tip* or *balloon help* (a little box that appears when the mouse pointer is pointing to the link), or the title might appear on the status bar. Currently, the only popular browser that makes use of the TITLE attribute in a link is IE 4, which displays it as a tool tip (as shown in Figure 7.1); Navigator should soon support these attributes.

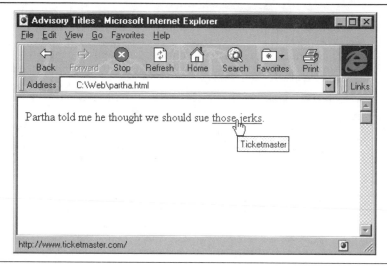

FIGURE 7.1: IE displays a tool tip for this link, thanks to the use of the TITLE attribute in the anchor element.

CHANGING THE STATUS BAR TEXT FOR YOUR LINKS

When you point to a link, Navigator and IE display the URL of the link's target in the status bar. A commonly used attribute (similar in intent to the TITLE attribute) changes the browser's status bar to display a specific phrase when pointing to the link.

Consider this code:

```
<TITLE>Text in the Status Bar</TITLE>
<BODY>
We buy all of our books from <AHREF="http://www.sybex.com/"
ONMOUSEOVER="window.status='Click Here For Computer
Books!'; return true">Sybex</A>.
```

continued ▶

When the mouse pointer crosses over the anchor text ("Sybex"), the status bar doesn't display the link's URL as it normally would. Instead, the phrase "Click Here For Computer Books!" is displayed, as shown here.

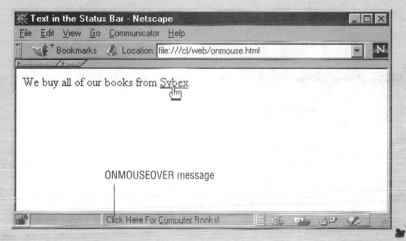

The attribute value for ONMOUSEOVER in the third line of the above HTML code (beginning with the word "window.status") is not HTML at all— instead, this line contains two JavaScript commands. JavaScript is a scripting language, created by Netscape, that can change how Web pages behave. This particular JavaScript code is fairly simple (just one line and two commands), and causes a visible change to the way that Web pages behave, so it's easy to understand why it is popular.

The ONMOUSEOVER attribute is one example of HTML 4.0's new event attributes; the event attributes can be used with many different elements, not just anchors. We'll see more about ONMOUSEOVER and its related attributes in Skill 15, which is about scripting languages.

We'll see more about JavaScript and its advantages and drawbacks in Skill 15 as well, but while we've mentioned this status bar example, we should point out that it has a major drawback: Many people like to see the URL of the links on a page, and they get annoyed when the URL is replaced with a different message in the status bar. (IE 4 combats this

continued ▶

problem a little by showing the URL as a tool tip.) In general, people should be able to use their browser normally when they view your page. Every time you change the normal behavior of the browser, you risk confusing or annoying people. Also, since many of the visitors to your page might not be able to see the JavaScript message, you shouldn't rely on conveying important information in the status bar.

One use of the TITLE attribute is to provide a description for links to images or other file types that don't have a full title. For example:

```
<P>You can see <A HREF="http://www.construct.net/images/goolnut.jpg"
TITLE="Construct's Hand Logo">a logo</A> that I admire.
```

Another use of the TITLE attribute is to set the subject of e-mail when you use a mailto link. If a user selects the following link:

```
<P>Send e-mail to the <A HREF="mailto:president@whitehouse.gov"
TITLE="Save the Whales!">president</A> today!
```

then the browser should start a new e-mail message with the subject "Save the Whales!" as indicated by the title.

Unfortunately, not all browsers support the TITLE attribute in this way for mailto links; some Web authors attempt the same thing with this construction:

```
Send e-mail to the
<A HREF="mailto:president@whitehouse.gov?Subject="Save
the Whales!">president</A> today!
```

However, many e-mail programs get confused by the ?Subject part, and think it's part of the e-mail address—which means the length won't work. Since the ?Subject modifier is not (yet) an accepted Internet standard and doesn't always work reliably, it's discouraged.

 NOTE   As we saw in Skill 5, the advisory TITLE attribute can apply to almost every HTML element, not just the anchor element.

The anchor element's TITLE attribute is not nearly as important as the HREF attribute, or the NAME attribute, which we will discuss next.

Labeling Sections of Your Document with the *NAME* Attribute

We've now seen two of the anchor element's attributes, HREF and TITLE. Another important attribute of the anchor element is the NAME attribute, which labels a section of an HTML document with a specific reference name.

The NAME attribute allows links to be able to point to a specific section within a document (instead of links always leading to the top of a document).

For example, suppose you want to link to the street directions on a particular page at your site. But the page is a long one, and the directions are near the bottom. If you link to the page itself, no one will see the directions unless they read all the way to the bottom of the document. Fortunately, you can link straight to the directions. It's a two-step process: First, you must edit the target document and give a name to the section where the directions begin, using the NAME attribute of the anchor element. Second, you must specify that name in your link.

The appropriate section of the page (where the street directions are located) can be named using this anchor element:

```
<A NAME="directions">Here are the directions to our office:</A>
```

NOTE   The anchor element here isn't supposed to affect this text's appearance, but some older browsers did change the enclosed text by making it bold.

Once this code has been added, you can link to the directions by taking a normal link tag and adding a number sign (#) and the name assigned (in this case, directions) to the URL. If the normal URL for the page is http://www.foo .com/, then you would specify the link for the directions name like this:

```
The<A HREF="http://www.foo.com/#directions">directions to our
office</A>are available
```

HTML 4.0 uses the term *fragment URLs* for these URLs that link to a named anchor section of a document.

TIP   You can only link to named sections; you can't arbitrarily link to the middle of a document unless the <A NAME="*name*"> and </A> tags have been added to that document.

Let's take a real-life example. Suppose you want to link to a particular poem in Shakespeare's play *The Tempest* (available from MIT at http://the-tech.mit.edu/ Shakesepare/works.html). Let's say the section you want occurs in Act I, Scene 2.

MIT has broken up each scene of *The Tempest* into a separate file, so the desired URL turns out to be `http://the-tech.mit.edu/Shakespeare/Comedy/tempest/thetempest.1.2.html`. But there are 593 lines in this scene and your poem is near the bottom.

Fortunately, MIT has added a NAME attribute anchor to each line of every Shakespeare play. The NAME attribute anchor is simply the line number, anchored around a word in that line. For example, the line you're interested in is line number 461 of this scene. (You can discover this by searching at the Shakespeare site for the word or phrase in which you're interested.) Here's the NAME attribute anchor that's used by MIT:

```
<A NAME="461">fathom</A>
```

So you can now link straight to your poem by adding #461 to end of the URL for the scene, which creates a fragment URL. You can use the fragment URL in your link like this:

```
<P>One of my favorite poems is sung by a character named Ariel in
William Shakespeare's <CITE>The Tempest</CITE>, at
<A HREF="http://the-tech.mit.edu/Shakespeare/Comedy/tempest/
➡thetempest.1.2.html#461">line 461 of Act I, Scene 2</A>. This verse was
used in a song by Laurie Anderson.
```

 **WARNING**   The fragment URL used here is very long; it must be typed in one continuous line, with no line-breaks or spaces at all. Remember, any white space in any URL will prevent it from working.

Now when someone clicks on the link text (<u>line 461 of Act I, Scene 2</u>), they'll see the poem at the top of the screen, with the rest of the play continued underneath. Figure 7.2 shows the result—note the extra information in IE's location bar URL, and you can judge by the vertical scroll bar how far down in the document this line occurs.

There's more to learn about named sections and using named links; we'll return to the topic of anchor names later in this Skill.

Changing Browser Windows with the *TARGET* Attribute

Another attribute you can use in an anchor element's <A> tag is TARGET. The TARGET attribute is normally used with frames (as we'll see in Skill 11). However, you can use the TARGET attribute even if you don't use frames.

When you specify a TARGET for your links, you indicate the name of a window where you'd like the linked page to appear. For example, a link can specified like this:

```
<A HREF="http://www.walrus.com/~gibralto/" TARGET="window2">Acorn
Mush</A>
```

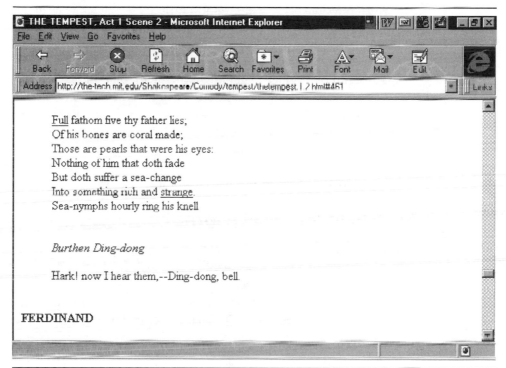

FIGURE 7.2: IE uses a fragment URL to fetch this verse from Shakespeare's *The Tempest*. The <u>Full</u> and <u>strange</u> links lead to a discussion of those words in a glossary.

When this link is followed, a new window (named internally "window2") is created, containing the Acorn Mush page.

The browsers that obey target attributes (including IE and Navigator) create new windows that look as if an extra copy of the browser is running. The old window is located behind the new window, and the old page that contained the link will still be visible, if the browser does not take up the full screen. If a browser does take up the full screen, then the only way to see the old window is for the user to switch windows and go back to the old page.

The new window, with the new page, functions like a normal copy of the browser in every respect. Eventually, the viewer will close the new window, revealing the old window again—which in effect guarantees that the viewer will return to the original site at some point.

Web designers like the idea of letting people follow a link from their site while still keeping their site visible somewhere.

The main drawback of the TARGET attribute is that some users can get confused by the unexpected behavior of their browsers when they follow a targeted link. Since each browser window maintains its own history of documents viewed, viewers can get confused when they can't seem to return to a recently visited page—until they notice their old window with their old history.

Also, if a viewer switches back to the old window while leaving the new window open but hidden, then any other links that they select with the same TARGET window (for example, a second link that also specifies TARGET="window2") will appear to be do *nothing at all*! The viewer will be confused about why links have stopped working in their browser. In reality, the links are working—but the link is only causing a change in a *hidden* window, so it *seems* like nothing is happening.

Using Other Anchor Attributes

There are several other attributes used in an anchor element's <A> tag. We saw the use of the first two other attributes in Skill 5: REL and REV.

Although rarely used, these two attributes can theoretically mark relationships between the current document and the resource in the link. Their use is identical in the anchor element as it is in the link element discussed in Skill 5. Here's an example from the specification of HTML 4.0:

```
<P>Thanks to <A REL="SPONSOR">Acme Inc</A> for support.</P>
```

This link specifies that "Acme Inc" has a "sponsor" relationship to the current document. The important thing to realize about this type of anchor is that it does *not* necessarily create a link to Acme or to any particular URL; you always have to use an HREF attribute if you want a link.

Every popular browser currently ignores these kind of relationship attributes, so there's not much point in using them yet.

HTML 4.0 allows several new attributes to be used with anchors. We'll see the use of the new ACCESSKEY and TABINDEX attributes, and after that we'll take a detailed look at how you can use HTML 4.0's generic attributes with the anchor element to produce some useful effects.

Specifying Keyboard Shortcuts for Links

One drawback with a graphical browser is that it is usually very mouse-dependent. For example, you have to click on links to follow them if you use Navigator 3 or earlier. (IE 3 and 4 and Navigator 4 all let you use the Tab key to select a link and then Enter to follow it.)

If a page has many links, then this keyboard method is a little cumbersome and can be difficult to use, especially for people with disabilities. HTML 4.0 addresses this problem by introducing two new attributes:

- The ACCESSKEY attribute lets you specify a shortcut key to be used to follow a link (for example, you can specify that a link should be followed whenever a user presses the A key).

- The TABINDEX attribute lets you specify a priority number for a link so that the Tab key will select that link earlier or later than other links. By using the TABINDEX attribute with a number of anchor elements, you can create a custom "tab order" that replaces the default top-to-bottom order.

Using the ACCESSKEY attribute with an anchor is simple: Specify a single character as an attribute value. When the surfer presses the equivalent keyboard shortcut command, the browser should automatically select and follow the link. For example, `<A HREF="http://www.yahoo.com/" ACCESSKEY="Y">Yahoo!</A>` specifies that the Y key should take your readers to Yahoo!'s URL. However, on Windows machines the reader will have to press Alt+Y, and on a Macintosh the user will need to press Command+Y to follow the Yahoo! link. Other systems may use different shortcuts, or perhaps allow the shortcut key to be used by itself (without a modifier key).

According to the HTML 4.0 specification, browsers should indicate the Y key as the shortcut in some fashion. It shouldn't be necessary for you to write "Press the Y key to visit Yahoo!" anywhere on your page (and nor would that description be accurate for all systems or browsers). However, you may need to include the name of the access key in the anchor text so that it can be highlighted. For example, if you want to use Z as the ACCESSKEY value for your Yahoo link, you may want to use anchor text such as "Z: Yahoo" or "Yahoo (Z)" so that there can be a visual indication that Z is the shortcut key.

 NOTE   Currently, only IE 4 supports the use of the ACCESSKEY attribute, but other browsers should introduce support for it shortly. However, IE does not indicate the shortcut key on screen at all.

The TABINDEX attribute is a little more complicated than ACCESSKEY. Both the ACCESSKEY and TABINDEX attributes can also be used with form elements. We'll see how to use the TABINDEX attribute after we've learned about forms in Skill 12.

In Skill 6, we described the generic HTML 4.0 attributes that can be used on almost every element; these generic attributes can be used with the anchor element to create interesting effects. First we'll take a look at the language attributes and then we'll see the style and reference attributes.

Using Language Attributes

The generic LANG and DIR attributes can be particularly useful with anchors, since you can indicate what language is being used in the linked document, as well as the direction (left-to-right or right-to-left) that is used in that document.

In addition, the anchor element allows a special CHARSET attribute to declare what character encoding (that is, what set of foreign language characters) is used in the linked-to resource. (For more information about character encoding, see Skill 3 and the end of Skill 5.)

For example:

```
<A HREF="http://www.jmas.co.jp/FAQs/" LANG="JP" CHARSET="euc-jp">Index
to various FAQs</A>
```

This is a link to a page on a server located in Japan. The language of the page is declared to be Japanese by the LANG attribute. The CHARSET attribute indicates that browsers should use a particular character encoding to display the Japanese characters that are used on the page. In this case, the character encoding is called "euc-jp" but other charsets are possible as well. Unfortunately, charsets are not yet in wide enough use for there to be a definitive list of them anywhere. More details about charsets can be found online (`ftp://ds.internic.net/rfc/rfc2045.txt`).

Using Reference, Style, and Script Attributes

In Skill 6, we briefly described three generic attributes that are commonly used with style sheets (ID, CLASS, and STYLE), and said that we'd see their use in Skill 14.

By defining a style sheet and applying one of these attributes to an anchor element, you can control a wide range of possibilities for the appearance of links and anchor text.

In addition, HTML 4.0 specifically allows the use of ID attribute values as a target for named anchors. So instead of using an anchor with a NAME attribute to label a particular part of your document, you can use an element's ID attribute. For example, you could name a section of bold text with the identity "Greg" as shown:

```
<B ID="greg">Greg Burrell</B> is an expert on this subject.
```

Later in your document (or in a different document), you can link to the "Greg" section using a fragment URL that ends with #greg.

 WARNING   Unfortunately, current browsers only support named anchors using the anchor element; they can't yet link to elements named with the ID attribute.

Using Events Attributes with Anchors

Earlier in this Skill, we saw the use of the ONMOUSEOVER attribute and a piece of JavaScript code to change the contents of the browser's status bar. There are a wide range of event attributes that can affect the contents or appearance of an attribute; we'll see the use of these attributes in Skill 15. One possible use is a message or confirmation dialog box to give the surfer some information about the link they're about to follow.

In the next section, we'll see how to use the anchor element with other elements (for example, to create a list of links).

Using Anchor Elements with Other HTML Elements

Before we proceed to some new uses of anchor elements, let's see how well the anchor element interacts with other tags. Specifically, we'll look at how the anchor element should be nested.

We've already stated that an anchor element cannot be nested within other anchor elements. So this use of an anchor element is illegal:

```
<A HREF="http://www.yahoo.com/">There are a whole range
of categories in Yahoo's listings, including general categories like
Computers and Entertainment, and specific categories for
<A HREF="http://www.yahoo.com/Entertainment/Actors_
➥and_Actresses/Bacon__Kevin/">Kevin Bacon</A> and Coca-Cola.</A>
```

Instead, separate your anchors into separate elements. Anchor text should be relatively short—a few words should be sufficient. Try this as a replacement for the previous listing:

```
There are a whole range of categories in
<A HREF="http://www.yahoo.com/">Yahoo's listings</A>,
including general categories like Computers and Entertainment, and
specific categories for
<A HREF="http://www.yahoo.com/Entertainment/Actors
➥_and_Actresses/Bacon__Kevin/">Kevin Bacon</A> and Coca-Cola.</A>
```

It's legal to put an anchor element inside a heading:

```
<H1><A HREF="http://www.jazzflavor.com/">It's About Jazz,
Daddyo!</A></H1>
```

The anchor here would take on the quality of the heading, as shown in Figure 7.3.

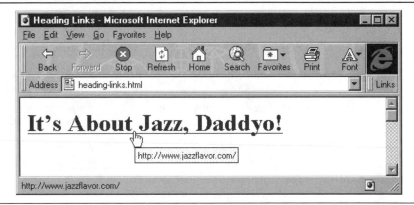

FIGURE 7.3: An anchor nested within a heading appears the same as a heading, but also with the qualities of a link.

Since headings are block-level elements and anchors are text-level elements, the heading must contain the anchor for a link and not vice versa. (Recall the rules of nesting from the end of Skill 2.)

 NOTE　In the next Skill, we'll show you how to use an image as an anchor's link.

Similarly, you can use text-level elements either inside or outside the anchor element to affect the quality of links. This allows you to color-code or otherwise flag certain links. Some Web sites use this technique to make a distinction between internal and external links.

For example, you can make a link appear in italics by enclosing it in the italic element:

```
<I><A HREF="http://www.sos.net/home/jef/">Jef's Home</A></I>
```

The order here doesn't matter, so this similar construction would also render the anchor text in italics:

```
<A HREF="http://www.sos.net/home/jef/"><I>Jef's Home</I></A>
```

As you can see from Figure 7.4, both these links appear the same way.

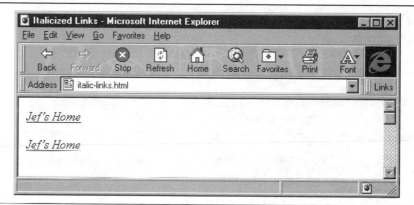

FIGURE 7.4: Two Italicized links, each nested in a different order but with an identical result displayed by IE

 NOTE

Actually, it's slightly preferable to put the anchor element *inside* the italic element so that any software that is using the anchor text to index or store links doesn't have any chance of getting confused by the italic element and storing the link as "I Jef's Home I" or "<I>Jef's Home</I>"

You can also color-code links, but the font element that contains the COLOR attribute must occur nested within the anchor element. If you put the font element outside the anchor element, then the default color of the link takes precedence over the font element. To see this in action, we'll see the following two links:

```
<FONT COLOR="GREEN">
    <A HREF="http://www.bway.net/~drkeith/hoot/">Hootenanny</A>
</FONT>
<P>
<A HREF="http://www.bway.net/~drkeith/hoot/">
    <FONT COLOR="GREEN">Hootenanny</FONT>
</A>
```

The first link will appear in blue, the default color for a link, because the inner anchor element has a default color that takes precedence over the outer font element. The second link will appear in green, as specified, since the inner font element takes precedence over the default link color.

NOTE If you color your links, make sure to choose colors that are consistent and easy to read. Some HTML style guides recommend against coloring individual links because it may be confusing to users who are used to seeing links in blue or the color they've specified for links. Others designers recommend you use style sheets if you do want to color links, since style sheets keep the presentation separate from the content. Since HTML is all about content and not really about formatting, this approach makes sense.

One issue to consider is that if you color a link, surfers won't be able to see if they've visited the link. Your color specification will override the browser's standard behavior of having two different link colors, one for visited links and another for unvisited links.

WARNING Although Navigator 4 and IE 4 can color links, earlier versions of these browsers have problems. IE 3 cannot display links in different colors at all. Navigator 3 only displays colored links if the anchor is within a table cell (see Skill 10 for the use of table cells).

For our final example of using anchors with other HTML tags, we'll see the use of lists of links. Since lists are a good way to organize information, they're a natural way of presenting a group of links.

For example, consider the following section of HTML code:

```
<P>There are several good HTML 3.2 references on the Web, but not yet any
good outside references for Cougar. Here are some recommended online
references:
<UL>
<LI><A HREF="http://www.htmlhelp.com/reference/wilbur/">WDG's HTML 3.2
Reference</A>
<LI><A HREF="http://www.eskimo.com/~bloo/html/index.html">Index Dot
HTML's Advanced HTML Reference</A>
<LI><A HREF="http://www.hut.fi/~jkorpela/HTML3.2/all.html">Learning
HTML 3.2 by Examples</A>
</UL>
```

This code would create a nice bulleted list of HTML references, as shown in Figure 7.5.

Feel free to experiment with other text-level elements and anchors; most of them work just as you might expect. For example, you can make a link bigger by surrounding it with the <BIG> and </BIG> tags:

```
<BIG><A HREF="http://www.levity.com/corduroy">Bohemian Ink</A></BIG>
```

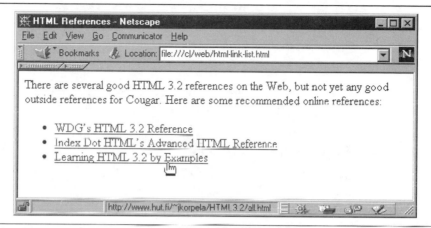

FIGURE 7.5: Each of these links is a list item in an unordered list, displayed by Navigator.

Creating an Internal Link

Now that we've seen external links, it's time to talk about internal links. As you'll recall, we defined internal links as those links that refer to pages within your own Web site.

Internal links behave identically to external links with one exception: You can use *relative URLs* for internal links, which saves typing. We'll see how relative URLs work in a moment. First we'll define the concept of absolute URLs.

Understanding Absolute URLs

Absolute URLs are simply the fully specified URLs that we learned about in Skill 1.

If your Web page's URL is `http://www.rupert.com/rupert-links.html`, then you can refer to other individual pages on your Web site with the appropriate absolute URL, as we've seen. Each page can be reached by simply changing the individual filenames at the end. In the sample file we saw in the previous section, there were several such absolute URLs. Take this example:

```
<A HREF="http://www.rupert.com/history.html">Rupert's History Page</A>
```

In the `history.html` file, there might be a link back to the Rupert's Recommend Links page with an element like this one:

```
<A HREF="http://www.rupert.com/rupert-links.html">Rubert's Recommend
Links</A>
```

These two URLs are called "absolute URLs" since the address is fully specified. The URL is 100 percent, absolutely complete.

Understanding Relative URLs

Both of the previous absolute URLs contain the same stuff at the beginning, `http://www.rupert.com/`. It's a pain to have to retype the full address every time. It's also more likely that you'll make a mistake if you have to type an absolute URL over and over; in addition, if your Web page ever moves for some reason (for example, from `www.rupert.com` to `www.t-shirts.com`) then you'll have to go through and correct every link.

Relative URLs prevent these problems. A relative URL simply drops the common part from the URL and lets the browsers automatically figure out the part that's missing.

For example, in the `http://www.rupert.com/rupert-links.html` file, instead of specifying

```
<A HREF="http://www.rupert.com/history.html">Rupert's History Page</A>
```

just specify the part that's different from the current page's URL:

```
<A HREF="history.html">Rupert's History Page</A>
```

Whenever anyone chooses the link to `history.html`, the browser will automatically change the relative URL into the fully specified absolute URL, `http://www.rupert.com/history.html`, and the correct page will be retrieved.

Relative URLs like this all assume that the files are in the same directory; in a moment, we'll see what to do if the files are in different directories on the same system. In general, when you create a link such as `<A HREF="joe.html">All About Joe Thomas</A>`, then choosing this link just causes the browser to look for a file named `joe.html` in the current directory.

As you might imagine, you can use relative URLs for all sorts of files, including images. For example, you can specify an inline image with an `<IMG>` tag that uses a relative URL, like this one:

```
<IMG SRC="pluto.gif">
```

If there's an image file in the current directory that is called "`pluto.gif`," then it will be displayed properly by this <IMG> tag.

Using Relative URLs with Different Directories

We'll assume you know how directories and subdirectories (also known as *folders*) work on your operating system. (If you don't, check with the documentation that came with your computer, or your operating system's online help.)

Suppose you have a subdirectory called `faculty`, and you want to link to a file in `faculty` called `smith.html`. If you were to use an absolute URL, it would be `http://www.rupert.com/faculty/smith.html` (assuming we're still using the `rupert.com` example from the previous two sections).

If you want to link to the `smith.html` file from `rupert links.html` (which is at the top level of the server), instead of having to use that absolute URL, you can just a relative URL like this one :

```
<A HREF="faculty/smith.html">Rupert's pal, Professor Smith</A>
```

 NOTE   As we saw in Skill 1, the slash used to separate folders is always a forward slash (/), never a backslash (\).

But how do we make a link that goes back to `rupert-links.html` in the `smith.html` file? We can't simply say <A HREF="`rupert-links.html`">Rupert's Links</A>, since these two files aren't in the same directory.

You could use the absolute URL, <A HREF="`http://www.rupert.com/rupert-links.html`">Rupert's Links</A>, but we've already learned that absolute URLs aren't as desirable as relative URLs, so it would be a shame to have to rely on this method.

Fortunately, there's an abbreviation that means "the directory above the current directory" (also know as the "parent" directory). This abbreviation is two periods (`..`).

If you're a DOS or UNIX user, you are probably familiar with this "dot-dot" notation; older versions of Windows also use the `..` abbreviation in directory lists.

NOTE   Periods are sometimes called *dots*.

Using this abbreviation, we can specify a relative URL in `smith.html` that leads to `rupert-links.html`:

```
<A HREF="../rupert-links.html">Rupert's Links</A>
```

 NOTE   You can even use multiple .. references. If you have a file deeply buried in a series of subdirectories, it can link to a file much higher up on the directory tree with a link like this one: `<A HREF="../../../icecream.html">Vanilla Ice Cream</A>`. This relative URL means, "go to the folder three levels above the current folder, and get the file there named `icecream.html`."

Relative URLs are commonly used, and we recommend you use them whenever possible.

Troubleshooting Relative URLs

If your relative URLs aren't working for some reason, you should try two things. First, when you type your URL into your browser, make sure you're using a slash at the end in the URL if it doesn't refer to a specific `.html` file—for example, make sure the URL you're using is `http://www.rupert.com/` (with a final slash) and not `http://www.rupert.com` (without a final slash).

You can also try using the `<BASE>` tag, as described in Skill 5. A `<BASE>` tag tells the browser the correct absolute URL of your document, which might fix the relative URLs used on that page. (If you already have a `<BASE>` tag, try removing it.) If the worst comes to the worst and the relative URLs still don't work (and you've checked to make sure the files are in same directory and are properly readable), then you can always use the absolute URL. If *that* doesn't work, then something is wrong with your server or your files, or else you're not using your URL correctly at all. In that case, it might be time to call in your ISP's technical support.

Using Default Pages

You might be puzzled by one thing we haven't explained before: Why does a URL that doesn't specify an `html` filename still retrieve an HTML file?

For example, when you type in a URL such as `http://www.yahoo.com/`, it's clear you're retrieving an HTML file of some kind. (If you don't believe us, just the view the page's source, and you'll definitely see HTML code in there.) But you didn't specify the name of this HTML file in your URL, as you would in a URL such as `http://www.yahoo.com/help.html`.

The answer to this puzzle is that each server is programmed to send a certain page if no other page is specified in the URL. The name of this default page is usually index.html.

 NOTE

The term "default" just means the usual or expected choice. If Scott *always* orders cappuccino whenever he's in a coffee shop, you can assume that if he doesn't specify his order, he still wants cappuccino. You could say that Scott orders cappuccino "by default." This terminology is used with computers and the Web all time.

Try it: Go visit http://www.yahoo.com/index.html and you'll notice that the page displayed is *exactly* the same as what's displayed with http://www.yahoo .com/. These two URLs both refer to the same file. When you leave off the index.html part, Yahoo!'s server still sends the index.html page—your browser just doesn't tell you in the address box exactly what happened.

Some HTTP servers use a different filename for the default page—for example, Default.html, default.htm, or index.htm instead of index.html. Other servers let you specify the default file independently for each directory so that you can specify that your bacon directory sends the kevin.html file by default. That would mean that, say, the http://www.foo.com/bacon/ and http://www.foo .com/bacon/kevin.html URLs would both display the same page.

When we get to the part of the book that teaches you how to publish your pages on your Web server (Skill 18), we'll give you some more tips about how you should name your pages to take advantage of the default page. After all, you want people to reach you with the shortest amount of typing possible, so it's good to take advantage of this feature—it can shorten your URL dramatically if your visitors don't have to enter a filename.

Skill 7

How to Make a Relative Link to an *INDEX.HTML* File without Using the Word *INDEX.HTML*

The last point we have to make here about the index.html default filename is that it can be a little tricky to link to it. You can always refer to it as index.html (with an element like <A HREF="index.html">Rupert's Main Page</A>), but then you might be pointing to the same file with two different names, which could be confusing. After all, the other name for

continued ▶

the same file is `http://www.rupert.com/` and your visitors (and search engines) might not know that you're talking about the same file.

If your `index.html` file is in a subdirectory called `faculty`, it's simple to refer to it: Just use a relative link like HREF="`faculty/`".

If you're linking back to your `index.html` file from a subdirectory, then you can just use the `..` shortcut that we saw earlier, with a relative link like HREF="`../`".

If your `index.html` file is in your main directory, then you have a choice. You can link to it with its absolute URL, like href="`http://www.rupert.com/`" (which is equivalent to `http://www.rupert.com/index.html` but shorter). Or you can use the special abbreviation for the current directory, a single period (`.`), which would make your relative URL look like this: HREF="`./`".

In all of these examples, it's not strictly necessary to include the final slash, but the correct name does include the slash—and using the correct name is a safer practice than leaving off the slash, since some servers and browsers can get confused if the final slash is missing.

Jumping to a Named Anchor with Internal Links

Now that we fully understand internal links, it's time to return to a topic we first brought up earlier in this Skill: named anchors. In this section, we'll expand on the concept of naming a section of your document by seeing how you can jump from one part of the document to another. This makes it easy, for example, to link from the top of the document to the bottom. In turn, this allows you to put a table of contents at the top of a particular document.

Before we see how to do this, however, we'll review the use of named anchor elements in light of what we've just learned about relative URLs.

Using Named Anchor Elements with Internal Links and Relative URLs

We saw earlier that you could link to a specific part of a document by adding its name to the URL after a "#" character. (We called this type of URL a *fractional URL*.) For example, linking to:

```
http://www.emf.net/~estephen/facts/lefthand.html#scientific
```

opens a file called `lefthand.html` and then jumps down to the "scientific" section.

These types of links will only work if the file has named a section with a named anchor element. For example, you'll need to use a tag like `<A NAME="scientific">` and then put an `</A>` tag at the end of the section's anchor text.

So when we see a fractional URL like the one above, we can assume that there is a section of the `lefthand.html` file that contains a section that has been named `scientific`. It turns out that there is such a file with a named anchor as described. The specific HTML code to name the section looks like this:

```
<H4><A NAME="scientific">Scientific Articles and Sites</A></H4>
```

Since you don't have control over whether a named anchor elements exists in an external file, sometimes you won't be able to link to a specific section of an external document. However, when you're linking to your own internal files, you'll always be able to add the necessary NAME attribute to an anchor element in the appropriate section of your document.

If you want to jump to a certain section within one of your documents, just use a relative URL with the label in your anchor. For example,

```
<P>Please <A HREF="mary.html#contact">contact Mary</A> for more
information.
```

To make this link work, just make sure that the `mary.html` file exists in the same directory as the file containing the previous code, and make sure that `mary.html` contains the following HTML code somewhere:

```
<A NAME="contact">My Contact Information</A>
```

NOTE   The specification for HTML says that the names should not be case sensitive. However, anchor names are case sensitive in IE 3 and Navigator 3 and 4, so you shoud not use `<A NAME="CONTACT">` if you later use `<A HREF="#contact">`. Instead, you should make sure that your name always uses the same case in the name anchor and the fractional URL.

 **WARNING**   Don't name your sections with illegal characters. Names should be unique in each document, and must consist of letters and numbers, without spaces or punctuation other than the period (.) and hyphen (-). Also, be careful not to leave off one of the quote marks in your anchor. Finally, don't use try to use an empty NAME anchor, like this: <A NAME="foo"></A>. Many browsers get confused by empty anchors, so you should always wrap the anchor around some text.

Linking to Different Parts of the Same Document

In addition to linking to other internal files, you can also use anchor elements to name and link to parts of the same document. For example, suppose you're creating a very long document. If there's important information that has to be at the bottom of the document, you might want to create a link that lets your viewers quickly jump to the bottom (without having to scroll all the way down).

At the bottom of your document, name a section with the following tag:

```
<P><A NAME="bottom">Here's the important information:</A>
<P>(Important information goes here.)
```

Now you can put a link at the top of the document that jumps down to the bottom of the document:

```
<P><A HREF="#bottom">Jump down to the bottom of this document</A> to
see some important information.
```

We mentioned earlier that you can't nest anchors inside other anchors. Sometimes you'll need to create an HREF link and a NAME at the same time, for the same text. This would be impossible without nesting, except for the fact that an anchor element can include both attributes, like this:

```
<A HREF="next.html" NAME="next-section">The next section describes
Monarch butterflies.</A>.
```

 **WARNING**   If your document is *really* long, then your viewers will have to wait a few moments, until the document is loaded, before they can jump down to the bottom. That's because browsers can't jump to a label if they haven't yet loaded the part of the document that contains the named label.

Creating a Table of Contents Using Named Anchors

Now that we've seen how to link to named anchors within the same file (which are sometimes known as *bookmarks*), we can create a table of contents.

If you create a long document, you can divide it up into sections with headers, as we've seen in Skill 6. It's a good idea to add an anchor element with the NAME attribute within each header element, and use a single-word name for each section that's a relevant keyword, like this:

```
<H2><A NAME="history">History of the Sonnet</A></H2>
```

This allows other documents to link straight to the history section, by adding #history to the URL.

TIP   Even if you don't plan on linking straight to a particular section yourself, perhaps other Web authors will want to, so they will appreciate it if you take the time to put in the NAME anchors.

The best reason to name each section is that it allows you to create a table of contents for your page. This table of contents can occur anywhere in the same document or in a different document.

Each item in the table of contents simply contains link that leads to the particular section, like this:

```
<A HREF="#history">History of the Sonnet</A>
```

If the table of contents is in a different file, then it has to include the filename in the URL, like this:

```
<A HREF="sonnets.html#history">History of the Sonnet</A>
```

Here's a simplified version of a real-life table of contents, based on a page at the Church Divinity School of the Pacific (http://www.cdsp.edu/). This example is a page that is simply a table of contents for a list of articles found in another document.

deanspage.html

```
<!DOCTYPE HTML PUBLIC "-//W3C//DTD HTML 3.2//EN">
<!--Copyright 1997 by CDSP.-->
<HTML>
<HEAD>
<TITLE>CDSP: Dean's Page</TITLE>
```

Skill 7

```
<LINK REV="MADE" HREF="mailto:Info@CDSP.edu">
</HEAD>
<BODY BGCOLOR="#FFCC33" TEXT="#000000" LINK="#0033FF" VLINK="#6600CC"
ALINK="#FFFFFF">
<H1>Dean's Page</H1>
<P>
The Dean's Page is published monthly and features reflections from Dean
Morgan,as well as short newsbriefs about CDSP faculty, students, staff,
the campus, and the Graduate Theological Union (GTU).

<P>
<FONT SIZE=5 COLOR="#FF0000">
<B>April 1997 Dean's Page</B>
</FONT>

<P>
<A HREF="dp-apr97.html#top">CDSP Announces Honorary Degree Recipients and
Speaker for 1997 Commencement</A><BR>
<A HREF="dp-apr97.html#israel">Israel Trip Planned for January
1998</A><BR>
<A HREF="dp-apr97.html#facilities">CDSP Engages GTU Schools in Facilities
Dialogue</A><BR>
<A HREF="dp-apr97.html#director">CDSP Announces New Director of Alumni/ae
and Church Relations</A><BR>
<A HREF="dp-apr97.html#third">Third-Year Students Gather for Final Class
Weekend</A><BR>
<A HREF="dp-apr97.html#reception">CDSP To Host Reception at General
Convention</A><BR>
<A HREF="dp-apr97.html#apparel">CDSP Launches New Apparel Line</A><BR>
<A HREF="dp-apr97.html#countryman">Beyond Inclusion with Bill
Countryman</A>
</P>

</BODY>
</HTML>
```

Figure 7.6 shows the previous HTML code displayed by Navigator. Each of the blue links leads to the appropriate article in the separate newsletter document.

The actual real-life page is quite a bit more attractive than our example, since it incorporates an attractive background image and some advanced layout techniques thanks to use of tables. But the table of contents is identical to our version. To give you a sneak peak of the sorts of documents that we can create once we learn about tables and images, Figure 7.7 shows the real CDSP page.

We've now seen just about every possible use of the anchor element. We'll round out this Skill with a look at some methods of making sure your links can be verified and maintained.

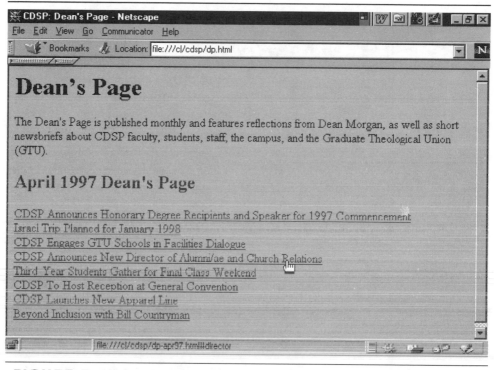

FIGURE 7.6: Our simplified table of contents for the Dean's Page newsletter.

Verifying and Maintaining Links

One of the problems Web authors face is that external links are beyond their control. If someone moves or removes their Web page, then your link to them will suddenly be broken—it will lead nowhere.

When someone tries to follow one of your links that leads to a missing page, they'll get an error message—usually the infamous "404 - Document Not Found" error message.

NOTE The numbers attached to Web error messages are assigned by the protocol specification for HTTP. An article at CNET's Web site explains these errors in plain English: http://www.cnet.com/Resources/Tech/Advisers/Error/.

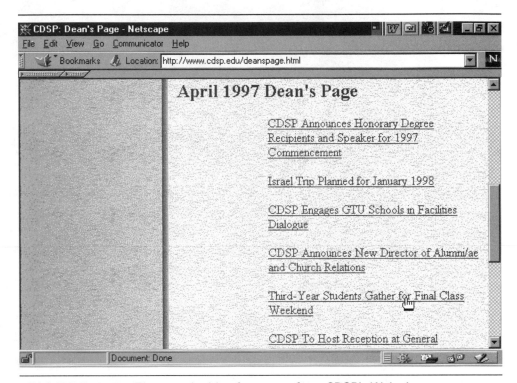

FIGURE 7.7: The actual table of contents from CDSP's Web site

For example, trying to view a non-existent page from the sonic.net Internet service provider results in the error message shown in Figure 7.8.

You can prevent having a lot of bad links in two ways. The first is to not link to any external sites at all. This is an extreme measure, and the drawback is that you can't link to a lot of useful material (and if you don't link to other people, it's less likely other people will want to link to you, unless your content is very compelling). The second way is to choose your external links with care, tending toward documents that have been around for a long time or are maintained by responsible people or by stable companies.

TIP   When you link to someone's Web page, it's polite (but not necessary) to write them a brief e-mail saying that you've linked to them. Send along your e-mail address and the URL of your page. That way, they are able to link back to you (if they want to), and they can let you know if they have to move or delete their page.

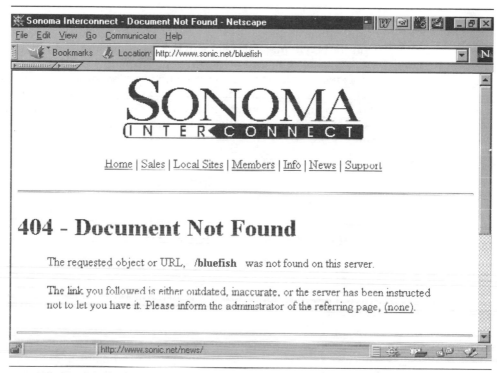

FIGURE 7.8: We tried to display a page called "bluefish" from sonic.nct, but it no longer exists. Instead we're greeted with this error message, a "404 - Document Not Found" error.

There really is no alternative but to check your links often and replace any bad links. You can replace a missing link with either a different resource, or you can try to search for the old resource to see if it's moved without leaving a forwarding address.

To verify the links on your pages, you should go through all of your external links and follow them to make sure the pages on the other side are still valid. You should try and do this at a regular interval, perhaps once a month. You might receive e-mail from people who have noticed that a link of yours is stale (bad links are sometimes called *cobwebs*), but don't count on people to tell you about bad links—most people are too busy to take the time to report every bad link they see.

When (not if) you do find a bad link, either remove it or replace it with something else that works. This is the process of maintaining your links.

Avoid putting an excessive number of links on your page; not only is it more difficult for you to maintain, but you risk overwhelming your audience and they won't know which links are useful. Lots of people have already tried the "link every single word on the page to something" experiment. However, it's worthwhile to create a link whenever you are using a technical term or abbreviation, or mentioning a person or institution that has a home page. Consider creating a "Further Information" section at the end of your document with relevant links.

Verifying and maintaining links is a time-consuming process. Fortunately, computers are quite adept at helping you out with this task. There are several good link verification tools that will help you weed out the bad links.

Using External Link Verification Tools

There are two types of tools that can verify your external links. One type is a Web page service where you indicate which of your pages need to have their links verified; the service will go through all of the links on your pages, and then create a report to let you know which links are bad.

This process is not foolproof. Sometimes a good link might be reported as bad because the link is not working temporarily. Sometimes a bad link will seem like it's good because the page on the other side is still present, but empty. Link verification tools can only check whether the external page exists—they don't tell you if a page is no longer worth a link.

Here are a couple of link verification tools available from the Web:

- NetMechanic (`http://www.netmechanic.com/`) can run an exhaustive check on the links in your site in the background, and when it's finished it can mail you a pointer to its report.

- Doctor HTML (`http://imagiware.com/RxHTML.cgi`) includes link verification as one of its tests of a page. (If you want the Doctor to check more than one page at a time, then you'll have to pay for the service.)

The second type of link verification tool is a program you run on your server or local computer that goes through the links. Some of these programs are freeware or shareware, while others are commercial software.

Here are some link verification tools you can download or purchase:

- MOMSpider, a robot that searches for bad links from your site and runs on UNIX-based systems (as long as they have the Perl language available).

Freeware from the University of California, Irvine (`http://www.ics.uci.edu/pub/websoft/MOMspider/`).

- Linklint, a fast HTML link checker available for DOS, UNIX, and Windows machines, but only if they have the Perl language interpreter available. By Jim Bowlin (`http://www.goldwarp.com/bowlin/linklint/`).

- Linkbot, a Windows-based commercial link checker from Tetranet Software (`http://www.tetranetsoftware.com/`). A demo version is available to download.

- MissingLink, a UNIX shareware program to check links, from Radical Solutions (`http://www.rsol.com/ml/`).

No matter what tool you use, you'll still want to check your links yourself from time to time.

 NOTE   In addition, page- and site-creation tools such as FrontPage include built-in link verification commands.

In this Skill, we saw just about everything there is to know about anchors and links, from external links to internal links, some general advice and examples on how to use the anchor element and its attributes, as well as how to create tables of contents. One area we didn't cover was how to make an image into a link. We'll see how to do that in the next Skill, which is all about creating and using images on your Web pages.

Are You Experienced?

Now you can...

- ☑ link to external sites, with the *HREF* anchor element's attribute
- ☑ format your links attractively
- ☑ name and link to specific parts of your documents
- ☑ create a table of contents for a page
- ☑ verify and maintain your links

Catching the Colors—
Adding Graphics

⊖ **Working with the image element and its attributes**

⊖ **Creating useful alternate text for images**

⊖ **Linking with images**

⊖ **Working with image formats and image files**

⊖ **Creating transparent, interlaced, and animated images**

Graphics, images, pictures, photographs—whatever you call them, a visual element makes your page more compelling and is the easiest way to give your page a unique look. In this Skill, we'll see all of the ways you can add images to your pages using the <IMG> tag and its many attributes. We'll also learn how to use images as links.

Toward the end of the Skill, we'll take a look at the different image formats and learn how you can create images (including interlaced images, transparent images, and animated images). Throughout this Skill, you'll find suggestions on how you can make your images useful and functional even when your page is viewed by a browser that doesn't display images.

Adding Graphics with the Image Element

The purpose of the image element (which consists of the <IMG> tag) is to include graphic images in the body of your Web page.

 NOTE   HTML 4.0 recommends using the object element (the <OBJECT> and </OBJECT> tags) instead of the image element. However, <IMG> is still common and HTML 4.0 fully supports it. We'll see the object element in Skill 9 and learn that it isn't as widely supported as the image element.

We first saw the image element back in Skill 2, when we created a sample page and added a graphic of a T-shirt. Our example <IMG> tag looked like this:

```
<IMG SRC="http://www.emf.net/~estephen/images/turtleshirt.jpg">
```

Recall that images are sometimes referred to as *inline images* because the images are inserted within a line of body text. (You may want to review "Comprehending the Example's Image" in Skill 2 about how images can affect a line's height.) We also saw that since the image element is a text-level element, it should be nested inside a paragraph or other block-level container, and it doesn't start a new paragraph automatically.

To make an image appear as a separate paragraph, enclose it within the paragraph element, like this:

```
<P><IMG SRC="http://www.emf.net/~estephen/images/turtleshirt.jpg"></P>
```

From our discussion of relative URLs in the previous Skill, we now know that if you have an image in the same directory as your HTML file, you can abbreviate the URL and use a tag like this:

```
<IMG SRC="turtleshirt.jpg">
```

This inserts an image called `turtleshirt.jpg` on a page, but it will work only if the `turtleshirt.jpg` file exists in the same directory as the HTML file.

 TIP Many Web authors like to keep their images together in one (or more) subdirectories, such as `images`, separate from their HTML files. This practice helps keep images organized. If you decide to do this, you can use a tag such as `<IMG SRC="images/turtleshirt.jpg">` to refer to your image files. See Skill 7 for more details about relative URLs.

For the first part of this Skill, don't worry too much about the format of image files or how you create them. For now, just remember that most graphical browsers can only display images if they are in a particular format. The two most popular image formats are GIF and JPEG (with the `.gif` and `.jpg` file extensions respectively). We'll learn more about these two image formats in the "Understanding Image Formats" section later in this Skill, as well as a newer image format called PNG.

Using Image Element Attributes

Now we're ready to learn how to use the image element. In this section, we'll expand on the possibilities of the `<IMG>` tag and see how its attributes work. The `<IMG>` tag's attributes are principally intended to tell a browser how the page should be laid out with the image so that text can flow properly around the image.

 **WARNING** Since HTML is about structure and not presentation, the HTML 4.0 specification recommends you use style sheets to control an image's appearance on a page, instead of using `<IMG>` appearance attributes.

Describing Images with Alternate Text

You should always use two attributes with any `<IMG>` tag: the SRC and ALT attributes, both of which are required. The ALT attribute is used to describe the image in some way. For any browser that isn't displaying images, the alternate text contained inside the ALT attribute is displayed instead. Here's an example of an image element using alternate text:

```
<IMG SRC="images/mickeymouse.jpg" ALT="Mickey Mouse">
```

If you use this tag, browsers can display the words "Mickey Mouse" instead of displaying an image of Walt Disney's famous rodent.

Here are five reasons why a browser would use the alternate text instead of the image itself:

- The browser is text-only and can't display images. If there is no ALT attribute in the <IMG> tag, a text-only browser like Lynx will display the word "[INLINE]" on the screen instead of the image itself. However, if alternate text is present, Lynx displays the alternate text in place of the image.

- The browser is programmed to read aloud the alternate text instead of displaying an image. In this way, the ALT attribute can explain your image to blind surfers or surfers who are using a speaking machine.

- The person using the browser has chosen not to display images. Since images are often large files that are slow to display, many people surf with their browser set to *not* Auto Load Images or View Pictures. Instead, browsers show an empty frame as a placeholder for the image, and the alternate text is displayed inside the frame (see Figure 8.1).

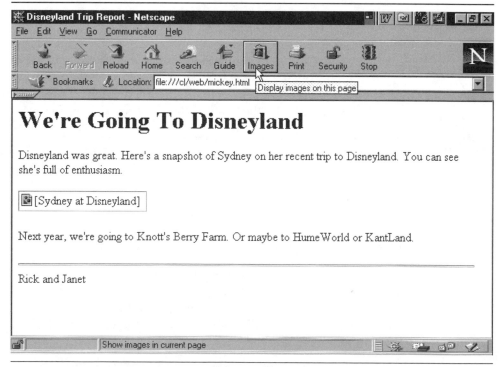

FIGURE 8.1: Navigator puts the alternate text for this image in a frame, with an icon to show there's a image not being displayed.

- Navigator and IE display an image's alternate text while the image is being loaded.

WARNING Some people use alternate text such as "Please switch on images" or "Please wait for this image to load." These descriptions don't actually describe the image, and they make assumptions about what browser is being used.

- Finally, IE 3 and IE 4 as well as Navigator 4 display the alternate text as a tool tip whenever you point your mouse cursor at the image for a few seconds. (If the <IMG> tag has an advisory TITLE attribute, that's shown instead.)

TURNING OFF IMAGES

Images are slow. To surf quickly (and avoid advertising banners in the process), set your browser so it doesn't automatically display images.

To set Navigator 4 to not load images automatically, follow these steps:

1. Select Edit ➤ Preferences.

2. Choose the Advanced category.

3. Deselect Automatically Load Images. (For Navigator 3, you can use the Options ➤ Auto Load Images.)

To quickly display all the images on a page, click on the Images button on the Navigation toolbar. To display an individual image, choose Show Image from the image's context menu. (To see a context menu, right-click on a PC or hold down the mouse button on a Mac.)

To tell Internet Explorer 4 not to display images automatically, follow these steps:

1. Choose View ➤ Options.

2. Deselect Show Pictures from the Advanced tab.

To quickly display an image, right-click on it and choose Show Picture.

Skill 8

For these five reasons, using alternate text is important. Fortunately, it's an easy task: Just put a meaningful description as the attribute value for ALT for every image (except for purely decorative images).

TIP   Some HTML style guides recommend using empty alternate text for purely decorative images (that is, putting nothing within the quotes for the alternate text: ALT=""). We agree, unless the image is being used as an anchor for a link, as we describe in "Using Images as Links." Using nonexistent alternate text will mean that users of text-only or text-to-speech browsers won't be distracted by your page's decorative borders, for example.

Here are some guidelines to follow when describing an image with alternate text:

- Put brackets around the description (for example, ALT="[Me at age 12.]") to distinguish the description from regular text.

- Leave off the words "image" or "picture." It's better to describe the image itself, rather than its media. "[President Lincoln at the White House]" is a more compact and useful description than "[Image of President Lincoln at the White House]".

- Don't be too vague. For your company logo, don't use ALT="[Company Logo]", for example. Instead, use ALT="[RadCo Spinning R Logo]".

- Remember that text-only and speech browsers place the alternate text wherever the image occurs in a sentence. So, be sure your alternate text is clear in context. "Another excellent Web site from [Picture of a Tree] [Company Logo]" will raise some eyebrows.

- Use the alternate text to duplicate the image's purpose. If you use an image of a yellow star next to several items in a list, don't use ALT="Pretty yellow star" but instead use ALT="*". For the alternate text for an image of a decorative horizontal line, try ALT="------------".

- Alternate text can subtly present two different versions of a page. If you've used ALT="[New!]" for a "new" icon, you can then explain at the top of your page, "New information is denoted by <IMG SRC="new.jpg" ALT="[New!]">. Users with graphics will see your new icon in the explanation; but users without graphics will also see an explanation that correctly matches their view of your page.

- Some art sites place copyright information along with the image's description; other sites put secret messages in an image's alternate text.

- You can use entities (such as ©, as we saw in Skill 3) in alternate text.

- For full compatibility, keep your alternate text on one unbroken line of your document since some browsers have problems with a carriage return in the middle of the alternate text.

You can't use tags inside ALT text, so ALT="[I'm <EM>beating</EM> Hemmingway at wrestling]" is not valid. However, the <IMG> tag, including the alternate text, is subject to whatever elements it's nested within. To make your alternate text bold, enclose the <IMG> tag within <B> and </B> tags, for example:

```
<B><IMG SRC="new.jpg" ALT="[New!]"></B>
```

Now that we've seen the use of alternate text, the next attribute we'll see determines how images are aligned on a page.

Placing Images with Alignment Attributes

When you align images with an alignment attribute (ALIGN), there are two entirely separate behaviors:

- Inline images occur in the middle of a line of text. If the image is a large one, then the line becomes very tall, and a lot of white space will appear.

- Floating images cause text to wrap around the image. Images can either be left-aligned or right-aligned. The paragraph will flow around the image for several lines, if the image is large.

The two different behaviors are caused by choosing the attribute value for ALIGN. We'll see the values for inline images first, then floating images.

 **WARNING**   Using ALIGN to place images is not recommend by HTML 4.0, since alignment is a presentational feature, not a structural feature. Instead, HTML 4.0 recommends style sheets (see Skill 14).

Aligning Inline Images

To align an image in a line, choose one of the following attributes for the image element:

```
ALIGN="TOP"
ALIGN="MIDDLE"
ALIGN="BOTTOM"
```

The default behavior is `ALIGN="BOTTOM"`, which means that the bottom of an image will align with the bottom of the line of text. By choosing `ALIGN="TOP"` you request that the browser display the top of your image so that it aligns with the top of the line of text. (This will push down the next line of text.) Similarly, by choosing `ALIGN="MIDDLE"` the browser will align the middle of the image with the middle of the line of text. Figure 8.2 shows an image aligned to the middle of its line of text.

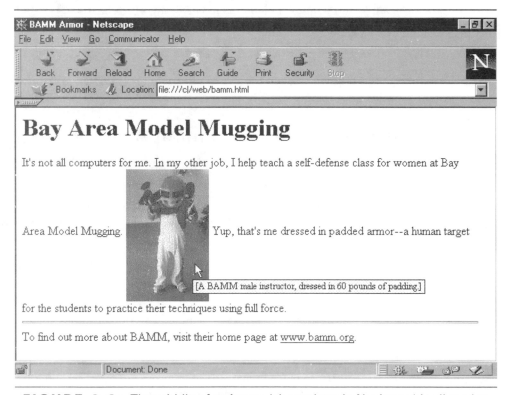

FIGURE 8.2: The middle of an image (shown here in Navigator) is aligned to the middle of the second line of text. The first and last line are pushed apart by the image. (Notice the alternate text appearing as a tool tip.)

The HTML code that produces the image in Figure 8.2 is fairly simple.

 **bamm.html**

```
<!DOCTYPE HTML PUBLIC "-//W3C//DTD HTML 4.0//EN">
<HTML LANG="EN">
  <HEAD>
    <TITLE>BAMM Armor</TITLE>
```

```
    </HEAD>
    <BODY>
      <H1>Bay Area Model Mugging</H1>
      <P>
        It's not all computers for me.  In my other job, I help teach a
        self-defense class for women at Bay Area Model Mugging.
        <IMG SRC="http://www.emf.net/~estephen/sbamm.jpg" ALIGN="middle"
        ALT="[A BAMM male instructor, dressed in 60 pounds of padding.]">
        Yup, that's me dressed in padded armor--a human
        target for the students to practice their techniques
        using full force.
      </P>
      <HR>
      <P>
        To find out more about BAMM, visit their home page at
        <a href="http://www.bamm.org/">www.bamm.org</a>.
    </BODY>
</HTML>
```

If we had used ALIGN="TOP" instead of ALIGN="MIDDLE", then the first and second lines would be next to each other and there'd be a large space between the second and third lines. If we had used ALIGN="BOTTOM" (or no ALIGN attribute at all), then there would have been a big space between the first and second lines. (Try these examples on your own; simply make the change to the ALIGN attribute in your editor, save the HTML file, switch to your browser, and reload the file using the Reload button.)

Creating Floating Images

To make an image "float" to the left or right side and cause paragraphs to wrap around the image, choose one of the following two attribute values for the ALIGN attribute:

```
ALIGN="LEFT"
ALIGN="RIGHT"
```

Choosing LEFT or RIGHT as the value for ALIGN causes the image to be placed directly against the left or right margin. Text after the <IMG> tag will flow around the image. Shown on the following page is the result of taking the code we used in the previous section and using ALIGN="RIGHT" as the alignment attribute.

Skill 8

Bay Area Model Mugging

It's not all computers for me. In my other job, I help teach a self-defense class for women at Bay Area Model Mugging. Yup, that's me dressed in padded armor--a human target for the students to practice their techniques using full force.

To find out more about BAMM, visit their home page at www.bamm.org.

This result might not be quite what we desire, so let's move the <IMG> tag up to the beginning of the first paragraph. Here's the result:

Bay Area Model Mugging

It's not all computers for me. In my other job, I help teach a self-defense class for women at Bay Area Model Mugging. Yup, that's me dressed in padded armor--a human target for the students to practice their techniques using full force.

To find out more about BAMM, visit their home page at www.bamm.org.

One drawback to this result is that the horizontal rule (from the <HR> tag) and the last paragraph are next to the picture. We might want to push these items down so they're below the image. In Skill 6, we mentioned that the line-break element has attributes that can be used to clear the margin. The line-break element is simply the <BR> tag. By itself, the <BR> tag won't do what we want (it will just create a single blank line that wouldn't be big enough to push the horizontal rule below the image). But if we use the CLEAR attribute and the appropriate margin value, then the horizontal rule and the last paragraph will be forced down below the image. Since the image is on the right margin, we want to use a <BR CLEAR="RIGHT"> tag (placed immediately before the <HR> tag or before the </P> tag). Shown here is the effect of the line-break element with a CLEAR attribute:

Bay Area Model Mugging

It's not all computers for me. In my other job, I help teach a self-defense class for women at Bay Area Model Mugging. Yup, that's me dressed in padded armor--a human target for the students to practice their techniques using full force.

To find out more about BAMM, visit their home page at www.bamm.org.

If your page has images on both the left and right sides, use <BR CLEAR="ALL"> to force the next line of text to appear below the lowest image.

Sizing an Image with *WIDTH* and *HEIGHT* Attributes

Two attributes are used with the <IMG> tag to specify an image's width and height. The WIDTH and HEIGHT attributes indicate the exact size of your image, in pixels. For example:

```
<IMG SRC="sbamm.jpg" WIDTH="109" HEIGHT="175"
ALT="[A BAMM male instructor, dressed in 60 pounds of padding.]">
```

TIP   To find out the size of an image in pixels, you'll have to use an image utility. See the "Using Image Tools" section later in this Skill. Or if you have access to Navigator, choose View Image from an image's context menu (right-click on a PC, hold down the button on a Mac)—once you're viewing an image, you'll see the image's width and height in the title bar.

One overwhelming advantage to adding the height and width to an <IMG> tag is that when you do specify the image size for all of your images, browsers take a lot less time to render your page. That's because the browser can determine the layout of the page without having to retrieve each image separately to find out what size it is.

However, there are two drawbacks to specifying the height and width:

- The height and width are presentational attributes, so they ideally belong in a style sheet instead of in your <IMG> tag.

- If you have a very small image and specify its height and width, then Navigator and IE won't be able to fit the alternate text inside the small image box for those users not displaying images.

Figure 8.3 shows the difference in IE between setting and not setting the HEIGHT and WIDTH attributes when images aren't displayed.

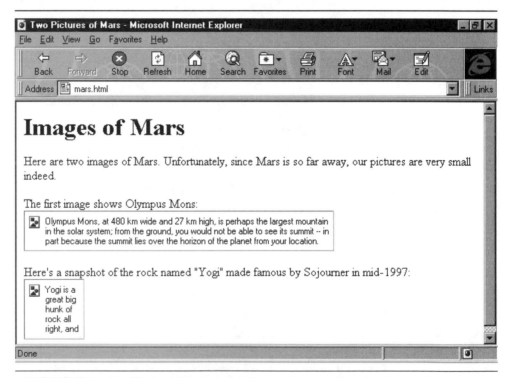

FIGURE 8.3: IE displays a page with two image areas displaying alternate text instead of the images; the first alternate text is fully displayed, but the second is cut off.

In Figure 8.3, the user has set IE to not display images. The first image does not have its height and width specified in the HTML code, so the entire alternate text is shown. For the second image, the height and width were specified (in the <IMG>

tag). If images were to be displayed, both would only be 80 pixels wide and fit the frame shown for the second image. However, since IE allocates the specified size for the second image even when the image itself is not displayed, the alternate text cannot fit inside this small area and so it is cut off by IE. (Navigator does the same thing, but displays none of the second image's alternate text at all.) Newer versions of both browsers would allow the alternate text to be seen via tool tips, but only if the mouse is pointed to the image area.

The speed advantages of setting the WIDTH and HEIGHT attributes may outweigh the two drawbacks, especially if you are not using small images with a lot of alternate text.

There's one other use of the HEIGHT and WIDTH attributes: to scale an image.

Scaling Images with *WIDTH* and *HEIGHT* Attributes

You can specify an image to have a particular height and/or width, even if the original dimensions of the image don't match. Navigator and IE will then scale your image, stretching it accordingly.

For example, if your original image's dimensions are 50 by 50, you can specify an <IMG> tag with a WIDTH of 200 and a HEIGHT of 25. Graphical browsers (that know how to scale images) will then stretch out the image's width to quadruple the normal size, while at the same time squeezing the image's height so that it's half as tall as normal.

You can create interesting and artistic effects with this technique, but not every browser knows how to scale images. Most browsers do a poor job (leaving jagged edges or strange distortions), so if you want to resize an image permanently, it's better to use an image tool for that purpose.

By specifying a WIDTH of 350 pixels and a HEIGHT of 100 pixels, we've distorted our sample image significantly, as shown here.

> **NOTE** To scale an image vertically, you can specify just the height and leave the width automatic. Or you can scale an image horizontally by specifying the width and leaving the height with its default value.

The HTML 4.0 specification recommends against using the HEIGHT and WIDTH attributes to scale images.

Setting an Image's Border Width

By default, no border appears around an image *unless* that image is a link (as we'll see in "Using Images as Links").

However, you can specify a border for an image. If you use the BORDER="1" attribute in an <IMG> tag, then a thin border will appear around the image. You can specify larger values for the BORDER attribute as well.

There's no need to specify BORDER="0" for a normal image since borders do not appear by default.

WARNING IE 3 does not display image borders and ignores the value of BORDER, unless the image is a link.

An image border will always be colored black in IE 4, while in Navigator it's the same color as the text color (see Skill 3 to learn how to set the text color with a <BODY> tag attribute).

If you use a style sheet (Skill 14), you can specify whatever color you desire for image borders, and you'll have far better control over the border's appearance. This practice is preferred by the HTML 4.0 specification over BORDER attributes.

An image's border width does not count toward determining an image's height or width. So if you specify an image to be 100 pixels wide (with WIDTH="100"), and have a border width of 10 (with BORDER="10"), then the image will take 120 pixels of horizontal space (because the border appears on both the left and right side of the image). In addition, the image will take a few pixels more than 120 because browsers will put a small amount of space between an image and text. The amount of space allocated is determined by the HSPACE and VSPACE attributes.

Adding White Space with *HSPACE* and *VSPACE*

IE and Navigator do not place images right next to text. Instead, they put a small margin of a few pixels in between text and an image. You can control the amount of horizontal space with the HSPACE attribute and the amount of vertical space with VSPACE attribute:

- The value of the VSPACE attribute sets the number of pixels of vertical white space around the image (both top and bottom).

- The value of the HSPACE attribute sets the number of pixels of horizontal white space around the image (both left and right).

For example, suppose we edit our bamm.html document to add 50 pixels of horizontal space around the image, by putting an HSPACE="50" attribute in the <IMG> tag. Figure 8.4 shows the result.

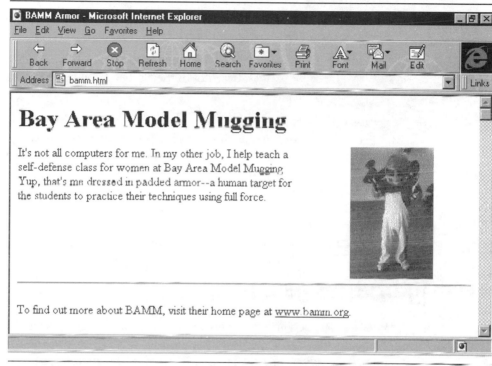

FIGURE 8.4: IE displays 50 pixels to both the left and right of the image thanks to the HSPACE attribute.

Using Other Attributes with Images

In addition to the image attributes, HTML 4.0 allows some generic attributes that apply to almost every element, including the image element:

- The LANG and DIR attributes (Skill 5) can be used to indicate what language an image's alternate text is written in, and which direction the alternate text should be displayed (either left-to-right or right-to-left).

- The STYLE, ID, and CLASS attributes can be used with an <IMG> tag to allow precise formatting and control over an image's appearance on a page (Skill 14).

- A new attribute, LONGDESC, points to a URL of the image's description. It is not yet supported.

- Several event attributes (such as ONCLICK and ONMOUSEOVER) can have a dramatic effect on images (Skill 15). In particular, you can use an ONMOUSEOVER attribute to change an image when someone points their mouse cursor to it. This special effect is quite common on the Web.

- The <IMG> tag takes a special attribute, NAME, when you are using an image as a button on a form (Skill 12).

- Image maps use two different attributes in the <IMG> tag: ISMAP and USEMAP. We'll see these two attributes in the "Creating Image Maps" section and this book's Web site.

- An advisory TITLE attribute can provide information about an image. Some browsers put this information in a tool tip, which would display instead of the alternate text. Since an image's advisory title is similar to its alternate text, there's not much need to use a TITLE attribute with an image. Just use the ALT attribute instead.

Now that we've seen all of the various attributes for images, we'll see how images can be used as the anchors for links.

Using Images as Links

When we learned about links using the anchor element (<A> and </A>) in the previous Skill, we only looked at examples where text was the content of the link anchor. However, images can also be used as the anchor for links.

For example, suppose we want to make the bamm.jpg image of the self-defense instructor take us to more information about BAMM when we click on it. Instead of using a text-anchored link, we can make the image itself a link:

```
<A HREF="http://www.bamm.org/"><IMG SRC="sbamm.jpg" ALT="[BAMM]"></A>
```

 NOTE   Using alternate text for an image is even more important if that image is being used as a link. Lynx displays the image link as just the word [LINK] if there's no alternate text for the image.

You can also have both text and image in a link anchor:

```
<A HREF="http://www.bamm.org/">Find out about BAMM! <IMG
SRC="bammlogo.gif" ALT="[Bamm's Logo]"></A>
```

By default, Navigator and IE place a blue border around image links to show that the image is clickable. Clicking the image would take you to the URL shown in the status bar, just as with a text link. (Users of non-graphical browsers can also follow image links, provided the alternate text is present.)

The blue border placed by Navigator and IE is normally two pixels wide. You can make the border width bigger, smaller, or nonexistent by specifying a value for the BORDER attribute that we saw earlier. Specifying an <IMG> tag with BORDER="0" means not to use any border at all.

 **WARNING**

Be cautious with the use of BORDER="0". If an image isn't surrounded with the customary border showing it's a link, then most of your audience will have no idea that the image is a link and won't click on it (unless the image looks like a button).

Figure 8.5 shows what happens when you set the BORDER to a large value for an image used as a link. We used the following code:

```
<A HREF="http://www.bamm.org/"><IMG SRC="sbamm.jpg" ALIGN="right"
BORDER="10" WIDTH="109" HEIGHT="175"
ALT="[A BAMM male instructor, dressed in 60 pounds of padding.]"></A>
```

FIGURE 8.5: A wide border around this image in the link color is a strong visual clue that it's a link.

 TIP

If you see an extraneous blue underlined space appearing next to your document's image links in IE and Navigator, make sure that the </A> tag that closes the anchor is right next to the <IMG> tag and not separated by a space or carriage return.

Skill 8

Creating Image Maps

We've just learned how clicking on an image can lead to a link. Imagine if you have an image of a map of the United States, with five different branch offices of your company highlighted in different states. It would be nice if, depending on where the user clicks, they saw information about a specific branch—the California branch if they click on California, or the Idaho branch if they click on Idaho.

That kind of image set up is called an *image map*. But image maps don't have to be geographic maps. You can create a custom image and divide it up into whatever regions you like.

In general, an image map is an image that contains *hot spots* or *active regions*. Your readers access your pre-defined hot spots by passing the mouse pointer over an area and then clicking the mouse. Just by passing the mouse over the hot area, the browser will usually display the URL of the hot spot in the status bar.

Image maps are useful for directing viewers to options in a menu bar image. You can create an image that names the major features of your Web site, and then use an image map to direct visitors to the appropriate place; these kinds of image maps are called *navigation image maps*.

Image maps were once fairly common on the Web but have become less common recently due to their drawbacks. You can always duplicate the effects of an image map by placing several linked images next to each other. Just make sure to set the HSPACE, VSPACE, and BORDER attributes of each image to zero, and if your images are on the same line, they'll be right next to each other, just like an image map.

Understanding Image Map Types

There are two distinct kinds of image maps. The older type of image map is called a *server-side image map*, because a Web server is responsible for determining where each region leads when you click on the image. The newer and more efficient kind of image map is called a *client-side image map*, because a client (that is, a viewer's Web browser) determines where each region is supposed to lead when you click on the image.

For both types of image maps, you must first create an image to use as a map. Next, divide it up into regions that lead to different URLs. For a server-side image map, you'll need to create a special map file and make sure that the server is set up to deal with image maps. For a client-side image map, you'll use special area and map elements.

Finally, in the image tag itself, you'll include a special attribute to indicate that the image is actually an image map. For a server-side image map, use the ISMAP attribute. For a client-side image map, use the USEMAP attribute with the name of a map element.

Since image maps are an advanced topic that are not really that useful, we won't discuss them in detail in this book. Instead, the Sybex Web site for this book has a detailed tutorial, step-by-step instructions, and several examples.

Working with Image Files

Now that we've seen the HTML code for using images, it's time to discuss the different image formats used on the Web, and how to create and edit images in those formats.

Entire books are written about creating images, and we're certainly not going to be able to tell you even a fraction of everything there is to know on this topic. However, we're certainly going to give you enough information to get you going by recommending some tools and approaches and pointing out some pitfalls to avoid.

Understanding Image Formats

Two different image formats are common on the Web: GIF and JPEG. We'll give them each a run-down, along with some less frequently seen formats.

GIF Images

GIF images (with a file extension of .gif) are the most common types of images used on the Web. *GIF* stands for Graphic Interchange Format and was developed by CompuServe (with the compression scheme patented by UNISYS) in the late '80s.

 NOTE   The word "GIF" is commonly pronounced with a hard g sound like the first part of the name "Gifford," but officially it's pronounced with a soft g as if it were spelled "Jif."

GIFs are used for all types of images, but GIF is an especially good format for line drawings, icons, computer-generated images, simple cartoons, or any images with big areas of solid colors. GIFs are compact, since the GIF format uses the same "LZW" compression routine found in zip files (which is why zipping GIFs is not effective).

The biggest limitation of GIFs is that they can only contain up to 256 different colors.

There are two common varieties of GIF: GIF87A and GIF89A. The difference won't normally be important to you, but basic GIF images are GIF87A and more complicated GIFs are usually in GIF89A format. (A third variety, GIF24, was proposed by CompuServe but has never become popular.)

One particular advantage of GIF images is their flexibility, since GIF89A images can be transparent, animated, or interlaced. (These three kinds of GIFs are defined in a later section.)

JPEG Images

JPEG images used on the Web are more formally known as JPEG JFIF images, but we'll follow standard usage and just call them JPEGs. JPEGs have a file extension of `.jpg` (or less commonly `.jpeg`) and are the second most common format for images on the Web.

 NOTE   The word "JPEG" is pronounced as "jay-peg." Don't bother trying to pronounce "JFIF."

JPEG stands for the Joint Photographic Experts Group, a committee organized to develop advanced image formats. JPEGs started becoming popular in 1993.

JPEG is a remarkably compact format, designed for photographs and other images without big patches of solid colors. JPEGs are *lossy*, which means that they achieve their amazing compression by eliminating data that the human eye does not perceive. When creating JPEGs, it's possible to specify an amount of lossiness. At the highest levels of lossiness, the image becomes visibly crude. At normal levels of lossiness, you probably won't be able to detect the difference between a GIF and a JPEG onscreen. You'll notice the file size difference, however, since a JPEG is usually one-fourth of the size of a GIF.

The largest difference between JPEGs and GIFs is that JPEG images are always 24-bit—in other words, they allow up to 16 million different colors in an image.

JPEGs are *not* very effective for icons or logos with lots of solid colors. Both GIFs and JPEGs have their role, and it's usually not too hard to decide which format to use. You'll probably end up using a mix of both GIF and JPEG images.

The biggest limitation of JPEGs (aside from the lossiness that can accumulate if you repeatedly compress and decompress a JPEG in the process of editing it) is that they can't be transparent or animated. A special type of JPEG called "progressive JPEG" is similar to an interlaced GIF, discussed a little later.

WARNING Don't convert GIFs to JPEGs without being very careful. GIFs are only 256 colors (8-bit) at most, while JPEGs use millions of colors (24-bit). If a photograph is already in GIF format, it has lost most of its color information, and may get worse if you convert it into a JPEG. To make the best JPEGs, start with a file format that has full 24-bit color information, such as a TIFF file. (TIFF files are a common format used when you scan a photograph into your computer using an image scanner.)

Other Image Formats

The only other image format that's a contender for Web popularity is the PNG format. *PNG* stands for Portable Network Graphics, and the format was devised in 1995 by the W3C and CompuServe in response to controversies over GIF licensing. PNG is superior to GIF in just about every way possible: PNGs are smaller, have more colors, and more capabilities. But two things hamper the PNG format:

- PNG images cannot be animated images (although a companion design promises to take care of that).

- Most important, the major browsers did not support PNG at all until recently. (Navigator 4.02 still does not support PNG without a special add-on called a *plug-in*, but future versions of Navigator promise PNG support. IE 4 supports PNG, but earlier versions do not.)

NOTE For more information about PNG, visit the PNG home page (http://www.wco .com/~png/) or W3C's information (http://www.w3.org/Graphics/PNG/ Overview.html).

Several other miscellaneous image formats are used infrequently on the Web, such as TIFF (Tagged Image File Format), XBM (Portable Bitmap), BMP (Windows Bitmap), PICT (Macintosh Bitmap), CGM (Computer Graphics Metafile), and Postscript (a common printing format). *Bitmap* is simply a generic term for an image, and many bitmap formats produce huge file sizes since the images aren't compressed.

It's not worth going into much more detail about any of these formats here since they aren't very popular or well-supported on the Web.

NOTE There's also PDF (Portable Document Format), advocated by Adobe for their Acrobat Reader, and we'll talk about that format in Skill 9.

Skill 8

Working with Special Image Formats

GIF images can have three special abilities: transparency (where one color of an image is invisible and reveals the background), interlacing (where the image is formatted so that it appears in stages), and animation (where two or more image frames appear in sequence). JPEGs can't be transparent or have animation, but they do feature a kind of interlacing called progressive JPEGs.

Creating Interlaced GIFs and Progressive JPEG Images

Since images are often large and therefore slow to load, it's annoying for viewers to have to wait a long time before they can see your image. Normally images load from top to bottom, a line at a time. However, if you use a special image format of GIF, you can *interlace* your image so that it loads in a mixed order of different segments instead of simply top-to-bottom. First the top line of the image appears, then every fifth line appears, on down to the bottom. Then the second line appears followed by the sixth line, and so on. Thus, the image appears in four passes. After the first pass, the viewer has a good idea of what the image will look like. The second pass adds more detail, the third pass even more detail, and the image is complete after the fourth pass.

To save your image in interlaced format, check with your image tool (we'll discuss image tools in "Using Image Tools to Create and Edit Images"). Usually you can select an option if you want your image interlaced. Interlacing makes your image's file size slightly larger (which makes it actually load slower), so not every image should be interlaced.

Progressive JPEGs are similar in theory to interlaced GIFs. To quote Tom Lane's JPEG frequently asked question file (or *FAQ*), which can be found online (`http://www.cis.ohio-state.edu/hypertext/faq/usenet/jpeg-faq/top.html`), a progressive JPEG "divides the file into a series of scans. The first scan shows the image at the equivalent of a very low quality setting, and therefore it takes very little space. Following scans gradually improve the quality. Each scan adds to the data already provided so that the total storage requirement is about the same as for a baseline JPEG image of the same quality as the final scan. (Basically, progressive JPEG is just a rearrangement of the same data into a more complicated order.)"

However, progressive JPEGs are not as widely supported as interlaced GIFs. Even though most browsers now know how to display progressive JPEGs, a lot of image tools don't know how to create them.

Creating Transparent GIF Images

HTML images are always square or rectangular. However, you can create the illusion that your image is shaped differently in several ways. For example, if your page has a white background, you can create an image of a dog on a white background. The white colors will blend and it will appear as if the image is dog shaped (and it will fit better with your page).

 **WARNING**   Not all white colors are the same. Be sure that the different whites match. A true white has an RGB value of #FFFFFF (which is equivalent to the decimal values of 255, 255, 255 for red, green, and blue). Some image tools use decimal values, others use hexadecimal values. Skill 3 teaches the use of hexadecimal.

An image with a white background does not match with a page with a gray background. If you assume that your background page color is white, you might end up with an ugly result if your page's background ends up a different color, such as the old default of gray. If that happens, you'll end up with the white and gray background color clash shown in Figure 8.6.

FIGURE 8.6: The "New!" image has a white background, while the page has a default gray background (common for users who haven't customized the default background color).

 **WARNING** You can't guarantee that your page's background will always be displayed with the color you select. Many surfers will override the default document color with their own preferences, particularly if they have vision problems or are color-blind. Therefore the background color of your images might not match the background color of your page.

When you have specified a background color or image for your page, you'll often want to ensure that the page background shows through the background parts of an image. The only way to do this is to make a transparent image. A transparent image has a color that has been set to be "invisible" so that whatever is behind the image shows through. Using a transparent image will save you from having to match an image's background with your page's background. Transparency is easier seen than explained, so examine Figure 8.7, which shows a transparent image compared to its non-transparent counterpart.

FIGURE 8.7: Two "New!" images on a cloud background; the color white in the left-hand image is transparent (allowing the cloud background to come forward) and the right-hand image is not transparent.

NOTE   The techniques for making GIFs transparent vary wildly from program to program, but only GIF89A format GIFs can have a transparent color—so make sure you're saving in the right format. Check your image tool's Help program and try searching for "Transparent" to find out how transparency works in your program.

Some image tools can only make transparent GIFs if the transparent color is black or white, while other image tools let you make any color transparent. However, only one color can be transparent. JPEGs cannot have a transparent color, and PNGs allow more complex types of transparency than GIFs.

 TIP   There are also pages on the Web that will make your image transparent as a free service (http://www.vrl.com/Imaging/ or http://www.inf.fu-berlin.de/~leitner/trans/english.html). Another excellent site that can help you with your GIFs is Gif Wizard (http://www.gifwizard.com/).

Creating Animated GIF Images

One type of image really jumps out on the Web: animated GIFs. An *animated GIF* is a series of two or more normal GIF images that have been combined into one file and are displayed by the browser frame by frame in the same space. This creates the illusion of animation.

Animated GIFs are popular because they don't require special software or a complicated program to display an animation. Any graphical browser from Navigator 2 or IE 2 on will show animated GIFs, although early browsers did have glitches. (The newer versions of Navigator and IE allow you to switch off animation.)

 **WARNING**   Some surfers become annoyed and distracted by animated images. Use them sparingly. Certain animated GIFs are in wide spread use (such as the spinning globe or the animated mailbox) and to use one of these animated GIFs on your page is cliché.

To create an animated GIF, you'll need to first create each frame of the animation as a separate image. Then, you use a special image tool to combine the images together and set the amount of delay between each frame.

Animating an image is a special art, and an exhaustive review of the technique is beyond the scope of this book. However, we'll list several GIF animation tools in the next section on image tools; each of the packages we mention will come with sufficient documentation to get you started.

Using Image Tools to Create and Edit Images

When it comes time to add an image to your page, you have two choices: either create your own images, or use and edit existing images. You'll also probably want to edit your images for different reasons (such as to change a color scheme, modify a design, or convert from one format to another).

No matter what you're doing with an image, you'll need an image tool. There are just as many image tools as there are HTML tools (and you already know from Skill 4 how many different HTML tools there are). You're already equipped with a fairly capable image tool: Your browser at least knows how to display images in several different formats, and it can also save images you see on the Web.

Since this book isn't really about images, we're not going to go into a lot of detail on the different image tools. We will take a brief look at some broad categories of image tools and name the major players.

Image Applications

Most people have heard of the popular image applications. The application that's probably mentioned most often is Photoshop, sold by Adobe. Photoshop was designed, as its name implies, to edit photographs. It features many advanced tools for creating and editing images (not just photographs), but it may not be as easy to use Photoshop to create logos and images as other tools; for example, there's no simple way to create a circle in Photoshop, and its text tools are not sophisticated. However, Photoshop's capabilities can be extended through the use of plug-ins.

 TIP   If you use Photoshop and want to work with more powerful text-editing features, you can give Extensis' PhotoTools plug-in a try. Visit their home page (http://www.extensis.com/) to download a trial version.

Photoshop is, unfortunately, extremely expensive. However, its powerful filters can apply professional effects to your images (just be careful not to overuse the "lens flare" filter, for example).

Illustrator is another expensive and powerful application sold by Adobe that's often used to create graphics. Illustrator's emphasis is more on creating images than Photoshop. However, both Photoshop and Illustrator are some of the more complicated applications in existence, and both will take you some time to learn.

Photoshop and Illustrator are both available for Windows PCs, Macintoshes, and UNIX systems. More information is available from Adobe (http://www.adobe.com/).

For Windows users, Paint Shop Pro is a popular shareware program used to edit and create images. Created and distributed by Jasc, Inc., more information and the shareware package can be found from their home page (`http://www.jasc.com/`).

ClarisDraw (sold by Apple's Claris Corporation) is an easy-to-use image application for Macintosh and Windows users. You can read more about it at Claris' home page (`http://www.claris.com/`).

CorelDRAW and related software packages are also popular image applications. Find out more from Corel's home page (`http://www.corel.com/`).

In addition, Deneba (`http://www.deneba.com/`) sells the popular Canvas application for Windows and Macintosh users, and for the Macintosh, UltraPaint can be purchased for under $20.

 TIP   FrontPage and some other HTML editors come with image editors. Most of the recent versions of FrontPage ship with the Microsoft Image Composer, which is a capable image tool. FrontPage itself can be a handy image tool, since it can make images transparent with a click of a button.

You may able to adapt your existing applications' drawing capabilities. Popular word processors such as WordPerfect and Microsoft Word have drawing tools, and Microsoft PowerPoint (normally used to create business presentations) may be able to handle your image needs. The main issue involved in using these tools is their inability to save the images in a useful Web format.

On the low end, you can always create images with a drawing program that may have been provided free with your operating system (such as the Paint program that comes with Windows). However, these simple drawing programs don't have a lot of features and often don't save files in GIF or JPEG format (so you'll have to use a utility or conversion tool before you can add your drawings to your Web pages).

The image applications usually know how to convert images fairly effectively, but aren't really optimized for creating images in GIF or JPEG formats (Photoshop especially). For that, you should check out an image utility.

Image Utilities and Conversion Tools

A large number of popular utilities are available; most of these utilities are shareware and can be downloaded from the Web.

All of these utilities can display images quickly, and convert images between GIF and JPEG formats as well as other popular image formats (some of the tools are solely designed for converting images from one format to another). Most of these utilities can also make simple and complex transformations to an image, such as changing an image's size, orientation, color, contrast, and rotation. Some of these utilities can handle more advanced editing, such as rearranging the image and changing the number of colors.

 NOTE   The process of reducing the number of colors in an image is called *dithering*, and it's usually wise to get a utility that's good at dithering if you want to convert a 24-bit image into GIF format.

For Windows, popular image utilities include LView Pro, WinGIF, ACDSee, and PolyView. One popular commercial image utility is HiJaak Pro.

For Macintosh, check out DeBabelizer, JPEGView, GIFConverter, Graphic-Converter, Giffer, and GifBuilder.

GIF Animators

The best-known GIF animator is Alchemy Mindwork's GIF Construction Set (available as shareware from `http://www.mindworkshop.com/`). This package is a little unconventional, but it contains everything you need to animate images, including an animation wizard to guide you through the process. It's a capable image utility as well, and it includes several shortcuts for creating animated images, such as a scrolling marquee image with a message you specify or a special transition between two images.

Other GIF animators include Microsoft's free (for now) Microsoft GIF Animator, as well as PhotoImpact GIF Animator, Animagic, VideoCraft, and WebImage.

Creating Images

Creating images is difficult work and requires a lot of time and energy—not to mention talent. There's no shortage of graphic designers and design firms who would be happy to design a coordinated series of images for you.

If you do create images yourself for your Web sites, you should use the best image tool available to you. Take the time to fully learn how your tool or application works (finish the online tutorials and look into computer training classes) and find out what it's capable of. Scour the Web for inspiration in the form of design ideas and fresh approaches—don't always rely on the drop shadows and neon effects that are so commonplace.

 TIP   If you're creating a simple image, it's often best to work on a version that's much larger than what you intend as your final size, and then rescale your work down to your desired size.

The easiest type of image for most people to create is a photograph. Using either a conventional camera or a newer digital camera, you can take a wide variety of photographs to help illustrate your page. You can scan in photographs, or have them developed onto CD-ROM and then converted into JPEG format. However, an amateur photograph with ineffective lighting or poor composition will hamper your page as much as a crudely drawn image will.

TIP   When you create images, decide if you're designing for 256 colors or 24-bit color. (We'll discuss the pros and cons in Skill 17.) If you're using 256 colors, try to see if your application has a Web-compatible palette of colors that won't dither—that is, colors that will be displayed as a solid that resembles the color you intend. Visit the browser safe palette page (http://www.lynda.com/hex .html) for a tutorial on the 216 "safe" colors and to pick up a Web palette for Photoshop.

If you're good at illustrating on paper (or know someone who is), then buy or rent a scanner to convert paper illustrations into computer files. (You can also find scanners at many copy stores and find scanning services in the Yellow Pages. Some scanners are sold with bundled image applications, such as Photoshop.)

However, if (like most of us) you're no artist, then it's time to consider using existing images.

Using Existing Images

You can take existing images and use them on your Web pages in several ways. Here are some methods:

- **Legacy material** Perhaps your organization has some image material that you can use (such as logos, street maps, slide presentations, or previously commissioned material) once you convert it into the correct format.

- **Clip art collections** There are a large number of commercial and shareware packages of clip art and stock photographs that are licensed for non-profit use on your Web pages. (Check the license of the package carefully before using a clipart image on your Web site.)

- **Public domain material** Certain illustrations and images are public domain and can be included on your Web page once you find (and convert if necessary) the image. However, be careful since most images are copyrighted and are not in the public domain.

- **Freely licensed material** Many companies create special images and logos (also known as *badges* or *banners*) for the express purpose of use on a Web page when you link to that company.

NOTE   For example, Netscape freely licenses the ubiquitous "Netscape Now" image that many people use to link to Netscape's site. Check a site that you want to link to and see if they have a logo page that explains their licensing and linking policies. Using a badge to link to a company is free advertising for them, so think twice before you send your audience away to their site.

- **Freeware collections and libraries** There are a number of collections of images (such as background images and common icons) where the artist has relinquished copyright or allows you to use their images on your Web pages with no restrictions (or sometimes simply in exchange for author credit and a link back to their site).

NOTE   Here are several freeware image collections of links (aside from the ones you can find at Yahoo!): Clipart.com (`http://www.clipart.com/`), Clip Art Review (`http://www.webplaces.com/html/clipart.htm`), and Gini Schmitz's "Cool Graphics on the Web" (`http://www.fishnet.net/~gini/cool/index.html`).

- **Material that you may use after you buy a license** Many Web artists display images in their online galleries and will sell an inexpensive image license. If you see an image that you wish to use on a Web page, it doesn't hurt to inquire if it is available for licensing.

WARNING   In the early days of the Web, fan sites used copyrighted material (like images of U2 album covers or pictures of Star Trek characters) unchecked. These days, corporate crackdowns on illegally used copyrighted material are common. You must assume that any image you see is copyrighted unless there is a specific statement to the contrary. U.S. copyright law grants copyright protection even if there is no explicit copyright statement.

It's all too easy to see an image, background, or icon that you like and save it to your hard drive. (Using Navigator or IE, all you have to do is use the save command on the image's context menu—right-click on the PC, or hold down the mouse button over an image with a Mac.) Once the image is saved on your hard drive, you can edit it and include it on your Web pages with little difficulty. However, just because you *can* use other people's images on your Web pages does not mean it's legal to do so. In general, this practice is quite widespread—and also quite immoral. Using another person's copyrighted work without their permission is a crime. (There are exceptions to copyright law for fair use or parody, but we're not lawyers, so you're on your own to determine what's fair use and parody.)

 **WARNING**   It's considered bad manners to include an <IMG> tag or BACKGROUND attribute that links to another site's image without their permission. You're just using their work without giving them credit. (Whether this practice is actually illegal hasn't been settled.)

If you own the material or if your license allows it, use the image tools we described earlier to modify existing images for your own purposes. Add your company name to a stock photograph of the Golden Gate Bridge, or change the contrast of the Mona Lisa and add your logo to replace her head. Be creative above all else, by trying things you *haven't* seen on other Web sites. The more unique your images are, the more likely your site will stand out. Our best advice is to start experimenting with images and practicing to feel comfortable with them.

Throughout this Skill, we've discussed a lot of information about images, certainly one of the more important things that you can include on your page. Some of the same principles that apply to working with images also apply to other types of files, such as sound files and movie files. We'll learn all about these types of multimedia objects in the next Skill, which discusses multimedia extensively.

You'll also see how images can be displayed by using HTML 4.0's new object element, and how the <OBJECT> tag uses many of the same attributes that we've learned in this Skill.

Are You Experienced?

Now you can...

- ☑ use the *<IMG>* tag with many different attributes, including *ALT*
- ☑ link to sites with images as the link anchor
- ☑ understand image formats and special image formats
- ☑ create and edit images using different image tools

Skill 8

PART 2

BEYOND THE BASICS

In Part I, we learned the basic features of HTML. In Part I, we'll learn how to include many advanced elements of HTML—that can help you make unique and powerful Web pages. Skill 9 teaches the use of multimedia (sound and movie clips), Skill 10 shows how to create tables of data, Skill 11 is concerned with how to divide the browser window into different frames, and Skill 12 shows how to make interactive Web pages that get information from the surfer by using forms.

The rest of Part II goes beyond HTML. Skill 13 shows the use of browser-specific proprietary extensions to HTML, Skill 14 teaches how to use HTML with a style sheet and introduces Cascading Style Sheets, and Skill 15 gives an overview of scripting languages and applets. We'll finish Part II in Skill 16 with a discussion of the exciting new future of HTML known as Dynamic HTML.

Making Your Pages Sing: Multimedia

- → Understanding how to use sound files
- → Creating sound files in different formats
- → Learning about multimedia software applications
- → Using video and other multimedia formats
- → Using the object element
- → Working with plug-ins

In this Skill, we'll take your pages into another dimension by teaching you how to add multimedia to your Web pages. *Multimedia* refers to "multiple mediums"— the ability to add bits of sound and moving pictures (*clips*) to your Web pages.

We'll see several different methods of how multimedia can be included in your page. The principal method used in HTML 4.0 is the object element; in this Skill, we'll see several examples of the object element's <OBJECT> tag, which can include a multimedia clip on your page in much the same way that an <IMG> tag can add an image to your page.

Since HTML 4.0's object element is new and not yet fully supported by browsers, we're also going to learn about some older and simpler methods of including multimedia on your Web site. We'll also see some HTML extensions that are still common because they work with a wide range of browsers and take a brief look at two popular plug-ins.

To begin this Skill, we'll learn some methods of getting multimedia to work on your computer, learn the different file formats, and see what tools you can use to create or edit multimedia files.

Getting Multimedia to Work with Your Browser

Audio and video files created for the Web can come in a variety of different file formats; we'll learn more about these formats in the next section.

Internet Explorer and Netscape Navigator are usually able to play some of these different audio and video file formats automatically, but it depends on your specific computer system and how the browser has been configured.

 NOTE   In general, you can't hear sound files on your PC unless you have a sound card and speakers. A few software programs, like Microsoft's speaker driver, may allow you to hear sounds through your PC's tinny built-in speaker.

Browsers retrieve multimedia files using server protocols such as HTTP and FTP (see Skill 1); both of these protocols can send any type of file. Once the browser has retrieved the file (which can take a long time since the files are generally large), then the browser can work out how it should display it. IE and Navigator generally include a built-in program called a *plug-in* to play a variety of multimedia files. By itself, a browser only has the ability to display a few file formats (such as HTML and plain text). A plug-in expands a browser's ability to display a particular file format. Many different plug-ins are available; each one is installed (or "plugged in") to the browser to teach it new tricks.

 **WARNING**   Sometimes you'll have to download the multimedia plug-ins of each browser separately. The minimum installed versions might not include the movie and sound players.

IE's built-in multimedia player is the ActiveMovie player (even though it plays sounds as well as video). Netscape includes its LiveAudio and LiveVideo plug-ins with most versions of Navigator. (LiveVideo is available for Windows only.) Both browsers will try to take advantage of the other browser's plug-in if they don't have a plug-in of their own.

 NOTE   Computer movies are still a new technology. Most computers are only fast enough to play video files using a tiny portion of the screen. To play full-screen video, you need special hardware or a very fast computer. Older computers are simply not powerful enough to play video clips at all.

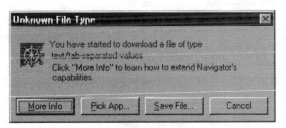

When your copy of Navigator downloads a specific multimedia file that it doesn't know how to display, you'll be given four options, as shown here.

The More Info button allows you to pick a plug-in from Netscape's Web site. (We'll see plug-ins in more detail toward the end of this Skill.) Once you've downloaded a plug-in that can display that file, you'll have to set your browser's preferences so it can automatically open and play the file.

The Pick App button will let you associate an external application with that type of file.

The Save File button will simply save the file without displaying it at all. You can then use the file with another software program or on a different computer that can play that specific file.

The Cancel button will stop Navigator from retrieving the file.

 NOTE   With IE, if you don't have a plug-in already installed, IE will prompt you to either try to open the file, save it, or cancel the download. If you try to open the unknown file type, then IE will try to use an external application to display the file, depending on how your operating system is set up.

The main difference between a plug-in and an external helper application is that a plug-in can be used to display an object that's part of a Web page, while external applications (or *helper apps*) run separately from the browser.

Skill 9

One important distinction is that IE tends to use a file's extension to recognize its file type, while Navigator tends to recognize a file by its MIME type.

UNDERSTANDING MIME TYPES

MIME refers to the categories of Multipurpose Internet Mail Extensions. Originally developed for describing mail attachments, MIME types have become useful for describing files on the Web.

MIME categories are divided into a major type (such as text, image, audio, or application), followed by a slash and then a code for a specific type (such as html, text, wav, or gif).

These category descriptions are fairly self-explanatory, but some of them use abbreviations (such as mid for MIDI files) or commonly understood conventions (such as audio/basic to mean .au format, or application/x-zip-compressed to mean a ZIP archive).

Here are some typical MIME types:

text/plain	audio/basic	application/msexcel
text/html	audio/mid	video/mpeg
image/jpeg	audio/wav	application/x-zip-compressed
image/gif	audio/aiff	video/x-msvideo

You can see an official list (which is not necessarily complete) created by the Internet Assigned Numbers Authority (http://www.isi.edu/in-notes/iana/assignments/media-types/media-types).

Knowing a little about MIME types is important because your Web server must correctly describe the MIME type of every file it sends, or else a browser won't know what to do with the file.

For example, if surfers complain that they cannot download zip files from your site, then you might need to contact your Web server administrator and have them update the MIME type configuration file, which associates different file extensions with different MIME types. It's usually a simple task for an administrator to tell the Web server that zip files should be sent as the application/x-zip-compressed MIME type.

Because the capabilities of the browser that will view your pages are unknown to you, it's impossible to be sure your audience can see or hear your multimedia. Using a well-known file format helps, but there are no guarantees.

We'll look at the common sound formats first and then see the formats used for video clips.

Understanding Sound Formats

The most common sound file formats used on the Web are Microsoft Wave sounds (or *waves*, with a .wav extension), basic audio (also known as Sun audio and UNIX audio, with an .au extension), and Macintosh audio (.aif, .aiffc, or .aiff).

Netscape's LiveAudio and Microsoft's ActiveMovie plug-ins should handle all of these formats. These formats are useful for general purpose sounds (speech, short music clips, and sound effects), but they are not particularly efficient—they don't usually compress well, and they're not optimized for any one purpose. In contrast, the MIDI format (.mid) is designed exclusively for musical notes arranged into a song, so MIDI files are very small. We'll discuss each of these types of files in a section of their own.

 NOTE In addition, the video formats that we'll see later can also play sounds.

Another sound file technology is *streaming audio*. Different companies, like Real-Audio and AudioActive, have developed sound formats that are tremendously compressed, allowing them to be downloaded to your computer rapidly. These formats allow your computer to begin playing the sound file before it is completely downloaded. This method of receiving sound files is called *streaming* because the sound is heard in real-time (or more typically, *almost* real-time) as your computer receives the stream of sound. RealAudio (http://www.realaudio.com/) and TrueSpeech offer free software plug-ins that allow you to hear these types of real-time sound files (with file extensions .ra, .ram, .rpm, and .rae for RealAudio, and .tsp for TrueSpeech). We'll see more about TrueSpeech later in this Skill.

Streamed sound files are also compressed so that each file is smaller than the same file would be if created in .au or .wav file format, for example. However, this compression also sacrifices some of the sound quality, sounding a bit like AM radio. Following the same logic with RealAudio, the sound files formatted to be received by 28.8 modems sound much better than those formatted for 14.4 modem speed because sound quality is sacrificed at the slower modem speed.

In general, the higher the quality of sound files, the larger the file size. Audio data is difficult to compress without sacrificing much of the sound quality.

Microsoft Windows comes bundled with various software applications that allow you to play, record, and edit various multimedia files. To take a look at these built-in programs, click on Start ➤ Programs ➤ Accessories ➤ Multimedia. If your browser doesn't have the appropriate built-in multimedia player, these external Windows applications can work with the multimedia files that you'll come across on the Web.

 NOTE   To create sounds, you'll need a microphone and a sound card. Also, you can use your sound card to record sounds from a CD, radio, or VCR, but the same points we made about copyright in the previous Skill also apply to multimedia files.

If you have a Macintosh computer, several applications are available for editing and creating sounds, some of which may be provided with your computer (depending on which software bundle came with your system). Popular sound editing shareware and freeware, such as SoundEffects and SoundStudio Lite, are available from MacUser (`http://www5.zdnet.com/mac/download.html`) or Macworld (`http:// www.macworld.com/software/`).

 NOTE   If your browser doesn't include a built-in application to play basic audio files, you'll need to get a plug-in or helper application. Most of the popular sound-editing programs work well as helper apps. Sound Machine for Apple is a shareware program that plays and records basic audio sound files for the Mac. GoldWave and Cool Edit are popular PC sound editors. For more PC and Macintosh sound programs, see TUCOWS (`http://www.tucows.com/`) and look under Audio Applications (after you've picked your location and system).

As long as you're prepared to license sounds or double-check that the sound is in the public domain, you can use the Web to search for existing sounds.

Searching for Sounds

The search engine Lycos (`http://www.lycos.com/`) has a function that allows you to search only for sound files. For example, a recent search for zebra sounds brought up files with the following partial URLs:

```
/~zebra/eterflam.mid          /~zebra/pianopw.mid
/zebra.wav                    /~zebra/miyahara_lab/sy1.au
/Zebra/zeb11m8w.wav           /sounds/swp7001-2.au
```

Notice the variety of file extensions that were found: `.mid`, `.wav`, and `.au`. Each type of sound file has its own characteristics. Other search engines allow searching for sounds and multimedia as well. We'll discuss each of these audio file formats in the next few sections.

A wide variety of sound libraries contain public domain sounds that you can use on your pages. You can try searching under Sounds at Yahoo!, or go to sites like the Audio Browser Sound Files collection (`http://www.webplaces.com/html/sounds.htm`) or even the Microsoft Sound Gallery (`http://www.microsoft.com/gallery/files/sounds/`).

Creating and Using Wave Sounds

Microsoft's wave format for sounds (with an extension of `.wav`) is probably the most commonly used format on the Web these days. Even though waves are a Windows format, most platforms have a wave player (and browsers on Macintosh and UNIX systems usually include a plug-in to play waves).

You can create wave sounds by taking existing sounds and converting them to wave format, or by recording your sound with a microphone and sound software, and then saving the file in wave format.

Another way to create a wave sound is to record your voice, music, or sound effect on a cassette tape. To transfer your sound to your computer, you'll need to play the sound from the cassette tape and record it onto your computer. You'll need both a program that records (which is usually provided with your computer or your sound card), as well as the proper cable to connect the output of the cassette player to the input jack of your computer or computer's sound card.

 NOTE   You can find the proper audio cables at many electronics stores, or one may have been provided with your computer or sound card.

When you've connected your recorder to your computer, open up a sound program. Play your tape and at the same time click on the program's Record button. Your computer will begin to create a digitized sound file of your tape recording. After your taped sound has finished playing, click on the Stop button of your sound software to stop recording. You should be able to save your sound file in wave format, with the `.wav` extension.

You'll probably want to edit your sound file, clipping any excess silence so your file is as small as possible; many sound programs allow you to change the volume, add echo, or apply other special effects. Some programs can compress the sound file into a smaller size as well.

TIP   Stereo files may sound better, but a mono sound file is half the size.

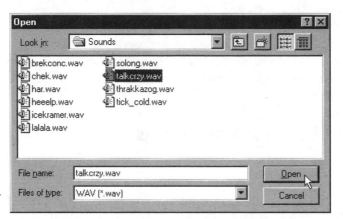

To test your wave file, see if you can open it in your browser. You should be able to use the normal File ➤ Open command and browse to the file. Make sure the Files of Type box is set appropriately, as shown here.

Alternately, you can create a test HTML page that includes a link to the wave sound. Then you can open the HTML page and follow the link to see if it plays properly. Here's how the HTML code looks for a simple link to a wave file:

```
You can <A HREF="hello.wav">hear me say hello</A>.
```

Clicking on the anchor text <u>hear me say hello</u> would cause your browser's sound plug-in or helper application to appear on top of your browser window. After the `hello.wav` file has loaded, the helper application should automatically play the sound file.

Creating and Using Other Sound Formats

The same recording method mentioned for creating wave files works for creating sounds in basic audio format and Macintosh's AIFF format.

At one point, the basic audio format (with `.au` as the extension, but you'll sometimes see `.snd` as well) was the most popular sound format on the Web. The format was created by Sun and NeXT to be a flexible format, but on the Web, basic audio format is an 8-bit mono format that's fairly low quality. On the other hand, `.au` files are compact and well-understood.

WARNING   Macintosh sound format (`.aiff`, which stands for Audio Interchange File Format) is not in general use on the Web, even though you can find plenty of `.aiff` files in different archives. It's probably best to pick one of the other two formats. There are many other sound formats as well, such as Creative Labs' `.voc` format, MPEG-layer3 audio (`.mp3`), or the Amiga `.mod` format. If your Web site has sounds in any of these formats, it's unlikely that most surfers will be able to hear them without needing to get special software.

After you record your sound file, save your file in the appropriate format, if your sound software supports it.

NOTE   You may need to download an audio tool, some of which we mentioned earlier. Check the normal software archives to find some audio tools, or go by the WWW Virtual Library: Audio (http://www.comlab.ox.ac.uk/archive/audio.html) for a list of software and audio resources. You can find some technical information on the various sound formats here.

If you've already created a sound file in one format and you need to use a different format, various sound file conversion programs are available for download on the Web. SOX (SOund eXchange Utility, http://www.spies.com/Sox/) is a basic sound file converter you can use, for example, to change a wave file into a basic audio file.

Creating and Using MIDI Sounds

MIDI, which stands for Music Instrument Digital Interface, is the format pioneered by Apple Computer in 1986 to digitize songs from electronic musical instruments such as synthesizers and keyboards. Janan's test MIDI file (http://www.sonic.net/web/NoExperienceRequired/test.mid) was created by connecting an electronic keyboard to a PC and then recording the music into a MIDI sound program.

MIDI is often used on the Web for background sounds, or to give a theme song to a Web page. Since most MIDI files are small, they don't take long to download.

NOTE   MIDI files will sound good on some computers and not so good on other computers. It depends on the quality of the sound card. On a PC, a Wave Table sound card will play MIDIs with much higher quality than a standard sound card. If possible, test your MIDI files on computers with both types of sound cards. Macintosh computers usually have no trouble playing MIDI sounds well.

Plenty of MIDI files are also available on the Web (just do a search for "MIDI archive" to get started). However, be sure that a particular MIDI file is not copyrighted before using it on your page. We'll see how to add a background MIDI sound toward the end of this Skill.

Streaming Your Sounds with RealAudio

The RealAudio encoder programs allows you to create compressed real-time digitized audio files. Real-time streaming means you can play the sound as it downloads. With basic audio and wave files, for example, you cannot hear the file until you've completely downloaded the sound file. With RealAudio sound files you can stop and start the sound, pause, move forward, and move backward somewhat like playing a tape-recorded sound. RealAudio files are highly compressed so they can be delivered quickly over a limited bandwidth.

However, using a RealAudio sound requires special software both to create the sound and to send the sound from your Web server. If you have a Web server and you purchase the RealAudio server software, you can offer a live audio signal from your Web pages. Many Web sites have become Internet radio stations using RealAudio sounds.

Incorporating Plug-in Sound Formats

At the end of this Skill, we'll give you an overview of a few fun sound and video plug-ins to get you started with exploring the current range of possibilities with Web multimedia.

Now that we know a little bit more about sound formats, we're ready to learn how to add sounds to a Web page. Before we do that, however, we'll learn about video formats.

Understanding Video Formats

Video on the Web is a bandwidth hog. Video files are usually large and have to be downloaded to be viewed with a browser plug-in or helper application. In most cases, the whole file must download completely before you can start viewing it, but streaming video files are becoming popular as well.

There are three popular formats for video clips: MPEG format (.mpg or .mpeg), Microsoft format (.avi), and QuickTime format (.mov or .qt). We'll learn more about these three types of videos in just a second.

The quality of movie viewing can be high, if you take the time to download a huge file. MPEG video is the highest quality video and can be shown full-screen at 30 frames per second. However, 30 seconds of video can require a file size of a megabyte or more.

It's difficult for most Web authors to create video files. You'll need access to a digital camera or special hardware and software that can capture output from a VCR, laser disk, or video camera. You'll need a fast computer with a huge amount of available hard disk space and memory. The software that creates movie files in one of the three standard formats can be expensive. And when you're done creating your movie, the end result may be a file that's too huge to be practical.

NOTE   It's a lot simpler to create an animated GIF file for simple animations. See Skill 8 for a brief overview of animated GIFs. We'll compare them to video files shortly. You can also create animations using Shockwave, which we'll discuss later.

In order to offer the best-quality, non-streamed video, there are a few ways to reduce file size. First of all, set your software to compress video files at the highest possible compression rate. (On a slow computer, the compression process might take you several hours or more, but the end result will be a much smaller file.) Second, experiment with using smaller frame sizes (for example, 160 by 120 pixels or a postage stamp–sized 60 by 50 pixels). The third method is to use a lower frame rate (such as 10 to 15 frames per second).

Using Streaming Video

Streamed video is a recent happening on the Web. For example, a company called netStream (`http://www.netvideo.com/netvideo/stream.html`) offers a combination of RealAudio/RealVideo and VDOLive technologies so video clips can play instantly (eight to 15 frames per second with a 28.8 modem) without a download delay.

Another approach to streaming video is to create a streaming JPEG image. No special software is required to view the resulting movie image. The drawback is that most servers require special setup to send a streaming JPEG file, and most software can't (yet) create movie files in streaming JPEG format.

NOTE   Streaming image files often employ a special type of dynamic document called *server push*, where a Web server is programmed to keep sending the different frames of an animation or movie. For more information about server push, see Mal's Server Push page (`http://www.emf.net/~mal/animate.html`) or Netscape's push documentation (`http://www.netscape.com/assist/net_sites/pushpull.html`).

We're not going to go into a lot of detail on the different video tools in this book. As with images in Skill 8, we'll list several tools in the next section on video creation; each of the packages we mention will come with enough documentation to get you started.

Comparing Animated Images to Video

We introduced you to animated images in Skill 8. We also talked about the GIF Construction Set and other tools for creating animated GIFs.

Alchemy Mindworks GIF Construction Set's Web site includes some samples of animated images (`http://www.mindworkshop.com/alchemy/gcsdemo.html`). Animated images usually have fewer frames per second than Web video. The most common type of animated images look like a cartoon characters, with a small range of movement. Animated images can also be used for slide-show presentations. Most Web search engines include animated advertising banners.

Since GIF animations will appear frame by frame as they're downloaded, they are much faster than a non-streamed video clip. You can also create a transparent animated GIF, whereas video images must always be rectangular.

For simple, low-quality animations, you'll find animated GIFs are easier to create and they work on a wider range of platforms with fewer problems. However, for longer clips or clips that involve realistic movement, the video formats are more appropriate.

 NOTE   The animated GIF tools mentioned in Skill 8 can convert video files into animated GIFs.

Using QuickTime Video

QuickTime is a format from Apple Computer, created in 1991 for the Macintosh. (By 1992, QuickTime was available for Windows platforms as well). A free program available from Apple Computer, QuickTime allows you to view movie files. The QuickTime plug-in for Web browsers was created in 1996. QuickTime movies (with either `.qt` or `.mov` extensions) can include sound, video, and animation. QuickTime employs compression to keep file sizes as small as possible; however, MPEG files tend to be smaller than QuickTime files.

QuickTime is included with the Macintosh as an operating system extension. PC and Macintosh users can download a free copy of the QuickTime plug-in for Navigator and IE from Apple Computer's QuickTime Software Web page (`http://www.quicktime.apple.com/sw/`). More information and some sample movies are available from "Descriptions of Multimedia" (`http://www.training.apple.com/online/fast/spfast/mult/multdesc.html`).

Here's one way you can play a video using QuickTime with Navigator on the PC:

1. Install the QuickTime plug-in by visiting Apple's site and following the instructions.

2. Find a Web page that has a link to a `.mov` file (for example, at the WWW Viewer Test page, `http://www-dsed.llnl.gov/documents/WWWtest.html`). Once you click on the QuickTime movie link, your browser will begin to download the QuickTime file to your computer.

3. As soon as the file is downloaded, a small QuickTime window will appear and your .mov file will begin to play.

Before you add QuickTime movies to your own page, consider if you want other surfers to go through the same process that you just did. Some surfers will have already installed the QuickTime plug-in, but many others have not—and quite a few of them won't be willing to go to any effort to see your movie.

NOTE   In addition, text-to-speech browsers and non-graphical browsers won't be able to do anything with a movie file except download it. If your movie contains critical information, consider having the narration transcribed into a text file.

The simplest way to include a video file on a page is to link to it. Here's an example of HTML code for a link to a QuickTime movie file named video.mov:

```
Our <A HREF="video.mov">training video</A> is available.
```

TIP   Since the QuickTime plug-in is freely available from Apple, it's more likely that people will have a plug-in for QuickTime than a plug-in for MPEG or Microsoft Video movies. Some versions of QuickTime software can also play MPEG movies.

Using MPEG Video

MPEG is a type of high-quality compressed audio and visual coding format for Web files. Pronounced "empeg," MPEG stands for Moving Pictures Experts Group. MPEG files can contain sound, video, or both.

When you surf the Web, you'll come across several different MPEG file extensions. MPEG video files have the extension .mpg or .mpeg, while MPEG audio files have the extension .mp2 or .mp3 depending on which "layer" (version) of MPEG audio the file uses. You will need to install a different MPEG player for both audio and video files, and you may need a separate player for layer 2 and layer 3 MPEG audio.

We're fond of the Web site MPEG.ORG (http://www.mpeg.org/), which is a comprehensive roadmap of MPEG resources. Their site links to a variety of MPEG audio and video players and recorder software applications as well as a lot of detailed technical information. You can also find links to different MPEG test files to see how well your system plays MPEG video and audio files.

Here's an example of the basic HTML code for links to MPEG video (.mpg) and audio (.mp2) files:

```
You can see an <A HREF="http://www.sonic.net/web/mpgvideo.mpg">MPEG
video sample</A> or listen to an <A HREF="http://www.sonic.net/web/
mpgaudio.mp2"> MPEG audio sample</A>.
```

While many MPEG viewers are available (from MPEG.ORG among other places), these viewers work as external helper applications and are not directly plugged into the browser itself. While there are one or two commercial MPEG plug-ins, there is not a wide variety of freely available MPEG plug-ins. For this reason, you may prefer to use QuickTime or AVI formats.

Using AVI Video

The Microsoft video format uses the `.avi` extension. AVI stands for Audio Video Interleave and is one of the most common formats for video and audio data on the PC. The sound data is usually 8 or 16-bit, stereo or mono, sampled at 11, 22, or 44.1 kHz (kilohertz). Video data in an AVI file can be formatted and compressed in a variety of ways to accommodate the bandwidth constraints of the Internet.

Of the three video formats, the AVI format is the least popular. Fewer surfers will be able to view your movie if you present it in AVI format; you should consider using MPEG or QuickTime formats instead, although Netscape's LiveVideo plug-in is available for AVI files (currently for Windows 95 and Windows NT only).

Microsoft sells its Microsoft Video product to let you create and edit AVI files, and this program also lets you convert images and other video formats into AVI format. In addition, there are several programs available from the Web:

- AVI Constructor (`http://henge1.henge.com/~caracena/`) is a PC program that allows you to quickly create AVI files from still frames (.bmp, .jpg, or .tga image files) and sound files (.avi or .wav files).

- HyperCam (`http://www.hyperionics.com/www/hypercam.htm`) captures the action from your PC screen and saves it to an AVI file.

Employing Other Multimedia Formats

A wide variety of other multimedia formats are available on the Web today. Let's take a brief look at some other formats so you can get a quick feel for the range of audio and visual uses possible on the Web:

CU-See-Me ("See you, see me") is a desktop video conferencing system developed by Cornell University that lets you see, hear, and speak directly with someone who also has the CU-See-Me software and hardware system. You'll need a video camera attached to your computer as well as special software. Information and pointers to software can be found at Cornell's site (`ftp://gated.cornell.edu/pub/video/html/Welcome.html`).

VDOLive (`http://www.vdolive.com/`) offers a software program where your Internet connection becomes your own personal video channel. The information you choose to receive can be personalized to you on a minute-to-minute basis. VDO-Live also offers video broadcasting on the Internet with a second component called "video telephony," a face-to-face audio and visual communication medium. The VDO player is free.

pwWebSpeak (`http://www.prodworks.com/pwwebspk.htm`) is a PC browser for people who are visually impaired, users with learning disorders, and people learning new languages. Speech and large character interpretation of the Web pages are provided so that a blind or low-vision user can use the software effectively.

VoxChat (`http://www.voxware.com`) provides simultaneous text and voice transmission over low bandwidth networks for social chat, conferencing, and distance learning.

TrueSpeech (`http://www.dspg.com/`) offers high-quality, low-bandwidth Internet audio that has real-time, streaming audio playback. TrueSpeech files, unlike RealAudio, can be created and played without the need for special server software. The TrueSpeech software is offered free from their Web site, and the Windows Sound Recorder can encode files in the TrueSpeech's special `.wav` format.

Adding Multimedia to Your Web Pages

In the previous sections on multimedia formats, we've seen a couple of pages that simply link to a multimedia file using the anchor element. A link has the advantage of being extremely simple to set up, and it won't distract surfers from the rest of the content of your page.

 TIP   You might want to include some information about the file format in the anchor text, such as `<A HREF="cornflake.mid">Cornflake Girl [MIDI format, 16k]</A>`. This lets surfers know what type of file is being referenced and gives them a rough idea of how long it will take to download.

Sometimes you'll want to embed a multimedia clip or other object directly on a part of your Web page. HTML 4.0 lets you include objects like these on a page with the new object element (using the `<OBJECT>` and `</OBJECT>` tags).

 NOTE   An *object* is a general-purpose computer term for data in a particular format. Almost everything, including an HTML document, can be an object.

In the previous Skill, we learned how to use the image element to include images on a Web page. We saw many uses of the image element's `<IMG>` tag and some image attributes. The same concepts, and many of the same attributes, apply to other objects, especially multimedia objects like sound or video clips.

Skill 9

In the next few sections, we'll learn how to use HTML 4.0's object element to include multimedia directly on a Web page. Since the object element is new, it's not yet widely understood by most browsers—so we'll also see some older and more compatible methods of including multimedia on a page.

 NOTE   The applet element, first mentioned in Skill 6, is another way to include multimedia on a page. Used exclusively for Java programs, we'll see more about this in Skill 15.

Using the Object Element

The object element can be a general-purpose way to include multimedia on a page. The object element can be used with many types of files, including all of the sound and video file types that we discussed earlier. In addition, you can use the object element to include active scripts (see Skill 15), applications, images, and even other HTML documents. In this Skill, we'll concentrate on the multimedia uses of the object element and discuss other uses in later Skills.

The object element must begin with the <OBJECT> tag. In that <OBJECT> tag go several attributes must appear; with multimedia objects, you must use attributes specifying both the location of the multimedia file (using the DATA attribute) as well as what type of file you want to include (using the TYPE attribute). After the <OBJECT> tag comes some alternate text that a browser will display if it can't display the object itself. Then the object element must end with an </OBJECT> end tag.

We'll see several examples of the object element, starting with audio files.

Playing a Sound with a Sound Object

Let's see an example of a simple object element that will play an audio file, in basic audio format:

```
<OBJECT DATA="hello.au" TYPE="audio/basic">Hello</OBJECT>
```

The DATA attribute specifies the URL of the object. (It's similar to the SRC attribute of the image element.) You can use either an absolute URL (as defined in Skill 1) or a relative URL (as defined in Skill 7).

The TYPE attribute specifies the MIME type of the object. This attribute is important since browsers won't always recognize what type of file an object is by its extension. (Review our discussion of MIME types earlier in this Skill for more information.)

TIP

The browser may stop loading your page to load the hello.au file, so you may want to put this element near the bottom of your page. That way, a surfer has something to read onscreen while the sound is downloading.

This HTML code will automatically play the hello.au file. If the browser can't play basic audio files, then the word "Hello" will appear onscreen instead.

WARNING

Navigator 3 and IE 3 ignore this sound object; Navigator 4 will not play it automatically. Preliminary versions of IE 4 played the sound automatically but did not display the rest of the page correctly. See the "Preventing Object Problems with Browsers" for some workarounds.

The content between the <OBJECT> and </OBJECT> tags should be considered as the alternate text, in much the same way as an image's ALT attribute. (Review the alternate text section in the previous Skill for more information.) For a sound, it's helpful to include a transcription or description of the sound file's content.

Including a Movie Object

This example of the object element will put a QuickTime movie onscreen:

```
<OBJECT DATA="whale.mov" TYPE="video/quicktime">[How not to blow up a
whale]</OBJECT>
```

For browsers that recognize the object element and have a plug-in that knows how to display QuickTime movies, the whale movie will play on the page, exactly as if it were an inline animated image.

For a browser that didn't understand the object element or didn't have an appropriate QuickTime plug-in available (or for browsers set to not auto-load objects), the words "[How not to blow up a whale]" would appear instead.

You can put all sorts of HTML elements inside the object element. (Remember, the object element's contents are only displayed if the object's data isn't displayed.) So here's an alternate version of the previous code that falls back to a static image (or even an animated image, if the GIF is an animated GIF). The <IMG> tag will only be displayed if the movie object itself can't be played:

```
<OBJECT DATA="whale.mov" TYPE="video/quicktime">
  <IMG SRC="whale.gif" ALT="[How not to blow up a whale]">
</OBJECT>
```

TIP

You might want to include a link to the QuickTime plug-in as the alternative content for a QuickTime movie, so that surfers can easily download the plug-in.

Specifying an Object's Attributes

The object element can be used with many of the same attributes used with images. For example, we can specify the width, height, alignment, border size, horizontal space, and vertical space of the object. (See Skill 8 if any of these attributes are unfamiliar.) Here's the previous example with these attributes specified:

```
<OBJECT DATA="whale.mov" TYPE="video/quicktime" WIDTH=200 HEIGHT=180
ALIGN="RIGHT" HSPACE="20" VSPACE="10">
  <IMG SRC="whale.gif" ALT="[How not to blow up a whale]">
</OBJECT>
```

This example floats the object to the right (thanks to the ALIGN attribute), and

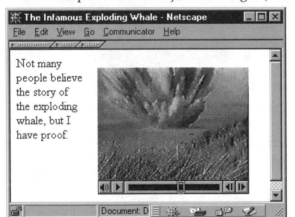

sets up a 200 by 150 image, with 20 pixels of space to the left and right, and 10 pixels of space above and below the object. Here's how this object would be displayed in Navigator, with a little bit of explanatory text added after the object element.

Using an ALIGN attribute with the "LEFT" or "RIGHT" values cause an object to float to the left or right margin, as described for images in the previous Skill. Text after the object will then appear next to the image, wrapped around it.

Some browsers can float objects to the center of the screen by specifying ALIGN="CENTER". Alternately, HTML 4.0 allows the ALIGN attribute to include several additional attributes:

- TOP The top of the object should be aligned with the top of the current line of text.

- MIDDLE The middle of the object should be aligned with the text's baseline.

- BOTTOM The bottom of the object should be vertically aligned with the bottom of the current text line.

The popular browsers do not yet support most of these alignment options.

You should always use the HEIGHT and WIDTH attributes with the object element since IE 4 and Navigator 4 won't display the object correctly without the height and width specified.

In addition to the attributes we've listed, the generic HTML 4.0 attributes (for language, style, and events) can be used with the object element. Some other attributes are reserved for applet objects (which we'll see in Skill 15), and some advanced attributes aren't yet supported by browsers, such as the DECLARE attribute that allows you to pre-load an object and then cause the object to play by a later object element, and the STANDBY attribute, which lets you specify a message to be displayed while the object is being loaded. See the appendix for a full list.

Nesting Object Elements

You can nest several object elements within each other to have a browser "negotiate" its way to the best type of object that it can display. For example, suppose you have several different formats of movies, and you want to allow a browser to display a QuickTime version. If the browser can't do that, you want to include an MPEG version, and if that doesn't work, then an animated GIF image. You might try embedding several object elements within each other, like this:

```
<OBJECT DATA="whale.mov" TYPE="video/quicktime">
  <OBJECT DATA="whale.mpg" TYPE="video/mpeg">
    <IMG SRC="whale.gif" ALT="[How not to blow up a whale]">
  </OBJECT>
</OBJECT>
```

Browsers that correctly understand HTML 4.0 should work their way through the object elements until they arrive at an object type that they can play; any other objects embedded within the object that gets displayed are ignored.

 WARNING   IE 4 and Navigator 4 don't display nested objects correctly.

Specifying Run Time Parameters

Different programs handle different objects. For example, Navigator uses LiveAudio to handle MIDI objects, and it uses LiveVideo to handle AVI movies.

However, if a surfer has installed a different plug-in, then that plug-in will handle the object. One popular plug-in is the Crescendo plug-in, which plays MIDI files.

Skill 9

There's no way to tell which plug-in is available to handle an object, so it's difficult to control the plug-in.

However, most plug-ins that handle a certain type of object, such as a MIDI sound, tend to have parameters. For example, normally a MIDI or movie object won't begin playing automatically. Instead, the surfer will have to click on a play button. But if you want to control the plug-in program, you can sometimes change its behavior by using a parameter. A *parameter* is a property name and value that can change the behavior of the plug-in program in certain ways. For example, the "AUTOSTART" parameter controls whether the object begins to play automatically.

To pass a parameter, include a param element within the object element. (The param element is an exception to the rule of items inside the object element being ignored if the object can be displayed.) The param element is an empty element, that normally looks like this:

```
<PARAM NAME="parameter name" VALUE="parameter value">
```

For example, Netscape's LiveAudio plug-in does not automatically play a sound file. You can force it to begin playing automatically by triggering its AUTOSTART parameter, with HTML such as this:

```
<OBJECT DATA="clouds.mid" TYPE="audio/midi">
  <PARAM NAME="AUTOSTART" VALUE="TRUE">
  [Soothing background sound.]
</OBJECT>
```

 NOTE   It's impossible to list which programs take parameters, and what the parameter names should be. There are just too many programs to discuss, and you can't guarantee that these programs are installed on the computers of everyone who visits your page. Therefore, you shouldn't depend on parameters unless you're sending a parameter to a program that you've installed on a Web server yourself. We'll see how in Skill 15 when we learn about applets.

There are several other possible variations to the parameter element, but since they aren't widely supported yet, we won't go into them here.

Inserting Image Objects

As we mentioned earlier, object is a general-purpose element intended to insert a wide variety of file types. One such type is an image. You can include an object element for either a GIF or JPEG image, using the object element in place of the image element discussed in the last Skill.

Instead of using a tag such as:

```
<IMG SRC="birdhouse.gif" ALT="[My birdhouse]">
```

HTML 4.0 allows:

```
<OBJECT DATA="birdhouse.gif" TYPE="image/gif">
[My birdhouse]
</OBJECT>
```

Unfortunately, most current browsers wouldn't display this at all. IE 4 can display an image object such as this, but it places an annoying scroll bar around the image, so it's hard to get the size correct.

Alternately, you can nest the object element around an <IMG> tag so that the <IMG> tag is displayed by browsers that don't understand image objects. However, since HTML 4.0 still endorses the use of the image element, you may as well simply use the image element instead of the object element.

Preventing Object Problems with Browsers

Since the object element is new, current browsers have a great deal of problems with its use. We've already seen a few problems in last few sections, but there are other problems as well.

Your first consideration should be that many people are using IE 3 and Navigator 3. Navigator 3 doesn't display the object element at all (although it does display the contents of the object element as an alternative). IE 3 uses object elements solely for ActiveX controls (which we'll see in Skill 15) and gets confused if you try to display other types of objects. It may erroneously issue warnings to people who view your page, or it may not display the object at all, depending on its current security settings.

Navigator 4 will only display an object if a plug-in is installed. MIDI and Quick-Time plug-ins are fairly common so it will display these two types of objects on many systems, along with other sound objects. (By default Navigator will require you to right-click or double-click on the object to make it play—this may be confusing to your page's viewers.) However, Navigator won't display image or HTML objects at all.

IE 4 has several quirks. Although it can display embedded images and HTML objects, it places a vertical scroll bar in the display, which makes it hard to work out the correct sizes for the object element's width and height attributes. Figure 9.1 shows IE's display of an embedded image and HTML object.

In addition, IE 4 may not display objects for a Web site at all, if its security levels are set high (which is the default) and the Web site does not have any special security certificates for which IE is looking. IE 4 may arbitrarily decide to display a sound clip in a separate window instead of inline on a page.

Finally, since IE uses ActiveMovie to display MIDIs while Navigator uses Live-Audio, it's difficult to find the proper settings for the width and height of a MIDI object. Netscape recommends you use a width of 144 pixels and a height of 60, but these are too short for a proper ActiveMovie display.

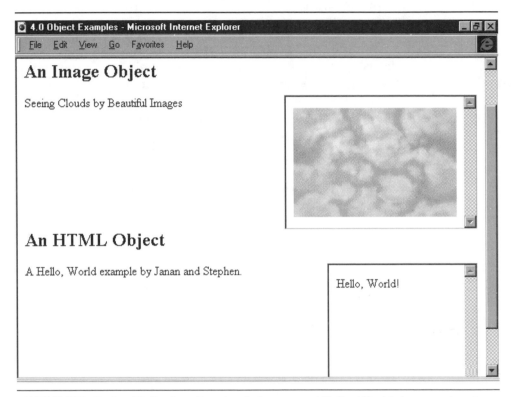

FIGURE 9.1: IE displays the clouds image and Hello, World document as two different objects. Note the border and scroll bar, which are displayed even if you set the BORDER attribute to zero.

 NOTE   We'll include an example HTML file that uses several different object elements on the Web site.

Given all of these problems with the object element, it may be safest for the moment to rely on anchors, or resort to some older methods used to include multimedia on a page.

Putting a Sound in the Background and Embedding Multimedia

If you're not going to use the object element or an anchor element, you have three easy options for putting a sound in the background of your Web page. These methods will make the sound load and play automatically with some browsers.

WARNING   Many surfers don't like sounds that play automatically, especially if they're working in a quiet office. If you do include a background sound, you should make sure that the volume of the sound is not louder than normal.

The oldest method is to use meta refresh (as we saw in Skill 5) in the head section of your document to refer to a background sound:

```
<!DOCTYPE HTML PUBLIC "-//W3C//DTD HTML 4.0//EN">
<HTML LANG="EN">
<HEAD>
     <TITLE>Including Background Sounds</TITLE>
     <META HTTP-EQUIV="REFRESH" CONTENT="5; URL=hello.au">
<HEAD>
<BODY>
<P>
In five seconds, you should hear me say hello.
</BODY>
</HTML>
```

This method works well for MIDI files as well.

A second method uses the Microsoft HTML Extension <BGSOUND>, which is a tag only recognized by IE. We'll see more about this extension in Skill 13.

A third technique uses the <EMBED> HTML tag, which is also an extension to HTML. The <EMBED> tag is recognized by IE and Navigator, but only if an appropriate plug-in is available. Unfortunately, Navigator and IE may not be able to play an embedded MIDI (or other multimedia file)—it depends solely on the plug-in's availability. If the plug-in is correctly working, than IE 3 and 4 as well as Navigator 3 and 4 should play the file correctly.

NOTE   The syntax for the <EMBED> tag for a background MIDI can allow for some interesting effects. LiveAudio can understand several attributes (we saw the use of the AUTOPLAY object parameter earlier; in the <EMBED> tag, you'd say AUTOPLAY= TRUE). Several other attributes (such as LOOP, HIDDEN, and CONTROLS) are also available; visit Netscape's LiveAudio documentation (http://home.netscape .com/comprod/products/navigator/version_3.0/multimedia/audio/how.htm) for some more possibilities.

There's not much harm in using the <EMBED> tag for background sounds. Your viewers who don't have a MIDI plug-in may simply miss out on the audio portion of your page. You can include a simple hypertext link to the sound for viewers for have a MIDI helper app. Here's an example of this use.

midibed.html

```
<!DOCTYPE HTML PUBLIC "-//W3C//DTD HTML 4.0//EN">
<HTML LANG="EN">
<HEAD>
      <TITLE>Embedding Background MIDI Sounds</TITLE>
<HEAD>
<BODY>
<EMBED SRC="test.mid" AUTOSTART="TRUE" LOOP="TRUE" CONTROLLER="FALSE"
VOLUME="50" WIDTH="0" HEIGHT="0">

<P>
If you don't already hear Daniel Platt (age seven) playing an electronic
keyboard, then the <A HREF="test.mid">MIDI sound file</A> is available.
</BODY>
</HTML>
```

Another option for the <EMBED> tag is to display a LiveAudio console (hidden in `midibed.html` by the `WIDTH` and `HEIGHT` attributes that were set to zero). This LiveAudio console contains Stop, Play, and Pause buttons as well as a volume control. This allows the person viewing your page to start the MIDI manually if they wish, by clicking the Play button. Figure 9.2 shows the LiveAudio console in action.

Here's the <EMBED> tag that would display the console shown in Figure 9.2:

```
<EMBED SRC="clouds.mid" TYPE="audio/midi" ALIGN="RIGHT" WIDTH="144"
HEIGHT="60">
```

NOTE   If another plug-in is installed to handle MIDI files, then its console will appear instead. Other plug-ins use different-sized consoles than Netscape's LiveAudio plug-in.

Don't worry too much about the attributes used in the <EMBED> tag in these two examples. Any attribute we haven't discussed is not a standard HTML attribute. There's no official list maintained by either Microsoft or Netscape of what attributes are available to the <EMBED> tag. We'll see more about the <EMBED> tag along with other non-standard HTML extensions in Skill 13.

TIP   The safest way to include a MIDI file is to simply link to it.

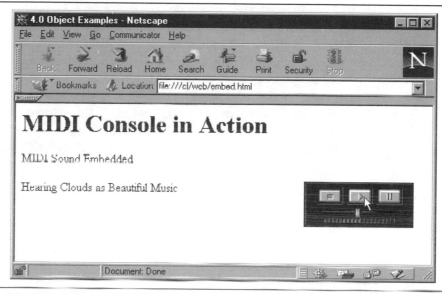

FIGURE 9.2: The Netscape LiveAudio plug-in console, displayed for sounds such as MIDI and basic audio. The same LiveAudio plug-in is used for both a MIDI object element or an <EMBED> tag for a MIDI file.

We can use the <EMBED> tag to embed other types of multimedia on a page, not just MIDI. We could substitute an <EMBED SRC="sf-tour.mpg"> file for an

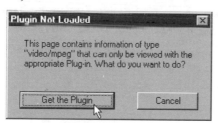

object element to include a MPEG file on a page. If you do this, Navigator will try to display the MPEG file inline, much like we saw for a/ multimedia object element. If Navigator doesn't have an MPEG plug-in, it will ask you for permission to retrieve one, as shown here.

NOTE   As soon as you leave the page that has the embedded MIDI or other multimedia, then it will stop playing. Some people use frames to keep a MIDI file playing for their entire site. You'll learn about frames in Skill 11.

Using Plug-Ins

There are a wide variety of plugs-ins that are available. Each plug-in extends the ability of the browser to display a new type of file. For example, using a special tool called Acrobat, you can create files in Adobe's Acrobat format (with the .pdf extension, for Portable Document Format). When you create a link to a .pdf file, it will only be displayed properly if the Acrobat plug-in is installed in the surfer's browser, or if the surfer saves the file and uses a helper app to view the PDF file.

Many plug-ins display different graphical formats, such as the movie files we saw earlier in this Skill or the PNG image files we discussed in Skill 8. In addition, special formats such as VRML (Virtual Reality Modeling Language) and Shockwave (discussed in the next section) can be handled by plug-ins. Other plug-ins handle sounds (including RealAudio and the other sound formats discussed in this Skill), speech, database browsing, animation, business presentations, and many other capabilities.

 TIP   If you're using Navigator, get a list of your currently installed plug-ins by using the Help ➤ About Plug-ins command. From there, a link will take you to Netscape's list of currently shipping plug-ins (more than 150 of them).

Since each plug-in is different and involves different tools to create files in the proper format, we won't go into much detail about most of the plug-ins. For each plug-in, you must balance the abilities of the file format with the inconvenience of forcing surfers to download a plug-in to see the files. Furthermore, you should test the plug-in to make sure it works in both IE and Navigator, and make sure that the plug-in is available for both Macintosh and PC users.

To find out more about plug-ins, visit Yahoo!'s Plug-Ins section (http://www .yahoo.com/Computers_and_Internet/Software/Internet/World_Wide_Web/ Browsers/Plug_Ins/) or Browser Watch's Plug-In Plaza (http://browserwatch .internet.com/plug-in.html).

Using Shockwave

One of the most popular formats for displaying animation, sound, and interactive games and programs is called *Shockwave*. Developed by Macromedia (http:// www.macromedia.com/), Shockwave is actually a group of related formats. To create Shockwave Director files, you must own Macromedia's Director (a big, expensive, and difficult-to-use program that creates complex presentations). Similarly, to create Shockwave Flash files (which are compact animations, similar to animated GIFs), you need the Flash program (available from Macromedia's Web site). There are other versions of Shockwave as well, including special tools such as Afterburner that convert and compress your presentations and animations so that they are appropriate for the Web.

The plug-ins to display Shockwave files are free and available from Macromedia (`http://www.macromedia.com/shockwave/download/`). To learn more about creating Shockwave files, visit Macromedia's developer center (`http://www.macromedia.com/support/centers.html`).

To display a Shockwave file on a Web page, you'll use an embed element.

Using Adobe Acrobat Documents on Your Web Page

Adobe Acrobat is a program that creates files in the PDF format (`http://www.adobe.com/prodindex/acrobat/`). For you to actually create files in this format, you'll need to own Acrobat, which costs $295. Its advantage is that it recreates the graphical appearance of a file almost completely, including fonts. You don't have to learn HTML or any other markup language to use Acrobat; instead, it converts files from many popular formats into the PDF format (making it easy, for example, to take a Word or Pagemaker document and publish it on the Web).

The biggest drawback to Acrobat, aside from its cost, is that surfers need to have the Acrobat Reader (which acts as a plug-in) in order to view your file. While the Reader is available free of charge from Adobe (`http://www.adobe.com/prodindex/acrobat/readstep.html`), not everyone will take the time to download a special tool just to see a file. While the PDF format is relatively popular, the file sizes can be large and the files are not as compatible (for example, with text-to-speech browsers) as HTML files, and it may not be convenient for your audience to work with files in this format.

But if you're taking existing newsletters, for example, it might be fastest to publish them on the Web in PDF format using Acrobat. You can link to a `.pdf` file, or embed it on the page with either the object or embed element.

In this Skill, we learned about MIDI and other multimedia and saw how it can be included on a page. In the next Skill, we'll learn about another advanced feature of HTML: the table element, which can be used to arrange tables of data.

Skill 9

Are You Experienced?

Now you can...

- ☑ understand how to use sound files in your Web pages
- ☑ incorporate video into your Web pages
- ☑ use anchors to create multimedia Web pages for most platforms
- ☑ include multimedia objects

Presenting Information in Tables

- ⊕ Understanding how and why to use tables
- ⊕ Looking at tables in action
- ⊕ Using the simple table model and the HTML 4.0 table model
- ⊕ Learning how to use elements and attributes for tables
- ⊕ Using tables for page layout (and why you shouldn't)

We briefly mentioned the table element in Skill 6. In this Skill, we'll learn a variety of ways to present your Web page data in table format. We'll cover all of the elements and attributes for tables in detail so you can become a master at using tables.

You'll learn about the advantages—and the limitations—to using tables. We'll show you many useful examples so you can learn how to create tables that organize your data. We'll also show you different ways you can use tables to enhance the layout of the text on your page. Tables are extremely popular on the Web because they are a flexible and attractive way of presenting information.

Understanding the Use of Tables

HTML tables mark up data that should be organized in a table structure, instead of in paragraphs or other block-level structures. With tables, you can present data organized in rows and columns. For example, two types of data that can easily be organized into a table structure are yesterday's high and low temperatures by city (see Table 10.1).

TABLE 10.1: Yesterday's Weather

City	High	Low	Wind
Alameda	70	53	south
Bakersfield	83	54	south
Barstow	93	65	south
Beaumont	89	52	west
Big Bear	72	40	south

Even though this isn't an HTML table, it's a good illustration of the concept of a table, and we can use it to establish some vocabulary:

- The *caption* is an optional description of the table. In Table 10.1, the caption is "Yesterday's Weather."

- A table's *rows* are the horizontal lines of data. Table 10.1 has six rows, starting with the "City" row and ending with the "Big Bear" row.

- The *columns* are the vertical lines of data. There are four columns in this example, starting with "City" and ending with "Wind."

- Each piece of data is at the intersection of a column and a row, and these intersections are called *cells*. Since there are six rows and four columns, Table 10.1 has 24 cells.

- Finally, the first four cells ("City," "High," "Low," and "Wind") show labels for the type of information in each column. These special cells are called *headings*.

Figure 10.1 shows how Internet Explorer would display the Yesterday's Weather table if it was created in HTML code. (We'll see the actual HTML code used to create this table in the "Creating an Example Table" section a little later.)

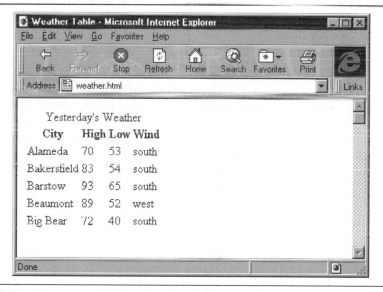

FIGURE 10.1: An HTML table showing yesterday's weather by city

Tables are sometimes used for general page layout; for example, to organize paragraphs into columns or to create margins. This has varying results, depending on which browser is used to view your pages. We'll talk about "Using Tables as a Layout Tool" later in this Skill, and we'll see some reasons why this is discouraged.

When you create a table in HTML, you'll use the table element. The table element starts with the <TABLE> tag and ends with a </TABLE> tag; in order to create a table, you'll need to understand the rules of what elements should appear between these two tags.

Understanding Table Models

The rules of which elements occur in a table (and in what order) is called a *table model*.

In this Skill, we'll present two important table models in HTML. Originally created by Netscape and later adopted by the W3C, the HTML 3.2 table model uses a fairly simple set of elements, and it has resulted in a widespread use of tables. Tables have become fully supported in all recent versions of Navigator, IE, Mosaic, and Lynx. Text-to-speech browsers and older versions of Lynx have trouble dealing with tables, however.

HTML 4.0 expands on the older, simple table model with new elements and attributes while still remaining compatible with the earlier table model. The main difference is that HTML 4.0 allows rows and columns to be grouped together and introduces several useful new attributes for alignment and cell borders. HTML 4.0's table model is designed to make tables richer, easier to import from spreadsheets, and more accessible to text-to-speech browsers. We'll see other differences in the "Using the HTML 4.0 Table Model" section. Fortunately, since the HTML 4.0 table model is completely backward-compatible with HTML 3.2's table model, you can use the simpler table model most of the time and only use the more complex HTML 4.0 table model if necessary.

Since the HTML 4.0 model is a lot more difficult, we're going to learn the older model first and see its relatively simple set of elements. Then we'll talk about the new HTML 4.0 table model after we've fully understood the basics of tables.

Introducing the Simple Table Model and Its Elements

For the simple table model, there are four elements that we will learn:

- The optional caption element consists of the <CAPTION> and </CAPTION> tags containing the table's description.

- The table row element (<TR> for "table row," with an optional </TR> end tag) creates a horizontal row of cells and contains the table headings and table data.

- The table data element uses the <TD> ("table data") tag (with an optional </TD> end tag) to create each individual cell. (The number of cells in a row determines how many columns will be displayed by the browser, so there is no separate element for table columns in the simple HTML table model.)

- The table heading (<TH> for "table heading" and optionally </TH>) element creates the heading cells.

We'll discuss each of these new elements in more detail later in this Skill, and we'll learn about their attributes and capabilities. For now, the next section will show these four elements in action by showing some code for our example table.

Creating an Example Table

Study the following HTML code to see how Figure 10.1 was created. To create this example on your own, type the code into your text editor and save it as weather .html, or visit the Sybex Web site to download the code.

 weather.html

```
<!DOCTYPE HTML PUBLIC "-//W3C//DTD HTML 4.0//EN">
<HTML LANG="EN">
<HEAD>
     <TITLE>Weather Table</TITLE>
</HEAD>
<BODY>

<TABLE>
   <!-- This is the table's caption. -->
   <CAPTION>
       Yesterday's Weather
   </CAPTION>

   <!-- This is the first row of the table. -->
   <TR>
       <TH>City</TH>
       <TH>High</TH>
       <TH>Low</TH>
       <TH>Wind</TH>
       <!-- Each of these four words is marked as a heading. -->
   </TR>

   <!-- This is the second row of the table. -->
   <TR>
       <TD>Alameda</TD>
       <TD>70</TD>
       <TD>53</TD>
       <TD>south</TD>
       <!-- Each of these pieces of information is a cell, or "table
       data." -->
   </TR>
```

```
<TR>
    <TD>Bakersfield</TD>
    <TD>83</TD>
    <TD>54</TD>
    <TD>south</TD>
</TR>

<TR>
    <TD>Barstow</TD>
    <TD>93</TD>
    <TD>65</TD>
    <TD>south</TD>
</TR>

<TR>
    <TD>Beaumont</TD>
    <TD>89</TD>
    <TD>52</TD>
    <TD>west</TD>
</TR>

<!-- This is the sixth and final row of the table.-->
<TR>
    <TD>Big Bear</TD>
    <TD>72</TD>
    <TD>40</TD>
    <TD>south</TD>
</TR>

</TABLE>
</BODY>
</HTML>
```

In this example, we've used indentations and comments to make this code easily comprehensible. We've also used the </TR>, </TD>, and </TH> closing tags for clarity. These end tags are optional and their absence shouldn't affect the table's appearance or function. (The </TABLE> end tag is always required.)

You'll see some HTML authors code table rows this way:

```
<TABLE>
<TR><TD>Beaumont<TD>89<TD>52<TD>west
<TR><TD>Big Bear<TD>72<TD>40<TD>south
</TABLE>
```

However, you may find this method a little harder to follow and edit.

TIP Older browsers (more than two years old) won't understand these table model elements at all. They would display all of the table data from the above sample in one big block—without any spaces at all. If you put a carriage return between each table cell when you're typing HTML source document, then older browsers will at least put a space between each piece of data, which is better than nothing. (If you put a <P> tag in the first cell of each row, then each row will appear on a separate line on older browsers, which will help out even more.)

Our example table does not have a border or any gridlines. We can use the BORDER attribute of the <TABLE> tag to cause a line to appear around each cell. By adding this one word to the <TABLE> tag, you can dramatically change the visual appearance of your table, as Figure 10.2 shows. (We'll see more about the BORDER attribute in the "Creating Border Lines with the BORDER Attributes" section.)

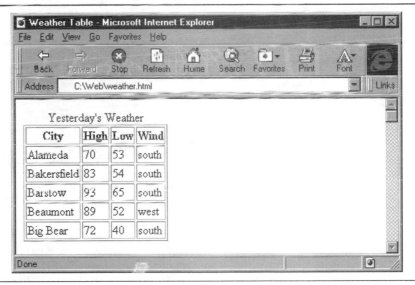

FIGURE 10.2: The same weather table now has a border. Notice that the caption appears outside the border.

You can use a table to highlight a particular paragraph with a border. Here's the HTML code for a one-celled table with a border:

```
<!DOCTYPE HTML PUBLIC "-//W3C//DTD HTML 4.0//EN">
<HTML LANG="EN">
<HEAD>
     <TITLE>Boxing "Hello, World"</TITLE>
</HEAD>
```

```
<BODY>
    <TABLE BORDER>
        <TR>
            <TD>
                Hello, World!
            </TD>
        </TR>
    </TABLE>
</BODY>
</HTML>
```

Figure 10.3 shows how Navigator renders this one-celled table with borders turned on.

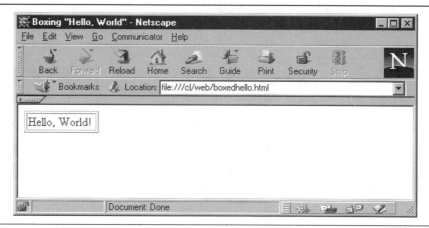

FIGURE 10.3: A bordered, one-celled table rendered in Navigator

 TIP   You may have noticed a small space between the exclamation point and the border. This is a consequence of putting the `</TD>` tag on the following line. To avoid that space, use `<TD>Hello, World!</TD>` on one line. (Review the rules of white space from Skill 3, especially "The Exception to the White Space Rules.")

 WARNING   Using a table for a boxed-paragraph effect can bring special attention to an important paragraph; however, the paragraph really doesn't belong in a table since it's not a table of information. Also, not every browser can display tables, so you will want to use an additional method of highlighting the paragraph, such as the Strong phrase element introduced in Skill 6 (which causes a paragraph to appear in bold or be read aloud with more emphasis, depending on the browser). If your only goal is to get a border around a paragraph, style sheets are better suited to that task (Skill 14).

The smallest table you can make has only one cell (that is, one row and one column), but there's no limit to how large you can make your tables. Although HTML does not impose any theoretical limits on how many rows or cells you can have, in practicality, more than 10 columns and you'll probably force the table to be wider than the window (and a horizontal scroll bar will appear in Navigator and IE).

TIP   Some Web artists have used very wide tables to create experimental pages that scroll horizontally, not vertically. For an example, see "That Rope" by Jef 'n' Gael (http://www.microaero.com/j'n'g/3-25.htm).

The only limit to the number of columns is how wide you want your table to be; there is no limit to the number of rows you can include in a table. There is also no limit to the number of separate tables that can appear on a page.

Advantages of Tables

One of the greatest advantages of tables is that your data is much easier to read when structured properly on the page. A properly designed table gives your readers a clear and quick way to evaluate your content. A table can contain many different types of content other than just text—such as lists, forms, nested tables (tables within tables), images, pre-formatted text, and paragraphs.

NOTE   You'll learn about tables inside of other tables in the "Nesting Tables" section.

The use of a table can also break up a plain page with an interesting visual feature (an attractive table is nicer to look at than just a bunch of numbers). We'll see some examples later in this Skill.

Limitations of Tables

One of the biggest limitations to tables is the amount of time it can take to create a complex table structure. A medium-sized table's HTML code can take up several pages if hand-coded properly for readability.

Making your tables easy to read is important so the data can be updated quickly later. With so many nested tags and attributes, there's more room for error when you're coding a table than other elements. It's harder to find errors, and if one tag is left off or put in the wrong place, the entire table may not appear.

Skill 10

Here's where it's useful to use an HTML editor to create the repetitive barebones of a table and to save some time. Then it's more fun to go back in and hand-code the details. We'll see how to use Netscape's Page Composer to create a table in the next section.

It's very tempting to try to use tables to solve a lot of your page layout challenges. First, you should consider your audience and decide whether most of your viewers will have access to browsers that can display tables (older versions of Navigator, Lynx, IE, and Mosaic don't know how to display tables at all). Second, be careful that your HTML coding follows the HTML standards for tables that we present in this Skill, and test that both Navigator and IE display your tables properly.

One example of using tables for layout is multiple columns of text (like the columns in a newspaper article). There's no standard HTML tag available to create multiple text columns. (However, there's an extension to HTML for columns that we'll see in Skill 13.) Web authors discovered they could duplicate the appearance of text columns in graphical browsers by using tables. Starting when Navigator 2 came out, tables were (and still are) often used (with borders turned off) to create the look of multicolumn text.

However, tables used for multiple text columns will produce extremely varied results. Web page designers might spend a long time trying to get the two columns to be exactly the same height. But this is a foolhardy quest. IE and Navigator don't always display fonts the same way. With multiple columns created in tables, depending on the font, the automatic line-breaks in IE may not render the same way in Navigator. Also, as soon as someone resizes the browser window, the line-breaks will readjust, and the bottom of the columns will probably not match, because of the relative lengths of the words in each column. Figure 10.4 shows how the bottom of two columns that were once even don't match up when we resize the Navigator window to a narrower width.

The moral here is that tables can't always be reliably used for multiple text columns, and you should be careful to check your tables with a few different browsers. This is a lesson in HTML's purpose: HTML elements are designed to indicate the structure of your document. Just because certain browsers happen to display some elements a certain way, that doesn't mean you should abuse the meaning of the tags to create a certain visual effect. If your document doesn't contain tables of data, it shouldn't have table elements.

Earlier versions of HTML had no way to change a page's layout without tables, so many Web designers (including us) ignored this advice. But now that HTML 4.0 and the new browsers are able to work with style sheets, you can always get the visual layout effects by using style sheets instead of tables. (We'll show you how in Skill 14.)

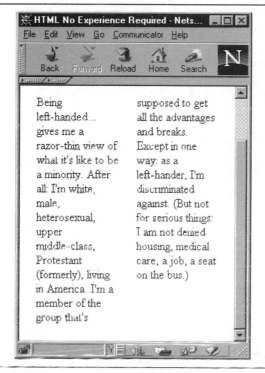

FIGURE 10.4: Navigator, with a reduced window width, renders our example of a two-column table of text in a less-than-desirable way.

Creating a Table with Netscape Composer

Some versions of Netscape Communicator include not only Navigator but also an HTML page-construction tool called Page Composer (often known simply as "Composer"). If you have Composer, switch to it now (Communicator ➤ Page Composer or Ctrl+4). We'll create the foundation for the table in Figure 10.5 and then save the file for future hand-editing.

Follow these steps to create this sample table:

1. From a new document in Composer, choose the Table button on the upper-right toolbar. The New Table Properties dialog box appears.

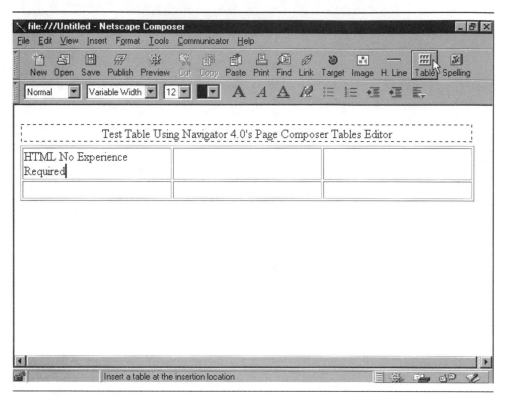

FIGURE 10.5: A simple two-row, three-column table created with the Composer table editor

2. Enter **2** in the Number of Rows box and type a **3** in the Number of Columns box.

3. Click the Apply button at the bottom of the page. In the background, you should be able to see the borders of an empty six-celled table.

4. Check the Include Caption field. Click OK.

5. Type **HTML No Experience Required** into the first cell. (Use the arrow keys to move between cells, or press Tab to move to the next cell.) Type **Test Table Using Navigator 4.0's Page Composer Tables Editor** inside the dotted box at the top of the table.

6. Save your file. Use the File ➤ Save command, navigate to your web directory, and save the file as `table.html`. Enter a sample title such as **Our Sample Table** when prompted for the page's title.

When you close Composer and switch to your regular text editor to retrieve `table.html`, you'll see some sample code similar to this:

```
<HTML>
<HEAD>
    <META HTTP-EQUIV="Content-Type" CONTENT="text/html; charset=
    iso-8859-1">
    <META NAME="Author" CONTENT="Stephen Mack and Janan Platt">
    <META NAME="GENERATOR" CONTENT="Mozilla/4.01 [en] (Win95; I)
    [Netscape]">
    <TTTLE>Our Sample Table</TITLE>
</HEAD>
<BODY>
 
<TABLE BORDER COLS=3 WIDTH="100%">
<CAPTION>Test Table Using Navigator 4.0's Page Composer Tables
Editor</CAPTION>

<TR>
<TD>HTML No Experience Required</TD>

<TD>cell 2</TD>

<TD>cell 3</TD>
</TR>

<TR>
<TD>cell 4</TD>

<TD>cell 5</TD>

<TD>and my cell 6</TD>
</TR>
</TABLE>
 
</BODY>
</HTML>
```

Notice that Composer inserts three <META> tags in the head section automatically. These three <META> tags respectively define the character set, author of the document, and which program was used. The rest of the tags are fairly self-explanatory and contain the simple table model's elements. Composer does a good job of inserting the <TABLE>, <TD>, <TR>, and <CAPTION> tags. It includes the BORDER attribute to the <TABLE> tag along with an attribute we'll see a little later, WIDTH="100%", and an advanced attribute, "COLS=3," which is part of the HTML 4.0 table model that we'll see at the end of this Skill.

However, the non-breaking spaces before and after the table (the   entity tags, as explained in Skill 3) are unnecessary, and it's a little strange that Composer puts them in. That's just another example of why it's important to hand-check HTML created by a page-composing tool.

It's your choice whether you want to use Composer or another page-composing tool to create a table for you. Regardless of how you start off your table, you'll probably end up coding the final parts of it by hand. For that reason, you need to know more details about the simple table model's elements and their attributes, which we'll discuss next.

Using the Simple Table Model's Elements and Attributes

The elements used in tables must all be nested within the beginning <TABLE> and ending </TABLE> tags. First we'll show you the <TABLE> tag and its attributes, then we'll show you all of the uses of the elements that create rows, cells, headings, and captions.

Defining Tables with the Table Element

The <TABLE> start tag and the </TABLE> end tag are both required for every table you create. All of the <TABLE> tag's attributes, however, are optional.

Even with the simple table model, the tables themselves can be very simple or very complex, as we've seen. Here's an example of the HTML code for an unbordered table that has one row (within the <TR> tags), one cell (within the <TD> tags that contain the words "Hello, World!"), and no attributes:

```
<TABLE><TR><TD>Hello, World!</TD></TR></TABLE>
```

If you exclude table attributes, the table's position defaults to left alignment, with no border. So this table would simply look like regular text, as we see in Figure 10.6.

However, you can make this table appear very differently using the table element's attributes.

Using the Table Element's Attributes

By using table attributes in the <TABLE> tags, you can determine the following formatting options for your table:

- Width of the entire table

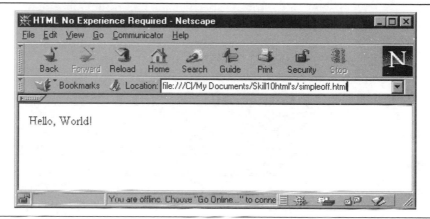

FIGURE 10.6: "Hello, World" inside a single-celled table with no attributes; it looks exactly like normal text.

- Alignment of the entire table
- Cell borders and table border width
- Spacing between each neighboring cell
- Padding within a cell (between the cell's content and the cell border)

Let's take a look at each <TABLE> tag attribute and try out some simple examples of tables created by hand. As you're reading along, you might want to experiment with a few more sample tables yourself. It's easiest to start with a basic table, such as the weather.html example we saw earlier, and try out the different attributes one at a time.

The <TABLE> tag can include any of following attributes, listed in any order: ALIGN, WIDTH, BORDER, CELLSPACING, CELLPADDING, and BGCOLOR.

We'll be discussing the BGCOLOR attribute (used to set a table's background color) a little later, in the "Coloring Parts of the Table with the BGCOLOR Attribute" section, but we'll talk about the rest of the table element's attributes in the next few sections, starting with the ALIGN attribute.

Positioning Tables with the *ALIGN* Attribute

There are three possible uses of the ALIGN attribute (left is the default):

```
<TABLE ALIGN="LEFT">
<TABLE ALIGN="CENTER">
<TABLE ALIGN="RIGHT">
```

The `ALIGN` attribute specifies the horizontal alignment of the table. This means that the table itself is aligned, not the contents of individual cells.

The weather table we saw in Figure 10.1 is shown here, except with the `ALIGN ="RIGHT"` attribute added.

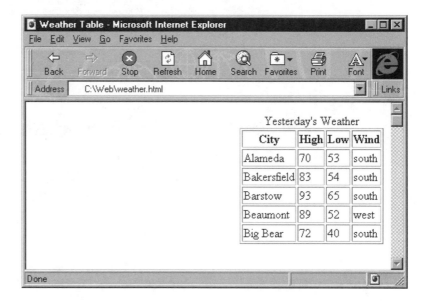

 **WARNING**   Navigator 3 and IE 3 both have a problem with the `ALIGN="CENTER"` attribute— they ignore it. The new versions of these browsers obey the `<TABLE ALIGN="CENTER">` tag. However, since there are still many users of the older versions, if you want your table centered it's best to surround it with a center or division element (see Skill 6).

Sizing Tables with the *WIDTH* Attribute

There are two ways to specify the width of a table using the `WIDTH` attribute:

```
<TABLE WIDTH="PERCENT">
<TABLE WIDTH="NUMBER">
```

If you don't specify the width, then the table will be only as wide as absolutely necessary.

You can force a table to take up more room if you don't like the way it displays. To do this, you either set the width of the table to a percentage of the window's horizontal width (for example, `WIDTH="50%"`), or you set `WIDTH` to a fixed pixel value (with an attribute such as `WIDTH="100"`) to make a table 100 pixels wide.

WARNING Don't leave off the percent sign if you want a table to be a certain percent of your page. There's a *big* difference between 100 *percent* (WIDTH="100%") and 100 *pixels* (WIDTH="100").

Figure 10.7 shows examples of two tables displayed in Navigator. The first table uses the table attribute WIDTH="150%". The second table uses the table attribute WIDTH="500". You can see how the first table is 50 percent larger than the horizontal width of the window (use the horizontal scroll bar to see the rest of the table). Specifying a percentage allows your table and its contents to adjust to fit the browser window whenever it is resized.

Creating Border Lines with the *BORDER* Attribute

There are two ways to use the BORDER attribute to make a table and its cells appear with lines:

```
<TABLE BORDER>
<TABLE BORDER="NUMBER">
```

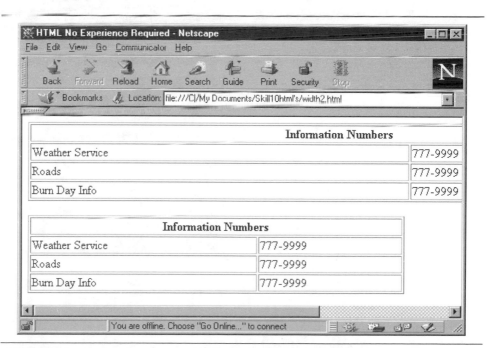

FIGURE 10.7: Navigator shows two examples of tables using the WIDTH attribute.

Earlier, we simply used <TABLE BORDER>. The default border size, if you don't specify a value, is one pixel width. So, using <TABLE BORDER> yields the same results as <TABLE BORDER="1">. Omitting the border tag or using BORDER="0" indicates no border. Really thick borders, such as <TABLE BORDER="5"> or <TABLE BORDER="10"> can produce interesting results.

WARNING   If you're using HTML 3.2, you must specify a value for the border width. Some older, but still popular, browsers get confused by <TABLE BORDER> without a value.

The border size *only* applies to the outside table border. If there is a border for your table, the inner cells will have a cell border that is always only one pixel thick, regardless of the setting of the BORDER attribute. There is no way to set the size of a cell's border yet.

If you specify a border of 50 pixels for the table in the weather.html example (with <TABLE BORDER="50">), you'll see a result similar to Figure 10.8.

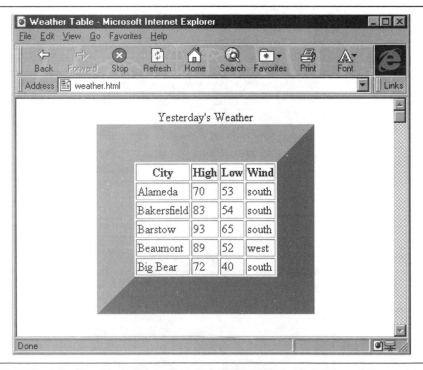

FIGURE 10.8: Your viewers won't be able to overlook this weather table with a 50-pixel border. IE (shown here) and Navigator give a three-dimensional appearance to the border, but not every browser does so.

Spacing Cells with the *CELLSPACING* Attribute

You can create more space in between each cell in your table by using the table element's CELLSPACING attribute, which looks like this:

```
<TABLE CELLSPACING="NUMBER">
```

The amount of cell spacing, indicated in pixels, is the common border width around each cell. For example, specifying CELLSPACING="5" in the <TABLE> tag would space each cell apart by 5 pixels (including 5 pixels between the first cell and the outside border).

The sample HTML fragment below creates a table with a border of 5 pixels and cell spacing of 50 pixels:

```
<TABLE BORDER="5" CELLSPACING="50")">
<TR>
    <TD>Sunday</TD>
    <TD>Monday</TD>
    <TD>Tuesday</TD>
</TR>
<TR>
    <TD>First</TD>
    <TD>Second</TD>
    <TD>Third</TD>
</TR>
</TABLE>
```

Figure 10.9 shows how IE would display this table.

The default value used by Navigator and IE for CELLSPACING is 2. If you specify a CELLSPACING of 0, then table cells will appear right next to each other, making the border appear to be solid instead of hollow.

Making Cells Bigger with the *CELLPADDING* Attribute

Within each cell, the data normally appears right next to the cell's border. You can increase the amount of space in between the cell border and the cell data with the CELLPADDING attribute:

```
<TABLE CELLPADDING="NUMBER">
```

The padding between each cell border and the cell contents is indicated in pixels, for example CELLPADDING="10".

The default value for CELLPADDING used by Navigator and IE is CELLPADDING="1", so you can squeeze each table cell down by specifying CELLPADDING="0" or you can make each cell larger by specifying a larger attribute value for CELLPADDING.

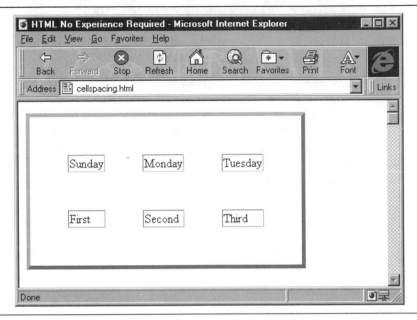

FIGURE 10.9: IE renders a six-celled table with the cell spacing between each cell (and the spacing between each cell and the table's border) equal to 50 pixels.

TIP   It's easy to confuse CELLSPACING and CELLPADDING. Remember, CELLSPACING determines the space *between* each cell, while cell padding determines the space *within* each cell.

Figure 10.10 shows various values for CELLPADDING in several different tables.

Putting All of the Table Element's Attributes Together

The following HTML code includes all of the <TABLE> tag's attributes listed previously and creates a basic table with two side-by-side cells. The left cell includes two lines of the text separated by a line-break. The right cell contains one line of text.

```
<!DOCTYPE HTML PUBLIC "-//W3C//DTD HTML 4.0//EN">
<HTML LANG="EN">
<HEAD>
      <TITLE>Two Competing Philosophies</TITLE>
</HEAD>
<BODY>

<TABLE ALIGN="CENTER" WIDTH="50%" BORDER="5" CELLSPACING="10"
CELLPADDING="5">
```

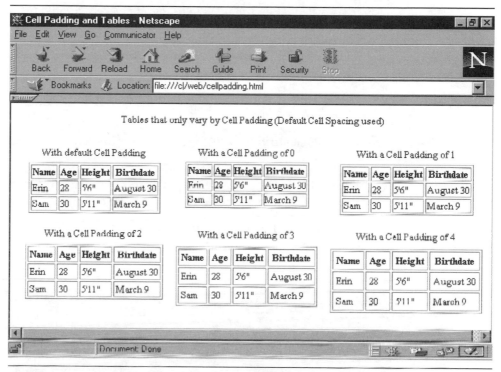

FIGURE 10.10: Six tables that only differ by how CELLPADDING is specified (shown in Navigator)

```
<TR>

<TD>
Make Love<BR>
Not War
</TD>

<TD>
Show Me The Money!
</TD>

</TR>

</TABLE>

</BODY>
</HTML>
```

Figure 10.11 shows the result of this code.

The two-celled table contains the following effects created by attributes:

- The ALIGN attribute makes the table (but not the table's contents) centered on the page. (It would have been better to put <CENTER> and </CENTER> tags around the table instead.)

- The WIDTH attribute makes the table width equal to 50 percent of the window's horizontal width.

- The BORDER attribute calls for cell borders and creates an outer border equal to 5 pixels.

- The CELLSPACING attribute puts 10 pixels of space between the two cells, and also 10 pixels of space between each cell border and the table's outer border.

- The CELLPADDING attribute puts 5 pixels of space between the cell data (the words) and the cell borders.

FIGURE 10.11: A simple two-column, one-row table using five table element attributes

Now that we've learned about the table element's attributes, it's time to learn more about the elements contained within the <TABLE> and </TABLE> tags. We were introduced to the four elements earlier in the Skill, but now we'll learn all about their uses and their attributes.

Using the Simple Table Model's Elements

The following elements are all nested within the <TABLE> and </TABLE> tags. These elements create captions, table rows, table data, and table headings. Their attributes can determine a variety of formatting options for the table and its individual cells.

Describing Tables with the Caption Element

The caption element (which requires both a <CAPTION> start tag and a </CAPTION> end tag) is used to create a caption on top of (the default) or below the table. This positioning is specified with the caption element's ALIGN attribute:

```
<CAPTION ALIGN="TOP">
<CAPTION ALIGN="BOTTOM">
```

As we've seen, the caption is displayed outside of the table's border. A caption will not make a table wider; instead, the contents of the caption element wrap within the available space (which will make the table taller).

 NOTE   HTML 4.0 allows you to specify ALIGN="LEFT" and ALIGN="RIGHT" for the caption, to place it to the left or right of the table. However, the popular browsers do not yet support these caption positions.

Only text and text-level elements are allowed within the caption element. The caption element must appear before the first row of the table, immediately after the <TABLE> tag.

Creating Rows with the Table Row Element

The table row element consists of a <TR> start tag and one or more table data elements or table head elements, optionally followed by a </TR> end tag. Each use of a table row element begins a new table row.

The <TR> tag can include several attributes: BGCOLOR, ALIGN, and VALIGN.

The BGCOLOR attribute determines the background color of the row (see the discussion of this attribute in "Coloring the Table Background with the BGCOLOR Attribute").

Since the ALIGN and VALIGN attributes can also be used with the <TD> and <TH> tags, we'll talk about them separately, after we learn more about the table heading and table data elements.

A row must contain at least one table data element or table heading element. Furthermore, the *only* two things that can legally be placed inside a table row element are table heading and table data elements. (The data itself must be contained in the cell, not the row.) We'll see how to use these cell elements in the next section.

Creating Cells with Cell Elements: Table Headings with *<TH>* and Table Data with *<TD>*

We've already learned that the table data element (<TD>) creates cells and the table heading element (<TH>) creates headings. These two elements are referred to as the *cell elements*. The end tags for both cell elements are optional.

The two cell elements are identical to each other except that a heading cell is specially marked. (We've seen that Navigator and IE display table heading text centered and in bold, but other browsers can use different methods.)

Cell elements can contain many different types of items, including text, images, and other tables. We'll see some examples of what you can put in a cell a little later in this Skill.

Cells may also be empty if you don't want them to contain data. (Simply use a <TD> tag followed immediately by a </TD> tag.) Navigator and IE will not display a cell border around the empty cell. If you want a cell to have a border but still be empty, put a non-breaking space inside the cell (<TD> </TD>).

There are several attributes for cells that can be used in the <TD> and <TH> tags; we'll see them in the next few sections.

Using Attributes with the Simple Table Model's Elements

In this section, we'll see the different attributes that can be used with table row elements and the cell elements. We'll also see how to use the BGCOLOR attribute to set the color of a table, row, or cell.

The attributes for cells include alignment (with ALIGN and VALIGN), background color (with BGCOLOR), the NOWRAP attribute to prevent word wrapping in a cell, and attributes to make a cell span one or more rows or columns (ROWSPAN and COLSPAN). You can also specify the WIDTH and HEIGHT of cells.

Aligning the Contents of Cells and Rows

The ALIGN attribute indicates the default horizontal alignment of cell data. The <TR>, <TD>, and <TH> tags can all include an ALIGN attribute. The possible values for HTML 3.2 are:

```
ALIGN="LEFT"
ALIGN="CENTER"
ALIGN="RIGHT"
```

As you may have noticed from all of the figures so far in this Skill, table data is left-aligned by default.

NOTE HTML 4.0 allows some new horizontal alignment choices. In addition to the three possibilities for HTML 3.2, you can use ALIGN="JUSTIFY". Also, there are attributes for aligning cell data on a particular character. We'll see this type of alignment when we learn about the HTML 4.0 table model later in this Skill.

You can also specify the vertical alignment of cell data with the VALIGN attribute, in the <TR>, <TD>, or <TH> tags. There are four choices for the VALIGN attribute's value:

```
VALIGN="TOP"
VALIGN="MIDDLE"
VALIGN="BOTTOM"
VALIGN="BASELINE"
```

WARNING Don't confuse the MIDDLE and CENTER attribute values. MIDDLE is for vertical alignment, while CENTER is for horizontal alignment.

The default value for the VALIGN attribute is MIDDLE. Since all the cells in a row will always have the same height, the vertical alignment only makes a difference if some cells in a row take up fewer lines than the biggest cell. (For example, look at Figure 10.11 and see how the "Show Me The Money!" line is halfway between the two text lines of its neighboring cell.)

NOTE The VALIGN="BASELINE" value is only subtly different from VALIGN="TOP". The difference is in the exact placement of the bottom of the first line of text in a cell; with the BASELINE value specified, the bottom of the first line of each cell will always line up, even if the font size used in different cells varies. When the TOP value is used, the bottoms of words in different cells won't necessarily line up.

If a cell and its row both include different ALIGN or VALIGN attribute values, then the cell's specified alignment take precedence. You can take advantage of this fact to make an entire row centered, and then make specific cells in that row right-aligned.

Coloring Parts of the Table with the *BGCOLOR* Attribute

You can change the background color of different parts of a table with the BGCOLOR attribute. You can change the background color of an entire table, a single row, or an individual cell, depending on where you specify the BGCOLOR attribute. Here are the possibilities:

```
<TABLE BGCOLOR="color name or color value">
```

```
<TR BGCOLOR="color name or color value">
<TD BGCOLOR="color name or color value">
<TH BGCOLOR="color name or color value">
```

In Skill 3, we learned how you can apply a background color to the body of your entire page by specifying a BGCOLOR attribute in the <BODY> tag. Using the BGCOLOR attribute in a table works exactly the same way.

NOTE   HTML 3.2 and earlier did not allow you to specify the BGCOLOR for a table although it was common practice (since Navigator and IE both understood the attribute as an extension to HTML). HTML 4.0 officially allows the BGCOLOR attribute to be used with some of the different elements of a table.

Although you can't change the color of a caption separately, if you specify the BGCOLOR in the <TABLE> tag, your background color applies to the entire table, including the caption.

See the appendix for a list of the valid color names, and review Skill 3 for a discussion of how color values work.

WARNING   All of the Warnings and Tips about setting colors that we mentioned in Skill 3 apply to coloring tables. In fact, it's somewhat more dangerous to color a table since current browsers don't let users override your table color choices, like they can with document colors. For example, if you specify a color that is hard to read, then people who are color-blind may not be able to read the contents of your table at all.

Disabling Word Wrapping with the *NOWRAP* Attribute

You can disable the default word wrapping of cell text with the NOWRAP attribute in a table cell (specified in either a <TD> tag or a <TH> tag). This means that the cell will be guaranteed to be displayed on one line. Here is how you can use the NOWRAP attribute:

```
<TD NOWRAP>
<TH NOWRAP>
```

Using the NOWRAP attribute is equivalent to changing all of the spaces in a cell to the non-breaking space entity, . (We learned about the non-breaking space in Skill 3.)

 **WARNING** You can make your table cell unnecessarily wide if you don't use the NOWRAP attribute carefully. Since style sheets can control word wrap more effectively, the use of NOWRAP is strongly discouraged by the HTML 4.0 specification.

Spanning Cells with the *COLSPAN* and *ROWSPAN* Attributes

The COLSPAN attribute can be used in a cell to make the cell's contents merge with another cell. You can use COLSPAN in either a table data cell or a table heading cell:

```
<TD COLSPAN="NUMBER">
<TH COLSPAN="NUMBER">
```

To span two columns, for example, specify COLSPAN="2". Naturally, the COLSPAN attribute value defaults to one cell.

The COLSPAN attribute is useful if you have a heading that you want to cover two different columns of data.

Similarly, the ROWSPAN attribute specifies how many rows a cell should take up:

```
<TD ROWSPAN="NUMBER">
<TH ROWSPAN="NUMBER">
```

Here's a fragment of HTML code for a two-row, three-column table, where the first cell is made two rows tall using ROWSPAN:

```
<TABLE>
<TR>
    <TD ROWSPAN="2">Burger Emperor
    <TD>Royale Burger
    <TD>690 calories

<TR>
    <TD>Royale with Cheese</TD>
    <TD>750 calories

</TABLE>
```

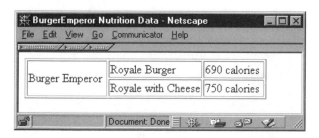

The first cell in the second row ("Royale with Cheese") is automatically moved over to make room for the spanned cell, as shown here.

Setting Cell Widths and Heights

We saw earlier that you can set the width of an entire table using the <TABLE> tag's WIDTH attribute. You can also specify the widths of individual cells in the simple table model.

When a browser displays a table constructed with the simple table model, each column will be as wide as the widest cell in that column. (Since it can take some time for a browser to retrieve the entire table and work out how wide each column should be, tables can sometimes be slow to display.) Each column will have a different width.

 NOTE   In HTML 4.0's table model, you can also specify column widths individually or by groups, using the new column elements that we'll see later in this Skill.

You can specify the minimum width of a column by using the WIDTH attribute on a cell. (Best results are achieved by specifying the widths for all the cells in the first row.) The width is specified in pixels, and the WIDTH attribute can only be used in a table data element or table heading element. For example:

```
<TD WIDTH="NUMBER">
<TH WIDTH="NUMBER">
```

The HEIGHT attribute is a new attribute in HTML 4.0. (However, Navigator and IE supported this attribute as an extension for quite a while.) It's important to remember that both the WIDTH and the HEIGHT attributes are recommmendations: Browser will often override your specified dimensions. The advantage to specifying the WIDTH and HEIGHT is that your tables will display much faster.

Putting Images and Other Elements Inside Cells

As a general rule, a cell can contain almost anything that you can put inside the body section of your document. This means that you can include:

- Text
- Block-level elements (including paragraphs, lists, pre-formatted text, and other tables)
- Text-level elements (including font and phrase elements, anchors, line-breaks, and images)

NOTE   When you use an image within a cell, it's a good idea to specify the height and width of the image (using the techniques we learned in Skill 8) and also specify the width of the image's cell (as we saw in the previous section). This will help your table display as quickly as possible.

Nesting Tables

Including a table inside another table's cell is called *table nesting*. One common use of table nesting is to create two tables that are side by side (normally each table would be in a separate paragraph).

Here's an example of the HTML code for two tables nested inside of another table:

toriamos.html

```
<!DOCTYPE HTML PUBLIC "-//W3C//DTD HTML 4.0//EN">
<TITLE>Tori Amos Music Catalog Numbers</TITLE>
<BODY>
<TABLE BORDER="0" CELLSPACING="20" BGCOLOR="#CCCCCC">
   <CAPTION>Tori Amos Album and Single Catalog Excerpt</CAPTION>
   <TR>
      <TD>
         <TABLE BORDER="10" CELLPADDING="4">
            <CAPTION>Albums</CAPTION>
            <TR><TD><I>Little Earthquakes</I>
               <TD>82358-2
            <TR><TD><I>Under the Pink</I>
               <TD>82567-2
            <TR><TD><I>Boys For Pele</I>
               <TD>82862-2
         </TABLE>
      </TD>

      <TD>
         <TABLE BORDER="10" CELLPADDING="4">
            <CAPTION>Singles</CAPTION>
            <TR><TD>"Crucify"
               <TD>82399-2
            <TR><TD>"God"
               <TD>85687-2
            <TR><TD>"Cornflake Girl"
               <TD>85655-2
            <TR><TD>"Caught A Lite Sneeze"
            <TD>85519-2
         </TABLE>
```

Skill 10

```
        </TD>
      </TR>
    </TABLE>
```

In Figure 10.12, IE renders this HTML code. The outer table contains no direct content of its own, it just specifies some attributes (including the light gray color) and contains a caption and two cells. Each cell contains a nested table. The inner tables have a 10-pixel border and a number of cells each (six for the left table, eight for the right table).

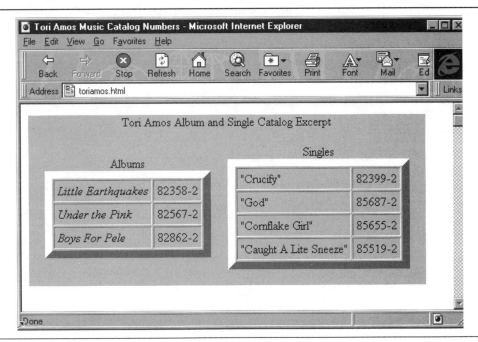

FIGURE 10.12: IE renders two tables nested within another table, allowing the two tables to exist side by side.

 NOTE   An earlier figure, Figure 10.10, was created by nesting six tables inside a larger table.

UNOFFICIAL HTML EXTENSIONS TO THE SIMPLE TABLE MODEL

A few other attributes can be used with the simple table model, but they aren't official HTML 3.2 or HTML 4.0 attributes—they're extensions to HTML. We'll learn more about extensions to HTML in Skill 13, but briefly, you can use a background image in a cell by specifying a BACKGROUND attribute, just like the one used in the body tag.

You can also specify the HEIGHT of an entire table; this will help your tables display more quickly.

Table widths can also be specified using percentage values as well as just pixels (for example, <TD WIDTH="33%">. If you specify a width for a table and then specify the width of a cell, you can request that another table cell be assigned the rest of the available width by using <TD WIDTH="*">.

These are useful extensions, but they are only understood by certain versions of IE and Navigator, so be sure your table does not depend on these attributes.

Once you've understood the simple table model and feel that the four basic table model elements make sense, you're ready to move on to the more complex HTML 4.0 table model.

Using HTML 4.0 Table Elements and Attributes

The HTML 4.0 table model builds on the simple table model and adds a few new elements and attributes to make tables richer and more capable, yet also more complex.

 TIP   If you're not comfortable with the simple table model from the first half of this Skill, you might want to work with it for a while before reading about the HTML 4.0 table model.

The changes in HTML 4.0's table model improve the simple table model in key areas. First, the simple table model resulted in slow display times for a large table since a browser had to read through the entire table before figuring out how wide each column needed to be. Second, it was difficult to import information from spreadsheets because the table models differed so much. Finally, it was impossible to group data by row or by column. To solve these problems, the HTML 4.0 table model introduces new elements for columns and groups of columns as well as groups of rows.

Here are some other changes in HTML 4.0's table model introduced by popular demand:

- The ability to align on a specific character such as "." or ":" (to allow numbers to be decimal aligned)

- More flexibility in specifying table borders, especially borders around individual row and column groups

- Better support for breaking tables across multiple pages when printing

- Setting the alignment of cells by column or by groups of rows

 WARNING   Currently, only IE 4 supports HTML 4.0's new table model.

To see how these changes work, we'll now discuss the HTML 4.0 table model's structure.

Understanding the HTML 4.0 Table Model Structure

In HTML 4.0, tables have the following structure:

- The required table element start tag (<TABLE>) must start a table, followed by an optional caption (with the caption element, same as the simple table model), followed by:

- One or more groups of columns (using the new column group and column elements), followed by:

- One or more *groups* of rows. You can have an optional table head row group, an optional table foot row group, and you must have one or more table body row groups (using the new <THEAD>, <TFOOT>, and <TBODY> tags).

- Each row group must consist of one or more rows (using the table row element, same as in the simple table model).

- Each row must consist of one or more cells (using the table data and table heading elements, same as in the simple table model).

- The required table element end tag (</TABLE>) must finish a table.

The new elements in the HTML 4.0 table model are the column group element (which uses the <COLGROUP> tag), the column element (which uses the <COL> tag), and the three new elements for row groups: table headers (the <THEAD> tag), table bodies (the <TBODY> tag), and table footers (the <TFOOT> tag).

Each table is assumed to have one column group and one table body row group, even if those elements are not explicitly specified with tags. (This is how the HTML 4.0 table model is able to stay backward-compatible with the simple table model.)

Since the new table model is backward-compatible, none of the five new elements are *required* if you want to make an HTML 4.0 table.

We'll see other new attributes and attribute values after we see the new elements for tables. There are five elements to consider; we'll start with the two new column group element, and then see the three new row group elements.

Creating Columns and Groups of Columns

HTML 4.0 tables always have at least one column group. If you don't specify your column group (using a <COLGROUP> tag), then every column in your table is assumed to make up the column group.

You can optionally define one or more groups of columns; each <COLGROUP> tag defines a new group. (There is an optional end tag, </COLGROUP>, but you can always leave it out.) Each column group must have one or more columns; we'll see how to define columns in the next section.

The <COLGROUP> tags are used immediately after the caption element, if there is one. If there's no caption, then the <COLGROUP> tags should be put after the <TABLE> tag.

The advantage to defining column groups is that you can apply attributes to every cell in the column group. For example, if you want to specify that every cell in a group of columns should be centered, you can simply use a <COLGROUP ALIGN="CENTER"> tag. In the simple table model, you would have had to apply the ALIGN attribute to every cell you wanted centered, one at a time.

Another advantage to column groups is that you can specify column widths. This allows browsers to begin displaying your table immediately, because they don't have to read through the entire table to find out how many columns there are and how wide they should be. For long tables, this can make a tremendous difference in the time it takes to display your document (especially for someone viewing your page on a slow Internet connection).

Skill 10

Using the Column Group Element

There are two ways to use the column group element, and you must use one or the other:

- Within the column group, you can use one or more column elements. The column element uses the <COL> tag. Each <COL> tag creates one column. We'll see how to use the column element in the next section.

- You can create a group of columns by using the <COLGROUP> tag with a SPAN attribute. The number of columns in the column group is equal to the attribute value of SPAN. For example, <COLGROUP SPAN="4"> creates a group of four columns. The SPAN attribute's value defaults to one. We'll see some examples of this method in this section.

In addition to the SPAN attribute, the <COLGROUP> tag can contain an ALIGN attribute, a VALIGN attribute, and a WIDTH attribute. The values for these attributes can be the same as the simple table model, or they can have new possibilities discussed later in this Skill, when we introduce the new HTML 4.0 table model's attributes.

Here are some examples of the <COLGROUP> tag. This first example creates a column group with only one column (because the SPAN attribute is not specified). Every cell in the column will be right-aligned:

```
<COLGROUP ALIGN="RIGHT">
```

This example creates a group of five columns, each one centered, top-aligned, and 100 pixels wide:

```
<COLGROUP SPAN="5" VALIGN="TOP" ALIGN="CENTER" WIDTH="100">
```

This example creates two groups of columns. The first group has eight columns which are fully justified, and the second group has four columns, each 50 pixels wide:

```
<COLGROUP SPAN="8" ALIGN="JUSTIFY">
<COLGROUP SPAN="4" WIDTH="50">
```

The WIDTH attribute is an important part of column groups. If you don't specify the width, then the browser will either divide all of the columns equally across the width of the screen, or else the browser will have to read through your entire table to determine the column widths.

We'll see other examples of the use of <COLGROUP> in our HTML 4.0 table examples in the next section and at the end of the Skill.

Using the Column Element

The column element uses a <COL> tag. The column element is empty, so there's no such thing as a </COL> end tag. The column element can only be placed inside a column group element. Each <COL> tag creates a column.

Like <COLGROUP>, you can use attributes in the <COL> tag to apply to each cell in a column. For example, you could begin a table like so:

```
<TABLE>
  <CAPTION>The "Six Columns of Fun" Table</CAPTION>
  <COLGROUP SPAN="2" ALIGN="CENTER" WIDTH="50">
  <COLGROUP ALIGN="RIGHT">
    <COL WIDTH="150">
    <COL WIDTH="100" VALIGN="TOP">
    <COL WIDTH="50">
    <COL WIDTH="*" ALIGN="LEFT">
  </COLGROUP>
```

Assuming you finished this example (with some table rows, cells, and a </TABLE> end tag), the code would define a table with six columns. The first two columns are created by the first <COLGROUP> tag (thanks to the SPAN="2" attribute). Both of these first two columns have their cell data centered and are 50 pixels wide. The next four columns are created by the four <COL> tags inside the second column group element. By default, these four columns will be right-aligned. The third column will be 150 pixels wide. The fourth column will be 100 pixels wide, and its cells are top-aligned. The fifth column is 50 pixels wide.

The sixth column uses a special width value, which means "give this column the rest of the available width"; we'll see more about the asterisk and its use in the new attributes section. The sixth column also specifies left-alignment for its cells, which will override the default of right-alignment set by the second <COLGROUP> tag.

When you complete the rest of the table, make sure not to include more than six cells in a row since you've already specified a maximum of six columns for this table. Browsers might not display any extraneous cells, or will possibly become confused.

Once you define your column groups and columns, you can next include elements that define one or more row groups.

Grouping Rows with Row Group Elements

In the simple table model, the table element simply contains an optional caption and one or more table row elements. In the HTML 4.0 table model, all of the table rows (and the <TR> tags) are contained in row groups. A *row group* is simply one or more table rows that are grouped together, for common formatting or positioning.

There are three types of row groups:

- An optional table head row group: <THEAD> tag (for the top of each page)

- An optional table foot row group: <TFOOT> tag (for the bottom of each page)

- At least one required table body row group: <TBODY> tag (for the bulk of the table's data)

The order of these row groups in a table is important.

- If there's a table head row group, it must occur before the table foot row group and the table body row group.

- If there's a table foot row group, it must occur before the table body row group.

- You can have one or more table body row groups. There's no limit to how many table body row groups your table can contain.

There is not actually much of a difference between these three types of row groups: Table head row groups go on the top of a table (and are repeated on the top of each page if a table is printed out), and table foot row groups go on the bottom of a table (and are repeated on the bottom of each page in a printout). Other than that, the main reason for these three row group sections is to allow you to conveniently assign attributes to groups of rows. The table head row group and table foot row group are completely optional.

If you want just one table body row group (without any table head or table foot row groups), you don't have to specify any row group elements at all—the presence of the table body row group element is assumed if there's not actually a <TBODY> tag in your table. For the required table body element, there's no difference between nesting the table row elements within plain <TBODY> and </TBODY> tags or not.

 NOTE   Remember, if you want a table head row group or table foot row group, then you have to use the <THEAD>, <TFOOT>, and <TBODY> tags (in that order).

It can be useful to specify a table body row group element in your table because (just like with columns and column groups) you can apply an attribute to the <TBODY> tag that will affect an entire group of rows (and the cells contained in those rows). For example:

```
<TABLE>
  <THEAD ALIGN="CENTER">
```

```
<TR>
    <TD>Br. 1<TD>Br. 2<TD>Br. 3<TD>Br. 4<TD>Br. 5<TD>Br. 6<TD>Br. 7
<TBODY ALIGN="RIGHT">
    <TR>
        <TD>1<TD>23<TD>04<TD>23<TD>232<TD>1<TD>91
    <TR>
        <TD>5<TD>39<TD>93<TD>104<TD>2<TD>22<TD>55
</TABLE>
```

This example creates a table with two row groups. The first row group (a table head row group) contains just one row, with all seven cells in that row center aligned. The second row group (a table body row group), contains two rows—and both of those rows will have right-aligned cells. In the simple table model, you would have had to apply the alignment attributes to the <TR> tags. In this example, with only three rows, it would not have been time-consuming to do so; but imagine a table where you want 700 right-aligned rows, and you'll understand the motivation for row groups.

 NOTE   One main idea behind row groups is to allow the display of a very large table within a scrolling frame region. The head section and foot section would stay constant at the top and bottom of the browser window, while the body section in between them would have a separate scroll bar. Alas, browsers have not yet implemented this approach.

 **WARNING**   Only the latest versions of IE and Navigator support the header and footer feature of tables when you're printing them out. Navigator 4.01 and earlier, and IE 4.0 and earlier, may not handle printed head and foot row groups properly.

Using the HTML 4.0 Table Model's Attributes

Several new attributes can be used in HTML 4.0 tables. Some of these attributes can only be used in the <TABLE> tag, while others can be used in a variety of different elements.

NOTE   In addition to these attributes, every element used in tables can take the standard HTML 4.0 attributes, such as the language attributes (LANG and DIR) and the advisory TITLE attribute discussed in Skill 5, the ID, CLASS, and STYLE attributes that will be discussed with style sheets in Skill 14, and the event attributes (ONMOUSEOVER and so on) that we'll see in Skill 15.

The first new attributes we'll see can be used in the <TABLE> tag: the COLS attribute to indicate the number of columns and the FRAME and the RULES attributes to specify borders more precisely.

Then we'll discuss some new values for the ALIGN attribute, see more about the WIDTH attribute, and finally learn about the new AXIS and AXES attributes (which can be used to label cells).

Specifying the Number of Columns with the *COLS* Attribute

Instead of using the column group and column elements we saw earlier, you can specify a COLS attribute in the <TABLE> start tag to indicate how many columns are in your table.

Navigator 4 understands this attribute and will display a table with the indicated number of columns, using a WIDTH="100%" (instead of the default width). You may have noticed earlier in "Creating a Table with Netscape Composer" that Composer automatically inserted this attribute.

IE 4 and earlier, along with earlier versions of Navigator, ignore this attribute. The specification for HTML 4.0 recommends that you use the column group elements to specify columns instead, since you can also use those elements to specify column widths, which speeds up display time.

Using Advanced Borders with the *FRAME* and *RULES* Attributes

The simple table model doesn't give you a lot of flexibility with your table borders: You either have a border or you don't; you can specify the width of the outside table border, but that's all you can specify. HTML 4.0 introduces the FRAME and RULES attributes for the <TABLE> tag to help improve the amount of control you have over borders.

NOTE   IE 3.0 and later versions recognize these FRAME and RULES attributes. Navigator 4.01 and earlier don't recognize them.

The FRAME attribute indicates which sides of the table's outside border are rendered.

WARNING   Don't confuse the FRAME attribute with the HTML frames feature; frames are used to subdivide the browser window with different documents (we'll see how in Skill 11).

There are a few possibilities for the FRAME attribute's value; they're shown in Table 10.2.

TABLE 10.2: Values for the FRAME Attribute and Their Meanings

FRAME Value	Effect
FRAME="ABOVE"	The top side
FRAME="BELOW"	The bottom side
FRAME="BORDER"	All four sides; this is the same as specifying the BORDER attribute
FRAME="BOX"	Same as FRAME="BORDER"
FRAME="HSIDES"	The top and bottom sides ("horizontal side")
FRAME="LHS"	The left-hand side
FRAME="RHS"	The right-hand side
FRAME="VOID"	No sides rendered (the default value)
FRAME="VSIDES"	The left and right sides ("vertical sides")

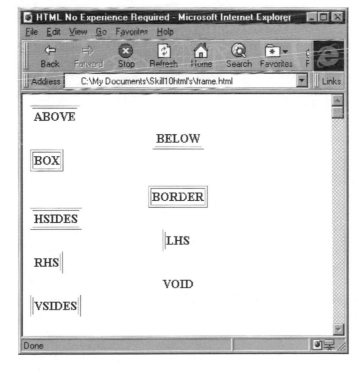

The result of using tables with each of these frame values is shown here using IE.

The FRAMES attribute applies to the outside of a table; alternately, the RULES attribute applies to which cell borders will appear between cells within a table.

There are a few possibilities for the FRAME attribute's value; they're shown in Table 10.3.

TABLE 10.3: Values for the RULES Attribute and Their Meanings

RULES Value	Effect
RULES="NONE"	No cell borders; this is the default value
RULES="GROUPS"	Cell borders will appear between row groups and column groups only
RULES="ROWS"	Rules will appear between rows only
RULES="COLS"	Rules will appear between columns only
RULES="ALL"	Rules will appear between all rows and columns (same as specifying the BORDER attribute)

The result of using tables with each of these frame values (and the BORDER attribute) is shown here, again using IE.

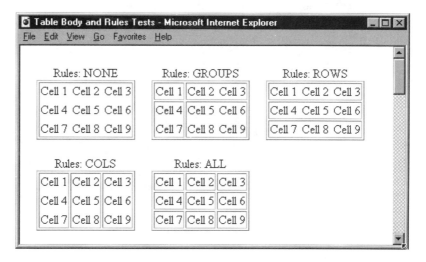

As you can see, the RULES attributes only apply to the inside of the table, not the outside border.

Since the BORDER attribute from the simple model is still available and overlaps with the use of FRAME and RULES, it's helpful to know that setting BORDER="0" is the same as RULES="NONE" and FRAME="VOID". Using BORDER="*NUMBER*" is the same as using FRAME="BORDER" and RULES="ALL". Using the attribute <TABLE BORDER> by itself is the same as using <TABLE BORDER="2" FRAME="BORDER" RULES="ALL">. However, IE 3 and 4 sometimes behave strangely unless the BORDER attribute is present along with the FRAME and RULES attributes.

New Alignment Attributes in HTML 4.0

HTML 4.0 adds ALIGN="JUSTIFY" so that you can use full justification on paragraphs inside table cells. See Skill 6 for a discussion of ALIGN="JUSTIFY".

HTML 4.0 also allows ALIGN="CHAR" to specify that cells should be aligned on a certain character. By default, the character is the decimal separator (which is a period if your document is in English). By specifying ALIGN="CHAR", you could cause a row of numbers to be aligned on their decimal points.

Two other alignment attributes new in HTML 4.0 are CHAR and CHAROFF. Using CHAR="$" along with ALIGN="CHAR" would allow you to justify on the dollar sign. You can specify any character you like.

The CHAROFF attribute specifies an offset (that is, distance) that the character alignment should be shifted.

Unfortunately, character alignment is not yet supported in the popular browsers.

Specifying the *ALIGN* Attribute in Multiple Places

The ALIGN attribute can be used in many different HTML 4.0 table model elements: the individual cells, the row groups, or the column groups.

NOTE   When you use the ALIGN attribute in the <TABLE> tag or the <CAPTION> tag, it applies only to the table itself or the caption itself, not the position of data in any cells.

The order of precedence (from highest to lowest) is the following:

1. An element within a cell's data (for example, <P ALIGN="CENTER">)
2. The cell (in the <TH> or <TD> tag)
3. A column or column group (<COL> and <COLGROUP>)
4. A row or row group (<TR>, <THEAD>, <TFOOT>, and <TBODY>)

For a VALIGN attribute, the order of precedence is:

1. The cell
2. The row or row group
3. The column or column group

In general, horizontal alignment is determined by columns in preference to rows, while it's the reverse for vertical alignment.

New Uses of the *WIDTH* Attribute

We saw earlier how the WIDTH attribute can be used in the column group and column elements to specify the width of a column.

In the simple table model of HTML 3.2, the only way to specify a width for a cell was in pixels. In HTML 4.0's table model, there are two additional ways to specify column widths: using percentages and using relative amounts with an asterisk.

The percentage amount of width is not complicated; simply specify a percentage for each column (for example <COL WIDTH="40%"> to give a column 40 percent of the available table width).

We also saw earlier that you could specify <COL WIDTH= "*"> to mean that a column should be given all of the available space. If two columns both specify the WIDTH="*" attribute, then the amount of space will be divided in half, with an equal amount of width for both columns.

HTML 4.0 allows additional possibilities involving these "relative amounts" of widths. The special value WIDTH="0*" means to use the minimum width possible for the contents of the column. You can also use a number with the asterisk to make a column use more of the available space. The bigger the number, the more proportional space the column will receive. (WIDTH="*" is the same as WIDTH="1*".)

Consider this example:

```
<TABLE>
  <COLGROUP SPAN="2" WIDTH="20">
  <COLGROUP SPAN="3" WIDTH="0*">
  <COLGROUP>
    <COL WIDTH="50">
    <COL WIDTH="20%"
    <COL WIDTH="1*">
    <COL WIDTH="2*">
```

(The rest of the table would follow here, with table row groups, table rows, data, and the </TABLE> tag.)

This example creates nine columns in three column groups. When determining the column widths, a browser will give the first two columns 20 pixels each. The next three columns will have a variable amount of width, the minimum possible to display their data. The sixth column has 50 pixels. The seventh column is given 20 percent of the table's total width (assuming that much is still available). The amount of remaining space for the table is divided into thirds. One-third is given to the eighth column, and two-thirds is given to the ninth column.

It's common to create a table with a total width of 100 percent and then assign a fixed pixel width to the first column. The remaining columns are often divided using relative amounts, with WIDTH="*".

NOTE   It's important to be flexible with table widths. Consider this warning from the HTML 4.0 specification: "A major consideration for the HTML table model is that the author does not control how a user will size a table, what fonts he or she will use, etc. This makes it risky to rely on column widths specified in terms of absolute pixel units. Instead, tables must be able to change sizes dynamically to match the current window size and fonts."

 WARNING   Browsers will disobey your column width whenever they feel it's necessary to override them.

Labeling Cells with *AXIS* and *AXES* Attributes

The other new attributes for HTML 4.0's table model are the AXIS and AXES attributes, which are used in the cell start tags (<TH> and <TD>) to help label the cells. The labels can be used for text-to-speech systems or for a table conversion program that imports or exports table data from a spreadsheet program or database.

The AXIS attribute should define an abbreviated name for a header cell. For example, if a cell falls under a header cell that contains "Last Name" then you might set an AXIS="lastname" attribute in the cell.

The AXES attribute is a comma-separated list of AXIS names, in order to specify the row and column headers that locate this cell.

The following example table creates a list of names and sets the value of the AXIS attribute to be the employee's last name. We also label the cell value as falling under the "Name" column.

```
<TABLE BORDER>
<CAPTION>Sick days used by employees</CAPTION>
<TR>
<TH>Name <TH>Sick Days Used
<TR>
<TD axis="Restrick" axes="Name">J. Restrick <TD>10
<TR>
<TD axis="Selan" axes="Name">P. Selan <TD>5
</TABLE>
```

 **WARNING**   Since these attributes are brand new to HTML 4.0, they are not yet widely supported by conversion programs. Browsers ignore them.

Skill 10

Putting the HTML 4.0 Table Model to Work: A Final Example

We've seen plenty of new features for HTML 4.0's table model; it's time to show a final example that will put it all together.

Here's an example of HTML code that uses the COLGROUP and TBODY elements to render a television schedule with three different column groups and two different row groups. Through the use of the new RULES elements, the cell borders effectively divide the table into different regions.

tvscout.html

```
<!DOCTYPE HTML PUBLIC "-//W3C//DTD HTML 4.0//EN">
<HTML LANG="EN">
<HEAD>
  <TITLE>TV Scout's TV Schedule</TITLE>
</HEAD>
<BODY>

<TABLE BORDER="5" RULES="GROUPS" FRAME="VOID" ALIGN="CENTER">
<CAPTION>Television Schedule for Monday</CAPTION>

<COLGROUP ALIGN="CENTER" WIDTH="75"> <!-- first column: headings -->
<COLGROUP> <!--columns 2 and 3: 6AM -->
  <COL ALIGN="CENTER" WIDTH="75">
  <COL WIDTH="*" ALIGN="LEFT">
<COLGROUP> <!--columns 4 and 5: 7AM -->
  <COL ALIGN="CENTER" WIDTH="75">
  <COL WIDTH="*" ALIGN="LEFT">

<THEAD VALIGN="BOTTOM" ALIGN="CENTER">
  <TR>
    <TH ROWSPAN="3">Channel</TH>
    <TH COLSPAN="4">Time</TH>
  <TR>
    <TH COLSPAN="2">6 AM</TH>
    <TH COLSPAN="2">7 AM</TH>
  <TR>
    <TH>Show</TH>
    <TH>Description</TH>
    <TH>Show</TH>
    <TH>Description</TH>

<TBODY ALIGN="CENTER">
  <TR>
    <TD>3
    <TD>CHiPS
    <TD>Ponch discovers some stolen Pentium processors.
```

```
        <TD>The Munsters
        <TD>Herman creates a family home page. The cops confiscate his
computer.
      <TR>
        <TD>7
        <TD>I Love Lucy
        <TD>Lucy surfs the Web and accidentally charges $50,000 to her VISA.
        <TD>The X-Files
        <TD>Scully and Mulder investigate some alien-infested table cells.
  </TABLE>
  </RODY>
  </HTML>
```

Figure 10.13 shows how this code will be displayed by IE 4 (and Navigator 4 in the background). Since Navigator 4 doesn't understand all of the HTML 4.0 table model, it displays the table a little differently—but at least all of the data is there. IE 3 handles this example more or less faithfully as well.

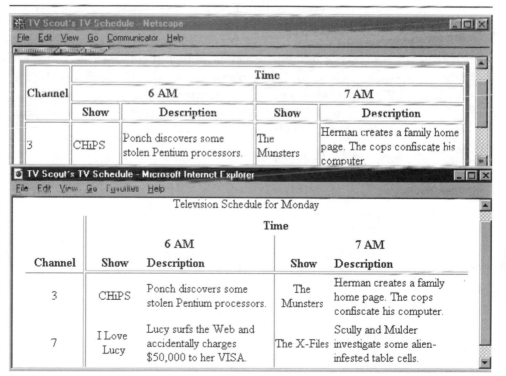

FIGURE 10.13: A table that uses the HTML 4.0 COLGROUP and TBODY elements displayed by IE, with Navigator's window behind IE's window

Using Tables as a Layout Tool

As we mentioned in Skill 1, HTML is not designed to be a page layout language. However, over the past two years, HTML has evolved to include a few layout elements. Style sheets were supposed to handle the rest of an author's layout needs, but style sheets were not in wide use until HTML 4.0 arrived. (We'll cover more about this in Skill 14.) In the meantime, many Web authors developed ways of laying out pages using tables.

Even though this is somewhat abusive of HTML's purpose (since, after all, you are not describing table data), it's a common practice, so we'll show you a few techniques for making tables perform as a layout tool.

Creating Page Margins with Tables

Sometimes it's nice to emphasize a paragraph with white space. The full width of a window can make it difficult to read long passages (we're used to reading magazines or books, which have thinner margins than most Web pages.)

To establish wider margins easily, you can create a simple one-celled table, borders off, and specify a table width or CELLPADDING. This will separate the text from the left and right margins of the page. The following HTML code (shown in Figure 10.14) uses text from "Sometimes You See Africa," the second part of a seven-part novella by Meg Wise-Lawrence (http://www.walrus.com/ ~gibralto/acorn/frag2.html):

```
<TABLE CELLPADDING="30">
<TR>
<TD>
<P>
Jack smiles his magazine smile. "I woke up on the beach this morning--"
He winks at Cal and signals that the bartender mix up some drinks-- the
usual. "When I woke up, I didn't know where I was for a minute. You
know that feeling? All I could see was this bright blue canvas above
me. I thought at first it was this blue blanket-- like a tent or
something. But it was the big empty sky. Beside me is a very beautiful
native woman. She leans over and says: 'Verte desnuda es recordar la
tierra'-- to see you naked is to remember the earth..."
</P>
</TD>
</TR>
</TABLE>
```

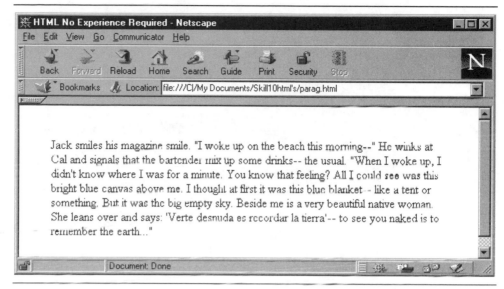

FIGURE 10.14: Navigator renders a one-celled table containing a paragraph of text emphasized with white space.

 TIP   It's easy to use style sheets to get even more control over margins.

Using Tables for Navigation Bars

Another nice way to use a table for page layout is to create a row with several columns that serves as a button navigation system. The most basic navigation bar can simply use a table with text in each cell (see Figure 10.15). (Some bars use an image in each cell.) Let's take a look at the HTML code for a simple text navigation bar:

```
<TABLE BORDER="3" FRAME="VSIDES" ALIGN="CENTER" CELLPADDING="5">
<TR>
    <TD BGCOLOR="AQUA"><A HREF="bodkin.html">Bodkin</A></TD>
    <TD BGCOLOR="AQUA"><A HREF="boliver.html">Boliver</A></TD>
    <TD BGCOLOR="AQUA"><A HREF="snimm.html">Snimm</A></TD>
    <TD BGCOLOR="AQUA"><A HREF="shadrack.html">Shadrack</A></TD>
    <TD BGCOLOR="AQUA"><A HREF="home.html">Home Page</A></TD>
</TR>
</TABLE>
```

Skill 10

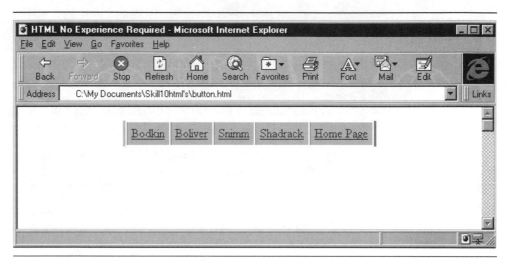

FIGURE 10.15: IE renders a table that serves as a text navigation bar.

As we saw earlier, Web authors sometimes try to create text columns using tables. Others use other tricks with tables (such as forcing a column to be a certain width by using transparent images); but in general, most of these effects can be much better achieved with style sheets. Some Web authors use tables to split a page into two halves, with navigation links on the left half and page content on the right half. In the next Skill we learn about frames, which are a more effective way of dividing the browser's screen into regions.

In this Skill, we've learned that using tables is an extremely powerful way to arrange data. Tables are both complex and useful, so it's worth taking the time to learn them and use them on your pages. Frames, in the next Skill, are also a powerful tool.

Are You Experienced?

Now you can...

- ☑ understand how to organize your data with tables
- ☑ masterfully use all of the table elements attributes
- ☑ use the simple table model
- ☑ create tables by hand or with a page editor
- ☑ use the HTML 4.0 table model
- ☑ change your page layout with tables

Dividing a Window with Frames

- ➔ Understanding the pros and cons of frames
- ➔ Presenting documents in multiple views
- ➔ Providing alternate content
- ➔ Using the frameset and frame elements
- ➔ Creating inline frames

In previous Skills, we've learned how to create HTML documents that take up the entire size of a browser window. But what if you want to create a document that divides the browser window into different parts and show more than one document at once? HTML 4.0 lets you use *frames* to do just that.

This Skill will teach you how to create a *frameset document*, which is a document that defines one or more frames by using the frameset and frame elements. You'll learn how to specify different sizes and properties for the frameset element, and how to target your links from one frame to another.

We'll consider the advantages and disadvantages of frames and also learn how to create alternate content for browsers that can't display frames. You'll also learn how to create inline frames, which is a region of an HTML document that contains another document.

Understanding the Use of Frames

Frames allow multiple HTML documents to be presented as independent windows (or subwindows) within one main browser window. This allows you to present two or more documents at once.

For example, a simple vertical frame is shown in Figure 11.1 as displayed by Netscape Navigator. A frameset document has declared that one HTML file should be shown on the left, and a different HTML file should be shown on the right.

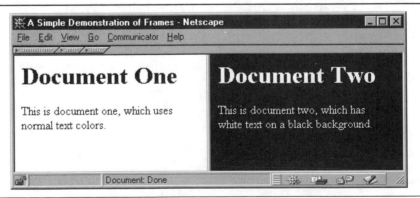

FIGURE 11.1: There are two frames here—one on the left, and one on the right.

In Figure 11.1, we're looking at three different files at once. The frameset document contains the main title element (you can see the title on the title bar) and creates the frames (the two different framed documents shown here). The contents of each frame, Document One and Document Two, are separate files.

Frames can also be horizontal, as shown here using Microsoft Internet Explorer.

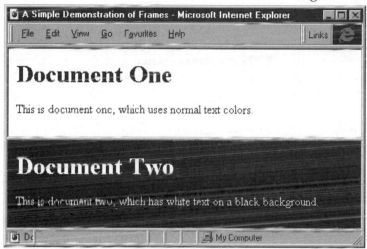

Each frame is resizable and scrolls separately by default (but later in this document we'll see how to change this behavior). You specify the initial size of each frame when you create the frameset document.

While our examples have just shown sample documents so far, you can probably see how frames can be useful. One frame can be used to keep some information static (such as a navigation bar or a site logo), while the other frame can contain the actual content of different sections of a Web site. We'll teach you to how to set up your links so that clicking on an item in one frame can change information in another frame.

You should only use frames if you have a good reason. If you don't feel confident with your Web design skills, adding frames can easily confuse your audience.

HTML 4.0 is the first version of HTML that officially includes frames. Despite the fact that HTML 4.0 has endorsed frames, there are still some limitations to using frames, which we'll see next.

Knowing the Limitations of Frames

Unfortunately, not all browsers support frames. (Browsers that can display frames are called *frames-enabled*, while those that can't are called *non-frames–enabled* browsers.)

Skill 11

Later in this Skill, we'll explain a few ways you can include alternate content for non-frames–enabled browsers by using the noframes element.

NOTE   Some surveys show that as many as 10 percent of surfers don't have frames-enabled browsers. It seems counterproductive to turn away that many potential customers.

Even among frames-enabled browsers like IE and Navigator, the browsers don't always display framed pages the same way. There are even significant differences between the Macintosh and Windows versions of the same browser.

For example, one platform's browser may center each frame so the text and images are easily viewable. But another browser may display a frame so the bottom of a line of text or an image is cut off. These limitations mean that framed pages must be tested thoroughly to ensure that your viewers won't become frustrated.

Since you don't know the size of the window being used to view your site (or if a screen is being used at all), it's hard to decide on the right size for each frame. You run the risk of having each frame be too small to display its content, forcing surfers to constantly scroll to read an entire line or see all of the options.

The user interface can also cause problems when a browser displays a frame page. After all, browsers were originally designed to display only one document at a time. The ability to show more than one document with frames was an afterthought. Because of this, browsers cannot assign a bookmark to an individual frame, only the entire frameset document.

Similarly, it's impossible to link to a particular set of framed pages after you've followed a link. You can only link to a document in an individual frame or to the initial frameset. Also, most browsers cannot print the entire frameset page, and some browsers can only print the first frame in a frameset. Furthermore, navigation using the Back button is confusing for anyone using Navigator version 2, which takes you back to the first non-frames page, ignoring any surfing you did within the framed pages. Even for other browsers, the Back and Forward buttons behave differently when used while viewing a frameset, which can make frame navigation confusing. It's also harder to view the source of framed pages.

The initial frames created by the frameset document will change as soon as someone follows a link (or if a page is updated dynamically, through meta refresh, for example). But the URL listed in the browser's location bar doesn't change, still pointing to the initial frameset and its default frames. The frameset document's source code no longer shows the true content of each frame. This is another source of confusion.

WARNING   Some search engines are also confused by frames and may not be able to index a framed site properly.

Before you give up on frames, however, try out their innovative interface. Some sites are improved with a frame-based design. If you're designing pages for an intranet (where you know what browser is being used by other employees in your organization), or if you make sure to offer both framed and non-framed alternatives, then frames might be right for your Web site. There are definitely some useful advantages to frames for navigation, as we'll see next.

Understanding the Advantages of Frames

Frames allow Web designers to present multiple documents in one window. In one frame, for example, you can present a static list of the sections of your site. This frame becomes a table of contents that's always available. Another frame might contain a logo and help button that won't scroll off the screen. Other frames can contain your site's content. Each frame can be scrolled through separately (allowing you to present and compare two documents side by side, for example), or you can replace the contents of each frame with a different page every time the surfer follows a link.

These navigation features are useful when a Web site contains many levels of pages and viewers might get lost searching through the content to find specific information. We'll learn how to use frames by creating a frameset document now.

Creating Frameset Documents

Frameset documents have a different structure than normal HTML documents. A regular HTML document has a head element and a body element, but a frameset document has a head element and a frameset element.

NOTE   When you create a frameset document, you must use a special DOCTYPE declaration on the first line. (Review our discussion of the DOCTYPE declaration in Skill 5 for more information about the purpose of this syntax.) Here's the DOCTYPE declaration you must use: <!DOCTYPE HTML PUBLIC "-//W3C/DTD HTML 4.0 Frameset//EN">.

As an example, consider the HTML code used in a frameset document to create the two simple frames shown in Figure 11.1:

```
<!DOCTYPE HTML PUBLIC "-//W3C//DTD HTML 4.0 Frameset//EN">
<HTML LANG="EN">
  <HEAD>
    <TITLE>A Simple Demonstration of Frames</TITLE>
  </HEAD>
  <FRAMESET COLS="50%,50%">
```

```
<FRAME SRC="document1.html">
<FRAME SRC="document2.html">
<NOFRAMES>
  <BODY>
    Your browser does not display frames. Please read
    <A HREF="document1.html">Document One</A>
    and
    <A HREF="document2.html">Document Two</A>.
  </BODY>
</NOFRAMES>
</FRAMESET>
</HTML>
```

NOTE   We'll discuss the new frameset element in the next section, and the frame element in a section that follows.

As you can see, the code doesn't contain a normal body element. Instead, the body element is contained in an optional noframes element, which is used for displaying alternate content for non-frames–enabled browsers. So, the noframes element's body section here is only displayed if the browser isn't displaying frames.

We'll learn more about how alternate content works near the end of this Skill, after we learn about the frameset and frame elements and their attributes.

Using the Frameset Element

The frameset element consists of the <FRAMESET> and </FRAMESET> tags, which contain one or more frame elements. The frameset element uses a couple of attributes (ROWS and COLS) that define the layout of the frames.

The frame element uses a SRC attribute to point to the document that you want to display in each frame; we'll discuss it in more detail a little later.

We'll see in an example a little later that you can nest one or more framesets to divide a page in a complex way.

We'll also learn that the frameset element can contain a noframes element if you want to present alternate text for non-frames–enabled browsers.

WARNING   Text and random HTML elements that appear before the frameset document's frameset element may be ignored or may prevent the frameset element from working properly.

This HTML code shows a simple two-column frames page with a navigation bar frame and a main content frame:

```
<!DOCTYPE HTML PUBLIC "-//W3C//DTD HTML 4.0 Frameset//EN">
<HTML LANG="EN">
  <HEAD>
    <TITLE>Frames - Two Columns</TITLE>
  </HEAD>
  <FRAMESET COLS="1*,3*">
    <FRAME SRC="navbar.html">
    <FRAME SRC="main.html">
  </FRAMESET>
</HTML>
```

Figure 11.2 shows the result of this code.

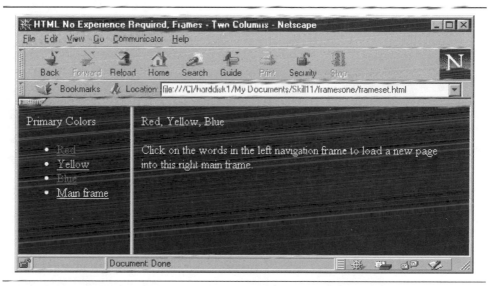

FIGURE 11.2: A two-column frames page with a navigation far frame (left) and a main content frame (right).

 **WARNING** This document would be completely blank for a non-frames–enabled browser. Always include a noframes element to display alternate content. We'll teach you how to use the noframes element near the end of this Skill.

You might notice from this example that instead of using percentages to size the frames, we used the asterisk width notation first introduced in the previous Skill.

Next we'll take a look at the COLS and ROWS attributes. Most frameset elements use one or the other of these attributes. If no columns or rows are defined, you can only have a single frame that takes up the entire page.

 NOTE The frameset element can also take an optional ONLOAD and/or ONUNLOAD attribute, which are used to trigger scripts. See Skill 15 for more details.

Creating Vertical Frames with the *COLS* Attribute

The COLS attribute is used within the frameset element's <FRAMESET> tag to specify the size of two or more vertical frames. Each column's width is a value separated by a comma.

 NOTE The default value for the COLS attribute is 100 percent, so if you don't specify a number of columns by giving each column a width, there will only be one column. If the COLS attribute is not used, each row is set to the entire width of the window.

Each column's width may be an absolute width (a percentage of the window or a number of pixels) or a relative width (a value followed by an asterisk, *) that assigns a part of the window in proportion to the amount requested.

Absolute values have highest priority and are assigned first, and then the remaining space is divided up among the columns with relative values next.

Let's take a look at some uses of the COLS attribute:

```
<FRAMESET COLS="25%,75%">
```

This element specifies two columns. The first column (on the left) takes 25 percent of the browser's window space. The second column (on the right) takes 75 percent of the browser's window space.

 **WARNING** The results are unpredictable if you specify percentages that don't add up to 100 percent, but the browser should adjust your percentages proportionally until they do add up to 100 percent.

This element also specifies two columns:

```
<FRAMESET COLS="1*,3*">
```

The first column takes the relative value of one part of the browser window. The second column takes the relative value of three parts of the browser window. Since there are a total of four parts requested, the first column will get one-quarter (or 25 percent) of the window's width, while the second column will get three-quarters (or 75 percent).

This element creates four columns:

```
<FRAMESET COLS="100, 25%, 2*, 3*>
```

If you have a window that's 500 pixels wide, this element will assign 100 pixels of space to the first column (which could be useful if you'd like to have the first frame contain an image that's exactly 100 pixels wide). The second column will get 25 percent of the total space, or 125 pixels. That leaves 275 pixels for the last two columns. Two-fifths of this remaining space will go to the third column (110 pixels). The last column will receive three-fifths of the remaining space (165 pixels).

 NOTE   Browsers will recalculate the space for each frame every time you resize the browser window.

Creating Horizontal Frames with the *ROWS* Attribute

The ROWS attribute works similarly to the COLS attribute, except for horizontal frames instead of vertical frames.

 NOTE   If you don't specify a ROWS attribute, each column will take up the entire height of the window.

Horizontal frames are created from top to bottom. Like the COLS attribute, you specify the height of frames using either absolute values (percentages or pixels) or relative values.

For example, this frameset

```
<FRAMESET ROWS="34%,33%,33%">
```

would create three horizontal frames, each of them taking up about one-third of the height of the window.

Creating Grids of Frames by Specifying Both Rows and Columns

You can use a frameset that specifies both the ROWS and COLS attributes in order to create a grid of frames.

For example:

```
<FRAMESET COLS="250,*" ROWS="50%,25%,25%">
```

This would create two columns and three rows, for a total of six frames. The frames appear from left to right, and then top to bottom. The first column is 250 pixels wide, while the second column gets the remaining space (* is equivalent to 1*). The first row is half of the window's height, while the second and third row are each a quarter of the window's height. The result is shown here.

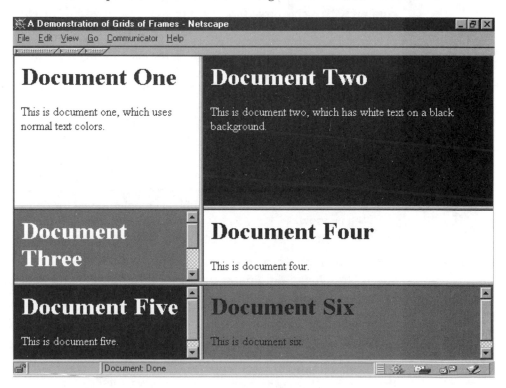

Nesting Framesets to Create Subdivided Frames

By nesting a frameset within another frameset, you can create complex frames. Each nested frameset replaces a single frame with two or more frames.

The following example uses a frameset to create a page with two rows. The lower row is a nested frameset, which splits the row into two equal frame columns, for a total of three frames:

```
<FRAMESET ROWS="25%,75%">
  <FRAME SRC="topnavbar.html">
  <FRAMESET COLS="50%,50%">
    <FRAME SRC="left.html">
    <FRAME SRC="right.html">
  </FRAMESET>
</FRAMESET>
```

Figure 11.3 shows a sample document created with the nested frames.

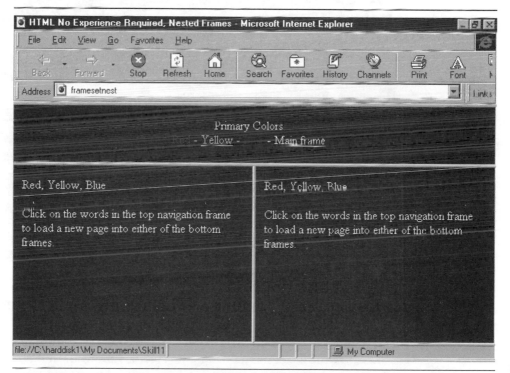

FIGURE 11.3: IE displays a frames page with two rows. The second row is split into two equal frames. This creates a total of three frames.

It's possible to use a series of nested framesets to continuously divide frames into more frames. This takes a lot of trial and error, however. It's possible to make documents with even more frames, like the nine frames we see on the following page.

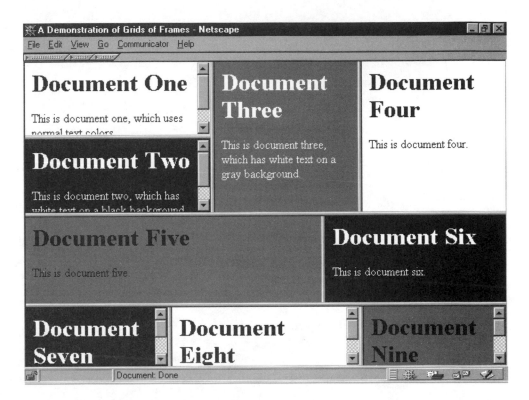

One way to make complex frames is to have more than one frameset document. If one of your frames contains a frameset document, then that frame will be subdivided into smaller frame windows. The first frameset document is called the *parent frameset* and the other embedded frameset documents are called *child frameset*.

Using the *BORDERCOLOR* Attribute

One other attribute is often used with the frameset element: The BORDERCOLOR attribute can set the color of a frame's border (instead of the default gray).

For example, <FRAMESET BORDERCOLOR="#FF0000"> sets the frame's border to red.

This attribute is not mentioned in the HTML 4.0 specifications—instead it's an extension to HTML that happens to be recognized by IE and Navigator.

All of the frameset document's frame border colors are universally set with this attribute value. (Border colors can also be set individually with the frame element's BORDERCOLOR attribute, another extension to HTML, as we'll see a little later.)

 **WARNING**   Be careful with this attribute since it produces invalid HTML that can't be easily checked for errors by a validation program. (Validation tools are discussed in Skill 17.) We'll see more about extensions to HTML and their drawbacks in Skill 13. Now that we've seen how the frameset element works, we'll learn about the frame element and its attributes.

Putting Documents Inside Frames with the Frame Element

The frame element's <FRAME> tag defines the contents of a single frame. The most important attribute for the frame element is the SRC attribute, which specifies the URL of the document inside the frame.

The frame contents must be located in a separate file. For example <FRAME SRC= "document1.html"> specifies that the document to be displayed inside this frame will be document1.html. You can use relative or absolute URLs. You don't have to link to HTML files; you can put any kind of file in a frame, including images and multimedia files.

You can use several other attributes with the frame element in order to change the frame's appearance and the way it works; we'll learn about them now.

Adding Frame Borders with the *FRAMEBORDER* Attribute

The FRAMEBORDER attribute determines if there is a separator border between the frame and its neighboring frames. The default behavior is for each frame to have a gray border. By specifying <FRAME SRC="document.html" FRAMEBORDER="0">, you can remove the border.

You can specify the FRAMEBORDER="1" to mean that a border should be visible, but this is the default value.

You must specify FRAMEBORDER="0" for both neighboring frames in order to remove a frame border. If one of the two frame elements doesn't include this attribute, then the border will appear.

The HTML code for one frame with borders on and one frame with no borders follows:

```
<FRAMESET ROWS="25%,75%">
    <FRAME FRAMEBORDER="0" SRC="topnavbar.html">
    <FRAMESET COLS="50%,50%">
```

Skill 11

```
         <FRAME FRAMEBORDER="0" SRC="left.html">
         <FRAME FRAMEBORDER="1" SRC="right.html">
      </FRAMESET>
   </FRAMESET>
</HTML>
```

NOTE   Navigator 3 and 4 as well as IE 4 treat the FRAMEBORDER attribute a little differently: FRAMEBORDER="YES" means to use a three-dimensional border, while FRAMEBORDER="NO" means a plain border. You can use a BORDER attribute in the frameset to set the frame's size (the default is BORDER="5" for a five-pixel frame border). These are all non-standard extensions to HTML.

Coloring Individual Frame Borders with the *BORDERCOLOR* Attribute

While we're talking about frame borders, you can use an HTML extension to specify the color of a frame's border. The latest versions of IE and Navigator recognize the BORDERCOLOR attribute, which you can use to color individual frame borders.

For example, <FRAME SRC="document.html" BORDERCOLOR="YELLOW"> would create a frame with a yellow border.

NOTE   As mentioned earlier, all of the frame border colors can be set at once with the BORDERCOLOR attribute in the frameset element.

Specifying Frame Margins with the *MARGINHEIGHT* and *MARGINWIDTH* Attributes

Two attributes can be used to set the margins of a frame. (Since regular documents can't have margins without style sheets, this is one advantage to using frames.)

The MARGINHEIGHT attribute determines the number of pixels (which must be greater than one pixel) between the frame's content and the frame's top and bottom edges.

Similarly, the MARGINWIDTH attribute determines the number of pixels between the frame's content and the frame's left and right edges.

For example:

```
<FRAME SRC="document2.html" MARGINHEIGHT="100" MARGINWIDTH="200">
```

This frame element would create a frame filled by the document2.html file, which would be displayed with a top and bottom margin of 100 pixels, and a left and right margin of 200 pixels.

Preventing Frame Sizing with the *NORESIZE* Attribute

Normally, each frame is resizable. By pointing your mouse at a frame border, you can drag the frame border to make a frame larger or smaller.

Sometimes, you will want to prevent surfers from being able to resize your frames. The NORESIZE attribute accomplishes this goal. For example, <FRAME SRC="document .html" NORESIZE> means that this frame window is not resizable.

 **WARNING**   Don't use the NORESIZE attribute without a good reason; surfers will have different screen resolutions and font sizes, and they will often need to be able to resize a frame to see all of its contents.

Removing Scroll Bars with the *SCROLLING* Attribute

Each frame will be displayed with a vertical or horizontal scroll bar (or both) if the contents of the frame won't all fit in the frame's current dimensions.

By default, these scroll bars only appear when necessary. Alternately, you can choose to always have the scroll bars appear or force them never to appear. These examples show the three possibilities:

```
<FRAME SRC="document.html" SCROLLING-"YES">
<FRAME SRC="document.html" SCROLLING-"NO">
<FRAME SRC="document.html" SCROLLING="AUTO">
```

The SCROLLING="AUTO" value is the default behavior.

By including a SCROLLING="YES" attribute, the frame's window will always include a scroll bar. Similarly, SCROLLING="NO" prevents a scroll bar from appearing, even when it's necessary to scroll to see a frame's contents.

 **WARNING**   You might already have predicted that we'd warn against using SCROLLING="NO" unless you have some compelling reason. Since you don't know what size window a surfer will have or what size fonts they use, there's really no way you can tell whether scrolling will be required to display a frame's entire contents.

Skill 11

Naming Frames for Targeting with the *NAME* Attribute

The NAME attribute sets a name for the frame. This name can then be used in links located in other frames to target the named frame.

For example, suppose we create a frameset document with two frames. We can name the second frame so that the links in the first frame will target it. Consider:

```
<!DOCTYPE HTML PUBLIC "-//W3C//DTD HTML 4.0 Frameset//EN">
<HTML LANG="EN">
<HEAD>
    <TITLE>Named Frames</TITLE>
</HEAD>
<FRAMESET COLS="1*,3*">
    <FRAME SRC="navbar.html">
    <FRAME SRC="main.html" NAME="main">
</FRAMESET>
```

The first frame, on the left, is static. It contains a document called navbar.html. Since this frame has not been named, links in other frames can't target this frame. The second frame, on the right, is given the name main.

 NOTE   Frame names must start with an alphanumeric character. It's safest to always use lowercase frame names since some browsers are confused by uppercase names. Also, frame names are case-sensitive in IE.

We'll see why naming a frame with the NAME attribute is useful in the next section.

Using Targeted Links

We first learned how to target links in Skill 7, where we used the TARGET attribute to cause links to create a new window. In this section, we'll learn how to have links target a particular frame.

We'll also learn about the use of the base element to set a default target, see a concrete example of how frames can be useful for large files, and then see how to use four special pre-defined target names.

Targeting Frames

Once we've named a frame, we can create links in one frame that target the named frame by using the TARGET attribute.

For this example, we'll use the HTML example we saw in the previous section about the NAME attribute (which created two frames, a navigation bar on the left and a document named main on the right).

We can create links in the left frame's document (navbar.html) that target the right frame. For example, any links in the navbar.html document can use the anchor element's TARGET attribute (as described in Skill 7) to cause the contents of the frame on the right to change whenever a link is followed.

A sample link in navbar.html might look like this:

```
Read <A HREF="page2.html" TARGET="main">page two</A> for more
information.
```

When anyone clicks on page two, the frame on the right will no longer display main.html, but will show page2.html instead. The navbar.html file will still be displayed in the left frame.

 NOTE   If most of the links in your document use the same target, you can set the default target by using a base element, as we'll explain in the next section.

Consider the frameset document shown in Figure 11.2. When the word Red in the left frame is clicked on, the page that was displayed on the right will change. Figure 11.4 shows how the left frame remains static but the right frame is replaced.

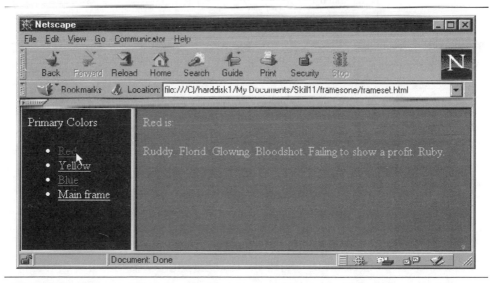

FIGURE 11.4: When the Red link in the left frame is clicked, the initial document in the right frame named main.html is replaced with the linked document named red.html.

The HTML code for navbar.html, contained in the first frame, includes the HTML code with targeted links to the frame named main:

```
<!DOCTYPE HTML PUBLIC "-//W3C//DTD HTML 4.0 Frameset//EN">
<HTML LANG="EN">
<HEAD>
    <TITLE>Frames Navigation Bar</TITLE>
</HEAD>
<BODY BGCOLOR="#000000" TEXT="#FFFFFF">
Primary Colors
<UL>
<LI><A HREF="red.html" TARGET="main">Red</A>
<LI><A HREF="yellow.html" TARGET="main">Yellow</A>
<LI><A HREF="blue.html" TARGET="main">Blue</A>
</UL>
</BODY>
</HTML>
```

Clicking on any of the four targeted links in navbar.html replaces the current document in the right frame, named main, with the linked page.

It's essential to use these targeted links if you want to keep a navigation element in one frame while having another frame's content change. If you don't specify a TARGET attribute in the link, then the current frame is replaced instead of a different frame.

 NOTE   Area elements and anchors in image map elements (Skill 8) and form elements (Skill 12) can also use the TARGET attribute to target different frames.

If you use a targeted link such as <A HREF="page2.html" TARGET="foo"> and there is no frame named foo, then the browser will create a new, full-sized window.

Using the Base Element to Set a Default Target

Sometimes a page will contain many links that you want targeted to a different frame. It's inconvenient to use the TARGET="*framename*" attribute in each link. Fortunately, we can use the base element (first introduced in Skill 5) to set the default target frame.

For example, putting a <BASE TARGET="main"> tag in the head of a document would make every link in that document change the contents of the frame named main.

To make this use clear, we'll create a longer example: You could create one frame with a long page full of alphabetized entries, and another frame with 26 links (one for each letter) that jump the first frame to the appropriate spot in the alphabet.

To do this, you'll need three HTML files: the frameset document (which we'll call `alphadict.html`), the first frame's long list of alphabetized entries (which we'll call `dictionary.html`), and the second frame's alphabet navigation page (`alphabet.html`).

The contents of `alphadict.html` might look like this:

```
<!DOCTYPE HTML PUBLIC "-//W3C//DTD HTML 4.0 Frameset//EN">
<HTML LANG="EN">
<HEAD>
    <TITLE>The Modern Hacker's Dictionary</TITLE>
</HEAD>
<FRAMESET ROWS="80%,20%">
    <FRAME SRC="dictionary.html" NAME="dictionary">
    <FRAME SRC="alphabet.html">
</FRAMESET>
</HTML>
```

This will create the two frames (one on top of the other), with the dictionary in the top frame (taking up 80 percent of the screen), and the alphabet links in the bottom frame (in the remaining 20 percent of the window's height). The top frame is given the name `dictionary` so that it can be targeted. (We could have used any name.)

The `dictionary.html` file will have to have 26 named anchors in the appropriate spots, such as:

```
<H2><A NAME="q">The Q Section</A></H2>
<H2><A NAME="r">The R Section</A></H2>
```

TIP   See Skill 7 for a thorough discussion of named anchors and partial URLs.

The `alphabet.html` document would have to have 26 targeted links that used partial URLs and a TARGET attribute, such as:

```
<A HREF="dictionary.html#q" TARGET="dictionary">Q</A>
<A HREF="dictionary.html#r" TARGET="dictionary">R</A>
```

Instead of using the TARGET attribute 26 times, you could simply create a head section in `alphabet.html` that includes a targeted <BASE> tag, and then you can leave out the TARGET attribute from the 26 links. The resulting `alphabet.html` file is shown here:

```
<!DOCTYPE HTML PUBLIC "-//W3C//DTD HTML 4.0//EN">
<HTML LANG="EN">
<HEAD>
    <TITLE>Index To The Modern Hacker's Dictionary</TITLE>
    <BASE TARGET="dictionary">
</HEAD>
<BODY>
<CENTER><BIG>
<A HREF="dictionary.html#a">A</A>
<A HREF="dictionary.html#b">B</A>
[The other twenty-four letters follow...]
</BIG></CENTER>
</BODY>
</HTML>
```

Here's how this setup might appear.

You can make this example more complex, if you like, by adding additional frames. Most agree that the advantages of being able to instantly jump from letter to letter while keeping the alphabet links constantly visible make this a handy use of frames. In this example, both `alphabet.html` and `dictionary.html` are given title elements, like any HTML document. However, Navigator and IE don't display the two frame's titles anywhere—only the frameset document's title is displayed in the title bar. However, the title element is still required for the frame documents, and the title will be displayed if the frame document ever becomes unframed.

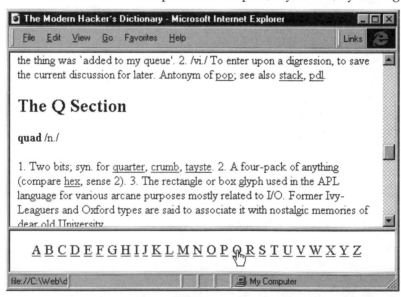

Using Special Target Names

We've seen how you can specify a TARGET attribute to change the contents of a particular frame, if that frame was named with the frame element's NAME attribute.

There are also four pre-defined names that can be targeted by an anchor. These four targets have special meanings. They all start with an underscore (_), which is normally an illegal character for a target name.

The _blank Target

By specifying TARGET="_blank", you can cause the document to be loaded into a new window.

For example:

```
<A HREF="document.html" TARGET="_blank">My document</A>
```

Clicking on <u>My document</u> would cause a new browser window to appear, containing the document.html file.

The _parent Target

The _parent target name refers to the parent frameset. Most of the time you won't have multiple framesets in separate files (so you won't have parent framesets or child framesets), but in the rare cases where you do have embedded framesets, you may need to refer to the parent frameset without using the frame's name.

If the current frame is part of a child frameset (that is, it is part of an embedded frameset in a separate file), then you can use the _parent target to dismantle the child frameset and target the frame from the initial frameset (before it was subdivided). One example of a site that makes use of _parent is Mark Napier's Potatoland (http://www.potatoland.org/) in the "Stolen" section.

For example:

```
<A HREF="document.html" TARGET="_parent">My document</A>
```

Clicking on <u>My document</u> in this case would cause the document.html file to appear in the parent frameset, if the parent had been defined in another file.

Skill 11

NOTE   If there is no parent, the document loads into the current frame.

The *_self* Target

The _self target loads the document into the current frame (the same frame as the HTML code that contains the anchor). Since this is the default behavior, the only reason that _self is useful is if you've used a base element to set a default target and want to make an exception.

For example, suppose you've previously declared <BASE TARGET="mary"> to have links target a frame named "mary" by default. You can use:

```
<A HREF="document.html" TARGET="_self">My document</A>
```

When someone clicks on <u>My document</u>, the file document.html will replace the current frame instead of the mary frame.

The *_top* Target

The most useful of the four special target names is _top, which removes frames altogether.

For example:

```
<A HREF="document.html" TARGET="_top">My document</A>
```

Clicking on <u>My document</u> would cancel all of the frames and replace the entire frameset with the document.html file.

 NOTE   You can use the browser's Back button to return to the frameset.

You can use the base element with any of the four special target names. For example, using <BASE TARGET="_top"> in a document's head section would cause any link on that page to cancel frames (thus "unframing" the page).

We'll see more about unframing documents a little later in this Skill.

Providing Alternate Content with the Noframes Element

The specification for HTML 4.0 strongly recommends that each frameset document include an alternate method of accessing the framed information.

Anyone using a non-frames–enabled browser will see a completely blank page if they view a frameset document that doesn't include alternate content. Therefore, it's imperative to use the noframes element to explain what's going on and allow people to access the content of your Web site.

The noframes element consists of the <NOFRAMES> and </NOFRAMES> tags, which contain the alternate content. The alternate content is *only* displayed by a browser that is not displaying frames.

Here's an example of how to include the noframes element in a frameset document:

```
<!DOCTYPE HTML PUBLIC "-//W3C//DTD HTML 4.0 Frameset//EN">
<HTML LANG="EN">
<HEAD>
    <TITLE>NOFRAMES Alternative Text Example</TITLE>
</HEAD>
<FRAMESET COLS="50%,50%">
    <FRAME SRC="document1.html">
    <FRAME SRC="document2.html">
    <NOFRAMES>
        <BODY>
            If you see this text, your browser does not support frames
            or is not configured to display frames. Please go to the
            <A HREF="noframes.html">alternate version</A>
            of this Web page.
        </BODY>
    </NOFRAMES>
</FRAMESET>
</HTML>
```

In Figure 11.5, we see how the non-frames–enabled browser Mosaic (a once-popular browser that inspired the design of both Navigator and IE) shows this page.

TIP   Some sites create two versions of their pages, one for frame-enabled browsers and one for non-frame–enabled browsers. However, this is a lot of work, and it's difficult to maintain two sets of pages accurately.

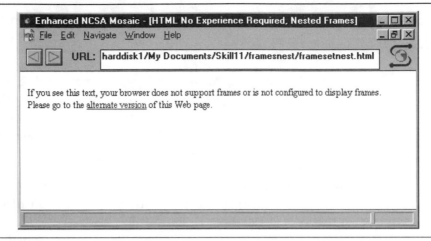

FIGURE 11.5: The 1994 version of Enhanced NCSA Mosaic (a browser that does not support frames) displays the alternate content.

HTML 4.0 allows you to include a noframes element in regular documents. The contents of the noframes element will be shown only if the document is not being displayed as part of a frameset. Unfortunately, this use of the noframes is not yet supported by any browser—so the contents of the noframes element will be displayed regardless.

NOTE In our example of the noframe element, we included the body element's <BODY> and </BODY> tags inside the noframe element, but these tags are not required here. Some browsers like to see it, however.

Many Web authors only include a brief "Get Navigator or IE" statement in the noframes element (sometimes they'll link to Netscape's or Microsoft's home page). But most surfers are aware that they need a frames-enabled browser to see frames, and even know where they can get such a browser—often, they've disabled frames by choice or are using a computer system where they can't possibly install a frames-enabled browser. No text-to-speech browsers can handle frames properly. So for any of these users, it's not polite to tell them to update their browser. Instead, you should link to the individual documents or an alternate document.

Using the Inline Frame Element to Create Inline Frames

The inline frame element is a brand new part of the HTML 4.0 specification that can show a separate document as part of a page. The inline frame element is related to frames, but they're actually two different things. So far, only IE 3 and 4 recognize this element.

The inline frame element uses the <IFRAME> and </IFRAME> tags, along with the same attributes used in the frame element, along with optional WIDTH, HEIGHT, and ALIGN attributes.

Inline frames can be included within a block of text and behave similarly to the object element discussed in Skill 9. Like the object element, the inline frame element should contain alternate text that is displayed only if the inline frame element can't be displayed.

The following HTML code inserts three inline frames centered within the document after the words "Primary Colors."

iframe1.html

```
<!DOCTYPE HTML PUBLIC "-//W3C//DTD HTML 4.0//EN">
<HTML LANG="EN">
<HEAD>
    <TITLE>First Inline Frames Example</TITLE>
</HEAD>
<BODY BGCOLOR="#000000" TEXT="#FFFFFF">

<P>
Primary Colors

<CENTER>

<IFRAME SRC="red.html" MARGINHEIGHT="0" FRAMEBORDER="10" WIDTH="300"
HEIGHT="25">
<P>The <A HREF="red.html">red</A> file is available.
</IFRAME>

<IFRAME SRC="yellow.html" MARGINHEIGHT="0" FRAMEBORDER="10" WIDTH="300"
HEIGHT="25">
<P>The <A HREF="yellow.html">yellow</A> file is available.
</IFRAME>

<IFRAME SRC="blue.html" MARGINHEIGHT="0" FRAMEBORDER="10" WIDTH="300"
HEIGHT="25">
<P>The <A HREF="blue.html">blue</A> file is available.
</IFRAME>
```

Skill 11

```
</CENTER>
</BODY>
</HTML>
```

Each inline frame defaults to automatic scrolling, just like regular frames. Figure 11.6 shows how these three inline frames would be displayed by IE.

> **NOTE** Just like with other frames, you'll have to create each of the files displayed by the inline frame element ahead of time. Figure 11.6 shows the contents of four different files.

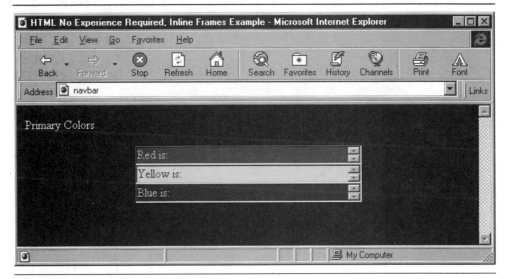

FIGURE 11.6: IE displays three centered inline frames.

On the other hand, Navigator, which doesn't recognize the iframe element, will show only the contents of each iframe element, as shown here.

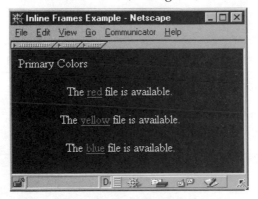

In Skill 9, we mentioned that the object element can be used to include an HTML file within another HTML file. The only difference between using an object element and an iframe element is that you can use the NAME attribute with an inline frame to enable you to create links that target the inline frame.

iframe2.html

```
<!DOCTYPE HTML PUBLIC "-//W3C//DTD HTML 4.0//EN">
<HTML LANG="EN">
<HEAD>
   <TITLE>Second Inline Frames Example</TITLE>
</HEAD>
<BODY

<P>
Primary Colors - pick one:
<A HREF="yellow.html" TARGET="centerframe"><FONT
COLOR="YELLOW">yellow</FONT></A>,
<A HREF="red.html" TARGET="centerframe"><FONT
COLOR="RED">red</FONT></A>, or
<A HREF="blue.html" TARGET="centerframe"><FONT
COLOR="BLUE">blue</FONT></A>.
</P>

<CENTER>
<IFRAME WIDTH="300" HEIGHT="75" NAME="centerframe">
<P>Choose a color from the list above.
</IFRAME>
</CENTER>

</BODY>
</HTML>
```

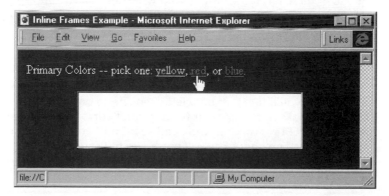

This example creates an empty inline frame in the center of the document, named `centerframe`. (We could have given it any legal name.) By clicking on any of the three links, the inline frame will display the appropriate document. The inline frame is initially empty, as shown here.

Skill 11

TIP   Since neither the iframe element nor the object element are widely supported yet, it might be better to just use frames to display more than one file at once.

Unframing Pages

It's easy to create a set of framed documents, but not so easy to remove them. Since the default action for a link is to replace only the current frame, a link to an external site might leave one or more of your frames still onscreen. That external site might have frames of its own, which will get added to your frames. Pretty soon the screen is cluttered with all sorts of frames containing menus and logos.

 **WARNING**   Another problem is that if one of the framed pages links to the frameset document without using a special target name, then the frameset will be repeated on screen—leaving you with two duplicate navigation bars displayed, for example.

To prevent this from happening, it's important to unframe pages for external links or internal links to frameset documents.

The easiest way to unframe pages is to use either the _blank or _top special targets presented earlier. If you're careful to always include a TARGET attribute with one of these targets for all of your external links (or internal links to pages that you want to display full-screen), then you'll never create a problem of too many frames onscreen. For example:

```
<A HREF="document.html" TARGET="_top"> see this document unframed.</A>
```

 TIP   Sometimes you'll find that people are linking to one of your pages as part of a frame. To make sure that their frames don't surround your page for long, put a `<BASE TARGET="_top">` in the head section of your document. The next link that's followed on your page will be shown full-screen.

 NOTE   To see three creative uses of frame on the Web, try Scot Hacker's Spong Classic (http://www.birdhouse.org/images/scot/spong/), Komninos: Poetry Juke Box (http://student.uq.edu.au/~s271502/jukebox.html), and Jef Morlan's Netage #2 (http://www.sos.net/home/jef/20_conta.html).

HOW TO UNFRAME A PAGE IN A BROWSER

Sometimes when you're surfing you'll want to unframe the pages that you see onscreen.

In order to view each separate document in a frames page, Navigator can open new browser windows for each document within a frames page.

This way, you can view each document "unframed," which will let you print or view source normally. To unframe a page in Navigator 4:

1. Click inside the frame you want to unframe to select it.

2. Click on the right mouse button (or hold the mouse button down if you're using a Macintosh) to make the context menu appear.

3. From the context menu, choose the Open Frame in New Window command.

Navigator will open a new window for that framed document.

IE doesn't have an easy way for you to unframe an individual page, although you can use a similar technique to open each link in a new window.

IE 4 does make it easy to print each separate frame document. In IE 4, click inside the frame you want to print, then choose the Print command. You'll have three options: as laid out on screen, only the selected frame, or all frames individually.

Are You Experienced?

Now you can...

☑ use frames to design Web pages with multiple views

☑ understand how to use all of the frames elements and attributes

☑ create frames pages that contain alternate, noframes content

☑ use targeted links and inline frames

Skill 11

Building Interactivity with Forms

- ➔ **Understanding forms and form-processing options**
- ➔ **Using the form element and its attributes**
- ➔ **Creating form controls**
- ➔ **Using CGI**
- ➔ **Considering security issues**

One of the interesting features of the Web is the interactive nature of Web pages—the ability to follow links to learn more about one aspect of a page or to skip past a section that's not interesting. Pages can also be interactive if they allow the surfer to contribute information or comments on a page (via a feedback form or sign-up sheet) or control the actions of a program (for example, indicating the terms you want to search for when you use a search engine). For both of these, Web pages make use of an HTML feature called forms.

In this Skill, we'll learn about the elements and attributes used to create a form. There are many different form controls, and we'll see examples of each control and how they're used.

We'll also learn a little bit about the separate programs that process forms and tabulate data, update databases or pages, or send automatic responses.

Forms are one of the most advanced features of HTML; be comfortable with the basics before tackling this Skill.

Understanding Forms

As a Web author, you may want to receive feedback, create mailing lists, get the information you need to complete a commercial transaction, or send information from a Web page to a custom program. For all these tasks, or to get any kind of information from a surfer, you need to use a form.

A *form* is simply a collection of fields of information. These fields of information come in many different varieties, such as text boxes, radio buttons, pull-down menus, and other elements (many of which may be familiar to you from the dialog boxes used in graphical user interfaces).

The more general term for a field in a form is a *control*. In this Skill we'll learn how to create all of the different types of controls by using the rich set of HTML elements and attributes.

However, the HTML you use to create a form on a Web page is only half of the battle. Think of creating a paper form: It's one thing to design a form with a word processor, but it's another to distribute the form, have it filled out, and then collect and summarize the results.

Similarly, HTML is only responsible for a few specific roles with forms. The rest of the job is handled by the browser, the Web server, and a custom program that you must ensure is in place and working correctly. Here's how the tasks are broken down:

- HTML elements are used within the form element to create and name the form controls, format their appearance and behavior, and determine default values (if any) for each control.

- An attribute in the form element tells the browser and Web server what program will process the form information.

- The browser displays the form and allows a surfer to fill it out, collects the information, and sends it to the Web server.

- The Web server sends the information to the indicated program.

- The specific program processes the form information (and usually displays a new Web page when it's done).

HTML itself cannot process a form at all. The general term for the program that processes a form is CGI.

Understanding CGI Programs

To process the information created by someone filling out a form, you'll usually need a separate program that is not written in HTML. These programs are known as *CGI* (Common Gateway Interface). There are two types of CGI: CGI programs and CGI scripts. The only difference is what programming language you use. If you use C, C++, Visual Basic, Java, or another compiled language, you'll create a CGI program. If you create a script using Perl, Tcl, AppleScript, a DOS batch file, or any of the various UNIX shell scripts (sh, csh, bash, tcsh, and so on) that runs on the Web server's computer, then you've created a CGI script. The programming language you use depends on what's available to run on the Web server's operating system.

TIP   Scripting languages, such as JavaScript and VBScript, can also be used to process some or all of a form. We'll discuss this at the end of this Skill and in Skill 15.

Usually CGI programs must be in a special directory on the Web server, often called `cgi-bin` (for "CGI binaries"). If you're running your own Web server, then the details of the CGI directory will depend on what server you're using.

NOTE   Some programming languages, like C, must be *compiled* (translated into machine code before it can be executed). Other languages, like Perl and scripts, are *interpreted* (each line of code is followed by an interpreter, one by one). Compiled programs, Perl scripts, and shell scripts belong in the `cgi-bin` directory, while the source code of a C program belongs in `cgi-src`.

Many ISPs do not allow users to create their own CGI programs. Some ISPs will carefully screen each CGI program for security holes before allowing you to use it. Other ISPs let you create your own CGI programs with few restrictions and allow you to create your own cgi-bin directory for your CGI programs. Check with your ISP if you're not sure about their policy.

Many books have been written about the languages used to create CGI and form-processing programs; we won't be able to teach you how to program a computer language in this book. However, we will teach a little about CGI programs used to process forms, and you'll see that there are often existing programs freely available that you can easily modify for your needs.

NOTE   CGI can be used for more than just processing a form. CGI can create pages "on-the-fly"—for example, you could write a CGI program to take information from a real-time database and create a custom HTML page with the latest information. The CGI program would send the HTML tags to the browser. See Skill 15 for an example.

You don't always have to use CGI. The most common alternative to CGI is a mail program. You can designate an e-mail address where the form's data should be sent by specifying a mailto URL (see Skill 1). Netscape Navigator can send the form's information to a designated e-mail address. However, Internet Explorer 3 cannot do so by default, which severely limits the usefulness of having responses handled by a mailto URL. (IE 4 can handle mailing a form, as long as a mail program is installed. IE 3 can mail a form, but only in certain formats and only if a mail program is specified as a Helper Application in the options.)

WARNING   There are other important limitations involved with using an e-mail program to process a form. We'll see some of the security risks and hazards in the "Considering Form Security" and "Using Mailto Processing" sections.

The best way to understand forms is to see them in action. So, we'll create two examples in the next two sections, then we'll go through and explain the different elements used.

Creating Simple Go Buttons

The simplest type of form is just a button that links to a URL (this type of button is sometimes called a *go button*). You might wonder what the difference is between this button and a normal link using an anchor tag. Other than the fact that this is a button and an anchor link is hypertext, there isn't much of a difference. Some people just like to put buttons on their pages sometimes.

Since there's no user input in this button, this type of form does not have to be processed at all; the browser and HTML can do all the work. Consider this HTML:

```
<FORM ACTION="http://www.antiweb.org/" METHOD="GET">
  <INPUT TYPE="SUBMIT" VALUE="- Go to Antiweb -">
</FORM>
```

This code is displayed as a button (shown here).
Clicking on the button would take you to Antiweb's home page.

This simple HTML code contains two elements: the form element and an input element nested within the form element. The form element sets up an area of the Web page for a form. The input element, in this case, creates a button in the form area.

When anyone clicks on the button, the form element's METHOD attribute tells the browser to "get" the page listed as the ACTION attribute's value.

You can specify any URL as the ACTION of the form element, and put any text you like as the text that goes inside the button (just change the input element's VALUE attribute to the text you desire).

> **NOTE** We'll discuss the form element and the input element used here, along with the attributes, in more detail in later sections of this Skill.

Creating a Fill-in Form Page

The example of a form in the previous section isn't really a form, although it did introduce us to the form element and the input element.

In this section, we'll use these same two elements to create a sample Web page with a slightly more complex form. We'll also add a couple of new elements that create different form controls.

Every form must use a form element (note the <FORM> and </FORM> tags that define where the form begins and ends), as well as some special elements for each control, such as the input element, select element, and textarea element. We'll define each of these elements and their attributes in more detail later in the Skill.

This example will use a mailto URL to process the form. Even though we don't recommend using mailto forms, it's the simplest approach. We'll learn more about the advantages and disadvantages in the "Using Mailto Processing" section at the end of this Skill.

The following form sends data in the form of an e-mail message to janan@sonic.net.

WARNING Change the e-mail address in this example from Janan's to yours. You don't want to send test mail to Janan accidentally.

comments.html

```html
<!DOCTYPE HTML PUBLIC "-//W3C//DTD HTML 4.0//EN">
<HTML LANG="EN">
<HEAD>
  <TITLE>Comment Form</TITLE>
</HEAD>
<BODY>

<P>Please send me your comments.

<FORM ACTION="mailto:janan@sonic.net" METHOD="POST"
ENCTYPE="TEXT/PLAIN">

<P>Your Name: <INPUT TYPE="TEXT" NAME="name">

<P>Your E-mail Address: <INPUT TYPE="TEXT" NAME="email">

<P>The URL of a Web Site you like:<BR>
<INPUT TYPE="TEXT" SIZE="60" NAME="url" VALUE="http://">

<P>Comments:<BR>
<TEXTAREA ROWS="5" COLS="60" NAME="comments">Please type your comments
here.</TEXTAREA>

<P>
<INPUT TYPE="SUBMIT" VALUE="Submit Comment"> <INPUT TYPE="RESET"
VALUE="Clear All">

</FORM>
```

Figure 12.1 shows the form, which contains four areas for a user to fill in information (name, e-mail address, URL, and comments), as well as two buttons: a *submit button*, which sends the information, and a *reset button*, which clears all of the user's entries by returning the fields back to their default values.

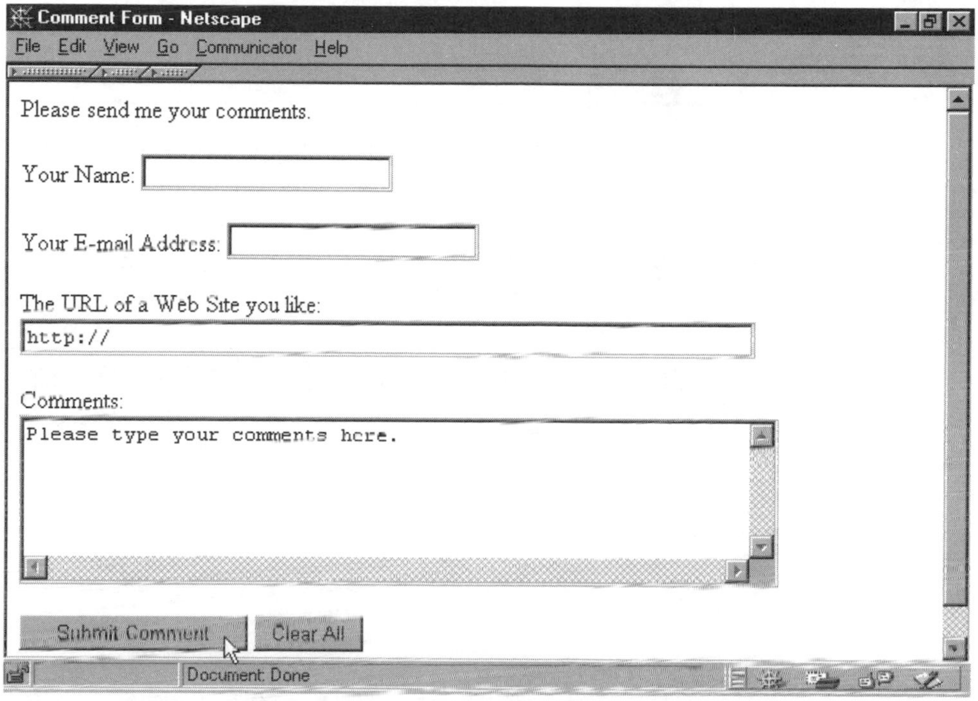

FIGURE 12.1: The form appears like this in Navigator; IE would display the form in a similar way.

Before we discuss the HTML used to create this form, let's take a look at some security issues and then see how this information will be received.

Considering Form Security

Security is a large concern on the Web, especially when credit card numbers are involved. In Skill 19, we'll talk a little about how you can set your site up to receive orders using a credit card. But long before you do that, you'll need to consider your form's security.

Information sent across the Internet, whether it's e-mail, an HTML file, or a form submission, is generally not protected. It's possible for someone to set up a "sniffer" program that reads Internet packets and looks for credit card numbers or passwords.

If you have access to a Web server that can use security measures (for example, a Netscape Commerce Server or Microsoft's Internet Information Server), then the packets of information will be encrypted to prevent anyone from being able to intercept and decode them. You'll need to put your form in an HTML file on the secure Web server. See Skill 19 for more information.

Skill 12

NOTE   Not every page should be put on a secure Web server since it's a lot slower to send a secure file than a normal one.

The e-mail form that we've used in `comments.html` is about the least secure type of transaction you can use. Even if you've placed your form on a secure server the e-mail will not be encrypted, so your security efforts will be compromised. After someone using Navigator fills out this form and clicks on the submit button, they'll see the warning shown in Figure 12.2.

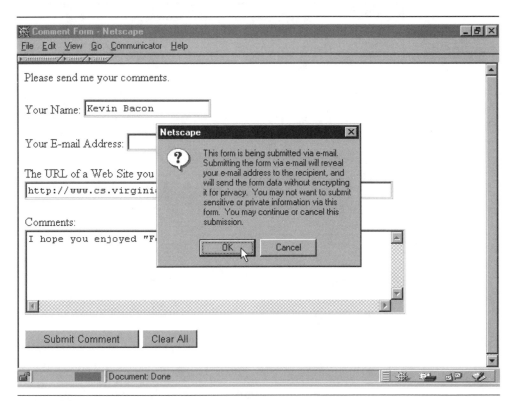

FIGURE 12.2: This warning appears when a form is submitted by mail. You can see the form being filled out in the background here.

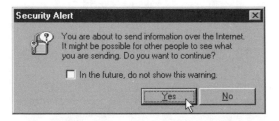

IE displays the warning shown here. These warnings only appear because the form is processed by a mailto URL; if a CGI program processed the form, then a different warning or no warning at all would be displayed by Navigator (depending on the security settings, as we'll see in a second).

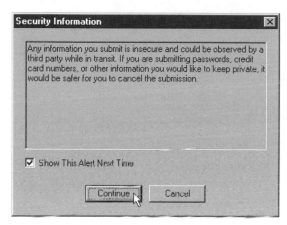

For Navigator, the presence of the warning depends on the settings of Communicator ➤ Security Info ➤ Navigator. If the option to show a warning before Sending Unencrypted Information to a Site is checked, then the warning shown here will be displayed.

If a secure Web server is used, then there's no need for a warning; instead, IE and Navigator indicate onscreen that you're viewing a secure page and warn you when you leave a secure area.

Receiving Feedback by Mail

When someone fills out the form in comments.html and clicks on the submit button, their e-mail program will send the form's information. Navigator sends the information automatically (after showing the warning in Figure 12.2). IE 4 makes the surfer filling out a form manually send the information using their e-mail program, as shown in Figure 12.3.

The e-mail will be sent to the address specified in the mailto URL in the form's ACTION attribute. The e-mail will look something like this:

```
Date: Tue, 22 Jul 1997 17:09:27 -0700
From: Stephen Mack <estephen@emf.net>
To: janan@sonic.net
Subject: Form posted from Mozilla

name=Kevin Bacon
email=
url=http://www.cs.virginia.edu/~bct7m/bacon.html
comments=I hope you enjoyed "Footloose."
```

Note that even though "Kevin Bacon" filled out the form and didn't include his e-mail address, the real e-mail address of the sender is shown in the headers. This is why both Navigator and IE show the security warnings for an e-mail form—it's hard to be anonymous.

Skill 12

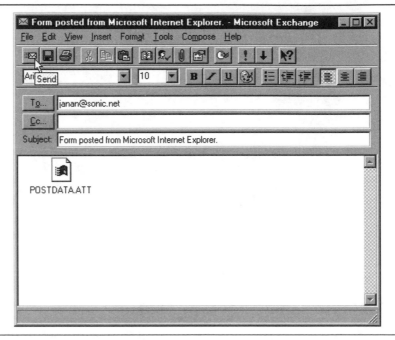

FIGURE 12.3: IE 4 posted the form's information using an e-mail program (Microsoft Exchange is shown here). You must click the Send button to actually submit the form's information.

NOTE

Note that any Navigator and IE user can put fake information as their real name and e-mail address when they set up their browser. You can learn about tracing e-mail at http://ddi.digital.net/~gandalf/spamfaq.html.

Our form in comments.html specified that we should receive the form's information as plain text (that's what the form element's ENCTYPE attribute is for). However, some browsers don't know how to send plain text. Instead, these browsers will send form information in the default format, which is called *URL-encoded text* (with a MIME type of application/x-www-form-urlencoded).

URL-encoded text sends the form's information in one long string, using special codes for certain characters. If we had not specified that we wanted to receive text/plain format information, or if we received form information from a browser that can't send in plain text format, then the previous information would have been received like this:

```
name=Kevin+Bacon&email=
```

```
&url=http%3A%2F%2Fwww.cs.virginia.edu%2F%7Ebct7m%2Fbacon.html
&comments=I+hope+you+enjoyed+%22Apollo+13.%22
```

Note that spaces are replaced by plus signs (+) and that each field is separated by ampersands (&). This format may be useful for CGI, but it's very hard for humans to interpret.

Understanding the Form Example

Now that we've seen how the form is used and filled out, there are several things worth discussing in comments.html that will help us understand forms in general.

The first thing to notice is that there is a form element that contains all of the form controls. The form element begins with the <FORM> tag (which causes a paragraph break). The <FORM> tag uses three attributes:

- The first attribute, ACTION, is used here to specify the e-mail address that should receive the form information. The word "mailto:" is required to make the ACTION a valid URL. (See Skill 1.)

- The second attribute, METHOD, specifies that the form information should be posted to the URL given in the ACTION attribute.

- The third attribute, ENCTYPE, indicates what MIME type should be used when the information is posted. (See the beginning of Skill 9 for more information about MIME types.)

The form element ends with the </FORM> tag, which also causes a paragraph break. Anything within these two tags is considered to be part of the form. Forms can contain normal text and form controls, as in comments.html. But form elements can also contain images, tables, or any other block-level or text-level elements, except for another form.

In comments.html there are a few pieces of normal text (such as "Your Name:" and "The URL of a Web Site you like:"). There are also a few paragraph element start tags (<P>) to create paragraph breaks, and line-break elements (<BR>) to create line-breaks.

There are six controls in comments.html. The first three controls are text boxes, the fourth control is a multi-line text area (for the comments themselves), and the last two controls are buttons (one to submit the form, and the other to reset the form).

For the first two controls (name and e-mail address), an input element is used with an attribute that specifies that the TYPE of input control should be a text control. A text control is simply a box that can have text entered into it. (In the "Creating Simple Go Buttons" section earlier in this Skill, we also used the input element, except we specified TYPE="SUBMIT" instead of TYPE="TEXT". We'll see later in this Skill that there are other types of input elements as well.)

The third control is also a text control—but unlike the first two, the third input element specifies a SIZE attribute to make the text box 60 characters wide. A VALUE attribute was also used to place a default value in the text box.

The fourth control is a textarea element to create a multi-line text input control. The number of rows and columns are specified with attributes (ROWS and COLS respectively). While the input element is an empty element (that is, no </INPUT> tag is used), the textarea element requires both a <TEXTAREA> start tag and a </TEXTAREA> end tag. The "Please type your comments here" text between these two tags is used as the default value for the multi-line text input control.

Note that a NAME attribute is used to give the first four controls a field name. The field name is used with the results when the form is submitted. (Check back to the e-mail result in the previous section and notice how the field names in comments.html correspond with each piece of information that was submitted.)

The submit button and reset button are standard elements for forms. Both buttons are created by an input element with an appropriate TYPE attribute. We could have used any text for the text that goes inside these buttons; we have chosen "Submit Comment" as the submit control's VALUE attribute and "Clear All" as the reset control's VALUE attribute.

Each form should have at least one submit button. (Note that the form in our go button example in the previous section contains a submit button and nothing else.) If you leave out the submit button, then there's no obvious way to send in the form's information for processing.

Now that we have a common vocabulary for talking about different parts of a form and we know what a form can do, it's time to learn more about the form element and its attributes. Then we'll see each of the elements used to create form controls.

Using the Form Element and Its Attributes

The form element is a block-level element that creates a form area. The form element's <FORM> and </FORM> tags contain the form's controls (along with other text and HTML elements).

Even though you cannot nest a form inside another form, you can have more than one form on a page as long as the form elements aren't nested.

The form element requires that the ACTION attribute be specified; in addition, you can specify the METHOD and ENCTYPE attributes we saw in our earlier examples. We'll talk more about the METHOD and ACTION attributes in the next section.

The ENCYTYPE attribute must be a valid MIME type, traditionally either application/x-www-form-urlencoded (the default), or text/plain. HTML 4.0 introduces the TARGET attribute to define a new window for a CGI program's output; check Skill 7 and Skill 11 for more information about using the TARGET attribute.

HTML 4.0 also allows a new ACCEPT attribute if your Web server accepts file uploads. We'll see how to use this attribute in the "Allowing File Uploads with File Controls" section.

We've seen the generic HTML 4.0 attributes in previous Skills. The form element (as well as every form control) can be used with the generic attributes:

- **Language attributes** Use the LANG and DIR attributes for language information about a form; you can also use the special ACCEPT-CHARSET form attribute to list different character encodings that might be used. For example, by specifying ACCEPT-CHARSET="ISO-8859-5" in the <FORM> tag, you can tell a CGI program that people filling out your form may be using Cyrillic characters. For more information about LANG, DIR, and character encodings, see Skill 5.

- **Style attributes** The CLASS, ID, and STYLE attributes for style sheet information can be specified in a form element if you are using a style sheet. We'll see some examples in Skill 14.

- **Event attributes** In addition to the normal event attributes that we'll see in Skill 15 (such as ONMOUSEOVER and ONCLICK), the form element can take the ONSUBMIT and ONRESET event attributes to trigger a script when a form is submitted or reset. (For example, you could use the ONSUBMIT attribute with a script to make sure that any required fields have been filled out before sending the form information by mail; we'll see such a script in Skill 15.)

- **Advisory title** The TITLE attribute can be used to give more information about a form element. We first saw this attribute in Skill 5.

Using the Method and Action Attributes

There are only two possible values for the METHOD attribute: METHOD="GET" or METHOD="POST". The default value is "GET". We've seen two examples of forms already in this Skill: The first example used the "GET" method, while the second example used the "POST" method.

Skill 12

In general, whenever you'll be e-mailing a form's contents, specify the `"POST"` method and use a mailto URL as the `ACTION` attribute value (just as we did in `comments.html`). The `"POST"` method passes the form information as a block of data; this block of data is pictured in Figure 12.3 (before it gets mailed off to the mail's recipient).

If you're going to use any kind of CGI program to process a form, you should specify the `"GET"` method and give the URL of the CGI program as the `ACTION` attribute value. The `"GET"` method adds the form's information to the URL so that a CGI program can see all of the form's data. (Some CGI programs can handle the `"POST"` method, but most cannot.)

For example, suppose you want to create a form on your site that asks for a search phrase, and then searches Yahoo!'s directory for sites relevant to that phrase. To do this, we'd add a simple form. Here we'll use an `ACTION` attribute that leads to the Yahoo! search program. The search term is requested using a text box control input element. The only other ingredient is a submit button to start the search. Here's the necessary code:

```
<FORM METHOD="GET" ACTION="http://search.yahoo.com/bin/search">
    <INPUT TYPE="TEXT" NAME="p">
    <INPUT TYPE="SUBMIT" VALUE="Go!">
</FORM>
```

NOTE   The only two tricky things here are knowing the URL for Yahoo!'s search program (`http://search.yahoo.com/bin/search`) and knowing what field name to give the search field text box. Yahoo! uses "p" for their search field name. To find out both pieces of necessary information, all we had to do was view the source of any Yahoo! page that has a search form on it. Alternately, Yahoo! offers instructions on making a slightly fancier version of this form online (`http://www.yahoo.com/docs/yahootogo/search/`).

When someone types in a search term and clicks on the Go! button, the browser will go to the URL listed under `ACTION`. The way Yahoo!'s search program knows what to search for is from information in the URL. Because we specified the GET method, the browser will add all of the form information to the end of the URL. First the browser adds a question mark, then the name of the field ("p" in this case), then an equals sign, and finally the data. So if you search for "kumquats," the URL will become:

```
http://search.yahoo.com/bin/search?p=kumquats
```

Yahoo!'s search engine is written to take the word "kumquats" from the URL and then search through its massive database for kumquat pages, and then return a list of categories and sites that match the term "kumquats."

Using Form Control Elements

The form element can contain eight different elements to create form controls. The most commonly used four elements are listed here:

- The input element is used to create a variety of controls, including text boxes and buttons.

- The textarea element is used to create multi-line text input controls, as we saw in the comments.html example.

- The select element contains one or more option elements. Together these two elements are used to create pull-down menus and multiple item controls.

HTML 4.0 introduces four new elements for forms:

- The button element creates button controls. It's similar to the input element with TYPE="BUTTON" specified—except that the button element is a container so it's a little more flexible.

- The label element can describe form controls, which helps text-to-speech browsers handle forms properly.

- The fieldset element is used to group different form controls together. The fieldset element can contain an optional legend element to describe the different groups.

We'll start by seeing more about the input element and its attributes, and then we'll look at the other different form control elements. After that, we'll see how we can use certain attributes for form controls to set the tab order and use keyboard shortcuts, and disable controls or make them read-only.

Creating Text Boxes, Buttons, and Other Form Controls with the Input Element

The input element is the most flexible and commonly used form control. We've seen several examples of <INPUT> tags that were used to create buttons and text boxes. In this section, we'll see some of the other possibilities for an input element.

The input element consists solely of an <INPUT> tag, along with the TYPE attribute (to specify what type of form control you want), the NAME attribute (to indicate the field name), and other optional attributes.

 If you leave out the NAME attribute, then the form control won't submit any data. The value of a name attribute should be descriptive and not contain any spaces or special characters.

The default TYPE for an input element is "TEXT", but there are a total of 10 different possibilities.

- "TEXT" Used to create the single-line text boxes we saw in comments.html.

- "PASSWORD" Similar to text, except the characters you type are not revealed onscreen. This type of input is often used for passwords or sensitive information.

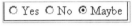

- "CHECKBOX" An on or off switch.

- "RADIO" Similar to a checkbox, except that in a group of radio buttons only one radio button can be on at a time.

- "SUBMIT" Submits a form to be processed (as we saw earlier).

- "IMAGE" Exactly the same as a submit button, except that you can specify any image instead of the normal gray button appearance.

- "RESET" Clears all of the input on a form, resetting it back to its default appearance (seen in the comments.html example earlier).

- "BUTTON" Creates a button similar in appearance to a submit button, except that this kind of button doesn't do anything in particular.

- "HIDDEN" A hidden input is not displayed onscreen at all. It's useful to send fixed information to a CGI program along with the form data.

- "FILE" Can be used to send a file from the surfer's computer along with the rest of the form data.

Some of these different types of form controls can use attributes in various ways, such as the SIZE, MAXLENGTH, VALUE, and CHECKED attributes. We'll see the use of each of these attributes when we discuss each of these 10 types of input form controls.

Using Text Form Controls

We saw several examples of the text form control in the comments.html example. (This type of form control is also known as a *text box*.) A text box is created like this:

```
Enter your music preference: <INPUT TYPE="TEXT" NAME="music">
```

You can specify a size for the text box (in characters) by using the SIZE attribute; for example, adding a SIZE="50" attribute to the <INPUT> tag would create a text box that's 50 characters wide.

To limit the text box so that only a certain number of characters can be entered, use the MAXLENGTH attribute. Adding MAXLENGTH="40" to an <INPUT> tag would only allow the surfer to enter in a maximum of 40 characters.

You can also add default text to the form control in a VALUE attribute. This default text will appear in the text box until the surfer changes it. For example:

```
Credit Card Type: <INPUT TYPE="TEXT" NAME="cardtype"
VALUE="Mastercard">
```

Finally, you can add a READONLY attribute to make a text box read-only, which means that its default value can't be changed, or add the DISABLED attribute to make a text box unavailable ("grayed out") until some other event makes the text box available. We'll discuss read-only and disabled form controls after we've seen all of the form control elements.

When a form is submitted, you (or the CGI program) will receive the name of the text box's field, followed by the value of the text entered by the surfer. For example, if someone filled out your form and put "alternative" as their music preference and left the credit card type as the default, you might receive: cardtype=Mastercard&music=alternative. If a text field is left blank, you'll just receive the fieldname and an equals sign with nothing else, such as music=.

> **NOTE**   If a form consists solely of a text box, the the Enter key will submit the form.

Using Password Form Controls

A password form control ("password box") is identical to a text box in every respect except one: When the surfer types in an entry in the password box, they won't see what they typed. Instead, they'll see a substitute character for each key that is typed.

This type of control is used for information that shouldn't be casually seen by someone who may be looking over the surfer's shoulder. There is no added security by using a password box, however, since the information typed by the surfer is submitted just like any other form control—that is, with no special encryption (unless a secure Web server is being used).

For example, here's an input element that creates a password box:

```
Credit Card Number: <INPUT TYPE="PASSWORD" NAME="CC">
```

Skill 12

When someone fills in this form control, Navigator and IE will substitute an asterisk for each number of their credit card that they enter, as shown here. The same attributes used for a text box can be used with a password box, and the same type of data will be received (such as cc=1234567812345555).

Using a Checkbox Form Control

A checkbox is simply an empty box by default. As with other form controls, you have to type your label next to the checkbox. For example:

```
<INPUT TYPE="CHECKBOX" NAME="MailList"> Please add me to your mailing
list.
```

To make the checkbox start off checked, add the CHECKED attribute.

When a form is submitted, the field name will be submitted only if the control is checked. With the previous example, you'll get MailList=on if the checkbox is checked, or nothing if it isn't checked.

You can control what data is sent by a checked checkbox by specifying a VALUE attribute. For example:

```
<INPUT TYPE="CHECKBOX" NAME="MailList" VALUE="Add"> Add me to your
mailing list.
```

If the field is checked, you'll receive MailList=Add when the form is submitted.

You can create several checkboxes with the same NAME attribute value. Each checkbox that is switched on will submit a name/value pair with the same field name. For example:

```
<INPUT TYPE="CHECKBOX" NAME="OPTIONS" VALUE="Rush"> Rush Service<BR>
<INPUT TYPE="CHECKBOX" NAME="OPTIONS" VALUE="FedEx"> Overnight
Delivery<BR>
<INPUT TYPE="CHECKBOX" NAME="OPTIONS" VALUE="Bill"> Send Billing Info
```

 NOTE   Remember that HTML runs everything together, ignoring your white space. If you don't include the <BR> tag to create a line-break, then all of your checkboxes will appear on the same line.

If all three of these checkboxes were checked, then you'd receive:

```
OPTIONS=Rush
OPTIONS=FedEx
OPTIONS=Bill
```

If you want to make the surfer choose only one of the three possible options, then use a radio button form control instead of three separate checkboxes.

Using Radio Button Form Controls

If you want to have a surfer choose one of several possible options, use a radio button. (The name "radio button" is derived from those old car radios with five station buttons: If you push in one of the buttons, the other buttons are pushed out—so only one button can be pushed in at a time.)

For example:

```
Choose a shipping option:
<INPUT TYPE="RADIO" NAME="Shipping" VALUE="PO" CHECKED> Post Office
<INPUT TYPE="RADIO" NAME="Shipping" VALUE="UPS"> United Parcel Service
<INPUT TYPE="RADIO" NAME="Shipping" VALUE="FedEx"> Federal Express
```

The default choice is indicated by using a CHECKED attribute. When the form is submitted, whichever one of the radio buttons is currently selected will send its field value. So if Federal Express is chosen, you'll receive Shipping=FedEx.

Including Submit Form Controls

We've already seen several examples of a submit button in this Skill, and we mentioned earlier that every form must have at least a submit button. (The only exception to this is when a form contains just a single text box. Enter acts as a submit button in this case.)

The label inside the submit button is taken from the VALUE attribute.

HTML 4.0 allows you to size the submit button (in pixels) by including a SIZE attribute. However, Navigator and IE don't obey this attribute's value. In practice, a submit button is about 20 pixels wider (on each side) than the VALUE text (the more text you have, the bigger the button), although browsers vary.

If you include a NAME attribute in a submit button, then the NAME and VALUE of the submit button will be included when the form is submitted.

A form can include more than one submit button. This allows the form to be submitted with different values, depending on which submit button is chosen. For example:

```
<FORM ACTION="form-processor">
Your name: <INPUT NAME="name">
```

```
<P>I have read the license and agree to abide by it.
<P><INPUT TYPE="SUBMIT" VALUE="I Agree" NAME="Choice">
<INPUT TYPE="SUBMIT" VALUE="I Disagree" NAME="Choice">
</FORM>
```

This example, shown in Figure 12.4, creates a text form control for a person's name, and then offers two different submit buttons, one labeled "I Agree" and the other labeled "I Disagree."

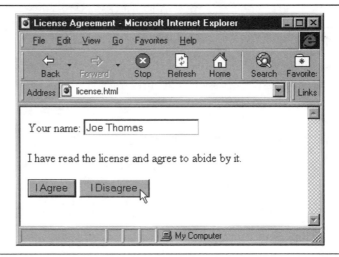

FIGURE 12.4: A form with a text box and two submit buttons, shown in IE

If the surfer in Figure 12.4 submits the form with the "I Agree" submit button, then the browser will GET the CGI program named form-processor and add ?name=Joe+Thomas to the URL as well as a &Choice=I+Agree. If "I Disagree" is clicked, the person's name is submitted along with &Choice=I+Disagree. You could set up your form-processor program to show one page for those who agree to the license and a different page for those who disagree.

If you want to use an image for a submit button, use TYPE="IMAGE" instead of (or along with) TYPE="SUBMIT".

Creating Image Submit Buttons

An input element with TYPE="IMAGE" creates an image button. An image button is similar in function to a submit button except that instead of a gray button with text, an image of your choice is displayed.

The attributes for an image button are similar to the attributes for the <IMG> tag that we saw in Skill 8. You must specify a SRC for the image, and you should specify an ALT attribute for alternate text. For example:

```
<INPUT TYPE="IMAGE" SRC="wow.gif" ALT="[Submit Me]" ALIGN="RIGHT">
```

This example creates a submit button that uses the wow.gif image as the face of the button. For browsers that aren't displaying images, a regular submit button with the text "[Submit Me]" will appear. The entire control is right-aligned (we'll see more about alignment later).

NOTE   One wrinkle is that a graphical browser will add X and Y coordinates when someone clicks on an image, making the image button similar to an image map (see Skill 8 and the Web site). However, it's not recommended that you use image maps with different URL responses as a submit button since non-graphical browsers won't be able to choose the different regions. Instead, just use several different submit images with appropriate alternate text.

Adding a Reset Button

We saw the use of a reset button earlier in this Skill, in the comments.html example. Like a submit button, the VALUE of a reset button is displayed in the button, and the SIZE attribute can control the width of a reset button.

A reset button's value is never submitted with a form; instead, the reset button will always just reset all of the form's controls to their initial values.

TIP   Since a reset button can undo a lot of work if someone presses it accidentally, make sure your reset button is well labeled and not placed before the submit button where it can be pressed inadvertently. Some Web authors never use reset buttons to avoid the risk of someone wiping out their input by accident.

Using Hidden Controls

Sometimes you'll want to set up a field name with a value that is always submitted along with a form and cannot be changed by the person filling out the form. (The field name and its value are known as *name/value pair*.)

Some CGI programs require that certain values be set by a form in order for the CGI program to work properly. For example, a form-to-mail gateway might require that you specify your e-mail address so that the form's data can be e-mailed to you after processing.

To create a name/value pair that is not displayed in the form area, use a hidden control by setting TYPE="HIDDEN" for the input element.

NOTE Hidden controls are not completely hidden, since a surfer can always view your source, and will see the name/value pair in the URL when the form is submitted (if you've used the GET method).

This example creates a hidden control with a field name of "destaddr" and a value of "billg@micr0soft.com":

```
<INPUT TYPE="HIDDEN" NAME="destaddr" VALUE="billg@micr0soft.com">
```

Creating Button Form Controls

The button input type is new in HTML 4.0, but it is well-supported since IE 3 and 4, as well as Navigator 3 and 4, understand this input type.

For example:

```
<INPUT TYPE="BUTTON" VALUE="Goober!">
```

creates a push button labeled "Goober!" that has no default behavior.

The only use of a button like this is when you use an event attribute that associates the button with an action (such as clicking the mouse button on the Goober! button). For example, the following code causes an active script named "doit( )" to be executed when a button labeled "Click Me" is clicked.

```
<INPUT TYPE="BUTTON" VALUE="Click Me" ONCLICK="doit()">
```

To learn more about event attributes and active scripts, see Skill 15.

Allowing File Uploads with File Controls

A file control lets a surfer submit a file on their computer along with the form. The file will be sent by the browser to the CGI program handling your form.

Receiving a file is a complex operation since it requires that the MIME type for the form and the file be set carefully, and that a complicated CGI program be ready to accept files.

If your CGI program can't receive every type of file, you should add an ACCEPT attribute to the <FORM> tag that lists the MIME types that your CGI program can handle (for example, <FORM ACTION="my_filer.pl" ACCEPT="audio/basic, text/plain,image/*">).

Here's another example of a form that asks for a person's name and then accepts a group of files. Note how the ENCTYPE attribute is set in the form element with a special MIME type to specify the file and other data:

```
<FORM ACTION="http://www.myserver.com/file_handler"
ENCTYPE="multipart/form-data"
METHOD="POST">
 What is your name? <INPUT NAME="name_of_sender">
 What files are you sending? <INPUT TYPE="FILE" NAME="name_of_files">
</FORM>
```

The hard part is having a CGI program named file_handler that can receive and process the files that are sent. Your ISP may already have set up such a program.

Using Input Element Attributes

In the course of describing the 10 different input controls, we saw several attributes, including VALUE, NAME, SIZE, MAXLENGTH, CHECKED, SRC, and ALT.

In addition, you can use the ALIGN attribute to specify that a form control's contents should be left-aligned, right-aligned, or centered, but in practice Navigator and IE ignore the ALIGN attribute for every input type except images.

We saw that text and password input element types could be set to be read-only with the READONLY attribute (although Navigator doesn't support read-only controls). In addition, every input type can be set to be disabled. We'll see more about read-only and disabled controls later in this Skill.

Every input form control can have also an ACCESSKEY keyboard shortcut and use a TABINDEX value to control when the tab key selects a control. We'll see more about ACCESSKEY and TABINDEX after we've learned about the other form control elements.

Finally, input and other form controls can use all of the generic HTML 4.0 attributes (for languages, styles, events, and advisory titles). As we saw in our discussion of the button control, the event attributes are particularly useful in order to associate a form control with a script action. Useful event attributes for form controls include the ONFOCUS, ONBLUR, ONSELECT, and ONCHANGE attributes. The use of these attributes is covered in Skill 15.

Now that we've seen the input element and its many different types of form controls, we'll take a look at the select element, which can create menus. After that we'll see the textarea element in more detail.

Skill 12

Creating Menu Controls with the Select Element

The select element creates a menu control. There are two formats for menu controls, and the one that's used depends on the attributes used in the select element.

The select element must contain one or more option elements. Each option element creates an item on the menu. The select element must begin with a <SELECT> tag with a required NAME attribute, and after the option element it must end with a </SELECT> tag.

To make this use clear, it's simplest to see an example:

```
<SELECT NAME="Users">
  <OPTION>John Restrick
  <OPTION>Sue Tully
  <OPTION>Mark Unger
  <OPTION>Lila Saks
  <OPTION>E.G. Yang
</SELECT>
```

This select element will create a drop-down menu control, as shown here.

 If you specify the optional SIZE attribute in the select element, then IE and Navigator will display a list box instead of a drop-down menu. So by using <SELECT NAME="Users" SIZE="5">, we'd see the list box shown here.

 You can specify a SIZE less than the number of options, in which case the browser will add a scroll bar, as we see here with a SIZE="3" attribute used.

 You can also use a SIZE greater than the number of options, which will leave one or more blank lines, as seen here, with SIZE="6".

 When the form is submitted, the currently selected option is sent along with the NAME of the select element. So for our example, if John Restrick's name is selected from the pull-down menu or list box, either you or the CGI program will receive Users=John Restrick when the form is submitted (or Users=John+Restrick if the ENCTYPE is not plain/text).

By default, only one item can be selected from the list. If you specify the optional MULTIPLE attribute, then more than one item can be selected. (Users will have to select their additional items by holding down the Ctrl key or command when they click, although different browsers use different techniques for multiple selections.)

Finally, an option element can have a VALUE attribute set to some text if you want to specify what text is submitted to you when the item is selected. You can also indicate the default menu item with a SELECTED attribute.

Here's an example of a more complex select element.

veggies.html

```
<!DOCTYPE HTML PUBLIC "-//W3C//DTD HTML 4.0//EN">
<HTML LANG="EN">
<HEAD><TITLE>Vegetable Selections</TITLE></HEAD>
<BODY>

<P>Choose your favorite vegetables.
(For multiple entries, hold down the control key and click
on each vegetable to highlight it.)

<FORM ACTION="mailto:janan@sonic.net" METHOD="POST"
ENCTYPE="TEXT/PLAIN">

<SELECT NAME="vegetable" SIZE="5" MULTIPLE>
  <OPTION>Carrots
  <OPTION>Lettuce
  <OPTION>Sprouts
  <OPTION SELECTED>Peppers
  <OPTION>Celery
  <OPTION VALUE="Brussel">Brussel Sprouts
  <OPTION>Squash
  <OPTION>Mushrooms
  <OPTION VALUE="RedT">Red Tomatoes
  <OPTION VALUE="YellowT">Yellow Tomatoes
</SELECT>

<P>
<INPUT TYPE="SUBMIT" VALUE="Submit My Information">

</FORM>

</BODY>
</HTML>
```

Figure 12.5 shows this form being used and three different vegetables being selected.

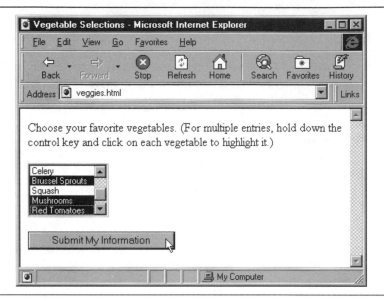

FIGURE 12.5: IE shows our `veggies.html` form and the user has selected three or more vegetables. (Vegetables that were selected before scrolling down the list will stay selected.)

When this form is submitted, each vegetable that's selected will be sent on a line by itself to the address specified in the ACTION attribute. So, Janan might receive something like:

```
vegetable=Brussel
vegetable=Mushrooms
vegetable=RedT
```

An option's value defaults to the option text, unless the VALUE attribute is specified. It's sometimes helpful to indicate alternate values (if your program deals with one word more easily than two words, for example).

Just like the input element, you can use generic HTML 4.0 attributes on a select element or option element. You can also have a select element disabled with the DISABLE attribute, or change its tab order with the TABINDEX element (described in more detail later).

The next type of form control is created by a textarea element.

Creating Multiple Text Line Input Controls with the Textarea Element

We saw the use of a textarea element in `comments.html` near the beginning of this Skill.

The textarea element creates a text box that's similar to an input element with TYPE="TEXT", except that an input element creates a single-line text box, and a textarea element can create a multiple-line text box.

To use a textarea element, you must begin with a <TEXTAREA> tag that must include a NAME attribute, and you must specify a number of rows and a number of columns with the ROWS and COLS attributes. You can then (optionally) include some default text that will appear inside the multi-line text box. You must finish the control with a </TEXTAREA> tag.

The default text is treated like pre-formatted text (see the pre-formatted element in Skill 6), so carriage returns and other white space are significant.

This example creates a multi-line text box control 10 rows tall by 60 columns wide, and contains three default lines of text (with a blank line in between each of the three lines):

```
<TEXTAREA rows="10" cols="60" NAME="feedback">
General Reaction:

Likes:

Dislikes:
</TEXTAREA>
```

This multiple-line form control will be created in IE as shown here

Just because you specify a certain number of columns and rows in a textarea element, that doesn't limit the user's input. The rows and columns just determine the size of the textarea control onscreen. Surfers can type text as wide as they like, and they can create as many lines as they like. Navigator and IE will use scroll bars to let the user move from place to place within the multi-line text control.

An Example Using Different Form Controls

Now that we've seen the most common form controls, here's another example that puts them together.

iceform.html

```
<!DOCTYPE HTML PUBLIC "-//W3C//DTD HTML 4.0//EN">
<HTML LANG="EN">
<HEAD>
  <TITLE>Six Flavors Ice Creame Shoppee</TITLE>
</HEAD>
<BODY>

<H1>Ice Cream Request Form</H1>

<P>Our simple ice cream request form can be used to indicate what kind
of ice cream cone you want. The information will be mailed to us. If
you're using a browser that can't mail forms (such as Internet
Explorer 3), please
<A HREF="mailto:estephen@emf.net">mail us</A> the information
instead of filling out this form.

<HR>

<FORM METHOD="POST" ACTION="mailto:estephen@emf.net"
ENCTYPE="TEXT/PLAIN">

Would you care for some ice cream?
<INPUT TYPE="RADIO" NAME="ICE" VALUE="Y" CHECKED>Yes
<INPUT TYPE="RADIO" NAME="ICE" VALUE="N">No

<BR>

Flavor:
<SELECT NAME="FLAVOR" SIZE="3">
  <OPTION VALUE="Van">Vanilla
  <OPTION VALUE="Choc">Chocolate
  <OPTION VALUE="Straw">Strawberry
  <OPTION VALUE="Coff" SELECTED>Coffee
  <OPTION VALUE="Pist">Pistachio
  <OPTION VALUE="Marb">Marble Fudge
</SELECT>

Cone:
<SELECT NAME="CONE">
<OPTION>Sugar
<OPTION>Plain
<OPTION>Waffle
</SELECT>

<BR>

Describe what you like about our ice cream:<BR>
<TEXTAREA NAME="COMMENTS" ROWS="4" COLS="40">
Thank you for your comments.
```

```
</TEXTAREA>

<BR>

Your Name:
<INPUT TYPE="TEXT" NAME="Name" SIZE=30>

<BR>

<INPUT TYPE="CHECKBOX" NAME="SPRINKLE" VALUE="Y" CHECKED>Sprinkles?
<BR>
<INPUT TYPE="CHECKBOX" NAME="DOUBLE" VALUE="Y">Two scoops?

<BR>

<INPUT TYPE="SUBMIT" VALUE="Serve It!">
<INPUT TYPE="RESET" VALUE="Reset My Responses">

</FORM>

<HR>

Thanks for taking the time to write us.

</BODY>
</HTML>
```

This example presents several different elements that we've seen in this Skill. In Navigator, it would appear as shown in Figure 12.6.

We could make this example more complex by using a table element or list elements to organize the different form controls, or by using images or hidden controls.

Another way we could add complexity is by using some of the new HTML 4.0 elements that can be used with forms, which we'll see next. We'll see the new button control, and the new label and fieldset/legend elements that can group form controls.

Creating Buttons with the Button Element

Earlier in this Skill, we learned about the input element and its TYPE="SUBMIT", TYPE="RESET", and TYPE="BUTTON" form controls.

HTML 4.0 introduces a new element that can be quite similar to these existing controls. The new button element is intended to be a little more flexible than the input element since it can contain images, lists, objects, multiple paragraphs, or other block-level and text-level elements. Anything contained between the <BUTTON> and </BUTTON> tags will be displayed as a button. (In contrast, an input element is not a container, so it can't have anything nested within it.)

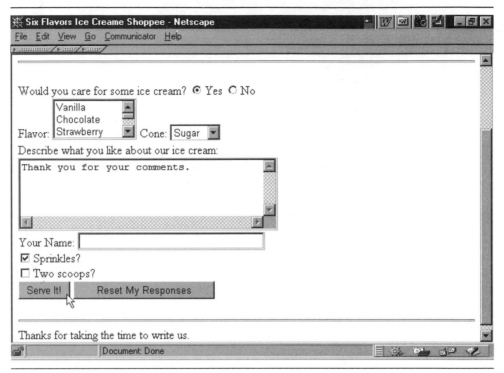

FIGURE 12.6: Our iceform.html example in Navigator

The button element can take a TYPE attribute, but it can only be set to TYPE=
"BUTTON", TYPE="RESET", and TYPE="SUBMIT". As you might expect, these
attributes make a regular button, a reset button, and a submit button. Their use
is the same as for the similar input element controls that we saw earlier.

NOTE One difference between the new button element and the input TYPE="IMAGE"
element that we saw earlier is that the button element does not send the X and
Y coordinates of where on the image the user clicks.

Since the button element is new, only the latest versions of IE 4 support it. In
the future, the button element will be a more popular way of creating submit
buttons that are images. For now, just stick with the input element.

Using the Label Element

One drawback to forms in earlier versions of HTML is that while a text label is often
near a control, no HTML element ties them together. This means that text-to-speech
browsers had difficulty in rendering a form control in a comprehensible way.

To rectify this shortcoming, HTML 4.0 introduces the label element, which nests the textual label along with its control. The label element must begin with a <LABEL> tag, contain one form control and its text label (which may be either before or after the control), and end with a </LABEL> tag. For example:

```
<LABEL>First Name: <INPUT TYPE="TEXT" NAME="first_name"></LABEL>
```

You can also use a FOR attribute with the <LABEL> tag to associate a label in one place with a form control in a different place. Suppose, for example, that you created a table in a form. You can place the label in one cell and the form control in a different cell:

```
<FORM ACTION="query">
<TABLE>
  <TR><TD><LABEL FOR="fname">First Name:</LABEL>
      <TD><INPUT TYPE="TEXT" NAME="first_name" ID="fname">
  <TR><TD><LABEL FOR="lname">Last Name:</LABEL>
      <TD><INPUT TYPE="TEXT" NAME="last_name" ID="lname">
</TABLE>
</FORM>
```

The advantage of putting labels in one column and fields in another column of a table is that it's easy to line up the different form controls. Here, the first column contains the controls' text labels (which have been marked with the label element), and the second column contains the text boxes. The FOR attribute requires that the input elements be labeled with an ID attribute. For more about tables, see Skill 10. The drawback to the label element is that it's so new that it is not yet widely supported.

Grouping Controls with the Fieldset and Legend Elements

The final new elements introduced by HTML 4.0 for forms are the fieldset element and its optional legend element. The fieldset element can be used to group one or more form controls together. The legend element applies a label to these grouped controls. A browser might choose to box the grouped elements together, or otherwise indicate that they belong together.

To use the fieldset element, simply put a <FIELDSET> start tag at the beginning of a group of controls, and then a </FIELDSET> end tag at the end of the group. Your form area can contain one or more fieldset elements, and they can even be nested within each other, but for maximum clarity, you should keep your fieldset elements separate.

The legend element should simply contain a description of the group. You can use an optional ALIGN attribute in the <LEGEND> tag to indicate where the

Skill 12

description should be placed (ALIGN="LEFT", ALIGN="RIGHT", ALIGN="TOP", and ALIGN="BOTTOM" are allowed by HTML 4.0). HTML 4.0 also allows an ACCESSKEY shortcut in a legend, to make it easier to select a fieldset. (We'll talk about ACCESSKEY attributes a little later.) The legend element can only occur inside a fieldset element, and although its actual placement doesn't matter, it should occur as the first element for clarity.

Here's a quick example of the fieldset and legend elements:

```
<FORM ACTION="http://www.emf.net/cgi-bin/test-cgi.sh" METHOD="GET">
  <FIELDSET>
    <LEGEND ALIGN="RIGHT">Personal Information</LEGEND>
    <LABEL>First Name: <INPUT NAME="fname"></LABEL><BR>
    <LABEL>Last Name: <INPUT NAME="lname"></LABEL>
  </FIELDSET>

  <P>

  <FIELDSET>
    <LEGEND ALIGN="RIGHT">Order Information</LEGEND>
    <LABEL>Product Name: <INPUT NAME="product"></LABEL><BR>
    <LABEL>Quantity: <INPUT NAME="quantity"></LABEL>
  </FIELDSET>
</FORM>
```

This example creates two different groups of form controls, one for personal information and one for order information. Each group could contain as many controls as we like, but here we've only used two each. The two fieldsets are each given a legend that's placed to the right. IE will group the controls as shown here.

Even though the presence of the label elements in this example doesn't affect the presentation, they help make it clear how the label text is related to the control, and text-to-speech browsers will appreciate the grouping.

┌──────────────── Personal Information ─┐
│ First Name: [   ]│
│ Last Name: [   ]│
│   │
│ ┌──────────── Order Information ─┐   │
│ Product Name: [   ]   │
│ Quantity: [   ]   │
└───────────────────────────────────────┘

NOTE   Navigator does not yet support the fieldset or legend elements at all, although the presence of these elements won't cause any problems.

As you can see, IE 4 supports the fieldset element by boxing the controls contained within the fieldset. The legend's contents are displayed onscreen, but unfortunately, IE cannot align the legend with the bottom of the fieldset box and it does not support the ACCESSKEY attribute.

Disabling Form Controls

We saw earlier in the Skill that every form control can be disabled, which prevents that form control from being submitted. IE 4 shows disabled elements as being grayed-out. HTML 4.0 describes disabled elements as being unable to take focus (that is, you can't tab to or click on disabled elements).

Since all versions of Navigator so far and the early versions of IE 3 and earlier don't support disabled controls, there's not much reason to disable a control yet. However, when this attribute is more widely supported, you'll be able to add scripts that make controls disabled, depending on what options are selected.

Read-Only Form Controls

Similarly, a read-only control is one that can't be changed. It's useful if you want to show and submit form information that you don't want the user to change.

You can make text and password boxes read-only, as well as textarea elements.

However, Navigator and IE 3 (and earlier) don't support the read-only attribute so you might find the text that you thought was read-only has been changed by the user after all, and a different value submitted to your CGI program than expected.

The only safe way to make sure that a value is always submitted without being changed is to make it a hidden control (see the input element's hidden type, earlier in the Skill).

Setting Tab Order and Access Keys

In Skill 7, we learned about the use of the ACCESSKEY attribute to create a keyboard shortcut for links. The same ACCESSKEY attribute can be used with input, button, label, and legend elements to create shortcut keys for form controls.

By assigning an ACCESSKEY="Z" attribute, for example, you can make a submit button or any other input form control trigger on a key press (Alt+Z in Windows, Cmd+Z in Macintosh, and other keyboard shortcuts on different platforms).

Unfortunately, while IE 4 supports these new shortcuts for input controls, it doesn't support them for labels or legend elements, and Navigator 4 doesn't support access key shortcuts at all.

Even without access key shortcuts, the latest versions of IE and Navigator let you use the Tab key to move through the controls in a form. (The Enter key or space bar trigger checkboxes and radio buttons, and the arrow keys can choose menu items.)

For a form with a lot of elements, it's sometimes inconvenient to have to hit the Tab key many times to work your way from control to control.

Skill 12

That's why HTML 4.0 lets you assign each control a number through a TABINDEX attribute in the control's element. This number can be high or low, negative or positive. The effect of a TABINDEX is to change the order of where the Tab key takes you. Higher numbers will receive focus earlier than lower numbers.

HTML 4.0 defines the following four rules for how elements should receive focus:

- Those elements that support the TABINDEX attribute and assign a positive value to it are navigated first. Navigation proceeds from the element with the lowest TABINDEX value to the element with the highest value. Values need not be sequential nor must they begin with any particular value. Elements that have identical TABINDEX values should be navigated in the order they appear in the document.

- Those elements that do not have a TABINDEX attribute defined (or do not support it) are navigated next. These elements are navigated in the order they appear in the document.

- Those elements that support the TABINDEX attribute and assign a negative value to it do not participate in the tabbing order.

- Elements that are disabled do not participate in the tabbing order.

It can be tricky to get the TABINDEX values in a useful order, and for a really long form that loads slowly, the order may be a little skewed until all of the form controls have been downloaded.

The elements that support the TABINDEX attribute are the anchor element, the object element, all of the input element variations, the select element, the textarea element, and the button element.

Processing Forms

Now that we've seen how to create forms and use form controls, it's time to take a brief look at the last half of the forms equation—how a form is processed. There are three ways to process a form: by using a CGI program, by using a mailto link, and by using a script.

Using Active Scripting to Process Forms

In Skill 15, we'll learn more about active scripting languages (such as JavaScript and VBScript) and see a little bit about how an active script can process a form.

Unfortunately, even the most comprehensive active script can't really do all the work. As we'll learn, active scripting languages are hampered by security considerations so they might not be able to handle what you need. If the form's data is only going to be manipulated in order to create a new page, then an active script might be fine. But if you need to compile the data somewhere and save it, then an active script can't handle that task since most active scripts can't save results at all.

TIP   An active script is often a good way to "pre-process" data—for example, make sure that information is valid and that required fields are filled out—before submitting the data to an e-mail address or a CGI program. See Skill 15 for an example.

Using Mailto Processing

In this Skill, we've seen several examples of how the POST method and a valid mailto URL can be used to send a form's data to a mail address. We saw the warnings displayed by IE and Navigator regarding the security risk inherent in someone sending data by e-mail (the principal risks being that a surfer has to reveal their e-mail address, and that e-mail is not secure so anyone can intercept a password or credit card number).

NOTE   You may want to review the "Considering Form Security" and "Receiving Feedback by Mail" sections at the beginning of this Skill.

In addition, since IE 3 doesn't usually support mailto actions, there's a good chance that surfers will go to some effort to fill out your form and try to submit it only to discover that their browser can't mail the results to you.

This doesn't mean that you can never receive results by e-mail, however. Secure Web servers usually include special secure CGI programs that can send encrypted e-mail to a designated address. This saves you from having to use a mailto URL for form processing.

A final consideration is that just mailing the results to someone doesn't do anything to compile or track statistics or accumulate data. The e-mail has to be responded to and dealt with before anything happens. It's time-consuming and painful to have to process e-mails by hand; you'll probably need a program that processes the e-mail—which means you're right back in the same dilemma where you started. You need a program to process forms. Usually, the best way to process a form is a CGI program.

Using CGI to Process Forms

At the beginning of this Skill, we took a look at CGI, defining the term and listing the languages that can be used to create CGI programs that will process your form.

By far the most popular CGI language currently is Perl, the Practical Extraction and Report Language—a free interpreted scripting language created by Larry Wall for manipulating text, among other things. The latest version is Perl 5.

If you are familiar with Perl programming, you can write your own CGI Perl script to handle your form's data. You can hire programmers to write it for you; or you can just dive in and modify an existing Perl script for your needs. If you use common sense and test your results thoroughly, then you should be fine.

By using CGI, you can have form information be sent to another Web page or e-mail address, you can update a guestbook, compile statistics, send back custom-generated feedback e-mail, or submit a credit card number to a bank.

Your ISP may be able to help you with "canned" scripts that you can insert into your Web pages. Many ISPs have already set up the basic scripts that you'll need (since many customers aside from you will have the same requirements).

If all else fails, though, and you know that you can put CGI programs on your Web server, then you should take a trip to Matt's Script Archive (`http://www.worldwidemart.com/scripts/`), which is a well-traveled resource for prewritten scripts. Most of the scripts archived at Matt Wright's site are written in Perl, and each of them are well-documented with step-by-step instructions for customizing the appropriate areas.

There are also good places on the Web to start learning how to create CGI programs, in Perl or another language. Try searching for "CGI" and "Perl" at Yahoo! or a search engine.

Using Tips and Tricks with Forms

Finally, although we don't recommend it in every case, you can create some special effects on a Web page by using controls out of the context of a normal form.

For example, Janan's personal Web page (`http://www.sonic.net/web/jpages/`) uses a pull-down menu to describe the page:

```
<FORM>
<CENTER>
<FONT SIZE=5>Janan Platt</FONT><BR>
and Her
<SELECT NAME="Nontoxic">
<OPTION>Drive-Thru<OPTION>Nonprofit<OPTION>Numinous<OPTION>Dangerous
<OPTION>All American
<OPTION>Flame-Retardant<OPTION>Headless<OPTION>Unscented
```

```
<OPTION>Maximum Security
<OPTION>Curmudgeonly<OPTION>Warm, Fuzzy<OPTION>Frothy<OPTION>Big-Time
<OPTION>Grand Central<OPTION>In-Your-Face
<OPTION>Menacing<OPTION>Lactose
Intolerant<OPTION>Monolithic<OPTION>Treadless
<OPTION>Fiscally Conservative<OPTION>Aesopian<OPTION>Nontoxic</SELECT>
Word Page</FONT>
</CENTER>
</FORM>
```

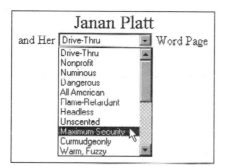

The effect of this form is shown here. This form doesn't have a submit button (or even an ACTION) so the value chosen from the pull-down menu won't be processed or sent anywhere. It's just for fun. Similarly, you can include form effects on parts of your pages.

 **WARNING**   Be careful; these uses of forms are not valid HTML or true to the intentions of the form element. Don't use them on pages that aren't experimental or for amusement.

In this Skill, we've learned the full variety of elements used to create form controls. At this point, we've learned every official element in HTML. In the next Skill, we'll look at some unofficial extensions to HTML, and in future Skills we'll look at other technologies that go hand in hand with HTML, such as style sheets (Skill 14), scripting languages and applets (Skill 15), and Dynamic HTML (Skill 16).

Are You Experienced?

Now you can...

- ☑ **create forms and form controls**
- ☑ **send the form's data to a CGI program or an e-mail address**
- ☑ **use the new HTML 4.0 form elements and groups**
- ☑ **create buttons, text boxes and other controls, as well as simple go buttons**

Skill 12

Experimenting with HTML Extensions

- ➔ Following the history of proprietary extensions
- ➔ Reviewing the current popular Web browsers
- ➔ Understanding how to use proprietary tags properly
- ➔ Creating excitement with Navigator and IE extensions

Now that the first 12 Skills have shown us all of the official elements and attributes of HTML 4.0, it's time to see some elements and attributes that are not officially part of HTML but are still in widespread use. When a browser vendor such as Netscape or Microsoft supports an unofficial element, tag, or attribute (that is, one not described by the World Wide Web Consortium's official HTML specification), it's known as an *extension* to HTML. If only one browser supports the extension, then it's often called a *proprietary extension*.

In this Skill, we'll examine the history and use of extensions. Some extensions are good ideas that have been endorsed by the W3C. Other extensions are poor ideas because they do not fit well with HTML's philosophy. Netscape and Microsoft are notorious for poorly documenting their extensions, so we'll teach you when it may be safe to use an extension and how each extension works.

Learning the History of Extensions

In 1995, Microsoft released the first version of Internet Explorer and tried to decrease Netscape's dominant market share. HTML authors have suffered from the fallout of this *browser war* between Microsoft and Netscape ever since (see Skill 20).

Part of the Microsoft and Netscape browser war strategy includes marketing an exciting (and often frustrating) array of proprietary extensions to the standard HTML specification. Browser marketers offer the proprietary tags to increase their market share.

This seemed to work for Navigator. Its earliest versions offered elements for centering text, changing font sizes, and making text blink. Since the other browsers available at the time couldn't do that, some people switched to Navigator. But most people switched because Navigator 1 was efficient, easy to get, free, and quite capable (combining a news reader, mail program, and browser into one package).

 NOTE   The browser war and the dominance of Netscape and Microsoft was enough to force many other browsers into extinction. In 1995 there were dozens of actively developed browsers. By early 1997, NCSA (originators of Mosaic) finally threw in the towel, no longer offering updates of their Mosaic Web browser. Lynx is now the third-most popular browser.

Microsoft tried the extension strategy as well. IE 2 and 3, for example, offered the <MARQUEE> tag and other extensions in hopes that people would switch from Navigator to IE so they could see the marquees and other extensions in action. (We'll discuss IE's extensions later in this Skill.)

The glut of proprietary extensions and the sometimes-confusing issues of which Web browsers could display which extensions threatened to cause a sort of Balkanization of the Web. Sites could be developed with extensions to "look good" for either Navigator or for IE, but not both.

Web authors have suffered through the fast and furious offerings of unstable beta versions of browsers—all claiming to include "New! Improved! Exciting!" extensions to HTML.

An End to Extensions?

In mid-1996, Microsoft issued an exciting and somewhat surprising pledge (http://www.microsoft.com/internet/html.htm) on HTML standards: "Previous proprietary HTML extensions from Microsoft and other vendors have confused the market, hampered interoperability, and been ill-conceived with respect to the design principles underlying HTML (and its SGML parent)."

Microsoft pledged not to introduce new extensions without first having them approved by the W3C. Along with this pledge, Microsoft also offers the question: "Microsoft agrees to hold itself to these standards. Will all the other Web browser vendors, including Netscape, also agree to this conduct of behavior?"

Netscape has not yet agreed to use only W3C-approved elements and attributes, but they are moving in that direction.

 NOTE   The W3C supports an independent Web Interoperability Pledge (WIP). The WIP campaign consists of Web authors who state, "I pledge to use only recommended HTML tags as defined by W3C." The W3C argues that "by pledging to support only official standards, users take away the incentive for vendors to 'cheat' by introducing proprietary extensions."

Why Should You Not Use Extensions to HTML?

The Web was designed to be a universal system that can deliver information to everyone without restricting its audience. This unity is one of the most useful features of the Web. Therefore, the main and obvious problem with HTML extensions is their failure to be cross-compatible among browsers.

Browsers can have different reactions to an extension. While most browsers simply ignore elements and attributes that they don't understand, the trouble comes when browsers each implement the extension in a slightly different way. The use of some proprietary extensions can cause a browser to have trouble displaying a page properly (or at all). In extreme cases, the extension may confuse the browser so much that it actually crashes.

Here are a few other reasons for not using extensions: Your pages will be invalid HTML, and therefore you won't be able validate your documents to check for errors (see Skill 17). You're at the mercy of the whims of the browser vendor. If they change their mind about how a particular extension works in a future version of their browser, then you may have to redo your page. The extensions are poorly documented and may behave in unexpected ways. Text-to-speech readers in particular may be confused by extensions.

"THIS SITE BEST VIEWED WITH NETSCAPE NAVIGATOR"

Surf the Web for long and you'll run into a lot of sites that say that they were designed for Navigator. This may be because the site uses extensions created by Netscape, or because the Web author has only tested the site with Navigator.

Some Web authors assert that they use Navigator-only extensions because "95 percent of our readers use Netscape browsers." But there are several problems with this argument.

First, it is difficult to accurately determine what browser is being used or how many people from a particular location are viewing a page. Most surfers won't bother to fill out an online survey if a site tries to ask them what browser they use. (Many people use more than one browser, so individual surveys may be misleading anyway.) Since most browsers are free or downloaded from the Web, it's not wise to rely on sales figures. No current polls on browser use are scientifically valid—and trends change too quickly for any poll to be reliable for long. Techniques for detecting the browser automatically are not 100 percent reliable. Second, the reason that a site designed for Navigator seems to attract mostly Navigator users could well be that non-Navigator users don't bother to access (or cannot access) a site that claims it is "best viewed with Netscape Navigator."

And finally, there are easily more than 200 different versions of Navigator (counting the many different official releases, interim releases, beta releases, preview releases, international versions, different platforms, and different options such as Gold, minimum, full, secure, and

continued ▶

other options). Even if an extension works with one version of Navigator, it's difficult to know which other versions will understand the extension. The safest and easiest thing to do is to not write your HTML code for a particular browser; instead, just use valid HTML to give your site the widest possible audience.

One issue to consider is whether an extension is backward-compatible. If other browsers are able to ignore the extension and still have the page display properly, than the extension is said to be one that *degrades gracefully*.

Style sheets (Skill 14) are a new way for Web designers to offer their viewers attractively designed documents without abusing HTML elements or resorting to extensions. Style sheets can be much more powerful than formatting elements. As you'll see in the next Skill, style sheets can be stored completely separately from the HTML document it formats. Users and browsers with special needs (such as search engine robots, the disabled, text-only browsers, color-blind users) can easily set their browser to ignore style sheets. As a result, style sheets degrade very gracefully.

Why Should You Use Extensions to HTML?

There are a few reasons to justify using extensions:

- **Knowing your audience** If you have done extensive studies and know exactly what browser your audience is using (a difficult task, as we saw just now), or if you are creating pages on an intranet and you know exactly what browser each user at your site is using, then it's probably safe to use an extension.

- **Degrading gracefully** If the extension degrades gracefully and its absence won't prevent access to the content of your page.

- **Axe grinding** Some designers really dislike a particular browser, and maliciously use extensions on a page to make it difficult for users of that browser to see their page.

- **Compelling content** Some extensions allow design effects or content that can't be achieved any other way. If the whole purpose of your page revolves around multiple columns, for example, or different layering effects, then there may be no other choice but to use Netscape's extension for multiple columns or layers.

If you've considered the drawbacks and you still want to use an HTML extension, you should test your HTML code under every reasonable condition. Cutting-edge extensions (such as Dynamic HTML) may crash a Web browser. Your audience will probably get frustrated and even fearful of your pages if they need to reboot their computer several times while trying to view your Web site.

Using Netscape's Non-Standard Extensions to HTML

The first versions of Navigator introduced extensions that the W3C eventually incorporated into different versions of HTML: Features such as center, font, tables, and frames were originally Netscape extensions.

 NOTE   Some people call Navigator-only extensions *Netscapisms*.

Some Netscape-proposed extensions have not been accepted by the W3C, either because they are too different from the intentions of HTML or because they are too new. In our discussion of Navigator extensions, we'll look at the blink element, the multicol element, the spacer element, and the new layer element. We'll end with some other miscellaneous Netscapisms.

Flashing Text with the Blink Element

Introduced with Navigator version 1, the blink element is a font element that makes text wink on and off continually. It's something of a Netscape trademark, reviled by many who call it "the dreaded blink tag."

 **WARNING**   IE has always ignored this element.

To use the blink element, start with a `<BLINK>` tag and include the text that you want to blink. End the blink element with a `</BLINK>` tag.

 **WARNING**   You should be extra careful with this element. Blinking text is hard to read. There's also the remote possibility that overuse of blinking text can trigger seizures in those with epilepsy.

To quote from the Suck e-zine (`http://www.suck.com/daily/95/09/07/daily.html`): "It's like stringing Christmas lights around a Picasso...very poor taste."

Creating Multiple Text Columns with the Multicol Element

The multiple column element displays text in multiple newspaper columns (also known as snaking columns). This element was introduced with Navigator 3.

 **WARNING**   Only Navigator 3 and 4 display multiple columns.

To use the multicol element, start with a `<MULTICOL>` tag and include the text you want displayed in multiple columns. End the columns with a `</MULTICOL>` tag. The multicol element has several attributes:

- The first attribute, `COLS`, is mandatory and defines how many columns the text or images will be split into.

- The `GUTTER` attribute defines the amount of space between columns in pixels (the default is 10 pixels).

- The `WIDTH` attribute determines the width of the entire multicol element (including all of the columns). You can specify the width in either pixels or a percentage of the window. By default, the columns will fill the entire window. All columns will always share the same column width.

Using the Spacer Element

Navigator's spacer element extension allows Web page designers to control vertical and horizontal white space. The spacer element uses a `<SPACER>` tag with several possible options; this element was introduced in Navigator 3.

 WARNING   IE and browsers other than Navigator 3 and 4 ignore the spacer element.

There are three possible uses of the spacer element, depending on its `TYPE` attribute. One of these three types is required:

- `TYPE="VERTICAL"`   Creates vertical white space (between lines of text, or above or below an image)

- TYPE="HORIZONTAL"   Creates horizontal white space (to create paragraph indents or to space apart words or images within the text-flow of a line)

- TYPE="BLOCK"   Creates a rectangle of white space (similar to an invisible image)

To use the spacer element, start with the text or images that will need some space. At the point where you want the white space created, insert a <SPACER> tag with the appropriate attributes. The spacer element does not require an end tag.

The spacer element has several other attributes:

- SIZE   For vertical or horizontal spacer types, this attribute indicates the amount of white space (in pixels) that should be created.

- WIDTH and HEIGHT   For TYPE="BLOCK" spacers, these two attributes control the horizontal and vertical dimensions of the rectangle of white space, in pixels.

- ALIGN   For TYPE="BLOCK" spacers, you can use any of the alignment attributes that can be used with an image (see Skill 8).

Using the Layer Element

The layer element is new to Navigator 4 and allows for absolute positioning of Web page design elements, including the ability to position one element on top of another element.

 NOTE   Netscape acknowledges that the layer element is beginning to look too propri-etary to have much use to most Web designers. Netscape is recommending that Web designers instead use Cascading Style Sheets and JavaScript to achieve the same effect as layering.

The layer element is a big part of Microsoft's Dynamic HTML strategy (which we'll see in Skill 16); the basic idea is that you use JavaScript to change which layers are visible and to animate the layers. We'll explain a bit about the layer element and its attributes here. For a more in-depth look at layers, you can visit the Netscape Web site and read their developer's notes for the layer element (http:// developer.netscape.com/library/documentation/communicator/layers/).

To use the layer element, start with a <LAYER> tag and nest the text or images that you want layered. End the layer element with a </LAYER> tag. You can also use an inflow layer element, with the <ILAYER> and </ILAYER> tags. The differ-ence is only that layer elements are absolutely positioned by you, while an inflow layer element is positioned by the natural flow of the page.

You can also use a SRC attribute with the layer element to include an external file as a layer (either an HTML document or an image). In this way, the layer element is somewhat similar to the inline frames element (iframe) that we learned in Skill 11.

Layers can be nested, and they can also be solid or transparent. Each layer element, and all the elements within the beginning and ending tags, creates a single layer of content that can be moved and altered as a unit.

The layer element has quite a few attributes:

- The ID attribute names the layer (so that it can be affected by active scripts and targeted links), for example <LAYER ID="joe">.

- The LEFT and TOP attributes specify the layer's initial position on the page (in pixels). For example, <LAYER LEFT="100" TOP="50"> positions a layer 100 pixels from the left margin, and 50 pixels down. For inflow layer elements, these two attributes can nudge a layer to the right or down.

- The Z-INDEX, ABOVE, or BELOW attributes determine the three-dimensional position of the layer, which results in whether the layer is underneath or on top of another layer. You can only use one of these three attributes. For example, if you give one layer a Z-INDEX="15" attribute and a second layer a Z-INDEX="5" attribute, then the first layer will be on top of the second one. (Normally, each layer goes on top of the previous layers.) Alternately, you can give a layer an ABOVE="joe" attribute, which puts this layer above the layer named joe.

- The WIDTH and HEIGHT attributes determine a layer's dimensions.

- The CLIP attribute is a set of four numbers that can define the visible boundaries of a layer. For example, an image that is normally 200 pixels wide and 100 pixels tall could be cropped with a CLIP="5,20,45,60" attribute. This would display a rectangular subset of the image, starting at the fifth pixel over and the 20th pixel down, and ending at the 45th pixel over and the 60th pixel down.

- The VISIBILITY attribute determines whether a layer is invisible. By default, layers are visible (VISIBILITY="SHOW"), but you can set VISIBILITY to either "HIDDEN" or "INHERIT" as well. VISIBILITY="HIDDEN" would make a layer invisible, while VISIBILITY="INHERIT" gives a layer the same visibility property as its parent layer (for nested layers only).

- The BGCOLOR and BACKGROUND attributes work the same for layers as they do for the body element, creating a background color or background image respectively. (By default, layers are transparent.)

All together, these attributes allow you to define precisely positioned, overlapping layers of transparent or solid content in a Web page. You can find an example of the layer element on the book's Web site.

NOTE A nolayer element displays some alternate content for those browsers that don't support the layer element. However, Netscape gives little documentation of its use. It appears that you can embed the nolayer element within a layer element; anything within the nolayer portion is only displayed if the layer can't be displayed.

Using Other Navigator Extensions

Navigator offers a few other extensions that we won't explain in detail. To summarize:

We saw in Skill 8 that the ALIGN attribute of and <IMG> tag can be set to "TOP", "MIDDLE", or "BOTTOM". Since some lines of text have elements of varying height, the results of these three ALIGN attributes might not always be what you expect. So Netscape introduces some other possibilities for image alignment: "ABSMIDDLE", "ABSBOTTOM", "TEXTTOP", and "BASELINE". You can use trial and error to see if these attributes will help, but remember that they are extensions to HTML and therefore won't be supported by every browser.

These attributes are also used in the input elements of forms (see Skill 12) when you've specified a submit button image and want to control its alignment. The same goes for the applet element (see Skill 15).

The no break element uses the <NOBR> and </NOBR> tags. When wrapped around a section of text, the text will not word wrap at all—it will be one continuous long line (causing horizontal scrolling if necessary). This is useful if there is a section of text that should be one continuous line. However, the non-breaking space ( ) introduced in Skill 3 is more accepted for this practice. If you have a long no break section and want to indicate a particular place where a line-break could occur if necessary, you can use Navigator's proprietary <WBR> tag. (To break a line unconditionally, just use the <BR> tag.) Both the <NOBR> and <WBR> tags are long-time Netscape extensions that have never caught on.

Navigator 4 introduces the concept of dynamic fonts and extends the font tag so you can use a POINT-SIZE attribute to specify an exact point size for a font. (For example, <FONT FACE="Baskerville" POINT-SIZE="18">.) You can also indicate how bold a font should be by specifying its *weight* (degree of boldness) with the Netscape's proprietary WEIGHT attribute: for example, you could use an attribute such as WEIGHT="600" (which is only useful for those fonts that have several different font weights, traditionally numbered in hundreds). Be careful with both of these attributes since they aren't well supported by browsers and because point sizes are notoriously variable from platform to platform. (There's a significant size difference between a 12-point font on a Macintosh and a 12-point font on a PC, for instance.)

NOTE   Two other Navigator-only extensions are rarely used. The keygen element (<KEYGEN>) can be used to verify a surfer's identity using encryption "keys" when you're using a secure server. The server element (<SERVER>) is used with Netscape's "LiveWire" technology to run a server-side script. You'll need to pick up a book on server security or LiveWire to learn about these elements.

Using Microsoft's Non-Standard Extensions to HTML

Although Microsoft has now pledged to not introduce any more proprietary extensions to HTML without first submitting them to the W3C, Microsoft previously introduced numerous extensions that worked only with IE.

NOTE   Some HTML 4.0 elements work a little differently in IE 3 than IE 4. For example, in IE 3, the object element was used only to insert ActiveX controls (we'll discuss ActiveX in Skill 15). IE 4 correctly allows different types of object elements, as specified by HTML 4.0.

We'll look at a few early proprietary IE elements that are still fully functional in IE 4. We'll start with the marquee element and then look at creating background sounds and colored rules.

Using the Marquee Element

The marquee element creates a region with scrolling text, similar to a live ticker tape from a stock brokerage firm. The marquee element originated in IE 2.

WARNING   Since Navigator and other browsers completely ignore the marquee element, and since the marquee element is a particularly display-oriented concept, we recommend that you avoid using it.

If you do want to use the marquee element, start with a <MARQUEE> tag and then include the text that you want scrolled across the screen. End the marquee element with a </MARQUEE> tag.

The marquee element has several attributes:

- ALIGN="TOP" or ALIGN="MIDDLE" or ALIGN="BOTTOM" for vertical alignment of the marquee text (relative to the text around the marquee)

- BEHAVIOR="SCROLL" or BEHAVIOR="SLIDE" or BEHAVIOR="ALTERNATE" to determine how the marquee behaves, either scrolling text like a ticker tape (the default behavior), flying text in, or having it move from side to side

- BGCOLOR to set the background color of the marquee (with a color name or an RGB value)

- DIRECTION="LEFT" or DIRECTION="RIGHT" to set the direction used with the BEHAVIOR attribute

- HEIGHT and WIDTH to set (in pixels or as a percentage of the window) the vertical and horizontal size of the marquee

- HSPACE and VSPACE to set the number of pixels of horizontal and vertical space around the marquee

- LOOP to set the number of times the marquee display will do its thing (the default behavior is LOOP="INFINITE")

- SCROLLAMOUNT with a number of pixels to determine how much the marquee text moves each time it scrolls

- SCROLLDELAY to set an amount of time (in milliseconds) between each successive scrolling of the marquee text

 NOTE   The Web site shows an example of a marquee.

Creating Background Sounds with the *<BGSOUND>* Tag

The <BGSOUND> tag causes a background sound to start playing when a document loads. To use the <BGSOUND> tag, specify a sound file and place the tag near the end of a document (so that your document has a chance to load before IE has to load the background sound).

The <BGSOUND> tag has two attributes: SRC and LOOP. The SRC attribute defines the URL of the sound file to be played. (Sound file formats were discussed in Skill 9.)

The LOOP attribute defines the number of times the sound file is to be played. You can specify a number of times to repeat the sound, or you can specify the keyword "INFINITE" to make it play as long as that page is displayed.

Here are two examples:

```
<BGSOUND SRC="sounds/solarwind.au" LOOP="5">
<BGSOUND SRC="silence.mid" LOOP="INFINITE">
```

 **WARNING**   See the end of Skill 9 for some discussions of background sounds and some warnings about their use.

Using IE's Attribute Extensions for Colored Rules

IE allows the use of the COLOR attribute with the horizontal rule element (the <HR> tag) to specify the color of the rule. Since this attribute is not an official HTML attribute for horizontal rules, this is an extension to HTML. However, since browsers that don't understand the COLOR attribute will ignore it, this attribute degrades very gracefully.

As with other COLOR attributes, you can either use an RGB color value or specify a color name.

The HTML code below creates one default gray rule and seven different colored rules:

```
<!DOCTYPE HTML PUBLIC "-//Microsoft//DTD Internet Explorer 3.0
HTML//EN">
<HTML>
<HEAD>
        <TITLE>IE and Colored Rules</TITLE>
</HEAD>
<BODY>

<HR SIZE="5">
<HR COLOR="VIOLET" SIZE="5">
<HR COLOR="#FF0000" SIZE="5">
<HR COLOR="BLUE" SIZE="5">
<HR COLOR="GREEN" SIZE="5">
<HR COLOR="YELLOW" SIZE="5">
<HR COLOR="BLACK" SIZE="5">
<HR COLOR="TEAL" SIZE="5">

</BODY>
</HTML>
```

Specifying Page Margins and Background Properties in IE

In IE 2 and later, you can add proprietary attributes to a document's <BODY> tag in order to apply a top and left margin. The TOPMARGIN attribute specifies (in pixels) how much of a top margin you'd like for a page. The LEFTMARGIN attribute specifies the left margin in pixels. For example:

```
<BODY TOPMARGIN="20" LEFTMARGIN="30">
```

This would create a left margin of 30 pixels and a top margin of 20 pixels. There's no way to specify a right margin or a bottom margin. And of course, no browser other than IE obeys these two attributes. (You can have much greater control over a document's margins by using a style sheet; see Skill 14.)

IE 2 and later also allow you to specify the BGPROPERTIES="FIXED" attribute. This prevents a background image from scrolling with the document. Some HTML tools call this kind of non-scrolling background a *watermark*. For example:

```
<BODY BACKGROUND="tree.jpg" BGPROPERTIES="FIXED">
```

Again, Navigator and other browsers ignore this unofficial extension to HTML. The image of the tree might be a watermark in IE, but it will scroll in every other browser.

Using Extensions Understood by Both Navigator and IE

Although not endorsed by the W3C, some extensions have been "cloned" by both browsers—one browser introduces the extension, and by the time the next version comes out, the other browser obeys it as well.

One example is the embed element, which can put inline multimedia on a page. Another example is the BACKGROUND attribute, which can put images in table cells.

Using the Embed Element to Include Multimedia

The embed element lets you insert plug-in elements into your Web pages, as seen in Skill 9. To use the embed element, start with an <EMBED> tag. Text and images may be included within the embed element; these will be displayed near the plug-in. End the embed element with an </EMBED> tag.

The EMBED element has several attributes that should be used:

- SRC to specify the embedded object's URL

- HEIGHT and WIDTH (specified in pixels)

Several additional attributes exist depending on the plug-in program.

Here's an example of the HTML code that embeds an audio player into an IE page and allows the surfer to play a sound:

```
<!DOCTYPE HTML PUBLIC "-//Microsoft//DTD Internet Explorer 3.0
HTML//EN">
<HTML>
<HEAD>
      <TITLE>The EMBED Proprietary Element</TITLE>
</HEAD>
<BODY>

<EMBED SRC="vacuum.au">
Click on the button above to listen to my vacuum.
</EMBED>

</BODY>
</HTML>
```

Figure 13.1 shows Active Movie, IE's embedded sound player (see Skill 9 for more information about sounds).

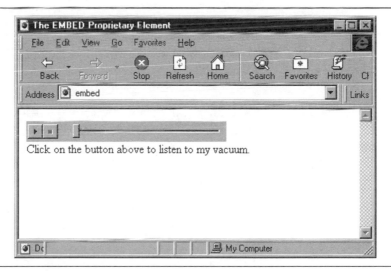

FIGURE 13.1: IE displays an embedded audio player.

IE supports the use of a noembed element nested inside the embed element in order to present alternate information to IE surfers who can't display the embed element (if they don't have the appropriate plug-in). Anything between the

<NOEMBED> and </NOEMBED> tags will only be displayed by IE if the embedded object itself can't be displayed. For example:

```
<EMBED SRC="disney.avi" HEIGHT="150" WIDTH="175">
  <NOEMBED>
    Your browser can't display in-line AVI movies, but you can still
    view this <A HREF="disney.avi">Disney movie</A>.
  </NOEMBED>
</EMBED>
```

Even though other browsers don't necessarily understand the noembed element, they will still show the correct thing if you use the above code (because other browsers will simply ignore the <NOEMBED> and </NOEMBED> tags).

Changing Heights and Displaying Background Images in a Table

In Skill 10, we learned how to create tables and table cells. We saw some extensions in that Skill. In addition, you'll want to include a particular image as the background of a cell (with the cell's data superimposed on the background image).

Navigator 4, IE 3, and IE 4 can place a background image in a cell. Simply add a BACKGROUND attribute to a table data tag (<TD>) or table heading tag (<TH>):

```
<TD BACKGROUND="URL">
<TH BACKGROUND="URL">
```

In addition, sometimes you'll want to specify the height of a cell or a table. IE 3 and 4 as well as Navigator 3 and 4 allow you to specify the number of pixels or a percentage of the window size for either a table's height or an individual cell's height.

Here's some sample HTML code for a colored table with a particular height:

```
<!DOCTYPE HTML PUBLIC "-//Microsoft//DTD Internet Explorer 3.0
HTML//EN">
<HTML>
<HEAD>
    <TITLE>Four Cells with Backgrounds</TITLE>
</HEAD>
<BODY>

<TABLE BORDER ALIGN="CENTER" HEIGHT="200" WIDTH="200" CELLSPACING="10"
CELLPADDING="5">
  <TR>
    <TH BGCOLOR="RED">Red cell</TH>
```

```
        <TH BACKGROUND="catwmn.gif">Catwoman, by Mark Napier</TH>
    </TR>
    <TR>
        <TH BACKGROUND="catwmn.gif">Catwoman, by Mark Napier</TH>
        <TH BGCOLOR="RED">Red cell</TH>
    </TR>
</TABLE>
</BODY>
</HTML>
```

This code would create a simple four-cell table that uses both the BGCOLOR and the BACKGROUND attributes to set the background. The cells are each about 100 pixels tall (because the entire table was set to be 200 pixels tall). The results are shown here in IE.

In addition, you can set the color of a table's border using proprietary extensions. IE 3 and 4 obey a BORDERCOLORLIGHT and BORDERCOLORDARK attribute to change a table border's color (for example, <TABLE BORDER BORDERCOLORLIGHT ="YELLOW" BORDERCOLORDARK ="RED">). Navigator 4 understands a BORDERCOLOR attribute to change the table's border color. Since the browser vendors have not reached a consensus here, a Web author has no real control over a table's border color (unless style sheets are being used).

While we don't recommend the use of extensions in general, they allow some interesting effects. As we'll see in the next Skill, style sheets offer more flexibility and are a better approach in most cases.

Are You Experienced?

Now you can...

☑ **understand the why and how of extensions**

☑ **create pages that use proprietary tags**

☑ **use extensions while offering cross-platform content**

Formatting Your Site with Cascading Style Sheets

- ➔ Understanding style sheets and Cascading Style Sheets, level one
- ➔ Creating style sheets and rules
- ➔ Using properties and values to change a document's appearance
- ➔ Attaching style sheets to HTML documents

Separating the *content* of a document from its *presentation* has many advantages. The main attraction is the ability to change your document's appearance without changing its substance. We've seen that HTML is used to display documents on many different kinds of systems, from personal computer screens to text-to-speech readers to cellular phones.

HTML was designed to classify the different parts of your document. By marking up the content, you let a browser do its job of presenting your document—whether the browser works on a computer screen or a telephone. Some Web authors are so concerned with their document's appearance that they use HTML elements incorrectly in order to force it to look nice on a certain browser and computer system. The drawback is that anyone using a different browser or a different platform may not be able to see or hear the content of the document.

HTML does have a few elements and attributes intended to help make a document look attractive (for example, the font element and the various attributes of the horizontal rule element)—but HTML 4.0 does not recommend these presentational features. Instead, HTML 4.0 endorses style sheets for better control over a document's appearance, in a way that doesn't interfere with the content of a document.

In theory, HTML lets you use any style sheet technology; in practice, the only type of style sheet that's well-supported is Cascading Style Sheets, level one (CSS1), a style sheet system developed by the W3C and supported by recent versions of Netscape Navigator and Microsoft Internet Explorer.

In this Skill, we'll show you how you can include CSS1 style sheets in your documents by using HTML elements and attributes. We'll introduce you to CSS1 and help you decide if CSS1 is right for your Web site. And we'll teach you enough of CSS1's syntax and properties to get you started.

Understanding Style Sheets

A *style sheet* is a collection of rules that affect the appearance of a document. Currently, the most common type of style sheet is Cascading Style Sheets (CSS). The first (and so far only) version of CSS is called "level one"; we'll use the term "CSS1" to mean Cascading Style Sheets, level one, throughout this Skill.

CSS1 is primarily concerned with how a document should appear onscreen, when the viewer is using a graphical browser (such as Navigator or IE). CSS1 uses style sheet rules to control about 50 different properties, such as color, background, font face, border appearance, margins, alignment, and character spacing. Here's an example of a CSS1 style sheet with one rule:

```
H1 { text-align: center }
```

This example rule centers every level-one heading element in an HTML document by default. As you can see, CSS1 style sheets use a completely different syntax than HTML.

 NOTE   While we'll do our best to show you some CSS1 properties and get you started using style sheets, read the official specification from W3C (http://www.w3.org/pub/WWW/TR/REC-CSS1) for a more in-depth discussion.

Seeing Style Sheets in Action

The easiest way to learn about style sheets is to use them in documents. We'll present two examples of how style sheets can change the appearance of a document. We'll start with a simple example of a CSS1 style sheet, then define some CSS1 terminology and syntax, and then look at a more complex CSS1 style sheet. After that we'll see how different browsers would display this complex style sheet. That will give us enough background information to start learning how HTML and CSS1 can work together. Then we'll see some more syntax of CSS1 and list a few of the more useful properties that CSS1 can control.

A Simple Example of CSS1

We'll create a CSS1 rule by using a style element (<STYLE> and </STYLE>) in the head section of an HTML document to change the appearance of all first-level headings:

```
<!DOCTYPE HTML PUBLIC "-//W3C//DTD HTML 4.0//EN">
<HTML LANG="EN">
  <HEAD>
    <TITLE>Cookbook for Jennie</TITLE>
    <STYLE TYPE="text/css">
     H1 { border: thick solid blue }
    </STYLE>
  </HEAD>
  <BODY>
    <H1>Jennie Chuang's Cookbook</H1>
    <P>This page will contain some of Jennie's favorite recipes.
  </BODY>
</HTML>
```

Copy from Style to Style then use the H1 anywhere [handwritten annotation]

This example would be displayed as a normal document in every respect *except* that any text enclosed within the <H1> and </H1> tags will be displayed with a thick border, as shown here in Navigator (IE's display would be similar).

Right away, you should be able to see one of the advantages of style sheets. This document doesn't contain any lengthy code for font or table elements; instead, the border is in the head section's style sheet, which consists of only one rule: H1 { border: thick solid blue }.

This rule simply says that level-one headings should have the "thick solid blue border" declaration. Rules consist of selectors and declarations, and declarations consist of properties and values. We'll define these terms in the next section.

 NOTE   The style element's <STYLE> tag used here has a TYPE attribute (TYPE= "text/css"), which declares that the style sheet is written in the Cascading Style Sheet language. This attribute or its equivalent is required so that your browser knows what style sheet language to use. We'll learn more about the style element and the TYPE attribute in the "Attaching a Style Sheet to an HTML Document" section later in this Skill.

Using CSS1 Terminology

Since CSS1 uses a different syntax than HTML, it also has different terminology. Instead of elements, tags, and attributes, CSS1 style sheets consist of rules, selectors, declarations, properties, and values. We'll now define these terms so that we can use a consistent vocabulary throughout this Skill.

The basic units of CSS1 are properties and values. A *property* is a browser behavior that can be affected by CSS1. For example, font-family, background, border, and text-align are all examples of properties. The properties that can be changed are listed in the CSS1 specification; as we said earlier, there are about 50 of them.

The *value* is whatever choice you can set for a property. For example, the font-family property's values can be font names such as arial, times, and courier, or one of the font-family properties we listed in Skill 6, such as serif or sans-serif. The CSS1 specification defines what the possible values are for each property.

A *declaration* is a property and its value (for example, `color: blue` is a declaration). To create a declaration, start with a property name (be sure to specify it exactly, including any hyphens), followed by a colon, followed by the value for the property. (A semicolon at the end of a single declaration is optional.)

A *selector* is the name of the HTML element to which you want to apply a declaration. For example, if you want to change the behavior of every blockquote element, then you would use BLOCKQUOTE as your selector. You can use simple selectors, which is simply the name of a single HTML element, or more complex *contextual selectors* that consist of several HTML elements; we'll learn about these in more detail later.

A *rule* is a selector plus a declaration. For example, P { `margin-left: 20%` } is a rule. The selector in this rule is the paragraph element (indicated by P), and the declaration is `margin-left: 20%`. The property being changed in this declaration is the `margin-left` property, which normally has a value of zero. We're changing the `margin-left` for every paragraph so that it has a value of 20% of the window's default width.

NOTE   Note the punctuation. In a rule, the selector is followed by the opening curly brace, then the declaration, and then a closing curly brace. (Curly braces are sometimes called *curly brackets* or *French braces*.)

You can group rules together. H1, H2 { `font-weight: normal` } groups two different selectors together to create two rules. Similarly, H1 { `background: black; color: white` } groups two different declarations together to create two rules. Grouped rules are called *rulesets*.

WARNING   When making a ruleset, be absolutely sure to separate selectors with commas and multiple declarations by semicolons. A single mistake (such as leaving out a comma) may cause the ruleset to have a completely different meaning or be ignored entirely.

A CSS1 *style sheet* consists of one or more rules or rulesets. The diagram in Figure 14.1 should help illustrate the terminology.

NOTE   By tradition, selectors are uppercase and declarations are lowercase. But this is only a tradition since CSS1 rules are not case-sensitive.

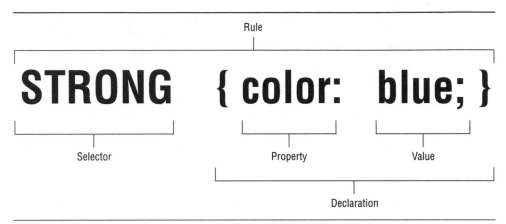

FIGURE 14.1: The terms used to define the parts of a CSS1 rule

A More Complex Example of CSS1

Before we get too hung up in learning about how CSS1's rules work, let's expand on the first example by making a few rulesets. This will give us a better idea of CSS1's capabilities and limitations. It may be worth your time to create this example yourself so that you can experiment with CSS1.

cookbook.html

```
<!DOCTYPE HTML PUBLIC "-//W3C//DTD HTML 4.0//EN">
<HTML LANG="EN">
<HEAD>
  <TITLE>Cookbook</TITLE>
  <STYLE type="text/css">
H1, H2 { font-family: monospace; }
BODY { color: white; background: black; }
P.warning {
  font-family: verdana, sans-serif;
  font-size: larger;
  text-align: center;
  color: red;
  background : cyan;
  border: thick groove gray;
}
  </STYLE>
</HEAD>
<BODY>
<H1>Rob's Cookbook</H1>
<P>This page contains some of Rob's favorite recipes.
<P CLASS="WARNING">Try not to burn yourself!</P>
```

```
<P>We'll start with a recipe for toast.
<H2>Toast</H2>
Ingredients:
<UL>
  <LI>Bread
  <LI>Toaster
</UL>
<HR>
<ADDRESS>Robert W. E. Mack</ADDRESS>
</BODY>
</HTML >
```

This HTML document contains a style sheet with 10 rules, in three sets of rule-sets. We'll briefly explain each of the rulesets.

The first ruleset is this: `H1, H2 { font-family: monospace; }`. There are two rules here: one for level-one headings, and the other for level-two headings. Both rules say the same thing: The font should be a monospaced font.

These two rules would be equivalent to using a font face element within each heading, for example `<H2><FONT FACE="Courier New,Courier">Toast</FONT></H2>`. Alternately, you could use the teletype element, `<H2><TT>Toast</TT></H2>`, but the teletype element often results in a slightly smaller font size when you use Navigator or IE. (See Skill 6 for more about the font and teletype elements.)

The second ruleset says: `BODY { color: white; background: black; }`. These two rules declare that the text color of the document should be white and the background color should be black. (This is equivalent to using body attributes to set text and background color, as we learned in Skill 3. For example, `<BODY TEXT="WHITE" BGCOLOR="BLACK">` would have the same effect.)

The third ruleset is more complex. It declares:

```
P.warning {
  font-family: verdana, sans-serif;
  font-size: larger;
  text-align: center;
  color: red;
  background : cyan;
  border: thick groove gray;
}
```

There are six rules here. Together they say that any paragraph element given the "warning" class should be displayed in the Verdana typeface, or a default sans-serif typeface if Verdana is not available (for example, Arial or Helvetica; the one that's chosen depends on the browser and what fonts are available). Also, the font size should be one size larger than normal, the paragraph should be centered, the text color should be red, the background color should be cyan, and a thick gray border should be around the paragraph in the "groove" border style.

There's no direct equivalent in HTML for all of these style sheet effects, but you could approximate the result by using a table (see Skill 10), along with some HTML elements that we covered in Skill 6, plus an HTML extension to get the border color right:

```
<TABLE BORDER="5" BORDERCOLOR="GRAY" ALIGN="CENTER" CELLPADDING="0"
CELLSPACING="0">
<TR>
<TD BGCOLOR="CYAN" ALIGN="CENTER">
<FONT SIZE="+1" COLOR="RED" FACE="verdana, helvetica, arial">Try not to
burn yourself!
</TD>
</TR>
</TABLE>
```

This code is invalid and illogical HTML. It pretends a paragraph is a table when it really isn't, it uses all sorts of visual formatting that has nothing to do with the content of the document, and it uses a proprietary HTML extension. More importantly, this code is bulkier and less efficient than a style sheet. Suppose you wanted a paragraph later in the document that says, "Don't eat raw pork!" to be displayed the same way as the paragraph about not burning yourself. With style sheets, we've defined the rule for how the "warning" class of paragraph should appear. To have another paragraph appear in this style, we could simply say <P CLASS= "WARNING">Don't eat raw pork!</P>. Without a style sheet, we'd have to repeat all of the table and font elements again.

 NOTE We're using the CLASS attribute, which is a generic HTML 4.0 attribute that can be applied to many different HTML elements. We'll discuss the CLASS attribute (and its close cousin the ID attribute) later in this Skill.

In the next section, we'll see how the cookbook.html document would be displayed by different versions of IE and Navigator.

How Various Browsers Display Style Sheets

Unfortunately, since style sheets are a new and emerging technology, different browsers react to them in different ways. Let's start by seeing how the latest versions of Navigator and IE display cookbook.html. Figure 14.2 shows how IE 4 will display this document.

Navigator 4 is the first release of Navigator that can display style sheets. Figure 14.3 shows how Navigator 4 displays cookbook.html.

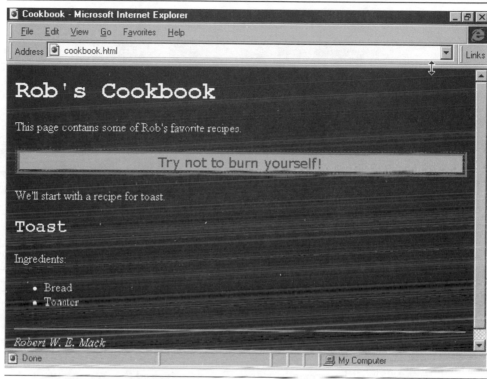

FIGURE 14.2: IE 4 follows the style sheet rules in a reasonable way.

NOTE   Future versions of both browsers will display this document slightly differently, since both Netscape and Microsoft have promised new versions of their browsers with better support for CSS1.

Some style sheet rules that Navigator 4 does follow correctly are not interpreted correctly by IE 4, and vice versa. Unfortunately, both browsers have numerous problems with style sheets (although IE has fewer problems than Navigator). A list of "known issues" (which is to say, *bugs*) is available from Netscape (`http://developer.netscape.com/support/bugs/known/css.html`). A comparison of the different browsers, showing which style sheet features are supported in each browser, is available from the W3C's CSS page (`http://www.w3.org/Style/CSS/#browsers`).

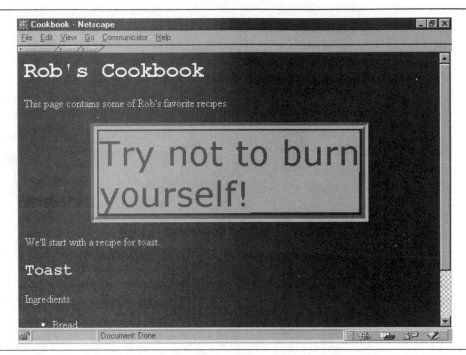

FIGURE 14.3: Navigator 4 has a lot of support for style sheets but is plagued by some serious misinterpretations. Here, Navigator is displaying the warning paragraph with too large of a font size, and the warning box should be the full width of the screen.

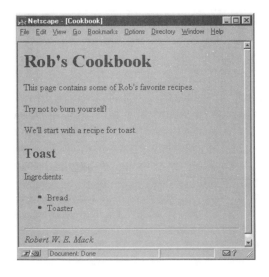

It's also important to remember that many people use older versions of Navigator and IE. Navigator 3 is extremely popular and has no support for style sheets at all. By design, your style sheets should only supplement a page's content, so Navigator users will be able to see your page, albeit without any style sheet information. Here's how Navigator 3 would display cookbook.html.

Another important consideration is that IE 3, still in popular use, has only partial support for style sheets.

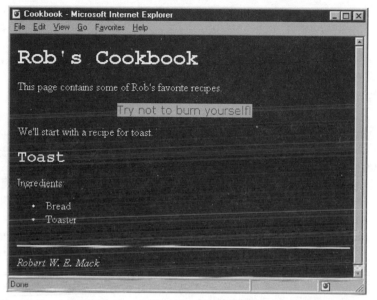

Most of the time, IE 3 safely ignores the style sheet properties that it doesn't understand. For example, IE 3 doesn't display borders, so as you can see here, `cookbook.html` is displayed with almost all of the rules intact, except for the border.

However, sometimes IE 3 can completely misunderstand some valid style sheet rules, leading to disastrous results.

Understanding CSS1's Advantages and Limitations

As you can tell, support of CSS1 is a mixed bag. CSS1 (and style sheets in general) have tremendous potential, but it's still a little early in their development. Safe use of CSS1 requires a lot of testing. CSS1 has a number of important advantages:

- You can write one style sheet with a number of different properties and attach this style sheet to every page on your site.

- If you do create a uniform style sheet for your site, you can revise that single file and give your entire Web site a facelift.

- You no longer have to rely on tricks and misuse of HTML elements to achieve some basic typographical effects.

- You can give your pages a distinct look—and a uniform, "branded" style—without the use of graphics.

- Style sheets are much more compact and specific than HTML formatting elements and can be reused more easily.

Already proposals and drafts have been written for future versions of CSS that will tackle more than what CSS1 currently aims to control. In the future, a W3C extension will help control the appearance of a printed HTML document, and Microsoft and Netscape are working together with the W3C to extend CSS1 to handle absolute positioning.

But CSS1 is specifically not intended to fulfill certain roles. CSS1 is *not* a layout language or page-description language. Unlike a word processor or desktop publishing program (such as Pagemaker or Framemaker), CSS1 cannot currently create layout effects like multiple newspaper columns or overlapping frames—nor can CSS1 force text to flow from one area to another.

CSS1 does *not* offer absolute control over a page's appearance. The Web is used all over the world, on hundreds of different platforms. Neither HTML nor CSS1 promise a designer absolute control over a document's appearance—in fact, you can be assured that your document *will* look different from platform to platform. Navigator and IE come in different versions and work differently on different computers. Furthermore, consider how your document will "appear" on a text-to-speech browser or a TV set. CSS1 allows you to hint at what your preferred fonts and appearance may be, but you can't guarantee a particular font will be available, nor can you know what screen resolution or window size will be used to view your page (or if a screen will be used at all).

CSS1 also *cannot* guarantee you any kind of absolute pixel control. Even with current work by Microsoft and Netscape extending CSS1 to allow absolute positioning, you will never be able to guarantee a particular image or line of text will be aligned at a particular point over a background image. (At best, you will be able to align objects absolutely for that small percentage of surfers who happen to be using the same screen resolution and window size with a CSS1-compliant browser.)

In some ways, HTML 4.0 uses style sheets as a promise of document appearance. But current implementations of CSS1 can't keep all of those promises yet. For example, HTML 4.0 recommends that you use style sheet properties to control the width, height, horizontal space, vertical space, and alignment of images, instead of using the WIDTH, HEIGHT, HSPACE, VSPACE, and ALIGN attributes in the <IMG> tag. However, Navigator and IE are not yet able to use these style sheet settings for images with any reliability at all.

 **WARNING** You'll definitely have to experiment with style sheet properties before being able to arrive at a style sheet that matches your intentions. It's essential that you test your style sheets in Navigator 4, IE 4, and IE 3.

> **NOTE** CSS is not the only style sheet technology. Although no current browser supports it, Document Style Semantics and Specification Language (DSSSL) is an advanced document transformation and style language. For more information, see Novell's specification (http://occam.sjf.novell.com:8080/dsssl/dsssl96). JavaScript Style Sheets (JSSS) uses JavaScript to change the appearance of a document. Navigator 4 can display documents using JSSS, but no other browser yet supports it. For more information, see Netscape's DevEdge (http://developer.netscape.com/library/documentation/communicator/dynhtml/index.htm).

Making HTML and CSS1 Work Together

Given CSS1's advantages and ability to offer better control over a document's appearance without damaging the document's content, it's worth experimenting with CSS1 in your HTML documents.

We'll first learn how you can use CSS1 within HTML elements and attributes. Don't worry too much about CSS1's syntax; we'll see some more examples later. In this section, we're interested in the elements and attributes used as *glue* to bind HTML and CSS1 together.

We need to discuss two types of glue: The first type is how you can attach a style sheet to an HTML document. The second type of glue is which HTML elements and attributes can help you work with style sheets.

After we see how to specify CSS1 as the style sheet language, we'll look at the first type of glue, which has four methods. Then we'll see how to specify style sheet names and apply style sheets to a particular media. Then we'll look at the second type of glue, which involves two HTML elements (the division and span elements introduced in Skill 6) and two generic attributes, CLASS and ID.

Setting the Default Style Sheet Language

Since there are several style sheet technologies, you must declare to browsers that you're using CSS1 as a document's style sheet language. There are two ways to do this:

- The first method is to include a TYPE="text/css" attribute with the style or link elements that attach a style sheet.

- The second method is to indicate the default style sheet language for the entire document by using a specific meta element anywhere in the head section: <META HTTP-EQUIV="Content-Style-Type" CONTENT="text/css">.

The second method is preferred because you can set the default style sheet language with just one tag, and you won't ever worry about needing to use the TYPE attribute in several different places.

We'll see more about where to use the TYPE attribute in the next few sections, when we learn about the link and style elements.

Attaching a Style Sheet to an HTML Document

There are four ways a Web author can associate a CSS1 style sheet with an HTML document. We'll talk about each method in the following sections.

Using Inline Style Declarations

There are times when you want to apply style declarations to an individual element in a particular HTML document. This is not an efficient way of using CSS1, since you have to repeat the declarations again if you want to apply the same effects to a different element. But if you only want a particular declaration in a single element, inline style declarations can be a useful approach.

NOTE   One drawback to this method is that it mixes your content with your presentation, which is what style sheets were designed to avoid.

TIP   If you just want to apply a particular style every now and then, you don't have to use an inline style declaration. Instead, you can use the CLASS or ID attributes (discussed a little later) to apply a particular style sheet.

The STYLE attribute can be included in just about any body section element (including the `<BODY>` tag itself). For example:

```
<BODY STYLE="background: yellow">
```

This would create a yellow background for the entire body of a particular HTML document. You can include any number of declarations; just separate each one by a semicolon. For example:

```
<P STYLE="font-weight: bolder; font-size: larger; color: yellow">He's
dead, Jim!</P>
```

This style declaration would make this particular paragraph bolder and larger than normal and also change the text color to yellow.

WARNING   When you use inline style sheets, be sure to specify the default style sheet language by using the `<META HTTP-EQUIV="Content-Style-Type" CONTENT="text/css">` tag in the head section.

Embedding a Style Sheet

As we've already seen, you can put a style sheet inside the style element in a document's head section. The style element contains a style sheet (consisting of one or more rules). The style element's `<STYLE>` tag should always contain a TYPE attribute to indicate what type of style sheet is included (unless you set the default style sheet language with the meta element we described).

NOTE   You can also specify a MEDIA attribute in the `<STYLE>` tag to indicate what media or medium this style sheet should apply to (see the "Applying Style Sheets to a Particular Media" section).

An optional advisory TITLE attribute can name a style sheet, and we'll discuss the meaning of titled style sheets in the "Naming External Style Sheets" section.

To create an embedded style sheet, you must always start with the `<STYLE>` start tag, then include the style sheet, and then finish with a `</STYLE>` end tag.

One important consideration for embedded style sheets is that older browsers (which are not aware of the style element) might get confused by the style elements contents and display the rules onscreen. To prevent this from happening, you should always comment out the style sheet by using the comment structure that we saw in Skill 6. CSS1-enabled browsers will still obey the style sheet, but other browsers will be able to safely ignore the content that it doesn't understand. To comment out the style sheet, put the `<!--` characters before the style sheet, and the `-->` characters after the style sheet, as shown here:

```
<HEAD>
<TITLE>Black and White TV Worship Page</TITLE>
<STYLE TYPE="text/css">
<!--
BODY { color: white; background: black }
TD { color: white; background: black }
-->
</STYLE>
</HEAD>
```

Importing a Style Sheet

Any style sheet can use a special `@import` notation to refer to an external style sheet. The external style sheet's rules are imported (that is, loaded) along with the main style sheet's rules, and both style sheets will apply to the HTML document's elements.

 NOTE   There are special rules about which style sheet's rules take priority; we'll learn about these priority rules in the "Inheriting Properties" section.

The `@import` statement must be placed at the top of the style sheet, before any rules. Use the word `url` with parentheses around the external style sheet's URL to indicate where the style sheet is located.

 TIP   You can give your external style sheets any filename you like, but it's best to give them a `.css` extension for consistency.

Here's an example:

```
@import url(hightech.css)
```

Here we've used a relative URL. The browser would retrieve the style sheet stored in a file named `hightech.css`. This file should be stored in the same directory as the style sheet file that contains the `@import` statement.

You can also use absolute URLs, like this:

```
@import url(http://www.emf.net/~estephen/css/library.css)
```

 **WARNING**   Navigator 4.01 on Windows 95 dies a horrible death when it encounters the `@import` statement. Newer versions of Navigator do not have this problem.

Linking to External Style Sheets

The best method of gluing an HTML document to a style sheet is to link to an external style sheet using the link element introduced in Skill 5.

The ability to link to an external style sheet is the most powerful option, since it means you can define a standard style sheet for your entire Web site. Each HTML file on your site can contain a link to that standard style sheet. If you then want to change the appearance of every page on your site at once, you just have to edit the external style sheet's file, and not bother changing each individual HTML file. There are three attributes that must be set, along with two optional attributes:

- The HREF attribute must point to the external style sheet file's URL (either relative or absolute).

- The REL attribute must have a value of either "STYLESHEET" or "ALTERNATE STYLESHEET".

- The TYPE attribute must be "text/css", unless you've set the default style sheet in the head section with a meta command (as we saw earlier in the "Setting the Default Style Sheet Language" section).

- Optionally, the TITLE attribute can indicate the name of the style sheet, if you want surfers to be able to disable it (see "Naming External Style Sheets" a little later)

- Optionally, the MEDIA attribute can indicate what media or medium this style sheet should apply to (see the "Applying Style Sheets to a Particular Media" section)

For example, this code will link to an external style sheet named elegant.css:

```
<LINK HREF="elegant.css" REL="STYLESHEET" TYPE="text/css"
TITLE="Meredith's Elegant Style Sheet">
```

Similarly, here's an example of a head element showing how to set the default style sheet language and link to a style sheet stored at an absolute URL:

```
<HEAD>
<TITLE>Marx Wacky Page</TITLE>
<META HTTP-EQUIV="Content-Style-Type" CONTENT="text/css">.
<LINK HREF="http://www.accesscom.com/~marx/psychedelic.css"
REL="STYLESHEET" TITLE="Mark's Psychedelic Groove Style Sheet">
</HEAD>
```

Structuring an External Style Sheet and Including Comments

When you create an external style sheet, it should simply be a text file with your rules and rulesets and no HTML elements at all. (As mentioned earlier, any @import statement should come first.)

NOTE   In particular, don't include <HTML> and <HEAD> tags, or any other HTML tags. In the early days of CSS1, some unclear examples of external style sheets encouraged this practice, so don't be confused if you run across an incorrect external style sheet.

CSS1 has a format for comments that's different than HTML. CSS1 comments begin with /* and end with */. For example:

```
/* This is a CSS1 comment */
```

It's a good idea to begin your style sheet with a comment that explains its purpose. Also, any rules that might be complex should be explained with a comment. Here's an example of an external style sheet.

stylish.css

```
/* CSS1 Style Sheet by Stephen Mack and Janan Platt */

@import url(ourdefaultfonts.css)
/* The ourdefaultfonts.css style sheet contains font settings */

BODY { background: black; color: white; margin-left: 10%; margin-left:
10% }

H1 { text-align: center }

TD { color: white; background: black }
/* Since Navigator 4 doesn't inherit properties to tables, you must
separately define the body rule for a table cell */

.WARNING {
  font-size: larger;
  font-weight: bolder;
  text-align: center;
  color: red;
  background : yellow;
  border: thick groove gray;
}

HR { text-align: center; margin-left: 25%; width: 50%; margin-right:
25%; }
```

Most of these rules should be fairly self-explanatory.

Here's how IE 4 would display a document about first aid with this style sheet applied to it.

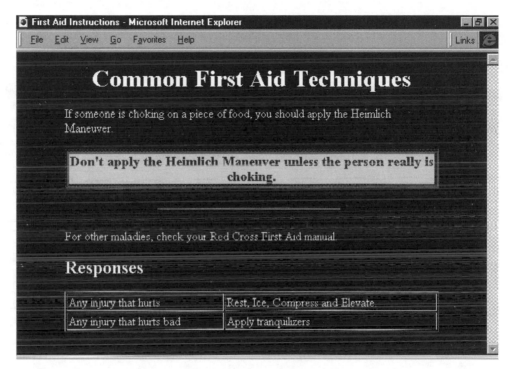

 WARNING   Unfortunately, IE 3 and Navigator 4 have problems displaying the same document. IE 3 has a bug where background images and colors specified for the BODY selector are ignored if they are in an external style sheet (although the background color is correctly applied if you use an embedded style sheet or inline style declaration). Navigator 4 gets confused by the style sheet's left and right margins. To see some screen shots, further examples and workarounds, visit the Web site for this book.

 **NOTE**   On the Web site for the book, we'll also collect some pointers to good external style sheets that you can safely use for your Web site.

Naming External Style Sheets

CSS1-enabled browsers should be able to show surfers a list of style sheets that have been applied to a document and allow surfers to disable any style sheets that they don't want to see. Unfortunately, no browser has yet implemented this useful feature.

Future browsers will allow surfers to disable a particular style sheet (as opposed to just switching off all style sheets completely, which IE 3 and Navigator 4 do allow). You'll give a name to each style sheet that you want to allow to be disabled.

We saw how to use the TITLE attribute to give a style sheet a name earlier. HTML 4.0 defines three types of style sheets:

- A *persistent style sheet* is always applied to a document. To create a persistent style sheet, don't give the style sheet a TITLE attribute.

- An *alternate style sheet* is only applied if a surfer selects it specifically. To create an alternate style sheet, use the REL="ALTERNATE STYLESHEET" attribute in the link element and give the style sheet a name with the TITLE attribute.

- A *default style sheet* is applied to a document when it is first loaded but can be disabled by the surfer. To create a default style sheet, use the REL="STYLESHEET" attribute in the link element and give the style sheet a name with the TITLE attribute.

The same value for a TITLE attribute can be applied to more than one external style sheet in two different link elements:

```
<LINK REL="ALTERNATE STYLESHEET" TITLE="Big Print" HREF="bigfonts.css">
<LINK REL="ALTERNATE STYLESHEET" TITLE="Big Print" HREF="bigmargins.css">
```

This would allow the two style sheets specified to both be named "Big Print" so they could be enabled or disabled together.

Applying Style Sheets to a Particular Media

In most cases, HTML does not care what type of platform (or *media*) is used to display an HTML document. It could be a computer screen, a TV screen, a telephone, a text-to-speech reading device, a Braille tactile device, or a printer. (Some HTML elements, like the button element or the bold element, are a little more specific to a particular device than most HTML elements.)

In contrast, style sheets are always designed for a particular medium or group of media. CSS1 is mostly concerned with computer screens that are capable of presenting colors and graphics. But you can also use CSS1 to optimize your document for printing, and draft extensions to CSS have special properties for text-to-speech readers (such as accent properties or volume properties).

For example, you might be interested in creating two separate style sheets, one for a computer screen and another for a printer. The link and style elements both allow you to specify a MEDIA attribute to indicate what destination medium you want to control with a style sheet.

TIP   Studies have found that it's easier to read a sans-serif font on a computer screen, but it's easier to read a serif font on paper. Using style sheets, you can suggest different fonts for each media.

Here are the potential values for the MEDIA attribute:

- SCREEN The default value, for computer screens (on any platform)
- PRINT For paged material and for documents viewed in print preview mode
- PROJECTION For projectors and large-screen devices.
- BRAILLE For Braille tactile devices
- SPEECH For a speech synthesizer, text-to-speech system, or telephone
- ALL For all devices

NOTE   HTML 4.0 allows you to specify a comma-delimited list of the media to which you want to have a style sheet apply (such as MEDIA="SCREEN,PROJECTION").

Future versions of HTML and CSS1 will expand on these media types. For right now, the two most practical choices are PRINT and SCREEN since most of the CSS1 properties apply to those two media. Suppose you create one external style sheet called myway.css that you want to use for the screen, and another external style sheet called myprint.css that you want to use for printouts.

Here's a head section that shows how you could link to these two style sheets:

```
<!DOCTYPE HTML PUBLIC "-//W3C//DTD HTML 4.0//EN">
<HTML LANG="EN">
<HEAD>
    <TITLE>Freaky Styley</TITLE>
    <META HTTP-EQUIV="Content-Style-Type" CONTENT="text/css">.
```

```
<LINK REL="STYLESHEET" HREF="myway.css" MEDIA="SCREEN">
<LINK REL="STYLESHEET" HREF="myprint.css" MEDIA="PRINT">
</HEAD>
```

WARNING Navigator 4 and IE 3 don't obey the MEDIA attribute. IE 3 simply ignores it. Navigator 4 ignores any media type other than MEDIA="SCREEN" (which means that a style sheet with MEDIA="ALL" or MEDIA="SCREEN,PROJECTION" will be ignored). Navigator 4 also has numerous problems printing pages that have style sheets.

Using HTML Attributes and Elements as Style Glue

In addition to the STYLE attribute used to create inline styles, there are two HTML attributes and two HTML elements that are simply glue for style sheets. We'll take a quick look at how to use each of these four pieces of HTML glue now.

Applying Styles to a Class with the *CLASS* Attribute

In the earlier section called "A More Complex Example of CSS1," we saw an example of a style sheet class and the CLASS attribute.

To create a style sheet class, use a period followed by the name you want for the class. You can create classes that only apply to particular HTML elements by specifying that element, or you can create generic classes that can apply to every HTML element. For example, here's a style sheet that creates three classes (we've named our example classes warning, note, and big, but you can use any descriptive word you like):

```
P { font-family: verdana, sans-serif }
P.warning { color: red; border: thick double black }
P.note { color: green; background: url(clouds.gif) }
.big { font-size: 150% }
```

This style sheet has four rulesets. The first ruleset applies to every paragraph element (it changes the font face to Verdana, or a generic sans-serif typeface if Verdana isn't available). The second ruleset applies to only those paragraph elements in the warning class (and changes the text-color to red and gives a thick border made of two lines). The third ruleset applies to those paragraph elements in the note class (and changes the text color to green with an image background). The fourth rule applies to any HTML element (including paragraph elements, blockquote elements, table data cell elements, and so on) but only if they are in the big class (and makes the paragraph 50 percent larger than normal).

In any HTML document attached to this style sheet, you can use the CLASS attribute with a body section element to select the appropriate rule:

```
<H3 CLASS="big">All About Jeff Goldblum, Who Is A Very Tall Man.</H3>
<P>Jeff Goldblum is a very popular actor.
<P CLASS="note">Jeff's first big role in a popular movie was in "The
Big Chill."
<P CLASS="warning">His movie "The Fly" is not for the squeamish.
<P CLASS="big">Jeff stars in the "The Tall Guy" which parodies another
movie, "The Elephant Man."
```

The big class can be used with any HTML element (we've used a paragraph element and a level-three heading element here). The note and warning classes can only be used with paragraph elements, so the following CLASS attribute will be ignored:

```
<H3 CLASS="note">Don't see "Transylvania 6-5000."</H3>
```

Here's how IE 4 will display a document with this style sheet and these HTML elements (along with a normal heading about Sylvester Stallone for contrast).

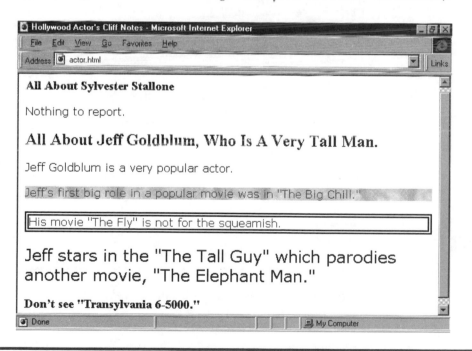

NOTE Because we didn't specify a value for padding between the border and the paragraph text, the sixth line (with the double border) does not look very attractive. See the end of this Skill for a list of properties, including padding.

Applying Styles to a Single Instance with an *ID* Attribute

The CLASS attribute can be used on many different HTML elements to reuse a rule over and over again. But sometimes you want to make a rule that applies to only a single HTML element. To do this, you can use the ID attribute.

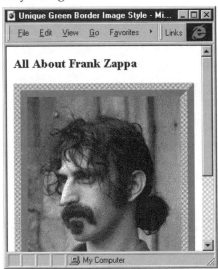

For example, suppose you want a particular image to have a fancy green border and you know that you'll never have another image in the same document use a green border.

You can define a style sheet rule like this: IMG#bord13 { border: 20px ridge green }. This rule creates a border around a particular image named bord13. The border will be 20 pixels wide, green, and in the "ridge" style. In an HTML document, you can tie this rule to the bord13 image by using an ID attribute like this: <IMG ID="bord13" SRC="zappa.jpg" ALT="Frank Zappa (Photo by Phil Franks)">. Shown here is how IE would display a page with such a border.

WARNING   Neither IE 3 nor Navigator 4 puts borders around images properly.

The selector's ID name must be a unique value. Always precede it with a number sign ("#"). ID names are a similar concept to named anchors (see Skill 7).

NOTE   The names used with the ID and CLASS attribute must be a word with no spaces or punctuation (except dashes). Also, the name can't begin with a number.

We could have left of the IMG part off the selector, like this:

```
#bord13 { border: 20px ridge green }
```

Both style sheets end up working the same way, although this second construction is slightly more flexible (since a different document could include something such as `<P ID="bord13">` to get a paragraph with a unique border instead of an image).

In practice, classes are more flexible than unique IDs, but there may be times when you really want a style sheet to apply uniquely to a single element.

Applying Styles to a Span

The span element is a generic text-level HTML element. The span element implies no meaning in and of itself; it is simply used as a place to stick generic attributes or identify where style sheet rules should apply. For example, you could have a style sheet with the following rule:

```
SPAN { text-decoration: blink }
```

You could then link the style sheet to a document and include the following line somewhere in the document:

```
<H2>News <SPAN>Flash!</SPAN></H2>
```

The word "Flash!" would blink on and off, just as if you had used the blink extension discussed in Skill 13. (Most of our warnings against the blink element apply equally to the `text-decoration: blink` declaration. Of course, you can use the span element with any CSS1 rule, we're just using `text-decoration` as one example.)

 **WARNING**   IE 3 and 4 ignore the `blink` value for the `text-decoration` property.

The span element is often combined with the CLASS or ID attributes. Rather than making every span element blink, you might want to set it up this way:

```
SPAN.blinky { text-decoration: blink }
```

This creates a class called `blinky`, and the rule could be invoked with:

```
<H2>News <SPAN CLASS="blinky">Flash!</SPAN></H2>
```

 NOTE   The span element can also be used with scripts, as we'll see in Skill 15.

The advantage of these uses of the span element is that they're completely ignored by browsers that don't display style sheets, which leaves your document's contents undisturbed, even for older browsers.

Applying Styles to a Division

The division element (<DIV> and </DIV>) can be used to apply a style sheet rule, just like the span element. The only difference is that the division element is a block-level element, so it can contain paragraphs and other block-level and text-level elements. (Since the span element is a text-level element, it can only contain text-level elements. See the "HTML's Rules of Nesting" section at the end of Skill 2 for more information.)

Learning How CSS1 Works

Up to now in this Skill, we've been more concerned with how HTML and CSS1 can work together rather than how CSS1 operates. In this section, we'll introduce you to CSS1's design.

Inheriting Properties

A CSS1 rule applies a declaration to a particular HTML element. That declaration will also apply to any elements nested inside that element. For example, suppose you've made paragraphs green:

```
P { color: green }
```

Consider an element nested inside another element, such as: <P>I am a <I>barrista</I></P>. The word "barrista" will appear both in italics and in green. This is an example of *inheritance*. The italics element here is said to "inherit" the green property from its *parent* element (which in this case is the paragraph element).

Other style properties will also be inherited, such as font-family and font-size. Some style properties are not inherited from the parent element to the child element. (Check with the CSS1 specification or a quick-reference to see if a property inherits.)

The best example we've seen of inheritance is applying declarations to the body element. With a style sheet such as:

```
BODY { color: white; background: url(marble.gif) black; }
```

(which sets the text color to white and the background to an image named marble.gif, or black if the image isn't available) every element in a document, including every heading and paragraph, will inherit the default text color.

 **NOTE**   This works even if the <BODY> tag is omitted since the presence of the body element is assumed even if there aren't explicit tags for it.

WARNING   In Navigator 4, tables don't inherit values from the body of a document since Navigator incorrectly considers tables to be separate from the body. You'll have to repeat your BODY rules for the TD and TH selectors to avoid problems. Otherwise, if you specify background black and text-color white, the table will end up being invisible (since this bug causes both the text color and the background to be black).

The background is a little more complicated since the background property does not inherit. However, the initial value for every element's background is "transparent," so the parent's background will shine through for each child element in the way that you'd expect.

Sometimes, the value of a property is a percentage that refers to another property. For example:

```
P { font-size: 10pt; line-height: 150% }
```

In this case, the line height will work out to 15 points, since it is one-and-a-half times the paragraph's font size of 10 points. Elements nested inside a paragraph element will inherit the 15-point line height.

Using Contextual Selectors

At the beginning of this skill, we defined the selectors used in CSS1 rules and stated that there were simple selectors and contextual selectors. All of the examples of CSS1 rules so far in this Skill (including the examples with CLASS and ID) have contained simple selectors.

A *contextual selector* creates a rule that only matches HTML elements based on their position in a document structure. To create a contextual selector, simply list two or more simple selectors.

For example, the selector H2 SPAN could be used to make sure a declaration only applied to a span element nested inside a level-two heading element. (The declaration would not apply to span elements elsewhere in the document.)

Suppose you want all level-one headings to be green and all emphasized text to be blue. You would use two rules:

```
H1 { color: green }
EM { color: blue }
```

But what would happen to an emphasized element that happened to be inside a level-one heading? Given the HTML code `<H1>Philip is a <EM>musician </EM>!</H1>`, it's hard to predict whether the word "musician" will be blue or green. It turns out it will be blue, since the style sheet's EM selector applies to every emphasis element, regardless of whether the emphasis is nested in another element.

To make sure that the emphasized element was green if it was inside a level-one heading element, you could use the following contextual selector:

```
H1 EM { color: green }
```

This rule only applies to emphasis elements nested inside a level-one heading. Level-one headings themselves are not affected, and emphasis elements elsewhere are also not affected. To cause the heading element to be green and also have any emphasis elements nested inside be green (but blue elsewhere), you'd need three rules. The order of these three rules doesn't matter:

```
H1 { color: green }
EM { color: blue }
H1 EM { color: green }
```

You can also use a style sheet that includes a contextual selector to select a third possibility for the emphasis element:

```
H1 { color: green }
EM { color: blue }
H1 EM { color: red }
```

This will cause the emphasis element to normally be blue, but it will appear in red if it's inside a level-one heading element.

 **WARNING** Be sure you don't confuse contextual selectors with rulesets. The only difference is a comma: `H1, EM { color: red}` is a grouped ruleset (with two rules) that makes both level-one headings and emphasis elements appear in red. By removing the comma, it becomes a contextual selector that makes only emphasis elements inside a level-one heading red; other emphasis elements and level-one headings are not affected.

You can make very complex contextual selectors. For example:

```
TD UL UL LI { font-size: smaller }
```

This rule will only apply to list-item elements embedded inside a nested unordered list (that is, a list inside a list) that is also inside a table cell.

You can combine contextual selectors together, or mix them with CLASS and ID attributes to create sophisticated results. For example, you might create rules such as:

```
P.fiction { text-indent: 5% }
DIV P.fiction { text-indent: 10% ; margin-left 10% }
```

Then any paragraphs in the fiction class (<P CLASS="FICTION">) would have their first line indented 5 percent—unless it was a paragraph inside a division element (<DIV><P CLASS="FICTION">), in which case the paragraph's left margin would be 10 percent of the screen width, and the first line would be indented a total of 15 percent.

Making Style Sheets Cascade

"Cascading" is the first word in the name of CSS, and it refers to the ability of multiple style sheets to work together to arrive at the document's final appearance. But we haven't yet talked about what "cascading" means and how conflicting style sheet rules are resolved.

As we saw earlier, you can specify a number of style sheets in the same document. In addition, IE 4 lets a user specify a default style sheet of their own.

NOTE   The idea that author and user style sheets should mesh together and negotiate to decide on the best presentation of a document (considering both the author's design and the user's display needs) is the main intention of CSS.

As we've seen in the earlier Skills of this book, every browser has a default behavior for rendering HTML elements (for example, headings are bold, and horizontal rules are two pixels high). The set of all of the default appearances is considered to be another style sheet—but the defaults apply only if no other style sheet rule affects an element's appearance.

WARNING   An element's default appearance should outweigh any properties that apply to that element by inheritance, but IE 4 and Navigator 4 differ in their interpretation. For example, the specification for CSS1 declares that setting a default font size in the body element shouldn't change the font size of headings. But IE 3 and Navigator 4 get this wrong. Prudent style sheet authors will therefore create a style sheet that defines properties for almost every element used in a document.

Suppose two different style sheets specify the color for level-one headings; the first style sheet says they should be red, and the second one says they should be blue. Here are the five levels of priority:

1. If no declarations apply to an element, then the inherited value is used. If there is no inherited value, then the browser's default behavior is used for that element. In this case, the default behavior (black text, unless the user has customized their browser's or operating system's colors) will be over-ridden by the declarations for blue and red text.

2. You can mark a declaration with !important to make that rule carry more weight than normal. (However, IE and Navigator ignore the !important notation so far.)

3. The Web author's style sheets outweigh any of the surfer's style sheets. Embedded style sheets and linked style sheets outweigh any style sheets that are imported. But any style sheet will outweigh the browser's default values.

4. The more specific the selector, the more weight it carries. Selectors with ID attributes are more specific than CLASS attributes, which are more specific than contextual selectors, which are more specific than simple selectors.

In a tie, the order counts. The later rules outweigh earlier rules. So in this case, the fifth rule will break the conflict, and headings will be blue. This system is complicated, so it's important to test your documents and make sure the rules are working as you expected.

Using Anchor Pseudo-Classes

A *pseudo-class* is a way of distinguishing between different types of a single element. There is only one pseudo-class in CSS1, and it is for the anchor element.

By default, three colors are used with anchor elements (as we saw in Skill 3): unvisited links are usually blue, visited links are usually purple, and active links (a link being clicked on) are usually red. (These colors are the default settings, although many surfers change the default colors.)

To be able to set the colors and other properties for these three types of links separately, CSS1 creates pseudo-classes for the anchor element: A:link can be used as a selector for unvisited links, A:visited refers to visited links, and A:active applies to active links. For example, you could set the colors for links with the following rules:

```
A:link { color: cyan }
A:visited { color: gray }
A:active { color: black }
```

WARNING   Early versions of IE 4 ignored the A:active pseudo-class.

 NOTE   A similar concept, called *pseudo-elements*, is defined by CSS1 to make rules that apply to the first line or first letter of text. Sadly, pseudo-elements are ignored by Navigator and IE.

Using CSS1 Units

CSS1 uses several different types of units (as you may have noticed from our examples so far in this Skill). There are two types of units: absolute units and relative units.

The common absolute units are:

- Inches, specified by in (for example, 0.5in means half an inch)

- Points, specified by pt (for example, 13pt means 13 points)

You can also use centimeters (cm), millimeters (mm), and picas (pc).

 NOTE   These are typographical terms. A *pica* is equal to 12 points, and 72 points is equal to an inch.

However, relative units are preferred since they scale better from one medium to another (and you don't have to make assumptions about a surfer's screen size or paper size). Here are the relative units:

- Pixels, specified by px (for example, 12px means 12 pixels)

- Ems, specified by em (where one *em* is equal to the element's font size, so 0.5em is half a line)

- Ex-heights, specified ex (where one *ex* is equal to the height of the lower-case letter x in the current font, so 2ex is twice the height of the letter x)

- Percentages, which are usually relative to the font-size (so 200% usually means twice the current font size of the element)

Pixels might not seem to be a relative unit at first glance. But in actuality, pixels can vary tremendously. The first case is for a printer: A screen is often 72 pixels per inch, but a printer is typically 300, 600, or 1200 "pixels" per inch. So browsers will scale pixel units appropriately when you print out a document, making pixel a relative term. Secondly and more importantly, the pixel size measurements for fonts are slightly different on Macintosh platforms than they are on Windows platforms. The difference is enough to cause problems, so pixel units should be avoided.

TIP   The safest two units are currently percentages and ems, so you should try to use these two units for measurements in your style sheets as much as possible.

Using Color Units in CSS1

Color units are usually one of 16 color names (aqua, black, blue, fuchsia, gray, green, lime, maroon, navy, olive, purple, red, silver, teal, white, and yellow), or an RGB value (such as #38B0DE, as defined by Skill 3).

NOTE   CSS1 also supports an abbreviated RGB value where you only use one hexadecimal digit for each color instead of two. You can also use percentages and decimal values. See the CSS1 specification for more details (http://www.w3 .org/pub/WWW/TR/REC-CSS1#color-units). Be careful, since Navigator and IE might not support the color notation you've chosen.

WARNING   Some Macintosh-style editors and HTML editors have real problems with named colors; if you have any trouble, use the RGB notation instead. See the appendix for a chart.

Using CSS1 Properties

In this last section, we'll list the different CSS1 properties by category. Although we don't have room to list or describe each one thoroughly, we've tried to give examples of the most useful properties throughout this Skill.

The CSS1 specification defines the behavior of the different properties and lists each possible value, and it describes the overall formatting model used by CSS1.

Visit the W3C CSS page (http://www.w3.org/Style/CSS/) for a list of CSS1 references and style sheet tools. One particularly useful tool that can check your style sheets for errors is CSSCheck, available from WDG's CSS1 and HTML reference site (http://www.htmlhelp.com/).

Understanding the Categories of Properties

There are five categories of properties that can be controlled by CSS1:

- **Font Properties** Properties that affect a font: font-family (which changes the font face), font-style (either normal, italic, or oblique), font-variant (normal or small-caps), and font-weight (which changes the boldness of a font). Also, the font-size property can specify text size (and in addition to the normal units of em, px, and percentage for setting sizes, there are some special values: larger and smaller are relative sizes, while you can also specify xx-small, x-small, small, medium, large, x-large, and xx-large). The font property is a shorthand property for all of these.

NOTE When you specify a font that has spaces in its name, you must put quotes around it. For example, { font-family: "New Century Schoolbook" }. Quotes should not be used in any other situation.

- **Color and Background Properties** Properties that describe the foreground color and background (image or color) as well as background image placement.

- **Text Properties** Properties that change text's appearance and placement, such as line-height, text-decoration, vertical-align, and text-align. The word-spacing and letter-spacing properties can make letters wider or squeezed more tightly next to each other. The text-transform property can be set to capitalize, uppercase, or lowercase.

- **Box Properties** Properties that set the margins, borders, and padding (between the margin and border) for an element. For example, you can set margin-top, margin-right, margin-bottom, or margin-left properties (or use the margin shorthand property to set all four at once). You can also set the width and height properties to control an element's size. The float property can make any element behave like a floating image.

- **Classification Properties** Properties that classify different elements by their behavior and control how elements such as list item elements work (for example, you can use the list-style-image property with an unordered list selector (UL) to change the list-item bullet to an image of your choice).

For a complete list of the properties, their initial values, whether the property inherits, what values can be used with each property, and how safe they are to use with different elements, check with the Web site for this book for an updated

URL, or see the Quick Reference to Cascading Style Sheets (`http://www.cwi.nl/` `~steven/www/css1-qr.html`).

Using Shorthand Properties

Some properties are simply *shorthand properties* for groups of other properties. For example, you can set the `font-style`, `font-variant`, `font-weight`, `font-size`, `line-height`, and `font-family` properties separately:

```
P { font-style: italic; font-variant: small-caps; font-weight: bold;
font-size: 120%; line-height: 150%; font-family: sans-serif }
```

Alternately, you can set the `font` property as a shortcut:

```
P { font: italic small-caps bold 120%/150% sans-serif }
```

These two style sheets are precisely equivalent.

Similarly, setting the rule BODY { `margin: 15%` } will create a margin of 15 percent of the window's size for all four margins, exactly as if the rule were BODY { `margin-left: 15%; margin-top: 15%; margin-right: 15%;` `margin-bottom: 15%` }.

Using Some Important Style Sheet Properties

We would like to end this Skill by demonstrating two important example style sheets that can improve your documents' appearance: `text-indent` and the body attributes.

Using the *Text-Indent* Property

The first example style sheet is useful for controlling indenting. As we saw back in Skill 3, there's no good HTML method for creating a paragraph indent (as is seen in books). However, you could use the following simple style sheet:

```
P.fiction { text-indent: 5% }
```

In your HTML documents, attach this style sheet normally, and for any paragraphs that you want indented, use a tag like <P CLASS="fiction">. The first line of each paragraph will be indented 5 percent of the window's width.

You can also remove the double-spacing between paragraphs and create extra left and right margins for the fiction class paragraphs with the following rule, a modification of the above:

```
P.fiction { text-indent: 5%; margin-top: 0; margin-bottom: 0; margin-
left: 10%; margin-right: 15%; }
```

Setting Colors without Using Body Attributes

Skill 3 introduced the use of the six body attributes to change a document's colors and background image. As we mentioned, HTML 4.0 does not recommend that these attributes be used.

Consider this <BODY> tag, which sets white text on a black background along with specific link colors and a background image:

```
<BODY BGCOLOR-"#000000" TEXT="#FFFFFF" LINK="#CC0000" ALINK="#777777"
VLINK="#990099" BACKGROUND="marble.gif">
```

Using a style sheet, the same effect could be accomplished with the following five rules:

```
BODY { background: #000 url(marble.gif) }
BODY { color: #FFF }
A:link { color: #C00 }
A:visited { color: #555 }
A:active { color: #909 }
```

The only tricky thing here is the background rule, which says to show the color black unless the marble.gif image is available. Also, these colors are expressed using three-digit RGB values instead of six-digit RGB values; CSS1 RGB colors can be stated either way, but HTML RGB colors must always be six digits.

Style sheets offer important advantages to Web authors. The possibilities are endless. While the current implementations are thorny and the differences between browsers will pose problems, the extra display capabilities make style sheets well worth learning. Style sheets are particularly powerful when combined with scripting. The next Skill will introduce you to scripting languages.

Are You Experienced?

Now you can...

- ☑ **create a CSS1 style sheet with rules**
- ☑ **embed and link to style sheets**
- ☑ **glue style sheet rules to your HTML documents**
- ☑ **understand the advantages of style sheets**
- ☑ **keep a document's content and formatting separate**

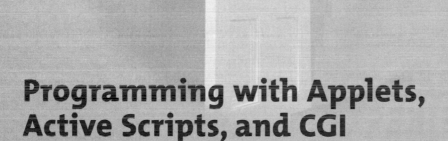

Programming with Applets, Active Scripts, and CGI

- ➔ Creating active scripts with JavaScript and VBScript
- ➔ Adding applets to a Web page with Java
- ➔ Using CGI scripts and programs
- ➔ Understanding the difference between JavaScript and Java

In this Skill, we'll show you how HTML can work with computer programs. Computer programs can make Web pages more dynamic and interactive: You can present specialized information from a database, offer games, verify form input, change the appearance of your Web page, or provide an interface to your existing specialized programs. We'll define each of the three types of programs used on the Web (applets, active scripts, and CGI programs) and see how to use them with HTML. We'll also concentrate on introducing two programming languages—JavaScript, which is the most popular language for active scripts, and Java, the most popular language for applets. These two languages are often confused; we'll compare and contrast them in this Skill.

After that, we'll show you how to include JavaScript on a page. We'll teach you what HTML elements you can use to work with active scripts and the various generic HTML event attributes. We'll briefly discuss other active script programming languages, such as VBScript.

We'll also take a detailed look at Java applets and a brief look at other applet programming languages and formats (such as ActiveX). We'll discuss more about CGI and the many different programming languages you can use with CGI.

At the end of this Skill, we'll compare the different programming languages and make sure you understand the difference between active scripts (JavaScript and VBScript), applets (Java and ActiveX), and CGI.

It's important to understand that applets, active scripts, and CGI are written using computer programming languages. These languages are very different from HTML (and much more complicated than HTML as well). To learn how to write an applet or a script, you'll need to learn about basic programming concepts such as variables, constants, loops and branching, control flow, operators, scope, functions, and so on. Since this book is about HTML, we can't teach you any of these concepts here—but we will show you a few examples of scripts and how to modify an existing script for your own use.

Understanding Active Scripts and Applets

Spend some time on the Web and you'll see enough references to "Java" to know that people aren't talking about coffee or the island. Instead, Sun developed a general-purpose programming language named Java—and it has become extremely popular on the Web as a language for making applets. *Applets* are little applications that run inside a rectangular region on a Web page. With applets, you can display animation, sound, games, and general utilities (such as calculators and search engines).

Applets don't have to be written in Java (although most of them are). Some applets are written in other programming languages and formats, such as ActiveX, Python, or C. However, Java applets are put on a page with the applet element; the other languages use the object element, which isn't as widely supported.

Such a buzz has built up around the Java programming language that when Netscape was preparing to release a scripting language for Netscape Navigator 2, they changed their script language's name from LiveScript to *JavaScript* and made the language itself more similar to Java. This turned out to be confusing since JavaScript is still very different from Java. (See the next section.)

Netscape licensed the name "Java" from Sun so they can use the name legally; however, Microsoft's version of JavaScript is *JScript*.

In contrast to an applet, which is a program running in a portion of a Web page, a *scripting language* creates or modifies Web pages in some way. For example, you can use a scripting language to put words anywhere on a page, display confirmation and message dialog boxes, change text color, modify the browser screen's appearance (by removing toolbars, for example), or present different text to surfers depending on what browser they're using.

There are two popular scripting languages: JavaScript and VBScript. Microsoft Internet Explorer 3 and 4 can interpret VBScript and JScript, while Navigator 2, 3, and 4 interpret only JavaScript. (For convenience in this Skill, from now on we'll say "JavaScript" when we're referring to both JavaScript and JScript, unless we talk about "Netscape JavaScript.")

Since both major browsers can understand JavaScript code, JavaScript is much more popular on the Web than VBScript—so we'll spend more time teaching you about JavaScript than VBScript here. (Most other browsers can't understand either scripting language.)

When you create an active script in a scripting language, it's usually added directly to the HTML page and run by the browser. In contrast, the CGI programs we learned about in Skill 12 are stored in a separate file from a Web page and are run by the Web server. Both scripting languages and CGI programs can use "scripts." To distinguish the two, we'll refer to JavaScript and VBScript scripts as *active scripts*, and CGI programs written in a scripting language as *CGI scripts*. (For more about CGI, see "Using CGI Programs and Scripts.") Examples in this Skill should help you keep them distinct in your mind, and we'll compare the two technologies at the end of this Skill.

Understanding the Differences Between Java and JavaScript

Other than the name and a similarity in programming *statements* (or commands), Java and JavaScript are very different. Java is a compiled language, while JavaScript is an interpreted language (we defined these terms at the beginning of Skill 12). Java applications can stand alone and be run outside Web pages, but JavaScript is always tied to a Web page and can never be run separately. JavaScript depends on HTML to work. Java applets are confined to a particular rectangle that's only part of a Web page; in contrast, JavaScript can control an entire Web page. Java applets sit in their rectangle and do their own thing, while JavaScript can be used to respond to form buttons and mouse movements anywhere on a page.

For security reasons, both JavaScript active scripts and Java applets do not allow file reading or writing. This severely limits their usefulness. While both Java applets and JavaScript are supposedly secure, both have a long history of security and privacy problems. Java applet security problems usually involve compromising secure networks, while JavaScript security problems usually involve invasions of privacy.

There are also significant internal differences between the two languages. We'll take a look at JavaScript's abilities and limitations first, and then we'll look at Java in some detail.

Understanding and Using JavaScript

JavaScript is a scripting language developed by Netscape that appeared with version 2 of Navigator. JavaScript is a programming language designed to be used only in the context of changing the way an HTML page behaves.

When JavaScript was first introduced, Web authors were excited at the prospect of being able to make pages more interactive. Since JavaScript is a programming language, it allows some powerful capabilities. You can write active scripts and add them to Web pages in order to make your page respond to events and only show selected information. You can use JavaScript to create pages that ask questions, change dynamically, and have interesting visual effects. The dialog box shown in Figure 15.1 was created by JavaScript. We'll show you how to do this in "Seeing JavaScript in Action."

Even if you don't know enough about programming to write your own active scripts, you can take existing ones and add them to your page. We'll show you how to do this, using the script element, in a little bit.

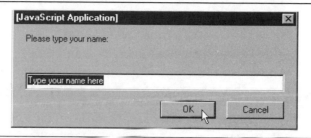

FIGURE 15.1: A JavaScript prompt that asks for information to be used on a Web page

JavaScript can also be used to extract data from small databases and present requested information onscreen. Often, JavaScript is used to present random images and information (useful for games or to keep your pages interesting). Perhaps most usefully, JavaScript can make sure that surfers are filling out forms correctly; we'll show you an example of this later.

Recognizing JavaScript's Limitations

With JavaScript's capabilities come some severe limitations:

- JavaScript is harder to learn and use than HTML.

- It's difficult to find accurate information about the latest version because JavaScript is developing so quickly.

- Many browsers aren't capable of interpreting JavaScript statements (*non-JavaScript–enabled*), so using JavaScript might limit your audience.

- Only Navigator 2, 3, and 4, as well as IE 3 and 4, are *JavaScript-enabled* (and even these browsers interpret JavaScript slightly differently).

- JavaScript is intentionally limited in power, due to security concerns.

Despite its security designs, JavaScript is associated with security risks (including the possibility of a surfer unknowingly sending files from their computer to a remote site, or having a site track which sites a surfer visits and secretly learn what Web passwords they use). Malicious Web authors can exploit these security risks to unearth private information about a surfer's computer. Netscape's JavaScript design and Microsoft's JScript design are both proprietary, and they have never been scrutinized or certified by security experts.

JavaScript is also misused by Web authors by creating annoying browser behaviors (far too many Web authors use the same tricks of scrolling messages in the status bar and flashing backgrounds). Many surfers consider these common uses of JavaScript to be irritating.

For both the security and annoyance factors, a lot of surfers who have JavaScript-enabled browsers have configured their browsers to disable JavaScript.

Disabling JavaScript in Your Browser

JavaScript (and Java) is enabled by default in every version of Navigator and IE. To avoid any possible security risk, you might want to disable JavaScript for yourself. Follow the instructions for your browser:

- For Navigator 3, use the Options ➤ Network Preference ➤ Languages command and deselect JavaScript.

- For Navigator 4, use the Edit ➤ Preferences command, and choose the Advanced category to see which features (including JavaScript) you can disable.

To disable JScript in IE, you must also disable VBScript:

- For IE 3, use View ➤ Options ➤ Security, and disable the Run ActiveX Scripts option.

- For IE 4, use the View ➤ Options ➤ Security command, then choose the Zone where you want to disable scripting (such as the Internet zone). Then change to Custom security, and click on the Settings button. Scroll down to the Scripting section, and choose Disable under Active Scripting.

 **WARNING** It's trivially simple for a malicious Web site to create a "denial of service" attack. Using JavaScript, the site simply uses JavaScript commands to begin opening hundreds of browser windows on your computer. Your computer will quickly become sluggish and eventually too slow to use. At that point, your computer might crash, losing any unsaved information.

Seeing JavaScript in Action

Thousands of Web sites use JavaScript to create interesting Web pages. We'll show you a brief example of JavaScript here and another few examples on our Web site.

The simplest way to include JavaScript in a page is to use one or more script elements. You can also include one or more event attributes in body section elements. We'll talk about how to use the script element, and then see a JavaScript example that prompts the surfer for information.

Using the Script Element

The script element contains active script statements. Start your active script with the <SCRIPT> tag, place all of the statements next, and then end the script element with the </SCRIPT> tag. The script element can be placed in the head section or body section of your document (or both). There's no limit to the number of script elements that can be placed in a document.

> **TIP**
>
> Use a comment to hide the active script statements from older browsers (which might otherwise display the statements literally, onscreen). The example in the next section demonstrates how to hide active script statements with HTML comments.

The <SCRIPT> tag also needs two attributes to define what script language you're using. When you use JavaScript, you should use both the LANGUAGE= "JavaScript" and TYPE="text/javascript" attributes. (For VBScript, use LANGUAGE="VBS" and TYPE="text/vbscript".)

Navigator and IE expect the LANGUAGE attribute and ignore the TYPE attribute. But HTML 4.0 recommends the TYPE attribute so future browsers will expect it. For now, it's safest to use both. (Alternately, you can declare a default scripting language using a meta element, as we'll see in the "Setting the Default Script Language" section later.)

You can use one other attribute with the script element: the SRC attribute, which can point to an external script. We'll see how to use external scripts in the "Using External Scripts and Comments" section.

A JavaScript Example: Prompting for Information

Our first example will prompt the surfer for their name (Figure 15.1), and then use this name in an HTML document. This HTML document contains two JavaScript script elements.

Create or download this HTML code, and try it out in IE and Navigator. Type a name such as **Harry** when you are prompted.

Skill 15

namescript.html

```html
<!DOCTYPE HTML PUBLIC "-//W3C//DTD HTML 4.0//EN">
<HTML LANG="EN">
<HEAD>
  <SCRIPT LANGUAGE="JavaScript" TYPE="text/javascript">
    <!-- Begin script
      function GetName() {
        username = prompt("Please type your name:","Type your name here");
        if (username == "Type your name here" || username == null ||
            username == "") {
          username = "anonymous visitor";
        }
        return (username);
      }
    // End script -->
  </SCRIPT>
  <TITLE>Greeting Script Test</TITLE>
</HEAD>
<BODY BGCOLOR="YELLOW">
  <H1>Names in Action</H1>
  <P>Hello,
  <SCRIPT LANGUAGE="JavaScript" TYPE="text/javascript">
    <!-- Begin script
      document.write (GetName()+"!");
    // End script -->
  </SCRIPT>
  <P>Welcome to the script test page.
</BODY>
</HTML>
```

The first script element causes a prompt to be displayed. Navigator 4's prompt

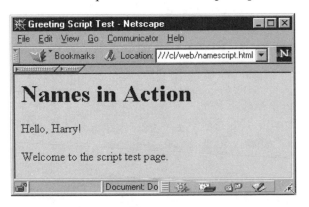

dialog box is shown in Figure 15.1 (Navigator 3's prompt and IE 3 and 4's prompt all look slightly different, but are equivalent).

The second script element causes the name that was entered to be written to the document, as shown here (if the surfer enters their name as "Harry").

If the surfer clicks on the Cancel button or presses the OK button without entering their name, the page will display the words, "Hello anonymous visitor."

While it's not necessary to understand the JavaScript statements here to use them on a page, it might help you to have each line of the script explained. If you'd rather learn about the noscript element, skip to the next section.

WARNING   It's not always safe to use programs you don't understand. A malicious programmer could intentionally hide undesirable effects into a long and complicated program. To combat this, make sure you use scripts from trusted sources and that each line of code is tested by you or well-explained by the author.

UNDERSTANDING THE *NAMESCRIPT.HTML* JAVASCRIPT EXAMPLE

We'll explain what we did in the two script elements of namescript.html. The first line of the first script element looks like this:

```
<!-- Begin script
```

This hides your JavaScript code so that the code isn't inadvertently displayed by a browser that isn't JavaScript-enabled.

The second line declares we are creating a function named GetName(). *Functions* are blocks of code that can be used to return a result. In this case, the HTML document uses the GetName() function to ask for the surfer's name. The parentheses, (and), are part

of the function's name. Any statements in between the curly braces after the name, { and }, define what the function does.

When you display namescript.html in your browser, notice that some of the document (like the heading) may appear onscreen before the browser asks you for your name. That's because even though the GetName() function appears in the document's head section, it does not actually get run until the function is requested by its name, later in the document. (Causing a function to be run is known as *calling a function*.)

The first line of the function looks like:

```
username = prompt("Please type your name:","Type your name
here");
```

continued ▶

This line creates a new variable called username. (Think of a *variable* as a box where data is stored temporarily.) Also, it displays a prompt. The text in the dialog box will say Please type your name: while the default text, inside the text box, is Type your name here. As soon as the surfer types anything, the default text will be replaced. We could have left the text box empty by using an empty value (" ") for the default text.

The next four lines constitute an *if statement*. The value of username is compared to three conditions. (The double vertical bars, ||, mean "or.") If any of the three conditions are true, then the username variable is set to the value "anonymous visitor."

To translate the if statement we used into plain English: *If* the user's name is equal to the default text "Type your name here" (which means the surfer didn't type anything), *or* if the user's name is non-existent (which means the surfer is using IE 4 or Navigator and clicked on the Cancel button), *or* if the user's name is an empty value (which means the surfer is using IE 3 and clicked on the Cancel button), *then* set the username variable to the words "anonymous visitor."

Note how the curly braces, { and }, are again used for grouping, and the double equals signs (==) is a comparison—but a single equals sign (=) changes the contents of a variable. (Also, each JavaScript statement should end with a semicolon.)

The final part of the GetName() function is return (username);. This code tells the function to return the value of the username variable as the result of the function. This allows you to call the function from later in your document, and get the surfer's name in return.

The last line of the first script element is an example of a JavaScript comment. To create a JavaScript comment, use two slashes (//), followed by the comment text. For example:

```
// The following code was inspired by Groucho Marx.
```

The particular comment we used at the end of the script element does double duty since it is both a JavaScript comment that tells us where the

continued ▶

end of the script is—and more importantly, it also closes the HTML comment with the `-->` characters.

Some JavaScript authors put their name in the final comment to indicate who wrote the code and when it was last modified, like this:

```
// by E. Stephen Mack and Janan Platt, 30-Nov-97 -->
```

Finally, the first script element ends with a `</SCRIPT>` tag. The body of the document is displayed, starting with the heading and the paragraph with the word "Hello." At that point, the second script element kicks in. This script element has only one line of real JavaScript code:

```
document.write (GetName()+"!");
```

This line writes to the HTML document. By using the name of the `GetName()` function, the function is called—which causes the prompt to be displayed. Whatever name the surfer types is returned by the function so that it can be written by the second element and made part of the document. This line actually writes two things to the document: the surfer's name, plus an exclamation point.

The rest of this second script element is just the same comment structure that we used before. You should use comments with every script element so that you always hide the JavaScript code from older browsers that would only be confused by it.

Seeing an Example of an Event Attribute

Later in this Skill, we'll see more about the HTML 4.0 event attributes that can be used to associate an active script with an HTML element. To introduce this concept, we'll show you a quick example right now.

Modify the `namescript.html` file by adding the following line of code to the end of the body section (right before the `</BODY>` tag):

```
<INPUT TYPE="BUTTON" VALUE="Change My Name"
ONCLICK="window.location='namescript.html'">
```

Skill 15

As you may remember from Skill 12, the input element can be used to create a form control. This particular control creates a button labeled with the words "Change My Name" (shown here).

 When the button is clicked, the ONCLICK event attribute kicks in, and the JavaScript code is executed. There's only one JavaScript statement here:

```
window.location='namescript.html'
```

This tells the browser to change its location to the URL `namescript.html`. Since that's the same as the document that's already displayed, in effect this simply reloads the current document—which will prompt the surfer for their name again.

⚠ **WARNING**   Unfortunately, Navigator can't display form controls unless they're within a form element. But you can't just add <FORM> and </FORM> tags, since HTML 4.0 requires an ACTION attribute in the <FORM> tag. We'll show you a solution in the next section.

Using the Noscript Element

For our `namescript.html` HTML example, anyone using a non-JavaScript–enabled browser would not see any prompts for their name, and the JavaScript code would be ignored. A surfer with a non-JavaScript–enabled browser would only see the word "Hello" and a comma. If you added the button from the previous section, then their confusion would be magnified by seeing a button that doesn't do anything at all.

By adding a noscript element, you can present alternate information for non-JavaScript–enabled browsers. Browsers that are not JavaScript-enabled (either because the browser doesn't understand JavaScript or because the surfer has switched it off) will display whatever is in between the <NOSCRIPT> and </NOSCRIPT> tags. For example, you could add this noscript element to `namescript.html`:

```
<NOSCRIPT>
   friend!
</NOSCRIPT>
```

If you add this element immediately after the second script element, then the word "friend!" will be displayed instead of the JavaScript-generated username.

So, JavaScript-enabled browsers will display "Hello" plus the surfer's name, and non-JavaScript–enabled browsers will display just "Hello, friend!"

However, if you added the button code, the button will still be displayed, regardless of whether the browser is JavaScript-enabled. It is confusing for older browsers to see buttons that don't do anything. One solution is to explain that the button doesn't do anything:

```
<NOSCRIPT>Don't worry about that button, it doesn't do
anything.</NOSCRIPT>
```

A better solution is to turn this button into a form-based go button (see Skill 12) that sends a surfer off to a different page if their browser is not JavaScript-enabled:

```
<FORM METHOD="GET" ACTION="noscript.html" ONSUBMIT="return false;">
  <INPUT TYPE="SUBMIT" VALUE="Change My Name"
  ONCLICK="window.location='namescript.html'">
</FORM>
```

This alternate version creates a button that appears identical to the earlier version. For surfers with JavaScript-enabled browsers, it acts the same as well, reloading the current page when it's clicked. But if a surfer with a non-JavaScript–enabled browser clicks on the button, then they will see a different page, noscript.html, thanks to the go button. (The trick here is the ONSUBMIT event; by using the JavaScript statement return false;, the form is not actually submitted when the surfer clicks on the button—instead the ONCLICK event kicks in.)

 NOTE   Normally, double quotes are used in JavaScript, (window.location="name-script.html"), but you can't put double quotes inside double quotes. Since the outer ONCLICK attribute is already using double quotes, the inner JavaScript statement here uses single quotes instead. Sometimes you'll have to use the " entity (see Skill 3) if you need more than two levels of quoting.

It's tremendously difficult to write an HTML document that uses JavaScript but still works equally well for a browser that isn't JavaScript-enabled. For this reason, some Web authors create two versions of important documents: a plain HTML version and an advanced version with JavaScript and other newer technologies.

You can use JavaScript code to redirect users to the JavaScript-enabled document:

```
<SCRIPT LANGUAGE="JavaScript" TYPE="text/javascript">
  <!--
  window.location = "mydoc-js.html";
  //-->
</SCRIPT>
```

Since this JavaScript statement is ignored by browsers that aren't JavaScript-enabled, you can make the rest of the document plain and put the JavaScript-specific scripts and buttons in `mydoc-js.html` (or whatever you want to call your document).

Setting the Default Script Language

If you want to use event attributes, HTML 4.0 recommends declaring the default script language for your document. This is done with a simple meta element in the head section, which looks like this:

```
<META HTTP-EQUIV="Content-Script-Type" CONTENT="text/javascript">
```

Using Event Attributes

In Skills 5 through 8 of the book, we've mentioned the generic event attributes that can be used with many different elements. We saw one example earlier in this Skill of an `ONCLICK` event attribute. Here is a list of the generic event attributes in HTML 4.0:

- `ONCLICK` The `ONCLICK` event occurs when the mouse is clicked on an element. This attribute is commonly used with buttons and links.

- `ONDBLCLICK` The `ONDBLCLICK` event occurs when the mouse is double-clicked on an element.

- `ONMOUSEDOWN` The `ONMOUSEDOWN` event occurs when the mouse button is pressed down while pointing over an element. (This is different from the `ONCLICK` event because a click occurs when the button is pressed and released; this is just the press, while `ONMOUSEUP` deals with the release of the button.)

- `ONMOUSEUP` The `ONMOUSEUP` event occurs when the mouse button is released while pointing over an element.

- `ONMOUSEOVER` The `ONMOUSEOVER` event occurs when the mouse pointer is moved over an element.

- `ONMOUSEMOVE` The `ONMOUSEMOVE` event is just about identical to `ONMOUSEOVER`. The only difference is that an `ONMOUSEOVER` event occurs at the instant a mouse pointer crosses from somewhere else to over an element but doesn't occur if the mouse moves while pointing at the element. The `ONMOUSEMOVE` event occurs any time the mouse moves, even if it's still pointing at the same element.

- ONMOUSEOUT The ONMOUSEOUT event occurs when the mouse pointer is moved away from an element.

- ONKEYPRESS The ONKEYPRESS event occurs when a key is pressed and released over an element.

- ONKEYDOWN The ONKEYDOWN event occurs when a key is pressed down over an element. This attribute may be used with most elements. (Again, this is similar to ONKEYPRESS; the only difference is that ONKEYDOWN occurs when the key is pressed but not yet released.)

- ONKEYUP The ONKEYUP event occurs when a key is released over an element.

In addition, there are two events that can be used only in the <BODY> or <FRAMESET> tag:

- ONLOAD The ONLOAD event occurs when the browser finishes loading the current document.

- ONUNLOAD The ONUNLOAD event occurs when the surfer moves to a different document. For example, you could use <BODY ONUNLOAD="alert ('Goodbye!')"> to say goodbye to people leaving your page.

There are also several events that are associated with forms (and we'll see an example in the next section). The first two events can be used with both forms and links, while the rest are for use with form elements.

- ONFOCUS The ONFOCUS event occurs when an element receives focus either by the mouse or by keyboard (for example, the Tab key).

- ONBLUR The ONBLUR event occurs when an element loses focus either by the mouse clicking somewhere else or by keyboard navigation.

- ONSUBMIT The ONSUBMIT event occurs when a form is submitted. It can only be use in a <FORM> tag.

- ONRESET The ONRESET event occurs when a form is reset. It only applies to a a <FORM> tag, and only if the form has a reset button (see Skill 12).

- ONSELECT The ONSELECT event occurs when a user selects some text in a text field. This attribute may be used with the input and textarea form control elements.

- ONCHANGE The ONCHANGE event occurs when a form control has its value changed, at the moment the control loses focus. This attribute can only be used with input, select, and textarea elements.

Skill 15

Some of these attributes are new and won't work with every browser. But Navigator 4 and IE 4 support all of these event attributes. Check out the example in the next section and on this book's Web site.

Checking Form Inputs

Perhaps the most useful application of JavaScript is to check the value of form input. For example, you can force a surfer to fill in a required field when they're filling out a form. (Review Skill 12 if you're hazy on forms and how form controls are created.) Here's a brief example of a document which requires that a field be filled out.

 formcheck.html

```html
<!DOCTYPE HTML PUBLIC "-//W3C//DTD HTML 4.0//EN">
<HTML LANG="EN">
  <HEAD>
    <TITLE>Form Validation Test</TITLE>
    <SCRIPT LANGUAGE="JavaScript" TYPE="text/javascript">
      <!--
        function require(field) {
          if (field.value.length > 0)
            return true;
          else {
            alert("Sorry, the " + field.name + " field is required.");
            field.focus();
            return false;
          }
        }
      // -->
    </SCRIPT>
  </HEAD>
  <BODY>
    <P>Please fill out our form, but don't forget your e-mail address.
    <FORM ACTION="formhandle.pl" ONSUBMIT="require(EMail)">
      Your Name: <INPUT NAME="UserName" TYPE="TEXT">
      <BR>
      E-Mail (Required): <INPUT NAME="EMail" TYPE="TEXT"
      ONBLUR="require(this)">
      <BR>
      <INPUT TYPE="SUBMIT">
    </FORM>
  </BODY>
</HTML>
```

This example uses one script element that contains a function called `require()`. Two different event attributes are used. The first event attribute, `ONSUBMIT`, checks that there's a value for the `EMail` field (note how the field is named with the `NAME` attribute) when the form is submitted. The second event attribute, `ONBLUR`, checks the `EMail` field whenever the field loses focus by the surfer tabbing or clicking elsewhere.

The `require()` function looks at the value of the field when it is called (so you can create a more complex example where several different fields are required). When the `require()` function checks a field, if the field's value is longer than zero characters, then the function assumes the field's value is okay. (A more robust version of this document might check to make sure the e-mail address contains an at sign, @.) If the value is empty, then a prompt is displayed and the focus returns to the `EMail` field.

This is only a simple example of form checking. You could do a lot more, such as requiring values within a certain range. For more examples of form checking, see Martin Webb's JavaScript No Content page (`http://www.btinternet.com/~martin.webb/`), Ask the JavaScript Pro (`http://www.inquiry.com/techtips/js_pro/`) under the Q&A Forms section, or the Netscape Authoring Guide (`http://home.netscape.com/eng/mozilla/Gold/handbook/javascript/index.html`).

Skill 15

Presenting Alternate Images

Another popular use of event attributes with image anchors is to show a different image whenever the mouse moves over an image. (This can create effects such as causing buttons appear to be pushed automatically, or images becoming highlighted when you point to them.) The JavaScript technique that accomplishes this will only work on Navigator 3 and 4 and IE 4 (not IE 3). We'll display some code and an example of this practice on the Web site for this book.

Excluding Illegal Tags from Your Scripts

Sometimes you'll want to include HTML tags inside a JavaScript statement. For example:

```
<SCRIPT TYPE="text/javascript" LANGUAGE="JavaScript">
  <!--
    document.write ("<STRONG>Warning!</STRONG>")
  // -->
</SCRIPT>
```

However, due to technical details having to do with SGML and how HTML defines the script element's content, it's illegal to include any end tags (the </ characters followed by any letter) anywhere inside the script element. That makes the </STRONG> tag here illegal.

To avoid this illegal tag, you must "escape" the end tag, so as not to confuse a browser or a validation program. (*Escaping* is the technical name for marking a character so that it doesn't have its normal effect.) The character that is used to escape end tags in JavaScript is the backslash, \.

So to make this example valid, you must put a backslash in the end tag, like this: <\/STRONG>. All of the JavaScript-enabled browsers understand this syntax. This will also help prevent older browsers from misunderstanding the embedded HTML in the script element.

WARNING   Some older browsers will still get confused, however, and end the comment whenever they see the > character. This will lead to your JavaScript statements being displayed onscreen. To avoid this problem in older browsers, use external scripts (see the next section) or avoid using tags in JavaScript statements. JavaScript has alternate ways of generating the effect of most HTML tags.

Using External Scripts and Comments

Navigator 3 and 4 as well as IE 3 and 4 can use the SRC attribute of the script element to point to an external script. *External scripts* are simply a separate file that contains an active script. External JavaScript files should use .js as their extension.

The advantage of an external script is that you can write a general script that you want to use on all of your pages and not have to copy the script to each separate HTML file. Instead, you can point to your external script quite simply. Just add something like the following script to each of your HTML documents:

```
<SCRIPT LANGUAGE="JavaScript" TYPE="text/javascript" SRC="myscript.js">
  <!-- Anything here is ignored if the external script is retrieved. -->
</SCRIPT>
```

The JavaScript statements in the myscript.js file can be anything that you would normally include inside the script element.

WARNING   You shouldn't put any HTML basic structure elements or tags in the external script file, like an <HTML> tag or title element at the beginning of the file, since external scripts are not HTML files. Only include JavaScript statements.

When you use an external script file, you don't have to worry about hiding the script with any HTML comments. It's still a good idea to include general comments, like:

```
// Copyright 1998 by Ron Eyal
```

to identify the author of the script and document how the script works. You can also use a different format for comments:

```
/* This is a comment format
that can stretch for several lines. */
```

The advantage to external scripts is that you can easily modify your site-wide JavaScript code without having to change a lot of files; instead, you just have to edit a single external script file. In addition, external scripts separate the HTML document from a script, which makes your document faster and safer for non-script–enabled browsers.

The only disadvantages to external script files are that it's slower to load two separate files than a single file, and that Navigator 2 doesn't understand external script files, ignoring the SRC attribute to the script element. Also, most Web servers must be specially configured to send the .js files properly.

 **WARNING**   IE 3 can sometimes crash if external scripts are used.

External script files don't have to be only for JavaScript. So far we've seen JavaScript exclusively, but in the next section we'll take a quick look at VBScript.

Understanding VBScript

Now that we've seen JavaScript in some detail, it's time to contrast it to Microsoft's alternative: VBScript.

VBScript, which stands for Visual Basic Scripting Edition, is a scripting language developed by Microsoft to be similar to Visual Basic. Visual Basic is a modern version of BASIC, the Beginner's All-purpose Symbolic Instruction Code, which is often the first computer programming language that many programmers learn.

As you might imagine, BASIC is a pretty simple programming language. Learning BASIC allows you to pick up the rudiments of programming concepts without a lot of complicated concepts or symbols. But as BASIC evolved into Visual Basic, it has become more powerful and popular.

The main limitation with Visual Basic is that it's a platform primarily for Windows users. VBScript has inherited part of that limitation, and it's harder to develop VBScript using the Macintosh or other platforms since the tools aren't as easy to find.

VBScript is similar to JavaScript in its capabilities and limitations. It also uses the script element and event attributes. Here's a quick example of a script element containing a VBScript statement:

```
<SCRIPT TYPE="text/vbs" LANGUAGE="VBScript">
  <!--
    MsgBox "Hello, sailor!"
  ' -->
</SCRIPT>
```

When this script element is put in an HTML file and displayed by IE, a message box is displayed onscreen, as shown here.

The most crippling problem facing VBScript is the fact that we mentioned earlier: Navigator and other browsers don't understand VBScript and will ignore script elements that contain it. Only IE 3 and 4 can interpret VBScript statements.

Notice that VBScript uses different values for the script element's TYPE and LANGUAGE attributes and a single apostrophe (') to end the comment.

TIP   Don't worry about VBScript unless the vast majority of your site's visitors use IE. One way you can be sure of that is if your site is on an intranet and your organization uses IE almost exclusively.

If you do want to learn more about VBScript, you should investigate Microsoft's VBScript FAQ (`http://www.microsoft.com/vbscript/us/techinfo/vbsfaq.htm`) and VBScript Tutorial (`http://www.microsoft.com/vbscript/us/vbstutor/vbstutor.htm`). Yahoo!'s VBScript section has some more VBScript resources.

NOTE   There are theoretically other scripting languages you can use to create active scripts, such as Tcl or Perl. However, browsers will only allow active scripts written in a programming language that they can interpret, which for now is only JavaScript and VBScript.

In the next section, we'll turn from active scripts to applets and begin our discussion of the Java programming language.

Understanding and Using Java

You can spend a lot of time learning and understanding the different Java technologies, with their strange names and abbreviations (such as JDK, AWT, JARS, and JavaBeans). Java is an intensely hyped technology; here we'll try to present a brief introduction to Java without the hype.

Java is a computer programming language. It was developed by Sun (http://www.sun.com/) independently of the Web. But when the Web became popular, Sun realized that Java could be used as a Web programming technology and soon released Java—along with HotJava, the first browser to integrate Java and HTML. Other browsers soon supported Java as well: Navigator 2 and later for the PC and UNIX (Navigator 3 and later on the Mac), as well as IE 3 and later.

You can use Java to create stand-alone applications that have nothing to do with the Web, or you can use it to create applets. Don't worry about stand-alone applications (unless you want to become a programmer); on your Web page, you can only use applets.

 TIP   To learn more about Java, pick up a book like *Java 1.1: No experience required*, also published by Sybex.

Understanding What Applets Can Do

As we said earlier in this Skill, a Java applet runs in a rectangular region of a Web page (see Figure 15.2).

Java applets run in their own world on the page; mouse-clicks outside the applet don't affect the applet, and the applet can't change the rest of the page. In addition, an applet must choose its own background and font; it's difficult to match an applet with the rest of the page. (You can't tell an applet to use a transparent background.)

As long as you remember that applets are independent programs running inside a Web page that can't normally save data, you won't expect applets to do too much.

 NOTE   New technologies, such as Netscape's LiveConnect, allow applets to interact with each other and with JavaScript. Another new technology called JavaBeans allows Java applets to work with ActiveX controls. But existing browsers isolate applets from each other and the rest of the page.

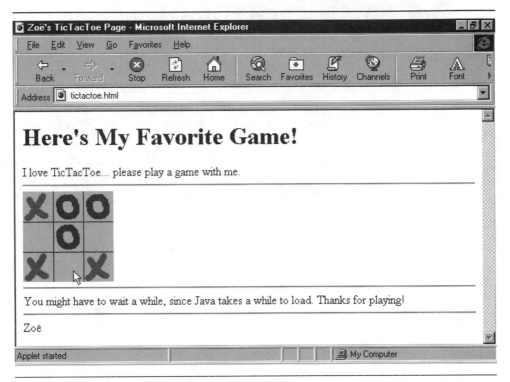

FIGURE 15.2: Sun's TicTacToe demonstration applet running on Zoë's Web page

Creating an Applet

To create an applet from scratch, you must go through several stages. Unlike JavaScript, Java code is developed using several separate files; only the last step involves HTML. First, you must create a file with the applet's *source code*, which is written in the Java language. (You can either write the Java code yourself, or use a development environment like Microsoft Visual J++ or Symantec Café.) Java source code is saved in a file with .java as the extension.

WARNING   You can't use Windows 3.1 or earlier with Java since Java requires long extensions for its filenames.

Second, you must compile the source code using Sun's Java compiler. The process of compiling creates one or more .class files from the .java file. Each .class file contains a special type of binary computer code called *bytecode*. The magic of bytecode is that it can be used on many different platforms so the same .class file can run on any computer platform that can run Java (including Windows, Macintosh, and UNIX platforms).

To compile an applet, you need the Java Development Kit, or *JDK*. The JDK is only available from Sun. Go to Sun's Java center (http://java.sun.com/), and click on the Download button.

Once you have a .class file, the third step is to add an applet element to a Web page that refers to the .class file. (You may have to transfer the .class file to a particular directory or publish it to your Web server first; see Skill 18 for information on publishing.) We'll see how to use the applet element later in this Skill.

The Web site for this book will show you how to accomplish these three steps by using a simple example. In the next section we'll see how to sidestep this process by adapting existing applets to your needs and how to use the applet element and the param element to control applets.

Documentation and tutorials about Java available from our Web site or Sun as part of the JDK will explain the applet creation and debugging process in more detail. Alternately, you can turn to the Web. Start with a search for "Java" at Yahoo!

Adapting an Applet for Your Uses

Since Java is a relatively difficult computer programming language to use, it's a lot of work to create an applet from scratch. It's much simpler to use someone else's existing applet and adapt it to your own needs.

 **WARNING**   Be sure that the applet is not copyrighted or restricted before changing it. While many applets are freely distributed, others are copyrighted or licensed in a way that prohibits you from making changes. Check with the author of the applet to be sure. Most .java files contain a copyright and license notice that explains what uses of the code are allowed.

You can adapt an applet either by changing the program or by using it "as is" on one of your Web pages.

The first method requires modifying the source code (changing anything in the .java file that you don't want). To do this, you'll need to understand enough about Java that you don't break the applet; then you'll have to go through the three-stage process of creating the .java file, compiling the .java file to create the .class file, and transferring the .class file to the proper directory where you can create an HTML file with an applet element that refers to the .class file.

Alternately, the second method lets you skip the first two steps and just use existing .class files. Many Web sites have collections of pre-compiled .class files that are ready for your use on a Web page. You can link to the existing .class file on the author's server (but only do this if you have their explicit okay, because it is rude to link to another person's image, multimedia file, or program without permission). It's better to copy the .class file to your computer or server and then use an applet element that refers to the local .class file.

For example, there is a public Java applet named Blink.class available from Sun (it's also distributed along with the JDK). This applet makes words blink in a variety of colors. If you use the full URL for the Blink.class file (http://www .javasoft.com/applets/Blink/1.0.2/Blink.class) then your browser will let you save it to your hard drive. Once it's saved, you can create an HTML file with the following applet element:

```
<APPLET CODE="Blink.class" WIDTH="400" HEIGHT="200">
   Sorry, you need a Java-enabled browser to see the blinking text.
</APPLET>
```

The Blink.class applet uses a parameter named lbl to determine what to display. (If you leave out the parameter, it will just display the word "Blink.") So if you want the words "Hello from the Berkeley Writer's Group" to appear in blinking colors, you'd use this param element:

```
<PARAM NAME="lbl" VALUE="Hello from the Berkeley Writer's Group">
```

Here's an example of the Blink.class applet using a longer lbl parameter:

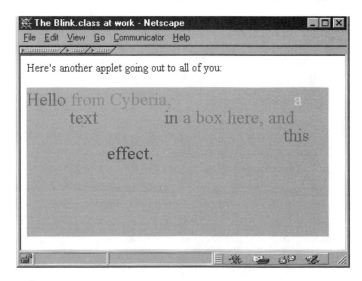

TIP   You can set the WIDTH and HEIGHT attributes to whatever size works for your page; make sure that the text fits inside the applet's rectangle.

By exploring some of the online Java applet collections, you can find some interesting examples of Java applets, most of which are free for non-commercial use. Start your search with Sun's public collection (http://www.javasoft.com/applets/js-applets.html). Another useful collection of news, tutorials, and applets is at Gamelan (http://www.gamelan.com/)—choose one of the categories at the bottom of the page, such as Tools and Utilities, Games, or Special Effects. Finally, you might want to check out the Java Applet Rating Service (http://www.jars.com/) or the Java Boutique (http://javaboutique.internet.com/).

Using the Applet Element

We've seen the applet element in use already in this Skill, but there are a few important details and attributes we haven't mentioned. It's important to remember that the applet element is a text-level element and behaves similarly to an image element. The <APPLET> tag starts an applet element and the </APPLET> tag ends the applet element. One or more optional param elements (using the <PARAM> tag, see the next section) can be placed after the <APPLET> tag to control the applet's behavior. Any text or other HTML elements in between the <APPLET> and </APPLET> tags are only displayed by non-Java–enabled browsers.

There are three required attributes in the <APPLET> tag: The CODE attribute must always point to a Java .class file containing the applet's bytecode. Furthermore, the WIDTH and HEIGHT attributes *must* be present in the <APPLET> tag in order to specify the dimensions of the applet's region. (In contrast, the image element does not require dimensions, as we saw in Skill 8.) You must use pixels, not percentages.

In addition, attributes used with images, such as HSPACE, VSPACE, and ALIGN, can also be used with the applet element. For an applet, you can use ALIGN="BOTTOM", ALIGN="MIDDLE", or ALIGN="TOP" to specify the applet's vertical placement relative to other elements on the same line, or you can specify ALIGN="LEFT" or ALIGN="RIGHT" to make an attribute float to the left or right. (See Skill 8 for more information about floating and the ALIGN attribute.)

You can name an applet with the NAME attribute; this is necessary if you want your applets to be able to communicate with each other using advanced Java techniques.

The ALT attribute can specify alternate text for an applet (but it's better to just put the alternate content in between the <APPLET> and </APPLET> tags since most browsers don't display the ALT attribute's value for an applet, although later versions of Lynx do.

The CODEBASE attribute can specify the directory where the .class file is located. This can be a relative URL to point to a local directory, or an absolute URL to a Java collection's directory somewhere on the Net.

For example, create a test file with the following applet element:

```
<APPLET CODEBASE="http://www.earthweb.com/java/Thingy/"
  CODE="Thingy.class" WIDTH="150" HEIGHT="150" ALIGN="RIGHT"
  ALT="[Thingy is hard to describe]" HSPACE="20" VSPACE="20">
  <STRONG>Sorry</STRONG>, there's a
  <A HREF="http://java.sun.com">Java</A>
  applet here that could not be displayed by your browser.
</APPLET>
```

This points to an example applet created by EarthWeb (the folks responsible for Gamelan). The Thingy.class Java applet is shown in Figure 15.3.

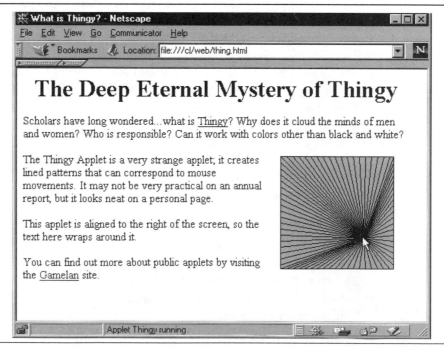

FIGURE 15.3: The Thingy applet is right-aligned and given some horizontal and vertical space so that text wraps around it.

Java applets may reference several other files (usually image or sound files). When you transfer a `.class` file to your server, make sure you take along any required helper files as well. All of the files should be placed in a directory referred to by the `CODEBASE` attribute, unless the applet requires the files to be in a different directory.

Two new HTML 4.0 attributes for the applet element are for advanced uses of Java applets. The `OBJECT` attribute may be needed instead of a `CODE` attribute if you refer to a Java applet in a special format, the "serialized applet" format. Don't worry about this since you probably won't be using serialized applets.

The second new attribute is the `ARCHIVE` attribute, supported by Navigator 3 and later as well as IE 4. This allows you to reference a JAR, or Java Archive. A JAR is a zip file that contains all of the class files needed by an attribute. (The zip format is a compressed archive; it merges several different files into one file and reduces their total file size. Visit Winzip, `http://www.winzip.com/`, if you need a zip program.) The advantage of the JAR format is that several class files can be downloaded at once, which will speed up an applet. For more information, see Sun's Javasoft page about JAR (`http://www.javasoft.com/products/jdk/1.1/docs/guide/jar/jarGuide.html`), Netscape's tutorial on optimizing Java downloads (`http://developer.netscape.com/library/technote/java/javaul.html`), or information on the Jar Installation Manager included with Navigator 4 (`http://developer.netscape.com/library/documentation/communicator/jarman/index.htm`).

Using the Param Element

As we saw in an earlier example, the param element can be used to pass parameter information to a Java applet. The applet must be specifically written to take advantage of parameters, and you will have to read the individual documentation for each Java applet to learn which parameters to use since every Java applet is different. (Viewing source is the best way to learn which parameters can be used with a particular applet.)

The param element is simply a `<PARAM>` tag used with two attributes: the `NAME` attribute, which gives the name of the parameter, and the `VALUE` attribute, which holds the value. For example, we showed you how to use the `Blink.class` applet earlier. You can specify two different parameters for this applet: the `lbl`, which is what text you want to display, and `speed`, to control how fast the text blinks.

To use both parameter elements, enclose them in the applet element, like this:

```
<APPLET CODE="Blink.class" WIDTH="400" HEIGHT="200">
```

```
<PARAM NAME="lbl" VALUE="Liz Phair was exiled from Guyville">
<PARAM NAME="speed" VALUE="1000">
Sorry, you need a Java-enabled browser to see the blinking text.
</APPLET>
```

The order of the param elements doesn't matter. Some applets use case-sensitive parameter names.

Using the Object Element for Applets

HTML 4.0 does not recommend the applet element. Instead, it recommends you use an object element (which we discussed in Skill 9). For example, if you used the following applet element

```
<APPLET CODE="Clock2.class" WIDTH="170" HEIGHT="150">
You can only dig this crazy clock with a Java-enabled browser.
</APPLET>
```

you could instead use the following eviqualent object element:

```
<OBJECT CODETYPE="application/octet-stream" CLASSID="java:Clock2.class"
WIDTH="170" HEIGHT="150">
You can only dig this crazy clock with a Java-enabled HTML 4.0 browser.
</OBJECT>
```

Navigator 4 can display the Java applet using either method, but IE 3 and 4 as well as Navigator 3 will only display a Java applet when you use an applet element.

WARNING   IE 3 and 4 don't display the alternate content for the object element; instead they just present an empty square. This is a severe problem with these versions of IE.

Since so much of your audience will be using these browsers, it's better to stick with the applet element for now. In the future, you'll be able to use the object element for Java with more confidence, which will have benefits because the object element is more flexible than the applet element.

NOTE   You can create applets using other programming languages, such as Python and ActiveX, and include them on a page using the object element.

TIP   If you're having trouble getting an applet to work, check the book's Web site for eight troubleshooting steps.

Understanding ActiveX Controls

We've now spent some time learning how Java applets work. A competing technology for applets is Microsoft's ActiveX. ActiveX is similar to Java in some ways, and Java can accomplish much of what ActiveX can accomplish. But there are differences. Instead of creating applets, ActiveX is used to create *controls*. A control is similar to an applet, but it can affect the operating system, any software installed on the computer including the browser, and how the Web page appears and works.

ActiveX only works with IE. Navigator users won't see your ActiveX controls at all. Since Netscape owns the majority of the browser market with Navigator, you should make sure that you have an alternate way of presenting your ActiveX controls— most likely with Java or JavaScript. This begs the question of why you'd spend time to develop an ActiveX control in the first place; it's only worth it if the vast majority of your audience uses IE.

The largest difference between an ActiveX control and a Java applet is that ActiveX can do all sorts of things with the local computer, including save files, open programs and documents, and change the behavior of Web pages. Unlike a Java applet, which has only a limited amount of capabilities so as to not compromise security, an ActiveX control has a lot of power. To control this power, Microsoft uses a different security model than Java: the *trusted source* model. The idea is that every developer who creates an ActiveX control will register with Microsoft, and that surfers will only download ActiveX controls from publishers they trust.

When a surfer encounters an ActiveX control that they have not downloaded previously, the browser will check to see if the control has been registered. If it hasn't, the surfer will be warned not to download the control (although a surfer can override these warnings if they are very trusting). If the control has been registered, then the publisher's certificate will be displayed (CNET's certificate is shown here in IE 3).

The certificate does not guarantee that the ActiveX control is safe, but it offers some accountability—so that if there is a problem, you can track down the author and alert them to the problem (or have their certificate revoked if they are being intentionally malicious).

> **WARNING**   By the time a malicious ActiveX control has been downloaded and has done its damage, it may be too late for your computer's data. To protect yourself, you should only download controls from large and well-known publishers. Most surfers will take the same approach; so if you create a custom ActiveX control of your own, you'll have to go to some effort to assure surfers that your control is safe and that you are trustworthy.

ActiveX is not strictly a programming language, like Java. Instead, it's a particular format for data that's an extension of two existing Microsoft technologies: OLE, or Object Linking and Embedding, and COM, the Component Object Model. *OLE* is used to allow programs to communicate with each other, and to hand off data to the program best equipped to deal with that data (for example, embedding a Microsoft Excel spreadsheet in a Web page, or linking from a PowerPoint presentation to a sales database). *COM* is a format for defining how objects can work together and communicate with each other.

ActiveX controls can be developed in Java, Visual Basic, C, C++, or other programming languages. Typically, an environment for developing an application (called a *software development kit*, or SDK) is used to create an ActiveX control. ActiveX controls are complicated to create (and you could fill several thick books with techniques). In addition, ActiveX usually involves some use of VBScript as a glue between ActiveX and HTML.

It's not easy to include a pre-developed ActiveX control on your page. ActiveX controls use files with .`ocx` extensions, and they can be downloaded from Microsoft's ActiveX Component Gallery (`http://www.microsoft.com/activex/controls/`) or from CNET's ActiveX site (`http://www.activex.com/`). But to add a control to your page, you'll need to use a special Microsoft tool called the Control Pad, which adds the proper code for the control to your HTML page. This is because each ActiveX control uses a long serial number for a URL, called a CLASSID. The object element can include an ActiveX control using the CLASSID attribute.

The best place to find out more about ActiveX is from Microsoft's general info (`http://www.microsoft.com/activex/actx-gen/faq.asp`) or Microsoft's information on the ActiveX Control Pad (`http://www.microsoft.com/workshop/author/cpad/newcpad-f.htm`). There's also a good definition of ActiveX and some important resources at the PC Webopaedia (`http://www.pcwebopaedia.com/ActiveX.htm`).

Using CGI Programs and Scripts

Make sure that you review the sections on CGI from Skill 12. We can't go into too much detail here since the use of CGI varies widely and the programming languages used are so different.

The main difference between CGI and the other types of programs we've seen in this Skill is that CGI scripts and programs always run on the Web server's computer, while active scripts and applets always run on the surfer's computer.

 NOTE   We hope it's not confusing to say that you could create a CGI program that's a server-side Java application; this is completely different from a Java applet that runs on the surfer's computer. New versions of JavaScript can also run on the server, but this is different from the active script uses we've seen in this Skill.

All CGI programs and scripts have a few limitations in common: First, CGI can be a source of huge security concerns. If the Web server has any kind of confidential information on it, a user of that Web server can accidentally or maliciously use CGI to allow surfers access to that confidential information. Second, since CGI involves the server for every action, CGI programs and scripts are not as responsive as an applet or an active script. Third, because of the security issues, many ISPs do not allow users to create their own CGI. Instead, you'll have to rely on the ISP's canned CGI, as we described at the end of Skill 12.

But CGI has a huge advantage over active scripts and applets: Since CGI runs on a server, it's compatible with every Web browser; that's because the server sends the results of the CGI, which is an ordinary HTML file or other type of file. As long as the CGI is written correctly and outputs its data in a valid format, then every browser can display the results. In addition, CGI can save results to the server, allowing you to collect information and statistics, or send information to a database (such as a sales database).

If you do have an ISP that lets you create your own CGI (or if you're running your own server), you can create CGI. You'll find that CGI is fairly simple, since most scripts and programs are not as complicated as Java applets or ActiveX controls.

Remember that the "G" in CGI stands for gateway. CGI is simply a rule for specifying how information from a script or program should be sent to a Web server. The actual gateway (the method of bridging the output from a script or program to a Web page) is simple indeed. The Web server runs your program whenever it is requested by its URL. You simply have your script or program output a special kind of data header. This header tells the Web server what kind of data to send to the browser.

Learn more about CGI from the NCSA (`http://hoohoo.ncsa.uiuc.edu/cgi/`) or the current CGI draft specification (`http://www.ast.cam.ac.uk/~drtr/cgi-spec.html`). All of the headers used by CGI are http headers. The more you know about http headers, the easier it will be write CGI. Unfortunately, we can't go into too much detail here, but you can read more about http at the official RFC (`http://www.ics.uci.edu/pub/ietf/http/rfc1945.html`) or the pointers and information at the W3C (`http://www.w3.org/Protocols/`).

The most common type of header declares what MIME type describes the data that your program creates. The header will look like one of these three examples:

```
Content-type: text/html
Content-type: text/plain
Content-type: image/jpeg
```

You can use any of the MIME types. We defined MIME types in Skill 9.

Alternately, you can use the `Location` header to specify where a file is located. (We'll see an example of this in the next section.)

The header *must* be followed by two carriage returns and then the appropriate type of data (that is, HTML, plain ASCII text, or a JPEG image to use the previous examples).

If your script or program begins its output with the proper header, then you create a virtual Web page or image. We'll see examples in the following sections.

Using Perl to Create CGI Scripts

The most popular language for CGI is Perl. If you want to learn more about Perl, check out a Web site such as the Perl Language Home Page (`http://www.perl.com/`) or the Perl Institute (`http://www.perl.org/`).

To get you started, here's a brief example of a Perl script that can be used to create a random background image or inline image:

```perl
#!/usr/bin/perl
# Random background display
srand(time ^ $$);
@files = ("image1.gif","image2.gif","back1.gif", "clouds.gif",
"marble.jpg");
$num = rand(@files);
print "Location: $files[$num]\n\n";
```

Create this file on your Web server's computer and save it as `random.pl` (Perl files typically use `.pl` as the extension).

NOTE   Some servers require that your CGI scripts and programs use a `.cgi` extension.

Briefly, here's how this script works. The first line of this script tells your system that this is a Perl script, and that it should interpret it with the Perl interpreter in the specified directory. (Your Web server may have Perl in a different directory; on a UNIX system, you can use the `which perl` command to find out where the `perl` interpreter is located.) The second line is a comment. Authors can put their name and a description of the script here, along with any copyright and usage information. The third line creates a random number seed based on the current time. The fourth line is a list of images (alter this line to create a list of your available images). The fifth line creates a random number from the list. The last line creates the actual CGI header that the server will use to retrieve the random file (using the `Location` http header). Note the two carriage returns (or "newlines") at the end of the header (\n\n). The two carriage returns are a strict requirement for every CGI header; the script won't work without them.

You can test the script from the command line; it should list a random image each time you run it. The last step is to simply include the script in an HTML document. You can use it to create a random inline image (`<IMG SRC="random.pl" ALT="[Random Image]">`) or a random background (`<BODY BACKGROUND="random.pl">`).

TIP   While JavaScript could be used for a similar effect, this CGI script will work with every browser (as long as the browser can display graphics, in this case).

As we recommended in Skill 12, Matt's Script Archive (`http://www.worldwidemart.com/scripts/`) can get you started with a number of useful Perl CGI scripts (including a more advanced version of this random image picker).

Using Other CGI Program Languages

The great advantage of CGI is that you can pick almost any computer programming language. As long as it runs on your Web server's operating system, and as long as you have the ability to create a program in the proper CGI directory, then all you need is to create a proper CGI header.

There are many popular languages used for CGI, including Tcl, Python, C, C++, and AppleEvents. Talk to your Web server administrator or ISP's technical support and find out what language they recommend for CGI on their system.

 TIP   Two further CGI script examples are available from this book's Web site.

Understanding Server Side Includes

A technology related to CGI is *server side includes* (SSI). SSI is a powerful technique that allows you to include a fragment of a separate file in your Web documents. For example, you could include some HTML code for a standard signature for each of your Web pages and store this code in a certain file (containing your name, e-mail address, and links to other pages at your site, for example). Then, you would include this signature block in every HTML file through SSI. If your e-mail address changes, then you can simply change that one file and all of your pages would update correctly.

Whether SSI is available on your system depends on what Web server software is being used and how it was installed. Popular Web servers such as Apache allow SSI, but only if the Web server administrator goes to some effort (we'll discuss the Apache server in Skill 18).

If SSI is enabled, you can use a special HTML comment structure, like this:

```
<!--#include file="test.txt"-->
```

The contents of `test.txt` (including any HTML tags) would be included in the page sent from your Web server to the surfer's browser. If they were to view the source, they would only see the included text, and not the special SSI comment above.

 NOTE   Some Web servers require that you use a .shtml extension instead of the normal .html file if you want to use SSI.

There is one drawback to SSI (aside from the fact that most Web servers don't support it): It's much slower for a Web server to process and send a file with SSI than a normal HTML document.

Some implementations of SSI are far more powerful than the simple example that we've listed here; on some Web servers, you can call CGI scripts using SSI, or execute any program on the server's computer. For more information, see NCSA's documentation of SSI (`http://hoohoo.ncsa.uiuc.edu/docs/tutorials/includes.html`)

or Matt Wright's explanation (`http://www.worldwidemart.com/scripts/faq/textclock/q1.shtml`).

Comparing Programming Technologies

Now that we've introduced and shown examples of active scripts (JavaScript and VBScript), applets (Java and ActiveX), and CGI programs, you may be wondering which of these types of programs you should include on your Web site.

The short answer may be: None of them. After all, each program technology is limited in its own way and requires a time investment to learn how to use it correctly. In most cases, active scripts and applets prevent full access to your pages since a significant portion of surfers won't be able to see the results. Millions of Web pages use only plain HTML without any programming technologies.

The long answer may be: All of them. If you are careful about compatibility and make sure that your site's content is still accessible (or if you're experimenting or don't mind limiting your audience), you'll find that each approach can create a unique result that can enhance your site.

NOTE It's important to emphasize that active scripts and applets are called *client-side solutions* since they depend on the Web client (that is, the surfer's browser) to work properly. CGI is a *server-side solution*, since the Web server does all of the work. CGI is much more compatible than active scripts and applets since it works with every browser.

Throughout this Skill, we've presented some significant problems of each technology as well as some positive uses. We've also shown how each technology has a different role. To help you decide which (if any) of these technologies to use, we'll help you compare their advantages and disadvantages (see Table 15.1).

TABLE 15.1: Web Program Technology Comparison

Technology	Advantages	Disadvantages
JavaScript active scripts	**Simple:** Relatively easy to program, as programming goes **Speed:** As a client-side solution, much faster than CGI **Utility:** Perfect for checking a surfer's input in a form; good for creating unique display effects and simple interactive games	**Security:** History of security holes that violate privacy **Compatibility:** Hard for developers to make sure their scripts work properly on all major browsers **Accessibility:** Many surfers don't have active script-enabled browsers **Limited:** Can't save information **Annoying:** Used to create annoying (and even dangerous) behaviors

TABLE 15.1 CONTINUED: Web Program Technology Comparison

Technology	Advantages	Disadvantages
VBScript active scripts	Same as JavaScript. In addition, many programmers are familiar with BASIC and new programmers find that VBScript's similarity to Visual Basic makes it easy to learn.	Same as JavaScript; however, compatibility problems are extreme since VBScript only works on IE 3 and 4.
Java applets	**Useful:** Unique visual animation effects, lightweight applications, and all types of interactive games and programs **Popular:** Knowing Java can enhance your résumé	**Difficult:** Programming in Java requires knowledge of advanced programming concepts **Slow:** With current Java implementations, applets take a long time to download and compile **High overhead:** Programs that are simple for active scripts are difficult with Java, since you must program the interface (such as the buttons and forms) yourself **Limited**: Can't save information, can't easily affect rest of page **Accessibility:** Many surfers don't have Java-enabled browsers **Security:** History of network security holes **Compatibility:** Java applets don't always work the same on every platform
ActiveX controls	**Useful:** ActiveX controls can interact with other programs on a surfer's computer, and display data from a database in useful ways	**Compatibility:** Huge issue, since only IE can display ActiveX controls. **Security:** Much more of a concern since ActiveX can save data and affect the operating system.
CGI programs	**Useful:** Can save data, act as a bridge for all sorts of programs, process forms, and much more **Highly compatible:** Works with every browser, since CGI looks identical to a normal Web page	**Slow:** Depends on the server for every action since the CGI program is run on the server's computer. Every action must be sent from the surfer to the server and back,which makes it highly vulnerable to a slow connection speed **Security:** Poorly written CGI programs make the server highly vulnerable **Accessibility:** Many ISPs do not allow users to create their own custom CGI programs

NOTE   Some limitations can be eased by combining technologies. For example, even though JavaScript, active scripts, and Java applets can't save information, they can pass data to a CGI program that saves data on the server's computer. Also, the maturing of these technologies will remove some limitations. For example, emerging Java developments from Sun and Netscape are making it more compatible, less limited, able to communicate better with other programs, and much faster.

On balance, we recommend that you start by investigating CGI programs and JavaScript in more detail. JavaScript has fairly wide compatibility and can be useful. CGI programs are much more compatible; as long as you have the ability to put a CGI program in place, you can create useful CGI programs with confidence that surfers will be able to access the results.

In the next Skill, we'll learn about Dynamic HTML, which is a new technology for vivid and interactive Web pages that is intimately connected to both style sheets and programming languages.

Are You Experienced?

Now you can...

- ☑ understand the difference between active scripts, applets, and CGI
- ☑ understand JavaScript and Java and their differences
- ☑ create simple JavaScript active scripts for your page
- ☑ validate forms using JavaScript
- ☑ use Java applets on your page
- ☑ include a CGI script or program on your Web server's computer

Modernizing Your Site with Dynamic HTML

- ➔ Learning about the Document Object Model and absolute positioning
- ➔ Seeing another example of JavaScript
- ➔ Learning about JavaScript Accessible Style Sheets
- ➔ Seeing Netscape's and Microsoft's versions of Dynamic HTML

In this Skill, we'll take a look at an emerging approach to Web design called Dynamic HTML. We'll show you the underlying technologies and see how Dynamic HTML is currently in an embryonic form.

Microsoft and Netscape each have their own approach to Dynamic HTML. We'll take a little time to show you the different technologies involved and the directions that Microsoft and Netscape are taking.

Along the way, this Skill will show you two examples of Dynamic HTML. The concepts in this Skill rely on a knowledge of style sheets (Skill 14) and active scripts (Skill 15), as well as a familiarity with basic HTML 4.0.

What Is Dynamic HTML?

Dynamic HTML is a new approach to creating Web pages that are highly visual, animated, interactive, and programmed to respond to the surfer's platform and actions.

The term "Dynamic HTML" is something of a misnomer since not much HTML is involved to make the pages dynamic. Instead, the three technologies that make up Dynamic HTML are:

- Cascading Style Sheets (CSS), to define the page's appearance—both Cascading Style Sheets, level one (CSS1) that we explored in Skill 14, as well as an emerging W3C extension to CSS called CSS-Positioning, which we'll discuss in this Skill.

- Active scripts, as defined in Skill 15, to make the page change—you can use either JavaScript or VBScript to create Dynamic HTML scripts (and you can also involve applets written in Java, or ActiveX controls).

- Document Object Model (DOM), to allow the scripts to change any HTML element and style sheet setting on the page—we'll define the DOM more closely in the next section.

HTML is simply used as a base to create the page's content (by marking up paragraphs and images normally) and as a glue to link the script and the style sheet to the page, most often using the event attributes seen in the previous Skill and the link element and style element that we saw in Skill 14.

One of the ideas behind Dynamic HTML is the idea that HTML elements will be created and changed "on the fly" after the page has been displayed. The DOM is what allows scripts to target parts of a Web page with great precision, as we'll see.

At the time of writing, these standards were not yet finalized—and in particular, the DOM was not available. Instead, both Microsoft and Netscape have their own interim approaches to Dynamic HTML—which are not compatible with each other. Microsoft calls their approach *Microsoft Dynamic HTML*, and it currently involves VBScript and ActiveX (Skill 15). Netscape's approach involves a new version of JavaScript, JavaScript 1.2. Later in this Skill, we'll look at the two approaches in more detail and give a brief example of Netscape's Dynamic HTML.

 **WARNING** Only Microsoft Internet Explorer 4 can display Microsoft Dynamic HTML, and only Netscape Navigator 4 can currently display Netscape's JavaScript techniques for Dynamic HTML. It is currently nearly impossible to use a single type of Dynamic HTML that works in both Navigator 4 and IE 4. Earlier versions of these browsers can't really display Dynamic HTML at all.

Of course, you don't really need the Dynamic HTML technologies to make pages that are "dynamic." As we saw in Skill 15, you can already create interactive pages using existing technologies. The form features of HTML, when combined with CGI, can create interactive pages that are compatible with the majority of browsers. To a lesser extent, JavaScript and Java applets are already creating dynamic Web pages. For example, we've seen in Skill 15 examples of scripts that change a Web page dynamically.

While Dynamic HTML means different things to different vendors currently, everyone agrees that there are a few technologies that are important. The DOM and CSS-Positioning technologies from the W3C are an essential part of Dynamic HTML, so we'll look at these two specifications first.

Understanding the W3C's Document Object Model (DOM)

The DOM is a World Wide Web Consortium (W3C) work in progress that aims to create a model for an HTML document. This *model* is a way of categorizing and organizing every part of a Web page: the basic structure, the head section elements, the body section elements, and any style sheets. The DOM builds on the specification of HTML 4.0 by creating a uniform model in a specific format that's compatible with active scripts; we'll see some examples of the DOM format later in this section.

With the DOM, each part of a page is considered to be an *object*: a page's image element creates an image object, a paragraph of text marked by <P> creates a paragraph object, and every other HTML element creates its own object. Other features are objects as well: the browser's toolbar buttons, scroll bars, the history of recently visited pages, and the browser window itself.

When a browser opens an HTML document, it can use the DOM to assign every element on that page to a category. Once this is done, active scripts and applets can use the model to access and control every HTML element and attribute on the page, as well as every CSS property and value.

The object model is *hierarchical*, which means that objects descend from other objects like people in a family tree. For example, a paragraph object is a *child object* of the body section object, which is a child of the entire page object, which in turn is a child of the browser window object (where the page is displayed). The DOM will probably number some of these objects and use periods to separate parent objects from their children. For example, the full name of a bold element object inside a paragraph element object might be `window[3].document.body .paragraph[4].bold[0]`.

TIP   You might not need to fully specify all of the object names when you want to refer to a specific object—if you leave names out, the browser will assume you're referring to the current document.

The attributes and properties of that paragraph might also be separated by a period, and an active script could change the value of a paragraph property by assigning a new value, perhaps like this:

```
hr[3].size = "10"
paragraph[4].bold[0].font-face = "arial"
paragraph[4].bold[0].color = "red"
```

The first example would change the fourth horizontal rule on a page to be 10 pixels high; the second and third examples together would change the first bold element of the fifth paragraph to be red and in the Arial font.

NOTE   Numbering starts at zero, so `paragraph[4]` refers to the fifth paragraph on a page, not the fourth paragraph.

Alternately, you can give a name to an element with HTML's ID attribute. Then you can refer to that element's name to change its properties. For example, if you use `<P ID="greets">Hello Rebecca!</P>` then you could use `greets.color ="red"` in an active script to change this paragraph's text color to red. Similarly, the DOM will allow you to refer to a group of elements that have the same class name. (See Skill 14 for a discussion of the CLASS attribute.)

WARNING Since the DOM has not been released yet, all of our examples in this section are theoretical. They're based on the current object models used by JavaScript and VBScript. For real life examples, read the later sections of this Skill.

The purpose of all of this is to allow you to write active scripts that can change any part of a page in whatever way you want—under whatever conditions you want. For example, you could create a group of buttons to change the font size and font color of your entire document. Or you could create a table of financial data that included cells with hidden paragraphs; then you could write a script that made the hidden paragraphs appear if the surfer's mouse point crossed over a particular phrase elsewhere in the document. Or you could make an image that randomly changed its dimensions every few seconds by writing a script that changed the image object's width and height properties.

Unfortunately, none of these examples are possible using Navigator 3 or IE 3. You must use either Navigator 4 *or* IE 4—but the same method won't work for both browsers. Once the DOM is complete and new browsers appear—with updated active scripting languages that incorporate the DOM—all of the three examples would be simple to create. When this happens, Dynamic HTML will be a general standard that will work with many browsers, including Navigator and IE.

NOTE Microsoft has stated that the current IE 4 object model methods (using VBScript) are just for demonstration purposes. When the DOM is finished, Microsoft will scrap its existing model and follow the W3C model. Similarly, Netscape has warnings that the current methods of manipulating objects using the layer element (see Skill 13) or other proprietary methods are subject to change, and that they will follow the W3C standard.

To keep up with the W3C's progress with the DOM, check the DOM activity page regularly (http://www.w3.org/MarkUp/DOM/). You can use a form at the bottom page to request to be automatically notified when the page has changed.

TIP While you're waiting for the DOM to be finished, it's worth concentrating on learning the technologies that are already here. To use the DOM, you'll need to be proficient with HTML, CSS1, JavaScript or VBScript (although JavaScript is more compatible), and CSS-Positioning.

Understanding CSS-Positioning

In Skill 14, we defined CSS1 and described its general use with HTML to control a Web page's appearance. We also briefly mentioned some work in progress by the W3C that will extend the capabilities of CSS1, including some control over how documents are printed (CSS-Printing), the ability to specify fonts with more accuracy (CSS-Fonts), and the ability to place an element with absolute positioning (CSS-Positioning or CSS-P).

Of these new CSS extensions, Netscape and Microsoft are most concerned with CSS-P; in fact, Microsoft and Netscape co-authored the draft specification for CSS-P, and Navigator 4 and IE 4 both support many of the properties (despite the fact that CSS-P is still a working draft).

 NOTE   CSS-P is an extension to CSS1 that simply adds new CSS properties and values. To understand CSS-P, you'll need to have an good working knowledge of CSS1.

CSS-P allows much more control of the positioning of HTML elements— including, for example, the following abilities:

- Defining the size and position of a rectangle where an element should appear. The `position` property can be set to `absolute` or `relative` to place an element at a particular coordinate (placing the upper-left edge of the element using the `left` and `top` properties and the size using the `width` and `height` properties).

- Layering different elements on top of each other (such as placing a heading on top of an image and placing both on top of a region of color); to do so, just use the positioning properties to place two or more elements in the same place on the page. By default, later elements are displayed on top of the earlier elements, but the `z-index` property can override this behavior.

- Choosing whether an element has a value of `visible` or `hidden` (with the `visibility` property).

- Clipping (otherwise known as *cropping*) an element to a particular size, and choosing whether elements larger than their normal region are scrolled, clipped, or just overflow normally (using the `clip` and `overflow` properties).

For example, the following style sheet in an HTML document will cause two different groups of elements to be placed side by side using absolute positioning.

C **comparison.html**

```
<!DOCTYPE HTML PUBLIC "-//W3C//DTD HTML 4.0//EN">
<HTML LANG="EN">
<HEAD>
  <TITLE>Side by Side Comparison of Two Singers</TITLE>
  <STYLE type="text/css">
  <!--
     H1 { text-align: center; }
     #container1 { position: absolute; left: 10%; width: 35%;
        border: thin solid black; padding: 0.5em; }
     #container2 { position: absolute; left: 55%; width: 35%;
        border: thin solid black; padding: 0.5em; }
  -->
  </STYLE>
</HEAD>
<BODY>
<H1>A Comparison of Singers</H1>

<DIV ID="container1">
  <H2>Tori Amos</H2>
  <P>Singer, songwriter. Composes her songs, writes her lyrics, plays
  piano.
  <UL>
    <LI>Emotional
    <LI>Confessional
    <LI>Profound
  </UL>
</DIV>

<DIV ID="container2">
  <H2>Alanis Morissette</H2>
  <P>Singer.
  <UL>
    <LI>Bitter
    <LI>Angry
    <LI>Popular
  </UL>
</DIV>

</BODY>
</HTML>
```

This example uses two division elements, which each contain a heading, a paragraph, and a list. The division elements are named using the ID attribute. The CSS properties in the embedded style sheet are tied to the ID attributes. The two rulesets use CSS-P properties to set the left position and width of the two groups, using percentages of the screen size. (To show where the rectangles are placed, we've also added an outline with some space using the CSS1 `border` and `padding` properties.) The result is shown here, using IE 4.

It's understandable, given that CSS-P is still a draft in progress, that IE 4 and Navigator 4 currently have great difficulty in displaying elements positioned absolutely. For example, there are problems in trying to layer elements on top of each other, using background colors, and numerous other quirks. You might notice that IE 4 is not displaying any padding around the border. Navigator 4 has its own problems with this example, as shown here.

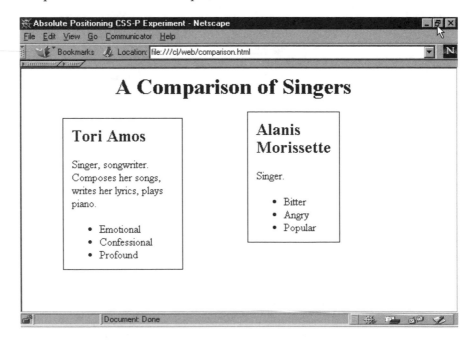

Using CSS-P currently guarantees that you will spend a lot of time using trial and error. It is absolutely essential that you test CSS-P using both Navigator and IE since their interpretations and supported properties differ tremendously. Later versions of IE 4 and Navigator 4 will not have as many problems.

Because we're using a style sheet to control the positioning of these elements, the example degrades very nicely. Older browsers that are not style sheet-enabled will have no problems displaying the content of this document; only the side-by-side presentation will be missing.

The best way to learn about CSS-P is to read the draft specification from the W3C (http://www.w3.org/TR/WD-positioning). Check with our Web site for updated news about CSS-P's progress and current implementations in IE and Navigator.

Using Netscape's Dynamic HTML

Netscape's Introducing Dynamic HTML page (part of Netscape's DevEdge online documentation) defines Dynamic HTML as a combination of style sheets, content positioning, and downloadable fonts. Netscape's original version of Dynamic HTML hinged on Navigator's use of the layer proprietary element (discussed in Skill 13). However, the layer element will never be an official part of HTML since the W3C has declared that it does not fit with the design of HTML. This means that IE will probably never support the layer element either.

Fortunately, Netscape documents show how to duplicate the effects of the layer element using CSS-P, but support for CSS-P is still sketchy in Navigator 4.

Netscape has moved away from the layer element and is now working to support CSS-P more completely (which can almost completely duplicate the effects of the layer element). The other key to Netscape's Dynamic HTML is their new version of JavaScript, which uses a document object model we'll see in the next section.

To find out more, visit Netscape's DevEdge online documentation (http://developer.netscape.com/library/documentation/communicator/dynhtml/index.htm).

Understanding JavaScript Versions and JavaScript's Object Model

There have been three versions of JavaScript; so far in this book, we've been discussing JavaScript 1.0, which is the version of JavaScript found in Navigator 2 and IE 3. JavaScript 1.1 offers improvements and refinements of the first version of JavaScript and is used in Navigator 3 and IE 4. The newest version of JavaScript is 1.2, which is used only by Navigator 4.

JavaScript 1.0 has a partial object model of a document; we saw this model in use in the previous Skill. For example, the section in Skill 14 that demonstrated how to verify form input used the "current value" for a particular text box. Similarly, the JavaScript example of a button that reloaded the page used the document's location. Both of these examples used the properties of an object. (The first example is the "value property" of a text box object; the second example is the "location property" of the browser window object.)

While JavaScript 1.0's document model is powerful, it's also limited. Only links, named anchors, forms, a page's background color, and a few other properties of a window or frame (such as its history of visited pages) are objects that are available to be changed and controlled by JavaScript 1.0. JavaScript 1.1 added images, applets, and image map areas to the document object model as well.

JavaScript 1.2 adds a much more complete document model using JavaScript Style Sheets. But only Navigator 4 supports JavaScript 1.2 and JavaScript Style Sheets.

The concepts for W3C's DOM apply to the JavaScript Style Sheets document object model as well. The technical name for this Netscape approach is *JavaScript Accessible Style Sheets*, or JASS. We'll see an example of JASS in the next section.

Using Absolute Positioning in Navigator

Navigator 4 implements some of CSS-P to allow absolute positioning (or you can use the layer element from Skill 13 to position items absolutely). Navigator 4's implementation of absolute positioning has a few quirks. For example, when the window is resized, things can look ugly unless the page is reloaded. Also, certain units, such as pixels, can't be used reliably for absolute positioning so it's best to use percentages (%) or inches (in) for specifying locations.

Here's a quick example of Navigator's JASS and CSS-P's ability to position objects so that they overlap. Suppose we have two images, but we only want to show one at a time. Using buttons, surfers can select which image they want to view. To accomplish this, we'll make one of the images initially hidden. (The browser will load both images at once, even though only one is displayed.)

C   dogs.html

```
<!DOCTYPE HTML PUBLIC "-//W3C//DTD HTML 4.0//EN">
<HTML LANG="EN">
<HEAD>
  <TITLE>Sam and Erin's Dogs</TITLE>
  <STYLE type="text/css">
  <!--
    #choose { position: absolute; top: 30%; }
    #dog1 { position: absolute; top: 0.2in; left: 1.5in; text-align: center; }
    #dog2 { position: absolute; top: 0.2in; left: 1.5in; text-align: center;
            visibility: hidden; }
  -->
  </STYLE>
  <SCRIPT TYPE="text/javascript" LANGUAGE="JavaScript">
  <!--
    function show1() {
      document.dog1.visibility = "visible";
      document.dog2.visibility = "hidden";
    }
    function show2() {
      document.dog1.visibility = "hidden";
      document.dog2.visibility = "visible";
    }
  // -->
  </SCRIPT>
</HEAD>
<BODY>

<DIV ID="choose">
<P>Choose a dog:</P>
<FORM>
   <INPUT TYPE="button" VALUE="Dharma" onClick='show1()'>
   <INPUT TYPE="button" VALUE="Djuna" onClick='show2()'>
</FORM>
</DIV>

<DIV ID="dog1">
   <IMG WIDTH="261" HEIGHT="301" SRC="dharma.gif">
   <P><B>Name:</B> Dharma<BR>
   <B>Breed:</B> Golden Retriever</P>
</DIV>

<DIV ID="dog2">
   <IMG WIDTH="275" HEIGHT="310" SRC="djuna.gif">
   <P><B>Name:</B> Djuna<BR>
   <B>Breed:</B> Chocolate Labrador</P>
</DIV>

</BODY>
</HTML>
```

Skill 16

This document will produce two buttons. Clicking on the buttons will alternate between a display of two different dogs, along with some information about the dogs. Figure 16.1 shows the result.

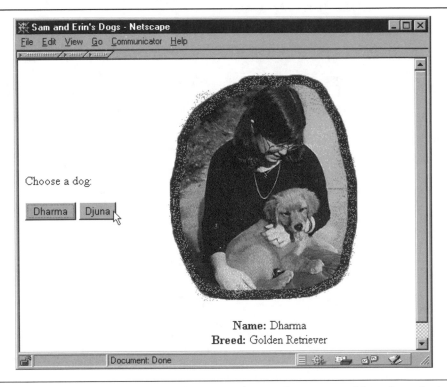

FIGURE 16.1: Navigator 4 shows one image that was positioned precisely on the page in dogs.html. The other image is currently hidden using the visibility property of CSS-P. Buttons toggle between the two images by simultaneously revealing the hidden image and hiding the visible image.

While this document works perfectly in Navigator 4, it produces problems in every other browser. Navigator 3 will show both images normally on the page (ignoring the positioning, since Navigator 3 is not style sheet–enabled). Clicking on either of the buttons results in an error. IE 3 will show both images, positioned properly at one-and-a-half inches from the left edge of the window (but not on top of each other since IE 3 doesn't implement CSS-P, only CSS1). Clicking on either button results in an error. IE 4 shows only one of the images (since the elements given the ID of "dog2" are hidden initially by the style sheet), and pressing either of the buttons results in the error shown here.

While the appearance of the error will vary from browser to browser, the reason for the error is the same. This error occurs in all three browsers because none of them understand the statements in the show1() and show2() functions.

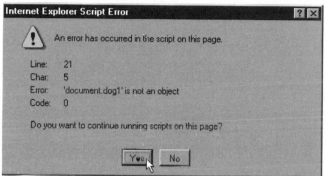

These statements are JASS features of JavaScript 1.2; they simply make one of the images invisible while making the other image visible.

There are several other tricks going on this document; study the rules in the style

sheets closely to see how the two images were positioned and formatted, and note the use of event attributes in the buttons to call the show1() and show2() functions.

Understanding Canvas Mode

In addition to JASS, JavaScript 1.2 adds another area of functionality: the ability to create windows that depend on the surfer's current resolution and color depth. By writing a script that examines the surfer's settings, you could choose whether to display a high-color or low-color image or set up the size of a table based on the height of the surfer's screen.

Several other possibilities are available as well; Netscape introduces *canvas mode*, which is the ability to create new browser windows without scroll bars, toolbars, or other user interface elements. Canvas mode, however, depends on JavaScript 1.2, which means that only Navigator 4 users will be able to see the proper effect; everyone else will receive a JavaScript error unless you're careful.

NOTE   You can use the LANGUAGE attribute of the script element to specify the version of JavaScript you want to use. For example, you could use a <SCRIPT LANGUAGE= "JavaScript 1.2"> tag to introduce a script that would only be run by browsers that understand JavaScript 1.2 (currently only Navigator 4). Other browsers would ignore the script. The possible values for the LANGUAGE attribute are JavaScript (which is equivalent to JavaScript1.0), JavaScript1.1, JavaScript 1.2, and VBScript. Watch out, IE will ignore a script element unless the LANGUAGE attribute is "JavaScript"; adding even 1.0 will prevent IE 3 and 4 from processing the script.

For more information on JavaScript features, see Netscape's JavaScript documentation (http://developer.netscape.com/one/javascript/index.html). Netscape has specific information on the changes in JavaScript 1.2 as well (http:// developer.netscape.com/library/documentation/communicator/ jsguide/js1_2.htm).

Understanding Dynamic Animation and Rendering

It's possible to use JavaScript 1.2 in combination with CSS-P settings to animate elements. The JavaScript code simply has to assign values to the position of elements in response to an event. Similarly, you can have elements change in response to any particular event (such as a surfer resizing their screen or moving the mouse). These capabilities depend on the event attributes that we saw in the previous Skill.

 **WARNING**   Bear in mind that most of these effects depend on JavaScript 1.2, so they only work in Navigator 4 for now.

When the W3C produces the DOM, it's likely that IE will support the effects and capabilities of JavaScript 1.2 that we've seen in this section and the previous two sections (although the syntax will change to reflect how the DOM works). However, as we'll find out next, Microsoft has its own strategies for Dynamic HTML.

Understanding Microsoft Dynamic HTML

Microsoft compares the emerging Dynamic HTML technologies of Microsoft and Netscape (http://www.microsoft.com/workshop/author/dhtml/dhtmlcc .htm) and naturally declares that Microsoft's implementation will be superior and less proprietary. But it's hard to learn from Microsoft exactly what their implementation will be like.

Microsoft says on their Frequently Asked Questions (FAQ) about Dynamic HTML page (http://www.microsoft.com/workshop/author/dhtml/dhtmlqa .htm) that Microsoft Dynamic HTML includes the DOM as well as CSS and CSS-P. But the FAQ leaves many questions unanswered, such as how Web authors can create Dynamic HTML documents for IE 4 given that the DOM does not yet exist. On this point, Microsoft simply says that Web authors can use any programming language.

But IE 4 can't rely on JavaScript 1.2's document object model (JASS) since IE 4 only supports JavaScript 1.1. Instead, IE 4 uses its own object model, using VBScript and ActiveX.

These two technologies are harder to learn than JavaScript, and since they aren't supported in Navigator at all (and most likely never will be), it's difficult for most Web authors to learn how to take advantage of Microsoft's Dynamic HTML.

As IE 4 matured, Microsoft made several tools available to help Web authors develop their pages for IE. The most important tool is the Internet Software Development Kit (InetSDK) for Microsoft Dynamic HTML, which includes a number of programs that can help a Web developer create VBScripts. More information is available from Microsoft's Authors page (`http://www.microsoft.com/ie/authors/`). An online workshop is also available from Microsoft's Web site (`http://www.microsoft.com/workshop/author/dhtml/`).

Microsoft Dynamic HTML aims to reach further than Netscape's method. Microsoft allows authors to combine HTML, scripts, style sheets, and database information together in complicated but useful ways. For example, a new feature of Microsoft Dynamic HTML is *databinding*, which allows a page to take its data from a database, and present the information organized in whatever way the surfer prefers. The data can be rearranged or re-sorted by the surfer without having to reload the data from a server. More information is available from the Microsoft Developer's Network documentation for the InetSDK (`http://www.microsoft.com/msdn/sdk/inetsdk/help/default.htm`).

We won't spend any more time in this Skill on Microsoft Dynamic HTML since it's less likely that your audience will be able to view the results (given that Navigator has such a market lead over IE). If you're interested, however, one starting point is the Inside Dynamic HTML Web site (`http://www.insidedhtml.com/`)—but you'll need IE 4 installed to read this site.

A site that's devoted to finding techniques that work in both Navigator 4 and IE 4 is the Dynamic HTML Zone (`http://www.dhtmlzone.com/`). Finally, a "toolkit" article presents some further resources on Dynamic HTML (`http://www8.zdnet.com/pcmag/iu/toolkit/html-dynamic-1.htm`).

Now that we've shown you the basics of Dynamic HTML and CSS-P, we've finished showing you all of the advanced features of HTML. In Part III, you'll learn about Web design and publishing.

Are You Experienced?

Now you can...

- ☑ **understand what Dynamic HTML means and how it's evolving**
- ☑ **use Cascading Style Sheets to control the position and visibility of a document**
- ☑ **change the background property of a document using a script**

PART 3

DESIGNING AND PROMOTING WEB SITES

We've covered both the basic HTML elements (in Part I) and the advanced HTML elements (in Part II), so you're ready to create pages that can contain a wide variety of text, tables, and multimedia. In Part III, we'll show you how to design attractive and accessible pages (Skill 17), publish your pages on the Web (Skill 18), publicize your Web site and orient it for business with advertising (Skill 19), and keep up with changes to the Web (Skill 20).

Wowing Them with Design

- ➔ Using logical, simple, and top-down design
- ➔ Creating a compatible design
- ➔ Designing for full accessibility
- ➔ Validating your pages

Now that we've spent most of the book teaching you the HTML elements, features, and tools you'll use to create Web pages, we'll give you perspective on the overall design process. The most successful approach to designing Web pages encompasses four key principles: Keep it logical, simple, compatible, and accessible.

You'll want to set your Web site apart from the pack and make it attractive, but you'll probably have to make some compromises along the way. HTML can't do everything, and there are some sensible reasons for keeping Web pages fairly simple. A good design places content above flashiness; the best Web sites have achieved a balance between attractiveness and simplicity.

Using Logical Design

One of HTML's weaknesses is that it will do exactly what you tell it to do. For example, if you accidentally omit a necessary portion of HTML, your page may not display at all, even if your text is perfectly ordered on the page. (At the end of this Skill, we'll talk about how to validate your pages in order to prevent errors like this from undermining all of your hard work.)

You can also easily create a Web site with pages that illogically connect to pages and pages and yet more pages, until your readers are lost in a confusing maze.

The simplest method for a first go-round with Web page design is to work with a logical structure. For most sites, this means using a top-down approach with clear subpages and then topic-level pages not more than four levels deep from your main page. Designing by these rules allows you and surfers more navigational control—a good trick to master from the outset. As you explore more complexity in your designs later on, you'll have mastered the skill of creating pages that appear simple but are actually rather complex.

Planning Your Web Site

Many excellent Web sites started as just a sketch on a napkin. Someone had a flash of inspiration and drew out their ideas for different pages and design elements. From there, they developed an outline of their site. Then they tied it all together by creating test pages and building the site from the top down.

You should do the same. Start by spending some time exploring the Web. Pay attention to what designs you like, which ones don't work, and why you think they fall short. The only way to know what's possible is to spend a lot of time surfing the Web.

If a flashy design technique is common on the Web, consider avoiding it because it's probably become a cliché. Far too many sites, for example, use a border of color on the left side containing a list of links—a practical design popularized by CNET (`http://www.cnet.com/`) and imitated by many.

Once you have some design ideas, you should set some objectives for your Web site by answering these questions: What do you want to accomplish? Who is your target audience? What elements are critical to include? Where do you foresee problems? How will you express your ideas clearly to your audience? What will be the scope of your Web site? Your design can, and should, evolve as you go along, but it's helpful to make some decisions before you even type a single HTML tag. To get started on your outline, try to answer this series of questions:

- Will your site have a consistent design for every page?
- If so, does this design include a background image?
- Does it involve a consistent color theme that's attractive, unique, and (most importantly) easy to read?
- What kind of navigation device will be used to help visitors move around your Web site (frames, a button bar, a textual list of links, a menu, a sidebar, or some combination of these)?
- How often will you update your site?
- How can you make surfers feel welcome?
- How will your design include interactivity (for example, forms, e-mail, chat rooms, scripting)?
- How will you generate design ideas to get your message across?
- Will your site have a consistent writing style?

You can achieve consistent formatting on your Web site by choosing a common theme in your backgrounds, menus, writing style, and other design elements. If you use the same background theme for all of your pages, for example, your readers will feel comfortable with the boundaries of your pages. Choosing an external link will lead to a different background image or theme—so your audience will immediately sense they've surfed beyond your pages. A consistent writing style is another way to make your readers feel more comfortable with your content.

These consistent elements don't need to be complex or time-consuming to create. You can gain control over your readers' comfort factor with a few simple and consistent formatting techniques. The Literary Kicks site (`http://www.charm.net/~brooklyn/`) uses a traditional and clean style with hyperlinks embedded in the text. Literary Kick's editor, Levi Asher, uses one simple bottom-of-the-page <u>menu</u> link that takes you back to the home page.

In contrast, HotWired (`http://www.hotwired.com/`) uses fresh, simple, and brightly monocolored backgrounds and text links along with simple graphics. Both sites value content over flashiness, and the choice of format is sympathetic to their content.

TIP   For information on how to create an interesting page that's not annoying, try Jay's Crafting A Nifty Personal Web Site (`http://www2.hawaii.edu/jay/styleguide/`). For what you *really* shouldn't do, check out Web Pages That Suck (`http://www.webpagesthatsuck.com/`). Some graphic design tutorials, like Lance Arthur's Design Tank (`http://www.glassdog.com/design-o-rama/designtank.html`) and the Yale Web Page Guide (`http://info.med.yale.edu/caim/manual/`) offer excellent page design techniques but neglect accessibility to a wide audience.

Drawing a Map

Your next step is to create an organizational map of some sort. This can be in the form of a list or a sketch that shows all of the levels and major sections of your Web site (see Figure 17.1).

For each type of page you plan to include, sketch it out on paper. When inspiration strikes, be sure to write your ideas down right away (a napkin will do fine).

Starting Simply

Starting simply keeps the process fun. After you've developed some basic objectives, created an outline, and sketched out a map, you may want to start with some of the ideas included in this book.

TIP   Keep in mind that commercial Web design is work, but personal Web design is often play. As Howard Rheingold of Electric Minds (`http://www.minds.com/`) wrote, "After a false start at HotWired, I went home and got sucked into updating my home page on a daily basis. It's hard to have more fun than that!"

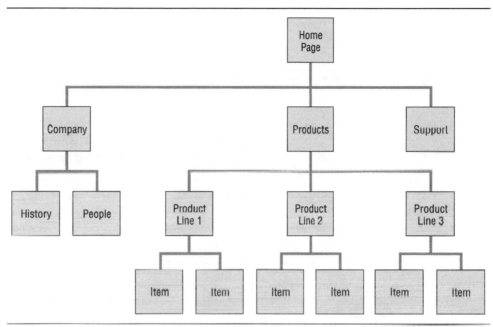

FIGURE 17.1: Drawing a map of your site

Your design should favor the top-down approach, where the more general pages lead you to the more specific (see the next section). You can also view the HTML source (see Skill 2) while you're Web surfing and try out someone else's Web page as if it were a template. If you use this technique, you'll want to resist the temptation to plagiarize.

You can always make your pages more complex later. A simple page can be redesigned with less effort later. Our favorite thing about simple page design is that it can usually handle browser upgrades and technology changes easily.

In many cases, a simple white background is much more attractive than a more complicated background image. Not only is a plain, white background faster, but it usually shows off your images more cleanly. People are used to reading black text on a white background.

TIP   Since older versions of popular browsers usually have a gray background, be sure to use the techniques discussed in Skill 3 or Skill 14 to explicitly specify the white background, along with black text and the link colors.

Also, a simple page is often quick to load. Surfers are extremely impatient; if they have to wait more than a few seconds to see your page, then you run the risk of them surfing on to the next site.

Using a Top-Down Approach

Most Web sites have a single *home page* that acts as an index to the rest of the site. You can think of this page as the front door or cover page that lets in visitors. Once inside, they can decide where to go next by choosing from the list of options. Each subpage has more choices, which lead to more and more specific pages. As each page is chosen, the surfer has gone from the top-level page of the Web site, which is general, down to lower and lower subpages, which are more specific.

As you can imagine, creating a complete Web site this way is a lot of work. You'll have to create one top-level page (and since it's the first page that most visitors will see, you'll want to give it the best design you can), and several level-two *subject pages*. For each subject page, you may need to subdivide into several specific level three *topic pages*. And each topic page may have several level four *item pages*.

There's no way to automate the creation of each of these four designs—you'll have to create the design yourself. Once you've created a sample page for each of the four designs, you should spend some time testing the design in several browsers; with trial and error you'll finalize your design.

Suppose you have four subjects, each with three topics, and each topic with five items. This means you'll create one home page, four subject pages, 12 topic pages, and 60 item pages, for a total of 77 pages. Bearing that in mind, you'll want to create a design that's simple enough to prevent you from spending too long on each page, yet complete enough that you have a compelling result and all of the information that each page needs to contain. Now you need to create the 77 pages...which can be extremely time-consuming.

TIP   To avoid frustration, set a time limit, or a session goal, when you start to work on your pages. Remember to try to have some fun—that way, you'll be motivated to come back to revise your pages when your readers need you.

You can investigate one of the HTML-creation tools (Skill 4) to automate some of the work of creating the pages. Alternately, you'll want to create a template (which we'll discuss later in this Skill).

Keeping It Flexible

After you've begun your basic design, it's a good idea to start to think about how you'll expand on this design so your pages will easily adapt to changes and new situations. Keeping your pages flexible will save you a lot of time when you update and redesign them. This also means using a basic design that is readable in different browsers.

You can also start to think about ways to generate new ideas to get your message across. Searching through a stack of magazines is a great way to get a feel for text styles, sizes, colors, and page formatting. Or you might find inspiration in nature. While taking a hike, you can get ideas for shapes and colors that appeal to your senses. You can experiment on your napkin sketch as you continue to develop your design. You can also find inspiration from some idea or process in your daily life. An office party discussion might give you new ideas for starting a chat area. Or maybe you'll create a new page design by reinterpreting the way the grocer stacks the cereal box display. Try breaking your idea down into its components so you can apply it to your design logically and effectively.

TIP One example of flexibility involves using the same background image for every page. That way, you can give your site an instant facelift by changing the image but keeping the filename the same.

Creating Attractive Pages

Everyone has different ideas about Web page design, and it's easy to become intimidated by the work of professional designers. However, there are a few simple ideas to keep in mind that will help make your pages attractive:

- **Employ white space** Empty space is a vital feature of every page. Don't crowd too much text or too many images into a small area. Instead, space everything out (use the </P> tag after each paragraph to make sure there's enough vertical space between elements; make sure to use CELLPADDING and CELLSPACING attributes in your tables with a generous value, as well as HSPACE and VSPACE attributes in your floating images). A style sheet that adds margins to a page (see Skill 14) will benefit a page's attractiveness and legibility tremendously.

- **Create balance** Too much white space in one part of the page, or huge fonts in one area but small fonts elsewhere, will create a page that looks unbalanced.

- **Use color sparingly** Too many colors on a single page can look garish. Instead of using many different colors, try to use only a few colors that harmonize well together.

- **Use fonts frugally** Most pages need only two fonts: one for headings, and another for body text. Perhaps a third font can be used in a logo, as long as it doesn't overwhelm the page. Use more fonts than this and your page risks looking like a ransom note.

- **Resist gratuitous decoration** Avoid any decorative horizontal rule or icon unless it adds real content to a page. Be particularly wary of pointless animation, unnecessary Java applets, irrelevant badges or logos, and other clutter. Some Web designers refer to page decorations like spinning globes and animated mailboxes as "dancing baloney."

Considering Other Web Design Metaphors

Some famous HTML designers advocate "third-generation HTML sites" that use different metaphors for navigation (circles within circles, multidimensional hubs, rings, and other new concepts that avoid the standard book-like metaphors often used for Web pages). Some approaches to Web design endorse the concept of tailoring your content to the audience so that a potential client sees a different set of choices and facts on your home page than, say, a relative or friend.

The Web rewards experimentation. But all of these considerations need to be tempered by practical considerations: Is your site comprehensible? Do the metaphors make sense? Will you lose part of your audience if they're confused by your site's ultra-modern design?

 **WARNING** Some of the new approaches to Web design are impersonal and sterile, as if the site had been designed by a committee instead of by a unique personality. One of the attractions of the Web is its personal face—after reading a technical paper or marketing report, you can usually find the author's home page and learn about their family, hobbies, and interests.

Creating Templates

A *template* is simply a file you use as a basis for creating pages. Templates can be mostly complete pages (where only a few words, paragraphs, or images need to change to reflect what the page is about)—such as the personal home page template or the résumé we present in the next two sections. Or a template can be just a basic skeleton of the requirements of a page. (Templates are sometimes called *stub files*.)

TIP On a Macintosh, you can specify that a document is a template by viewing the template's document information (Command+i) and checking the Stationery box located at the bottom of the info window. On a PC, just make sure to have a backup copy of your template, and save each page that's based on the template with a different filename (using the File ➤ Save As command).

Here's a minimum template that uses the recommended HTML elements for every page.

template.html

```
<!DOCTYPE HTML PUBLIC "-//W3C//DTD HTML 4.0//EN">
<HTML LANG="EN">
<HEAD>
  <TITLE>[Title of Page Here]</TITLE>
  <LINK REV="made" HREF="mailto:[Your E-Mail Address Here]">
  <META NAME="DESCRIPTION" CONTENT="[Describe this page]">
  <META NAME="KEYWORDS" CONTENT="[List keywords, separated by commas,
to ease searching]">
</HEAD>
<BODY BGCOLOR="#FFFFFF" TEXT="#000000">

<H1 ALIGN="CENTER">[Level One Heading of Page Here]</H1>

<P>
[Content of Page Here]
</P>

<HR>
<ADDRESS>
[Your Name Here]<BR>
[Date of Last Change Here]<BR>
<A HREF="mailto:[Your E-Mail Address Here]">[Your E-Mail Address
Here]</A>
</ADDRESS>
</BODY>
</HTML>
```

You'll want to modify this basic template by customizing your name and e-mail address, then save it in your web directory. Once you've gotten the basic template working, try creating a color scheme, adding a logo image, or using a navigation bar. After you've created your basic template for your Web site, start any new page by opening the template and customizing it for the individual page you want to create.

Using a Personal Home Page Template

Here's a typical template for a personal home page that you can use as a basis for your own page.

 personal.html

```
<!DOCTYPE HTML PUBLIC "-//W3C//DTD HTML 4.0//EN">
<HTML LANG="EN">
<HEAD>
  <TITLE>[Your Name]'s Home Page</title>
  <LINK REV="made" HREF="mailto:[Your E-Mail Address Here]">
  <META NAME="DESCRIPTION" CONTENT="[Describe your page]">
  <META NAME="KEYWORDS" CONTENT="[List your name and variants, as well
as any nicknames]">
</HEAD>
<BODY>

<P>
<FONT ALIGN="LEFT" FACE="ARIAL" SIZE="+1">Your Name Goes Here</FONT>

<IMG HSPACE="20" ALIGN="RIGHT" WIDTH="150" HEIGHT="200" SRC="photo.jpg"
ALT="[complete description here]">

<P>
You can put some text here about yourself. You can write a few
paragraphs about your <A HREF="bio.html">personal</A> and your
<A HREF="professional.html">professional</A> life with lower-level
links to more detailed pages. This design is structured to be
printable so it has the same look as the on-screen document.
</P>

<P>
A few of your favorite Web sites:

<UL>
<LI><A HREF="http://www.xxx.com/xxx.html">First favorite site</A>
<LI><A HREF="http://www.xxx.com/xxx.html">Second favorite site</A>
</UL>

<P>
Send mail to: <A HREF="mailto:[Your E-Mail Address Here]">Your name</A>
<BR>
Copyright &copy; 1998, Your name
```

```
</BODY>
</HTML>
```

WARNING   This template is intentionally boring. Jazz it up with whatever makes you unique and will interest your friends, family, co-workers, and random surfers.

Using a Résumé Template

Similarly, here's a template for a résumé, which you can customize for your own needs.

resume.html

```
<!DOCTYPE HTML PUBLIC "-//W3C//DTD HTML 4.0//EN">
<HTML LANG="EN">
<HEAD>
  <TITLE>[Your Name]'s R&eacute;sum&eacute;</TITLE>
  <LINK REV="made" HREF="mailto:[Your E-Mail Address Here]">
  <META NAME="DESCRIPTION" CONTENT="[Describe your page]">
  <META NAME="KEYWORDS" CONTENT="[List your name and its variants, as
  well as any nicknames, separated by commas]">
</HEAD>
<BODY>

<CENTER>
<TABLE ALIGN="CENTER" WIDTH="600" CELLSPACING="10">

  <TR>
    <TD WIDTH="100"><IMG ALIGN="LEFT"
    SRC="photo.jpg" HEIGHT="75" WIDTH="100" ALT="[Your photo]">

    <TD ALIGN="CENTER" WIDTH="500"><FONT SIZE="+2">Your Name</FONT>

  <TR>
    <TD ALIGN="RIGHT"><P><BIG>Objective:<BIG></P>

    <TD><P>To work as a Web page designer.</P>

  <TR>
    <TD ALIGN="RIGHT" VALIGN="TOP"><P><BIG>Education:</BIG></P>

    <TD><P><EM>Bachelor of Science</EM>, <STRONG>University of
    California at Berkeley</STRONG>, Berkeley, CA, 1992.<BR>
    Business Administration, Human Resources.</P>
```

```
<TR>
  <TD ALIGN="RIGHT" VALIGN="TOP"><P><BIG>Experience:</BIG></P>

  <TD><P><EM>City of Redding</EM>, <STRONG>Director of
  Administration &amp; Human Resources</STRONG>, 1992 to
  present.<BR>
  Involved in policy and procedure development, strategic
  planning, training and personnel relations.</P>

<TR>
  <TD ALIGN="RIGHT" VALIGN="TOP"><P><BIG>Contact<BR>
  Information:</BIG></P>

  <TD><P>1594 Court Street<BR>
  Redding, CA 96001<BR>
  Phone: (916) 555-9768<BR>
  Fax: (916) 555-9767<BR>
  E-mail: <A HREF="mailto:[Your E-Mail Address]">[Your E-Mail
  Address]</A></P>

</TABLE>

<P>
<SMALL>References available upon request</SMALL>
</P>

</CENTER>

<HR NOSHADE SIZE="1">

<ADDRESS>
Your Name<BR>
Last updated: April 23rd, 1999
</ADDRESS>
</BODY>
</HTML>
```

 NOTE   This résumé uses a table for layout, which is sort of cheating (although you could argue that a résumé is really a type of table). Unfortunately, until style sheets are more widely implemented, the use of tables for layout purposes will continue.

The unaltered résumé template is shown in Figure 17.2.

Revising, Testing, Reading

Now that you've gotten a good start on your basic design, it's time to take a more objective look at your writing and typing. Your readers will appreciate your pages more if all of your links are fresh (no dead-end links) and entered correctly. It's amazing how many good sites have typing errors in their linked URLs. It's a good idea to always double-check your links; review Skill 7 for some tips on this process.

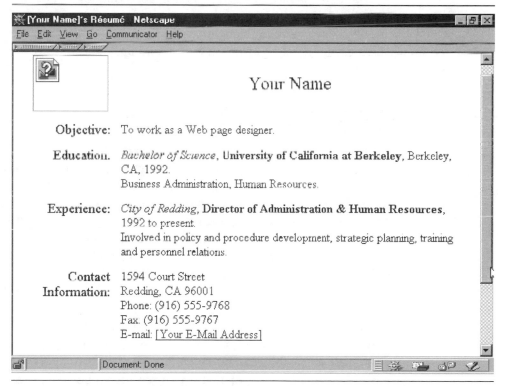

FIGURE 17.2: The résumé template as displayed by Netscape Navigator (make sure to put your photo in place to avoid this missing image icon)

Try to find another set of human eyes to check your grammar and spelling (spelling checkers can't catch everything). After you've finished testing your pages, you can always set them aside for a day or two, and then take a fresh look. Try to honestly eyeball your pages for a word, phrase, graphic, or other design element you personally love, but you know isn't effective. Try taking off the first element that catches your eye. Sometimes this trick works to get rid of that last stubborn "little lovely." In this manner, you are able to stay true to your writing without any element overshadowing your content.

Before you publish your pages on the Web (a process covered in the next Skill), it's important to test the pages under different hardware and software conditions. Try to view your pages in many different browsers and on many different types of computer platforms.

We've found it really helps to "idea surf" the Internet on a regular basis. This way, you'll be able to build on your skill base gradually. You'll also be developing your design voice by seeing and understanding more of what you do and don't like about the Web.

Always keep in mind that your Web pages are living documents. Unlike a printed page, you should expect to visit and update your pages on a regular schedule.

Creating a Compatible Design

Tim Berners-Lee, the principal designer of HTML and the Web, remarked in 1996 that the practice of putting a "This page is best viewed with browser X" label on a Web page "is done by those who are anxious to take the community back to the dark ages of computing when a floppy from a PC wouldn't read on a Mac, and a WordStar document wouldn't read in WordPerfect, or an EBCDIC file wouldn't read on an ASCII machine. It's fine for individuals whose work is going to be transient and who aren't worried about being read by anyone." The beauty of the Web is its widespread interoperability. A valid HTML document is truly cross-platform. (Remember from Skill 1 that *cross-platform* means the ability to work on many different types of computers and operating systems.)

While most people using the Web currently use either Navigator or IE, there are still many other browsers in use, on many different types of computers. Older computers, such as a Commodore Amiga, and powerful workstations, like an SGI Indy, all use a wide range of different browsers. Millions of people still use Lynx, a text-only browser. Other popular browsers still in use include Mosaic and various browsers included with America Online's software. Any of these browsers will display a standard HTML document just fine. There are even browsers that work on tiny handheld computers or using a telephone touch-tone pad.

Because so many designers use Navigator or IE, they tend to forget about all the different browsers. If you follow their bad example and rely on platform-specific tricks or the proprietary extensions to HTML (discussed in Skill 13), you may be excluding a significant portion of your audience. That's why it's important to consider all of the different ways in which your page may be viewed.

There are four main areas that are important to consider: color depth, screen resolution, browser features, and bandwidth.

Designing for Different Color Depths

Color depth refers to how many different colors can be displayed on screen at one time (see Table 17.1).

TABLE 17.1: Popular Computer Color Depths

Number of Different Colors	Comments
2	A black and white system
16	4-bit color—in use on the majority of Windows 3.1 systems and older Macintosh systems
256	8-bit color—the default for Windows 95 and older Macintosh systems (for technical reasons, only 216 different colors may be available to the browser)
65,536	16-bit color (also known on Mac systems as "thousands of colors," and on PC systems as "High Color")
16,777,216	24-bit color (also known on Mac systems as "millions of colors," and on PC systems as "True Color")

In Skill 8, we learned about the two most commonly used formats for images on the Web: GIF and JPEG. GIFs can have a maximum of 256 different colors, while JPEGs are always 24-bit. Color depth can make a huge difference in how a page appears.

So what can you do to accommodate the varying color depths that your audience will be using to read your page? First of all, you have to have some faith in the browser. Navigator and IE will do quite a lot of dithering automatically, and they do a fair job at making every image viewable. As long as you have enough contrast in your images to support black-and-white systems, you shouldn't have to worry too much.

 NOTE   *Dithering* is the process of adjusting an image to be displayed on a screen with fewer colors than the image contains. Dithering works by substituting the closest available colors and by mixing pixels of different colors to make up an approximation of the original color.

Second, consider making any navigation buttons and logos using GIF files. That way, they're already 256 colors. When you're designing a GIF image from scratch, always use the browser-safe 216-color palette that we mentioned in Skill 8.

Third, always have a text alternative to navigation images somewhere on the page, or as an ALT attribute to the image itself (see Skill 8 for more details).

Fourth and most important, it's essential to test your design on black-and-white and 16-color systems *before* you create every page on your entire site. Make sure the essential features of your page still come across. It doesn't matter that the image doesn't look *as* good with fewer colors—as long as the images are comprehensible at 16 colors, you should be fine.

Fifth, try printing out your page. The majority of printers in use around the world are black and white, so your images should be designed accordingly. Since printing out important information is a common activity, this is one practical application of designing enough contrast into your images.

Another point to bear in mind is that graphics usually appear brighter and better on Macintosh screens than on PC screens. So if you use one platform but not the other, make sure to at least borrow a friend's or co-worker's computer (or try to find a library or copy store where they have both PCs and Macs). Monitors vary widely, so the bottom line to consider is that you'll never be able to exactly reproduce the way your Web site appears on your screen on anyone else's computer.

Designing for Different Resolutions

Windows users and Macintosh users can set their monitors to display any of a number of different screen resolutions. If your design is for a specific browser on a screen of a particular resolution with a certain number of colors, then the vast majority of surfers (or potential customers) who visit your page will not see what you may have intended. Table 17.2 lists four commonly used resolutions.

TABLE 17.2: Common Screen Resolutions for PCs and Macs

Resolution	Comments
640 by 480	The default resolution for Windows and Macintosh users; on a PC, this resolution is known as "VGA"
800 by 600	A very common resolution; on a PC, this resolution and the higher resolutions below are sometimes called "SuperVGA" or "SVGA"
1024 by 768	The highest resolution in common use on a PC
1280 by 1024	Possible with newer monitors and graphic cards; popular with designers who are using very large monitors. Many UNIX workstations use resolutions far higher than this

WARNING If you don't take resolution into account, your audience may not be able to view your page properly.

Just as different color depths alter the appearance of images, different screen resolutions can vastly affect the layout of your page. That's why it's so important to have a flexible design and to test your design at different resolutions.

 **TIP** On the smaller end, a laptop may have lower resolution than a desktop PC, and a handheld computer such as the Newton or the Pilot has a resolution of only a few hundred pixels.

The best way to design to accommodate different resolutions is to always specify sizes for horizontal rules, frames, table cells, and style sheet units using percentages. That way, the browser will scale the page appropriately for the resolution of the screen.

Considering Browser Differences

Not only do Navigator and IE have different strengths and approaches to laying out a page, but you also have to consider different versions of Navigator and IE. Early versions of these browsers don't support all of the features of the later versions.

For that reason, we've warned throughout this book which HTML 4.0 features are new and not widely accommodated by earlier versions of Navigator and IE.

Don't get us wrong—there is definitely a good reason to learn about the latest additions to HTML and to use them when you need them. If everyone designed for the lowest common denominator, the Web would never advance. But if your page is rich in graphics, applets, frames, and proprietary HTML, you should be aware that a significant part of your audience won't be able to view your page. For these types of pages, you should strongly consider having text-only pages as an alternative.

 TIP You can use JavaScript (Skill 15) or meta refresh (Skill 5) to automatically take users of newer browsers to a page that's designed specially for them, while leaving the older browsers looking at the current page.

Accommodating Limited Bandwidth

For at least the next few years, the Internet will probably be too slow to render the big images of print magazines, the full-motion video of TV, and the dynamic sounds that we're used to enjoying from a stereo, television, or radio.

A surfer's typical *bandwidth* (a measure of how much data can be transferred through an ISP's connection) isn't always able to transfer its full capacity of data because the load on most ISP's computers is heavy. Also, most modems are too slow to receive the bigger data files quickly, even if the ISP's bandwidth is fast enough to support full-motion, full-screen video.

Because servers are often busy, they can be slow to respond. These response time problems can cause delays that affect the viewing quality of your pages. The most crucial aspect of adding graphics to your page design is addressing the bandwidth problem. You'll need to learn how to keep your image's file sizes to a minimum while keeping the viewing quality to a maximum. Most surfers, who use 28.8 modems, won't want to wait for more than a total of 50–75K of images per page.

Designing for Full Accessibility

Most Web designers assume their audience can read—but should they? The newest proposals for Cascading Style Sheets discuss auditory properties for text-to-speech browsers. These types of browsers are useful for all sorts of people in all sorts of situations:

- People who are blind or visually impaired

- People whose hands and eyes are occupied but still need to get data from the Web (for example, someone driving a car who wants to hear directions to your location, or a surgeon who's operating on you and needs your medical records)

- People who are illiterate

- Any surfer who prefers to have information read aloud

 TIP   Another consideration is making sure people who are deaf or hearing-impaired can still access any information in your multimedia files. Consider having text transcriptions of any speeches or interviews that are only available from your site as audio files.

How can you design your pages to be accessible to all people, to the greatest extent possible, without the need for adaptation or specialized design? To design for full accessibility, try applying the following universal principles:

- Maximize legibility (avoid color schemes with poor contrast, don't rely on shades of red and green for contrast, and don't use small fonts or extreme font size changes)

- Adapt to your reader's pace: Split long sections off into separate pages and offer a choice of length (summary, basic information, full information)

- Use a simple, intuitive, consistent design

- Don't abuse HTML elements or use proprietary extensions just to get a particular visual effect

- Validate pages to minimize errors (see the next section)

- Minimize repetitive actions (for example, don't make a surfer always return to a table of contents to move to the next section in a long document; instead, be sure to allow navigation from each section of your document, even if it's three simple buttons for next, previous, and introduction)

You must always trust browsers to do the right thing. If you use valid HTML, then a good text-to-speech browser should be able to render your page properly. But if you rely on a lot of tricks or extensions, then you may start receiving complaints from surfers.

Validating Your Work

The best HTML design is a legal HTML page since most browsers will be able to deal with it. An invalid page will be treated differently by every browser. You can use a few simple tools to *validate* your pages (that is, check to make sure your pages use valid HTML).

There are two ways to check pages. The first is to go to an online validation site that checks your Web pages (after they've been published on the Web). The second method is to use a local software program that can check the HTML documents on your computer.

We'll look at the online validation tools first. They're simple to use: Go to the tool's URL and simply fill in the form, indicating what the URL of your page is—the tool will do the work from there. There are two popular and useful online validators.

- WebTech's Validation Service (`http://www.webtechs.com/html-val-svc/index.html`)

- A Kinder, Gentler HTML Validator (`http://ugweb.cs.ualberta.ca/~gerald/validate/`)

As its name indicates, the Kinder, Gentler Validator (KGV) has error reports that are a little more helpful, but WebTech's service is a little more flexible (for example, it can check more than one page at once and check fragments of HTML).

In addition, Doctor HTML (`http://www2.imagiware.com/RxHTML/`) can offer all sorts of useful advice, but it isn't as sophisticated at catching HTML mistakes as the other two validators (since they use an advanced SGML-based tool called `sgmls` to catch mistakes). Doctor HTML is similar in concept to WebLint (`http://www.cre.canon.co.uk/~neilb/weblint/lintform.html`), which can also point out problems and HTML errors.

There are several useful lists of validation tools, such as the Chicago Computer Society's Suite of Validation Suites (`http://www.ccs.org/validate/`).

NOTE   A new service for validation is NetMechanic (`http://www.netmechanic.com/`), which offers a background error check service for your entire Web site's HTML files. Just leave your e-mail address and NetMechanic will send you a report when it's finished.

A few shareware or freeware programs can check the HTML files on your computer. One option is to use the HTML tools we saw in Skill 4, and another option is to view the source in Navigator (it highlights invalid code by making it blink, although it doesn't catch everything). A more comprehensive tool is the Spyglass HTML Validator (`http://www.spyglass.com/products/validator/`), available for Windows systems.

TIP   Validate your HTML files religiously. These tools will catch mistakes that might otherwise make your page completely invisible.

In this Skill, we've learned several important approaches to Web page design. We've seen how to create simple, flexible, and attractive pages that are also compatible and accessible. The more you create pages, the better your eye will be for design. In the next Skill, we'll teach you how to publish your HTML documents on the Web.

Are You Experienced?

Now you can...

- ☑ use a logical structure to plan, outline, and map your Web site
- ☑ work with a simple method to design your pages
- ☑ create your pages using templates
- ☑ design your site for universal accessibility
- ☑ validate your HTML files

Getting Connected and Publishing Your Web Site

- Getting connected
- Setting up your publishing tools
- Publishing your pages
- Adding fun doodads to your pages
- Protecting your pages with a password

Up until now, we've shown you how to create HTML pages, but you've only saved them and tested them on your local computer. In this Skill, we'll teach you how to *publish* your pages so that they are part of the World Wide Web. The only way to create a Web site is to publish pages to a Web server. To do this, you need to use the File Transfer Protocol (FTP) to copy the files from your computer to the proper place.

Since you'll need some kind of Internet connection to read and publish pages on the Web, we'll discuss how to choose an Internet service provider (ISP) in this Skill. We'll also use this Skill to show you how to give your page a few decorations and ornaments, such as hit counters, guest books, and badges. Finally, we'll look at how to password protect your pages.

Understanding Your Publishing Options

To publish on the Web, you'll need an Internet account. For a fee, you can connect to the Internet with an ISP. Review Skill 1 to learn about the different types of accounts that ISPs can give you and what it means to be connected to the Internet.

Most of the time, your ISP will offer you Web space as part of a package deal. But if not (or if your needs go beyond what your ISP can offer), you'll need an Internet presence provider (IPP). We'll talk more about IPPs in Skill 19.

You can, within limits, publish on the Web for free. Geocities (`http://www.geocities.com/`) is a company with a good reputation that offers free Web home pages and e-mail on the Web. Many other free Web services are available; search for "Free Web Pages" at Yahoo! to find a long list.

 **WARNING**   Some free Web page services don't care about customer service or only offer you a tiny amount of space. Other companies operate on a shoestring. Almost all of them will try to put their advertisements somewhere on your page.

Some organizations and companies that you're associated with (your school or your employer perhaps) may let you have some free space as well—but that will probably only be for professional or research information and only a little bit of your personal information.

If you want to spend big bucks, you can get your own Web server and connect it full-time to the Internet. We'll see a little bit more about this option later.

Alternately, you can install Web server software on your personal computer, and any time that you're connected to the Internet, people will be able to read Web pages on your computer. But if you're not connected, your Web site won't be available (and unless your personal computer has its own IP address and its network name listed by a name server, people won't know how to find your page). We don't recommend this approach.

Choosing an Internet Service Provider

If you have free Internet access through an organization (such as a library, college, or employer), you may want to get your own account with an ISP as well. That way, you can have a private account to experiment with, and you won't have to change e-mail addresses if you change jobs or graduate. If you don't have Internet access already, you'll certainly want to consider signing up with an ISP.

The easiest way to find an ISP is to search the Web for a local or national provider, and comparison shop. Most ISPs offer information about themselves—just go to their home page (for example, Netcom's home page is http://www.netcom.com/). Many ISPs even let you sign up online.

NOTE   You may wonder how you can sign up with an ISP if you don't already have access to the Internet. There are several things you can try. First, you'll need a modem or another connection to the Internet. Your modem should include some trial software that can get you started. Alternately, if you don't want to sign up on a temporary basis, go to your local library, university, cyber café, or copy shop to work online for an hour or two. That should be all the time you need to find an ISP that's right for you.

Local ISPs typically offer more personal service and lower overall fees than national ISPs. Local ISPs are often comfortably intimate with local businesses and computer groups.

National ISPs are sometimes able to provide more consistent service than some local ISPs because they have the big money necessary to continue service during various types of temporary emergencies such as poor weather conditions, power cuts, or equipment failure. If you travel a lot or move around, a national ISP makes sense since you can usually dial a local access number anywhere in the United States without having to call long-distance.

TIP   You can check around to see how a local ISP has handled these sorts of challenges in the past so you can decide if their service will be reliable and consistent enough to meet your needs.

To find a local ISP, look in the phone book Yellow Pages under computer dealers or computer Internet services. Phone each local ISP, talk with a service technician, and ask for price and service information. For a monthly fee (usually around $20), most ISPs will offer you an Internet connection, any software you need to get started, your own e-mail address, some amount of Web space on their server, and technical support.

Many ISPs charge a setup fee. You can watch for promotional membership drives when ISPs will often temporarily waive the setup fee. Some ISPs offer a trial membership for a reduced fee.

Most ISPs let you sign up for an account over the phone if you allow them to charge you a monthly fee using a credit card. Your account should only take an hour or two to create (but you may need to wait a few days for the software and setup instructions to arrive). If you're a Windows 95 user and you're proficient with its networking options, you won't need to wait for special software— Windows 95 (and the latest Macintosh operating systems) provides you with everything you need to get started, as long as you know how to answer the technical questions that the setup procedure will ask you.

Since the setup procedure varies tremendously depending on your operating system and ISP, we can't give you step-by-step instructions here, but part of the ISP's responsibility is to teach you how to get started; if they're committed to customer service, they shouldn't mind helping you out over the phone. If they balk, it's time to turn elsewhere.

Make sure to negotiate for Web space. HTML files and text files don't use much space, but the standard 5MB of Web space may not be enough if you plan to include a lot of graphics, multimedia, or an extensive database.

Watch out for hourly fees for online time. Some ISPs don't offer unlimited Internet access for a fixed monthly fee. These providers charge extra hourly fees if your monthly usage exceeds a certain amount of time (typically 90 to 150 hours per month). It's better to comparison shop and find an ISP that offers unlimited use of the Internet for a standard fixed monthly charge. That way you won't feel like you need to constantly watch the clock.

WARNING Even "unlimited" accounts don't allow you to stay connected 24 hours a day. Some ISPs will automatically disconnect you after a certain amount of time (especially if you're not using the connection). As a responsible citizen of the Internet (or *netizen*), you should disconnect whenever you don't need to be online.

Setting Up Your Own Server

As we saw in Skill 1, a server is a computer that sends information in response to requests. More specifically, a Web server sends files over the Internet in response to requests from Web clients (that is, a Web browser). These files are sent using the http protocol defined in Skill 1.

If you have a powerful computer, you can set it up to be a Web server and then you have complete control over your files. But Web server computers need lots of memory, lots of speed, a constant connection to the Internet, Web server software—and you'll need some expertise in setting it all up. The most expensive ingredient over time will be your monthly fees for a high-speed Internet connection. If you physically put your server at your ISP's office to take advantage of their high-speed connection (which is called *co-locating*), you can expect to pay from $200 to $500 per month. If you want to keep your server in your office, you can expect to pay even more for your high-speed Internet connection.

 NOTE
There are several types of high-speed Internet connections. Connection speeds are typically measured in kilobits per second (such as the four current speeds for modems: 14.4 kbps, 28.8 kbps, 33.3 kbps, and 56 kbps). Individuals and small businesses may be able to get by with ISDN (Integrated Services Digital Network), which offers speeds of 64 kbps or 128 kbps. Most businesses will need a full-time frame relay (256 kbps or 512 kbps) or T1 connection (1,544 kbps).

In 1995, the most popular Web server software in use was the NCSA httpd Web server, a public domain package developed in 1994 by the National Center for Supercomputing Applications at the University of Illinois, Urbana-Champaign. When the NCSA discontinued development of that program in 1995, a group of programmers used the NCSA's final version (NCSA httpd 1.3) as a base to create a new server program, called Apache, which is currently the number one server program on the Web today. It's powerful, free, and available from Apache's Web site (http://taz.apache.org/). However, to use Apache, your computer must be running UNIX as its operating system.

If you want to set up your own Web server, a number of other server software packages are available for you to download:

- Quid-Pro-Quo is a powerful Macintosh Web server from Social Engineering, Inc. (http://www.socialeng.com/). It's free.

- Microsoft's Personal Web Server (PWS) is included with some Microsoft products (such as FrontPage) or freely available as an add-in for IE (http://www.microsoft.com/ie/download/). The PWS is powerful

enough for a small intranet or a low-traffic Web site, running either
Windows 95 or Windows NT.

- For a step up from PWS, Microsoft's Internet Information Server (IIS) is a
  general-purpose Web server that's quite popular (`http://www.microsoft
  .com/iis/`). IIS requires Windows NT Server but doesn't cost extra.

- The next level from Microsoft is the Site Server (`http://backoffice
  .microsoft.com/products/siteserver/`), which is powerful but costs
  $1,500. The Enterprise Edition version of Site Server (for Internet commerce
  and advanced site management) costs more than $5,000.

- FastTrack Server ($300 and up) is Netscape's entry-level Web server for
  many different platforms, which is easy to use and manage (`http://home
  .netscape.com/comprod/server_central/product/fast_track/`).
  FastTrack includes almost everything you need to establish a Web server,
  except it doesn't include the extra complexity of a commercial enterprise
  environment.

For more information about Netscape's other server software programs you
can go to Netscape's Server Central (`http://home.netscape.com/comprod/
server_central/`).

Since most people won't have the need for a Web server of their own, we're not
going to go into more details about Web servers, or any of the arcane knowledge
required to set up a Web server correctly (you can buy thick books on these subjects). Instead, we're going to assume that you're publishing on an existing Web
server. The next section teaches you how to do that.

Publishing to the Web

Once you've created and tested your HTML document (using all of the skills
we've taught you so far in this book), you're ready to publish your document and
turn it from a file on your computer into a page on the Web.

Publishing a Web page involves a number of simple steps. First, make sure the
HTML document and any image files are all named correctly. Second, transfer
the file (or files) to the correct directory on your Web server. To do this, you'll use
FTP, the File Transfer Protocol introduced in Skill 1. Third, make sure that the
permissions are correct.

We'll see these three steps in the next few sections.

NOTE Alternately, if your ISP gives you a UNIX shell and you know how to use a UNIX text editor (such as vi or emacs), you can bypass the publishing process by creating your Web files in the proper directory. You'll still need to know where your Web directory is located as well as what to call your files, which we cover next. You'll also have to make sure your finished files are readable by the world. (Learn about the chmod program to change file permissions by using the man chmod command; this will teach you how to make your files readable.)

Naming Your Files Correctly

Before you start to publish your files, it's important to understand how to name them correctly. Although you can name your files almost anything you want (depending on your operating system), Web pages have particular naming requirements. The main rules are that you can't use any spaces or illegal punctuation. Since it's hard to remember which punctuation is legal, we recommend you don't use *any* punctuation except for a hyphen (-). Even a hyphen should not be used unless it's necessary. (You'll always include a period between the filename and the file's extension, of course.)

TIP It's best if your filenames are as short as possible (eight letters is a good rule of thumb) and descriptive of the page's content.

We recommend using only lowercase letters since it's easier for surfers to remember your URL if all the letters are in lowercase. (Some operating systems use filenames that are not case-sensitive, so it may be a moot point.)

Using the Default Filename

When you create your first Web file, it will usually be the main home page that introduces the rest of your pages. You should call this file index.html (unless your Web server uses a different default filename). The index.html file will link to the other pages in your site. (Refer to Skill 7 for a refresher on this topic. If your Web server's default page isn't called index.html, find out from your Web provider what the default filename is and use that instead; this may involve some trial and error or a call to your ISP's technical support.)

Each subdirectory you create should also have a Web page named index.html that introduces the rest of the files in that directory.

If you don't have an `index.html` file in a directory, then anyone requesting that directory's URL will usually see a somewhat-ugly list of all of the files in that directory. This can be a useful way of listing your files—if the contents of a directory frequently change, then you won't have to worry about maintaining a list of links to the files in that directory. You can just rely on the server to generate a list of links for you. However, it's important that you test this feature and make sure you are happy with how your Web server lists files. (There's not much you can do to customize the directory list if you don't like it, short of taking advanced courses in server management, or always creating your own `index.html` that lists your files the way you prefer.)

 TIP   If you have organized all of your images into an `images` directory, then anyone can see a list of all your image files by using the URL for your image directory (for example, `http://www.yoururl.com/images/`)—*unless* you create an `index.html` file in your `images` directory. What you put in that `index.html` file is up to you, but it could give details about how people can license your images from you if they want to use them on their own pages.

Naming your files to take advantage of the `index.html` default name can be tricky. Try these tips:

- If you're creating one page about your favorite hobby, baking cookies, and you have other content, then put the cookies page in your main directory and call it `cookies.html`. Put a link to `cookies.html` in your main index.

- If your *only* page at your Web site is about baking cookies, then call it `index.html`. If you later develop other pages, you can always move the cookies information from `index.html` to another file.

Sometimes you'll need to decide if it's worth creating a subdirectory to hold all of your files about a particular topic. Subdirectories can be a pain to manage (since you'll have to use different relative URLs). But it may be worth creating a subdirectory to keep topics separated:

- If you have lots of pages about baking cookies but little other content, then you won't need a subdirectory. Instead, it's probably best to put all of your HTML files in your main directory.

- If you do have lots of different content and you want one part of your Web site to be about baking cookies (with a lot of files about this topic), then it's best to create a separate area for your cookie files, in a `cookies` subdirectory. That way your cookie files don't get mixed up with the rest of your files. Make sure to put the introductory file about cookies in an appropriately named subdirectory (the `cookies` subdirectory would be best) and call this introduction file `index.html`.

Learning Where Your Files Go

When you open an account with an ISP that includes Web space, they will create a URL on their server that anyone can use to view your Web pages. The URL will look something like:

```
http://www.server.net/~login/
```

The word `login` here refers to the name you use to log in to your account (also known as the account name, as we saw in Skill 1; remember that the tilde character, ~, means "the home of"). The `server.net` part refers to your ISP's domain name (such as `netcom.com` or `sonic.net`).

TIP   Instead of using your ISP's URL with your account name, you can purchase a custom domain name for yourself. We'll tell you how in Skill 19 and see why doing so may be worth the price.

However, this URL is not the same address you'll use to transfer your files. Your Web files will have to go to a particular FTP URL that is usually different from the normal URL. This FTP address is only needed when your publish your pages. That FTP address varies from ISP to ISP. Some ISPs will create (or make you create) a directory called `public_html` for your Web pages, while other ISPs use a directory named www or web. The result is that your FTP address will usually look something like one of these URLs:

```
ftp://ftp.server.net/login/public_html/
ftp://ftp.server.net/login/web/
ftp://ftp.server.net/login/www/
```

NOTE   Your actual FTP URL may need an extra directory name, if required by your ISP, such as user, usr, or accounts.

You access your FTP URL using your FTP client. We'll show you how to use an FTP client a little later, after we talk about what tools to use in the next section. (Remember from Skill 1 that a browser can act as an FTP client as well.)

If you use Netscape Navigator as an FTP client, you'll need to indicate your login name, and often you'll have to use a period in the URL:

```
ftp://login@ftp.server.net/./public_html/
```

```
ftp://login@ftp.server.net/./web/
ftp://login@ftp.server.net/./www/
```

(For all of these URLs, replace `login` with your account name and `server.net` with your ISP's domain name. Some ISPs don't use the `ftp` machine name; your ISP will need to tell you what machine name to use if it's not `ftp`.)

NOTE Don't forget your password, since you'll always need it to reach an FTP URL with a username. You can add your password to the FTP URL by following your account name with a colon. However, your password is part of the URL, so you'll need to keep it a secret.

TIP When you sign up with your ISP, ask them to send you the FTP URL you'll use to publish your files straight away. That will prevent head-scratching later.

Once you use your FTP client to transfer a file from your local computer to the FTP directory, then your page is published.

Publishing to a Subdirectory (A Real Life Example)

If you're using subdirectories, you'll have to make sure you switch to that subdirectory or add it to the FTP URL before transferring your files. For example, Stephen has a subdirectory called posi-web.

His normal URL is http://www.emf.net/~estephen/. To refer to this posi-web subdirectory (in a link or when a surfer is typing in a URL), we add the name of the subdirectory to the URL:

> http://www.emf.net/~estephen/posi-web/

Normally, Stephen publishes (via FTP) to the following FTP URL:

> ftp://estephen@ftp.emf.net/./public_html/

When Stephen publishes a new page to the posi-web subdirectory, he uploads the file via FTP to this URL:

> ftp://estephen@ftp.emf.net/./public_html/posi-web/

Setting Up Tools for Publishing

You'll need a tool that can handle FTP in order to publish. Some FTP clients are command-line clients (where you type commands to transfer your files), while some FTP clients are graphical clients (where you drag files from one place to another, or click on buttons and use menu commands to start a transfer). Browsers like Microsoft Internet Explorer and Navigator are graphical FTP clients, although they're a little limited (IE more so than Navigator).

 NOTE   IE can only transfer files from a remote FTP server to your local computer. IE can't log in to an FTP server using a login name. Navigator is a better FTP client because it can transfer files in both directions and can log in to FTP servers using a login name.

Some of the HTML tools that we saw in Skill 4 (such as Netscape Navigator Gold, Netscape Composer, and Microsoft FrontPage) know how to use FTP to publish your files. Once you've set up the FTP URL for publishing, then the tool will take care of publishing files automatically from that point on. Another tool, Microsoft's Web Publishing Wizard, can also publish files to your site using FTP. We'll talk a bit about each of these tools next.

Using FTP to Publish Your Files

As we said, there are two types of FTP clients: command-line and GUI (Graphical User Interface). With either client, you'll need to know the name of your FTP directory for publishing to the Web.

You may already have an FTP client. If not, you can visit TUCOWS or Stroud's (we saw the URLs for these two software archives in Skill 4) to download one. Another software archive for FTP clients is Dave Central's complete list (`http://www.davecentral.com/ftpclnt5.html`). We'll cover a few of the most popular clients now.

Using a Command-Line FTP Client

Windows 95 includes a built-in command-line FTP client. To use it, select Start ➤ Run. In the Run box, type in **ftp**, then click on OK or press Enter. Windows 95 will open the FTP client for you. You'll see a big black window and a prompt for your next command.

At this point, you'll need to type a series of FTP commands to open the remote FTP server and transfer your files. These commands are not well documented; mostly people know these commands because of their previous experience using a UNIX command-line FTP program like ftp or nsftp. But you can type **help** at the FTP prompt to get a quick overview.

As an example, here are the commands we used to reach the FTP area of Janan's server (sonic.net). We typed open sonic.net to connect to the host FTP server. The server prompted us to input Janan's user name (janan) and her password (which is a secret). Then we typed cd (for change directory) and the location of Janan's Web files (home/WWW_pages/janan)—but this directory name will be different for every ISP and every user. Then we typed cd and the name of a subdirectory. We used the dir command to list the files that were here (don't worry about the . and .. entries; every directory has those). Figure 18.1 shows the results of these commands.

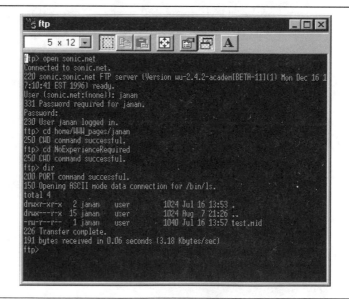

FIGURE 18.1: Using the Windows 95 command-line FTP client, we logged in and learned that the test.mid file is already published. We could publish more files at this point.

At this point, we could issue a put command to transfer files from the local computer to the remote FTP server. This would publish a file. Or we could use the get command to download a file. There are other commands, such as rename and delete, as well.

If you're thinking that the command line looks difficult, you're right. It's much easier and quicker to use a GUI FTP client (and there are no commands to memorize).

 **WARNING**   Images and multimedia files *must* be transferred in binary mode. ASCII files (such as plain HTML files with no international characters) should be transferred in text or ASCII mode. Graphical FTP clients will usually handle this automatically. But if you're using a command-line client, you will have to issue a `binary` command manually before using the `put` or `get` commands to transfer a file.

Using a GUI FTP Client

There are lots of different GUI FTP clients. WS_FTP (`http://www.gabn.net/junodj/ws_ftp32.htm`) is a popular and user-friendly Windows FTP client. CuteFTP (`http://www.cuteftp.com/`) is a shareware FTP client for Windows only. CuteFTP is intended for novice users; it offers a user-friendly graphical interface instead of the less friendly command-line interface. Fetch (`http://www.dartmouth.edu/pages/dartsoft.html`) is a Mac FTP client created by Dartmouth College.

With any GUI FTP client, you'll need to indicate the name of the FTP server that you want to log in to, along with the username, password (and optionally the local and remote directories that you want to use). Figure 18.2 shows how we set up WS_FTP for publishing to Stephen's Web site.

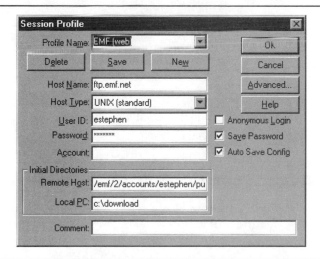

FIGURE 18.2: WS_FTP lets you set up session profiles for each of the FTP servers you want to use. The hardest part is finding out what remote directory you need to log in to; leave it blank and browse around, or ask your ISP for help.

Once you've logged in, you can simply select the files that you want to transfer. You can drag the files from one side to another, or use a transfer button. Figure 18.3 illustrates this process in WS_FTP.

When you've transferred the HTML files, make sure to also transfer any images and multimedia files that are needed by your page.

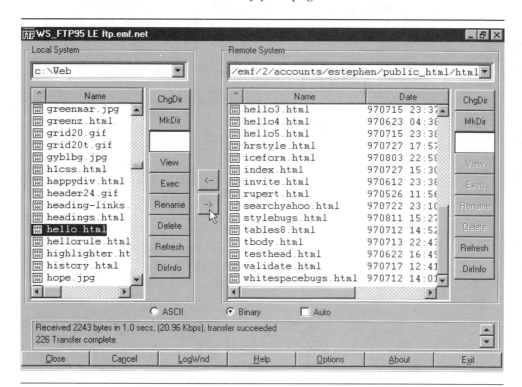

FIGURE 18.3: Clicking on the arrow button in the middle will transfer hello.html from the local system (on the left) to the remote system (on the right). Once the file is transferred, it's published to the Web.

Using Netscape Composer to Publish Your Files

Netscape Composer (and similarly Navigator Gold) has a "one-button publishing" feature (but it always takes at least two button pushes).

After you create your page, you can indicate where your page should be published. You'll need to know the full directory for publishing. One boon to using this publishing technique is that Composer takes care of transferring all of the associated image and multimedia files.

Netscape Composer is shown here in the process of publishing a simple file.

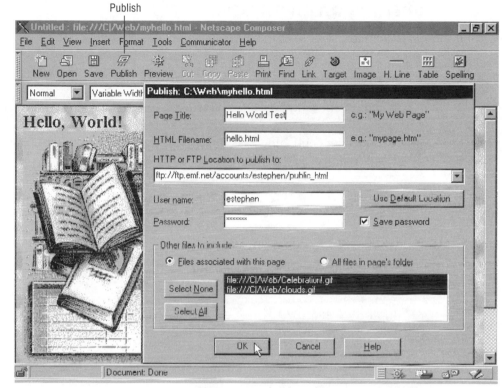

Using Microsoft's Web Publishing Wizard

Microsoft's Web Publishing Wizard is a simple-to-use tool (included with FrontPage and some versions of IE 4) that simplifies the process of publishing a Web site. The Wizard will ask you for the normal and FTP URLs of your site, and test to make sure it can transfer the files. The Wizard can publish many files quickly and efficiently, and it will ask you which files you want to publish.

Since there are several versions of the Web Publishing Wizard and each asks different questions depending on what type of Web server you're using, you'll have to follow its instructions and click on Help if you get stuck. Like any other publishing tool, it will only work if you know the publishing directory's FTP URL. You'll need to get your specific FTP information from your ISP.

Publishing on an Intranet

Intranets, as we saw in Skill 1, are corporate networks. Publishing on an intranet is usually the same process as publishing to the Internet. With intranet Web publishing, you use your computer, a Web browser, and other Web publishing tools to take company documents (like an employee manual, for example) and place them on your company's Web server's computer system in a particular directory.

For example, you could simply upload your employee manual files to a particular intranet publishing directory. The actual directory and publishing procedure depends on your intranet and what Web server is used. (Some intranet managers set up special publishing procedures.)

With Composer (or Navigator Gold) or FrontPage, users on corporate intranets can easily create HTML documents that can be published to a company's internal Web server. These HTML tools allows users to transfer the files (text, images, multimedia, and so on) they use to create a Web page onto the intranet at the press of a button.

Alternately, you can often use your operating system's normal copying commands and procedures to copy your files from your computer to the Web server's publishing directory.

The main difference between publishing to the Web and publishing to an intranet is that Web publishing almost always will require the use of an FTP URL.

Keeping a Copy of Your Files

One problem that Web authors can encounter is that once they've published their files, there are now two copies. If someone makes a change to the local copy, they must publish the files again in order to see those changes on the Web.

When you upload your file, it will replace the old version on the Web server. Make sure that you don't make changes in both places, because it's very difficult to synchronize these changes—inevitably, you'll end up losing a change in one place or the other.

Make sure to establish your procedure for making changes. Either always make changes directly to the file on the Web server (a process called "live updating"), or always make your changes to your local copy and re-publish them whenever you make a change.

 TIP   When you do update your page, include the date of the change somewhere on the page. See Skill 19 for more information about "freshness dating."

Making Sure the Files Are Readable

The FTP process should be fairly straightforward and take care of any technical details (such as converting the files from PC or Mac format to UNIX format and making the files readable).

If you've transferred your files and they are not readable on the Web, you'll have to troubleshoot the process. Are the files being transferred at all? Are both URLs (the Web URL and the FTP URL) correct? Is the error 404 (file not found) or some other error?

If you get a 401 (access denied) or 403 (unauthorized) error, the problem may be with file permissions or password protection. You may need to work with your ISP to resolve these errors.

NOTE   Normally, FTP transfers files so that they are readable by anyone looking in your directory. Some ISPs set up their system so that files are not readable by default—which means surfers won't be able to read your Web documents. If you have access to the UNIX shell, you can use the chmod command to change file permissions. Otherwise, your ISP will have to change the default behavior.

Skill 18

Keeping Transfers Quick and File Sizes Small

One of the quickest things that will turn off a surfer is having to wait. Surfers have notoriously short attention spans.

TIP   When you choose your ISP, it's a good idea to consider the speed of their Web server. Test their pages beforehand. If it's slow to read about the ISP itself, you can bet that your pages will be slow too.

The only way to make your pages fast is to use small file sizes. Review Skill 8 to see how to keep image sizes small: The smaller the image's dimensions, the smaller its file size will be. If you're offering large multimedia files, you might want to consider using a zip archive. Browsers usually know how to transmit zip files correctly, without getting confused and trying to display the zip file onscreen (which can sometimes occur for unzipped files).

Adding Fun Doodads

Once you've published a page on a server, you can add the scripts, applets, and other things discussed in previous Skills. You can also add the popular doodads we mention next, like a counter or a guest book.

Watching Hits with a Hit Counter

One of the most popular ways to track the number of *hits* (or accesses) your pages receive is to set up a page counter.

You can use CGI to add your own page counter. Matt's Script Archive (`http://worldwidemart.com/scripts/`) offers a graphical counter, for example. Many ISPs will have local counters available for their customers; check with your ISP's home page or see what your fellow customers are doing.

Not everyone is eager to include hit counters on their Web pages. Philip Greenspun (`http://www-swiss.ai.mit.edu/wtr/100-things.html`) recommends that you "delete the hit counter" because it slows down the loading of your page. And as we saw in Skill 13, counters are notoriously unreliable. If you really want to use a counter and can't use CGI (if your ISP doesn't let you use custom CGI and hasn't set up a site-wide counter for their customers' use) you can turn to a counter service.

The counter services are Web sites that will keep track of accesses for you, sometimes in exchange for showing an advertisement or for a small price. WebCounter (`http://www.digits.com/usage.html`) offers a free, fast public counter so you don't have to run a CGI counter from your server. You can find other counters from Yahoo! (search under "Access Counters").

We'll see a better way of tracking accesses using server logs in Skill 19.

Signing Surfers In with a Guest Book

Guest books allow your readers to leave comments on your Web site. Entries are usually left with the most recent at the top, and one can scroll down to read previous comments. Some guest book programs allow HTML codes in the comments, so surfers can leave links to their pages, or images, e-mail links, formatted text, and so on.

Just like width counters, there are two approaches: You can use CGI to run your own guest book or sign up with a guest book service.

Alternately, your ISP may have a guest book CGI program already set up and available to you.

If not, you may have to turn to a guest book service. There are several of them; some show advertisements, others have bad reputations for being unreliable. You can give Dreambook (`http://www.dreambook.com/`) or LPage (`http://www.lpage.com/`) a try.

Adding Badges and Banners

Sometimes Web designers want to use their Web pages to exchange links or promote causes. The LinkExchange (`http://www.linkexchange.com/`) is one popular service that allows you to exchange links by including banners on your site. We'll see LinkExchange in more detail in Skill 19.

Some Web sites include logos so that if you want to link to that site, you can use an image instead of a plain link. Netscape's ubiquitous "Netscape Now" logo is one example.

If your site is recognized for an award of some kind, then you'll often be given a badge to display on your page. The badge usually is linked back to the site that gave you the award.

 **WARNING** Some awards are meaningless—the sites behind the award are just handing out awards to drum up interest and get people to link back to them.

Including badges on your Web site is also a simple and effective way to promote a favorite cause. One recent and popular use of badges can be illustrated with the widespread use of a Free Speech image on home pages across the world. The Free Speech On-line Blue Ribbon Campaign (`http://www.eff.org/blueribbon.html`), sponsored by the non-profit Electronic Frontier Foundation.

Password Protecting Your Pages

Sometimes you will want to make a page available only to those surfers who know the proper password. You can do this to limit your page's audience to your friends or co-workers who know a password that you distribute by e-mail, or you can create a subscription-only page, where customers pay you for the password needed to read the page.

Password-protection is only available on certain Web servers. If your ISP uses the NCSA or Apache Web servers, then it's a fairly simple process to protect a directory (you can't protect individual files, only entire subdirectories).

You'll need to create two files: one file, called .htaccess, tells the server that a directory is password-protected. The .htpasswd file contains a list of users and their passwords.

 NOTE   Any UNIX file that begins with a period is a special, hidden file.

The format of these two files is fairly technical. Since the details vary from Web server to Web server, you'll need to check with the specific server's documentation. You'll also need to know the full pathname for the Web directory that you want to password protect.

For information and step-by-step instructions for Apache servers, check online (http://newman-data-services.com/howto/Password.html or http://www.apacheweek.com/features/userauth).

Now that we've seen how to publish pages and add some fun details to your published pages, you should be ready to start creating a commercial site that sells products or information. Even if you're not selling anything, you'll want to publicize your pages. The next Skill tells you how to orient your site for business and a wider exposure.

Are You Experienced?

Now you can...

- ☑ **get connected to the Internet**
- ☑ **set up a publishing tool**
- ☑ **publish your pages**
- ☑ **add fun doodads to your pages**
- ☑ **protect your pages with a password**

Orienting Your Site for Business

- ➔ Establishing your site
- ➔ Getting the word out
- ➔ Selling your products and services
- ➔ Keeping your customers happy

If you are creating a Web site for your own business or for another organization, you'll be interested in selling products from your site.

In this Skill we'll show you some methods to develop the level of service you'll want to provide for your customers, such as choosing an IPP and taking credit card orders. We'll show you how you can attract customers to your Web site, take advertisements and make commissions, and sell your products and services. We'll give you some ideas for how you can keep your customers happy and keep them coming back for more. (Of course, many of these strategies apply for personal pages as well as businesses.)

Choosing a Level of Service

In the previous Skill, we saw how to get connected to the Internet with an Internet service provider (ISP). Most ISPs will offer you Web space for your home page. For a small- or medium-sized business, this level of service may be all you need.

 **WARNING** Be sure to check with your ISP's terms of agreement; some ISPs only let you use their Web space for personal pages, prohibiting commerce.

If your business has special requirements that your ISP might not be able to handle affordably (such as a custom domain name, a secure server for credit card transactions, or a RealAudio server), or your site is too big or too busy for your ISP, then you'll need to turn to an Internet presence provider (IPP). IPPs specialize in giving your business a "presence" on the Web by hosting your Web site.

 NOTE Setting up your own Web server is another option; check Skill 18 for a brief overview.

We'll look at how to choose an IPP and see some of the services that they offer, such as custom domain names and access logs.

Choosing an Internet Presence Provider

There are many different nationwide and regional IPPs, and most of the big-name nationwide ISPs (such as Netcom, IBM, and MCI) also offer Web hosting services as IPPs.

Local IPPs offer competitive rates and often provide more personal service than the nationwide IPPs. This means that local IPPs may offer you more Web page space at less cost, personal technical support, free design services, and a close relationship with the local community.

It's important to shop around when you're looking for an IPP. You can find a listing of local IPPs at budgetweb (`http://www.budgetweb.com/`), theblade (`http://www.theblade.org/`), or see Yahoo!'s listing (search under "Web Services"). Some lists are organized geographically (but there's no reason why your IPP must be physically close to you). Alex Chapman also maintains a list and discussion of IPPs at the National Center for Supercomputing Applications, or NCSA (`http://union.ncsa.uiuc.edu/HyperNews/get/www/leasing.html`).

NOTE Most local ISPs typically offer a flat rate service with unlimited PPP Internet access, one e-mail address, and 5MB for your Web pages, FTP access, free software, and free technical support to get you started. But they may put limits on the Web space, such as preventing CGI. Local IPPs will often offer you 25MB of Web space and usually allow CGI as well as the other benefits we'll describe in the next few sections.

A good IPP will have a support staff that can help you with your decision-making process (and most will offer to sell you their Web design services). You'll need to be able to answer questions such as:

- What's the total file size for all of your site's files (including multimedia)?

- How much traffic will your site get?

- Do you need ongoing technical support? Does your business need specialized Web design or programming services?

- Does your site need special servers, such as a streaming video or RealAudio server? Will a secure commerce server be needed for credit card transactions?

In Skill 1, we mentioned that you can realistically maintain a small to medium professional-looking Web site with hundreds of pages for as little as $20 per month. The price does vary from provider to provider; the nationwide IPPs charge a lot more for Web hosting than most local IPPs.

WARNING It's important to find out whether the charges are flat-rate (the same each month no matter how much traffic you get), or if you are charged extra if your site is accessed by a lot of people.

If your Web site will demand a high level of traffic, IPPs usually charge extra money for the extra load on their system. If other customers share your IPP's Web server with you, then their busy sites might slow things down for your site. Check out the Web sites created by the IPP's existing clients to see how fast they are. The IPP should be able to provide you with daily, weekly, and monthly statistics of traffic flow on their host server (and be able to indicate how fast file requests are fulfilled). You'll want to make sure your customers can receive consistent and quick access to your Web site.

Registering a Domain Name

For any business Web site, it's essential to have a custom domain name. Customers will place much more faith in a business with its own URL. Even personal Web sites can benefit from their own domain names.

Most ISPs will give you a URL based on *their* domain name (so if Rupert gets an account at Best, his URL will be http://www.best.com/~rupert/ as we saw in Skill 1). With a custom domain name such as http://www.rupert.com/, Rupert's customers won't know if Rupert has his own Web server or if he uses an IPP.

Not only is a custom domain name more professional and credible, it's usually easier to type and remember. Perhaps most beneficial of all, domain names can be transferred from one ISP or IPP to another, if you decide to switch to a different provider. That means that even though your Web site's files will move to a different host computer, your URL doesn't have to change.

All domain names that end in .com, .org, .net, .edu, or .gov must be registered through the InterNIC (http://www.internic.net/). (Geographical domains like .uk, .jp, and .us are handled by individual country registries.) Your domain name for a U.S. business should end in .com; if you're a non-profit organization (officially or unofficially), your domain name should end in .org. InterNIC requires a contact person and their name, phone number, and address for each domain. If you register your domain through an IPP or ISP, they'll usually take care of filling out InterNIC's forms for you.

WARNING   Don't confuse internic.net with internic.com; the latter is an unofficial private company that intentionally imitates InterNIC—and they charge a $150 premium for their domain registration service.

NOTE   If you have a network that's already connected to the Internet and two computers that act as domain name servers, then you can fill in InterNIC's forms yourself. But you'll need to know some technical information: the numerical IP address for the two domain name servers, and you'll need to add your domain name to the name server's name table (a technical task best accomplished by the system administrator).

The first step is to find out if your desired domain name is still available. Visit InterNIC's whois service (http://rs.internic.net/cgi-bin/whois) and follow the instructions on the page to check for your desired domain name's availability.

WARNING   Don't type in a URL or machine name—just type the domain name (for example, rupert.com). Many domains are already taken. Remember, domains can only contain letters, numbers, and a hyphen; other punctuation (including spaces) are not allowed. In addition, domain names can only be 26 letters—and after the period and three letters for com or org, that only leaves you 22 letters.

The best names are short, easy to spell and pronounce, and don't have hyphens or numbers. These domain names are much easier for your customers to remember. If the domain name matches your business's name exactly (for example, Smith & Jones Inc. becomes smithjones.com) then customers might be able to guess your Web site if they're looking for it. You might need to purchase more than one domain to cover all of the likely guesses (such as smith-jones.com, smithandjones.com, and smithjonesinc.com).

Once you find an available domain name, you'll have several forms to fill out. Rather than do this yourself, the easiest way to register a domain name with InterNIC is through your ISP or IPP. This is a service that most Internet providers offer their customers. The setup fee can range from $20–200. In addition, InterNIC charges $100 for the first two years, and then $50 per year after that; you will always have to pay these fees and they are not negotiable. Your ISP or IPP may charge a monthly or yearly fee on top of the InterNIC charges. But shop around, since many ISPs will register a domain name for a small fee when you sign up for Internet access and won't charge any other fees in addition to the InterNIC fees.

For example, Stephen recently registered zeigen.com through his ISP. His ISP charged him a one-time setup fee of $50 (while InterNIC charged him $100 for the first two years, as they do for every domain). Figure 19.1 shows his "under construction" placeholder page.

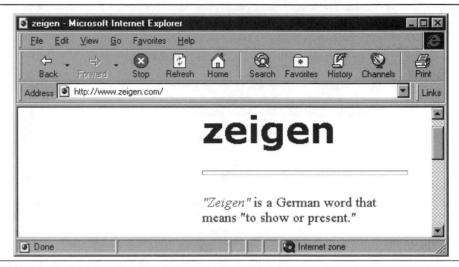

FIGURE 19.1: Stephen's new domain, `zeigen.com`. Who knows what he's going to do with it.

Now if Stephen moves to Bora Bora, he can transfer his domain name from his current ISP to a different ISP or IPP, and his customers won't know the difference (except during the day or two that it takes to transfer a domain). Surfers won't have to suffer through a "Sorry this site has moved" message since his domain name can move with the owner.

As we saw in Skill 7, "we've moved" pages are a preventable nuisance. Surfers may not bother to follow you from one ISP to another, and people who link to you will be upset. It's far better to prevent the problem by purchasing a custom domain name from the beginning. Figure 19.2 shows how many different "we've moved" pages are out there.

Keeping Track of Hits

Each file or page accessed by a surfer is called a *hit*. Therefore, if one person visits your site and views 15 pages and five images, that's 20 hits. Or if 10 surfers visit your site and each views one page and one image, that's also 20 hits. Page counters (as we saw in Skill 18) can only measure the number of hits for a particular page, and there are many problems trusting the reliability of hit counters.

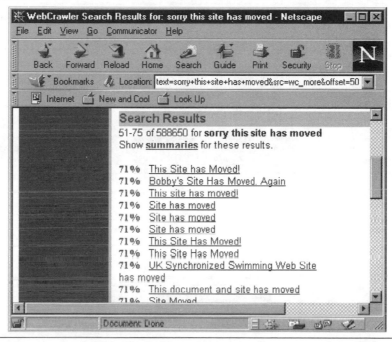

FIGURE 19.2: WebCrawler finds more than one-half million URLs for people who are sorry their site has moved.

Fortunately, every Web server will always keep a log of accesses. Many ISPs offer advice as to how you can use the server logs to keep track of the number of times your customers load specific pages on your Web site. Most ISPs and IPPs will offer you more detailed accounting methods for determining the number of separate visitors that your site has received, and can compile these numbers into daily, monthly, or yearly reports.

NOTE   If your site receives an average of 2,000 hits a day, that will probably result in more than one gigabyte (1GB, or 1,024MB) of data being transferred by your Web server. Many IPPs charge extra for traffic over 1GB. Since it's in your IPP's interest to charge you for this traffic, they'll offer you an accurate hit report.

Server reports are more reliable and less intrusive than the page counters we saw in Skill 18. Since access tracking techniques vary widely, ask your ISP or IPP for more information about their reporting services.

Skill 19

WARNING   These methods are still not foolproof, since there may be many more viewers to your site than are counted in the access logs (due to temporary caches).

There are free programs available that create reports based on the server logs. One popular program is wwwstat, and an excerpt from the middle of one of its monthly reports is shown here.

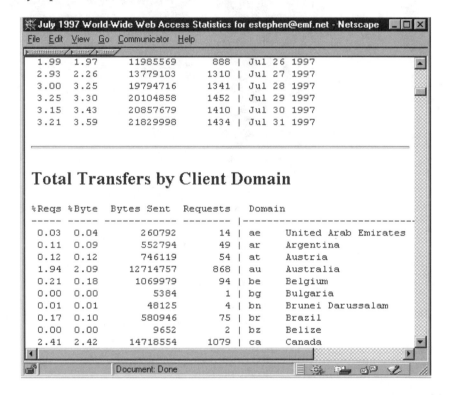

Your ISP may offer you wwwstat reports, or you can set up the software yourself—see their site for details (http://www.ics.uci.edu/pub/websoft/wwwstat/).

Another way to track hits is to pay for a third-party Internet service to track your hits for you. WatchWise (http://www.internetwise.com/), for example, creates real-time statistical reports that can give you the feedback you may need to develop your Web site over time, based on customer response to individual page performance.

Selling Goods and Services

The potential for selling services and goods over the Web is exciting. Web commerce should continue to grow and thrive as long as the transfer of money is secure and accurate and the transfer of goods is fair, legal, and timely—and as long as customer service is high enough to instill customer confidence. Bookstores like Amazon.com (http://www.amazon.com/) and CD vendors like CDnow (http://www.cdnow.com/) appear to be big winners at the moment because they were able to pioneer a field and establish reputations for large selection and good customer service.

TIP   Before you start selling goods and services, you should try out the process for yourself: Buy something via the Web. Make sure that the vendor is using a secure server so that your credit card number is protected. Choose a business that seems responsible, stable, and reliable. Pay attention to what happens during the purchase. See what parts of the experience were enjoyable and which parts could have been improved.

There are many ways to take money online—for example, DigiCash (http://www.digicash.com/) has created a system where surfers buy "e-cash" credits that can be spent at Web sites; a similar service is offered by CyberCash (http://www.cybercash.com/). But although many surfers are understandably reluctant to give away their credit card information online, consumer confidence has increased thanks to secure servers. Currently, by far the most popular way to buy things online is with a credit card.

Taking Credit Card Orders

Most banks offer an Internet merchant credit card program. You'll want to shop around because service and price vary. You sign a contract to purchase, lease, or connect online to a software program that connects your computer with a real-time credit card verification service. Your orders are approved online singly or in batches. Within a few days, the customer's funds are electronically transferred into your business account. Your software program provides reports to track your customer purchases. Most credit card merchant services charge a mix of fixed and variable fees for the use of their service and software, based on your volume of transactions per month.

 **WARNING**   Some merchant credit card services do not want to offer their services to home businesses.

One place to start for information is The Credit Card Network (http://www .creditnet.com ccs/ccn-resources.html), which lists dozens of links to the

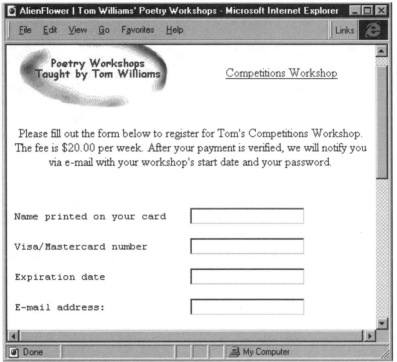

following types of Web sites: credit bureaus, digital cash businesses, consumer credit resources, credit card merchant services, and bank Web sites.

To get credit card information from your customers, you'll need to create a form (see Skill 12). Shown here is a sample credit card form, from the Albany Poetry Workshop.

Making Your Web Site Secure

As we discussed in Skill 12, information sent back and forth over the Internet is not usually protected. It's technically possible for someone to set up a "packet sniffer" that can eavesdrop on e-mail and Web pages, including credit card data and passwords. To increase security, browsers and Web servers can encrypt the data that is transferred.

NOTE *Encryption* is the process of scrambling data using advanced mathematical techniques so that only trusted parties who know the "key" can decrypt the code. Anyone else intercepting the encrypted data will see gibberish (although with enough time and computer horsepower, they can probably break the code). Because of U.S. export restrictions, the encryption used in the general versions of Navigator and IE is not as strong as the U.S.-only versions. (Look for the 128-bit versions of Navigator and IE; this refers to the strength of the encryption. You'll have to certify that you're a U.S. citizen.)

TIP The most popular personal encryption and digital signature technology is called *PGP* (for "Pretty Good Privacy"). PGP is a little complicated when you get started, but its encryption is much more powerful than ordinary Web browsers. PGP can be used to certify or encrypt e-mail as well as Web pages. Surfers will need your key to view your encrypted Web pages. To learn more about PGP, visit their Web site (`http://www.pgp.com/`).

To secure your Web site for commerce, you'll want to make sure that your ISP or IPP can give you space on a secure Web server. Each ISP and IPP has their own procedure for moving pages to the secure site (and these procedures depend on what type of Web server is being used and what encryption tools are available on the server's platform).

As we said in Skill 12, not every page needs to be secure. Typically, only those pages that ask for credit card information or passwords should use a secure server (since secure servers are much slower than normal servers).

Often the URL for a secure page will begin with `https` (an extra "s" for secure) instead of `http`. Some ISPs and IPPs set up their secure server on the same computer as their normal Web server, so the only change you need to make is to a page's URL when you link to it. Other servers require a more complicated process of "checking in" a secure page so that it gets moved to the secure server.

Some credit card authorization methods take care of the secure server for you, allowing you to create your order form on their site. Other credit card vendors will tell you not to worry about using a secure Web server. However, your customers will feel more confident if their credit card information is protected.

NOTE While dangers are definitely involved with using your credit card on the Internet, the same risks apply to buying goods over the phone from a catalog merchant or using your credit card at a restaurant. No transaction is ever completely safe, either on or off the Net.

Publicizing Your Business

The best type of publicity is free. If your pages are designed properly, search engine robots will be able to pull information from your pages automatically to advertise your site to its best advantage.

 TIP The more unique pages you create, the more likely that you'll generate a hit for your site.

The first text on your home page should describe your pages in a few complete, concise sentences. This will help both the robots and surfers who come by your site for the first time.

In Skill 5, we talked about describing your page for search engines using the meta element and the title element. Describing your site carefully with these two elements will give you greater control over how the search engines index your site. Meta elements are especially important if your index pages use frames, forms, image maps, or JavaScript, because most search engine robots can't pick up useful information about your site or follow links if your pages use these features.

Microsoft offers a search service from Microsoft Internet Explorer's starting page (`http://home.microsoft.com/`) that lists the most popular search engines as Excite, Yahoo!, Infoseek, AOL NetFind, and Lycos. You can also search HotBot, WebCrawler, and AltaVista from Microsoft's home page. From Netscape's start page, Navigator's Net Search lists the search engines Yahoo!, Excite, Infoseek, Lycos, SEARCH.COM, HotBot, LookSmart, WebCrawler, and AOL NetFind. It's a good bet that you should target these popular services first. In the next section, we'll show you how to add your Web site's URL to these search engines.

But there are other ways to publicize your business. Marketing your Web site is an ongoing process. Schedule a routine amount of time to get out and make your site known. Here are a few ideas for marketing your site:

- Participate in chat sites, newsgroups, and e-mail mailing lists with interests complementary to your Web business.

- Share links with other Web sites, and run ad banners on other Web sites.

- Hold events from your Web site, or offer a newsletter or notification service.

- Advertise your URL offline (on your business cards, newsletters, advertisements, and stationery).

- Create a press release that coincides with the unveiling of a major (and hopefully useful) feature of your site.

Another low-key and inexpensive way to advertise your site is to include your URL and a brief description of your Web site in the signature of all your e-mail correspondence and Usenet posts.

 **WARNING**   Before you begin promoting your site, make sure it's polished and complete. Anyone coming by an unfinished site with little content will surf away, most likely never to return.

Adding Your Site to a Search Engine

Every search engine and Web directory allows you to submit your Web site for inclusion in their database or catalog. The process is similar for each site: Go to the site's home page, find the Add Your Site or similar link, fill out the form with the pertinent information about your Web site, and wait for the site to add you to the database. You should eventually find that your hits have increased.

Let's use Digital's AltaVista as an example. Here are step-by-step instructions on how to add your site to AltaVista's database:

1. Start by going to AltaVista's main page. In the Location box for your browser, enter **http://www.altavista.digital.com** and press Enter.

2. Find the Add/Remove URL link at the bottom of the page and follow this link.

3. Read through the instructions for the page. At the bottom of the page, enter your URL in the text entry box.

4. Click on the Submit URL button. AltaVista will try to retrieve your page to make sure that you've entered the URL correctly. If it can retrieve the page, you'll be added to AltaVista's database. Furthermore, AltaVista's robot, nicknamed Scooter, will come by within the next few days to index every page it can find (by following links at your site).

You can repeat this process for other search engines and directories. Some directories, like Yahoo!, don't use indexing robots. You have to go to the directory and submit your information to them manually; otherwise, they will not generally seek your site out in order to list it. The registration form for a directory is usually longer to fill out. You may need to decide on a category or categories where you want your site to appear.

Search engines differ from directories in that they usually list less information about your site, and it's harder to predict when a search engine will list your page. Directories usually offer fairly straight-forward alphabetical lists organized by category or geographic region.

 NOTE
Yahoo! is definitely the most effective place to list your site since it's one of the most popular pages on the Internet and often a starting point for surfers. Yahoo! offers free listings, but you should take some time to familiarize yourself with Yahoo!'s categories. Each of your Web pages can only be listed in a maximum of two different Yahoo! categories. Yahoo! will take a while to add your site since they usually check each URL personally.

Since it's time-consuming to visit many directories and catalogs, you may want to use one of the services that we describe in the next section.

Getting Listed in Prominent Places

There are a number of free promotion services on the Web. These promotion services can help you in the submission process. We'll list three to get you started:

- **Multi-Submit** The Multi-Submit page (`http://users.boone.net/yinon/multisub/default.html`) is a free service that lists the most popular search engines and directories, using frames, making it easier to navigate to the appropriate submission page for each site. (But you have to submit your site manually to each service.)

- **Add It!** Add It! (`http://www.liquidimaging.com/submit/`) is a free service that submits your site to 20 popular search engines and directories automatically, once you fill out their form.

- **Submit It!** Since February 1995, the Submit It! service (`http://www.submit-it.com/`) has offered a free Web site announcement service to directories and search engines. Currently, the free service includes Infoseek, WebCrawler, and AltaVista, as well as 17 lesser-known sites. A pay service announces your site to more directories (including Excite, Magellan, Yahoo!, and so on), search engines (Lycos, AltaVista, HotBot, and others), as well as Award or Review sites (such as Cool Site of the Day, CNET's Best of the Web, and Cybertown's Site of the Week, among others).

Some submission services will list your site at an announcement site. Announcement sites list new Web pages or Web site content for a limited time. Often your announcement is archived so users can look your site up at a later date.

For more Web promotion sites, go to Yahoo! and search for "Promotion" to find the Web Services: Promotion category.

Exchanging Links

You can devote a section of your Web site for links to complementary sites. On a regular basis, you can correspond with other Web sites that share a common bond with your business or Web site's subject matter. Send individualized, personal, and friendly e-mail messages asking if specific sites will consider linking to your site in exchange for your link to their site.

Alternately, you can agree to exchange advertising with another site. You allow the other site to advertise at your Web site, and you create a banner ad of your own that will be advertised at their site.

One popular advertising exchange service is Link Exchange (http://www .linkexchange.com/). This free service for small and large businesses and personal sites claims to be the Web's largest advertising network. Web sites (both commercial and non commercial) advertise on each other's sites. Every time a surfer views the link exchange ad on your page, you'll earn half a credit. Each credit will cause your own banner ad to appear on another LinkExchange member's site. If your banner ad is compelling, you can attract more of an audience.

 TIP   Even if you don't use LinkExchange, it's a great idea to create a banner or graphic for your site that you freely make available for other Webmasters to use if they want to link back to you.

Skill 19

Advertising Your Site

LinkExchange is one place that accepts paid advertisements that will be displayed by many different sites. You can also sponsor a particular page or investigate advertising rates at a premium site, such as Netscape, Yahoo!, AltaVista, or other popular search engines, directories, and starting points.

Accepting Sponsorship Advertising

Many Web sites offer compelling content available nowhere else. Sometimes a page that began as a hobby site has attracted such a large audience that the creators are able to go professional and begin making money through advertising. (Popular sites such as Yahoo! and Mr. Showbiz began this way.)

Often, an interesting site has unique and compelling content solely because the Web author is an enthusiastic hobbyist or an expert on the topic (or has good inside connections, sources, and a lot of free time). Pages that offer unique information (or repackage other sites' information in a useful and attract format) soon attract an audience—as long as the field is not already too crowded. Since 1995, Web authors have been wondering how they can make money in exchange for all of the hours they have spent developing their site. The answer is usually advertising, if money is to be made at all.

In the real world, experts often sell their information by packaging it as a magazine article, or a book, or by working as a consultant. Those who collect useful information (such as stock market tips or short stories) can often gain subscribers if they create a paper 'zine or newsletter.

But on the Internet, the subscription model rarely works. Too much free information competes against a subscription-only site, so most surfers will not want to subscribe to a site's content—especially if there's no way for them to judge the quality of the information or entertainment available.

 NOTE If a Web site gives out useful information as a free sample to show that the site is worth subscribing to, then many surfers will take the free information and not bother to purchase the pay-only information. Finding the right balance between what to give away as a teaser and what to keep reserved for paying customers is a difficult task.

Only a few sites have made large amounts of money by using a subscription model. (The sites that do make money this way are typically well-known news providers, such as the *New York Times* and *Sports Illustrated*, gaming sites with state-of-the-art online multiplayer games, or quasi-legal sites that offer access to adult material or gambling.) Many well-known sites and magazines have "lost" tremendous amounts of money at their Web site (but many consider this money well-spent in exchange for prestige and the ability to provide information and brochures about their company).

Instead of wasting time trying to pursue a subscription model, you'll probably want to focus on an advertising strategy. If your site has unique and compelling content and you've spent some time publicizing your site, you'll soon be attracting a sizable audience. Once you've reached a certain target audience, you can solicit one or more sponsors to advertise on your pages.

The most popular type of advertising is a banner ad (which is usually of a certain dimension, such as 468 by 60 or 400 by 40). Your sponsors will want this ad to be displayed prominently on your site (usually at the top). It's not enough to simply display the ad: You must also deliver a certain number of *clickthroughs* (the number of surfers who actually click on the ad). So, the most successful sites are not just those that attract lots of visitors—they also somehow convince visitors to click on the ad.

There are several ways to find advertisers. You can find sponsors by soliciting companies that advertise online directly (good luck!). You can display a "Your Advertisement Here" banner and hope that someone comes across this banner who wants to advertise on your page. You can negotiate with an advertising agency to have them pay you a flat fee for displaying various advertising banners. Or you can contact an advertising broker or advertising representative, who will act as your agent and obtain advertising clients for your site (in exchange for a percentage of the advertising fee you charge). An advertising exchange network (like LinkExchange, which we saw in the previous section), is another alternative.

Some of the premium advertising brokers, like DoubleClick (`http://www`
`.doubleclick.net/`), will only be interested in negotiating with you if you can prove you receive a million different surfers a month. Other advertising brokers will work with smaller sites and pay different rates depending on how many "impressions" (unique visitors) and clickthroughs that you can deliver.

All of these options are listed and discussed in Mark Welch's informative advertising page (`http://www.markwelch.com/bannerad.htm`). As he points out, it's important to realize ahead of time that some deals sound too good to be true—because they are. There have already been a number of companies that have made outrageous promises for advertising dollars that they couldn't keep and have gone out of business as a result. And some advertising firms have cheated Web authors out of thousands of dollars of promised advertising revenue.

 NOTE   For some discussion of why you might not want to bother selling ads, read Philip Greenspun's "Making Money from Your Web Site" (`http://www-swiss.ai.mit.edu/wtr/dead-trees/53002.htm`). He also offers some useful metaphors for how a Web site can expand the barriers of commerce and possibly make money in the long run, if the site is clever enough and uses good technology.

Sell Related Products like Books or CDs

Another way to make money or find a sponsor for your page is to sell products related to your page. But even if you don't have any products of your own, you can become an *associate* of an online vendor and receive commissions for customers that you bring to the vendor.

Perhaps the most popular vendor association currently is to sell books from your page though an alliance with an online bookseller, like Amazon.com (http://www.amazon.com/). For example, suppose you have a popular page about cats. You can list several pet books that you recommend and use special links to a description of these books at Amazon.com (or other booksellers like Barnes and Noble). These vendors will describe the book, list its price, and offer a "Buy this book" button. If the surfer does buy a book that you recommended, you'll receive a commission check at the end of the month. (The commissions can be as large as 15 percent.)

Similarly, if you have a page about a musician or music-related topics, you can sell CDs through an associate relationship with CD vendors like CD Universe (http://www.cduniverse.com/) and Music Blvd. (http://www.musicblvd .com/). The commission rates for CDs are usually 5 percent currently.

You can also associate yourself with T-shirt stores, software companies, ISPs, and many other vendors that offer commissions.

Popular pages that are clever in recommending a few key best-selling items related to their topic can make decent amounts of money through sales commissions.

 **WARNING** Vendors have frequent problems with accurately crediting you with customers that you lead to the remote site. You may end up sending thousands of visitors away from your pages in exchange for a mere $10 or $15 per month (since most surfers look at the vendors' pages but don't usually purchase anything right away).

For information about becoming an associate, check with the vendors' Web sites. For Amazon.com, choose the <u>Associates</u> link in the Partners section; for CD Universe, see their Partners page (http://www.cduniverse.com/htdocs/ partner.htm). For other commission deals, check Mark Welch's reviews (http:// www.markwelch.com/bannerad.htm#_other).

Keeping Them Coming Back for More

Give your customers a reason to bookmark your site. Weekly updates, promotions, and beneficial events encourage repeat traffic. Create so much content that surfers can't read everything in one sitting. Give your site a compelling title (see Skill 5) so that surfers will remember the site and want to come back when they see it in their bookmarks.

 **WARNING**   Many sites include a page of instructions to tell surfers how to bookmark your page. But this is difficult to do correctly since there are many different browsers and platforms—which means that you'll have to create lots of different sets of instructions.

You can create a form for surfers to "subscribe" to your site. They'll submit their e-mail addresses, which you can collect into a mailing list. Then you can periodically mail out information to all of your subscribers about changes to your site whenever you've added new material.

 TIP   URL-Minder is a free service from NetMind (http://www.netmind.com/ URL-minder/) that allows surfers to sign up to be notified when a page changes. (The notification message from NetMind will have an advertisement in it; that's how they support the free service.) You can add a link to NetMind on your page to make it easier for surfers to sign up with NetMind and receive an e-mail message telling them when your page changes.

You can expand on this idea by sending out tips, news, and other information as a mailing list. These types of newsletters, as long as they're not intrusive, can vastly increase interest in your site.

 **WARNING**   Be sure that you know how to set up a mailing list correctly. Either use a mailing list program like majordomo, or use the blind carbon copy (BCC) feature of your mailing program so that you keep your subscribers' e-mail addresses confidential. Make sure you include prominent instructions on how people can be removed from your list. You don't want your message to look like spam, so don't try to sell anything in this newsletter.

Strategies for Increasing Your Web Audience

Never underestimate the old-fashioned power of word-of-mouth and customer satisfaction to increase your Web audience over the long run. If your Web site includes an unusual, specialized bit of content, other Web sites will eventually turn to your site for information about your specialization.

Hosting an event from your Web site is a good way to increase your Web audience. The Internet News Bureau (http://www.newsbureau.com/) issues press releases of your Web events (for a small fee) and shows you how you can track media coverage of your Web site events.

The best strategy is unique content (the "if you build it, they will come" strategy). Give away as much as you possibly can: a demo of your program, a few chapters of your book, tips, advice, humor—anything that surfers and customers will find worthwhile to read and recommend to others.

For example, if you just list your company's services and its phone number, few people will be interested. Adding a portfolio is a little better. But adding newsletters, tips, expert articles, real advice, chat forums, interactivity—things that are available nowhere else—will turn your site from ho-hum to something that really could be a "Cool Site of the Day."

Freshness Dating for Fun and Profit

Another simple technique that keeps your customers happy is to keep your content fresh, and to date your page every time you update. Freshness dating is useful especially for technical sites with time-dependent content. It's frustrating to your visitors when they spend 15 minutes reading technical information that they think is current, only to discover that it was written in April 1995. If your page's information can become stale with time, you owe it to your readers to freshness date your pages every time you update, and to list the date of last revision prominently.

Another consideration is that your readers will come back again and again if they realize that your fascinating site is updated regularly. Freshness dating is a simple way to let your readers know that your content is new, live, and kicking. Of course, simply slapping a current date on old information isn't what we're talking about here.

 TIP Adding a discussion forum, chat service, or guest book to a page can allow discussions that keep your Web page current for you, but you may have to edit out an occasionally obscene or irrelevant post.

Increasing Customer Satisfaction

Customer service is critical to customer satisfaction on the Web, just like it is off the Web. The old saying, "the customer is always right" applies on the Web. It never hurts to respond to your customer e-mail messages in a timely and courteous manner.

Your Web pages should aim to delight, as well as satisfy, your customers. Chat forums are a great way to keep an open line of communication between you and your customers. You may want to hold periodic events (a guest speaker, a free or low-cost seminar) through a conferencing forum.

Creating Customer Forums

Chat services are a popular way for customers to get together over the Internet. We'll mention three chat software programs to get you started:

- PowWow (`http://www.tribal.com/powwow/`) is a Windows program that lets up to nine people chat, download files, surf the Internet together as a group, and more.

- Motet (`http://www.sonic.net/~foggy/motet/`) is a conferencing software program that allows for online written group discussions to occur.

- Hotline (`http://www.hotline.com/`) is chat software for a Macintosh server.

For more chat services and conferencing solutions, see Yahoo!'s Chat section in the Business and Economy: Companies: Computers: Software: Internet category.

Responding to Customer Inquiries

To help keep customers happy, you should send an automated response that promises a personal reply within 24 hours to every customer query. Then make sure you have the staff or personal dedication to keep that promise. Display your business's phone number (preferably an 800 number) in every piece of e-mail your company sends, right next to your URL. (Since the Internet is international, indicate if the 800 number is for U.S. residents only and provide an international number.) Make sure that e-mail is smoothly integrated into your existing customer service channels and that your staff is well-trained to reply to e-mail inquiries.

Highlight your commitment to customer service on your Web page. Offer unsolicited customer testimonials, and make sure your Web site is never neglected. Don't make your Web site a neglected secondary concern.

Now that you've seen how to publish your Web site and attract an audience, you're almost on your own. The last Skill of this book will take a look at what you can expect in the Web's future.

Are You Experienced?

Now you can...

- ☑ **establish your Web site Internet service**
- ☑ **advertise your Web site, and sell your services and products**
- ☑ **keep your customers coming back for more**

Skill 19

Looking to the Future: Changes to HTML and the Web

- ➔ Understanding the direction of HTML and the Web
- ➔ Keeping up with the W3C
- ➔ Understanding XML, push, and other emerging technologies

In this book, we've taken you from the basics of HTML to the more advanced features. You should now be able to create, publish, and maintain your site on the Web.

In this last Skill, we'll discuss some trends on the Web and make some predictions about HTML's future. We'll discuss the implications of the browser war, show you two new technologies that may change the Web, and talk about how you can evaluate new elements and attributes from future versions of HTML.

Predicting the Future of the Web

The Web will keep evolving—that is one thing we can guarantee. It's already a cliché to talk about "Web years" in the same way as people talk about dog years—that one year of normal time is equivalent to 12 years of Web developments. (If that's true, then this book took more than four Web years to write. Yikes!) The Web's immense popularity and relative youth means there are plenty of competing opinions about how the Web should work and what it will be like in the future. Don't worry too much about rumors or any one company's vision of what the Web will be like; instead, try to stay informed about what's actually happening. Be neither the first nor the last to follow the latest trends. Just create your Web site, see how well it works and how well it compares to other sites, and build from there.

 NOTE The Web is still young. The pace of change on the Web is daunting—even to computer industry professionals. Surfing the Web, simply for pleasure's sake, is one of the easiest ways to keep a reasonable perspective on trends and new technology.

We'll start with a look at one of most volatile areas of Web development: new browser versions from Microsoft and Netscape.

Sheltering Yourself from the Browser War

In Skill 13, we talked about the browser war being fought by Netscape and Microsoft, who create new versions of browsers at a frenzied pace in order to win market share.

Microsoft is fighting to increase market share for Internet Explorer, while Netscape is struggling to preserve Navigator's huge lead (which appears to be dwindling slowly but steadily in response to Microsoft's onslaught). Microsoft is a huge company that can afford to throw plenty of resources into developing IE and give it away. Netscape's advantages are its huge brand recognition, good performance, and history of innovation.

The war has meant an increase in the normal software development pace, with four major versions of Navigator and IE in only two-and-a-half years. The browser companies are now on a pace that produces a major browser version every year. Compare that to the development of popular word processors, which typically appear every other year (see Table 20.1).

TABLE 20.1: Browser Development Compared to Word Processor Development

	IE	Navigator	Microsoft Word	WordPerfect for Windows
Version 1 Date	July 95, as part of Microsoft Windows 95 CD and Plus! package	December 94 (October 94)	January 90	January 1992 as "WordPerfect for Windows 5.1"
Version 2 Date	November 95 (October 95)	March 96 (October 95)	October 91	January 1993 as "WordPerfect for Windows 5.2"
Version 3 Date	August 96 (March 96)	August 96 (April 96)	October 93, as "Word 6.0" instead of 3.0	October 93 as "Word-Perfect 6.0" and November 94 as "Novell WordPerfect 6.1 for Windows/PerfectOffice 3"
Version 4 Date	September 97 (April 97)	June 97 (December 96)	July 95 as "Word 95"	May 96 as "Corel WordPerfect 7"
Version 5 Date	Unknown, but probably Summer 98	Unknown, but probably Summer 98	January 97 as "Word 97"	June 97 as "Corel Word-Perfect 8"

NOTE   These dates refer to when the final (non-beta) release of the Windows version was first made available in the United States. The date of the first beta release is sometimes given in parentheses. For more complete browser dates, see Index Dot HTML's browser history (http://www.eskimo.com/~bloo/html/history .htm) or the BrowserWatch News Room (http://browserwatch.internet .com/news.html).

Because browser vendors use a "rolling development" schedule, the beta for the next version is often announced immediately after the current version is shipped.

Initially, one might think that this rapid pace of development is beneficial for Web users and Web authors. In fact, there are many drawbacks to the rapid pace of browser development. Documentation quickly becomes out of date and is difficult to maintain. Training classes lose their value rapidly, and users must be constantly retrained. Corporations that purchase software in large blocks must spend significantly more money each year, if they want the latest browser version for their employees (and there will always be many users who want the latest version, no matter how little improvement it offers).

 NOTE   Our book has a Web site to keep its information up-to-date (not to mention new editions of this book).

More importantly, the relentless development pace has led to a serious problem: The quality of the browser software has decreased. Harmful bugs and critical security holes are not discovered until long after a browser has been released and distributed—because there isn't time for in-depth testing and quality assurance. Instead, the tremendous pressure to rush a browser to market, particularly if the competition has just released a new version, guarantees that some corners are cut.

Many users simply give up and stick with an older browser version that more or less works for them. Meanwhile, a lot of Web surfers don't have any ability to upgrade their browser, because they're using a company or library computer and are not allowed to install software on their own, for example. Sometimes they can't upgrade because they're using an older computer that can't support the latest version's requirements, or because they lack the technical knowledge of how to download a new browser, uninstall the old one, and install the new one with the correct settings. This fractures the browser market tremendously, making it impossible for Web authors to predict what browsers will be used to view their site, and it makes new developments and Web technologies extremely unstable. Microsoft and Netscape are compounding the problem by not agreeing on new standards.

Each new browser version introduces new wrinkles in HTML support, and new and inexperienced Web authors understandably don't realize that their site, which looks fine in the browser that they happen to use, is unviewable in many other popular browsers.

The only solution is to write HTML for as broad an audience as possible and realize that any new technologies (including Dynamic HTML, style sheets, multimedia, and active scripting languages) will only be available to a fraction of your audience at any given time.

By writing valid HTML, you shelter yourself from browser changes. You can be sure that a valid HTML document that uses the HTML elements correctly, without a lot of tricks or abuse of an element's intent, will be equally accessible to

Navigator 4 and IE 4—but more importantly, still viewable five years from now on Navigator 9 and IE 9.

 TIP Even better, by writing valid HTML you can be assured that your site is accessible to those with disabilities. It's usually true that the newest technologies hyped on the Web are "disabling technologies" because they are not widely supported, backward-compatible, nor accessible to those using text-to-speech browsers. Style sheets and HTML 4.0 are notable exceptions, since they take strides to improve accessibility.

Keeping an Eye on the W3C

While the browser war rages on and new browsers become more and more different, the W3C is getting nearer to "finishing" HTML. While there will probably be several versions of HTML in the future, HTML itself is now fairly stable. New elements from W3C are increasingly rare, and when Web authors make proposals for new elements, they are often told that their proposal can be better handled by style sheets or other "extensible" technologies.

In the Director's Perspective that accompanied the first draft of HTML 4.0, Tim Berners-Lee (the inventor of the Web, as we saw in Skill 1) said, "But the crazy feature rush may be slowing. HTML 4.0 has a powerful object element which allows extensions to be incorporated without changing HTML; Cascading Style Sheets (CSS), a W3C Recommendation released December 1996, accommodates a variety of format, layout, and desktop publishing features that were making an awkward entry into HTML; and W3C's Extensible Markup Language (XML) naturally supports a variety of applications which could compromise the design of HTML. So while you can read HTML 4.0 as being the next frame in an adventure movie being played faster than feels comfortable, it may mark the beginning of a maturity. HTML may one day be a closed book, a key to many new formats which build on it but don't threaten its interoperability."

 NOTE We'll talk about the Extensible Markup Language (XML) a little later in this Skill.

Still, if the past is any guide, we can expect the W3C to propose HTML 5 or 6 around the dawn of the new millenium. It's hard to predict what future versions of HTML will include, but we know that future versions of HTML will be, on the whole, similar to what exists now in HTML 4.0. The existing elements will not be changed, by and large—except that formatting elements like the font element will

Skill 20

eventually become obsolete, replaced by style sheets. Expect that few new elements will be added to HTML 5 and that some presentational elements will disappear.

There are some areas of HTML that can be improved and are likely bets for HTML 5:

- **Frames** The ability to link to particular framesets (that is, the arrangement of documents in frames after links have been followed, changing the initial frameset) may involve a change to URLs or the introduction of a new element used inside the anchor element.

- **Dynamic HTML** As we saw in Skill 16, HTML 4.0's Dynamic Object Model (DOM) is new, and the glue for dynamic events is not as developed as the browser vendors would like. While HTML itself might not change, the DOM will definitely tie active scripts to HTML 4.0's new event attributes, and new extensions to Cascading Style Sheets will be more dynamic.

- **Forms** The HTML 4.0 specification notes that the range of form field types, although wide, is limited in comparison to modern user interfaces. While graphical operating systems' dialog boxes include such things as sliders and spinners for entering numbers, these cannot currently be duplicated in HTML. Future versions of HTML will fix this problem. In addition, the W3C would like to create HTML methods for tabular data entry and multiple pages for forms.

Many Web authors (especially graphic designers) are pushing for more formatting support, including better control of fonts, kerning (micro-adjustments of the spacing between individual letters), and the ability to specify the precise position of an image or text on top of other elements. These things are being supported by current and future versions of Cascading Style Sheets, with new properties. As we saw in Skill 14, as well as Skill 16, work is currently being done in the areas of fonts, speech properties, printing, and absolute positioning. Proposals for such visual effects as blurring, shadows, and scaling are underway.

Absolute positioning is an important draft extension to style sheets; the W3C's draft page on this subject (`http://www.w3.org/TR/WD-positioning`) is written by Netscape and Microsoft. As we saw in Skill 16, this draft is not yet finished and the support for absolute positioning is not quite in place with the current browsers. But future browsers will depend on absolute positioning as Dynamic HTML becomes more popular.

Furthermore, work is in progress to allow Web authors to specify a particular font that should be downloaded in order to display their Web page. This will be accomplished by a statement in a style sheet, an `@font-face` rule. For more information, see the Working Draft on fonts (`http://www.w3.org/TR/WD-font`). At the moment, no browser supports this rule properly, but this will change shortly.

Another new possibility will be the emergence of a single programming language endorsed by the W3C for use with active scripts. Currently, JavaScript is popular, but there are differences between Netscape's version of JavaScript and Microsoft's version, JScript (see Skill 15). JavaScript was recently certified by a European standards organization, ECMA. Perhaps in the future JavaScript will become ECMAScript, and the W3C will standardize it so that Web authors can use one scripting language with confidence.

In general, the most exciting and influential changes to the Web are not being proposed for HTML (now that HTML 4.0 has appeared), but instead involve new levels and extensions to Cascading Style Sheets or entirely new technologies.

Considering Emerging Technologies

Several technologies emerging on the Web are not covered in this book. We'll discuss two of these technologies briefly: XML and push.

Understanding XML

If anything will supplant HTML as the language of the Web, the most likely candidate at the moment seems to be the Extensible Markup Language (XML). XML is another simplified application of SGML (see Skill 1) that allows you to create your own document types to define new elements, tags, and attributes for your own purposes.

For example, suppose you're a musician and need specialized ways of displaying and classifying musical notation. Using XML, you could define a set of elements for musical notation and teach an XML browser how those elements should be displayed.

To quote from the XML FAQ (http://www.ucc.ie/xml/), "XML will allow groups of people or organizations to create their own customized markup languages for exchanging information in their domain (music, chemistry, electronics, hill-walking, finance, surfing, linguistics, knitting, history, engineering, rabbit-keeping, etc.)."

XML is a W3C project. To find out more about XML, visit W3C's XML page (http://www.w3.org/XML/). The specification for XML is still in draft format (http://www.w3.org/TR/WD-xml). No commercial browser supports XML…yet. But Microsoft's Channel Definition Format (see the next section) is written in XML, as are some other current proposals submitted to the W3C.

Skill 20

NOTE   XML is actually fairly compatible with HTML (you'll certainly see the similarities when you view XML code), and most HTML documents can be turned into XML with little effort.

Understanding Push Technology

When you build a Web page in HTML or XML, it's stored on a Web server, and a surfer has to actually visit its URL to retrieve it. Because people visit sites instead of the other way around, the Web is considered to be *pull* technology. You visit a Web site and "pull" its contents to your computer manually. When you want information, you go out and get it.

In contrast, there is more and more interest in applications of *push* technology: information that comes to your computer automatically.

The earliest examples of push technology are e-mail subscription services. You sign up with an information service that sends you specific data by e-mail. For example, you can sign up with a stock reporting system and tell them to send you e-mail when a certain company's stock rises above or falls below a particular value. That way, you don't have to watch the company's stock price all day; you know that you'll receive e-mail if anything important happens.

The best-known example of current push technology comes from the PointCast Network (http://www.pointcast.com/). Users install PointCast's custom software. The software downloads news, weather, sport scores, and other information from PointCast's wire services and affiliated information providers. (You can set up the software to say what kinds of information you're interested in and tell the software to retrieve this information automatically at certain times each day, or if you are on a corporate network, it can retrieve the information throughout the day.)

The PointCast software displays this information in two different ways: First, you can manually read different news articles or sports scores. Second and most useful, the information can be automatically displayed on your computer screen after a certain amount of idle time, as a screen saver. News and feature stories, weather maps, horoscopes, and other information is displayed in the main part of the screen (next to a flashy advertisement), while stock prices, sports scores, and headlines are displayed as a scrolling marquee. This information is "pushed" to you and displayed (somewhat haphazardly) throughout the day.

The first versions of PointCast had several different news and information services. Version 2 of PointCast, recently released, allows individual Web authors to create their own "push channels" (called *connections*) and become "Webcasters"—PointCast users can subscribe to your Web channel and have your Web site's content delivered to them automatically. The process is fairly simple and described by PointCast in detail (`http://www.pointcast.com/connections/webcaster/`). The result will be a Channel Definition Format file (a file with a `.cdf` extension that defines the connection).

 NOTE

> To be able to Webcast effectively, your content should be of wide interest and constantly updated. PointCast and other Webcasting technologies tend to rely on a newspaper metaphor, where each Web page you publish becomes an "article" broadcast to your subscribers.

Microsoft and Netscape have both produced push technology as part of their browser packages. Netscape's Netcaster is available as part of the Communicator package. A guide to developing channels for Netcaster is available (`http://developer.netscape.com/one/netcaster/index.html`). Microsoft's Active Channel technology is integrated into IE 4, and content creators can easily define channels for surfers to subscribe to (and automatically receive updates). Microsoft has prepared a channel-creation guide called Channels 101 (`http://microsoft.com/workshop/prog/ie4/channels/cdf1-f.htm`).

Microsoft's Channel Definition Format (`http://microsoft.com/standards/cdf-f.htm`) is similar to PointCast's CDF format, but it differs significantly from Netscape's method for defining channels (which relies on JavaScript). Only time will tell which types of channels survive and thrive in this unstable technology area.

Keeping an Eye on Our Web Site

At Sybex's Web site (`http://www.sybex.com/`), you'll find an area devoted solely to this book. We'll try to keep you updated on new technologies that affect HTML. We'll also present pointers to tutorials for significant new technologies and let you know how well the browsers have adopted HTML 4.0.

From Sybex's main page, choose the No Experience Required icon, choose the HTML 4.0 book, and then view the Related Links section for a list of online tutorials, demonstrations, news items, and updates.

Learning New Elements and Attributes

If future versions of HTML include new elements and attributes, the first and best place to find out how they work is from the W3C (`http://www.w3.org/`). While other places might present tutorials, the only official and reliable place to find out how the new attributes work is from the W3C's HTML activity page. If the extension or attribute is not described there, then chances are that you're looking at a proprietary extension that won't be compatible with many browsers.

The second place to turn is our Web site, where we'll document the new element or attribute's level of support and any implementation problems that may exist. This should give you enough information to decide whether to start using it.

Deciding When and How to Update Your Site's HTML

When you create an HTML document, make sure it's valid (use the validators discussed in Skill 17). Once you've created a valid HTML document, you're safe—whether you use HTML 2.0, 3.2, or 4.0, future browsers should not have any problems displaying a valid HTML document for any of these three versions. It's in the interests of browser vendors to make sure that they're backward-compatible with existing versions of HTML since so many existing pages are written in these versions of HTML (and users will be upset if a new browser does not let them view the bulk of existing or legacy documents).

So even if new elements and attributes are introduced, you are not required to change your entire site. Even if the font element becomes obsolete and is removed from HTML 5.0, you're still allowed to keep the font element in your HTML 4.0 or HTML 3.2 documents (just make sure that your DOCTYPE declaration, as defined in Skill 5, correctly describes the version of HTML you're using).

If the newest version of HTML has an element that you want to use, then you should make the switch. Be sure to study the new elements and attributes and see if your site would really benefit from using them (also check to see that at least one or two other sites are using these new elements, without significant problems). But be sure to test the element with existing browsers. Many people still use the earliest versions of Navigator and IE, and many people use special browsers that fulfill their needs.

New versions of HTML, even when they've become official recommendations, take some time to filter down to the browsers in use by the general public. There's no reason to force your audience to upgrade their browsers (and no reason to expect that anyone will change browsers or change their current browser's settings just to view your site). Unless there's a compelling reason to use a new feature, you should stick to established HTML elements and attributes. And even then, always test to make sure your content is still accessible by older browsers. Even if not every aspect of your presentation is displayed properly, make sure that the content, including any critical data, is fully available.

Making Sweeping Changes to a Site

If you decide to change the way your site works, you'll probably want to change many pages of your site at once. (Be sure to create a test page first, and make sure that everything works as you expect.) It's time-consuming to change pages one by one, by hand—instead, look at the ability of the HTML tools discussed in Skill 4, many of which can make sweeping changes to a site by performing a global search-and-replace across multiple files.

Predicting the Future of HTML

No one can really predict the future of HTML or the Web. There are always new developments, and even the most polished crystal ball gets distinctly hazy when you try to peer ahead more than a few years.

But the Web has revolutionized publishing and information distribution. Over a billion Web pages already exist. These pages will not disappear overnight; instead, they will persist for quite some time—and browser vendors will not turn their backs on this huge existing legacy of the Web. While the Web can change surprisingly quickly, it is also acquiring a huge mass, and Web authors cannot change every page in existence at once. This means you can comfortably predict that practices valid in 1997 will still be valid in 1998 and 1999. Even better, a page that you create today will probably be viewable.

Some people draw a comparison between HTML and ASCII: They are both basic standards that are universal and revolutionary, which created a little order out of the previous chaos of multiple standards. An ASCII document created in 1975, for example, is still viewable today. While HTML is not as stable as ASCII, we are hopeful that the documents we have taught you how to create in this book will be useful and viewable for dozens of years to come.

Skill 20

Are You Experienced?

Now you can...

- ☑ **predict changes to HTML and the Web**
- ☑ **keep pace with the browser war**
- ☑ **understand new technologies such as XML and push**

Comprehensive HTML Quick Reference

- → Specifying colors by RGB codes
- → Inserting character and numerical entity codes
- → Using the HTML element and attribute reference
- → Summarizing case-sensitivity

Everyone needs a good HTML reference, and we've made this one as compact and convenient as possible. Here you'll find a list of the RGB color codes you can use, several lists of the special HTML characters you can include in your HTML documents (either by the entity's name or number), and an alphabetical list of HTML elements, including the start and end tags, attributes, description, and any warnings.

Specifying Color Names and RGB Values

As we discussed in Skill 3, you can use colors by name (<FONT COLOR="RED">) or by RGB code (<BODY TEXT="#FF0000">). Several HTML elements use colors: the <FONT> tag and <BASEFONT> tag can include a COLOR attribute to set the font color, and the <BODY> tag can specify background color, text color, and three types of link colors. (See Skill 3 for examples of these elements.) Tables also specify background (see Skill 10).

In addition, some style sheet properties such as COLOR and BACKGROUND can use color names or RGB codes for a value (see Skill 14 for details). HTML 4.0 recommends you use a style sheet to set colors instead of HTML attributes.

 NOTE   Some HTML tools and older browsers have difficulty with color names, so it's safest to always use the RGB code. The RGB code is a hexadecimal number preceded by a number sign (surrounded by quotes). See Skill 3 to learn how these RGB codes work and how to use hexadecimal numbers.

Table A.1 shows the 16 colors named in HTML 3.2 and HTML 4.0. These 16 colors come from the names and colors used on the IBM PC.

TABLE A.1: The 16 Named Colors of HTML 3.2 and HTML 4.0

COLOR NAME	RGB CODE	COLOR NAME	RGB CODE	COLOR NAME	RGB CODE	COLOR NAME	RGB CODE
black	"#000000"	green	"#008000"	maroon	"#800000"	navy	"#000080"
silver	"#C0C0C0"	lime	"#00FF00"	red	"#FF0000"	blue	"#0000FF"
gray	"#808080"	olive	"#808000"	purple	"#800080"	teal	"#008080"
white	"#FFFFFF"	yellow	"#FFFF00"	fuchsia	"#FF00FF"	aqua	"#00FFFF"

 **WARNING**   All colors vary by computer system. The shade of red you see on your screen can be different from what your audience will see. Also, many systems are black and white (including most printers).

Table A.2 is a longer list of color names. These color names, which are always without spaces, are recognized by Netscape Navigator 3 and Microsoft Internet Explorer 3 (and later versions), but not by any other browsers. They are not official HTML color names, so you should *always* use the RGB code instead of the color name shown in Table A.2. However, it's helpful to be able to look up a color by name, even if some of these names are a little strange ("blanchedalmond"?).

TABLE A.2: The 125 Named Colors Supported by Navigator and IE, with Their Equivalent RGB Code

COLOR NAME	RGB CODE	COLOR NAME	RGB CODE	COLOR NAME	RGB CODE
aliceblue	"#F0F8FF"	gainsboro	"#DCDCDC"	mintcream	"#F5FFFA"
antiquewhite	"#FAEBD7"	ghostwhite	"#F8F8FF"	mistyrose	"#FFE4E1"
aquamarine	"#7FFFD4"	gold	"#FFD700"	moccasin	"#FFE4B5"
azure	"#F0FFFF"	goldenrod	"#DAA520"	navajowhite	"#FFDEAD"
beige	"#F5F5DC"	greenyellow	"#ADFF2F"	oldlace	"#FDF5E6"
bisque	"#FFE4C4"	honeydew	"#F0FFF0"	olivedrab	"#6B8E23"
blanchedalmond	"#FFEBCD"	hotpink	"#FF69B4"	orange	"#FFA500"
blueviolet	"#8A2BE2"	indianred	"#CD5C5C"	orangered	"#FF4500"
brown	"#A52A2A"	indigo	"#4B0082"	orchid	"#DA70D6"
burlywood	"#DEB887"	ivory	"#FFFFF0"	palegoldenrod	"#EEE8AA"
cadetblue	"#5F9EA0"	khaki	"#F0E68C"	palegreen	"#98FB98"
chartreuse	"#7FFF00"	lavender	"#E6E6FA"	paleturquoise	"#AFEEEE"
chocolate	"#D2691E"	lavenderblush	"#FFF0F5"	palevioletred	"#DB7093"
coral	"#FF7F50"	lawngreen	"#7CFC00"	papayawhip	"#FFEFD5"
cornflowerblue	"#6495ED"	lemonchiffon	"#FFFACD"	peachpuff	"#FFDAB9"
cornsilk	"#FFF8DC"	lightblue	"#ADD8E6"	peru	"#CD853F"
crimson	"#DC143C"	lightcoral	"#F08080"	pink	"#FFC0CB"
cyan	"#00FFFF"	lightcyan	"#E0FFFF"	plum	"#DDA0DD"
darkblue	"#00008B"	lightgoldenrodyellow	"#FAFAD2"	powderblue	"#B0E0E6"
darkcyan	"#008B8B"	lightgreen	"#90EE90"	rosybrown	"#BC8F8F"
darkgoldenrod	"#B8860B"	lightgrey	"#D3D3D3"	royalblue	"#4169E1"
darkgray	"#A9A9A9"	lightpink	"#FFB6C1"	saddlebrown	"#8B4513"
darkgreen	"#006400"	lightsalmon	"#FFA07A"	salmon	"#FA8072"
darkkhaki	"#BDB76B"	lightseagreen	"#20B2AA"	sandybrown	"#F4A460"
darkmagenta	"#8B008B"	lightskyblue	"#87CEFA"	seagreen	"#2E8B57"
darkolivegreen	"#556B2F"	lightslategray	"#778899"	seashell	"#FFF5EE"
darkorange	"#FF8C00"	lightsteelblue	"#B0C4DE"	sienna	"#A0522D"
darkorchid	"#9932CC"	lightyellow	"#FFFFE0"	skyblue	"#87CEEB"
darkred	"#8B0000"	limegreen	"#32CD32"	slateblue	"#6A5ACD"
darksalmon	"#E9967A"	linen	"#FAF0E6"	slategray	"#708090"
darkseagreen	"#8FBC8F"	magenta	"#FF00FF"	snow	"#FFFAFA"
darkslateblue	"#483D8B"	maroon	"#800000"	springgreen	"#00FF7F"
darkslategray	"#2F4F4F"	mediumaquamarine	"#66CDAA"	steelblue	"#4682B4"
darkturquoise	"#00CED1"	mediumblue	"#0000CD"	tan	"#D2B48C"
darkviolet	"#9400D3"	mediumorchid	"#BA55D3"	thistle	"#D8BFD8"
deeppink	"#FF1493"	mediumpurple	"#9370DB"	tomato	"#FF6347"
deepskyblue	"#00BFFF"	mediumseagreen	"#3CB371"	turquoise	"#40E0D0"
dimgray	"#696969"	mediumslateblue	"#7B68EE"	violet	"#EE82EE"
dodgerblue	"#1E90FF"	mediumspringgreen	"#00FA9A"	wheat	"#F5DEB3"
firebrick	"#B22222"	mediumturquoise	"#48D1CC"	whitesmoke	"#F5F5F5"
floralwhite	"#FFFAF0"	mediumvioletred	"#C71585"	yellowgreen	"#9ACD32"
forestgreen	"#228B22"	midnightblue	"#191970"		

TIP   Our Web site will show these colors so you can see what they look like on your system.

If you're designing a GIF image with regions of solid color, you shouldn't use any of the RGB color values in Table A.1 or A.2 since they might dither (see Skill 8) on a system that only displays 256 colors (see Skill 17). Instead, you'll want to use a special 216-color palette that consists of RGB codes that only include 00, 33, 66, 99, CC, or FF. See Lynda Weinman's Browser Safe Color Palette page (http://www.lynda.com/hex.html).

Referencing an Entity List

For a review of entities, see Skill 3. You can use either the numerical entity code or the named entity code. For example, either ë or ë would display an e with an umlaut (ë), a character used in words like Zoë or Noël.

ASCII Table in Entity Format

ASCII is the American Standard Code for Information Interchange, consisting of 128 codes used by most computers, as formalized by the American National Standards Institute (ANSI) in 1968. The first 32 codes (numbered from #0 to #31) as well as the 128th code (#127) are not used in HTML since they are control characters with no specified visual appearance. The rest of the codes, from 32 to 126, correspond to commonly used keyboard characters (see Table A.3). These characters are universally supported.

 NOTE   Only the ASCII characters with a special meaning in HTML (&, <, >, and ") have an entity name. Be sure to review Skill 3 for a warning of why you should use either the numeric or name entity code instead of the &, >, and < characters in your documents.

TABLE A.3: ASCII Character Chart in HTML Entity Format

ASCII Character Number	Appearance	Numerical Entity Code	Name (Comments) and Named Entity Code, if any
32	N/A	&#32;	space
33	!	&#33;	exclamation mark
34	"	&#34;	quotation mark (double quote) **Named Entity Code:** "
35	#	&#35;	number sign (hash, pound sign)
36	$	&#36;	dollar sign
37	%	&#37;	percent sign
38	&	&#38;	ampersand **Named Entity Code:** &
39	'	&#39;	apostrophe (single quote)
40	(	&#40;	left parenthesis (open parenthesis)
41	)	&#41;	right parenthesis (close parenthesis)
42	*	&#42;	asterisk
43	+	&#43;	plus sign
44	,	&#44;	comma

TABLE A.3 CONTINUED: ASCII Character Chart in HTML Entity Format

ASCII Character Number	Appearance	Numerical Entity Code	Name (Comments) and Named Entity Code, if any
45	-	`&#45;`	hyphen-minus (dash)
46	.	`&#46;`	full stop (period)
47	/	`&#47;`	solidus (forward slash)
48	0	`&#48;`	digit zero
49	1	`&#49;`	digit one
50	2	`&#50;`	digit two
51	3	`&#51;`	digit three
52	4	`&#52;`	digit four
53	5	`&#53;`	digit five
54	6	`&#54;`	digit six
55	7	`&#55;`	digit seven
56	8	`&#56;`	digit eight
57	9	`&#57;`	digit nine
58	:	`&#58;`	colon
59	;	`&#59;`	semicolon
60	<	`&#60;`	less-than sign **Named Entity Code:** `&lt;`
61	=	`&#61;`	equals sign
62	>	`&#62;`	greater-than sign **Named Entity Code:** `&gt;`
63	?	`&#63;`	question mark
64	@	`&#64;`	commercial at (at sign)
65	A	`&#65;`	Latin capital letter A
66	B	`&#66;`	Latin capital letter B
67	C	`&#67;`	Latin capital letter C
68	D	`&#68;`	Latin capital letter D
69	E	`&#69;`	Latin capital letter E
70	F	`&#70;`	Latin capital letter F
71	G	`&#71;`	Latin capital letter G
72	H	`&#72;`	Latin capital letter H
73	I	`&#73;`	Latin capital letter I
74	J	`&#74;`	Latin capital letter J
75	K	`&#75;`	Latin capital letter K
76	L	`&#76;`	Latin capital letter L
77	M	`&#77;`	Latin capital letter M
78	N	`&#78;`	Latin capital letter N
79	O	`&#79;`	Latin capital letter O
80	P	`&#80;`	Latin capital letter P
81	Q	`&#81;`	Latin capital letter Q
82	R	`&#82;`	Latin capital letter R
83	S	`&#83;`	Latin capital letter S
84	T	`&#84;`	Latin capital letter T
85	U	`&#85;`	Latin capital letter U

TABLE A.3 CONTINUED: ASCII Character Chart in HTML Entity Format

ASCII Character Number	Appearance	Numerical Entity Code	Name (Comments) and Named Entity Code, if any
86	V	&#86;	Latin capital letter V
87	W	&#87;	Latin capital letter W
88	X	&#88;	Latin capital letter X
89	Y	&#89;	Latin capital letter Y
90	Z	&#90;	Latin capital letter Z
91	[	&#91;	left square bracket (open bracket)
92	\	&#92;	reverse solidus (backslash)
93	]	&#93;	right square bracket (close bracket)
94	^	&#94;	circumflex accent (caret, exponent)
95	_	&#95;	low line (underscore, underline)
96	`	&#96;	grave accent
97	a	&#97;	Latin small letter a
98	b	&#98;	Latin small letter b
99	c	&#99;	Latin small letter c
100	d	&#100;	Latin small letter d
101	e	&#101;	Latin small letter e
102	f	&#102;	Latin small letter f
103	g	&#103;	Latin small letter g
104	h	&#104;	Latin small letter h
105	i	&#105;	Latin small letter i
106	j	&#106;	Latin small letter j
107	k	&#107;	Latin small letter k
108	l	&#108;	Latin small letter l
109	m	&#109;	Latin small letter m
110	n	&#110;	Latin small letter n
111	o	&#111;	Latin small letter o
112	p	&#112;	Latin small letter p
113	q	&#113;	Latin small letter q
114	r	&#114;	Latin small letter r
115	s	&#115;	Latin small letter s
116	t	&#116;	Latin small letter t
117	u	&#117;	Latin small letter u
118	v	&#118;	Latin small letter v
119	w	&#119;	Latin small letter w
120	x	&#120;	Latin small letter x
121	y	&#121;	Latin small letter y
122	z	&#122;	Latin small letter z
123	{	&#123;	left curly bracket (left French brace)
124	|	|	vertical line (vertical bar)
125	}	&#125;	right curly bracket (right French brace)
126	~	&#126;	tilde

Latin-1 Entities

The Latin-1 characters are available as character number 160 up to character number 255 (see Table A.4). Many foreign languages require the characters in Latin-1; many of the special symbols will be useful for your documents (see Skill 3).

 **WARNING**   Don't use the characters numbered from 127 to 159. Although a particular character may appear on your system, it will not be the same on other systems. In particular, Macintosh and PC systems have different characters in this range.

TABLE A.4: Latin-1 Character Chart with Name and Numerical Entity Codes

Latin-1 Character Number	Appearance	Numerical Entity Code	Named Entity Code	Name (Comments)
160	N/A			non-breaking space (see Skill 3)
161	¡	&#161;	&iexcl;	inverted exclamation mark
162	¢	&#162;	&cent;	cent sign
163	£	&#163;	&pound;	pound sterling sign
164	¤	&#164;	&curren;	general currency sign
165	¥	&#165;	&yen;	yen sign
166	¦	&#166;	&brvbar;	broken (vertical) bar
167	§	&#167;	&sect;	section sign
168	¨	&#168;	&uml;	umlaut (dieresis)
169	©	&#169;	&copy;	copyright sign
170	ª	&#170;	&ordf;	ordinal indicator, feminine
171	«	&#171;	&laquo;	angle quotation mark, left
172	¬	&#172;	&not;	not sign (logical not sign)
173		&#173;	&shy;	soft hyphen
174	®	&#174;	&reg;	registered sign (registered trademark)
175	¯	&#175;	&macr;	macron
176	°	&#176;	&deg;	degree sign
177	±	&#177;	&plusmn;	plus-or-minus sign
178	²	&#178;	&sup2;	superscript two
179	³	&#179;	&sup3;	superscript three
180	´	&#180;	&acute;	acute accent
181	µ	&#181;	&micro;	micro sign
182	¶	&#182;	&para;	pilcrow (paragraph sign)
183	·	&#183;	&middot;	middle dot
184	¸	&#184;	&cedil;	cedilla
185	¹	&#185;	&sup1;	superscript one
186	º	&#186;	&ordm;	ordinal indicator, masculine
187	»	&#187;	&raquo;	angle quotation mark, right
188	¼	&#188;	&frac14;	fraction one-quarter
189	½	&#189;	&frac12;	fraction one-half
190	¾	&#190;	&frac34;	fraction three-quarters
191	¿	&#191;	&iquest;	inverted question mark
192	À	&#192;	&Agrave;	capital A, grave accent
193	Á	&#193;	&Aacute;	capital A, acute accent
194	Â	&#194;	&Acirc;	capital A, circumflex accent
195	Ã	&#195;	&Atilde;	capital A, tilde

TABLE A.4 CONTINUED: Latin-1 Character Chart with Name and Numerical Entity Codes

Latin-1 Character Number	Appearance	Numerical Entity Code	Named Entity Code	Name (Comments)
196	Ä	&#196;	&Auml;	capital A, dieresis or umlaut mark
197	Å	&#197;	&Aring;	capital A, ring
198	Æ	&#198;	&AElig;	capital AE diphthong (ligature)
199	Ç	&#199;	&Ccedil;	capital C, cedilla
200	È	&#200;	&Egrave;	capital E, grave accent
201	É	&#201;	&Eacute;	capital E, acute accent
202	Ê	&#202;	&Ecirc;	capital E, circumflex accent
203	Ë	&#203;	&Euml;	capital E, dieresis or umlaut mark
204	Ì	&#204;	&Igrave;	capital I, grave accent
205	Í	&#205;	&Iacute;	capital I, acute accent
206	Î	&#206;	&Icirc;	capital I, circumflex accent
207	Ï	&#207;	&Iuml;	capital I, dieresis or umlaut mark
208	Ð	&#208;	&ETH;	capital Eth, Icelandic
209	Ñ	&#209;	&Ntilde;	capital N, tilde
210	Ò	&#210;	&Ograve;	capital O, grave accent
211	Ó	&#211;	&Oacute;	capital O, acute accent
212	Ô	&#212;	&Ocirc;	capital O, circumflex accent
213	Õ	&#213;	&Otilde;	capital O, tilde
214	Ö	&#214;	&Ouml;	capital O, dieresis or umlaut mark
215	×	&#215;	&times;	multiply sign
216	Ø	&#216;	&Oslash;	capital O, slash
217	Ù	&#217;	&Ugrave;	capital U, grave accent
218	Ú	&#218;	&Uacute;	capital U, acute accent
219	Û	&#219;	&Ucirc;	capital U, circumflex accent
220	Ü	&#220;	&Uuml;	capital U, dieresis or umlaut mark
221	Ý	&#221;	&Yacute;	capital Y, acute accent
222	Þ	&#222;	&THORN;	capital THORN, Icelandic
223	ß	&#223;	&szlig;	small sharp s, German (sz ligature)
224	à	&#224;	&agrave;	small a, grave accent
225	á	&#225;	&aacute;	small a, acute accent
226	â	&#226;	&acirc;	small a, circumflex accent
227	ã	&#227;	&atilde;	small a, tilde
228	ä	&#228;	&auml;	small a, dieresis or umlaut mark
229	å	&#229;	&aring;	small a, ring
230	æ	&#230;	&aelig;	small ae diphthong (ligature)
231	ç	&#231;	&ccedil;	small c, cedilla
232	è	&#232;	&egrave;	small e, grave accent
233	é	&#233;	&eacute;	small e, acute accent
234	ê	&#234;	&ecirc;	small e, circumflex accent
235	ë	&#235;	&euml;	small e, dieresis or umlaut mark
236	ì	&#236;	&igrave;	small i, grave accent
237	í	&#237;	&iacute;	small i, acute accent
238	î	&#238;	&icirc;	small i, circumflex accent
239	ï	&#239;	&iuml;	small i, dieresis or umlaut mark
240	ð	&#240;	&eth;	small eth, Icelandic
241	ñ	&#241;	&ntilde;	small n, tilde
242	ò	&#242;	&ograve;	small o, grave accent
243	ó	&#243;	&oacute;	small o, acute accent
244	ô	&#244;	&ocirc;	small o, circumflex accent
245	õ	&#245;	&otilde;	small o, tilde
246	ö	&#246;	&ouml;	small o, dieresis or umlaut mark
247	÷	&#247;	&divide;	divide sign

TABLE A.4 CONTINUED: Latin-1 Character Chart with Name and Numerical
Entity Codes

Latin-1 Character Number	Appearance	Numerical Entity Code	Named Entity Code	Name (Comments)
248	ø	&#248;	&oslash;	small o, slash
249	ù	&#249;	&ugrave;	small u, grave accent
250	ú	&#250;	&uacute;	small u, acute accent
251	û	&#251;	&ucirc;	small u, circumflex accent
252	ü	&#252;	&uuml;	small u, dieresis or umlaut mark
253	ý	&#253;	&yacute;	small y, acute accent
254	þ	&#254;	&thorn;	small thorn, Icelandic
255	ÿ	&#255;	&yuml;	small y, dieresis or umlaut mark

WARNING   All named entity codes are case-sensitive.

NOTE   Portions of Tables A.4 and A.5 are Copyright © International Organization for Standardization 1986: Permission to copy in any form is granted for use with conforming SGML systems and applications as defined in ISO 8879, provided this notice is included in all copies.

New HTML 4.0 Language, Symbol, and Math Entities

HTML 4.0 adds several new named entity codes that are available from the Unicode character set. Many of these entity names are for symbols (available through a Symbol font or a Unicode font); some are for mathematical symbols or foreign languages. (Note that the named Greek entities here are for math, not the Greek language.)

In Table A.5, we list the Unicode number in hexadecimal so that you may check its appearance at the Unicode home page (http://www.unicode.org/). While future browsers will allow you to use the hexadecimal number, for now all of the browsers require the (decimal) numerical entity code.

WARNING   Because these entity names are new, support is currently mixed. Older browsers can't display these entity names properly at all.

If you use any of the named entities from Table A.5, Navigator 4 and earlier and IE 3 and earlier won't display them. Instead, your named entity itself will be displayed literally (that is, you'll see the letters "√" instead of the square root/radical symbol).

If you use the numerical entities, IE 3 displays the wrong character. Navigator 3 and earlier display only a question mark for any of the characters in Table A.5. (Navigator 4 can display some of them.)

IE 4 displays both the numerical and named entity codes perfectly (with the two exceptions noted)—as long as the Universal Alphabet Font (UTF-8) font is selected from the View ➤ Fonts command. If the default Western font is used, then only some of these symbols are displayed correctly.

TABLE A.5: New HTML 4.0 Named Entities from the Unicode Character Set

Unicode Hexadecimal Number	Appearance	Numerical Entity Code	Named Entity Code	Name (Comments)
&#x0152;	Œ	&#338;	&OElig;	Latin capital ligature OE
&#x0153;	œ	&#339;	&oelig;	Latin small ligature oe
&#x0160;	Š	&#352;	&Scaron;	Latin capital letter S with caron
&#x0161;	š	&#353;	&scaron;	Latin small letter s with caron
&#x0178;	Ÿ	&#376;	&Yuml;	Latin capital letter Y with dieresis
&#x0192;	ƒ	&#402;	&fnof;	Latin small f with hook (function, florin)
&#x02C6;	^	&#710;	&circ;	modifier letter circumflex accent
&#x02DC;	~	&#732;	&tilde;	small tilde
&#x0391;	A	&#913;	&Alpha;	Greek capital letter Alpha
&#x0392;	B	&#914;	&Beta;	Greek capital letter Beta
&#x0393;	Γ	&#915;	&Gamma;	Greek capital letter Gamma
&#x0394;	Δ	&#916;	&Delta;	Greek capital letter Delta
&#x0395;	E	&#917;	&Epsilon;	Greek capital letter Epsilon
&#x0396;	Z	&#918;	&Zeta;	Greek capital letter Zeta
&#x0397;	H	&#919;	&Eta;	Greek capital letter Eta
&#x0398;	Θ	&#920;	&Theta;	Greek capital letter Theta
&#x0399;	I	&#921;	&Iota;	Greek capital letter Iota
&#x039A;	K	&#922;	&Kappa;	Greek capital letter Kappa
&#x039B;	Λ	&#923;	&Lambda;	Greek capital letter Lambda
&#x039C;	M	&#924;	&Mu;	Greek capital letter Mu
&#x039D;	N	&#925;	&Nu;	Greek capital letter Nu
&#x039E;	Ξ	&#926;	&Xi;	Greek capital letter Xi
&#x039F;	O	&#927;	&Omicron;	Greek capital letter Omicron
&#x03A0;	Π	&#928;	&Pi;	Greek capital letter Pi
&#x03A1;	P	&#929;	&Rho;	Greek capital letter Rho
&#x03A3;	Σ	&#931;	&Sigma;	Greek capital letter Sigma
&#x03A4;	T	&#932;	&Tau;	Greek capital letter Tau

TABLE A.5 CONTINUED: New HTML 4.0 Named Entities from the Unicode Character Set

Unicode Hexadecimal Number	Appearance	Numerical Entity Code	Named Entity Code	Name (Comments)
&#x03A5;	Υ	&#933;	&Upsilon;	Greek capital letter Upsilon
&#x03A6;	Φ	&#934;	&Phi;	Greek capital letter Phi
&#x03A7;	X	&#935;	&Chi;	Greek capital letter Chi
&#x03A8;	Ψ	&#936;	&Psi;	Greek capital letter Psi
&#x03A9;	Ω	&#937;	&Omega;	Greek capital letter Omega
&#x03B1;	α	&#945;	&alpha;	Greek small letter alpha
&#x03B2;	β	&#946;	&beta;	Greek small letter beta
&#x03B3;	γ	&#947;	&gamma;	Greek small letter gamma
&#x03B4;	δ	&#948;	&delta;	Greek small letter delta
&#x03B5;	ε	&#949;	&epsilon;	Greek small letter epsilon
&#x03B6;	ζ	&#950;	&zeta;	Greek small letter zeta
&#x03B7;	η	&#951;	&eta;	Greek small letter eta
&#x03B8;	θ	&#952;	&theta;	Greek small letter theta
&#x03B9;	ι	&#953;	&iota;	Greek small letter iota
&#x03BA;	κ	&#954;	&kappa;	Greek small letter kappa
&#x03BB;	λ	&#955;	&lambda;	Greek small letter lambda
&#x03BC;	μ	&#956;	&mu;	Greek small letter mu
&#x03BD;	ν	&#957;	&nu;	Greek small letter nu
&#x03BE;	ξ	&#958;	&xi;	Greek small letter xi
&#x03BF;	o	&#959;	&omicron;	Greek small letter omicron
&#x03C0;	π	&#960;	&pi;	Greek small letter pi
&#x03C1;	ρ	&#961;	&rho;	Greek small letter rho
&#x03C2;	ς	&#962;	&sigmaf;	Greek small letter final sigma
&#x03C3;	σ	&#963;	&sigma;	Greek small letter sigma
&#x03C4;	τ	&#964;	&tau;	Greek small letter tau
&#x03C5;	υ	&#965;	&upsilon;	Greek small letter upsilon
&#x03C6;	φ	&#966;	&phi;	Greek small letter phi
&#x03C7;	χ	&#967;	&chi;	Greek small letter chi
&#x03C8;	ψ	&#968;	&psi;	Greek small letter psi
&#x03C9;	ω	&#969;	&omega;	Greek small letter omega
&#x03D1;	ϑ	&#977;	&thetasym;	Greek small letter theta symbol
&#x03D2;	ϒ	&#978;	&upsih;	Greek upsilon with hook symbol
&#x03D6;	ϖ	&#982;	&piv;	Greek pi symbol
	N/A			en space (a space as wide as the letter N)
	N/A			em space (a space as wide as the letter M)
	N/A			thin space

TABLE A.5 CONTINUED: New HTML 4.0 Named Entities from the Unicode Character Set

Unicode Hexadecimal Number	Appearance	Numerical Entity Code	Named Entity Code	Name (Comments)
&#x200C;	N/A	&#8204;	&zwnj;	zero width non-joiner (used in foreign languages such as Arabic and Persian to prevent characters from joining each other)
&#x200D;	N/A	&#8205;	&zwj;	zero width joiner (used in foreign languages such as Arabic and Persian when a character must join with another, but no character is available due to context)
&#x200E;	N/A	&#8206;	&lrm;	left-to-right mark (see also Skill 5 and the DIR attribute)
&#x200F;	N/A	&#8207;	&rlm;	right-to-left mark (see also Skill 5 and the DIR attribute)
&#x2013;	–	&#8211;	&ndash;	en dash (dash as wide as the letter N)
&#x2014;	—	&#8212;	&mdash;	em dash (dash as wide as the letter M)
&#x2018;	'	&#8216;	&lsquo;	left single quotation mark
&#x2019;	'	&#8217;	&rsquo;	right single quotation mark
&#x201A;	‚	&#8218;	&sbquo;	single low-9 quotation mark
&#x201C;	"	&#8220;	&ldquo;	left double quotation mark
&#x201D;	"	&#8221;	&rdquo;	right double quotation mark
&#x201E;	„	&#8222;	&bdquo;	double low-9 quotation mark
&#x2020;	†	&#8224;	&dagger;	dagger
&#x2021;	‡	&#8225;	&Dagger;	double dagger
&#x2022;	•	&#8226;	&bull;	bullet (black small circle)
&#x2026;	…	&#8230;	&hellip;	horizontal ellipsis (three dot leader)
&#x2030;	‰	&#8240;	&permil;	per mille sign
&#x2032;	′	&#8242;	&prime;	prime (minutes, feet)
&#x2033;	″	&#8243;	&Prime;	double prime (seconds, inches)
&#x2039;	‹	&#8249;	&lsaquo;	single left-pointing angle quotation mark
&#x203A;	›	&#8250;	&rsaquo;	single right-pointing angle quotation mark
&#x203E;	‾	&#8254;	&oline;	overline (spacing overscore)
&#x2044;	/	&#8260;	&frasl;	fraction slash
&#x2118;	℘	&#8472;	&weierp;	script capital P (power set, Weierstrass p)
&#x2111;	ℑ	&#8465;	&image;	black letter capital I (imaginary part)
&#x211C;	ℜ	&#8476;	&real;	black letter capital R (real part symbol)
&#x2122;	™	&#8482;	&trade;	trademark sign (**NOTE**: IE 3 understands this entity name)
&#x2135;	ℵ	&#8501;	&alefsym;	alef symbol (first transfinite cardinal)
&#x2190;	←	&#8592;	&larr;	leftwards arrow
&#x2191;	↑	&#8593;	&uarr;	upwards arrow
&#x2192;	→	&#8594;	&rarr;	rightwards arrow
&#x2193;	↓	&#8595;	&darr;	downwards arrow

TABLE A.5 CONTINUED: New HTML 4.0 Named Entities from the Unicode Character Set

Unicode Hexadecimal Number	Appearance	Numerical Entity Code	Named Entity Code	Name (Comments)
&#x2194;	↔	&#8596;	&harr;	left right arrow
&#x21B5;	↵	&#8629;	&crarr;	downwards arrow with corner leftwards (used to symbolize the carriage return)
&#x21D0;	⇐	&#8656;	&lArr;	leftwards double arrow
&#x21D1;	⇑	&#8657;	&uArr;	upwards double arrow
&#x21D2;	⇒	&#8658;	&rArr;	rightwards double arrow
&#x21D3;	⇓	&#8659;	&dArr;	downwards double arrow
&#x21D4;	⇔	&#8660;	&hArr;	left right double arrow
&#x2200;	∀	&#8704;	&forall;	for all
&#x2202;	∂	&#8706;	&part;	partial differential
&#x2203;	∃	&#8707;	&exist;	there exists
&#x2205;	∅	&#8709;	&empty;	empty set (null set, diameter)
&#x2207;	∇	&#8711;	&nabla;	nabla (backward difference)
&#x2208;	∈	&#8712;	&isin;	element of
&#x2209;	∉	&#8713;	&notin;	not an element of
&#x220B;	∋	&#8715;	&ni;	contains as member
&#x220F;	∏	&#8719;	&prod;	*n*-ary product (product sign)
&#x2211;	∑	&#8721;	&sum;	*n*-ary summation
&#x2212;	−	&#8722;	&minus;	minus sign
&#x2217;	∗	&#8727;	&lowast;	asterisk operator
&#x221A;	√	&#8730;	&radic;	square root (radical sign)
&#x221D;	∝	&#8733;	&prop;	proportional to
&#x221E;	∞	&#8734;	&infin;	infinity
&#x2220;	∠	&#8736;	&ang;	angle
&#x2227;	∧	&#8743;	&and;	logical and (wedge)
&#x2228;	∨	&#8744;	&or;	logical or (vee)
&#x2229;	∩	&#8745;	&cap;	intersection (cap)
&#x222A;	∪	&#8746;	&cup;	union (cup)
&#x222B;	∫	&#8747;	&int;	integral
&#x2234;	∴	&#8756;	&there4;	therefore
&#x223C;	∼	&#8764;	&sim;	tilde operator (varies with, similar to)
&#x2245;	≅	&#8773;	&cong;	approximately equal to
&#x2248;	≈	&#8776;	&asymp;	almost equal to (asymptotic to)
&#x2260;	≠	&#8800;	&ne;	not equal to
&#x2261;	≡	&#8801;	&equiv;	identical to
&#x2264;	≤	&#8804;	&le;	less-than or equal to
&#x2265;	≥	&#8805;	&ge;	greater-than or equal to
&#x2282;	⊂	&#8834;	&sub;	subset of

TABLE A.5 CONTINUED: New HTML 4.0 Named Entities from the Unicode Character Set

Unicode Hexadecimal Number	Appearance	Numerical Entity Code	Named Entity Code	Name (Comments)
&#x2283;	⊃	&#8835;	&sup;	superset of
&#x2284;	⊄	&#8836;	&nsub;	not a subset of
&#x2286;	⊆	&#8838;	&sube;	subset of or equal to
&#x2287;	⊇	&#8839;	&supe;	superset of or equal to
&#x2295;	⊕	&#8853;	&oplus;	circled plus (direct sum)
&#x2297;	⊗	&#8855;	&otimes;	circled times (vector product)
&#x22A5;	⊥	&#8869;	&perp;	up tack (orthogonal to, perpendicular)
&#x22C5;	·	&#8901;	&sdot;	dot operator
&#x2308;	⌈	&#8968;	&lceil;	left ceiling (apl upstile)
&#x2309;	⌉	&#8969;	&rceil;	right ceiling
&#x230A;	⌊	&#8970;	&lfloor;	left floor (apl downstile)
&#x230B;	⌋	&#8971;	&rfloor;	right floor
&#x2329;	⟨	&#9001;	&lang;	left-pointing angle bracket ("bra") **WARNING:** IE 4 does not display this symbol
&#x232A;	⟩	&#9002;	&rang;	right-pointing angle bracket ("ket") **WARNING:** IE 4 does not display this symbol
&#x25CA;	◊	&#9674;	&loz;	lozenge
&#x2660;	♠	&#9824;	&spades;	black spade suit
&#x2663;	♣	&#9827;	&clubs;	black club suit (shamrock)
&#x2665;	♥	&#9829;	&hearts;	black heart suit (valentine)
&#x2666;	♦	&#9830;	&diams;	black diamond suit

Alphabetical Summary of HTML 4.0 Elements, Tags, and Attributes

In this section, we'll list the 91 valid HTML 4.0 elements with their tags and attributes. We won't list any extensions to HTML (covered in Skill 13). Any elements that are new to HTML 4.0 will be marked as so. Everything else is valid in HTML 3.2 as well as HTML 4.0.

NOTE   Elements only introduced in HTML 3.0 are not listed here since HTML 3.0 was never approved. Other versions of HTML before 4.0 included only three elements that are not listed here: the listing, plaintext, and xmp elements (all three of which behaved similarly to the pre-formatted text element). HTML 4.0 has made these elements obsolete; use <PRE> and </PRE> instead.

Table A.6 is alphabetical by start tag. Included for each of the 91 elements are several items:

- The element's description (sometimes including an example or a warning) and where in this book it's discussed

- The element's start tag, and whether it's optional or required

- For elements with end tags, the tag is listed and we indicate whether the end tag is optional or required. For elements without end tags (such as <IMG>), we'll list "forbidden (empty element)."

- The element's attributes, if any. All attributes are optional unless marked as required.

- What type of content is allowed within the element, if anything (the special term *DATA* refers to ordinary characters and entities, called "CDATA" by the HTML 4.0 specification)

- The element's category

There are several possible categories for an element. Elements are either part of HTML's basic structure (Skill 2), the head section, or the body section's block-level and text-level elements (see Skill 2 and Skill 6 for a discussion and comparison), or a special category. In addition, some elements only occur inside another element. Here's how the elements break down (listed by start tag):

- Basic structure elements: <BODY>, <HEAD>, <HTML>, and <TITLE>

- Head section elements: <BASE>, <ISINDEX>, <LINK>, <META>, <SCRIPT>, and <STYLE>

- Block-level elements: <ADDRESS>, <BLOCKQUOTE>, <CENTER>, <DIV>, <FIELDSET>, <FORM>, <H1>, <H2>, <H3>, <H4>, <H5>, <H6>, <HR>, <ISINDEX>, <NOFRAMES>, <NOSCRIPT>, <P>, <PRE>, and <TABLE>

- Block-level list elements: <DL>, <DIR>, <MENU>, <OL>, and <UL>

- Text-level special elements: <A>, <APPLET>, <BASEFONT>, <BDO>, <BR>, <FONT>, <IFRAME>, <IMG>, <MAP>, <OBJECT>, <Q>, <SCRIPT>, <SPAN>, <SUB>, and <SUP>

- Text-level phrase elements: <ACRONYM>, <CITE>, <CODE>, <DFN>, <EM>, <KBD>, <SAMP>, <STRONG>, and <VAR>

- Text-level font elements: <B>, <BIG>, <I>, <S>, <SMALL>, <STRIKE>, <TT>, and <U>

- Text-level form controls: <BUTTON>, <INPUT>, <LABEL>, <SELECT>, <TEXTAREA>.

- Special hybrid elements: <DEL> and <INS>

- Special SGML constructs: <!DOCTYPE> and <!--

- Special frame structure: <FRAMESET>

- Table model elements: <CAPTION>, <COL>, <COLGROUP>, <TBODY>, <TD>, <TFOOT>, <TH>, <THEAD>, and <TR>

- Child elements: The definition list element contains <DD> and <DT>. Other types of list elements contain <LI>. The select element contains <OPTION>. The map element contains <AREA>. The frameset element contains <FRAME>. The fieldset element contains <LEGEND>. Finally, the applet and object elements contain <PARAM>.

 NOTE   The script element is both a head section element and a text-level element. The isindex element is both a head section element and block-level element.

You'll notice that many elements can use the "generic 4.0 attributes." These are the language attributes (LANG and DIR; see Skill 5), the advisory TITLE attribute (see Skill 5), the style and identification attributes (CLASS, ID, and STYLE; see Skill 14), and the event attributes (see Skill 15 for a list and discussion).

TABLE A.6: Alphabetical List of HTML 4.0 Elements

Element	Description
<!DOCTYPE> **document type declaration**	Declares the precise version of HTML you are using (Skill 5). For example: <!DOCTYPE HTML PUBLIC "-//W3C//DTD HTML 4.0//EN">
Category:	special SGML construct; can only occur in the very beginning of an HTML document, before any tags
Starting Tag:	<!DOCTYPE>, required
Ending Tag:	forbidden (empty element)
Attributes:	special; see Skill 5
Content:	none (empty element)
<!-- **comment**	Inserts comments into an HTML document that won't be displayed by a browser (unless the surfer views source); see Skill 3. Also used to hide style sheets and active scripts from older browsers (see Skill 14 and Skill 15)
Category:	special SGML construct
Starting Tag:	<!--, required
Ending Tag:	-->, required
Attributes:	none
Content:	Any DATA except for two dashes (--). Also, greater-than signs (>) can cause problems and are not recommended inside a comment

TABLE A.6 CONTINUED: Alphabetical List of HTML 4.0 Elements

Element	Description
<A> **anchor element**	Inserts hyperlink anchors and can name a section of a document (Skill 2 and Skill 7)
Category:	text-level element (special)
Starting Tag:	<A>, required
Ending Tag:	</A>, required
Attributes:	HREF to create a link, NAME to create a named section (either an HREF or NAME attribute, or both, is required), CHARSET to indicate the character encoding used at the other end of the link, TARGET to indicate where the link should be displayed (see Skill 7 and Skill 11), REL and REV to indicate relationships (not commonly used in anchors; see the link element in Skill 5), ACCESSKEY and TABINDEX to define a keyboard shortcut and tab order for the link (see Skill 7 and Skill 12), SHAPE and COORDS to define an image map (see the Web site), plus generic 4.0 attributes (including ONFOCUS and ONBLUR; see Skill 15)
Content:	DATA and/or text-level elements (excluding other anchor elements)
<ACRONYM> **acronym/abbreviation element**	Indicates that the enclosed text is an acronym or abbreviation (Skill 6)
Category:	text-level element (phrase)
Starting Tag:	<ACRONYM>, required
Ending Tag:	</ACRONYM>, required
Attributes:	none except generic 4.0 attributes
Content:	DATA and/or text-level elements
<ADDRESS> **address element**	Indicates the author's address (Skill 6)
Category:	block-level element
Starting Tag:	<ADDRESS>, required
Ending Tag:	</ADDRESS>, required
Attributes:	none except generic 4.0 attributes
Content:	DATA, paragraph elements, and/or text-level elements
<APPLET> **applet element**	Inserts a Java applet (Skill 15) **NOTE:** This element is not recommended by HTML 4.0 in favor of the object element, but for now you should continue to use the applet element since it is currently compatible with more browsers
Category:	text-level element (special)
Starting Tag:	<APPLET>, required
Ending Tag:	</APPLET>, required

TABLE A.6 CONTINUED: Alphabetical List of HTML 4.0 Elements

Element	Description
Attributes:	CODE, to indicate the .class filename of the applet (this attribute should be used in most cases), ARCHIVE to indicate the location of a .jar format Java Archive, OBJECT to indicate a special serialized-format applet (at least one of CODE, OBJECT, or ARCHIVE is required), CODEBASE to indicate the directory URL where the applet is located, WIDTH and HEIGHT to size the applet (both of these attributes are required), ALIGN to place the applet in relation to the rest of the line (either "BOT-TOM", "MIDDLE", "TOP", "LEFT", or "RIGHT"), HSPACE and VSPACE to determine the amount of pixels of space around the applet's region, ALT to provide a text description of the applet for browsers that are not Java-enabled, and NAME to give the applet a name (useful if two applets on a page need to communicate with each other), plus the ID, CLASS, STYLE, and TITLE generic attributes
Content:	One or more param elements (to control the applet's behavior), followed by DATA and/or text-level elements (used as alternate content for browsers that can't display the applet)
\<AREA\> **area element**	Defines a clickable hot spot in an image map (see Skill 8 and Web site)
Category:	child element: can only be used in a map element
Starting Tag:	\<AREA\>, required
Ending Tag:	forbidden (empty element)
Attributes:	SHAPE (to set the shape of the hot spot; either "RECT", "POLYGON" or "CIRCLE"), COORDS (the x and y coordinates of the hot spot; see Web site for format and example), HREF (the URL for the hot spot's link), TARGET (where the link should be targeted, see Skill 7), NOHREF (to declare a hot spot region with no link), ALT (required, to describe the resource being linked to), and TABINDEX (to control the hotspot's position in the tab key navigation order), ACCESSKEY (for a keyboard shortcut), plus generic 4.0 attributes
Content:	none
\<B\> **bold element**	Makes enclosed text bold (Skill 2 and 6) **WARNING:** \<STRONG\> is preferred over \<B\>
Category:	text-level element (physical font)
Starting Tag:	\<B\>, required
Ending Tag:	\</B\>, required
Attributes:	none except generic 4.0 attributes
Content:	DATA, and text-level elements
\<BASE\> **base element**	Indicates the location of a document (Skill 5) and can set a default link target (Skill 11)
Category:	head section element

TABLE A.6 CONTINUED: Alphabetical List of HTML 4.0 Elements

Element	Description
Starting Tag:	<BASE>, required
Ending Tag:	forbidden (empty element)
Attributes:	HREF (required, to indicate the full URL of the current document; see Skill 5), TARGET (to indicate the default targeted location of all links in the current document, see Skills 7 and 11)
Content:	none (empty element)
<BASEFONT> **basefont element**	Indicates the default font settings for the rest of the document (Skill 3 and Skill 6) **WARNING:** This element is not recommended by HTML 4.0; use a style sheet instead
Category:	text-level element (special)
Starting Tag:	<BASEFONT>, required
Ending Tag:	forbidden (empty element)
Attributes:	SIZE (required, to set the font size—must be a number from "1" to "7"), COLOR (to set the font color), and FACE (to specify the desired font face; use a comma-delimited list, for example FACE="Verdana, Helvetica, Arial"), plus the generic ID attributes
Content:	none (empty element)
<BDO> **bdo element (bi-directional text override element)**	Overrides the current direction of text (either right-to-left or left-to-right), only useful when working with documents written in a language that reads from right-to-left such as Hebrew (Skill 5) **WARNING:** This element is not yet widely supported
Category:	text-level element (special)
Starting Tag:	<BDO>, required
Ending Tag:	</BDO>, required
Attributes:	DIR (required, to indicate the direction of text; must be either DIR="RTL" for right-to-left text or DIR="LTR" for left-to right text), and LANG (to indicate the language used for the bdo element's content, see Skill 5), plus the ID, CLASS, STYLE, and TITLE generic attributes
Content:	DATA and/or text-level elements
<BIG> **big element**	Makes enclosed text one size larger (Skill 3 and Skill 6)
Category:	text-level element (physical font)
Starting Tag:	<BIG>, required
Ending Tag:	</BIG>, required
Attributes:	none except generic 4.0 attributes

ew

TABLE A.6 CONTINUED: Alphabetical List of HTML 4.0 Elements

Element	Description
Content:	DATA and/or text-level elements
<BLOCKQUOTE> **blockquote element**	Indicates a quotation from another source (Skill 6); often the quote is indented but not every browser does this
Category:	block-level element
Starting Tag:	<BLOCKQUOTE>, required
Ending Tag:	</BLOCKQUOTE>, required
Attributes:	CITE (to indicate the URL of the quote's source) plus generic 4.0 attributes
Content:	DATA, block-level elements, and/or text-level elements
<BODY> **body element**	Contains the body section of an HTML document (Skill 2)
Category:	basic structure element
Starting Tag:	<BODY>, optional
Ending Tag:	</BODY>, optional
Attributes:	BACKGROUND (to set a background image), BGCOLOR (to set a background color), TEXT (to set the text color), LINK (to set the link color), ALINK (to set the active link color), and VLINK (to set the visited link color); see Skill 3 for examples of these attributes, which set the appearance of the entire document. HTML 4.0 recommends the use of a style sheet instead. In addition the <BODY> tag can use the ONLOAD and ONUNLOAD event attributes (see Skill 15), plus generic 4.0 attributes
Content:	DATA, block-level elements, text-level elements, plus ins and del elements
** ** **line-break element**	Creates a line-break (Skill 2 and Skill 6)
Category:	text-level element (special)
Starting Tag:	 , required
Ending Tag:	forbidden (empty element)
Attributes:	CLEAR (either "LEFT", "RIGHT", "ALL", or "NONE") to determine how far down the line-break should move (see Skill 8), plus the ID, CLASS, STYLE, and TITLE generic 4.0 attributes (not the language or event generic attributes)
Content:	none (empty element)
<BUTTON> **button element**	Creates a button form control (Skill 12) **WARNING:** The button element is not yet widely supported
Category:	form control element
Starting Tag:	<BUTTON>, required

new

TABLE A.6 CONTINUED: Alphabetical List of HTML 4.0 Elements

Element	Description
Ending Tag:	</BUTTON>, required
Attributes:	VALUE (to give the button a value that's passed to the form processor when the form is submitted), NAME (to give the button a name for use with a script), TYPE (either "SUBMIT" or "RESET" to make this button submit or reset the form), DISABLED (to make this button "grayed out" and unavailable by default), TABINDEX (to control this button's position in the tab key navigation order), ACCESSKEY (for a keyboard shortcut), plus generic 4.0 attributes, including the special ONFOCUS and ONBLUR event attributes (see Skill 15)
Content:	DATA, text-level elements, and/or block-level elements (except for anchor elements, form elements, fieldset elements, and form control elements)
<CAPTION> **caption element**	Creates a caption for a table (Skill 10)
Category:	table model element
Starting Tag:	<CAPTION>, required
Ending Tag:	</CAPTION>, required
Attributes:	ALIGN (to indicate where the caption should go; either "TOP", "BOTTOM", "LEFT", or "RIGHT" although most browsers only support top and bottom), plus generic 4.0 attributes
Content:	DATA, and/or text-level elements
<CENTER> **center element**	Horizontally centers its content (Skill 2 and 6); identical to <DIV ALIGN="CENTER"> **WARNING:** This element is not recommended in HTML 4.0. Use a style sheet instead
Category:	block-level element
Starting Tag:	<CENTER>, required
Ending Tag:	</CENTER>, required
Attributes:	none except generic 4.0 attributes
Content:	DATA, block-level elements, and/or text-level elements
<CITE> **cite element**	Indicates a source that is being used as a citation (Skill 6)
Category:	text-level element (phrase)
Starting Tag:	<CITE>, required
Ending Tag:	</CITE>, required
Attributes:	none except generic 4.0 attributes
Content:	DATA and/or text-level elements

TABLE A.6 CONTINUED: Alphabetical List of HTML 4.0 Elements

Element	Description
<CODE> **code element**	Indicates that the contents is computer code (Skill 6)—browsers will often render a code element in a fixed-width font
Category:	text-level element (phrase)
Starting Tag:	<CODE>, required
Ending Tag:	</CODE>, required
Attributes:	none except generic 4.0 attributes
Content:	DATA and/or text-level elements
new **<COL>** **column element**	Creates a column or range of columns in a table (Skill 10)
Category:	table model element
Starting Tag:	<COL>, required
Ending Tag:	forbidden (empty element)
Attributes:	SPAN (to indicate the number of columns to create), WIDTH (to specify the width of the columns in pixels, a percentage of the table width, or the special asterisk notation; see Skill 10), horizontal cell alignment attributes: ALIGN (to set the default alignment of the cell data, either "LEFT", "CENTER", "RIGHT", "JUSTIFY", or on a particular character with "CHAR"), CHAR (to specify which alignment character to use if ALIGN="CHAR"), CHAROFF (to specify a length in pixels or percentage of the column's width to use as an offset for determining the character alignment), and vertical cell alignment: VALIGN (to specify the vertical position of cell data: "TOP", "MIDDLE", "BOTTOM", or "BASELINE"), plus generic 4.0 attributes **WARNING:** Character alignment is not yet supported in the popular browsers
Content:	none (empty element)
new **<COLGROUP>** **column group element**	Creates groups of columns in a table, allowing many columns to be formatted together with one set of attributes (Skill 10)
Category:	table model element
Starting Tag:	<COLGROUP>, required
Ending Tag:	</COLGROUP>, optional
Attributes:	Same as for the column element (see <COL>)
Content:	One or more column elements (see <COL>)
<DD> **definition element**	Creates a definition in a definition list (Skill 6)
Category:	child element: can only be used in a definition list
Starting Tag:	<DD>, required

TABLE A.6 CONTINUED: Alphabetical List of HTML 4.0 Elements

Element	Description
Ending Tag:	</DD>, optional
Attributes:	none except generic 4.0 attributes
Content:	DATA, text-level elements, and/or block-level elements
<DEL> **del element**	Indicates elements and text that are considered removed from a document (Skill 6) **WARNING:** Not yet widely supported
Category:	special hybrid element (used in the body section, similar to a block-level element except doesn't cause a paragraph break)
Starting Tag:	<DEL>, required
Ending Tag:	</DEL>, required
Attributes:	CITE (with a URL explaining why the contents were removed), DATETIME (to indicate when the contents were removed; this attribute's value must use the special date and time format explained in Skill 6), plus generic 4.0 attributes
Content:	DATA, text-level elements, and/or block-level elements
<DFN> **definition element**	Indicates that the contents is a definition (Skill 6)
Category:	text-level element (phrase)
Starting Tag:	<DFN>, required
Ending Tag:	</DFN>, required
Attributes:	none except generic 4.0 attributes
Content:	DATA and/or text-level elements
<DIR> **directory list element**	Creates a list in the "directory" style (Skill 6) **WARNING:** This element is not recommended; use an ordered list or unordered list instead
Category:	block-level element (list)
Starting Tag:	<DIR>, required
Ending Tag:	</DIR>, required
Attributes:	COMPACT (to indicate that the list should be reduced in size; ignored by most browsers and not recommended) plus generic 4.0 attributes
Content:	One or more list item elements (see <LI>)
<DIV> **division element**	Divides a document into logical sections (Skill 6); useful when used with style sheets (see Skill 14)
Category:	block-level element

ew

TABLE A.6 CONTINUED: Alphabetical List of HTML 4.0 Elements

Element	Description
Starting Tag:	<DIV>, required
Ending Tag:	</DIV>, required
Attributes:	ALIGN (for horizontal alignment; possible values are "LEFT", "RIGHT", "CENTER", or "JUSTIFY", but this attribute is not recommended; use style sheets instead) plus generic 4.0 attributes
Content:	DATA, text-level elements, and/or block-level elements
<DL> **definition list element**	Creates a definition list (Skill 6)
Category:	block-level element (list)
Starting Tag:	<DL>, required
Ending Tag:	</DL>, required
Attributes:	COMPACT (to indicate that the list should be reduced in size; ignored by most browsers and not recommended), plus generic 4.0 attributes
Content:	One or more definition terms (see <DT>) and/or one or more definitions (see <DD>); however it is recommended that each term be followed by a definition
<DT> **definition term element**	Creates a term that can be defined in a definition list (Skill 6)
Category:	child element: can only be used in a definition list element
Starting Tag:	<DT>, required
Ending Tag:	</DT>, optional
Attributes:	none except generic 4.0 attributes
Content:	DATA and/or text-level elements
<EM> **emphasis element**	Indicates that the contents should be emphasized, often displayed using italics (Skill 6)
Category:	text-level element (phrase)
Starting Tag:	<EM>, required
Ending Tag:	</EM>, required
Attributes:	none except generic 4.0 attributes
Content:	DATA and/or text-level elements
<FIELDSET> **fieldset element**	Groups one or more form controls (Skill 12); you should usually use a fieldset element only within a form element
Category:	block-level element

new

TABLE A.6 CONTINUED: Alphabetical List of HTML 4.0 Elements

Element	Description
Starting Tag:	<FIELDSET>, required
Ending Tag:	</FIELDSET>, required
Attributes:	none except generic 4.0 attributes
Content:	a legend element, followed by form controls (including DATA, block-level elements, and/or text-level elements)
<FONT> **font element**	Sets the font size, font color, and/or font face (Skill 3 and Skill 6) **WARNING:** This element is not recommended by HTML 4.0; use a style sheet instead.
Category:	text-level element (special)
Starting Tag:	<FONT>, required
Ending Tag:	</FONT>, required
Attributes:	SIZE (to set the font size—must be a number from "1" to "7"), COLOR (to set the font color), and FACE (to specify the desired font face; use a comma-delimited list, for example FACE="Verdana, Helvetica, Arial"), plus the ID, CLASS, STYLE, and TITLE generic attributes
Content:	DATA and/or text level elements
<FORM> **form element**	Marks an area containing an interactive form (consisting of one or more form controls); attributes indicate how the form is to be processed using CGI, e-mail, or an active script (Skill 12)
Category:	block-level element
Starting Tag:	<FORM>, required
Ending Tag:	</FORM>, required
Attributes:	ACTION (required, to indicate the URL of the form handler that will process the form when it's submitted), METHOD (either "GET" or "POST", see Skill 12), ENCTYPE (to indicate what MIME type should be used to send the data), TARGET (to indicate where the results of the form should appear), ACCEPT-CHARSET (to indicate what character encodings the form processor can understand), plus generic 4.0 attributes—as well the special ONSUBMIT and ONRESET event attributes
Content:	DATA, block-level elements, and/or text-level elements (except for other form elements: a form cannot be nested inside another form) **NOTE:** Form elements should contain one or more fieldset elements and one or more form controls (button elements, input elements, label elements, select elements, and/or textarea elements)
<FRAME> **frame element**	In a frameset document, indicates the file the URL used as the contents of a frame (Skill 11)
Category:	child element: can only be used in a frameset element
Starting Tag:	<FRAME>, required

TABLE A.6 CONTINUED: Alphabetical List of HTML 4.0 Elements

Element	Description
Ending Tag:	forbidden (empty element)
Attributes:	SRC (a URL for the frame's content), NAME (the name of the frame for targeting purposes), MARGINWIDTH and MARGINHEIGHT (the distance in pixels between the frame's border and the content), FRAMEBORDER ("0" for no border, "1" for a border), NORESIZE (to indicate whether the frame can be resized by the surfer), and SCROLLING ("YES", "NO", or "AUTO" to determine whether or not a scroll bar is present), plus the generic ID attributes
Content:	none (empty element)
<FRAMESET> **frameset element**	Creates a frameset that defines how multiple documents can appear in different frames of a browser's window (Skill 11)
Category:	special frame structure element; replaces the body element in the basic structure
Starting Tag:	<FRAMESET>, required
Ending Tag:	</FRAMESET>, required
Attributes:	Either ROWS or COLUMNS is a required attribute to define the number of frames, or use both to create a grid (see Skill 11 for the format of the attribute); in addition, you can use the ONLOAD or ONUNLOAD events (see Skill 15)
Content:	Any number of frame elements and any number of frameset elements. Also you should use a noframe element (not required but highly recommended)
<H1> **heading level-one element**	Creates a first-level heading (Skill 2 and Skill 6)
Category:	block-level element
Starting Tag:	<H1>, required
Ending Tag:	</H1>, required
Attributes:	ALIGN (for horizontal alignment; either "LEFT", "RIGHT", "CENTER", or "JUSTIFY", although this attribute is not recommended in favor of style sheets), plus generic 4.0 attributes
Content:	DATA and/or text-level elements
<H2> **heading level-two element**	Creates a second-level heading (Skill 2 and Skill 6)
Category:	block-level element
Starting Tag:	<H2>, required
Ending Tag:	</H2>, required
Attributes:	ALIGN (for horizontal alignment; either "LEFT", "RIGHT", "CENTER", or "JUSTIFY", although this attribute is not recommended in favor of style sheets), plus generic 4.0 attributes
Content:	DATA and/or text-level elements

≡new

TABLE A.6 CONTINUED: Alphabetical List of HTML 4.0 Elements

Element	Description
<H3> **heading level-three element**	Creates a third-level heading (Skill 6)
Category:	block-level element
Starting Tag:	<H3>, required
Ending Tag:	</H3>, required
Attributes:	ALIGN (for horizontal alignment; either "LEFT", "RIGHT", "CENTER", or "JUSTIFY", although this attribute is not recommended in favor of style sheets), plus generic 4.0 attributes
Content:	DATA and/or text-level elements
<H4> **heading level-four element**	Creates a fourth-level heading (Skill 6)
Category:	block-level element
Starting Tag:	<H4>, required
Ending Tag:	</H4>, required
Attributes:	ALIGN (for horizontal alignment; either "LEFT", "RIGHT", "CENTER", or "JUSTIFY", although this attribute is not recommended in favor of style sheets), plus generic 4.0 attributes
Content:	DATA and/or text-level elements
<H5> **heading level-five element**	Creates a fifth-level heading (Skill 6)
Category:	block-level element
Starting Tag:	<H5>, required
Ending Tag:	</H5>, required
Attributes:	ALIGN (for horizontal alignment; either "LEFT", "RIGHT", "CENTER", or "JUSTIFY", although this attribute is not recommended in favor of style sheets), plus generic 4.0 attributes
Content:	DATA and/or text-level elements
<H6> **heading level-six element**	Creates a sixth-level heading (Skill 6)
Category:	block-level element
Starting Tag:	<H6>, required
Ending Tag:	</H6>, required
Attributes:	ALIGN (for horizontal alignment; either "LEFT", "RIGHT", "CENTER", or "JUSTIFY", although this attribute is not recommended in favor of style sheets), plus generic 4.0 attributes

TABLE A.6 CONTINUED: Alphabetical List of HTML 4.0 Elements

Element	Description
Content:	DATA and/or text-level elements
<HEAD> **head element**	Contains the head section of a document (Skill 2 and Skill 5)
Category:	basic structure element
Starting Tag:	<HEAD>, optional
Ending Tag:	</HEAD>, optional
Attributes:	The generic 4.0 attributes for language (LANG and DIR) and the PROFILE attribute (see Skill 5)
Content:	Must contain exactly one title element. In addition, can contain one isindex element and/or one base element. Can also contain multiple script elements, style elements, meta elements, and link elements
<HR> **horizontal rule element**	Inserts a horizontal line to divide two different sections (Skill 2 and Skill 6)
Category:	block-level element
Starting Tag:	<HR>, required
Ending Tag:	forbidden (empty element)
Attributes:	ALIGN (to determine the horizontal alignment of the rule; either "LEFT", "CENTER", or "RIGHT"), SIZE (to specify the height of the rule in pixels), WIDTH (to specify the width of the rule in pixels or as a percentage of the window's size), NOSHADE (to indicate that the rule should be solid, and not given the default shading and three-dimensional appearance), plus the generic 4.0 attributes (except for the two language attributes, LANG and DIR). HTML 4.0 recommends using style sheets instead of the ALIGN, SIZE, or WIDTH attributes.
Content:	none (empty element)
<HTML> **html element**	Contains the head element and body element of a document (Skill 2); if frames are used (see Skill 11), then a frameset element can be substituted for the body element
Category:	basic structure element
Starting Tag:	<HTML>, optional
Ending Tag:	</HTML>, optional
Attributes:	generic 4.0 attributes for language (LANG and DIR, see Skill 5), plus a VERSION attribute (to indicate the version of HTML you're using; not recommended—use a DOCTYPE declaration instead, see <!DOCTYPE>)
Content:	One head element, and either a body element or a frameset element

TABLE A.6 CONTINUED: Alphabetical List of HTML 4.0 Elements

Element	Description
\<I> **italics element**	Makes the enclosed text italic (Skill 2 and Skill 6) **WARNING:** \<EM> is preferred over \<I>
Category:	text-level element (physical font)
Starting Tag:	\<I>, required
Ending Tag:	\</I>, required
Attributes:	none except generic 4.0 attributes
Content:	DATA and/or text-level elements
\<IFRAME> **iframe element**	Creates an inline frame—that is, a region containing a different HTML document (Skill 11) **WARNING:** Not supported by Navigator 4 or earlier
Category:	text-level element (special)
Starting Tag:	\<IFRAME>, required
Ending Tag:	\</IFRAME>, required
Attributes:	SRC (a URL for the frame's content), NAME (the name of the frame for targeting purposes), HEIGHT and WIDTH (to set the frame's size in pixels or a percentage), ALIGN to place the frame in relation to the rest of the line (either "BOTTOM", "MIDDLE", "TOP", "LEFT", or "RIGHT"), MARGINWIDTH and MARGINHEIGHT (the distance in pixels between the frame's border and the content), FRAMEBORDER ("0" for no border, "1" for a border), and SCROLLING ("YES", "NO", or "AUTO" to determine whether or not a scroll bar is present)
Content:	DATA, text-level elements, and/or block-level elements (used as alternate content for browsers that cannot display inline frames)
\<IMG> **image element**	Inserts an inline image (Skill 2 and Skill 8)
Category:	text-level element (special)
Starting Tag:	\<IMG>, required
Ending Tag:	forbidden (empty element)
Attributes:	SRC (required, with the URL of the image), ALT (required for the alternate text of the image, displayed by browsers that don't display images), LONGDESC (for a URL to a longer description of the image), ALIGN to place the image in relation to the rest of the line (either "BOTTOM", "MIDDLE", "TOP", "LEFT", or "RIGHT"), HEIGHT and WIDTH (to determine the dimensions of the image, in pixels), BORDER (to determine the image's border width, in pixels), HSPACE and VSPACE (to determine the space between the image and the text around it, in pixels), and USEMAP and ISMAP (for use with image maps, see the Web site), plus generic 4.0 attributes
Content:	none (empty element)

TABLE A.6 CONTINUED: Alphabetical List of HTML 4.0 Elements

Element	Description
\<INPUT> **input element**	Creates one of several types of form controls, including text boxes, radio buttons, and submit buttons (Skill 12)
Category:	form control element
Starting Tag:	\<INPUT>, required
Ending Tag:	forbidden (empty element)
Attributes:	TYPE (to indicate what type of form control to create; either "TEXT", "PASSWORD", "CHECKBOX", "RADIO", "SUBMIT", "RESET", "FILE", "HIDDEN", "IMAGE", or "BUTTON"), VALUE (determines the value of a radio button, the text label used in a button, or the default text in a textbox; required for the "RADIO" and "CHECKBOX" types), NAME (required for most input types, to give the form control a value that's passed to the form processor when the form is submitted and to give the form control a name for use with a script), SIZE (to determine how large a text box is or indicate the size of a button in pixels), CHECKED (for radio buttons and check boxes to indicate the control's initial state), MAXLENGTH (to limit the text box entries to a particular number of characters), ACCEPT (a list of MIME types that the file input type can accept, indicating what types of files your CGI can process), DISABLED (to make this button "grayed out" and unavailable by default), READONLY (to prevent changes from being made to the text in a text box), TABINDEX (to control this button's position in the tab key navigation order), ACCESSKEY (for a keyboard shortcut), ALIGN (to determine where the control is placed relative to its surroundings; either "TOP", "MIDDLE", "BOTTOM", "LEFT", or "RIGHT"), a number of attributes to control buttons that are images (SRC, ALT, and USEMAP: see the image element and Skill 14), plus generic 4.0 attributes, including the special ONFOCUS, ONSELECT, ONCHANGE, and ONBLUR event attributes (see Skill 15)
Content:	none (empty element)
\<INS> **ins element**	Indicates elements and text that are considered inserted into a document (Skill 6) **WARNING:** Not yet widely supported
Category:	special hybrid element (used in the body section, similar to a block-level element except doesn't cause a paragraph break)
Starting Tag:	\<INS>, required
Ending Tag:	\</INS>, required
Attributes:	CITE (with a URL explaining why the contents were inserted), DATETIME (to indicate when the contents were insert; this attribute's value must use the special date and time format explained in Skill 6), plus generic 4.0 attributes
Content:	DATA, text-level elements, and/or block-level elements
\<ISINDEX> **isindex element**	Indicates that the document is a searchable index (Skill 5); requires that you set up CGI to handle the search (see Skill 15) **WARNING:** No longer recommended; use forms instead (see Skill 12)
Category:	head section element (HTML 4.0 now allows it to be block-level element as well)

new

TABLE A.6 CONTINUED: Alphabetical List of HTML 4.0 Elements

Element	Description
Starting Tag:	<ISINDEX>, required
Ending Tag:	forbidden (empty element)
Attributes:	PROMPT attribute for a search prompt (see Skill 5), plus generic 4.0 attributes (but not the event attributes)
Content:	none (empty element)
<KBD> **keyboard element**	Indicates that the contents is a keyboard command, often displayed using bold text (Skill 6)
Category:	text-level element (phrase)
Starting Tag:	<KBD>, required
Ending Tag:	</KBD>, required
Attributes:	none except generic 4.0 attributes
Content:	DATA and/or text-level elements
<LABEL> **label element**	Associates a text label with a form control (Skill 12); for example: <LABEL>Name: <INPUT TYPE="TEXT" NAME="yourname"></LABEL> **WARNING:** This element is not widely supported
Category:	form control element
Starting Tag:	<LABEL>, required
Ending Tag:	</LABEL>, required
Attributes:	ACCESSKEY (to create a keyboard shortcut for the control), DISABLED (to make the label and its contents disabled or "grayed-out" initially), FOR (to associate this label with a form control elsewhere in the document that has a matching ID name), plus generic 4.0 attributes, including the special ONFOCUS and ONBLUR events (see Skill 15)
Content:	DATA and/or text-level elements (excluding another label); mostly will be used to contain a single form control
<LEGEND> **legend element**	Adds a legend (caption) to a fieldset (Skill 12)
Category:	child element: can only be used in a fieldset element
Starting Tag:	<LEGEND>, required
Ending Tag:	</LEGEND>, required
Attributes:	ALIGN (to specify where in the fieldset the legend should appear: use "TOP", "BOTTOM", "LEFT", or "RIGHT"), ACCESSKEY (to set a shortcut key; see Skill 12), plus generic 4.0 attributes
Content:	DATA and/or text-level elements

TABLE A.6 CONTINUED: Alphabetical List of HTML 4.0 Elements

Element	Description
<LI> **list item element**	Creates a list item in an ordered list, unordered list, menu list, or dir list (Skill 6)
Category:	child element: can only be used in a ul element, ol element, menu element, or dir element
Starting Tag:	<LI>, required
Ending Tag:	</LI>, optional
Attributes:	TYPE (to indicate the list item style; for list items in unordered lists, can be one of the bullet types, and for list items in ordered lists, can be one of the numbering styles; see the unordered list element and ordered list element), VALUE (for list items in ordered list, used to set a specific number; see example in Skill 6) plus generic 4.0 attributes
Content:	DATA, text-level elements, and/or block-level elements (except dir and menu lists cannot contain list items that contain block-level elements)
<LINK> **link element**	Creates link relationships to other documents and resources such as the author's e-mail address (Skill 5), and links to external style sheets (Skill 14). For example: `<LINK REL="next" HREF="chapter2.html">` or `<LINK REV="made" HREF="mailto:estephen@emf.net">` or `<LINK REL="stylesheet" HREF="mystyle.css" TYPE="text/css" MEDIA="screen" TITLE="My Style Sheet">` **WARNING:** The relationships other than style sheets are not well supported
Category:	head section element
Starting Tag:	<LINK>, required
Ending Tag:	forbidden (empty element)
Attributes:	REL or REV (one of these are required) with a relationship name (see Skill 5), HREF (the URL of the linked resource), TARGET (where the linked resource should be displayed), TYPE (for the style sheet language), MEDIA (defining when to use the style sheet), CHARSET (to indicate a character encoding for foreign languages), plus generic 4.0 attributes (including the TITLE attribute for the style sheet's title)
Content:	none (empty element)
<MAP> **map element**	Creates a collection of hotspots for use with a client-side image map (Skill 8 and Web site)
Category:	text-level element (special)
Starting Tag:	<MAP>, required
Ending Tag:	</MAP>, required
Attributes:	NAME (to name the map, for reference via an image's USEMAP attribute) plus generic 4.0 attributes
Content:	One or more area elements

TABLE A.6 CONTINUED: Alphabetical List of HTML 4.0 Elements

Element	Description
\<MENU\> **menu list element**	Create a list in the "menu" style (Skill 6) **WARNING:** This element is not recommended; use an ordered list or unordered list instead.
Category:	block-level element (list)
Starting Tag:	\<MENU\>, required
Ending Tag:	\</MENU\>, required
Attributes:	COMPACT (to indicate that the list should be reduced in size; ignored by most browsers and not recommended) plus generic 4.0 attributes
Content:	One or more list item elements (see \<LI\>)
\<META\> **meta element**	Defines information about the document (Skill 5); can be used to help indexing robots, to define the document's default style sheet language (Skill 14), scripting language (Skill 15), or for meta refresh (Skill 5). For example: \<META NAME="Description" CONTENT="Meredith's page about The Simpsons"\>
Category:	head section element
Starting Tag:	\<META\>, required
Ending Tag:	forbidden (empty element)
Attributes:	NAME or HTTP-EQUIV (to define the type of meta information you're specifying) along with a CONTENT attribute (required, with the actual information), SCHEME (to indicate the type of information system being used, see Skill 5), plus the generic 4.0 language attributes (LANG and DIR)
Content:	none (empty element)
\<NOFRAMES\> **noframes element**	Marks content that should only be displayed when the browser is not frames-enabled (Skill 11) **NOTE:** This element has two uses. The first use is inside the frameset element of a frameset document, where the noframes element should contain a body element. The second use is in any document, when you want to display any section (such as a navigation bar) only in the event that the document is not being displayed in a frame. The second use is not widely supported yet, but the first use is very important.
Category:	block-level element
Starting Tag:	\<NOFRAMES\>, required
Ending Tag:	\</NOFRAMES\>, required
Attributes:	none except generic 4.0 attributes
Content:	First use: body element (which may in turn contain DATA, block-level elements, and/or text-level elements) Second use: DATA, block-level elements, and/or text-level elements

TABLE A.6 CONTINUED: Alphabetical List of HTML 4.0 Elements

Element	Description
new <NOSCRIPT> **noscript element**	Marks content that should only be displayed if the browser is not active script-enabled (Skill 15)
Category:	block-level element
Starting Tag:	<NOSCRIPT>, required
Ending Tag:	</NOSCRIPT>, required
Attributes:	none except generic 4.0 attributes
Content:	DATA, block-level elements, and/or text-level elements
<OBJECT> **object element**	Inserts an object of some kind, such as a sound, image, applet, movie object, text file, or another HTML document (Skill 9 and Skill 15)
Category:	text-level element (special)
Starting Tag:	<OBJECT>, required
Ending Tag:	</OBJECT>, required
Attributes:	DATA (the object's URL), HEIGHT and WIDTH (to define the object's size, in pixels or a percentage), TYPE (the MIME type of the object), ALIGN to place the object in relation to the rest of the line (either "TOP", "MIDDLE", "BOTTOM", "LEFT", or "RIGHT"), HSPACE and VSPACE (space in pixels between the object and the surrounding text), BORDER (size in pixels of the object's surrounding border), NAME (to give the object or applet a name), TABINDEX (where the object fits in the tab key navigation order, see Skill 12), CLASSID (to identify the URL and CLSID implementation of ActiveX controls), CODEBASE (the URL of the applet's source code), CODETYPE (the MIME type of the applet's source code), STANDBY (a message to show while the object is loading), DECLARE (to indicate that an applet should be loaded but not beginning running immediately), ARCHIVE (to indicate the location of an applet file), plus generic 4.0 attributes
Content:	One or more param elements (to control an applet object's behavior), followed by DATA, text-level elements, and/or block-level elements (used as alternate content for browsers that can't display the object); notably you can nest several objects within each other to allow the browser to negotiate for an object it is able to display
<OL> **ordered list element**	Creates an ordered list (Skill 6), with numbers preceding each list item
Category:	block-level element (list)
Starting Tag:	<OL>, required
Ending Tag:	</OL>, required

TABLE A.6 CONTINUED: Alphabetical List of HTML 4.0 Elements

Element	Description
Attributes:	COMPACT (to indicate that the list should be reduced in size; ignored by most browsers and not recommended), TYPE (to indicate the numbering style: "1" for numbers: 1 2 3..., "A" for capital letters: A B C..., "a" for small letters: a b c..., "I" for large Roman numerals: I II III..., and "i" for small Roman numerals: i ii iii...), START (to indicate what number to start at, for example <OL TYPE="A" START="9"> would create a list where the numbering will start with "I" then "J" and so on), plus generic 4.0 attributes
Content:	One or more list item elements (see <LI>)
<OPTION> **option element**	Creates menu items for a select element form control (Skill 12)
Category:	child element: can only be used in a select element
Starting Tag:	<OPTION>, required
Ending Tag:	</OPTION>, optional
Attributes:	VALUE (to indicate the default value for this menu item when it is selected and submitted to the form processor; by default, it's equal to the contents; see Skill 12), SELECTED (to indicate that this menu item is initially selected as the default value), DISABLED (to make this menu item "grayed out" and unavailable by default), plus generic 4.0 attributes
Content:	DATA
<P> **paragraph element**	Creates a paragraph (Skill 2 and Skill 6)
Category:	block-level element
Starting Tag:	<P>, required
Ending Tag:	</P>, optional
Attributes:	ALIGN (for horizontal alignment; either "LEFT", "RIGHT", "CENTER", or "JUSTIFY", although this attribute is not recommended in favor of style sheets), plus generic 4.0 attributes
Content:	DATA and/or text-level elements
<PARAM> **param element**	Passes a parameter to an applet element or object element; this parameter controls the applet's behavior (Skill 9 and Skill 15)
Category:	child element: can only be used in an applet element or object element
Starting Tag:	<PARAM>, required
Ending Tag:	forbidden (empty element)

TABLE A.6 CONTINUED: Alphabetical List of HTML 4.0 Elements

Element	Description
Attributes:	NAME (required, the name of the parameter as dictated by the applet; varies from applet to applet), VALUE (the data content for the parameter; usually data of some kind such as a name or number), VALUETYPE (not used often, but indicates whether the VALUE attribute contains data, with VALUETYPE="DATA", as is the default; or a URL, with VALUETYPE="REF"; or the specific ID name of another applet or HTML element, with VALUETYPE="OBJECT"), and TYPE (to indicate the MIME type of the file given in the VALUE URL if VALUETYPE is "REF"), plus the generic ID attributes
Content:	none (empty element)
<PRE> **pre-formatted text element**	Creates a block of preformatted text (in which the normal rules of collapsing white space do not apply) so that you can arrange lines in a particular way and create text art (Skill 6) **NOTE:** Most browsers will display the pre element using a monospaced font, such as Courier
Category:	block-level element
Starting Tag:	<PRE>, required
Ending Tag:	</PRE>, required
Attributes:	WIDTH to indicate the number of characters the widest line of the preformatted text has (but this attribute is not widely supported) plus generic 4.0 attributes
Content:	DATA and/or text-level elements (except for the img, big, small, sub, sup, basefont, font, applet, and object elements)
<Q> **quote element**	Creates inline quotes (Skill 6) **NOTE:** This element is not widely supported yet; it's similar to the blockquote element, but the quote element is a text-level element while blockquote is a block-level element
Category:	text-level element (special)
Starting Tag:	<Q>, required
Ending Tag:	</Q>, required
Attributes:	CITE (to indicate the URL of the quote's source) plus generic 4.0 attributes
Content:	DATA and/or text-level elements
<S> **strike element**	Makes the enclosed text appear with a strike-out through the middle (Skill 6); see also <STRIKE> (which is more widely supported than <S>) **WARNING:** HTML 4.0 does not recommend the use of this element; use the del element or a style sheet instead
Category:	text-level element (physical font)
Starting Tag:	<S>, required
Ending Tag:	</S>, required
Attributes:	none except generic 4.0 attributes
Content:	DATA and/or text-level elements

TABLE A.6 CONTINUED: Alphabetical List of HTML 4.0 Elements

Element	Description
\<SAMP\> **sample element**	Indicates that the contents is a sample output from a computer program, often displayed using a fixed-width font (Skill 6)
Category:	text-level element (phrase)
Starting Tag:	\<SAMP\>, required
Ending Tag:	\</SAMP\>, required
Attributes:	none except generic 4.0 attributes
Content:	DATA and/or text-level elements
\<SCRIPT\> **script element**	Contains an active script (Skill 15)
Category:	head section element; also text-level element (special)
Starting Tag:	\<SCRIPT\>, required
Ending Tag:	\</SCRIPT\>, required
Attributes:	TYPE and LANGUAGE, to specify the scripting language (HTML 4.0 recommends using the TYPE attribute, but current browsers expect the LANGUAGE attribute, so both methods are currently necessary, see Skill 15), plus SRC to specify an external active script file
Content:	DATA that's an active script written in a scripting language (such as JavaScript or VBScript); be sure to surround the script with an HTML comment so older browsers don't display it inadvertently (see Skill 15)
\<SELECT\> **select element**	Creates a selection menu form control, either as a drop-down menu or list box (Skill 12)
Category:	form control element
Starting Tag:	\<SELECT\>, required
Ending Tag:	\</SELECT\>, required
Attributes:	NAME (required, to give the form control a value that's passed to the form processor when the form is submitted, and to give the form control a name for use with a script), SIZE (to determine how many items are displayed at once; if this attribute is omitted, most browsers will display a drop-down menu, but if it's included, you'll get a list box instead—see Skill 12), MULTIPLE (if you want to allow the surfer to select more than one item from a list box), DISABLED (to make this form control "grayed out" and unavailable by default), TABINDEX (to control this form control's position in the tab key navigation order), plus generic 4.0 attributes, including the special ONFOCUS, ONCHANGE, and ONBLUR event attributes (see Skill 15)
Content:	One or more option elements

TABLE A.6 CONTINUED: Alphabetical List of HTML 4.0 Elements

Element	Description
<SMALL> **small element**	Makes the enclosed text one size smaller (Skill 3 and Skill 6)
Category:	text-level element (physical font)
Starting Tag:	<SMALL>, required
Ending Tag:	</SMALL>, required
Attributes:	none except generic 4.0 attributes
Content:	DATA and/or text-level elements
<SPAN> **the span element**	A generic text-level element, useful for indicating where style sheets should be applied (Skill 14), to give a name to section using the generic CLASS or ID attributes (Skill 6), or to assign a language to a section (Skill 5); for example: <SPAN LANG="FR" CLASS="foreign">Bonjour!</SPAN>
Category:	text-level element (special)
Starting Tag:	<SPAN>, required
Ending Tag:	</SPAN>, required
Attributes:	none except generic 4.0 attributes
Content:	DATA and/or text-level elements
<STRIKE> **strike element**	Makes the enclosed text appear with a strike-out through the middle (Skill 6); see also <S>, but <STRIKE> is more widely supported than <S> **WARNING:** HTML 4.0 does not recommend the use of this element; use the del element or a style sheet instead
Category:	text-level element (physical font)
Starting Tag:	<STRIKE>, required
Ending Tag:	</STRIKE>, required
Attributes:	none except generic 4.0 attributes
Content:	DATA and/or text-level elements
<STRONG> **strong emphasis element**	Indicates that the contents should be given a strong emphasis, usually displayed with bold (Skill 6)
Category:	text-level element (phrase)
Starting Tag:	<STRONG>, required
Ending Tag:	</STRONG>, required
Attributes:	none except generic 4.0 attributes
Content:	DATA and/or text-level elements

TABLE A.6 CONTINUED: Alphabetical List of HTML 4.0 Elements

Element	Description
<STYLE> **style element**	Creates an embedded style sheet (Skill 14)
Category:	head section element
Starting Tag:	<STYLE>, required
Ending Tag:	</STYLE>, required
Attributes:	TYPE (required, to specify the style sheet language's MIME type such as TYPE="text/css" for Cascading Style Sheets), MEDIA (to specify what display the style sheet should be used with, see Skill 14), and TITLE (to name the style sheet); you may also use the generic HTML 4.0 language attributes (LANG and DIR) to specify the language used in the TITLE attribute
Content:	DATA that's a style sheet written in a style sheet language (such as Cascading Style Sheets); be sure to surround the style sheet with an HTML comment so older browsers don't display it inadvertently (see Skill 14)
<SUB> **subscript element**	Used to indicate a subscripted section (Skill 6); for example: H<SUB>2</SUB>0
Category:	text-level element (special)
Starting Tag:	<SUB>, required
Ending Tag:	</SUB>, required
Attributes:	none except generic 4.0 attributes
Content:	DATA and/or text-level elements
<SUP> **superscript element**	Used to indicate a superscripted section (Skill 6); for example: E=MC<SUP>2</SUP>
Category:	text-level element (special)
Starting Tag:	<SUP>, required
Ending Tag:	</SUP>, required
Attributes:	none except generic 4.0 attributes
Content:	DATA and/or text-level elements
<TABLE> **table element**	Creates a table of data (Skill 10)
Category:	block-level element
Starting Tag:	<TABLE>, required
Ending Tag:	</TABLE>, required

TABLE A.6 CONTINUED: Alphabetical List of HTML 4.0 Elements

Element	Description
Attributes:	ALIGN (for the table position, "LEFT", "RIGHT", or "CENTER"), BGCOLOR (for the table's background color), WIDTH (in pixels or percentage, for the table's width), COLS (the number of columns in the table), BORDER (to create a visible border; use BORDER="SIZE" to determine how big the border is in pixels), FRAME (which sides of the table will have a border, either "VOID", "ABOVE", "BELOW", "HSIDES", "LHS", "RHS", "VSIDES", "BOX", or "BORDER"), RULES (to determine which sides of the whole table will have a border, either "NONE", "GROUPS", "ROWS", "COLS", or "ALL"), CELLSPACING (how much space between cells, in pixels), CELLPADDING (how much space between the edge of the cell and the cell's contents, in pixels) plus generic 4.0 attributes
Content:	An optional caption element, followed by any number of optional colgroup and/or col elements, followed by an optional thead element, followed by an optional tfoot element, followed by one or more tbody elements (the <TBODY> and </TBODY> tags are optional if there's no thead element, no tfoot element, and only one tbody element). One tbody element is required. The tbody element contains one or more table row elements (see the <TR> tag), and each row contains one or more cells of data
<TBODY> **table body row group element** **(tbody element)**	Creates a group of rows in a table, used as the body of the table; convenient for setting the attributes of many rows of data at once (Skill 10)
Category:	table model element
Starting Tag:	<TBODY>, optional (required if a thead or tfoot element is present in the table)
Ending Tag:	</TBODY>, optional
Attributes:	horizontal cell alignment attributes: ALIGN (to set the default alignment of the cell data, either "LEFT", "CENTER", "RIGHT", "JUSTIFY", or on a particular character with "CHAR"), CHAR (to specify which alignment character to use if ALIGN="CHAR"), CHAROFF (to specify a length in pixels or percentage of the column's width to use as an offset for determining the character alignment), and vertical cell alignment: VALIGN (to specify the vertical position of cell data: "TOP", "MIDDLE", "BOTTOM", or "BASELINE"), plus generic 4.0 attributes **WARNING:** Character alignment is not yet supported in the popular browsers
Content:	one or more table rows (see <TR>)
<TD> **table data element**	Creates a cell of data in a table (Skill 10)
Category:	table model element
Starting Tag:	<TD>, required
Ending Tag:	</TD>, optional

TABLE A.6 CONTINUED: Alphabetical List of HTML 4.0 Elements

Element	Description
Attributes:	BGCOLOR (background color for the cell), ROWSPAN and COLSPAN (number of rows or columns spanned by the data, see Skill 10), NOWRAP (to indicate that the cell's data shouldn't be word wrapped), AXIS and AXES (to set up the cell's name and coordinates, see Skill 10), horizontal cell alignment attributes: ALIGN (to set the default alignment of the cell data, either "LEFT", "CENTER", "RIGHT", "JUSTIFY", or on a particular character with "CHAR"), CHAR (to specify which alignment character to use if ALIGN="CHAR"), CHAROFF (to specify a length in pixels or percentage of the column's width to use as an offset for determining the character alignment), and vertical cell alignment: VALIGN (to specify the vertical position of cell data: "TOP", "MIDDLE", "BOTTOM", or "BASELINE"), WIDTH and HEIGHT (in pixels, to specify a cell's minimum dimensions), plus generic 4.0 attributes **WARNING**: Character alignment is not yet supported in the popular browsers
Content:	DATA, text-level elements, and/or block-level elements
<TEXTAREA> **textarea element**	Creates a textarea form control, displayed as a box where the surfer can type information (Skill 12)
Category:	form control element
Starting Tag:	<TEXTAREA>, required
Ending Tag:	</TEXTAREA>, required
Attributes:	NAME (required, to give the textarea form control a value that's passed to the form processor when the form is submitted, and to give the textarea form control a name for use with a script), ROWS and COLS (both required, to set the size of the textarea box), DISABLED (to make this form control "grayed out" and unavailable by default), READONLY (to make the contents of the textarea form control unchangeable by default), TABINDEX (to control this form control's position in the tab key navigation order), plus generic 4.0 attributes, including the special ONFOCUS, ONSELECT, ONCHANGE, and ONBLUR event attributes (see Skill 15)
Content:	DATA (the default information in the textarea control)
<TFOOT> **table foot row group** **element (tfoot element)**	Creates a row group in a table that's used as the table's footer, repeated on the bottom of each page of a printout (Skill 10)
Category:	table model element
Starting Tag:	<TFOOT>, required
Ending Tag:	</TFOOT>, optional
Attributes:	Same as for the tbody element (see <TBODY>)
Content:	one or more table rows (see <TR>)

ew

TABLE A.6 CONTINUED: Alphabetical List of HTML 4.0 Elements

Element	Description
\<TH> **table heading element**	Creates a cell with table heading data, usually centered and in bold (Skill 10)
Category:	table model element
Starting Tag:	\<TH>, required
Ending Tag:	\</TH>, optional
Attributes:	Same as for the table data element (see \<TD>)
Content:	DATA, text-level elements, and/or block-level elements
\<THEAD> **table head row group** **element (thead element)**	Creates a row group in a table that's used as the header for the table, repeating on each page of a printout (Skill 10) **WARNING:** This element is not yet widely supported
Category:	table model element
Starting Tag:	\<THEAD>, required
Ending Tag:	\</THEAD>, optional
Attributes:	Same as for the tbody element (see \<TBODY>)
Content:	one or more table rows (see \<TR>)
\<TITLE> **title element**	Creates the document's title (Skill 2 and Skill 5). Every HTML document requires a title
Category:	head section element that's part of the basic structure
Starting Tag:	\<TITLE>, required
Ending Tag:	\</TITLE>, required
Attributes:	none except the generic HTML 4.0 language attributes (LANG and DIR, see Skill 5)
Content:	DATA
\<TR> **table row element**	Creates a row of cells in a table (Skill 10)
Category:	table model element
Starting Tag:	\<TR>, required
Ending Tag:	\</TR>, optional
Attributes:	Same as for table body row groups (see \<TBODY>), plus BGCOLOR can be used to set the row's background color
Content:	One or more cells; cells can be table data elements (see \<TD>) or table heading elements (see \<TH>) or a mixture of both

TABLE A.6 CONTINUED: Alphabetical List of HTML 4.0 Elements

Element	Description
<TT> **teletype element**	Makes enclosed text appear in a fixed-width, typewriter-style font, such as Courier (Skill 6)
Category:	text-level element (physical font)
Starting Tag:	<TT>, required
Ending Tag:	</TT>, required
Attributes:	none except generic 4.0 attributes
Content:	DATA and/or text-level elements
<U> **underline element**	Makes enclosed text appear with an underline (Skill 6) **WARNING:** HTML 4.0 does not recommend the use of this element at all; underlined text is easily confused with a link
Category:	text-level element (physical font)
Starting Tag:	<U>, required
Ending Tag:	</U>, required
Attributes:	none except generic 4.0 attributes
Content:	DATA and/or text-level elements
<UL> **unordered list element**	Creates an unordered list (Skill 6), with bullets preceding each list item
Category:	block-level element (list)
Starting Tag:	<UL>, required
Ending Tag:	</UL>, required
Attributes:	COMPACT (to indicate that the list should be reduced in size; ignored by most browsers and not recommended), TYPE (to indicate the bullet style, either "DISC" for a normal solid bullet, "SQUARE" for a solid square, or "CIRCLE" for a hollow bullet), plus generic 4.0 attributes
Content:	One or more list item elements (see <LI>)
<VAR> **variable element**	Indicates that the contents is a computer program variable or user-specified piece of information (Skill 6)
Category:	text-level element (phrase)
Starting Tag:	<VAR>, required
Ending Tag:	</VAR>, required
Attributes:	none except generic 4.0 attributes
Content:	DATA and/or text-level elements

Summary of Case-Sensitivity

To end this appendix, we'll summarize case-sensitivity in HTML.

- Tags are *not* case-sensitive (<B> and <b> are the same).

- The attribute names are *not* case-sensitive (HREF and href are the same).

- The values for attributes are generally *not* case-sensitive (COLOR="RED" is the same as COLOR="red"), but there are a few exceptions. For example, ordered list types *are* case-sensitive (TYPE="a" is different from TYPE="A"), as are URLs, general text (for example, alternate content with the ALT attribute or the meta element's CONTENT attribute), and embedded active scripts used with the event attributes (see Skill 15).

- Some browsers treat anchor and target names as case-sensitive (<A NAME= "ROXANNE"> is different from <A NAME="Roxanne"> in some browsers, despite HTML's declaration that they should not be different).

- Names of entities are *always* case-sensitive (© won't display a copyright symbol, only © will).

- The four special target names from Skill 11 are case-sensitive.

- Some parts of URLs are *not* case-sensitive: the protocol is not case-sensitive (HTTP: and http: are the same), and the domain name is *not* case-sensitive (WWW.IBM.COM and www.ibm.com are the same), but everything else in a URL *is* usually case-sensitive (depending on the Web server's operating system). Skill 1 has more information.

- The components of a <!DOCTYPE> declaration *are* case-sensitive (for example, dtd html 4.0 and DTD HTML 4.0 are not the same).

- Cascading Style Sheet rules are *not* case-sensitive except for URLs and some font family names. To be safe, you should treat CLASS and ID attribute names as if they were case-sensitive since some browsers treat them that way (incorrectly).

- Most active script statements *are* case-sensitive (exactly how much so depends on the programming language; for example, JavaScript is case-sensitive).

That concludes this appendix, so we'll take this chance to wave goodbye to you before the index and the end of the book. Be sure to catch up with us on the book's Web site, where we'll tell you about any changes to HTML that you need to know. Thanks for reading our book, and we sincerely hope you have a lot more knowledge of HTML now than when you started.

Index

Note to the Reader: First-level entries are in **bold**. Page numbers in **bold** indicate the principal discussion of a topic or the definition of a term. Page numbers in *italic* indicate illustrations.

X

Y

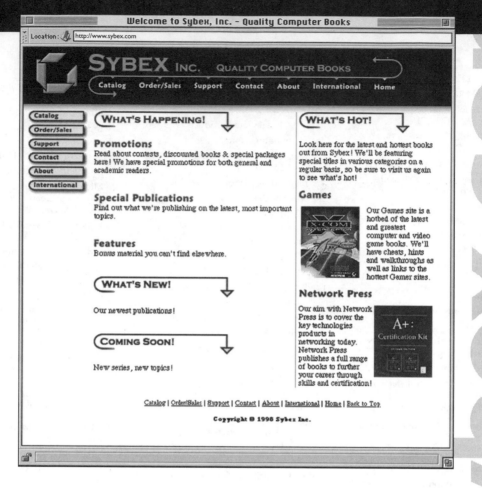